CENSUS OF INDIA 1931

Owing to the antiquity and rarity of this book, certain pages are regrettably absent, and readability is compromised due to the blurring of the original text. If you possess any insights regarding the availability of these missing sections, kindly inform us. Your assistance is crucial in ensuring the completion of this significant work for the benefit of future generations.

CENSUS OF INDIA, 1931

VOLUME - XXIV

JAMMU & KASHMIR STATE

PART II, III - IMPERIAL & STATE TABLES

RAI BAHADUR, PT. ANANT RAM
&
PT. HIRA NAND RAINA

GYAN

Published by

Gyan Publishing House
5, Ansari Road
Daryaganj, New Delhi-110002
Phone: 011-47034999, 9811692060
E-mail: books@gyanbooks.com

Distribution Network
gyanbooks.com
India, USA, Canada, UK, Australia

ISBN: 978-81-212-7123-3 (Set) 28 Vols. In 52 Bindings

ISBN: 978-81-212-7517-0 (PB) Vol. XXIV, Pt. II, III

First Published, 1933

2nd Impression 2024

Printed at: Gyan Press, Delhi.

CENSUS OF INDIA 1931

Census of India, 1931

VOLUME XXIV

JAMMU & KASHMIR STATE

PART II

Imperial & State Tables

BY

RAI BAHADUR, PT. ANANT RAM, B. A.

Director of Land Records, State Property in British India, Devasthan and Dharmarth, and

Census Commissioner

His Highness' Government, Jammu and Kashmir

AND

PT. HIRA NAND RAINA, B. SC., LL. B.

Assistant Census Commissioner.

JAMMU :

Printed under the supervision of

J. Sharma, C. P. C. Tech., M. P. G. (Manchester), Superintendent The Ranbir Govt. Press.

1933.

TABLE OF CONTENTS.

CORRIGENDA.

Serial No.	Page.	Table.	Column and Reference.	Line.	Read.	For.
1	17	V	14—Jains Female ..	3	269	219
2	19	,,	15—Buddhist Persons ..	6	1,689	,6f9
3	22	VI	4—Fopulation ..	19	13,889	13,898
4	24	,,	34—Females ..	2 from the bottom	2	9
5	24	,,	,, ..	last	9	2
6	28	,,	1—District etc. Part C. ..	51	Europe	Eurodo
7	45	VII	7—Unmarried Males ..	1	66,187	56,187
8	47	,,	13—Widowed Males ..	1	271	27
9	53	,,	3—Persons ..	13	19,007	19,07
10	53	,,	14—Widowed Females ..	16	7,238	7,230 intelligible
11	65	,,	Title ..	......	Delete " Continued " after Ladakh District.	
12	67	,,	4—Populaticn Males ..	7 from the bottom	2,083	2,83
13	78	VIII	5—Total ..	last	24	4
14	132	X	Title ..	......	Group 123	Grorp 98
15	170	XI	6—Males ..	11	25,839	25,838
16	170	,,	2—Traditional Occupaticn ..	11	Agriculture	after State service.
17	218	XIV	8—Persons ..	5	33,230	33,:30
18	241	XV-II	5—Females ..	3	147,234	1,47,23
19	260	,,	6—Persons ..	5	54	45
20	281	XVII	Title ..	......	Kamanghar	Kumanghar
21	284	,,	204—Females ..	2	7,915	7,95
22	287	,,	269—Males ..	5	185	135
23	291	,,	359—Males ..	2	13,484	13,448
24	292	,,	Title ..	......	Tarkhan	Tharkhan
25	302	XX	11-1921 ..	12	165	164
26	312	*II	6—Males ..	4	293	29
27	331	*VII	2—Occupation ..	3	thatchers	that he s

* State Table.

TABLE I.

AREA, HOUSES AND POPULATION.

Jammu and Kashmir Census 1931.

1. The Bhadrawah Jagir which at previous censuses used to be shown as a separate district of the Jammu Province ceases to exist as a separate administrative unit and has been amalgamated with the Udhampur District with which its totals have consequently been incorporated.

2. The totals of Chenani Jagir were included in Udhampur District in the past but the Jagir being a separate administrative unit its totals have been shown separately under the proper head "Jagirs".

3. The three districts of Kashmir North, Kashmir South and Muzaffarabad make up the Provincial Total of Kashmir Province. At the last census an additional heading of "Kashmir Valley" was included in the tables which simply represented the totals of "Kashmir North" and "Kashmir South". This heading being superfluous has been deleted from the present tables.

4. The figures of area of the Jammu and Kashmir Provinces are based on the information supplied by the Survey Department of the Government of India. The area figures of the Frontier Province have been repeated from 1921 Census Table.

5. The total number of villages is exclusive of 154 uninhabited villages besides 15 inhabited villages which constitute the towns of Kathua, Parol, Pampur and Skardu.

6. The population of 3 villages of Karlup Jagir of the Raja Sahib of Poonch is included in the population of the Jammu District as was done in 1921.

NOTE.—Remarks against items 1 to 3 apply to other tables also.

TABLE I.

Area, Houses and Population.

Jammu and Kashmir Census 1931.

District or State.	Area in square miles.	Towns.	Villages.	Occupied Houses.			Population.								
							Persons.			*Males.*			*Females.*		
				Total.	In towns.	In villages.	Total.	Urban.	Rural.	Total.	Urban.	Rural.	Total.	Urban	Rural.
1	2	3	4	5	6	7	8	9	10	11	12	13	14	15	16
Jammu and Kashmir State ..	84,471	39	8,903	671,638	60,942	610,696	3,646.243	342,314	3,303,929	1,938,338	192,199	1,746,139	1,707,905	150,115	1,557,790
I. **Jammu Province (including *Jagirs*)**	12,378	20	4,544	350,928	21,041	329,887	1,788,441	99,239	1,689,202	942,815	53,300	884,515	845,626	40,939	804,687
(*a*) *Total Districts* ..	*10,656*	*19*	*4,004*	*282,009*	*19,551*	*262,458*	*1,390,132*	*91,087*	*1,299,045*	*738,267*	*53,394*	*681,873*	*651,865*	*37,693*	*614,172*
1. Jammu District (including City)	1,147	5	1,160	78,717	10,190	68,527	375,240	50,798	324,442	205,719	31,317	174,402	169,521	19,481	150,040
2. Kathua ..	1,023	3	561	34,101	2,470	31,631	161,232	10,351	150,881	85,993	5,757	80,236	75,239	4,594	70,645
3. Udhampur (including Bhadrawah).	5,070	4	938	50,381	2,539	47,842	273,668	11,767	261,901	143,514	6,506	137,008	130,154	5,261	124,893
4. Reasi ..	1,789	3	647	42,479	1,168	41,311	235,245	5,220	230,025	124,210	2,913	121,297	111,035	2,307	108,728
5. Mirpur ..	1,627	4	698	76,331	3,184	73,147	344,747	12,951	331,796	178,831	6,901	171,930	165,916	6,050	159,866
(*b*) *Total Jagirs* ..	*1,722*	*1*	*540*	*68,919*	*1,490*	*67,429*	*398,309*	*8,152*	*390,157*	*204,548*	*4,906*	*199,642*	*193,761*	*3,246*	*190,515*
6. Chenani (*Jagir*) ..	95	..	57	2,338	....	2,338	10,925	....	10,925	5,930	....	5,930	4,995	....	4,095
7. Punch (*Jagir*) ..	1,627	1	483	66,581	1,490	65,091	387,384	8,152	379,232	198,618	4,906	193,712	188,766	3,246	185,520
II. **Kashmir Province** ..	8,539	15	3,542	267,016	37,767	229,249	1,569,218	232,660	1,336,558	847,022	127,706	719,316	722,196	104,954	617,242
8. Baramulla District (including Langot) or Kashmir North ..	3,317	4	1,390	92,290	2,941	89,349	559,828	24,343	535,485	301,397	13,357	288,040	258,431	10,986	247,445
9. Srinagar District (including City) or Kashmir South ..	2,814	9	1,381	136,896	33,765	103,131	771,943	203,121	568,822	419,190	111,224	307,966	352,753	91,897	260,856
10. Muzaffarabad ..	2,408	2	771	37,830	1,061	36,769	237,447	5,190	232,251	126,435	3,125	123,310	11,012	2,071	108,941
III. **Frontier Districts** ..	63,554	4	817	53,694	2,134	51,560	288,584	10,415	278,169	148,501	6,193	142,308	140,083	4,222	135,861
11. **Ladakh** ..	45,762	2	468	37,053	1,312	35,741	192,138	5,510	186,628	96,259	2,914	93,345	95,879	2,596	93,283
12. **Gilgit** ..	3,112	2	79	5,144	822	4,322	31,902	4,905	26,997	17,752	3,279	14,473	14,150	1,626	12,524
13. **Frontier Ilaqas** ..	14,680	..	270	11,497	....	11,497	64,544	....	64,544	34,490	....	34,490	30,054	....	30,054

TABLE II.

VARIATION IN POPULATION DURING LAST FIFTY YEARS.

Jammu and Kashmir Census 1931.

1. The first two regular censuses of 1871 and 1881 were not extended to this State and the columns of population and variation relating to these two Censuses have, therefore, been omitted.

2. The population of Jammu, Udhampur, Riasi, Mirpur, Kashmir North and Kashmir South has been adopted after incorporating the changes brought about by inter-transfer of area during the decade 1921-1931.

TABLE

Variation in Population

Jammu and Kashmir

District or State.	Persons.					Variation. Increase (+) Decrease (—).			
	1931.	1921.	1911.	1901.	1891.	1921 to 1931.	1911 to 1921.	1901 to 1911.	1891 to 1901.
1	2	3	4	5	6	7	8	9	10
Jammu and Kashmir State ..	**3,646,243**	**3,320,518**	**3,158,126**	**2,905,578**	**2,543,952**	**+325,725**	**+162,392**	**+252,548**	**+361,626**
I. Jammu Province including Jagirs	**1,788,441**	**1,640,259**	**1,597,865**	**1,516,450**	**1,434,686**	**+148,182**	**+42,394**	**+81,415**	**+81,764**
(a) Total Districts ..	*1,390,132*	*1,277,858*	*1,252,883*	*1,211,962*	*1,166,078*	*+112,274*	*+24,975*	*+40,921*	*+45,884*
1. Jammu District (including City)	375,240	337,544	329,283	....	....	+37,696	+8,261	——	——
2. Kathua ..	161,232	154,209	151,802	154,213	151,518	+7,023	+2,407	—2,411	+2,695
3. Udhampur (including Bhadrawah)	273,668	245,255	242,648	34,311	32,433	+28,413	+2,607	+3,201	+1,878
4. Riasi ..	235,245	223,652	205,912	....	....	+11,593	+17,740	——	——
5. Mirpur ..	344,747	317,198	323,238	....	....	+27,549	—6,040	——	——
(b) Total Jagirs —	*398,309*	*362,401*	*344,982*	*304,488*	*268,608*	*+35,908*	*+17,419*	*+40,494*	*+35,880*
6. Chenani Jagir ..	10,925	10,620	10,589	——	——	+305	+31	——	——
7. Poonch .. —	387,384	351,781	334,393	304,488	268,608	+35,603	+17,388	+29,905	+35,880
II. Kashmir Province —	**1,569,218**	**1,407,086**	**1,295,201**	**1,157,394**	**949,041**	**+162,132**	**+111,885**	**+137,807**	**+208,353**
8. Kashmir North / Baramulla (including Langet)	559,828	502,216	460,518	——	....	+57,612	+41,701	——	——
9. Kashmir South / Srinagar (including City)	771,943	688,761	639,481	——	....	+83,182	+49,280	——	——
10. Muzaffarabad —	237,447	216,109	195,205	168,198	134,800	+21,338	+20,904	+27,007	+33,398
III. Frontier Districts —	**288,584**	**273,173**	**265,060**	**231,784**	**160,225**	**+15,411**	**+8,113**	**+33,326**	**+71,509**
11. Ladakh —	192,138	183,476	186,656	——	....	+8,662	—3,180	——	——
12. Gilgit —	31,902	28,706	23,969	60,885	....	+3,196	+4,737	+17,519	——
13. Frontier Ilaqas —	64,544	60,991	54,435		....	+3,553	+6,556		——

II.

DURING LAST FIFTY YEARS.

Census 1931:

Net Variation in period 1891 to 1931 Increase (+) Decrease (—)	Males.					Females.				
	1931.	1921.	1911.	1901.	1891.	1931.	1921.	1911	1901.	1891.
11	12	13	14	15	16	17	18	19	20	21
+1,102,291	**1,938,338**	**1,757,122**	**1,674,367**	**1,542,057**	**1,353,229**	**1,707,905**	**1,563,396**	**1,483,759**	**1,363,521**	**1,190,723**
+353,755	**942,815**	**859,619**	**846,790**	**805,415**	**767,864**	**845,626**	**780,640**	**751,075**	**711,035**	**666,822**
+*224,054*	*738,267*	*672,546*	*667,546*	*644,736*	*625,919*	*651,865*	*605,312*	*585,337*	*567,226*	*540,169*
....	205,719	184,071	181,979	....	....	169,521	153,473	147,304	——	——
+9,714	85,993	82,467	81,375	82,391	81,434	75,239	71,742	70,427	71,822	70,084
+241,235	143,514	128,637	127,178	....	....	130,154	116,618	115,470	——	——
——	124,210	118,094	108,571	....	——	111,035	105,558	97,341	——	——
——	178,831	159,277	168,443	——	....	165,916	157,921	154,795	——	——
+*129,701*	*204,548*	*187,073*	*179,244*	*160,679*	*141,945*	*193,761*	*175,328*	*165,738*	*143,809*	*126,663*
——	5,930	5,725	5,674	....	....	4,995	4,895	4,915	——	——
+118,776	198,618	181,348	173,570	160,679	141,945	188,766	170,433	160,823	143,809	126,663
+620,177	**847,022**	**757,824**	**691,780**	**616,887**	**502,345**	**722,196**	**649,262**	**603,421**	**540,507**	**446,696**
——	301,397	269,538	244,488	——	——	258,431	232,678	216,027	——	——
——	419,190	372,606	342,984	——	——	352,753	316,165	296,497	463,038	384,777
+102,647	126,435	115,680	104,308	90,729	72,881	111,012	100,429	90,897	77,469	61,919
+128,359	**148,501**	**139,679**	**135,797**	**119,755**	**83,020**	**140,083**	**133,494**	**129,263**	**111,979**	**77,205**
——	96,259	91,258	93,220	——	....	95,879	92,218	93,436	——	——
——	17,752	15,880	13,299	33,778	——	14,150	12,826	10,670	27,107	——
——	34,490	32,541	29,278		——	30,054	28,450	25,157		——

TABLE III.

Towns and Villages classified by Population.

Jammu and Kashmir Census 1931.

1. Towns consisting of more than one village unit have been dealt with as a single unit and their total population has been taken as the basis of classification for this table.

2. The unclassed population shown under column 22 of this table comprises the Railway and water-borne persons and their total has been excluded from the population of towns and villages under the various categories.

TABLE III.

TOWNS AND VILLAGES CLASSIFIED BY POPULATION

Jammu and Kashmir Census 1931.

District or State.	Total No. of inhabited towns & villages.	Population	Under 500.		500—1,000.		1,000—2,000.		2,000—5,000.		5,000—10,000.		10,000—20,000.		20,000—50,000.		50,000-100,000.		100,000 & over.		Encampments, boats and Railway Population unclassed.
			Number.	Population.	Number.	Population.	Number.	Population.	Number.	Population.	Number.	Population.	Number.	Population.	Number.	Population.	Number.	Population.	Number.	Population.	
1	2	3	4	5	6	7	8	9	10	11	12	13	14	15	16	17	18	19	20	21	22
Jammu and Kashmir State ..	**8,942**	**3,646,243**	**6,914**	**1,383,302**	**1,377**	**955,878**	**520**	**701,349**	**118**	**309,288**	**9**	**55,779**	**2**	**21,439**	**1**	**38,474**	..	....	**1**	**166,592**	**14,142**
I. Jammu Province (including *Jagirs*) ..	**4,584**	**1,788,441**	**3,553**	**677,362**	**644**	**450,228**	**290**	**397,363**	**70**	**187,066**	**6**	**37,734**	..	....	**1**	**38,474**	..	....	..	....	**214**
(a) Total Districts ..	*4,023*	*1,390,132*	*3,276*	*608,831*	*514*	*357,046*	*190*	*259,891*	*37*	*96,094*	*5*	*29,582*	..	....	*1*	*38,474*	..	....	..	....	*214*
1. Jammu District (including City) ..	1,165	375,240	1,017	189,997	106	74,522	30	42,290	11	29,743	..	....	..	....	1	38,474	..	....	..	....	214
2. Kathua District ..	564	161,232	480	85,630	65	45,059	16	20,192	2	5,108	1	5,243	..	....	..	....	..	....	..	....	....
3. Udhampur, including Bhadarwah	942	273,668	796	140,570	111	75,104	28	39,138	7	18,856	..	....	..	....	..	....	..	....	..	....	....
4. Riasi District ..	650	235,245	500	95,901	105	72,943	40	52,660	4	8,622	1	5,119	..	....	..	....	..	....	..	....	....
5. Mirpur ,, ..	702	344,747	483	96,733	127	89,418	76	105,611	13	33,765	3	10,220	..	....	..	....	..	....	..	....	....
(b) Total Jagirs ..	*541*	*398,309*	*277*	*68,531*	*130*	*93,182*	*100*	*137,472*	*33*	*90,972*	*1*	*8,152*	..	....	..	....	..	....	..	....	....
6. Chenani (*Jagir*) ..	57	10,925	54	8,503	2	1,358	1	1,004	..	....	..	....	..	....	..	....	..	....	..	....	....
7. Punch (*Jagir*) ..	484	387,384	223	59,968	128	91,824	99	136,468	33	90,972	1	8,152	..	....	..	....	..	....	..	....	....
II. Kashmir Province ..	**3,557**	**1,569,218**	**2,713**	**574,165**	**600**	**414,814**	**198**	**260,018**	**40**	**100,222**	**3**	**18,045**	**2**	**21,439**	..	....	..	....	**1**	**166,592**	**13,928**
1. Baramulla District (including Langet) or Kashmir North ..	1,394	559,828	1,070	229,966	217	150,391	91	121,169	13	33,848	2	12,600	1	10,703	..	....	..	....	..	....	1,151
2. Srinagar District (including City) or Kashmir South ..	1,390	771,943	1,004	218,960	271	187,649	89	114,853	23	54,931	1	5,445	1	10,736	..	....	..	....	1	166,592	12,777
3. Muzaffarabad ..	773	237,447	639	125,239	112	76,774	18	23,991	4	11,443	..	....	..	....	..	....	..	....	..	....	....
III. Frontier Districts ..	**821**	**288,584**	**648**	**131,775**	**133**	**90,836**	**32**	**43,973**	**8**	**22,000**	..	....	..	....	..	....	..	....	..	....	....
1. Ladakh ..	470	192,138	349	79,212	89	60,659	26	36,948	6	15,319	..	....	..	....	..	....	..	....	..	....	....
2. Gilgit ..	81	31,902	62	14,849	17	11,506	1	1,073	1	4,474	..	....	..	....	..	....	..	....	..	....	....
3. Frontier Ilaqas ..	270	64,544	237	37,714	27	18,671	5	5,952	1	2,207	..	....	..	....	..	....	..	....	..	....	....

TABLE IV.

Towns classified by population with variation since 1891.

Jammu and Kashmir Census 1931.

1. The names of places which have been treated as towns at the current Census but were not treated as such at previous Censuses are given below :—

1921.	1911.	1901.		1891.	
Katra.	Badamibagh Cantt.	Sopore.	Bhadrawah.	Kathua.	Shopyan.
Uri.		Anantnag.	Pattan.	Gilgit.	Verinag.
Machhbhavan.		Poonch.	Skardu.	Bijbehara.	Manawar.
Gilgit.		Mirpur.	Doru.	Muzaffarabad.	Riasi.
Badamibagh.		Baramulla.	Shopyan.	Jammu Cantt.	Basohli.
		Kathua.	Rampur.	Pampur.	Ranbirsinghpura.
		Gilgit.	Verinag.	Cherar Sharif.	Bhimber.
		Bijbehara.	Manawar.	Udhampur.	Ramnagar.
		Muzaffarabad.	Riasi.	Kishtwar.	Kotli.
		Pampur.	Basohli.	Leh.	Katra.
		Cherar Sharif.	Ranbirsinghpura.	Parol.	Badamibagh Cantt.
		Udhampur.	Bhimber.	Machhbhavan.	Uri.
		Kishtwar.	Ramnagar.	Akhnoor.	Gilgit.
		Leh.	Kotli.	Samba.	
		Parol.	Badamibagh.	Bhadrawah.	
		Machhbhavan.	Uri.	Pattan.	
		Akhnoor.	Gilgit.	Skardu.	
		Samba.		Doru.	

2. There are no towns in class II. Srinagar city falls in class I., Jammu in class III. There are two towns in class IV and 4 in class V.

3. The total Urban population in columns 5 to 8 represents population returned as such during the past Censuses.

4. The increase in the population of Srinagar City besides being natural is also attributable to the transfer of the following villages to the Municipality after 1921 :—

Zunimar, Sonwar, Bonamsar, Bagh Nandsingh, Shivpura, Rathpura, Lachhmanpura, Batmalna (Part).

The total increase in 1921 and 1911 figures is of 10617 and 16365 persons respectively.

	1921.	1911.
Males ...	5780	8839
Females	4837	7526

The figures of Military population shown as sub-totals under Srinagar Municipality have been deducted and transferred to their respective columns against Badamibagh Cantonment.

5. The increase in the population of Sopore is also due to the transfer of the villages of Arampura, Chinkipura, Hamilna and Bagat to the newly constituted Notified area.

6. The increase in the population of Udhampur is similarly partly ascribable to the portions of Baharian and Umara villages having been incorporated in the recently constituted Notified Area.

7. The figures of Jammu City and Ranbirsinghpura town include the Railway Population of their adjacent stations in conformity with the instructions of the Census Commissioner for India. The Railway population of Jammu Cantonment Station has not, however, been included in the Cantonment figures.

Statement showing the net variation during the decade 1921-1931 in the places treated as towns at both Censuses.

Province State or Agency.	Places treated as Towns in 1921 but now omitted. No.	Places treated as Towns in 1921 but now omitted. Aggregate Population in 1921.	Places now treated as Towns which were not so treated in 1921. No.	Places now treated as Towns which were not so treated in 1921. Aggregate Population in 1931.	Net Variation in decade 1921-1931, due to differences in the list of Towns.	Variation in aggregate population of places which were treated as towns at both Censuses.
1	2	3	4	5	6	7
Kashmir State ..	3	9,637	4	5,357	—4,280	+54,901

TABLE

Towns classified by population,

Jammu and Kashmir

Name of Town.	District or State.	Description of town (Municipality, suburbs, Cantonments, etc.)	Population. 1931.	1921.	1911.	1901.	1891.
1	2	3	4	5	6	7	8
Total Urban Population ..	..	..	*342,314*	*291,693*	*300,879*	*158,748*	*197,743*
Total Cities ..	..	..	*212,186*	*171,026*	*155,966*	*158,748*	*197,743*
						Class I.	—100,000
1. Srinagar ..	Kashmir South ..	Municipality ..	173,573	139,520	124,240	122,618	118,960
						Class III.	—20,000
2. Jammu ..	Jammu ..	Do. ..	38,613	31,506	31,726	36,130	34,542
						Class IV.	—10,000
3. Sopore ..	Kashmir North ..	Do. ..	10,982	8,524	8,514	..	8,410
4. Anantnag ..	Do. South ..	....	10,736	9,464	9,019	..	10,227
						Class	V.—5,000
5. Poonch ..	Poonch Jagir ..	....	8,152	7,026	7,564	..	7,489
6. Mirpur ..	Mirpur ..	Notified area ..	7,274	6,490	6,640	..	7,253
7. Baramulla ..	Kashmir North ..	Do. ..	6,886	6,744	6,599	..	5,656
8. Kathua ..	Kathua ..	....	5,243	5,072	5,240	..	..
							Class VI.—
9. Gilgit ..	Gilgit ..	....	4,474	4,393	3,562	..	..
10. Bijbehara ..	Kashmir South ..	....	4,438	4,270	4,424	..	..
11. Muzaffarabad ..	Muzaffarabad ..	....	4,236	3,579	3,462	..	..
12. Jammu Cantonment ..	Jammu ..	Cantonment ..	4,181	2,969	3,201	..	..
13. Pampur ..	Kashmir South ..	....	3,869	3,494	3,348	..	..
14. Chorar Sharif ..	Do. North ..	....	3,784	3,342	3,380	..	..
15. Udhampur ..	Udhampur ..	Notified area ..	3,633	2,390	2,360	..	..
16. Kishtwar ..	Do. ..	....	3,335	2,546	2,378	..	..
17. Leh ..	Ladakh ..	....	3,093	2,401	2,895	..	..
18. Parol ..	Kathua ..	....	3,016	2,158	1,678	..	..
19. Machhbhawan ..	Kashmir South ..	....	3,016	..	..	..	..
20. Akhnoor ..	Jammu ..	....	3,007	2,905	3,033	..	..
21. Samba ..	Do. ..	....	2,917	2,418	2,307	..	..
22. Bhadrawah ..	Udhampur ..	....	2,895	2,603	2,563	..	..
23. Pattan ..	Kashmir North ..	....	2,691	2,243	1,903	..	..
24. Skardu ..	Ladakh ..	....	2,417	2,282	2,197	..	..
25. Doru ..	Kashmir South ..	....	2,252	2,177	2,202	..	..
26. Shopyan (Hiragam) ..	Do. ..	....	2,217	2,236	2,114	..	..
27. Rampur Rajouri ..	Riasi ..	....	2,164	2,253	2,192	..	....

IV.

WITH VARIATION FOR FIFTY YEARS.

Census 1931.

Variation Increase (+) Decrease (—).				Variation in period 1891 to 1931. Increase (+) Decrease (—)	Males.			Females.		
1921 to 1931.	1911 to 1921.	1901 to 1911.	1891 to 1901.		1931.	1921.	1911.	1931.	1921.	1911.
9	10	11	12	13	14	15	16	17	18	19
+50,621	*—9,186*	*+142,131*	*—38,995*	*+144,571*	*192,199*	*161,919*	*167,028*	*150,116*	*129,774*	*133,851*
+41,160	*+15,060*	*—2,782*	*—38,995*	*+14,443*	*118,154*	*94,273*	*86,356*	*94,032*	*76,753*	*69,610*
and over.										
+34,053	+15,280	+1,622	+3,658	+54,613	94,793	75,152	66,994	78,780	64,368	57,246
to 30,000.										
+7,107	—220	—4,404	+1,588	+4,071	23,361	19,121	19,362	15,252	12,385	12,364
to 20,000.										
+2,458	+10	....	....	+2,572	5,956	4,610	4,465	5,026	3,914	4,049
+1,272	+445	....	....	+509	6,103	5,303	4,937	4,633	4,161	4,082
to 10,000.										
+1,126	—538	....	....	+663	4,906	4,103	4,662	3,246	2,923	2,902
+784	—150	....	....	+21	3,840	3,251	3,441	3,434	3,230	3,199
+142	+145	....	....	+1,230	3,780	3,691	3,586	3,106	3,053	3,013
+171	—168	....	....	....	3,002	2,948	3,008	2,241	2,124	2,232
under 5,000.										
+81	+831	....	....	....	2,848	2,947	2,301	1,626	1,446	1,261
+168	—154	....	....	....	2,462	2,311	2,360	1,976	1,959	2,064
+657	+117	....	....	....	2,506	2,131	2,015	1,730	1,448	1,447
+1,212	—232	+1,950	....	....	3,626	2,567	2,847	555	402	354
+375	+146	....	....	....	2,114	1,941	1,851	1,755	1,553	1,497
+442	—38	....	....	....	2,136	1,894	1,853	1,648	1,448	1,527
+1,243	+30	....	....	....	2,065	1,373	1,311	1,568	1,017	1,049
+789	+168	....	....	....	1,874	1,396	1,277	1,461	1,150	1,101
+692	—494	....	....	....	1,571	1,182	1,464	1,522	1,219	1,431
+858	+480	....	....	....	1,661	1,209	917	1,355	949	761
....	....	....	....	....	1,603	....	....	1,413	....	....
+102	—128	....	....	....	1,608	1,496	1,550	1,399	1,409	1,483
+499	+111	....	....	....	1,524	1,263	1,210	1,393	1,155	1,097
+292	+40	....	....	....	1,538	1,369	1,348	1,357	1,234	1,215
+448	+340	....	....	....	1,485	1,236	1,018	1,206	1,007	885
+135	+85	....	....	....	1,343	1,246	1,137	1,074	1,036	1,060
+75	—25	....	....	....	1,192	1,163	1,157	1,060	1,014	1,045
—19	+122	....	....	....	1,187	1,223	1,161	1,030	1,013	953
—89	+61	....	....	....	1,225	1,214	1,203	939	1,039	989

TABLE

TOWNS CLASSIFIED BY POPULATION,

Jammu and Kashmir

Name of Town.	District or State.	Description of town (Municipality, suburbs, Cantonments, etc.)	Population.				
			1931.	1921.	1911.	1901.	1891.
1	2	3	4	5	6	7	8
28. Verinag ..	Kashmir South ..	....	2,134	2,156	2,095	....	....
29. Manawar ..	Mirpur ..	....	2,120	1,966	2,057	....	....
30. Riasi ..	Riasi ..	....	2,106	1,940	1,905	....	....
31. Basohli ..	Kathua ..	....	2,092	1,914	1,954	....	....
32. Sri Ranbirsinghpura ..	Jammu ..	....	2,080	1,611	1,336	....	....
33. Bhimber ..	Mirpur ..	....	2,020	1,709	1,438	....	....
34. Ramnagar ..	Udhampur ..	....	1,904	1,977	2,073	....	....
35. Kotli ..	Mirpur ..	....	1,537	1,563	1,584	....	....
36. Uri (*i. e.* Pirsthan) ..	Muzaffarabad ..	....	960	....	544	....	....
37. Katra ..	Riasi ..	....	950	....	828	....	....
38. Badamibagh Cantonment ..	Kashmir South ..	....	886	2,215	2,104	....	....
39. Gilgit Cantonment ..	Gilgit ..	....	431	....	....	....	....

IV.

WITH VARIATION FOR FIFTY YEARS.

Census 1931.

Variation Increase (+). Decrease (—).				Variation in period 1891 to 1931. Increase (+) Decrease (—)	Males.			Females.		
1921 to 1931.	1911 to 1921.	1901 to 1911.	1891 to 1901.		1931.	1921.	1911.	1931.	1921.	1911.
9	10	11	12	13	14	15	16	17	18	19
—22	+61	....	....	....	1,045	1,103	1,063	1,089	1,053	1,032
+154	—91	....	....	....	1,133	1,078	1,142	987	888	915
+166	+35	....	....	....	1,193	1,073	1,062	913	867	843
+178	—40	....	....	....	1,094	979	1,003	998	935	951
+469	+275	....	....	....	1,198	890	761	882	721	575
+311	+271	....	....	....	1,121	931	777	899	778	661
—73	—96	....	....	....	1,029	1,061	1,107	875	916	966
—26	—21	....	....	....	807	813	825	730	750	759
....	....	....	....	....	619	....	298	341	....	246
....	....	....	....	....	495	....	443	455	....	385
—1,329	+111	....	....	....	725	1,452	1,384	161	763	720
....	....	....	....	....	431	....	....	....	....	....

TABLE V.

TOWNS ARRANGED TERRITORIALLY WITH POPULATION BY RELIGION.

Jammu and Kashmir Census 1931.

1. The population shown under "others" in the Jammu Municipality comprises 5 Sansi females.

2. Aryas and Brahmos are included under "Hindus" in this Table.

3. The Civil and Military population of Cantonments is given below :—

Name of Cantonment.	Population.					
	Military.			*Civil.*		
	Total.	Males.	Females.	Total.	Males.	Females.
Jammu ..	2,884	2,884	——	1,297	742	555
Badamibagh ..	642	633	9	244	92	152
Gilgit ..	411	411	——	20	20	——
Total ..	3,937	3,928	9	1,561	854	707

TABLE

Towns arranged territorially

Jammu and Kashmir

District or State.	Town, Municipality, Suburbs, Cantonments, etc.	Population.			Hindu.			Sikh.		
		Persons.	Males.	Females.	Persons.	Males	Females.	Persons.	Males.	Females.
1	2	3	4	5	6	7	8	9	10	11
Jammu and Kashmir State ..	......	342.314	192,199	150,115	99,148	57,013	42.135	4,664	2,851	1,813
I. Jammu Province ..	......	99,239	58,300	40,939	57,503	33,559	23.944	3,016	1,699	1,317
Jammu District ..	......	50,798	31,317	19.481	31,263	19,177	12,085	1,415	823	592
1. Jammu City ..	Municipality.	38.613	23,361	15,252	24,102	14,354	9,748	1,296	757	539
2. Jammu Cantonment ..	Cantonment.	4,181	3,626	555	2,797	2,488	309	21	10	11
3. Akhnoor ..	......	3,007	1.608	1,399	1,611	845	766	45	23	22
4. Samba ..	......	2.917	1,524	1,393	1.752	914	838	36	19	17
5. Sri Ranbirsinghpura ..	......	2,080	1.198	882	1.000	576	424	17	14	3
Kathua District ..	......	10.351	5.757	4.594	6,796	3,766	3,030	77	45	32
6. Kathua ..	......	5,243	3.002	2,241	3.191	1.837	1,354	71	41	30
7. Parol ..	......	3,016	1,661	1,355	1,951	1,069	882	2	2	....
8. Basohli ..	......	2,092	1,094	998	1,654	860	794	4	2	2
Udhampur District ..	......	11.767	6,506	5,261	6.673	3,654	3,019	34	24	10
9. Udhampur ..	......	3,633	2.065	1,568	2,906	1,582	1,324	23	14	9
10. Kishtwar ..	......	3,335	1,874	1,461	989	567	422	6	6	....
11. Bhadrawah ..	......	2,895	1,538	1.357	1.096	605	491	5	4	1
12. Ramnagar ..	......	1.904	1,029	875	1.682	900	782	....	....	....
Riasi District ..	......	5,220	2.913	2,307	3.032	1,670	1.362	21	18	3
13. Rampur Rajouri ..	......	2.164	1,225	939	815	463	352	14	12	2
14. Riasi ..	......	2,106	1.193	913	1.402	779	623	7	6	1
15. Katra ..	......	950	495	455	815	428	387	....	....	....
Mirpur District ..	......	12.951	6.901	6,050	7,191	3,797	3,394	1,107	582	525
16. Mirpur ..	......	7,274	3.840	3,434	3,777	2,007	1,770	706	366	340
17. Manawar ..	......	2,120	1.133	987	996	510	486	288	148	140
18. Bhimber ..	......	2,020	1,121	899	1,125	622	503	87	55	32
19. Kotli ..	......	1.537	807	730	1,293	658	635	26	13	13
Poonch Jagir ..	......	8,152	4.906	3.246	2.549	1,495	1,054	362	207	155
20. Poonch ..	......	8,152	4.906	3.246	2,549	1,495	1,054	362	207	155
II. Kashmir Province ..	......	232,660	127.706	104.954	40,828	22,720	18,108	1,533	1,083	450
Kashmir North (Baramulla) ..	......	24,343	13,357	10,986	2,034	1,172	862	84	66	18
21. Sopore ..	......	10.982	5,956	5,026	896	509	387	12	12	....
22. Baramulla ..	......	6,886	3.780	3,106	1.012	578	434	35	26	9
23. Cherar Sharif ..	......	3,784	2,136	1,648	1	1	....	1	1	....
24. Pattan ..	......	2,691	1,485	1,206	125	84	41	36	27	9
Kashmir South (Srinagar) ..	......	203,121	111,224	91,897	37.396	20,721	16.675	1,016	727	289
25. Srinagar City ..	......	173,573	94,793	78,780	33,670	18,447	15,223	870	634	236
26. Anantnag ..	......	10.736	6.103	4.633	1,469	881	588	18	16	2
27. Bijbehara ..	......	4.438	2.462	1,976	381	214	167	7	4	3
28. Pampur ..	......	3,869	2.114	1,755	104	58	46	1	1	....
29. Machhbhavan ..	......	3,016	1,603	1,413	682	318	364	108	63	45
30. Doru ..	......	2,252	1,192	1,060	46	30	16	2	2	....
31. Shopiyan ..	......	2,217	1,187	1,030	52	39	13	5	3	2
32. Verinag ..	......	2.134	1,045	1,089	312	178	134	....	....	....
33. Badamibagh ..	......	886	725	161	680	556	124	5	4	1

V.

WITH POPULATION BY RELIGION.

Census 1931.

Jain.			Buddhist.			Muslim.			Christian.			Zoroastrain.			Others.		
Persons.	Males.	Females.	Persons.	Males.	Females.	Persons.	Males.	Females.	Persons.	Males.	Females.	Persons.	Males.	Females.	Persons.	Males.	Females.
12	13	14	15	16	17	18	19	20	21	22	23	24	25	26	27	28	29
594	317	277	1,707	850	857	234,915	130,497	104,418	1,277	668	609	4	3	1	5	—	5
591	314	277	9	4	5	37,183	22,218	14,970	932	511	421	—	—	—	5	—	5
578	309	219	9	4	5	16,876	10,649	6,227	653	355	298	—	—	—	5	—	5
563	297	266	9	4	5	12,036	7.621	4.415	602	328	274	—	—	—	5	—	5
9	8	1	....	....	....	1,347	1,118	229	7	2	5	—	—	—	—	—	—
6	4	2	....	....	....	1,345	736	609	..	..	..	..	—	—	—	—	—
—	..	..	....	....	....	1,129	591	538	—	..	..	..	—	..	—	—	—
..	..	..	....	....	....	1,019	583	436	44	25	19	—	..	..	—	—	—
—	..	..	....	....	....	3,333	1,862	1,471	145	84	61	..	..	—	—	—	—
—	..	..	....	....	....	1,899	1,072	827	82	52	30	..	..	..	—	..	—
—	..	..	....	....	....	1,000	558	442	63	32	31	..	..	..	..	—	—
..	..	..	....	....	....	434	232	202	..	..	..	..	—	..	—	—	—
2	1	1	....	....	....	5,027	2,808	2,219	31	19	12	..	—	..	—	—	—
2	1	1	....	....	....	699	466	233	3	2	1	..	..	—	—	—	—
—	—	..	....	....	....	2,340	1,301	1,039	..	..	..	..	..	..	—	—	—
—	—	..	....	....	....	1,794	929	865	..	..	..	..	..	..	—	—	—
—	—	..	....	....	....	194	112	82	28	17	11	..	..	..	—	—	—
—	—	..	....	....	....	2,143	1,212	931	24	13	11	..	..	..	—	—	—
—	..	..	....	....	....	1,335	750	685	..	..	..	..	..	..	—	..	—
—	—	..	....	....	....	691	404	287	6	4	2	..	..	..	—	—	—
—	..	..	....	....	....	117	58	59	18	9	9	..	..	..	—	—	—
8	3	5	....	....	....	4,585	2,488	2,097	60	31	29	..	..	..	..	—	—
8	3	5	....	....	....	2,782	1,464	1,318	1	..	1	..	..	..	..	—	—
—	—	..	....	....	....	791	447	344	45	28	17	..	..	..	..	—	..
—	—	..	....	....	....	795	441	354	13	3	10	..	..	..	..	.	—
—	..	..	....	....	....	217	136	81	1	..	1	..	..	..	..	..	..
3	1	2	....	....	....	5,219	3,194	2,025	19	9	10	..	..	..	..	..	..
3	1	2	....	....	....	5,219	3,194	2,025	19	9	10	..	..	..	..	..	..
3	3	..	5	5	....	190,029	103,773	86,256	258	119	139	4	3	1	—	—	—
—	—	..	....	....	....	22.225	12.119	10.106	..	..	..	—	..	—	—	—	—
—	—	..	....	....	....	10,074	5,435	4.639	..	..	..	..	—	—	—	—	—
—	—	..	....	....	....	5.839	3,176	2,663	..	..	..	..	..	..	—	—	—
—	—	..	....	....	....	3.782	2,134	1,648	..	..	..	..	..	..	—	—	—
—	—	..	....	....	....	2.530	1.374	1.156	..	..	..	..	..	..	—	—	—
3	3	..	5	5	....	164,439	89,646	74,793	258	119	139	4	3	1	—	—	—
3	3	..	5	5	....	138.764	75.583	63.181	257	118	139	4	3	1	—	—	—
..	—	..	....	....	....	9.249	5,206	4,043	..	..	..	..	..	..	—	—	—
..	—	..	....	....	....	4,050	2,244	1,806	..	..	..	..	..	..	..	—	—
..	..	..	....	....	....	3,764	2,055	1,709	..	..	..	..	—	—	—	..	..
..	..	—	....	....	....	2,226	1,222	1,004	..	..	..	..	—	..	—	—	—
..	..	..	....	....	....	2,204	1,160	1,044	..	..	—	—	..	..	—	..	—
—	..	..	....	....	....	2,160	1,145	1,015	..	..	—	..	—	—	—	..	—
..	..	..	....	....	....	1,822	867	955	..	..	..	..	—	—	—	..	—
..	..	..	....	....	....	200	164	36	1	1	..	..	—	..	..	..	—

TABLE

Towns arranged territorially

Jammu and Kashmir

District or State.	Town, Municipality, Suburbs, Cantonments, etc.	Population. Persons.	Population. Males.	Population. Females.	Hindu. Persons	Hindu. Males.	Hindu. Females.	Sikh. Persons.	Sikh. Males.	Sikh. Females.
1	2	3	4	5	6	7	8	9	10	11
Muzaffarabad District ...	...	5,196	3,125	2,071	1,398	827	571	433	290	143
34. Muzaffarabad ...	...	4,236	2,506	1,730	1,191	693	498	355	233	122
35. Uri (i. e. Pirstan) ...	...	960	619	341	207	134	73	78	57	21
III. Frontier Districts ...	...	10,415	6,193	4,222	817	734	83	115	69	46
Ladakh District ...	...	5,510	2,914	2,596	218	194	24	60	34	26
36. Leh ...	...	3,093	1,571	1,522	91	84	7	1	1	...
37. Skardu ...	...	2,417	1,343	1,074	127	110	17	59	33	26
Gilgit District ...	...	4,905	3,279	1,626	599	540	59	55	35	20
38. Gilgit ...	...	4,474	2,848	1,626	192	133	59	53	33	20
39. Gilgit Cantonment ...	...	431	431	...	407	407	...	2	2	...

V.

WITH POPULATION BY RELIGION.

Census 1931.

Jain.			Buddhist.			Muslim.			Christian.			Zoroastrian.			Others.		
Persons.	Males.	Females.	Persons.	Males.	Females.	Persons.	Males.	Females.	Persons.	Males.	Females.	Persons.	Males.	Females.	Persons.	Males.	Females.
12	13	14	15	16	17	18	19	20	21	22	23	24	25	26	27	28	29
—	—	—	—	—	—	3,365	2,008	1,357	—	..	..	—	—	—	—	—	—
—	—	—	—	—	—	2,690	1,580	1,110	..	—	..	—	—	—	..	..	—
—	—	—	—	—	—	675	428	247	..	—	—	—	..	..	—	..	—
—	—	—	1,693	841	852	7,703	4,511	3,192	87	38	49	—	—	—	—	—	—
—	—	—	1,693	841	852	3,462	1,811	1,651	77	34	43	—	..	..	—	..	—
—	—	—	,689	837	852	1,235	615	620	77	34	43	—	..	—	—	—	..
—	—	—	4	4	—	2,227	1,196	1,031	—	—	—	—	—	—	—	—	—
—	—	—	—	—	—	4,241	2,700	1,541	10	4	6	—	—	—	—	—	..
—	—	—	—	—	—	4,219	2,678	1,541	10	4	6	—	..	—	—	—	—
—	—	—	—	—	—	22	22	—	..	—	—	—	—	—	—	—	—

TABLE VI.

Birth Place.

Jammu and Kashmir Census 1931.

The population of the Jammu Railway Station has been included in the District figures for purposes of this table.

2. The totals shown against "French and Portuguese Settlements" and against "India unspecified" are not included in II (b).

3. Asia and Africa unspecified have been shown as separate sub-heads to "Born in Asia or Africa" and their figures are not included in (ii) outside British Dominions.

TABLE

BIRTH

Jammu and Kashmir

District, State, Province or Country where born.	Population of the State.			District, Jagir, Ilaqa or City where enumerated. Jammu District.			Kathua District.		
	Persons.	Males.	Females.	Persons.	Males.	Females.	Persons.	Males.	Females.
1	2	3	4	5	6	7	8	9	10
Kashmir State ..	36,46,243	19,38,338	17,07,905	3,36,766	1,82,491	1,54,275	1,61,232	85,993	75,239
A.—Born in India ..	36,43,236	19,36,284	17,06,952	3,36,638	1,82,398	1,54,240	1,61,167	85,942	75,225
I. Born in District Ilaqa or Jagirs within the State territories ..	35,82,047	19,08,041	16,74,006	3,13,933	1,73,722	1,40,211	1,51,327	81,576	69,751
Jammu Province.									
(a) Districts.									
Jammu ..	3,43,295	1,90,474	1,52,821	3,02,967	1,68,689	1,34,278	3,396	1,478	1,918
Kathua ..	1,49,049	79,988	69,061	2,265	775	1,490	1,44,894	78,237	66,657
Udhampur (including Badhrawah) ..	2,75,441	1,44,101	1,31,340	2,226	1,028	1,198	2,740	1,633	1,107
Riasi ..	2,32,696	1,22,495	1,10,201	2,728	1,144	1,584	65	41	24
Mirpur ..	3,56,499	1,86,978	1,69,521	2,542	1,199	1,343	70	58	12
Total Districts (a) ..	*13,56,980*	*7,24,036*	*6,32,944*	*3,12,728*	*1,72,835*	*1,39,893*	*1,51,165*	*81,447*	*69,718*
(b) Jagirs.									
Poonch ..	3,67,277	1,88,062	1,79,215	143	88	55	14	9	5
Chenani ..	9,307	5,081	4,226	21	13	8	1	1	....
Total Jagirs (b) ..	*3,76,584*	*1,93,143*	*1,83,441*	*164*	*101*	*63*	*15*	*10*	*5*
Total Jammu Province ..	*17,33,564*	*9,17,179*	*8,16,385*	*3,12,892*	*1,72,936*	*1,39,956*	*1,51,180*	*81,457*	*69,723*
Kashmir Province.									
Baramulla (Kashmir North) ..	5,55,521	2,99,712	2,55,809	23	19	4	3	3	....
Srinagar ,, South) ..	7,72,749	4,20,574	3,52,175	942	709	233	135	108	27
Muzaffarabad ..	2,34,825	1,24,586	1,10,239	26	18	8	5	4	1
Total Kashmir Province ..	*15,63,095*	*8,44,872*	*7,18,223*	*991*	*746*	*245*	*143*	*115*	*28*
Frontier Districts.									
Ladakh ..	1,92,367	96,368	95,999	14	8	6	2	2	....
Gilgit ..	29,995	16,106	13,898	36	32	4	2	2	....
Frontier Ilaqas ..	63,026	33,516	29,510	....	....	....	....	....	....
Total Frontier Districts ..	*2,85,388*	*1,46,990*	*1,39,398*	*50*	*40*	*10*	*4*	*4*	....
II.—Provinces and States in India beyond the Province of enumeration ..	61,172	28,226	32,946	22,704	8,675	14,029	9,840	4,366	5,474
(a) Adjacent Provinces and States.									
N. W. F. Province ..	6,384	3,759	2,625	42	27	15	11	6	5
Districts ..	6,384	3,759	2,625	42	27	15	11	6	5
Contiguous ..	4,453	2,527	1,926	11	6	5	....	....	....
Hazara ..	4,453	2,527	1,926	11	6	5	....	....	....
Non-contiguous ..	1,931	1,232	699	31	21	10	11	6	5
Bannu ..	22	18	4	1	1	....	....	....	....
Dera Ismail Khan ..	46	38	8	6	5	1	2	1	1
Kohat ..	27	19	8	....	....	....	....	....	....
Peshawar ..	636	505	131	22	13	9	6	3	3
N. W. F. P. Unspecified ..	1,200	652	548	2	2	....	3	2	1
Punjab.									
Districts ..	52,366	22,934	29,432	22,403	8,467	13,936	9,487	4,185	5,302
Contiguous ..	46,363	19,250	27,113	21,230	7,763	13,467	9,027	3,966	5,061
Gujrat ..	7,522	2,750	4,772	1,208	518	690	15	9	6
Gurdaspur ..	12,043	5,130	6,913	3,503	1,165	2,338	7,849	3,579	4,270
Jhelum ..	2,006	1,096	910	67	45	22	12	10	2
Kangra ..	2,070	798	1,272	659	88	571	736	163	573
Rawalpindi ..	2,287	1,413	874	85	50	35	17	11	6
Sialkot ..	20,435	8,063	12,372	15,708	5,897	9,811	398	194	204
Non-contiguous ..	6,003	3,684	2,319	1,173	704	469	460	219	241
Ambala ..	57	31	26	8	3	5	2	2	....
Amritsar ..	902	529	373	105	59	46	62	37	25
Campbellpur (Attock) ..	259	165	94	3	2	1	6	5	1
Dera Ghazi Khan ..	20	12	8	....	....	....	....	....	....
Ferozepur ..	103	55	48	9	6	3	7	3	4
Gujranwala ..	1,009	610	399	194	109	85	23	11	12
Gurgaon ..	9	3	6	1	1	....	1	....	1
Hissar ..	31	20	11	2	2	....	1	1	....
Hoshiarpur ..	722	425	297	192	133	59	221	73	148
Jhang ..	49	37	12	7	5	2	2	2	....
Jullunder ..	452	317	135	79	59	20	39	27	12
Karnal ..	54	41	13	6	3	3	3	3	....
Lahore ..	784	445	339	180	89	91	39	21	18
Lyallpur ..	281	153	128	144	78	66	18	11	7
Ludhiana ..	79	56	23	17	13	4	2	1	1
Mianwali ..	26	16	10	1	1	....	....	....	....
Montgomery ..	52	34	18	29	19	10	6	3	3
Multan ..	94	60	34	26	13	13	6	5	1
Muzaffargarh ..	14	7	7	2	2	....	....	....	....
Rohtak ..	37	32	5	13	11	2	4	4	....
Sargodah ..	297	186	111	73	42	31	4	4	....
Shahpur ..	55	28	27	....	....	....	....	....	....
Shiekhupura ..	122	76	46	60	33	27	7	5	2
Simla ..	90	49	41	4	3	1	7	1	6
Punjab unspecified ..	405	297	108	18	18	....	....	....	....

VI.

Place.

Census 1931.

District, Jagir, Ilaqa or City where enumerated.											
Udhampur District.			*Riasi District.*			*Mirpur District.*			*Jammu City.*		
Persons.	Males.	Females.	Persons.	Males.	Females.	Persons.	Males.	Females.	Persons.	Males.	Females.
11	12	13	14	15	16	17	18	19	20	21	22
2,73,668	**1,43,514**	**1,30,154**	**2,35,245**	**1,24,210**	**1,11,035**	**3,44,747**	**1,78,831**	**1,65,916**	**38,474**	**23,228**	**15,246**
2,73,627	**1,43,480**	**1,30,147**	**2,35,197**	**1,24,172**	**1,11,025**	**3,44,696**	**1,78,803**	**1,65,893**	**38,369**	**23,146**	**15,223**
2,72,119	**1,42,480**	**1,29,639**	**2,34,176**	**1,23,486**	**1,10,690**	**3,34,354**	**1,75,024**	**1,59,330**	**32,498**	**19,533**	**12,965**
2,381	1,270	1,111	3,362	1,485	1.877	2,103	651	1,452	26,740	15,198	11,542
1,138	449	689	75	52	23	37	28	9	394	276	118
2,63,717	1,37,889	1,25,828	2,324	1,017	1,307	116	91	25	1,225	868	357
1,717	697	1,020	2,22,050	1,17,344	1,0,4706	1,430	456	974	837	531	306
157	119	38	2,887	1,580	1,307	3,27,373	1,71,522	1,55,851	855	707	148
2,69,110	*1,40,424*	*1,28,686*	*2,30,698*	*1,21,478*	*1,09,220*	*3,31,059*	*1,72,748*	*1,58,311*	*30,051*	*17,580*	*12,471*
542	287	255	1,614	831	783	2,206	1,304	902	118	87	31
490	232	258	13	5	8	1	1	....	17	9	8
1,032	*519*	*513*	*1,627*	*836*	*791*	*2,207*	*1,305*	*902*	*135*	*96*	*39*
2,70,142	*1,40,943*	*1,29,199*	*2,32,325*	*1,22,314*	*1,10,011*	*3,33,266*	*1,74,053*	*1,59,213*	*30,186*	*17,676*	*12,510*
101	72	29	110	94	16	659	644	15	113	42	71
1,705	1,344	361	1,461	885	576	353	267	86	1,997	1,643	354
62	45	17	263	182	81	64	55	9	54	43	11
1,868	*1,461*	*407*	*1,834*	*1,161*	*673*	*1,076*	*966*	*110*	*2,164*	*1,728*	*436*
95	66	29	....	....	....	4	2	2	85	80	5
14	10	4	17	11	6	8	3	5	63	49	14
....	....	....	....	....	....	....	....	....	....	....	....
109	*76*	*33*	*17*	*11*	*6*	*12*	*5*	*7*	*148*	*129*	*19*
1,508	**1,000**	**508**	**1,021**	**686**	**335**	**10,342**	**3,779**	**6,563**	**5,871**	**3,613**	**2,258**
78	45	33	216	136	80	160	131	29	296	248	48
78	45	33	216	136	80	160	131	29	296	248	48
50	30	20	189	121	68	42	30	12	33	22	11
50	30	20	189	121	68	42	30	12	33	22	11
28	15	13	27	15	12	118	101	17	263	226	37
....	....	....	....	....	....	3	3	....	9	7	2
....	....	....	1	....	1	11	10	1	19	17	2
1	....	1	....	....	....	6	5	1	12	8	4
13	11	2	12	6	6	98	83	15	223	194	29
14	4	10	14	9	5	....	....	....	....	....	....
1,198	790	408	680	474	206	9.973	3.535	6,443	5.103	3,084	2,069
928	604	324	516	364	152	9,389	3,181	6,208	3,226	1,926	1,300
53	38	15	229	185	44	5,426	1,635	3,791	390	234	165
160	88	72	26	16	10	97	24	73	300	185	115
15	11	4	18	8	10	1,279	642	637	152	86	66
314	260	54	24	18	6	22	12	10	134	95	39
32	27	5	60	36	24	1,043	549	494	212	123	89
354	180	174	159	101	58	1,522	319	1,203	2,029	1,203	826
270	186	84	164	110	54	589	354	235	1.877	1,108	769
4	2	2	1	1	....	7	3	4	19	12	7
46	33	13	19	11	8	51	28	23	325	170	155
3	2	1	7	7	....	12	9	3	27	16	11
....	....	....	....	....	....	2	2	....	9	6	3
3	2	1	1	1	....	33	18	15	32	17	15
23	14	9	43	29	14	110	69	41	506	304	202
....	....	....	....	....	....	3	1	2	4	1	3
3	1	2	1	1	....	19	13	6	1	....	1
47	33	14	13	10	3	22	10	12	111	70	41
2	2	....	....	....	....	4	2	2	33	25	8
34	21	13	11	6	5	52	38	14	148	101	47
3	3	....	1	1	....	24	18	6	14	11	3
36	22	14	27	18	9	37	18	19	363	196	167
2	2	....	7	2	5	51	25	26	49	28	21
9	8	1	1	1	....	10	7	3	21	10	11
....	....	....	....	....	....	12	8	4	9	4	5
1	1	....	....	....	....	7	5	2	7	5	2
3	3	....	16	10	6	8	5	3	24	14	10
1	1	....	....	....	....	5	2	3	6	2	4
....	....	....	....	....	....	7	6	1	9	8	1
11	7	4	11	8	3	71	41	30	121	83	38
....	....	....	....	....	....	....	....	....	....	....	....
4	4	....	2	2	....	16	9	7	28	19	7
30	21	9	3	2	1	3	2	1	13	6	7
5	4	1	....	....	....	23	15	8	....	....	....

TABLE

BIRTH

Jammu and Kashmir

District, State, Province or Country where born.	Poonch Jagir.			Chenani Jagir.			Baramulla including Langet. Kashmir North.			Srinagar Kashmir South.		
	Persons.	Males.	Females.	Persons.	Males.	Females.	Persons.	Males.	Females.	Persons.	Males.	Females.
	23	24	25	26	27	28	29	30	31	32	33	34
Kashmir State ..	3,87,384	1,98,618	1,88,766	10,925	5,930	4.995	5,59,828	3,01,397	2,58,431	5,98,370	3,24,397	2,73,973
A.—Born in India ..	3,87,358	1,98,602	1,88.756	10,924	5,929	4.995	5,59,760	3.01,362	2,58,398	5,97,814	3,24,071	2,73,743
I. Born in District Ilaqa or Jagir within the State territories ..	3,86,222	1,97,815	1,88,407	10.772	5,802	4.970	5.57.592	3.00.171	2,57,421	5,95,761	3,22,927	2,72,834
Jammu Province.												
(a) Districts												
Jammu ..	457	260	197	132	81	51	84	54	30	385	297	88
Kathua ..	8	6	2	38	15	23	8	6	2	46	33	13
Udhampur including Badhrawah) ..	37	20	17	1,609	704	905	35	22	13	1,047	560	487
Riasi ..	2,142	1,135	1,007	53	33	20	51	38	13	1,361	841	520
Mirpur ..	22,279	11,542	10,737	7	5	2	77	48	29	69	59	10
Total Districts (a) ..	*24,923*	*12,963*	*11,960*	*1,839*	*838*	*1,001*	*255*	*168*	*87*	*2,908*	*1,790*	*1,118*
(b) Jagirs												
Poonch ..	3,60,705	1,84,449	1,76,256	46	29	17	657	383	274	285	153	132
Chenani ..	....	....	....	8,758	4,817	3,941	....	....	....	2	....	2
Total Jagirs (b) ..	*3,60,705*	*1,84,449*	*1,76,256*	*8,804*	*4,846*	*3,958*	*657*	*383*	*274*	*287*	*153*	*134*
Total Jammu Province ..	*3,85,628*	*1,97,412*	*1,88,216*	*10,643*	*5,684*	*4,959*	*912*	*551*	*361*	*3,195*	*1,943*	*1,252*
Kashmir Province.												
Baramulla(Kashmir North)..	77	50	27	11	6	5	5,50,736	2,96,311	2,54,425	1,031	575	456
Srinagar (,, South)..	247	173	74	108	106	2	4,536	2,572	1,964	5,90,770	3,19,962	2,70,808
Muzaffarabad ..	220	132	88	6	3	3	1,299	668	631	392	219	173
Total Kashmir Province ..	*544*	*355*	*189*	*125*	*115*	*10*	*5,56,571*	*2,99,551*	*2,57,020*	*5,92,193*	*3,20,756*	*2,71,437*
Frontier Districts.												
Ladakh ..	21	21	....	1	..	1	38	26	12	272	171	101
Gilgit ..	29	27	2	3	3	....	64	39	25	81	45	36
Frontier Ilaqas ..	....	....	....	....	..	....	7	4	3	20	12	8
Total Frontier Districts ..	*50*	*48*	*2*	*4*	*3*	*1*	*109*	*69*	*40*	*373*	*228*	*145*
II. Provinces and States in India beyond the Provinces of enumeration ..	1,136	787	349	152	127	25	2.167	1,190	977	2,053	1,144	909
(a) Adjacent Provinces and States												
N. W. F. Province ..	161	108	53	17	11	6	1,569	795	774	1,805	970	835
Districts ..	161	108	53	17	11	6	1,569	795	774	1,805	970	835
Contiguous ..	117	74	43	14	8	6	1,533	769	764	659	350	309
Hazara ..	117	74	43	14	8	6	1,533	769	764	659	350	309
Non-contiguous ..	44	34	10	3	3	....	36	26	10	1,146	620	526
Bannu ..	2	1	1	....	..	....	....	....	....	....	....	....
Dera Ismail Khan ..	....	....	....	....	..	....	1	1	....	....	....	....
Kohat ..	6	4	2	....	..	....	1	1	....	....	....	....
Peshawar ..	36	29	7	3	3	....	34	24	10	9	5	4
N. W. F. P. Unspecified ..	....	....	....	....	..	....	....	....	....	1,137	615	522
Punjab.												
Districts ..	903	630	273	94	80	14	533	349	184	212	142	70
Contiguous ..	790	556	234	77	68	9	233	161	72	85	52	33
Gujrat ..	61	47	14	2	2	....	27	19	8	20	13	7
Gurdaspur ..	22	14	8	12	8	4	3	3	....	3	3	....
Jhelum ..	277	185	92	4	1	3	51	32	19	12	7	5
Kangra ..	28	17	11	47	47	....	4	3	1	10	7	3
Rawalpindi ..	359	265	94	4	3	1	127	88	39	20	16	4
Sialkot ..	43	28	15	8	7	1	21	16	5	20	6	14
Non-contiguous ..	113	74	39	17	12	5	300	188	112	127	90	37
Ambala ..	....	....	....	1	..	1	....	....	....	....	....	....
Amritsar ..	12	8	4	4	4	....	55	28	27	25	13	12
Campbelpur (Attock) ..	28	19	9	....	..	....	94	56	38	....	....	....
Dera Ghazi Khan ..	....	....	....	....	..	....	....	....	....	....	....	....
Ferozepur ..	....	....	....	1	1	....	....	....	....	1	....	1
Gujranwala ..	19	14	5	3	..	3	13	9	4	5	3	2
Gurgaon ..	....	....	....	....	..	....	....	....	....	....	....	....
Hissar ..	1	1	....	....	..	....	....	....	....	....	....	....
Hoshiarpur ..	10	5	5	....	..	....	5	4	1	4	4	....
Jhang ..	....	....	....	1	1	....	....	....	....	....	....	....
Jullundur ..	7	4	3	3	3	....	7	6	1	29	21	8
Karnal ..	....	....	....	....	..	....	1	1	....	....	....	....
Lahore ..	13	8	5	3	3	....	6	6	....	14	13	1
Lyallpur ..	2	2	....	....	..	....	1	....	1	1	1	....
Ludhiana ..	1	1	....	....	..	....	2	2	....	9	7	2
Mianwali ..	2	1	1	....	..	....	2	2	....	....	....	....
Montgomery ..	....	....	....	....	..	....	....	....	....	....	....	....
Multan ..	2	2	....	....	..	....	3	3	....	1	1	....
Muzaffargarh ..	....	....	....	....	..	....	....	....	....	....	....	....
Rohtak ..	....	....	....	....	..	....	....	....	....	....	....	....
Sargodah ..	6	1	5	....	..	....	....	....	....	....	....	....
Shahpur ..	....	....	....	....	..	....	16	8	8	....	....	....
Shiekhupura ..	2	2	....	....	..	....	2	....	2	....	....	....
Simla ..	3	1	2	1	..	1	1	1	....	4	2	9
Punjab unspecified ..	5	5	....	....	..	....	92	62	30	34	25	2

VI—*(continued)*.

PLACE.

Census 1931.

District, Jagir, Ilaqa or City where enumerated.														
Muzaffarabad District.			*Ladakh District.*			*Gilgit District.*			*Frontier Ilaqas.*			*Srinagar City.*		
Persons.	Males.	Females.	Persons.	Males.	Females.	Persons.	Males.	Females.	Persons.	Males.	Females.	Persons.	Males.	Females.
35	36	37	38	39	40	41	42	43	44	45	46	47	48	49
2,37,447	1,26,435	1,11,012	1,92,138	96,259	95,879	31,902	17,752	14,150	64,544	34,490	30,054	1,73,573	94,793	78,780
2,37,390	1,26,396	1,10,994	1,91,977	96,122	95,855	31,051	17,058	13,993	64,038	34,202	29,836	1,73,230	94,601	78,629
2,34,943	1,24,803	1,10,140	1,91,844	96,027	95,817	30,820	16,903	13,917	63,591	33,911	29,680	1,72,095	93,861	78,234
94	71	23	41	39	2	417	388	29	194	140	54	542	373	169
20	14	6	13	9	4	33	28	5	79	60	19	1	....	1
45	29	16	59	44	15	74	69	5	122	78	44	65	49	16
26	18	8	43	41	2	106	106	....	52	52	....	35	18	17
67	45	22	8	5	3	53	49	4	20	15	5	35	25	10
252	*177*	*75*	*164*	*138*	*26*	*683*	*640*	*43*	*467*	*345*	*122*	*678*	*465*	*213*
806	343	463	1	1	....	28	28	....	4	4	....	108	66	42
......	....	....	....	....	....	....	....	....	....	....	....	4	3	1
806	*343*	*463*	*1*	*1*	....	*28*	*28*	....	*4*	*4*	....	*112*	*69*	*43*
1,058	*520*	*538*	*166*	*139*	*26*	*711*	*668*	*43*	*471*	*349*	*122*	*790*	*534*	*256*
989	731	258	10	7	3	161	135	26	5	2	3	1,492	1,021	471
729	550	179	241	182	59	128	102	26	73	44	29	1,69,324	91,927	77,397
2,32,143	1,22,987	1,09,156	4	3	1	10	10	....	3	....	3	274	217	57
2,33,861	*1,24,268*	*1,09,593*	*255*	*192*	*63*	*299*	*247*	*52*	*81*	*46*	*35*	*1,71,090*	*93,165*	*77,925*
5	4	1	1,91,393	95,677	95,716	259	200	59	55	30	25	123	81	42
9	7	2	31	19	12	29,547	15,784	13,763	5	....	5	86	75	11
10	4	6	....	....	....	4	4	....	62,979	33,486	29,493	6	6	....
24	*15*	*9*	*1,91,424*	*95,696*	*95,728*	*29,810*	*15,988*	*13,822*	*63,039*	*33,516*	*29,523*	*215*	*162*	*53*
2,447	**1,593**	**854**	**133**	**95**	**38**	**230**	**154**	**76**	**447**	**291**	**156**	**1,121**	**726**	**395**
1,735	1,064	671	....	....	....	71	56	15	157	121	36	66	41	25
1,735	1,064	671	....	....	....	71	56	15	157	121	36	66	41	25
1,691	1,033	658	....	....	....	33	24	9	58	49	9	23	11	12
1,691	1,033	658	....	....	....	33	24	9	58	49	9	23	11	12
44	31	13	....	....	....	38	32	6	99	72	27	43	30	13
1	1	....	....	....	....	....	....	....	5	5	....	1	....	1
......	....	....	....	....	....	....	....	....	2	2	....	4	2	2
1	1	....	....	....	....	....	....	....	....	....	....	....	....	....
25	18	7	....	....	....	35	32	3	92	65	27	28	19	9
17	11	6	....	....	....	3	....	3	....	....	....	10	9	1
624	464	160	120	89	31	115	75	40	92	61	31	824	559	265
420	320	100	34	16	18	63	44	19	59	42	17	286	187	99
39	26	13	1	....	1	....	....	....	5	4	1	37	20	17
38	25	13	2	2	....	9	6	3	2	1	1	17	11	6
37	23	14	23	8	15	17	10	7	2	1	1	40	27	13
72	72	....	5	3	2	2	2	....	3	3	....	10	8	2
194	151	43	3	3	....	7	5	2	4	2	2	120	84	36
40	23	17	....	....	....	28	21	7	43	31	12	62	37	25
204	144	60	86	73	13	52	31	21	33	19	14	538	372	166
....	....	....	1	1	....	2	1	1	....	....	....	12	6	6
15	12	3	2	1	1	13	8	5	....	....	....	168	117	51
72	43	29	4	4	....	1	1	....	....	....	....	2	1	1
....	....	....	....	....	....	8	3	5	....	....	....	1	1	....
7	5	2	....	....	....	....	....	....	....	....	....	9	2	7
16	10	6	1	1	....	12	8	4	....	....	....	41	29	12
....	....	....	....	....	....	....	....	....	....	....	....	....	....	....
3	1	2	....	....	....	....	....	....	....	....	....	....	....	....
36	32	4	29	28	1	....	....	....	1	1	....	31	22	9
....	....	....	....	....	....	....	....	....	....	....	....	....	....	....
11	11	....	2	1	1	5	2	3	....	....	....	25	17	8
....	....	....	....	....	....	1	1	....	....	....	....	1	....	1
17	12	5	2	1	1	....	....	....	....	....	....	47	38	9
5	3	2	1	1	....	....	....	....	....	....	....	....	....	....
1	1	....	3	2	1	2	2	....	....	....	....	1	1	....
....	....	....	....	....	....	....	....	....	....	....	....	....	....	....
....	....	....	....	....	....	....	....	....	....	....	....	2	1	1
1	1	....	1	1	....	....	....	....	....	....	....	3	2	1
....	....	....	....	....	....	....	....	....	....	....	....	....	....	....
....	....	....	1	1	....	....	....	....	....	....	....	3	2	1
....	....	....	....	....	....	....	....	....	....	....	....	....	....	....
8	4	4	2	1	1	4	3	1	4	2	2	21	10	11
1	1	....	....	....	....	....	....	....	....	....	....	2	1	1
1	....	1	5	2	3	....	....	....	3	3	....	12	5	7
10	8	2	32	28	4	4	2	2	25	13	12	157	117	40

TABLE

Birth

Jammu and Kashmir

District, State, Province or Country where born.	Population of the State.			District, Jagir, Ilaqa or City where enumerated.					
				Jammu District.			Kathua District.		
	Persons.	Males.	Females.	Persons.	Males.	Females.	Persons.	Males.	Females.
1	2	3	4	5	6	7	8	9	10
II. Feudatory States ..	**756**	**437**	**319**	**35**	**26**	**9**	**287**	**138**	**149**
N. W. F. P. States ..	88	49	39	....	....	....	....	....	....
Bhawalpur ..	8	5	3	....	....	....	....	....	....
Chamba ..	459	242	217	8	5	3	278	133	145
Bilaspur ..	1	....	1	....	....	....	....	....	....
Jind ..	5	3	2	2	....	2	....	....	....
Kapurthala ..	52	31	21	12	10	2	1	....	1
Mundi ..	55	53	2	1	....	1	2	2	....
Nabha ..	15	10	5	....	....	....	....	....	....
Patiala ..	71	42	29	12	11	1	6	3	3
Soket ..	2	2	....	....	....	....	....	....	....
(b) Other Provinces and States in India ..	**1,539**	**1,026**	**513**	**199**	**148**	**51**	**55**	**37**	**18**
I. British territory ..	**1,369**	**903**	**466**	**178**	**131**	**47**	**45**	**31**	**14**
Ajmer Morwara ..	6	4	2	1	....	1	1	....	1
Assam ..	7	2	5	....	....	....	....	....	....
Balochistan ..	93	54	39	....	....	....	1	1	....
Bengal ..	111	67	44	16	11	5	6	3	3
Bihar and Orissa ..	23	15	8	6	4	2	....	....	....
Bombay ..	180	109	71	19	10	9	2	1	1
Burma ..	29	14	15	2	1	1	3	3	....
C. P. and Berar ..	45	32	13	6	4	2	3	2	1
Delhi ..	83	57	26	16	12	4	4	2	2
Madras ..	33	25	8	3	3	....	....	....	....
U. P. of Agra and Oudh ..	759	524	235	109	86	23	25	19	6
II. Feudatory States ..	**170**	**123**	**47**	**21**	**17**	**4**	**10**	**6**	**4**
Baroda ..	22	15	7	2	1	1	....	....	....
Bombay States ..	19	12	7	2	1	1	3	....	3
C. I. Agency ..	11	8	3	....	....	....	....	....	....
Gowalior ..	22	19	3	5	4	1	5	5	....
Hyderabad ..	19	14	5	....	....	....	....	....	....
Mysore ..	2	2	....	....	....	....	....	....	....
Rajputana Agency ..	64	50	14	12	11	1	2	1	1
Sikkim State ..	2	1	1	....	....	....	....	....	....
U. P. States ..	9	2	7	....	....	....	....	....	....
(c) French and Portuguese Settlements ..	**17**	**17**	....	**1**	**1**	....	....	....	....
(d) India unspecified ..	**127**	**70**	**57**	**25**	**7**	**18**	....	....	....
B. Born in other Asiatic Countries ..	**2,786**	**1,961**	**825**	**127**	**93**	**34**	**65**	**51**	**14**
I. Within British Dominions ..	**6**	**5**	**1**	....	....	....	....	....	....
Ceylon ..	5	4	1	....	....	....	....	....	....
Straits Settlements and Malaya ..	1	1	....	....	....	....	....	....	....
II. Outside British Dominions ..	**2,779**	**1,956**	**823**	**127**	**93**	**34**	**65**	**51**	**14**
Afganistan ..	1,607	1,026	581	30	29	1	1	1	....
China ..	5	1	4	....	....	....	....	....	....
Nepal ..	974	765	209	97	64	33	64	50	14
Elsewhere ..	193	164	29	....	....	....	....	....	....
III. Asia unspecified ..	**1**	....	**1**	....	....	....	....	....	....
C. Born in Europe ..	**183**	**84**	**99**	**1**	....	**1**	....	....	....
I. United Kingdom and Ireland	**146**	**64**	**82**	**1**	....	**1**	....	....	....
II. British possessions in Europe	**1**	....	**1**	....	....	....	....	....	....
III. Continental Europe ..	**32**	**17**	**15**	....	....	....	....	....	....
IV. Europe unspecified ..	**4**	**3**	**1**	....	....	....	....	....	....
D. Born in Africa ..	**9**	**2**	**7**	....	....	....	....	....	....
I. Within British Dominions ..	**1**	**1**	....	....	....	....	....	....	....
Cape Colony ..	1	1	....	....	....	....	....	....	....
II. Outside British Dominions ..	**1**	**1**	....	....	....	....	....	....	....
Elsewhere ..	1	1	....	....	....	....	....	....	....
III. Africa unspecified ..	**7**	....	**7**	....	....	....	....	....	....
E. Born in America ..	**12**	**4**	**8**	....	....	....	....	....	....
I. Within British Dominion ..	**10**	**3**	**7**	....	....	....	....	....	....
Canada ..	10	3	7	....	....	....	....	....	....
II. Outside British Dominion ..	**2**	**1**	**1**	....	....	....	....	....	....
United States ..	2	1	1	....	....	....	....	....	....
F. Born in Australasia ..	**17**	**3**	**14**	....	....	....	....	....	....
I. Within British Dominions ..	**17**	**3**	**14**	....	....	....	....	....	....
Australia ..	12	3	9	....	....	....	....	....	....
New-zealand ..	3	....	3	....	....	....	....	....	....
Tasmania ..	2	....	2	....	....	....	....	....	....

VI—*(continued)*.

PLACE.

Census 1931.

District, Jagir, Ilaqa or City where enumerated.											
Udhampur District.			*Riasi District.*			*Mirpur District.*			*Jammu City.*		
Persons.	Males.	Females.	Persons.	Males.	Females.	Persons.	Males.	Females.	Persons.	Males.	Females.
11	12	13	14	15	16	17	18	19	20	21	22
168	110	58	10	4	6	39	22	17	71	43	28
....	....	....	....	....	....	....	....	....	....	....	....
....	....	....	....	....	....	5	2	3	2	2	....
142	86	56	9	4	5	1	1	....	11	8	3
....	....	....	1	....	1	....	....	....	....	....	....
....	....	....	....	....	....	....	....	....	1	1	....
2	2	....	....	....	....	6	4	2	24	13	11
22	22	....	....	....	....	....	....	....	....	....	....
....	....	....	....	....	....	7	2	5	7	7	....
2	....	2	....	....	....	20	13	7	26	12	14
....	....	....	....	....	....	....	....	....	....	....	....
64	55	9	111	69	42	165	91	74	401	288	113
59	51	8	105	63	42	144	77	67	338	240	98
1	1	....	....	....	....	....	....	....	2	2	....
....	....	....	....	....	....	2	....	2	....	....	....
4	3	1	27	11	16	1	....	1	27	17	10
4	4	....	....	....	....	6	3	3	31	20	11
....	....	....	1	1	....	3	1	2	3	2	1
4	4	....	37	16	21	17	10	7	10	7	3
....	....	....	1	1	....	13	4	9	4	2	2
....	....	....	4	3	1	9	4	5	6	6	....
7	7	....	4	2	2	6	2	4	26	17	9
2	2	....	....	....	....	8	4	4	5	3	2
37	30	7	31	29	2	79	49	30	224	164	60
5	4	1	6	6	....	21	14	7	63	48	15
....	....	....	1	1	....	3	1	2	15	11	4
2	2	....	....	....	....	2	2	....	7	5	2
....	....	....	....	....	....	....	....	....	....	....	....
1	1	....	1	1	....	2	1	1	4	4	....
....	....	....	....	....	....	2	1	1	12	8	4
....	....	....	....	....	....	....	....	....	....	....	....
2	1	1	4	4	....	12	9	3	25	20	5
....	....	....	....	....	....	....	....	....	....	....	....
....	....	....	....	....	....	....	....	....	....	....	....
....	....	....	....	....	....	....	....	....	....	....	....
....	....	....	4	3	1	....	....	....	....	....	....
40	33	7	47	37	10	31	25	6	94	75	19
1	1	....	....	....	....	....	....	....	3	2	1
1	1	....	....	....	....	....	....	....	3	2	1
....	....	....	....	....	....	....	....	....	....	....	....
39	32	7	47	37	10	31	25	6	91	73	18
14	14	....	19	13	6	16	16	....	29	22	7
1	1	....	....	....	....	2	....	2	....	....	....
22	15	7	28	24	4	10	7	3	62	51	11
2	2	....	....	....	....	3	2	1	....	....	....
....	....	....	....	....	....	....	....	....	....	....	....
1	1	....	1	1	....	3	2	1	8	6	2
....	....	....	1	1	....	3	2	1	6	5	1
....	....	....	....	....	....	....	....	....	....	....	....
....	....	....	....	....	....	....	....	....	....	....	....
1	1	....	....	....	....	....	....	....	2	1	1
....	....	....	....	....	....	....	....	....	....	....	....
....	....	....	....	....	....	7	....	7	....	....	....
....	....	....	....	....	....	....	....	....	....	....	....
....	....	....	....	....	....	....	....	....	....	....	....
....	....	....	....	....	....	....	....	....	....	....	....
....	....	....	....	....	....	....	....	....	....	....	....
....	....	....	....	....	....	7	....	7	....	....	....
....	....	....	....	....	....	....	....	....	3	1	2
....	....	....	....	....	....	....	....	....	3	1	2
....	....	....	....	....	....	....	....	....	3	1	2
....	....	....	....	....	....	....	....	....	....	....	....
....	....	....	....	....	....	....	....	....	....	....	....
....	....	....	....	....	....	10	1	9	....	....	....
....	....	....	....	....	....	10	1	9	....	....	....
....	....	....	....	....	....	8	1	7	....	....	....
....	....	....	....	....	....	2	....	2	....	....	....
....	....	....	....	....	....	....	....	....	....	....	....

TABLE

BIRTH

Jammu and Kashmir

District, State, Province or Country where born.	District, Jagir, Ilaqa or City where enumerated.											
	Poonch Jagir.			*Chenani Jagir.*			*Baramulla including Langet.* *Kashmir North.*			*Srinagar.* *Kashmir South.*		
	Persons.	Males.	Females.	Persons.	Males.	Females.	Persons.	Males.	Females.	Persons.	Males.	Females.
	23	24	25	26	27	28	29	30	31	32	33	34
II. Feudatory States ..	10	9	1	32	28	4	2	1	1	....	....	....
N. W. F. P. States ..	....	....	....	....	....	....	....	....	....	....	....	....
Bhawalpur ..	....	....	....	....	....	....	....	....	....	....	....	....
Chamba ..	....	....	....	8	4	4	....	....	....	....	....	....
Bilaspur ..	....	....	....	....	....	....	....	....	....	....	....	....
Jind ..	....	....	....	....	....	....	1	1	....	....	....	....
Kapurthala ..	....	....	....	1	1	....	1	....	1	....	....	....
Mundi ..	8	7	1	21	21	....	....	....	....	....	....	....
Nabha ..	....	....	....	....	....	....	....	....	....	....	....	....
Patiala ..	....	....	....	2	2	....	....	....	....	....	....	....
Soket ..	2	2	....	....	....	....	....	....	....	....	....	....
(b) Other Provinces and States in India ..	62	40	22	9	8	1	47	35	12	34	30	4
I. British territory ..	58	36	22	9	8	1	44	32	12	31	27	4
Ajmer Merwara ..	....	....	....	....	....	....	....	....	....	....	....	....
Assam ..	....	....	....	....	....	....	....	....	....	....	....	....
Balochistan ..	3	3	....	....	....	....	15	9	6	....	....	....
Bengal ..	2	2	....	2	2	....	5	4	1	2	2	....
Bihar and Orissa ..	1	1	....	1	1	....	....	....	....	1	1	....
Bombay ..	15	9	6	1	1	....	2	2	....	1	1	....
Burma ..	1	....	1	....	....	....	....	....	....	2	2	....
C. P. and Berar ..	1	....	1	....	....	....	9	7	2	1	1	....
Delhi ..	1	1	....	....	....	....	1	....	1	1	1	....
Madras ..	....	....	....	....	....	....	1	1	....	4	3	1
U. P. of Agra and Oudh ..	34	20	14	5	4	1	11	9	2	19	16	3
II. Feudatory States ..	4	4	....	....	....	....	3	3	....	3	3	....
Baroda ..	....	....	....	....	....	....	....	....	....	....	....	....
Bombay States ..	....	....	....	....	....	....	....	....	....	....	....	....
C. I. Agency ..	....	....	....	....	....	....	2	2	....	1	1	....
Gowalior ..	....	....	....	....	....	....	....	....	....	1	1	....
Hyderabad ..	4	4	....	....	....	....	....	....	....	1	1	....
Mysore ..	....	....	....	....	....	....	1	1	....	....	....	....
Rajputana Agency ..	....	....	....	....	....	....	....	....	....	....	....	....
Sikkim State ..	....	....	....	....	....	....	....	....	....	....	....	....
U. P. States ..	....	....	....	....	....	....	....	....	....	....	....	....
(c) French and Portuguese Settlements ..	....	....	....	....	....	....	1	1	....	....	....	....
(d) India unspecified ..	....	....	....	....	....	....	16	10	6	2	2	....
B. Born in other Asiatic Countries ..	19	13	6	1	1	....	45	28	17	550	324	226
I. Within British Dominions ..	1	1	....	....	....	....	1	1	....	....	....	....
Ceylon ..	....	....	....	....	....	....	1	1	....	....	....	....
Straits Settlements and Malaya ..	1	1	....	....	....	....	....	....	....	....	....	....
II. Outside British Dominions ..	18	12	6	1	1	....	44	27	17	550	324	226
Afganistan ..	17	12	5	1	1	....	30	18	12	350	174	176
China ..	....	....	....	....	....	....	....	....	....	....	....	....
Nepal ..	....	....	....	....	....	....	13	8	5	194	144	50
Elsewhere ..	1	....	1	....	....	....	1	1	....	6	6	....
III. Asia unspecified ..	....	....	....	....	....	....	....	....	....	....	....	....
C. Born in Eurode ..	1	1	....	....	....	....	23	7	16	4	2	2
I. United Kingdom and Ireland	1	1	....	....	....	....	11	5	6	3	1	2
II. British possessions in Europe	....	....	....	....	....	....	....	....	....	....	....	....
III. Continental Europe ..	....	....	....	....	....	....	12	2	10	1	1	....
IV. Europe unspecified ..	....	....	....	....	....	....	....	....	....	....	....	....
D. Born in Africa ..	....	....	....	....	....	....	....	....	....	....	....	....
I. Within British Dominions ..	....	....	....	....	....	....	....	....	....	....	....	....
Cape Colony ..	....	....	....	....	....	....	....	....	....	....	....	....
II. Outside British Dominions ..	....	....	....	....	....	....	....	....	....	....	....	....
Elsewhere ..	....	....	....	....	....	....	....	....	....	....	....	....
III. Africa unspecified ..	....	....	....	....	....	....	....	....	....	....	....	....
E. Born in America ..	6	2	4	....	....	....	....	....	....	....	....	....
I. Within British Dominions ..	6	2	4	....	....	....	....	....	....	....	....	....
Canada ..	6	2	4	....	....	....	....	....	....	....	....	....
II. Outside British Dominions ..	....	....	....	....	....	....	....	....	....	....	....	....
United States ..	....	....	....	....	....	....	....	....	....	....	....	....
F. Born in Australasia ..	....	....	....	....	....	....	....	....	....	....	....	....
I. Within British Dominions ..	....	....	....	....	....	....	....	....	....	2	....	2
Australia ..	....	....	....	....	....	....	....	....	....	2	....	2
New-zealand ..	....	....	....	....	....	....	....	....	....	....	....	....
Tasmania ..	....	....	....	....	....	....	....	....	....	2	....	2

VI.—(*concluded*).

PLACE.

Census 1931.

District, Jagir, Ilaqa or City where enumerated.														
Muzaffarabad District.			*Ladakh District.*			*Gilgit District.*			*Frontier Ilaqas.*			*Srinagar City.*		
Persons.	Males.	Females.	Persons.	Males.	Females.	Persons.	Males.	Females.	Persons.	Males.	Females.	Persons.	Males.	Females.
35	36	37	38	39	40	41	42	43	44	45	46	47	48	49
8	7	1	...	...	...	8	6	2	79	42	37	7	1	6
1	1	...	...	...	...	8	6	2	79	42	37	...	...	...
1	1	...	...	...	...	...	...	...	...	...	...	...	...	...
2	1	1	...	...	...	...	...	...	...	...	...	...	...	...
...	...	...	...	...	...	...	...	...	...	...	...	...	...	...
1	1	...	...	...	...	...	...	...	...	...	...	...	...	...
1	1	...	...	...	...	...	...	...	...	...	...	4	...	4
...	...	...	...	...	...	...	...	...	...	...	...	1	1	...
1	1	...	...	...	...	...	...	...	...	...	...	...	...	...
1	1	...	...	...	...	...	...	...	...	...	...	2	...	2
...	...	...	...	...	...	...	...	...	...	...	...	...	...	...
75	54	21	11	5	6	29	13	16	104	56	48	173	97	76
74	53	21	7	2	5	23	12	11	99	53	46	155	87	68
...	...	...	...	...	...	...	...	...	...	...	...	1	1	...
...	...	...	...	...	...	1	1	...	...	...	...	4	1	3
4	1	3	...	...	...	...	...	...	5	5	...	6	4	2
2	...	2	...	...	...	2	2	...	1	1	...	32	13	19
...	...	...	...	...	...	...	...	...	...	...	...	7	4	3
19	17	2	...	...	...	5	2	3	39	22	17	9	7	2
...	...	...	...	...	...	...	...	...	...	...	...	3	1	2
6	5	1	...	...	...	...	...	...	...	...	...	...	...	...
3	3	...	1	...	1	1	...	1	...	...	...	12	10	2
...	...	...	...	...	...	...	...	...	...	...	...	10	9	1
40	27	13	6	2	4	14	7	7	34	25	29	71	37	34
1	1	...	4	3	1	6	1	5	5	3	2	18	10	8
...	...	...	...	...	...	...	...	...	...	...	...	1	1	...
...	...	...	...	...	...	...	...	...	...	...	...	3	2	1
1	1	...	2	1	1	...	...	...	1	1	...	4	2	2
...	...	...	...	...	...	...	...	...	...	...	...	3	2	1
...	...	...	...	...	...	...	...	...	...	...	...	...	...	...
...	...	...	...	...	...	1	1	...	...	...	...	...	...	...
...	...	...	2	2	...	...	...	...	...	...	...	5	2	3
...	...	...	...	...	...	...	...	...	...	...	...	2	1	1
...	...	...	...	...	...	5	...	5	4	2	2	...	...	...
...	...	...	...	...	...	1	1	...	...	...	...	14	14	...
5	4	1	2	1	1	7	4	3	15	11	4	51	28	28
45	31	14	151	131	20	843	692	151	496	281	215	232	146	86
...	...	...	...	...	...	...	...	...	...	...	...	...	...	...
...	...	...	...	...	...	...	...	...	...	...	...	...	...	...
...	...	...	...	...	...	...	...	...	...	...	...	...	...	...
45	31	14	151	131	20	842	692	150	496	281	215	232	146	86
41	29	12	...	...	...	514	371	143	496	281	215	49	45	4
...	...	...	1	...	1	...	...	...	...	...	...	1	...	1
1	1	...	1	1	...	312	311	1	...	...	...	170	89	81
3	1	2	149	130	19	16	10	6	...	...	...	12	12	...
...	...	...	...	...	...	1	...	1	...	...	...	...	...	...
12	8	4	9	5	4	8	2	6	9	6	3	103	43	60
6	3	3	3	1	2	8	2	6	9	6	3	94	37	57
...	...	...	...	...	...	...	...	...	...	...	...	1	...	1
5	4	1	6	4	2	...	...	...	...	...	...	6	5	1
1	1	...	...	...	...	...	...	...	...	...	...	2	1	1
...	...	...	1	1	...	...	...	...	...	...	...	1	1	...
...	...	...	1	1	...	...	...	...	...	...	...	...	...	...
...	...	...	1	1	...	...	...	...	...	...	...	...	...	...
...	...	...	...	...	...	...	...	...	...	...	...	1	1	...
...	...	...	...	...	...	...	...	...	...	...	...	1	1	...
...	...	...	...	...	...	...	...	...	...	...	...	...	...	...
...	...	...	...	...	...	...	...	...	...	...	...	3	1	2
...	...	...	...	...	...	...	...	...	...	...	...	1	...	1
...	...	...	...	...	...	...	...	...	...	...	...	1	...	1
...	...	...	...	...	...	...	...	...	...	...	...	2	1	1
...	...	...	...	...	...	...	...	...	...	...	...	2	1	1
...	...	...	...	...	...	...	...	...	1	1	...	4	1	3
...	...	...	...	...	...	...	...	...	1	1	...	4	1	3
...	...	...	...	...	...	...	...	...	1	1	...	3	1	2
...	...	...	...	...	...	...	...	...	...	...	...	1	...	1
...	...	...	...	...	...	...	...	...	...	...	...	...	...	...

TABLE VII.—Age, Sex and Civil Condition.

Jammu and Kashmir Census 1931.

1. This table has been divided into three parts each showing the distribution of population by Age, Sex and Civil condition.

Part (i) gives the details for the entire State and the different Provinces constituting it.

Part (ii) gives the details by Districts.

Part (iii) shows the civil condition for the two Cities (Jammu and Srinagar).

2. The Frontier Ilaqas which were excluded from this table at the last Census have been included in the current Census.

3. 134 persons (78 males and 56 females) classed as 'others' though not shown as a separate religion are included in the total population of the State in the column for 'All Religions'.

TABLE VII.—Age, Sex and Civil Condition.

Jammu and Kashmir Census 1931.

Religion.	Age	Population.			Unmarried.			Married.			Widowed.		
		Persons.	Males.	Females.	Persons.	Males.	Females.	Persons.	Males.	Females.	Persons.	Males.	Females.
1	2	3	4	5	6	7	8	9	10	11	12	13	14
							Entire State.						
All Religions.	*Total*	*3.646.243*	*1.938.338*	*1,707.905*	*1,715.299*	*1,025.160*	*690.139*	*1,633.533*	*799.073*	*834.460*	*297.411*	*114.105*	*183,306*
	0—1	115,930	58.323	57.607	115,930	58,323	57,607	....	....	....	....	....	....
	1—2	118,293	59.284	59.009	118.293	59,284	59.009	....	....	....	....	....	....
	2—3	117,890	59.099	58.791	117.889	59.099	58.790	1	....	1	....	....	....
	3—4	115,806	58.525	57.281	115.790	58.523	57,267	16	2	14	....	....	....
	4—5	111,623	56,700	54,923	111.446	56,617	54.829	166	82	84	11	1	10
	Total 0—5	*579,542*	*291,931*	*287.611*	*579,348*	*291,846*	*287,502*	*183*	*84*	*99*	*11*	*1*	*10*
	5—10	469,120	253,182	215,938	455,159	248,562	206,597	13,567	4,512	9,056	394	108	286
	10—15	429,988	234,021	195,967	374,136	221,797	152,339	54,482	11,877	42,605	1.370	347	1,023
	15—20	350,597	178,694	171,903	151,060	120,218	30.842	193.591	56.165	137.426	5.946	2,311	3.635
	20—25	364,687	182,675	182,012	87,522	80,253	7,269	266,638	97,466	169,172	10,527	4,956	5,571
	25—30	323,912	167,877	156,035	29,274	27,278	1,996	276,472	131,202	145,270	18,166	9,397	8,769
	30—35	287,468	156,681	130,787	15,810	14,456	1,354	249,499	131,227	118,272	22,159	10,998	11,161
	35—40	215,654	120,001	95,653	7.267	6,560	707	180.313	102,282	78,051	28,074	11,159	16,918
	40—45	164,794	91,981	72,813	5,015	4,562	453	130,852	77.013	53,839	28,927	10,406	18,521
	45—50	127,624	72,028	55,596	3,367	3,054	313	90,308	57.823	32,485	33,949	11,151	22,798
	50—55	101,362	57,413	43,949	2,499	2,263	236	67,345	44,767	22,578	31,518	10,383	21,135
	55—60	76,943	43,698	33,245	1,721	1,549	172	42,232	30,984	11,248	32,990	11,165	21,825
	60—65	64,878	36,427	28,451	1,364	1,231	133	33,100	24,897	8,203	30,414	10,299	20,115
	65—70	31,348	18,084	13,264	630	552	78	13,821	11,059	2,762	16,897	6,473	10,424
	70 & over	58,326	33,645	24,681	1,127	979	148	21,130	17,715	3,415	36,069	14,951	21,118
Hindu—(Brahmanic).	*Total*	*642,273*	*343,349*	*298,924*	*287,157*	*181,882*	*105,275*	*272,236*	*136,324*	*136,911*	*82,881*	*26,143*	*56,738*
	0—1	19,774	9,956	9,818	19,774	9,956	9,818	....	....	....	....	....	....
	1—2	17,843	8,918	8,925	17,843	8,918	8,925	....	....	....	....	....	....
	2—3	17,736	8,934	8,802	17,736	8,934	8,802	....	....	....	....	....	....
	3—4	17,939	8,979	8,960	17,939	8,979	8,960	....	....	....	....	....	....
	4—5	17,890	8,554	9,336	17,829	8,536	9,293	51	17	34	10	1	9
	Total 0—5	*91,182*	*45,341*	*45,841*	*91,121*	*45,323*	*45,798*	*51*	*17*	*34*	*10*	*1*	*9*
	5—10	73,797	39,362	34,435	70,009	38,046	31,963	3,646	1,281	2,365	142	35	107
	10—15	69,020	36,973	32 047	57,382	34,681	22,701	11,177	2,207	8,970	461	85	376
	15—20	60,138	30,954	29,184	26,303	22,815	3,488	32,147	7,760	24,387	1,688	379	1,309
	20—25	61,787	31,729	30,058	18,111	17,588	523	40,877	13,419	27,458	2,799	722	2,077
	25—30	55,390	29,596	25,794	8,284	7,969	315	42,109	20,053	22,056	4,997	1,574	3,423
	30—35	50,227	28,012	22,215	5,497	5,230	267	38,534	20,734	17,800	6,196	2,048	4,148
	35—40	39,477	21,982	17,495	2,862	2,804	58	28,576	16,765	11,811	8,039	2,413	5,626
	40—45	33,711	18,706	15,005	2,108	2,062	46	23,001	14,101	8,900	8,602	2,543	6,059
	45—50	28,199	15,984	12,215	1,589	1,558	31	16,935	11,455	5,480	9,675	2,971	6,704
	50—55	23,205	13,359	9,846	1,262	1,241	21	12,882	9,226	3,656	9,061	2,892	6,169
	55—60	18,576	10,513	8,063	974	950	24	8,459	6,649	1,810	9,143	2,914	6,229
	60—65	15,456	8,668	6,788	777	762	15	6,539	5,298	1,241	8,140	2,608	5,532
	65—70	8,165	4,627	3,538	331	324	7	3,041	2,604	437	4,793	1,699	3,094
	70 & over	13,943	7,543	6,400	547	529	18	4,261	3,755	506	9,135	3,259	5,876
Hindu—(Arya).	*Total*	*93,944*	*50,346*	*43,598*	*42,046*	*25,676*	*16,370*	*41,978*	*20,928*	*21,050*	*9,920*	*3,742*	*6,178*
	0—1	3,127	1,565	1,562	3,127	1,565	1,562	....	....	....	....	....	....
	1—2	2,805	1,424	1,381	2,805	1,424	1,381	....	....	....	....	....	....
	2—3	2,878	1,459	1,419	2,878	1,459	1,419	....	....	....	....	....	....
	3—4	2,803	1,411	1,392	2,803	1,411	1,392	....	....	....	....	....	....
	4—5	2,668	1,418	1,250	2,651	1,401	1,250	17	17	....	....	....	....
	Total 0—5	*14,281*	*7,277*	*7,004*	*14,264*	*7,260*	*7,004*	*17*	*17*	....	....	....	....
	5—10	11,428	6,173	5,255	10,876	6,050	4,826	508	114	394	44	9	35
	10—15	10,775	5,722	5,053	8,963	5,401	3,562	1,735	303	1,432	77	18	59
	15—20	9,156	4,585	4,571	3,795	3,081	714	5,148	1,424	3,724	213	80	133
	20—25	9,206	4,668	4,538	2,251	2,095	156	6,602	2,417	4,185	353	156	197
	25—30	8,311	4,478	3,833	794	731	63	6,918	3,461	3,457	599	286	313
	30—35	7,485	4,244	3,241	445	429	16	6,271	3,481	2,790	769	334	435
	35—40	5,544	3,108	2,436	184	174	10	4,375	2,562	1,813	985	372	613
	40—45	4,560	2,517	2,043	130	126	4	3,397	2,043	1,354	1,033	348	685
	45—50	3,698	2,086	1,612	92	87	5	2,451	1,624	827	1,155	375	780
	50—55	2,896	1,659	1,237	96	95	1	1,735	1,205	530	1,065	359	706
	55—60	2,248	1,299	949	64	61	3	1,086	847	239	1,098	391	707
	60—65	1,801	1,044	757	35	34	1	825	658	167	941	352	589
	65—70	892	543	349	19	18	1	363	301	62	510	224	286
	70 & over	1,663	943	720	38	34	4	547	471	76	1,078	438	640

TABLE VII.—AGE, SEX AND CIVIL CONDITION.

Jammu and Kashmir Census 1931.

Religion.	Age.	Population.			Unmarried.			Married.			Widowed.		
		Persons.	Males.	Females.	Persons.	Males.	Females.	Persons.	Males.	Females.	Persons.	Males.	Females.
1	2	3	4	5	6	7	8	9	10	11	12	13	14
Hindu—(Brahmo).	*Total*	*5*	*4*	*1*	*2*	*2*	....	*2*	*1*	*1*	*1*	*1*	....
	0—1	....	....	....	....	....	....	....	....	....	....	....	....
	1—2	....	....	....	....	....	....	....	....	....	....	....	....
	2—3	....	....	....	....	....	....	....	....	....	....	....	....
	3—4	....	....	....	....	....	....	....	....	....	....	....	....
	4—5	....	....	....	....	....	....	....	....	....	....	....	....
	Total 0—5	....	....	....	....	....	....	....	....	....	....	....	....
	5—10	....	....	....	....	....	....	....	....	....	....	....	....
	10—15	1	1	....	1	1	....	....	....	....	....	....	....
	15—20	1	1	....	1	1	....	....	....	....	....	....	....
	20—25	....	....	....	....	....	....	....	....	....	....	....	....
	25—30	....	....	....	....	....	....	....	....	....	....	....	....
	30—35	2	1	1	....	....	....	2	1	1	....	....	....
	35—40	....	....	....	....	....	....	....	....	....	....	....	....
	40—45	....	....	....	....	....	....	....	....	....	....	....	....
	45—50	....	....	....	....	....	....	....	....	....	....	....	....
	50—55	1	1	....	....	....	....	....	....	....	1	1	....
	55—60	....	....	....	....	....	....	....	....	....	....	....	....
	60—65	....	....	....	....	....	....	....	....	....	....	....	....
	65—70	....	....	....	....	....	....	....	....	....	....	....	....
	70 & over	....	....	....	....	....	....	....	....	....	....	....	....
Sikh.	*Total*	*50,662*	*26,457*	*24,205*	*25,199*	*14,729*	*10,470*	*21,609*	*10,324*	*11,286*	*3,854*	*1,404*	*2,450*
	0—1	2,002	1,033	969	2,002	1,033	969	....	....	....	....	....	....
	1—2	1,837	916	921	1,837	916	921	....	....	....	....	....	....
	2—3	1,828	913	915	1,828	913	915	....	....	....	....	....	....
	3—4	1,802	920	882	1,801	920	881	1	....	1	....	....	....
	4—5	1,770	869	901	1,763	865	898	6	4	2	1	....	1
	Total 0—5	*9,239*	*4,651*	*4,588*	*9,231*	*4,647*	*4,584*	*7*	*4*	*3*	*1*	....	*1*
	5—10	7,087	3,856	3,231	6,906	3,808	3,098	173	46	127	8	2	6
	10—15	6,224	3,359	2,865	5,456	3,237	2,219	748	119	629	20	3	17
	15—20	4,730	2,236	2,494	1,954	1,528	426	2,704	682	2,022	72	26	46
	20—25	4,692	2,156	2,536	978	911	67	3,604	1,189	2,415	110	56	54
	25—30	4,139	2,068	2,071	267	247	20	3,651	1,715	1,936	221	106	115
	30—35	3,697	2,011	1,686	150	136	14	3,258	1,751	1,507	289	124	165
	35—40	2,688	1,477	1,211	78	68	10	2,247	1,286	961	363	123	240
	40—45	2,139	1,197	942	51	46	5	1,710	1,021	689	378	130	248
	45—50	1,713	971	742	43	29	14	1,226	800	426	444	142	302
	50—55	1,300	745	555	31	20	11	878	599	279	391	126	265
	55—60	979	566	413	19	18	1	534	405	129	426	143	283
	60—65	815	472	343	15	15	....	401	316	85	399	141	258
	65—70	449	265	184	9	8	1	199	161	38	241	96	145
	70 & over	771	427	344	11	11	....	269	230	39	491	186	305
Jain.	*Total*	*597*	*319*	*278*	*322*	*188*	*134*	*216*	*104*	*112*	*59*	*27*	*32*
	0—1	14	10	4	14	10	4	....	....	....	....	....	....
	1—2	14	9	5	14	9	5	....	....	....	....	....	....
	2—3	20	11	9	20	11	9	....	....	....	....	....	....
	3—4	17	9	8	17	9	8	....	....	....	....	....	....
	4—5	13	7	6	13	7	6	....	....	....	....	....	....
	Total 0—5	*78*	*46*	*32*	*78*	*46*	*32*	....	....	....	....	....	....
	5—10	73	32	41	72	31	41	1	1	....	....	....	....
	10—15	74	34	40	71	34	37	3	....	3	....	....	....
	15—20	59	30	29	35	23	12	22	6	16	2	1	1
	20—25	57	32	25	24	18	6	30	12	18	3	2	1
	25—30	52	30	22	14	12	2	37	17	20	1	1	....
	30—35	44	22	22	9	8	1	31	13	18	4	1	3
	35—40	35	21	14	5	5	....	24	15	9	6	1	5
	40—45	32	15	17	5	4	1	20	9	11	7	2	5
	45—50	33	19	14	4	4	....	17	10	7	12	5	7
	50—55	28	18	10	2	2	....	17	11	6	9	5	4
	55—60	14	8	6	2	1	1	8	5	3	4	2	2
	60—65	7	4	3	....	....	....	4	3	1	3	1	2
	65—70	5	3	2	....	....	....	1	1	....	4	2	2
	70&over	6	5	1	1	....	1	1	1	....	4	4	....

TABLE VII.—Age, Sex and Civil Condition.

Jammu and Kashmir Census 1931.

Religion.	Age.	Population.			Unmarried.			Married.			Widowed.		
		Persons.	Males.	Females.	Persons.	Males.	Females.	Persons.	Males.	Females.	Persons.	Males.	Females.
1	2	3	4	5	6	7	8	9	10	11	12	13	14
Buddhist.	*Total*	*38,724*	*19,287*	*19,437*	*17,605*	*8,772*	*8,833*	*17,658*	*9,258*	*8,400*	*3,461*	*1,257*	*2,204*
	0—1	948	480	468	948	480	468	....	....	....	....	....	....
	1—2	800	400	400	800	400	400	....	....	....	....	....	....
	2—3	876	405	471	876	405	471	....	....	....	....	....	....
	3—4	928	429	499	928	429	499	....	....	....	....	....	....
	4—5	825	398	427	825	398	427	....	....	....	....	....	....
	Total 0—5	*4,377*	*2,112*	*2,265*	*4,377*	*2,112*	*2,265*	....	....	....	....	....	....
	5—10	4,038	2,014	2,024	4,034	2,013	2,021	4	1	3	....	....	....
	10—15	3,746	1,852	1,894	3,667	1,827	1,840	73	24	49	6	1	5
	15—20	3,108	1,524	1,584	1,890	886	1,004	1,157	616	541	61	22	39
	20—25	3,282	1,620	1,662	1,283	593	690	1,902	987	915	97	40	57
	25—30	3,119	1,556	1,563	597	294	303	2,382	1,208	1,174	140	54	86
	30—35	2,853	1,449	1,404	421	224	197	2,281	1,170	1,111	151	55	96
	35—40	2,561	1,290	1,271	271	154	117	2,080	1,062	1,018	210	74	136
	40—45	2,316	1,172	1,144	258	151	107	1,830	943	887	228	78	150
	45—50	2,147	1,098	1,049	220	138	82	1,589	849	740	338	111	227
	50—55	1,993	1,006	987	189	118	71	1,454	770	684	350	118	232
	55—60	1,595	786	809	122	79	43	1,063	568	495	410	139	271
	60—65	1,465	732	733	109	72	37	920	510	410	436	150	286
	65—70	905	457	448	72	45	27	450	259	191	383	153	230
	70& over	1,219	619	600	95	66	29	473	291	182	651	262	389
Zoroastrian.	*Total*	*5*	*3*	*2*	*1*	*1*	....	*4*	*2*	*2*	....	....	....
	0—1	....	....	....	....	....	....	....	....	....	....	....	....
	1—2	1	1	....	1	1	....	....	....	....	....	....	....
	2—3	....	....	....	....	....	....	....	....	....	....	....	....
	3—4	....	....	....	....	....	....	....	....	....	....	....	....
	4—5	....	....	....	....	....	....	....	....	....	....	....	....
	Total 0—5	*1*	*1*	....	*1*	*1*	....	....	....	....	....	....	....
	5—10	....	....	....	....	....	....	....	....	....	....	....	....
	10—15	....	....	....	....	....	....	....	....	....	....	....	....
	15—20	1	....	1	....	....	....	1	....	1	....	....	....
	20—25	1	....	1	....	....	....	1	....	1	....	....	....
	25—30	....	....	....	....	....	....	....	....	....	....	....	....
	30—35	1	1	....	....	....	....	1	1	....	....	....	....
	35—40	....	....	....	....	....	....	....	....	....	....	....	....
	40—45	....	....	....	....	....	....	....	....	....	....	....	....
	45—50	....	....	....	....	....	....	....	....	....	....	....	....
	50—55	1	1	....	....	....	....	1	1	....	....	....	....
	55—60	....	....	....	....	....	....	....	....	....	....	....	....
	60—65	....	....	....	....	....	....	....	....	....	....	....	....
	65—70	....	....	....	....	....	....	....	....	....	....	....	....
	70 &over	....	....	....	....	....	....	....	....	....	....	....	....
Muslim.	*Total*	*2,817,636*	*1,497,252*	*1,320,384*	*1,341,763*	*793,219*	*548,544*	*1,278,816*	*622,590*	*656,226*	*197,057*	*81,443*	*115,614*
	0—1	89,960	45,223	44,737	89,960	45,223	44,737	....	....	....	....	....	....
	1—2	94,926	47,580	47,346	94,926	47,580	47,346	....	....	....	....	....	....
	2—3	94,485	47,347	47,138	94,484	47,347	47,137	1	....	1	....	....	....
	3—4	92,246	46,736	45,510	92,231	46,734	45,497	15	2	13	....	....	....
	4—5	88,368	45,392	42,976	88,276	45,348	42,928	92	44	48	....	....	....
	Total 0—5	*459,985*	*232,278*	*227,707*	*459,877*	*232,232*	*227,645*	*108*	*46*	*62*	....	....	....
	5—10	372,408	201,588	170,820	362,980	198,460	164,520	9,229	3,067	6,162	199	61	138
	10—15	339,907	185,953	153,954	298,381	176,496	121,885	40,722	9,217	31,505	804	240	564
	15—20	273,180	139,253	133,927	116,977	91,814	25,163	152,301	45,643	106,658	3,902	1,796	2,106
	20—25	285,425	142,345	143,080	64,802	58,995	5,807	213,467	79,376	134,091	7,156	3,974	3,182
	25—30	252,669	130,021	122,648	19,279	17,999	1,280	221,195	104,652	116,543	12,195	7,370	4,825
	30—35	222,964	120,825	102,139	9,262	8,414	848	198,967	103,983	94,984	14,735	8,428	6,307
	35—40	165,195	92,033	73,162	3,847	3,345	502	142,900	80,523	62,377	18,448	8,165	10,283
	40—45	121,925	68,316	53,609	2,452	2,168	284	100,813	58,852	41,961	18,660	7,296	11,364
	45—50	91,735	51,810	39,925	1,409	1,233	176	68,025	43,040	24,985	22,301	7,537	14,764
	50—55	71,868	40,588	31,280	914	786	128	50,327	32,926	17,401	20,627	6,876	13,751
	55—60	53,474	30,492	22,982	532	436	96	31,048	22,487	8,561	21,894	7,569	14,325
	60—65	45,286	25,471	19,815	422	345	77	24,382	18,086	6,296	20,482	7,040	13,442
	65—70	20,912	12,180	8,732	196	157	39	9,758	7,728	2,030	10,958	4,295	6,663
	70 &over	40,703	24,099	16,604	433	339	94	15,574	12,964	2,610	24,696	10,796	13,900

TABLE VII.—Age, Sex and Civil Condition.

Jammu and Kashmir Census 1931.

Religion.	Age.	Population.			Unmarried.			Married.			Widowed.		
		Persons.	Males.	Females.	Persons.	Males.	Females.	Persons.	Males.	Females.	Persons.	Males.	Females.
1	2	3	4	5	6	7	8	9	10	11	12	13	14
Christian.	*Total*	*2,263*	*1,243*	*1,020*	*1,124*	*645*	*479*	*972*	*517*	*455*	*167*	*81*	*86*
	0—1	95	49	46	95	49	46	....	....	....	....	....	....
	1—2	65	34	31	65	34	31	....	....	....	....	....	....
	2—3	62	28	34	62	28	34	....	....	....	....	....	....
	3—4	66	38	28	66	38	28	....	....	....	....	....	....
	4—5	85	60	25	85	60	25	....	....	....	....	....	....
	Total 0—5	*373*	*209*	*164*	*373*	*209*	*164*	....	....	....	....	....	....
	5—10	273	150	123	268	148	120	5	2	3	....	....	....
	10—15	223	117	106	198	110	88	23	7	16	2	....	2
	15—20	208	103	105	94	64	30	106	32	74	8	7	1
	20—25	224	116	108	66	48	18	150	63	87	8	5	3
	25—30	218	120	98	37	24	13	169	91	78	12	5	7
	30—35	185	111	74	24	14	10	147	90	57	14	7	7
	35—40	150	87	63	20	10	10	108	66	42	22	11	11
	40—45	109	57	52	11	5	6	79	43	36	19	9	10
	45—50	92	56	36	9	5	4	62	42	20	21	9	12
	50—55	67	34	33	5	1	4	50	28	22	12	5	7
	55—60	57	34	23	8	4	4	34	23	11	15	7	8
	60—65	43	31	12	6	3	3	25	22	3	12	6	6
	65—70	20	9	11	3	....	3	9	5	4	8	4	4
	70 & over	21	9	12	2	....	2	5	3	2	14	6	8

TABLE VII.—Age, Sex and Civil Condition.

Jammu and Kashmir Census 1931.

Part I.—Jammu Province.

Religion.	Age.	Population.			Unmarried.			Married.			Widowed.		
		Persons.	Males.	Females.	Persons.	Males.	Females.	Persons.	Males.	Females.	Persons.	Males.	Females.
1	2	3	4	5	6	7	8	9	10	11	12	13	14
All Religions.	*Total*	*1,788,441*	*942,815*	*845,626*	*838,158*	*504,929*	*333,229*	*777,938*	*378,354*	*399,584*	*172,345*	*59,532*	*112,813*
	0—1	60,417	30,229	30,188	60,417	30,229	30,188	....	....	....	....	....	....
	1—2	56,734	28,324	28,410	56,734	28,324	28,410	....	....	....	....	....	....
	2—3	56,596	28,282	28,314	56,596	28,282	28,314	....	....	....	....	....	....
	3—4	56,075	28,117	27,958	56,074	28,117	27,957	1	....	1	....	....	....
	4—5	54,545	27,266	27,279	54,407	27,190	27,217	127	75	52	11	1	10
	Total 0—5	*284,367*	*142,218*	*142,149*	*284,228*	*142,142*	*142,086*	*128*	*75*	*53*	*11*	*1*	*10*
	5—10	228,570	122,969	105,601	218,939	119,655	99,284	9,314	3,233	6,081	317	81	236
	10—15	210,032	113,832	96,200	178,417	106,551	71,866	30,664	7,069	23,595	951	212	739
	15—20	169,800	85,644	84,156	73,891	59,422	14,469	92,461	25,054	67,407	3,448	1,168	2,280
	20—25	170,325	84,365	85,960	43,307	40,205	3,102	121,231	41,872	79,359	5,787	2,288	3,499
	25—30	152,836	78,465	74,371	15,680	14,824	856	126,741	59,096	67,645	10,415	4,545	5,870
	30—35	136,781	73,577	63,204	9,051	8,420	631	114,937	59,829	55,108	12,793	5,328	7,465
	35—40	102,046	55,754	46,292	4,311	4,029	282	81,579	46,401	35,178	16,156	5,324	10,832
	40—45	82,532	45,088	37,444	3,054	2,869	185	62,404	36,913	25,491	17,074	5,306	11,768
	45—50	66,682	37,212	29,470	2,178	2,043	135	45,068	29,231	15,837	19,436	5,938	13,498
	50—55	53,000	29,843	23,157	1,678	1,578	100	33,427	22,673	10,754	17,895	5,592	12,303
	55—60	41,862	23,564	18,298	1,217	1,145	72	21,929	16,361	5,568	18,716	6,058	12,658
	60—65	35,499	19,807	15,692	967	912	55	17,444	13,341	4,103	17,088	5,554	11,534
	65—70	18,709	10,670	8,039	436	402	34	8,030	6,555	1,475	10,243	3,713	6,530
	70 & over	35,400	19,807	15,593	804	732	72	12,581	10,651	1,930	22,015	8,424	13,591
Hindu—(Brahmanic).	*Total*	*571,870*	*303,364*	*268,506*	*252,591*	*159,132*	*93,459*	*244,812*	*121,083*	*123,729*	*74,467*	*23,149*	*51,318*
	0—1	18,258	9,170	9,088	18,258	9,170	9,088	....	....	....	....	....	....
	1—2	16,066	8,024	8,042	16,066	8,024	8,042	....	....	....	....	....	....
	2—3	15,857	7,988	7,869	15,857	7,988	7,869	....	....	....	....	....	....
	3—4	16,021	7,980	8,041	16,021	7,980	8,041	....	....	....	....	....	....
	4—5	15,983	7,533	8,450	15,923	7,515	8,408	50	17	33	10	1	9
	Total 0—5	*82,185*	*40,695*	*41,490*	*82,125*	*40,677*	*41,448*	*50*	*17*	*33*	*10*	*1*	*9*
	5—10	65,507	35,083	30,424	61,775	33,778	27,997	3,593	1,270	2,323	139	35	104
	10—15	61,410	32,917	28,493	50,360	30,693	19,667	10,606	2,144	8,462	444	80	364
	15—20	53,248	26,926	26,322	22,730	19,657	3,073	28,967	6,929	22,038	1,551	340	1,211
	20—25	54,353	27,415	26,938	15,381	14,894	487	36,440	11,876	24,564	2,532	645	1,887
	25—30	48,639	25,539	23,100	6,939	6,632	307	37,266	17,535	19,731	4,434	1,372	3,062
	30—35	44,201	24,261	19,940	4,591	4,328	263	34,099	18,142	15,957	5,511	1,791	3,720
	35—40	34,923	19,202	15,721	2,357	2,301	56	25,407	14,811	10,596	7,159	2,090	5,069
	40—45	29,774	16,335	13,439	1,709	1,664	45	20,458	12,482	7,976	7,607	2,189	5,418
	45—50	25,124	14,182	10,942	1,309	1,278	31	15,280	10,322	4,958	8,535	2,582	5,953
	50—55	20,690	11,912	8,778	1,053	1,032	21	11,689	8,368	3,321	7,948	2,512	5,436
	55—60	16,744	9,468	7,276	821	797	24	7,797	6,118	1,679	8,126	2,553	5,573
	60—65	14,040	7,833	6,207	661	646	15	6,064	4,888	1,176	7,315	2,299	5,016
	65—70	7,634	4,324	3,310	289	282	7	2,908	2,488	420	4,437	1,554	2,883
	70 & over	13,398	7,272	6,126	491	473	18	4,188	3,693	495	8,719	3,106	5,613
Hindu—(Arya).	*Total*	*93,372*	*49,981*	*43,391*	*41,750*	*25,485*	*16,265*	*41,733*	*20,771*	*20,962*	*9,889*	*3,725*	*6,164*
	0—1	3,114	1,559	1,555	3,114	1,559	1,555	....	....	....	....	....	....
	1—2	2,788	1,416	1,372	2,788	1,416	1,372	....	....	....	....	....	....
	2—3	2,861	1,449	1,412	2,861	1,449	1,412	....	....	....	....	....	....
	3—4	2,790	1,402	1,388	2,790	1,402	1,388	....	....	....	....	....	....
	4—5	2,647	1,408	1,239	2,630	1,391	1,239	17	17	....	....	....	....
	Total 0—5	*14,200*	*7,234*	*6,966*	*14,183*	*7,217*	*6,966*	*17*	*17*	....	....	....	....
	5—10	11,348	6,128	5,220	10,798	6,005	4,793	506	114	392	44	9	35
	10—15	10,706	5,682	5,024	8,898	5,361	3,537	1,731	303	1,428	77	18	59
	15—20	9,097	4,549	4,518	3,760	3,053	707	5,124	1,416	3,708	213	80	133
	20—25	9,153	4,632	4,521	2,231	2,076	155	6,570	2,401	4,169	352	155	197
	25—30	8,243	4,432	3,811	784	721	63	6,862	3,427	3,435	597	284	313
	30—35	7,427	4,201	3,226	441	425	16	6,220	3,444	2,776	766	332	434
	35—40	5,513	3,084	2,429	184	174	10	4,346	2,539	1,807	983	371	612
	40—45	4,533	2,496	2,037	129	125	4	3,377	2,027	1,350	1,027	344	683
	45—50	3,675	2,069	1,606	92	87	5	2,435	1,611	824	1,148	371	777
	50—55	2,888	1,654	1,234	96	95	1	1,730	1,200	530	1,062	359	703
	55—60	2,240	1,294	946	61	61	3	1,083	844	239	1,093	389	704
	60—65	1,797	1,042	755	34	33	1	824	658	166	939	351	588
	65—70	891	542	349	19	18	1	362	300	62	510	224	286
	70 & over	1,661	942	719	37	34	3	546	470	76	1,078	438	640

TABLE VII.—Age, Sex and Civil Condition.

Jammu and Kashmir Census 1931.

Part I.—Jammu Province—(continued).

Religion.	Age.	Population.			Unmarried.			Married.			Widowed.		
		Persons.	Males.	Females.	Persons.	Males.	Females.	Persons.	Males.	Females.	Persons.	Males.	Females.
1	2	3	4	5	6	7	8	9	10	11	12	13	14
Hindu (Brahmo).	*Total*	*4*	*3*	*1*	*2*	*2*	....	*2*	*1*	*1*	....	....	....
	0—1	....	....	....	....	....	....	....	....	....	....	....	....
	1—2	....	....	....	....	....	....	....	....	....	....	....	....
	2—3	....	....	....	....	....	....	....	....	....	....	....	....
	3—4	....	....	....	....	....	....	....	....	....	....	....	....
	4—5	....	....	....	....	....	....	....	....	....	....	....	....
	Total 0—5	....	....	....	....	....	....	....	....	....	....	....	....
	5—10	....	....	....	....	....	....	....	....	....	....	....	....
	10—15	1	1	....	1	1	....	....	....	....	....	....	....
	15—20	1	1	....	1	1	....	....	....	....	....	....	....
	20—25	....	....	....	....	....	....	....	....	....	....	....	....
	25—30	....	....	....	....	....	....	....	....	....	....	....	....
	30—35	2	1	1	....	....	....	2	1	1	....	....	....
	35—40	....	....	....	....	....	....	....	....	....	....	....	....
	40—45	....	....	....	....	....	....	....	....	....	....	....	....
	45—50	....	....	....	....	....	....	....	....	....	....	....	....
	50—55	....	....	....	....	....	....	....	....	....	....	....	....
	55—60	....	....	....	....	....	....	....	....	....	....	....	....
	60—65	....	....	....	....	....	....	....	....	....	....	....	....
	65—70	....	....	....	....	....	....	....	....	....	....	....	....
	70 &over	....	....	....	....	....	....	....	....	....	....	....	....
Sikh.	*Total*	*29,282*	*15,197*	*14,085*	*14,383*	*8,428*	*5,955*	*12,442*	*5,933*	*6,509*	*2,457*	*836*	*1,621*
	0—1	1,233	647	586	1,233	647	586	....	....	....	....	....	....
	1—2	1,042	512	530	1,042	512	530	....	....	....	....	....	....
	2—3	1,003	491	512	1,003	491	512	....	....	....	....	....	....
	3—4	1,000	509	491	999	509	490	1	....	1	....	....	....
	4—5	1,006	496	510	1,000	493	507	5	3	2	1	....	1
	Total 0—5	*5,284*	*2,655*	*2,629*	*5,277*	*2,652*	*2,625*	*6*	*3*	*3*	*1*	....	*1*
	5—10	4,037	2,213	1,824	3,901	2,173	1,728	128	38	90	8	2	6
	10—15	3,598	1,931	1,667	3,084	1,839	1,245	495	89	406	19	3	16
	15—20	2,680	1,244	1,436	1,103	842	261	1,526	386	1,140	51	16	35
	20—25	2,571	1,148	1,423	553	507	46	1,948	611	1,337	70	30	40
	25—30	2,339	1,125	1,214	172	162	10	2,021	902	1,119	146	61	85
	30—35	2,165	1,170	995	101	97	4	1,869	1,002	867	195	71	124
	35—40	1,600	883	717	53	48	5	1,305	762	543	242	73	169
	40—45	1,278	711	567	36	31	5	997	599	398	245	81	164
	45—50	1,023	587	436	35	22	13	725	481	244	263	84	179
	50—55	788	457	331	28	17	11	532	368	164	228	72	156
	55—60	626	358	268	15	14	1	342	255	87	269	89	180
	60—65	512	293	219	12	12	....	246	191	55	254	90	164
	65—70	299	168	131	7	6	1	132	103	29	160	59	101
	70& over	482	254	228	6	6	....	170	143	27	306	105	201
Jain.	*Total*	*591*	*314*	*277*	*320*	*186*	*134*	*212*	*101*	*111*	*59*	*27*	*32*
	0—1	13	9	4	13	9	4	....	....	....	....	....	....
	1—2	14	9	5	14	9	5	....	....	....	....	....	....
	2—3	20	11	9	20	11	9	....	....	....	....	....	....
	3—4	17	9	8	17	9	8	....	....	....	....	....	....
	4—5	13	7	6	13	7	6	....	....	....	....	....	....
	Total 0—5	*77*	*45*	*32*	*77*	*45*	*32*	....	....	....	....	....	....
	5—10	73	32	41	72	31	41	1	1	....	....	....	....
	10—15	73	33	40	70	33	37	3	....	3	....	....	....
	15—20	58	29	29	35	23	12	21	5	16	2	1	1
	20—25	56	31	25	24	18	6	29	11	18	3	2	1
	25—30	50	29	21	14	12	2	35	16	19	1	1	....
	30—35	44	22	22	9	8	1	31	13	18	4	1	3
	35—40	35	21	14	5	5	....	24	15	9	6	1	5
	40—45	32	15	17	5	4	1	20	9	11	7	2	5
	45—50	33	19	14	4	4	....	17	10	7	12	5	7
	50—55	28	18	10	2	2	....	17	11	6	9	5	4
	55—60	14	8	6	2	1	1	8	5	3	4	2	2
	60—65	7	4	3	....	....	....	4	3	1	3	1	2
	65—70	5	3	2	....	....	....	1	1	....	4	2	2
	70&over	6	5	1	1	....	1	1	1	....	4	4	....

TABLE VII.—Age, Sex and Civil Condition.

Jammu and Kashmir Census 1931.

Part I.—Jammu Province—(concluded).

Religion.	Age.	Population. Persons.	Population. Males.	Population. Females.	Unmarried. Persons.	Unmarried. Males.	Unmarried. Females.	Married. Persons.	Married. Males.	Married. Females.	Widowed. Persons.	Widowed. Males.	Widowed. Females.
1	2	3	4	5	6	7	8	9	10	11	12	13	14
Buddhist.	*Total*	*507*	*253*	*254*	*213*	*114*	*99*	*252*	*124*	*128*	*42*	*15*	*27*
	0—1	14	8	6	14	8	6	...	...	...	...	...	...
	1—2	14	7	7	14	7	7	...	...	...	...	...	...
	2—3	12	5	7	12	5	7	...	...	...	...	...	...
	3—4	12	5	7	12	5	7	...	...	...	...	...	...
	4—5	10	5	5	10	5	5	...	...	...	...	...	...
	Total 0—5	*62*	*30*	*32*	*62*	*30*	*32*	...	...	...	...	...	...
	5—10	59	31	28	58	30	28	1	1	...	...	...	...
	10—15	58	29	29	54	29	25	3	...	3	1	...	1
	15—20	40	20	20	20	12	8	19	8	11	1	...	1
	20—25	44	19	25	7	4	3	35	14	21	2	1	1
	25—30	55	27	28	5	4	1	47	21	26	3	2	1
	30—35	41	20	21	5	3	2	35	17	18	1	...	1
	35—40	31	16	15	1	1	...	26	12	14	4	3	1
	40—45	31	15	16	...	...	...	26	12	14	5	3	2
	45—50	23	11	12	...	...	...	17	10	7	6	1	5
	50—55	17	9	8	...	...	...	13	8	5	4	1	3
	55—60	16	8	8	...	...	...	11	6	5	5	2	3
	60—65	14	8	6	...	...	...	10	7	3	4	1	3
	65—70	7	5	2	...	...	...	4	4	...	3	1	2
	70 & over	9	5	4	1	1	...	5	4	1	3	...	3
Muslim.	*Total*	*1,091,021*	*572,699*	*518,322*	*528,021*	*311,062*	*216,959*	*477,722*	*229,936*	*247,787*	*85,278*	*31,702*	*53,576*
	0—1	37,695	18,788	18,907	37,695	18.788	18,907	...	...	...	...	...	...
	1—2	36,757	18,329	18,428	36,757	18,329	18,428	...	...	...	...	...	...
	2—3	36,789	18,313	18,476	36,789	18,313	18,476	...	...	...	...	...	...
	3—4	36,174	18,176	17,998	36,174	18,176	17,998	...	...	...	...	...	...
	4—5	34,810	17,762	17,048	34,755	17,724	17,031	55	38	17	...	...	...
	Total 0—5	*182,225*	*91,368*	*90,857*	*182,170*	*91,330*	*90,840*	*55*	*38*	*17*	...	...	...
	5—10	147,312	79,356	67,956	142,108	77,515	64,593	5,079	1,807	3,272	125	34	91
	10—15	133,991	73,139	60,852	115,781	68,502	47,279	17,802	4,526	13,276	408	111	297
	15—20	104,492	52,785	51,707	46,169	35,783	10,386	56,701	16,278	40,423	1,622	724	898
	20—25	103,957	51,022	52,935	25,072	22,674	2,398	76,065	26,898	49,167	2,820	1,450	1,370
	25—30	93,347	47,220	46,127	7,753	7,282	471	80,371	37,118	43,253	5,223	2,820	2,403
	30—35	82,765	43,817	38,948	3,898	3,554	344	72,564	37,137	35,427	6,303	3,126	3,177
	35—40	59,840	32,483	27,357	1,705	1,496	209	50,394	28,211	22,183	7,741	2,776	4,965
	40—45	46,811	25,474	21,337	1,173	1,044	129	37,472	21,751	15,721	8,166	2,679	5,487
	45—50	36,743	20,307	16,436	736	650	86	26,555	16,770	9,785	9,452	2,887	6,565
	50—55	28,551	15,771	12,780	499	432	67	19,420	12,702	6,718	8,632	2,637	5,995
	55—60	22,188	12,406	9,782	311	268	43	12,672	9,122	3,550	9,205	3,016	6,189
	60—65	19,103	10,606	8,497	257	218	39	10,284	7,582	2,702	8,562	2,806	5,756
	65—70	9,863	5,621	4,242	121	96	25	4,619	3,656	963	5,123	1,869	3,254
	70 & over	19,833	11,324	8,509	268	218	50	7,669	6,339	1,330	11,896	4,767	7,129
Christian.	*Total*	*1,753*	*987*	*766*	*865*	*512*	*343*	*749*	*399*	*350*	*149*	*76*	*73*
	0—1	87	47	40	87	47	40	...	...	...	...	...	...
	1—2	53	27	26	53	27	26	...	...	...	...	...	...
	2—3	53	25	28	53	25	28	...	...	...	...	...	...
	3—4	60	36	24	60	36	24	...	...	...	...	...	...
	4—5	75	55	20	75	55	20	...	...	...	...	...	...
	Total 0—5	*328*	*190*	*138*	*328*	*190*	*138*	...	...	...	...	...	...
	5—10	228	124	104	223	122	101	5	2	3	...	...	...
	10—15	187	96	91	162	89	73	23	7	16	2	...	2
	15—20	177	87	90	68	49	19	101	31	70	8	7	1
	20—25	188	97	91	38	32	6	142	60	82	8	5	3
	25—30	160	92	68	13	11	2	136	76	60	11	5	6
	30—35	135	85	50	6	5	1	116	73	43	13	7	6
	35—40	102	63	39	6	4	2	75	49	26	21	10	11
	40—45	72	41	31	2	1	1	53	32	21	17	8	9
	45—50	60	37	23	2	2	...	39	27	12	19	8	11
	50—55	35	20	15	...	...	...	25	15	10	10	5	5
	55—60	34	22	12	4	4	...	16	11	5	14	7	7
	60—65	26	21	5	3	3	...	12	12	...	11	6	5
	65—70	10	7	3	...	...	...	4	3	1	6	4	2
	70 & over	11	5	6	...	...	...	2	1	1	9	4	5

TABLE VII.—Age, Sex and Civil Condition.

Jammu and Kashmir Census 1931.

Part I.—Kashmir Province.

Religion.	Age.	Population.			Unmarried.			Married.			Widowed.		
		Persons.	Males.	Females.	Persons.	Males.	Females.	Persons.	Males.	Females.	Persons.	Males.	Females.
1	2	3	4	5	6	7	8	9	10	11	12	13	14
All Religions.	*Total*	*1,569,218*	*847,022*	*722,196*	*742,540*	*444,687*	*297,853*	*722,306*	*354,569*	*367,737*	*104,372*	*47,766*	*56,606*
	0—1	45,950	23,264	22,686	45,950	23,264	22,686	....	....	....	....	....	....
	1—2	52,800	26,662	26,138	52,800	26,662	26,138	....	....	....	....	....	....
	2—3	52,444	26,583	25,861	52,444	26,583	25,861	....	....	....	....	....	....
	3—4	50,933	26,088	24,845	50,920	26,086	24,834	13	2	11	....	....	....
	4—5	48,852	25,296	23,556	48,815	25,290	23,525	37	6	31	....	....	....
	Total 0—5	*250,979*	*127,893*	*123,086*	*250,929*	*127,885*	*123,044*	*50*	*8*	*42*	— —	— —	— —
	5—10	204,953	111,418	93,535	201,330	110,221	91,109	3,567	1,181	2,386	56	16	40
	10—15	188,108	103,048	85,060	166,653	98,718	67,935	21,119	4,227	16,892	336	103	233
	15—20	156,157	80,331	75,826	64,735	52,446	12,289	89,409	26,939	62,470	2,013	946	1,067
	20—25	166,206	84,380	81,826	36,566	34,410	2,156	125,791	47,707	78,084	3,849	2,263	1,586
	25—30	145,983	76,858	69,125	10,821	10,346	475	128,572	62,222	66,350	6,590	4,290	2,300
	30—35	128,069	71,552	56,517	5,390	5,053	337	114,694	61,419	53,275	7,985	5,080	2,905
	35—40	95,344	54,732	40,612	2,282	2,097	185	82,719	47,360	35,359	10,343	5,275	5,068
	40—45	71,320	40,867	30,453	1,533	1,417	116	59,120	34,765	24,355	10,667	4,685	5,982
	45—50	49,912	29,287	20,625	864	801	63	36,505	23,779	12,726	12,543	4,707	7,836
	50—55	37,148	21,773	15,375	549	510	39	25,108	17,013	8,095	11,491	4,250	7,241
	55—60	26,248	15,444	10,804	334	298	36	14,319	10,726	3,593	11,595	4,420	7,175
	60—65	21,881	12,811	9,070	252	228	24	10,950	8,526	2,424	10,679	4,057	6,622
	65—70	9,125	5,553	3,572	111	96	15	3,975	3,235	740	5,039	2,222	2,817
	70 & over	17,785	11,075	6,710	191	161	30	6,408	5,462	946	11,186	5,452	5,734
Hindu—(Brahmanic).	*Total*	*68,827*	*38,551*	*30,276*	*33,940*	*22,188*	*11,752*	*26,544*	*13,435*	*13,109*	*8,343*	*2,928*	*5,415*
	0—1	1,502	717	725	1,502	777	725	....	....	....	— —	— —	— —
	1—2	1,765	884	881	1,765	884	881	— —	....	....	— —	— —	— —
	2—3	1,863	938	925	1,863	938	925	....	....	....	— —	— —	....
	3—4	1,906	993	913	1,906	993	913	....	— —	....	....	— —	— —
	4—5	1,895	1,015	880	1,894	1,015	879	1	— —	1	....	— —	— —
	Total 0—5	*8,931*	*4,607*	*4,324*	*8,930*	*4,607*	*4,323*	*1*	....	*1*	....	— —	— —
	5—10	8,241	4,251	3,990	8,185	4,240	3,945	53	11	42	3	— —	3
	10—15	7,572	4,033	3,539	6,984	3,965	3,019	571	63	508	17	5	12
	15—20	6,673	3,824	2,849	3,442	3,028	414	3,097	760	2,337	134	36	98
	20—25	7,120	4,018	3,102	2,565	2,529	36	4,295	1,419	2,876	260	70	190
	25—30	6,413	3,739	2,674	1,248	1,240	8	4,619	2,313	2,306	546	186	360
	30—35	5,728	3,467	2,261	845	841	4	4,213	2,383	1,830	670	243	427
	35—40	4,418	2,652	1,766	494	492	2	3,057	1,848	1,209	867	312	555
	40—45	3,863	2,300	1,563	396	395	1	2,478	1,556	922	989	349	640
	45—50	3,049	1,777	1,272	276	276	....	1,636	1,115	521	1,137	386	751
	50—55	2,504	1,437	1,067	208	208	....	1,185	851	334	1,111	378	733
	55—60	1,827	1,041	786	153	153	....	660	530	130	1,014	358	656
	60—65	1,414	833	581	116	116	....	475	410	65	823	307	516
	65—70	530	302	228	42	42	....	132	115	17	356	145	211
	70 & over	544	270	274	56	56	— —	72	61	11	416	153	263
Hindu—Arya.	*Total*	*468*	*295*	*173*	*245*	*158*	*87*	*199*	*125*	*74*	*24*	*12*	*12*
	0—1	10	4	6	10	4	6	— —	— —	— —	— —	— —	— —
	1—2	13	6	7	13	6	7	— —	— —	— —	— —	— —	— —
	2—3	11	8	3	11	8	3	— —	— —	— —	— —	— —	— —
	3—4	12	8	4	12	8	4	— —	— —	— —	— —	— —	— —
	4—5	17	8	9	17	8	9	— —	— —	— —	— —	— —	— —
	Total 0—5	*63*	*34*	*29*	*63*	*34*	*29*	— —	— —	— —	— —	— —	— —
	5—10	65	36	29	64	36	28	1	— —	1	— —	— —	— —
	10—15	63	36	27	59	36	23	4	— —	4	— —	— —	— —
	15—20	50	31	19	30	24	6	20	7	13	— —	— —	— —
	20—25	44	30	14	17	16	1	26	13	13	1	1	— —
	25—30	52	34	18	7	7	— —	45	27	18	— —	— —	— —
	30—35	44	31	13	3	3	— —	39	27	12	2	1	1
	35—40	24	18	6	— —	— —	— —	23	17	6	1	1	— —
	40—45	23	17	6	1	1	— —	18	14	4	4	2	2
	45—50	20	15	5	— —	— —	— —	13	11	2	7	4	3
	50—55	7	4	3	— —	— —	— —	4	4	— —	3	— —	3
	55—60	7	5	2	— —	— —	— —	3	3	— —	4	2	2
	60—65	4	2	2	1	1	— —	1	— —	1	2	1	1
	65—70	1	1	— —	— —	— —	— —	1	1	— —	— —	— —	— —
	70 & over	1	1	— —	— —	— —	— —	1	1	— —	— —	— —	— —

TABLE VII.—Age, Sex and Civil Condition.

Jammu and Kashmir Census 1931.

Part I.—Kashmir Province—(continued).

Religion.	Age.	Population.			Unmarried.			Married.			Widowed.		
		Persons.	Males.	Females.	Persons.	Males.	Females.	Persons.	Males.	Females.	Persons.	Males.	Females.
1	2	3	4	5	6	7	8	9	10	11	12	13	14
Sikh.	*Total*	*21,190*	*11,135*	*10,055*	*10,723*	*6,246*	*4,477*	*9,073*	*4,323*	*4,750*	*1,394*	*566*	*828*
	0—1	758	379	379	758	379	379	....	....	....	....	....	....
	1—2	789	400	389	789	400	389	....	....	....	....	....	....
	2—3	817	419	398	817	419	398	....	....	....	....	....	....
	3—4	795	408	387	795	408	387	....	....	....	....	....	....
	4—5	760	371	389	759	370	389	1	1	....	....	....	....
	Total 0—5	*3,919*	*1,977*	*1,942*	*3,918*	*1,976*	*1,942*	*1*	*1*	....	....	....	....
	5—10	3,026	1,630	1,396	2,981	1,622	1,359	45	8	37	....	....	....
	10—15	2,609	1,417	1,192	2,355	1,387	968	253	30	223	1	....	1
	15—20	2,035	980	1,055	846	681	165	1,169	290	879	20	9	11
	20—25	2,103	997	1,106	422	401	21	1,641	570	1,071	40	26	14
	25—30	1,775	929	846	91	83	8	1,609	801	808	75	45	30
	30—35	1,513	897	686	46	38	8	1,374	737	637	93	52	41
	35—40	1,074	582	492	24	19	5	929	513	416	121	50	71
	40—45	852	478	374	15	15	....	704	414	290	133	49	84
	45—50	683	378	305	8	7	1	494	313	181	181	58	123
	50—55	510	286	224	3	3	....	344	229	115	163	54	109
	55—60	351	207	144	4	4	....	191	149	42	156	54	102
	60—65	302	178	124	3	3	....	154	124	30	145	51	94
	65—70	149	96	53	2	2	....	66	57	9	81	37	44
	70 & over	289	173	116	5	5	....	99	87	12	185	81	104
Buddhist.	*Total*	*5*	*5*	....	*4*	*4*	....	*1*	*1*	....	....	....	....
	0—1	....	....	....	....	....	....	....	....	....	....	....	....
	1—2	....	....	....	....	....	....	....	....	....	....	....	....
	2—3	....	....	....	....	....	....	....	....	....	....	....	....
	3—4	....	....	....	....	....	....	....	....	....	....	....	....
	4—5	....	....	....	....	....	....	....	....	....	....	....	....
	Total 0—5	....	....	....	....	....	....	....	....	....	....	....	....
	5—10	....	....	....	....	....	....	....	....	....	....	....	....
	10—15	....	....	....	....	....	....	....	....	....	....	....	....
	15—20	1	1	....	1	1	....	....	....	....	....	....	....
	20—25	2	2	....	2	2	....	....	....	....	....	....	....
	25—30	2	2	....	1	1	....	1	1	....	....	....	....
	30—35	....	....	....	....	....	....	....	....	....	....	....	....
	35—40	....	....	....	....	....	....	....	....	....	....	....	....
	40—45	....	....	....	....	....	....	....	....	....	....	....	....
	45—50	....	....	....	....	....	....	....	....	....	....	....	....
	50—55	....	....	....	....	....	....	....	....	....	....	....	....
	55—60	....	....	....	....	....	....	....	....	....	....	....	....
	60—65	....	....	....	....	....	....	....	....	....	....	....	....
	65—70	....	....	....	....	....	....	....	....	....	....	....	....
	70 & over	....	....	....	....	....	....	....	....	....	....	....	....
Zoroastrian.	*Total*	*5*	*3*	*2*	*1*	*1*	....	*4*	*2*	*2*	....	....	....
	0—1	....	....	....	....	....	....	....	....	....	....	....	....
	1—2	1	1	....	1	1	....	....	....	....	....	....	....
	2—3	....	....	....	....	....	....	....	....	....	....	....	....
	3—4	....	....	....	....	....	....	....	....	....	....	....	....
	4—5	....	....	....	....	....	....	....	....	....	....	....	....
	Total 0—5	*1*	*1*	....	*1*	*1*	....	....	....	....	....	....	....
	5—10	....	....	....	....	....	....	....	....	....	....	....	....
	10—15	....	....	....	....	....	....	....	....	....	....	....	....
	15—20	1	....	1	....	....	....	1	....	1	....	....	....
	20—25	1	....	1	....	....	....	1	....	1	....	....	....
	25—30	....	....	....	....	....	....	....	....	....	....	....	....
	30—35	1	1	....	....	....	....	1	1	....	....	....	....
	35—40	....	....	....	....	....	....	....	....	....	....	....	....
	40—45	....	....	....	....	....	....	....	....	....	....	....	....
	45—50	....	....	....	....	....	....	....	....	....	....	....	....
	50—55	1	1	....	....	....	....	1	1	....	....	....	....
	55—60	....	....	....	....	....	....	....	....	....	....	....	....
	60—65	....	....	....	....	....	....	....	....	....	....	....	....
	65—70	....	....	....	....	....	....	....	....	....	....	....	....
	70 & over	....	....	....	....	....	....	....	....	....	....	....	....

TABLE VII.—Age, Sex and Civil Condition.

Jammu and Kashmir Census 1931.

Part I.—Kashmir Province—(continued).

Religion.	Age.	Population.			Unmarried.			Married.			Widowed.		
		Persons.	Males.	Females.	Persons.	Males.	Females.	Persons.	Males.	Females.	Persons.	Males.	Females.
1	2	3	4	5	6	7	8	9	10	11	12	13	14
Christian.	*Total*	*339*	*166*	*173*	*172*	*81*	*91*	*154*	*81*	*73*	*13*	*4*	*9*
	0—1	3	....	3	3	....	3	....	....	....	....	....	....
	1—2	4	3	1	4	3	1	....	....	....	....	....	....
	2—3	3	2	1	3	2	1	....	....	....	....	....	....
	3—4	1	....	1	1	....	1	....	....	....	....	....	....
	4—5	5	3	2	5	3	2	....	....	....	....	....	....
	Total 0—5	*16*	*8*	*8*	*16*	*8*	*8*	....	....	....	....	....	....
	5—10	25	16	9	25	16	9	....	....	....	....	....	....
	10—15	23	15	8	23	15	8	....	....	....	....	....	....
	15—20	21	9	12	18	9	9	3	....	3	....	....	....
	20—25	25	12	13	21	11	10	4	1	3	....	....	....
	25—30	35	16	19	16	7	9	19	9	10	....	....	....
	30—35	31	16	15	12	5	7	19	11	8	....	....	....
	35—40	35	15	20	11	4	7	23	10	13	1	1	....
	40—45	28	12	16	7	3	4	19	8	11	2	1	1
	45—50	25	15	10	6	2	4	17	12	5	2	1	1
	50—55	25	11	14	5	1	4	18	10	8	2	....	2
	55—60	18	9	9	4	....	4	14	9	5	....	....	....
	60—65	15	8	7	3	....	3	11	8	3	1	....	1
	65—70	8	1	7	3	....	3	4	1	3	1	....	1
	70 & over	9	3	6	2	....	2	3	2	1	4	1	3
Jain.	*Total*	*3*	*3*	....	*1*	*1*	....	*2*	*2*	....	....	....	....
	0—1	....	....	....	....	....	....	....	....	....	....	....	....
	1—2	....	....	....	....	....	....	....	....	....	....	....	....
	2—3	....	....	....	....	....	....	....	....	....	....	....	....
	3—4	....	....	....	....	....	....	....	....	....	....	....	....
	4—5	....	....	....	....	....	....	....	....	....	....	....	....
	Total 0—5	....	....	....	....	....	....	....	....	....	....	....	....
	5—10	....	....	....	....	....	....	....	....	....	....	....	....
	10—15	1	1	....	1	1	....	....	....	....	....	....	....
	15—20	1	1	....	....	....	....	1	1	....	....	....	....
	20—25	1	1	....	....	....	....	1	1	....	....	....	....
	25—30	....	....	....	....	....	....	....	....	....	....	....	....
	30—35	....	....	....	....	....	....	....	....	....	....	....	....
	35—40	....	....	....	....	....	....	....	....	....	....	....	....
	40—45	....	....	....	....	....	....	....	....	....	....	....	....
	45—50	....	....	....	....	....	....	....	....	....	....	....	....
	50—55	....	....	....	....	....	....	....	....	....	....	....	....
	55—60	....	....	....	....	....	....	....	....	....	....	....	....
	60—65	....	....	....	....	....	....	....	....	....	....	....	....
	65—70	....	....	....	....	....	....	....	....	....	....	....	....
	70 & over	....	....	....	....	....	....	....	....	....	....	....	....
Hindu—(Brahmo).	*Total*	*1*	*1*	....	....	....	....	....	....	....	*1*	*1*	....
	0—1	....	....	....	....	....	....	....	....	....	....	....	....
	1—7	....	....	....	....	....	....	....	....	....	....	....	....
	2—3	....	....	....	....	....	....	....	....	....	....	....	....
	3—4	....	....	....	....	....	....	....	....	....	....	....	....
	4—5	....	....	....	....	....	....	....	....	....	....	....	....
	Total 0—5	....	....	....	....	....	....	....	....	....	....	....	....
	5—10	....	....	....	....	....	....	....	....	....	....	....	....
	10—15	....	....	....	....	....	....	....	....	....	....	....	....
	15—20	....	....	....	....	....	....	....	....	....	....	....	....
	20—25	....	....	....	....	....	....	....	....	....	....	....	....
	25—30	....	....	....	....	....	....	....	....	....	....	....	....
	30—35	....	....	....	....	....	....	....	....	....	....	....	....
	35—40	....	....	....	....	....	....	....	....	....	....	....	....
	40—45	....	....	....	....	....	....	....	....	....	....	....	....
	45—50	....	....	....	....	....	....	....	....	....	....	....	....
	50—55	1	1	....	....	....	....	....	....	....	1	1	....
	55—60	....	....	....	....	....	....	....	....	....	....	....	....
	60—65	....	....	....	....	....	....	....	....	....	—1	....	....
	65—70	....	....	....	....	....	....	....	....	....	....	....	....
	70 & over	....	....	....	....	....	....	....	....	....	....	....	....

TABLE VII.—AGE, SEX AND CIVIL CONDITION.

Jammu and Kashmir Census 1931.

Part I.—Kashmir Province—(concluded).

Religion.	Age.	*Population*			*Unmarried.*			*Married.*			*Widowed.*		
		Persons.	Males.	Females.	Persons.	Males.	Females.	Persons.	Males.	Females.	Persons.	Males.	Females.
1	2	3	4	5	6	7	8	9	10	11	12	13	14
Muslim.	*Total*	*1,478,287*	*796,802*	*681,485*	*697,397*	*415,970*	*281,427*	*686,300*	*336,582*	*349,718*	*94,590*	*44,250*	*50,340*
	0—1	43,670	22,098	21,572	43,670	22,098	21,572	....	—..	——	——	——	——
	1—2	50,226	25,366	24,860	59,226	25,366	24,860	....	....	..—	....	..—	..—
	2—3	49,746	25,214	24,532	49,746	25,214	24,532	....	—...	—..	—..	——	..—
	3—4	48,215	24,676	23,539	48,202	24,674	23,528	13	2	11	—..	——	....
	4—5	46,172	23,897	22,275	46,137	23,892	22,245	35	5	30	——	——	——
	Total 0—5	*238,029*	*121,251*	*116,778*	*237,981*	*121,244*	*116,737*	*48*	*7*	*41*	——	——	——
	5—10	193,586	105,480	88,106	190,065	104,302	85,763	3,468	1,162	2,306	53	16	37
	10—15	177,830	97,540	80,290	157,221	93,308	63,913	20,291	4,134	16,157	318	98	220
	15—20	147,366	75,480	71,886	60,392	48,699	11,693	85,115	25,880	59,235	1,859	901	958
	20—25	156,900	79,312	77,588	33,533	31,446	2,087	119,820	45,701	74,119	3,547	2,165	1,382
	25—30	137,695	72,131	65,564	9,456	9,006	450	122,271	59,067	63,204	5,968	4,058	1,910
	30—35	120,743	67,205	53,538	4,482	4,165	317	109,042	58,257	50,785	7,219	4,783	2,436
	35—40	89,791	51,464	38,327	1,753	1,582	171	78,686	44,971	33,715	9,352	4,911	4,441
	40—45	66,553	38,060	28,493	1,114	1,003	111	55,900	32,773	23,127	9,539	4,284	5,255
	45—50	46,129	27,098	19,031	573	516	57	34,342	22,325	12,017	11,214	4,257	6,957
	50—55	34,100	20,033	14,067	333	298	35	23,556	15,918	7,638	10,211	3,817	6,394
	55—60	24,045	14,182	9,863	173	141	32	13,451	10,035	3,416	10,421	4,006	6,415
	60—65	20,141	11,785	8,356	129	108	21	10,305	7,980	2,325	9,707	3,697	6,010
	65—70	8,437	5,153	3,284	64	52	12	3,772	3,061	711	4,601	2,040	2,561
	70& over	16,942	10,628	6,314	128	100	28	6,233	5,311	922	10,581	5,217	5,364

TABLE VII.—Age, Sex and Civil Condition.

Jammu and Kashmir Census 1931.

Part 1.—Frontier Districts.

Religion.	Age.	Population.			Unmarried.			Mairred.			Widowed.		
		Persons.	Males.	Females.	Persons.	Males.	Females.	Persons	Males.	Females.	Persons.	Males.	Females.
1	2	3	4	5	6	7	8	9	10	11	12	13	14
All Religions.	*Total*	*288,584*	*148,501*	*140,083*	*134,601*	*75,544*	*59,057*	*133,289*	*66,150*	*67,139*	*20,694*	*6,807*	*13,887*
	0—1	9,563	4,830	4,733	9,563	4,830	4,733	—	—	—	—	—	—
	1—2	8,759	4,298	4,461	8,759	4,298	4,461	....	—	—	—	—	—
	2—3	8,850	4,234	4,616	8,849	4,234	4,615	1	—	1	—	—	—
	3—4	8,798	4,320	4,478	8,796	4,320	4,476	2	—	2	—	—	—
	4—5	8,226	4,138	40,88	8,224	4,137	4,087	2	1	1	—	—	—
	Total 0—5	*44,196*	*21,820*	*22,376*	*44,191*	*21,819*	*22,372*	*5*	*1*	*4*	—	—	—
	5—10	35,597	18,795	16,802	34,890	18,686	16,204	686	98	588	21	11	10
	10—15	31,848	17,141	14,707	29,066	16,528	12,538	2,699	581	2,118	83	32	51
	15—20	24,640	12,719	11,921	12,434	8,350	4,084	11,721	4,172	7,549	485	197	288
	20—25	28,156	13,930	14,226	7,649	5,638	2,011	19,616	7,887	11,729	891	405	486
	25—30	25,093	12,554	12,539	2,773	2,108	665	21,159	9,884	11,275	1,161	562	599
	30—35	22,618	11,552	11,066	1,369	983	386	19,868	9,979	9,889	1,381	590	791
	35—40	18,264	9,515	8,749	674	434	240	16,015	8,521	7,494	1,575	560	1,015
	40—45	10,942	6,026	4,916	428	276	152	9,328	5,335	3,993	1,186	415	771
	45—50	11,030	5,529	5,501	325	210	115	8,735	4,813	3,922	1,970	506	1,464
	50—55	11,214	5,797	5,417	272	175	97	8,810	5,081	3,729	2,132	541	1,591
	55—60	8,833	4,690	4,143	170	106	64	5,984	3,897	2,087	2,679	687	1,992
	60—65	7,498	3,809	3,689	145	91	54	4,706	3,030	1,676	2,647	688	1,959
	65—70	3,514	1,861	1,653	83	54	29	1,816	1,269	547	1,615	538	1,077
	70& over	5,141	2,763	2,378	132	86	46	2,141	1,602	539	2,868	1,075	1,793
Hindu—(Brahmanic).	*Total*	*1,576*	*1,434*	*142*	*626*	*562*	*64*	*879*	*806*	*73*	*71*	*66*	*5*
	0—1	14	9	5	14	9	5	....	—	—	—	—	—
	1—2	12	10	2	12	10	2	....	....	—	—	—	—
	2—3	16	8	8	16	8	8	....	....	....	—	—	—
	3—4	12	6	6	12	6	6	....	—	—	—	—	—
	4—5	12	6	6	12	6	6	....	....	—	—	—	—
	Total 0—5	*66*	*39*	*27*	*66*	*39*	*27*	....	....	—	—	—	—
	5—10	49	28	21	49	28	21	....	....	....	—	—	—
	10—15	38	23	15	38	23	15	....	—	....	—	—	—
	15—20	217	204	13	131	130	1	83	71	12	—	—	—
	20—25	314	296	18	165	165	....	142	124	18	3	3	—
	25—30	338	318	20	97	97	....	224	205	19	7	7	....
	30—35	298	284	14	61	61	....	222	209	13	17	16	1
	35—40	136	128	8	11	11	....	112	106	6	15	14	1
	40—45	74	71	3	3	3	....	65	63	2	13	11	2
	45—50	26	25	1	4	4	....	19	18	1	6	5	1
	50—55	11	10	1	1	1	....	8	7	1	3	3	—
	55—60	5	4	1	....	....	....	2	1	1	2	2	—
	60—65	2	2	....	....	....	....	....	—	—	3	3	—
	65—70	1	1	....	....	....	....	1	1	—	2	2	—
	70&over	1	1	....	....	....	....	1	1	—	—	—	—
Hindu—(Arya).	*Total*	*104*	*70*	*34*	*51*	*33*	*18*	*46*	*32*	*14*	*7*	*5*	*2*
	0—1	3	2	1	3	2	1	—	....	—	....	—	—
	1—2	4	2	2	4	2	2	—	....	—	....	—	—
	2—3	6	2	4	6	2	4	....	....	—	....	—	—
	3—4	1	1	—	1	1	....	....	....	....	....	—	—
	4—5	4	2	2	4	2	2	—	—	....	....	....	—
	Total 0—5	*18*	*9*	*9*	*18*	*9*	*9*	....	....	....	—	....	—
	5—10	15	9	6	14	9	5	1	....	1	....	—	—
	10—15	6	4	2	6	4	2	—	....	—	....	—	—
	15—20	9	5	4	5	4	1	—	—	—	....	—	—
	20—25	9	6	3	3	3	....	4	1	3	....	—	—
	25—30	16	12	4	3	3	....	6	3	3	—	—	—
	30—35	14	12	2	1	1	....	11	7	4	2	2	—
	35—40	7	6	1	....	....	....	12	10	2	1	1	—
	40—45	4	4	....	....	....	—	6	6	....	1	—	1
	45—50	3	2	1	....	....	....	2	2	....	2	2	—
	50—55	1	1	....	....	....	....	3	2	1	—	....	—
	55—60	1	....	1	....	....	....	1	1	—	—	—	—
	60—65	....	....	....	....	....	....	....	—	—	1	—	1
	65—70	....	....	....	....	....	....	....	....	—	—	—	—
	70&over	1	....	1	1	....	1	....	....	—	—	—	—

TABLE VII.—Age, Sex and Civil Condition.

Jammu and Kashmir Census 1931.

Part I.—Frontier Districts—(continued).

Religion.	Age.	*Population.* Persons.	Males.	Females.	*Unmarried.* Persons.	Males.	Females.	*Married.* Persons.	Males.	Females.	*Widowed.* Persons.	Males.	Females.
1	2	3	4	5	6	7	8	9	10	11	12	13	14
Sikh.	*Total*	*190*	*125*	*65*	*93*	*55*	*38*	*94*	*68*	*26*	*3*	*2*	*1*
	0—1	11	7	4	11	7	4	....	....	....	....	....	....
	1—2	6	4	2	6	4	2	....	....	....	....	....	....
	2—3	8	3	5	8	3	5	....	....	....	....	....	....
	3—4	7	3	4	7	3	4	....	....	....	....	....	....
	4—5	4	2	2	4	2	2	....	....	....	....	....	....
	Total 0—5	*36*	*19*	*17*	*36*	*19*	*17*	....	....	....	....	....	....
	5—10	24	13	11	24	13	11	....	....	....	....	....	....
	10—15	17	11	6	17	11	6	....	....	....	....	....	....
	15—20	15	12	3	5	5	....	9	6	3	1	1	....
	20—25	18	11	7	3	3	....	15	8	7	....	....	....
	25—30	25	14	11	4	2	2	21	12	9	....	....	....
	30—35	19	14	5	3	1	2	15	12	3	1	1	....
	35—40	14	12	2	1	1	....	13	11	2	....	....	....
	40—45	9	8	1	....	....	....	9	8	1	....	....	....
	45—50	7	6	1	....	....	....	7	6	1	....	....	....
	50—55	2	2	....	....	....	....	2	2	....	....	....	....
	55—60	2	1	1	....	....	....	1	1	....	1	....	1
	60—65	1	1	....	....	....	....	1	1	....	....	....	....
	65—70	1	1	....	....	....	....	1	1	....	....	....	....
	70&over	....	....	....	....	....	....	....	....	....	....	....	....
Jain.	*Total*	*3*	*2*	*1*	*1*	*1*	....	*2*	*1*	*1*	....	....	....
	0—1	1	1	....	1	1	....	....	....	....	....	....	....
	1—2	....	....	....	....	....	....	....	....	....	....	....	....
	2—3	....	....	....	....	....	....	....	....	....	....	....	....
	3—4	....	....	....	....	....	....	....	....	....	....	....	....
	4—5	....	....	....	....	....	....	....	....	....	....	....	....
	Total 0—5	*1*	*1*	....	*1*	*1*	....	....	....	....	....	....	....
	5—10	....	....	....	....	....	....	....	....	....	....	....	....
	10—15	....	....	....	....	....	....	....	....	....	....	....	....
	15—20	....	....	....	....	....	....	....	....	....	....	....	....
	20—25	....	....	....	....	....	....	....	....	....	....	....	....
	25—30	2	1	1	....	....	....	2	1	1	....	....	....
	30—35	....	....	....	....	....	....	....	....	....	....	....	....
	35—40	....	....	....	....	....	....	....	....	....	....	....	....
	40—45	....	....	....	....	....	....	....	....	....	....	....	....
	45—50	....	....	....	....	....	....	....	....	....	....	....	....
	50—55	....	....	....	....	....	....	....	....	....	....	....	....
	55—60	....	....	....	....	....	....	....	....	....	....	....	....
	60—65	....	....	....	....	....	....	....	....	....	....	....	....
	65—70	....	....	....	....	....	....	....	....	....	....	....	....
	70&over	....	....	....	....	....	....	....	....	....	....	....	....
Buddhist.	*Total*	*38.212*	*19.029*	*19.183*	*17.388*	*8,654*	*8.734*	*17.405*	*9.133*	*8.272*	*3,419*	*1.242*	*2.177*
	0—1	934	472	462	934	472	462	....	....	....	....	....	....
	1—2	786	393	393	786	393	393	....	....	....	....	....	....
	2—3	864	400	464	864	400	464	....	....	....	....	....	....
	3—4	916	424	492	916	424	492	....	....	....	....	....	....
	4—5	815	393	422	815	393	422	....	....	....	....	....	....
	Total 0—5	*4.315*	*2,082*	*2,233*	*4,315*	*2.082*	*2.233*	....	....	....	....	....	....
	5—10	3,979	1,983	1,996	3,976	1,983	1,993	3	....	3	....	....	....
	10—15	3,688	1,823	1,865	3,613	1,798	1,815	70	24	46	5	1	4
	15—20	3,067	1,503	1,564	1,869	873	996	1,138	608	530	60	22	38
	20—25	3,236	1,599	1,637	1,274	587	687	1,867	973	894	95	39	56
	25—30	3,062	1,527	1,535	591	289	302	2,334	1,186	1,148	137	52	85
	30—35	2,812	1,420	1,383	416	221	195	2,246	1,153	1,093	150	55	95
	35—40	2,530	1,274	1,256	270	153	117	2,054	1,050	1,004	206	71	135
	40—45	2,285	1,157	1,128	258	151	107	1,804	931	873	223	75	148
	45—50	2,124	1,087	1,037	220	138	82	1,572	839	733	332	110	222
	50—55	1,976	997	979	189	118	71	1,441	762	679	346	117	229
	55—60	1,579	778	801	122	79	43	1,052	562	490	405	137	268
	60—65	1,451	724	727	109	72	37	910	503	407	432	149	283
	65—70	898	452	446	72	45	27	446	255	191	380	152	228
	70&over	1,210	614	596	94	65	29	468	287	181	648	262	386

TABLE VII.—Age, Sex and Civil Condition.

Jammu and Kashmir Census 1931.

Part 1.—Frontier Districts—(concluded).

Religion.	Age.	Population.			Unmarried.			Married.			Widowed.		
		Persons.	Males.	Females.	Persons.	Males.	Females.	Persons.	Males.	Females.	Persons.	Males.	Females.
1	2	3	4	5	6	7	8	9	10	11	12	13	14
Muslim.	*Total*	*248,328*	*127,751*	*120,577*	*116,345*	*56,187*	*50,158*	*11,4,794*	*66,073*	*58,721*	*17,189*	*5,491*	*11,698*
	0—1	8,595	4,337	4,258	8,595	4,337	4,258	....	—	—	—	—	—
	1—2	7,943	3,885	4,058	7,943	3,885	4,058	....	—	—	—	—	—
	2—3	7,950	3,820	4,130	7,949	3,820	4,129	1	—	1	—	—	—
	3—4	7,857	3,884	3.973	7,855	3,884	3,971	2	....	2	—	—	—
	4—5	7,386	3,733	3,653	7,384	3,732	3,652	2	1	1	—	—	—
	Total 0—5	*39,731*	*19,659*	*20,072*	*39,726*	*19,658*	*20,068*	*5*	*1*	*4*	—	—	—
	5—10	31,510	16,752	14,758	30,807	16,643	14,164	682	98	584	21	11	10
	10—15	28,086	15,274	12,812	25,379	14,686	10,693	2,629	557	2,072	78	31	47
	15—20	21,322	10,988	10,334	10,416	7,332	3,084	10,485	3,485	7,000	421	171	250
	20—25	24,568	12,011	12.557	6,197	4,875	1,322	17,582	6,777	10,805	789	359	430
	25—30	21,627	10,670	10,957	2,070	1,711	359	18,553	8,467	10,086	1,004	492	512
	30—35	19,456	9,803	9.653	882	695	187	17,361	8,589	8,772	1,213	519	694
	35—40	15,564	8,086	7,478	389	267	122	13,820	7,341	6,479	1,355	478	877
	40—45	8,561	4,782	3,779	165	121	44	7,441	4,328	3,113	955	333	622
	45—50	8,863	4,405	4,458	100	67	33	7,128	3,945	3,183	1,635	393	1,242
	50—55	9,217	4,784	4,433	82	56	26	7,351	4,306	3,045	1,784	422	1,362
	55—60	7,241	3,904	3,337	48	27	21	4,925	3,330	1,595	2,268	547	1,721
	60—65	6,042	3.080	2,962	36	19	17	3,793	2,524	1,269	2,213	537	1,676
	65—70	2,612	1,406	1,206	11	9	2	1,367	1,011	356	1,234	386	848
	70&over	3,928	2,147	1,781	37	21	16	1,672	1,314	358	2,219	812	1,407
Christian.	*Total.*	*171*	*90*	*81*	*97*	*52*	*45*	*69*	*37*	*32*	*5*	*1*	*4*
	0—1	5	2	3	5	2	3	....	—	....	—	—	—
	1—2	8	4	4	8	4	4	....	....	—	—	—	—
	2—3	6	1	5	6	1	5	....	....	....	—	....	—
	3—4	5	2	3	5	2	3	....	....	....	—	—	....
	4—5	5	2	3	5	2	3	....	....	....	—	....	....
	Total 0—5	*29*	*11*	*18*	*29*	*11*	*18*	....	....	....	—	—	—
	5—10	20	10	10	20	10	10	....	....	....	—	—	—
	10—15	13	6	7	13	6	7	....	....	....	—	—	....
	15—20	10	7	3	8	6	2	2	1	1	—	—	—
	20—25	11	7	4	7	5	2	4	2	2	—	—	—
	25—30	23	12	11	8	6	2	14	6	8	1	—	1
	30—35	19	10	9	6	4	2	12	6	6	1	—	1
	35—40	13	9	4	3	2	1	10	7	3	—	—	—
	40—45	9	4	5	2	1	1	7	3	4	—	—	—
	45—50	7	4	3	1	1	....	6	3	3	—	—	—
	50—55	7	3	4	....	....	....	7	3	4	....	—	—
	55—60	5	3	2	....	....	....	4	3	1	1	....	1
	60—65	2	2	....	....	....	....	2	2	—	—	....	—
	65—70	2	1	1	....	....	....	1	1	....	1	....	1
	70 & over	1	1	....	....	....	....	—	—	....	1	1	—

TABLE VII.—Age, Sex and Civil Condition.

Jammu and Kashmir Census 1931.

Part II.—Jammu District.

Religion.	Age.	Population. Persons.	Population. Males.	Population. Females.	Unmarried. Persons.	Unmarried. Males.	Unmarried. Females.	Married. Persons.	Married. Males.	Married. Females.	Widowed. Persons.	Widowed. Males.	Widowed. Females.
1	2	3	4	5	6	7	8	9	10	11	12	13	14
All Religions.	*Total*	*375,240*	*205,719*	*169,521*	*170,512*	*105,302*	*65,210*	*163,211*	*84,149*	*79,062*	*41,517*	*16,268*	*25,249*
	0—1	13,121	6,542	6,579	13,121	6,542	6,579	....	....	....	....	....	....
	1—2	11,192	5,618	5,574	11,192	5,618	5,574	....	....	....	....	....	....
	2—3	10,880	5,538	5,342	10,880	5,538	5,342	....	....	....	....	....	....
	3—4	11,227	5,552	5,675	11,227	5,552	5,675	....	....	....	....	....	....
	4—5	11,513	5,325	6,188	11,490	5,312	6,178	21	13	8	2	....	2
	Total 0—5	*57,933*	*28,575*	*29,358*	*57,910*	*28,562*	*29,348*	*21*	*13*	*8*	*2*	....	*2*
	5—10	45,551	24,887	20,664	42,361	23,387	18,974	3,104	1,471	1,633	86	29	57
	10—15	42,525	23,465	19,060	34,532	21,026	13,506	7,743	2,358	5,385	250	81	169
	15—20	36,137	19,328	16,809	15,743	13,149	2,594	19,551	5,838	13,713	843	341	502
	20—30	68,467	37,591	30,876	13;940	13,360	580	50,675	22,463	28,212	3,852	1,768	2,084
	30—40	50,396	29,097	21,299	3,484	3,365	119	39,805	22,855	16,950	7,107	2,877	4,230
	40—50	33,161	18,874	14,287	1,334	1,286	48	22,672	14,306	8,366	9,155	3,282	5,873
	50—60	21,947	12,762	9,185	740	715	25	12,076	8,669	3,407	9,131	3,378	5,753
	60& over	19,123	11,140	7,983	468	452	16	7,564	6,176	1,388	11,091	4,512	6,579
Hindu—(Brahmanic).	*Total*	*173,346*	*94,683*	*78,663*	*77,246*	*49,187*	*28,059*	*73,753*	*37,853*	*35,900*	*22,347*	*7,643*	*14,704*
	0—1	5,901	2,974	2,927	5,901	2,974	2,927	....	....	....	....	....	....
	1—2	4,892	2,460	2,432	4 892	2,460	2,432	....	....	....	....	....	....
	2—3	4,658	2,385	2,273	4,658	2,385	2,273	....	....	....	....	....	....
	3—4	5,077	2,407	2,670	5,077	2,407	2,670	....	....	....	....	....	....
	4—5	5,682	2,275	3,407	5,680	2,275	3,405	....	....	....	2	....	2
	Total 0—5	*26,210*	*12,501*	*13,709*	*26,208*	*12,501*	*13,707*	....	....	....	*2*	....	*2*
	5—10	19,522	10,830	8,692	17,970	10,015	7,955	1,497	795	702	55	20	35
	10—15	18,132	10,326	7,806	14,457	9,225	5,232	3,532	1,058	2,474	143	43	100
	15—20	16,358	8,819	7,539	7,433	6,539	894	8,482	2,153	6,329	443	127	316
	20—30	31,646	17,190	14,456	7,390	7,206	184	22,184	9,308	12,876	2,072	676	1,396
	30—40	23,787	13,542	10,245	2,095	2,046	49	17,775	10,205	7,570	3,917	1,291	2,626
	40—50	16,575	9,339	7,236	861	845	16	10,697	6,868	3,829	5,017	1,626	3,391
	50—60	11,315	6,561	4,754	506	490	16	5,900	4,383	1,517	4,909	1,688	3,221
	60& over	9,801	5,575	4,226	326	320	6	3,686	3,083	603	5,789	2,172	3,617
Hindu—(Arya).	*Total*	*43,710*	*24,059*	*19,651*	*20,235*	*12,357*	*7,878*	*19,106*	*9,803*	*9,303*	*4,369*	*1,899*	*2,470*
	0—1	1,623	813	810	1,623	813	810	....	....	....	....	....	....
	1—2	1,389	698	691	1,389	698	691	....	....	....	....	....	....
	2—3	1,382	705	677	1,382	705	677	....	....	....	....	....	....
	3—4	1,346	692	654	1,346	692	654	....	....	....	....	....	....
	4—5	1,279	685	594	1,266	672	594	13	13	....	....	....	....
	Total 0—5	*7,019*	*3,593*	*3,426*	*7,006*	*3,580*	*3,426*	*13*	*13*	....	....	....	....
	5—10	5,571	3,077	2,494	5,331	3,019	2,312	232	84	178	8	4	4
	10—15	5,184	2,852	2,332	4,408	2,692	1,716	755	151	604	21	9	12
	15—20	4,202	2,183	2,019	1,785	1,441	344	2,328	705	1,623	89	37	52
	20—30	7,883	4,238	3,645	1,296	1,232	64	6,172	2,782	3,390	415	224	191
	30—40	5,914	3,447	2,467	240	229	11	4,899	2,849	2,050	775	369	406
	40—50	3,724	2,137	1,587	78	74	4	2,660	1,692	968	986	371	615
	50—60	2,322	1,383	939	58	57	1	1,273	934	339	991	392	599
	60& over	1,891	1,149	742	33	33	....	774	623	151	1,084	493	591
Hindu—(Brahmo).	*Total*	*4*	*3*	*1*	*2*	*2*	....	*2*	*1*	*1*	....	....	....
	0—1	....	....	....	....	....	....	....	....	....	....	....	....
	1—2	....	....	....	....	....	....	....	....	....	....	....	....
	2—3	....	....	....	....	....	....	....	....	....	....	....	....
	3—4	....	....	....	....	....	....	....	....	....	....	....	....
	4—5	....	....	....	....	....	....	....	....	....	....	....	....
	Total 0—5	....	....	....	....	....	....	....	....	....	....	....	....
	5—10	....	....	....	....	....	....	....	....	....	....	....	....
	10—15	1	1	....	1	1	....	....	....	....	....	....	....
	15—20	1	1	....	1	1	....	....	....	....	....	....	....
	20—30	....	....	....	....	....	....	....	....	....	....	....	....
	30—40	2	1	1	....	....	....	2	1	1	....	....	....
	40—50	....	....	....	....	....	....	....	....	....	....	....	....
	50—60	....	....	....	....	....	....	....	....	....	....	....	....
	60& over	....	....	....	....	....	....	....	....	....	....	....	....

TABLE VII.—Age, Sex and Civil Condition.

Jammu and Kashmir Census 1931.

Part II.—Jammu District—(continued).

Religion.	Age.	Population.			Unmarried.			Married.			Widowed.		
		Persons.	Males.	Females.	Persons.	Males.	Females.	Persons.	Males.	Females.	Persons.	Males.	Females.
1	2	3	4	5	6	7	8	9	10	11	12	13	14
Sikh.	*Total*	*6,854*	*3,677*	*3,177*	*3,329*	*1,968*	*1,361*	*2,869*	*1,438*	*1,431*	*656*	*27*	*285*
	0—1	321	157	164	321	157	164	— —	— —	— —	— —	— —	— —
	1—2	230	113	117	230	113	117	....	— —	— —	— —	— —	— —
	2—3	215	116	99	215	116	99	....	— —	— —	— —	— —	— —
	3—4	212	114	98	212	114	98	....	— —	— —	— —	— —	— —
	4—5	205	100	105	205	100	105	....	— —	— —	— —	— —	— —
	Total 0—5	*1,183*	*600*	*583*	*1,183*	*600*	*583*	— —	— —	— —	— —	— —	— —
	5—10	906	484	422	879	479	400	25	5	20	2	— —	2
	10—15	803	433	370	701	411	290	89	21	68	13	1	12
	15—20	628	312	316	264	199	65	339	102	237	25	11	14
	20—30	1,186	598	588	207	189	18	912	364	548	67	45	22
	30—40	916	535	381	52	50	2	758	438	320	106	47	59
	40—50	528	300	228	19	18	1	383	240	143	126	42	84
	50—60	366	212	154	15	14	1	219	151	68	132	47	85
	60& over	338	203	135	9	8	1	144	117	27	185	78	107
Jain.	*Total*	*578*	*309*	*269*	*314*	*184*	*130*	*205*	*98*	*107*	*59*	*27*	*32*
	0—1	12	9	3	12	9	3						
	1—2	14	9	5	14	9	5	— —	— —	— —	— —	— —	— —
	2—3	20	11	9	20	11	9	....	— —	— —	— —	— —	— —
	3—4	16	8	8	16	8	8	....	— —	— —	— —	— —	— —
	4—5	13	7	6	13	7	6	....	— —	— —	— —	— —	— —
	Total 0—5	*75*	*44*	*31*	*75*	*44*	*31*	— —	— —	— —	— —	— —	[illegible]
	5—10	71	32	39	70	31	39	1	1	— —	— —	— —	— —
	10—15	71	32	39	68	32	36	3	— —	3	— —	— —	— —
	15—20	57	29	28	35	23	12	20	5	15	2	1	1
	20—30	104	59	45	38	30	8	62	26	36	4	3	1
	30—40	77	42	35	14	13	1	53	27	26	10	2	8
	40—50	65	34	31	9	8	1	37	19	18	19	7	12
	50—60	40	25	15	4	3	1	23	15	8	13	7	6
	60& over	18	12	6	1	....	1	6	5	1	11	7	4
Buddhist.	*Total*	*9*	*4*	*5*	*5*	*2*	*3*	*4*	*2*	*2*	— —	— —	— —
	0—1	1	....	1	1	....	1						
	1—2	....	....	....	....	....	....	....	....	— —	— —	— —	— —
	2—3	1	....	1	1	....	1	....	....	— —	— —	— —	— —
	3—4	....	....	....	....	....	....	....	....	— —	— —	— —	— —
	4—5	....	....	....	....	....	....	....	....	— —	— —	— —	— —
	Total 0—5	*2*	....	*2*	*2*	....	*2*	....	....	— —	— —	— —	— —
	5—10	2	1	1	2	1	1	....	....	....	— —	— —	— —
	10—15	....	....	....	....	....	....	....	....	....	....	— —	....
	15—20	2	1	1	1	1	....	1	....	1	....	— —	....
	20—30	2	1	1	....	....	....	2	1	1	....	....	....
	30—40	....	....	....	....	....	....	....	....	....	....	....	....
	40—50	1	1	....	....	....	....	1	1	....	....	....	....
	50—60	....	....	....	....	....	....	....	....	— —	....	....	....
	60 &over	....	....	....	....	....	....	....	....	— —	....	— —	....
Muslim.	*Total*	*149,336*	*82,202*	*67,134*	*68,699*	*41,200*	*27,499*	*66,675*	*34,637*	*32,038*	*13,962*	*6,365*	*7,597*
	0—1	5,192	2,550	2,642	5,192	2,550	2,642	....	....	....	— —	— —	— —
	1—2	4,620	2,316	2,304	4,620	2,316	2,304	....	....	....	— —	— —	— —
	2—3	4,559	2,299	2,260	4,559	2,299	2,260	....	....	....	....	— —	....
	3—4	4,530	2,304	2,226	4,530	2,304	2,226	....	....	....	....	— —	....
	4—5	4,270	2,210	2,060	4,262	2,210	2,052	8	....	8	— —	— —	— —
	Total 0—5	*23,171*	*11,679*	*11,492*	*23,163*	*11,679*	*11,484*	*8*	....	*8*	— —	— —	— —
	5—10	19,299	10,366	8,933	17,935	9,748	8,187	1,344	614	730	20	4	16
	10—15	18,192	9,750	8,442	14,769	8,598	6,171	3,350	1,124	2,226	73	28	45
	15—20	14,755	7,920	6,835	6,171	4,908	1,263	8,305	2,851	5,454	279	161	118
	20—30	27,369	15,357	12,012	4,974	4,674	300	21,116	9,872	11,244	1,279	811	468
	30—40	19,511	11,414	8,097	1,075	1,020	55	16,166	9,240	6,926	2,270	1,154	1,116
	40—50	12,161	7,001	5,160	363	338	25	8,819	5,438	3,381	2,979	1,225	1,754
	50—60	7,843	4,543	3,300	153	147	6	4,626	3,163	1,463	3,064	1,233	1,831
	60 &over	7,035	4,172	2,863	96	88	8	2,941	2,335	606	3,998	1,749	2,249

TABLE VII.—Age, Sex and Civil Condition.

Jammu and Kashmir Census 1931.

Part II.—Jammu District—(concluded).

Religion.	Age.	Population.			Unmarried.			Married.			Widowed.		
		Persons.	Males.	Females.	Persons.	Males.	Females.	Persons.	Males.	Females.	Persons.	Males.	Females.
1	2	3	4	5	6	7	8	9	10	11	12	13	14
Christian.	*Total*	*1,362*	*765*	*597*	*659*	*394*	*265*	*583*	*310*	*273*	*120*	*61*	*59*
	0—1	68	38	30	68	38	30	....	....	....	....	....	....
	1—2	47	22	25	47	22	25	....	....	....	....	....	....
	2—3	44	22	22	44	22	22	....	....	....	....	....	....
	3—4	45	27	18	45	27	18	....	....	....	....	....	....
	4—5	63	48	15	63	48	15	....	....	....	....	....	....
	Total 0—5	*267*	*157*	*110*	*267*	*157*	*110*	....	....	....	....	....	....
	5—10	174	95	79	170	93	77	4	2	2	....	....	....
	10—15	134	67	67	121	63	58	13	4	9	....	....	....
	15—20	127	60	67	48	35	13	74	21	53	5	4	1
	20—30	271	146	125	34	29	5	222	108	114	15	9	6
	30—40	186	114	72	8	7	1	149	93	56	29	14	15
	40—50	105	61	44	4	3	1	74	47	27	27	11	16
	50—60	58	36	22	4	4	....	34	22	12	20	10	10
	60 & over	40	29	11	3	3	....	13	13	....	24	13	11

TABLE VII.—Age, Sex and Civil Condition.

Jammu and Kashmir Census 1931.

Part II.—Kathua District.

Religion.	Age.	Population.			Unmarried.			Married.			Widowed.		
		Persons.	Males.	Females.	Persons.	Males.	Females.	Persons.	Males.	Females.	Persons.	Males.	Females.
1	2	3	4	5	6	7	8	9	10	11	12	13	14
All Religions.	*Total*	*161,232*	*85,993*	*75,239*	*71,776*	*44,825*	*26,951*	*69,349*	*34,407*	*34,942*	*20,107*	*6,761*	*13,346*
	0—1	5,151	2,553	2,598	5,151	2,553	2,598	....	....	—	—	—	—
	1—2	4,680	2,417	2,263	4,680	2,417	2,263	....	....	—	—	—	—
	2—3	4,657	2,402	2,255	4,657	2,402	2,255	....	....	—	—	—	—
	3—4	4,492	2,300	2,192	4,492	2,300	2,192	....	....	—	—	—	—
	4—5	4,258	2,240	2,018	4,249	2,231	2,018	9	9	—	—	—	—
	Total 0—5	*23,238*	*11,912*	*11,326*	*23,229*	*11,903*	*11,326*	*9*	*9*	—	—	—	—
	5—10	19.576	10,402	9,174	18,402	10,130	8,272	1.137	258	879	37	14	23
	10—15	18,914	9,943	8,971	15,396	9,265	6,131	3.387	648	2,739	131	30	101
	15—20	16,125	8.225	7,900	6,516	5,492	1,024	9,130	2,590	6,540	479	143	336
	20—30	29.508	15,471	14.037	5,541	5,377	164	21,932	9.366	12,566	2,035	728	1,307
	30—40	21,469	11,928	9,541	1,468	1,453	15	16,465	9,311	7,154	3,536	1,164	2,372
	40—50	14,327	8.001	6,326	657	649	8	9,369	6,006	3,363	4,301	1,346	2,955
	50—60	9,347	5.271	4,076	337	332	5	4,747	3,517	1,230	4,263	1,422	2,841
	60& over	8,728	4,840	3,888	230	224	6	3,173	2,702	471	5,325	1,914	3,411
Hindu—(Brahmanic).	*Total*	*104,667*	*55,242*	*49,425*	*46,039*	*29,281*	*16,758*	*43,628*	*21,360*	*22,268*	*15,000*	*4,601*	*10,399*
	0—1	3,308	1,677	1,631	3,308	1,677	1,631	....	—	—	—	—	—
	1—2	2,933	1,518	1,415	2,933	1,518	1,415	....	—	....	....	—	—
	2—3	2,841	1,470	1,371	2,841	1,470	1,371	....	—	....	....	....	....
	3—4	2,762	1,426	1,336	2,762	1,426	1,336	....	—	....	....	—	—
	4—5	2,609	1,368	1,241	2,609	1,368	1,241	....	—	—	—	—	—
	Total 0—5	*14.453*	*7.459*	*6.994*	*14.453*	*7.459*	*6.994*	....	—	—	—	—	....
	5—10	12,146	6,459	5,687	11,557	6,362	5,195	571	89	482	18	8	10
	10—15	11.718	6,117	5,601	9,726	5,847	3,879	1,919	259	1,660	73	11	62
	15—20	10,108	5.046	5,062	4,232	3,630	602	5.554	1,347	4,207	322	69	253
	20—30	19,008	9,738	9.270	3,942	3,870	72	13.578	5,450	8,128	1,488	418	1,070
	30—40	14,310	7.819	6,491	1,163	1,155	8	10,462	5,883	4,579	2,685	781	1,904
	40—50	9,881	5,414	4,470	482	477	5	6.153	4,001	2,152	3,249	936	2,313
	50—60	6,725	3,776	2,949	279	277	2	3.227	2,444	783	3,219	1,055	2,164
	60& over	6,315	3,414	2,901	205	204	1	2.164	1,887	277	3,946	1,323	2,623
Hindu—(Arya).	*Total*	*16,271*	*8,766*	*7,505*	*7,347*	*4,541*	*2,806*	*7,228*	*3,607*	*3,621*	*1,696*	*618*	*1,078*
	0—1	520	255	265	520	255	265	....	....	....	....	....	....
	1—2	487	247	240	487	247	240	....	....	....	....	....	....
	2—3	506	259	247	506	259	247	....	....	....	....	....	....
	3—4	483	243	240	483	243	240	....	....	....	....	....	....
	4—5	483	267	216	483	267	216	....	....	—	....	....	....
	Total 0—5	*2,479*	*1,271*	*1,208*	*2,479*	*1,271*	*1,208*	....	....	....	....	....	....
	5—10	1,999	1,077	922	1,880	1,048	832	116	29	87	3	....	3
	10—15	1,943	1,031	912	1,580	966	614	253	62	291	10	3	7
	15—20	1,754	892	862	721	597	124	987	277	710	46	18	28
	20—30	3,153	1,697	1,456	518	497	21	2,444	1,111	1,333	191	89	102
	30—40	2,137	1,190	947	104	102	2	1,736	982	754	297	106	191
	40—50	1,390	804	586	38	38	....	962	637	325	390	129	261
	50—60	776	426	350	16	14	2	398	301	97	362	111	251
	60& over	640	378	262	11	8	3	232	208	24	397	162	235
Sikh.	*Total*	*478*	*268*	*210*	*241*	*143*	*98*	*205*	*109*	*96*	*32*	*16*	*16*
	0—1	21	8	13	21	8	13	....	....	....	....	....	....
	1—2	17	6	11	17	6	11	....	....	....	....	....	....
	2—3	14	6	8	14	6	8	....	....	....	....	....	....
	3—4	11	5	6	11	5	6	....	....	....	....	....	....
	4—5	16	6	10	16	6	10	....	....	....	....	....	....
	Total 0—5	*79*	*31*	*48*	*79*	*31*	*48*	....	....	....	....	....	....
	5—10	67	37	30	63	37	26	4	....	4	....	....	....
	10—15	59	33	26	48	31	17	11	2	9	....	....	....
	15—20	51	26	25	25	19	6	25	7	18	1	....	1
	20—30	78	47	31	19	18	1	58	29	29	1	....	1
	30—40	62	38	24	6	6	....	52	30	22	4	2	2
	40—50	41	31	10	....	....	....	34	25	9	7	6	1
	50—60	26	15	11	....	....	....	16	12	4	10	3	7
	60& over	15	10	5	1	1	....	5	4	1	9	5	4

TABLE VII.—Age, Sex and Civil Condition.

Jammu and Kashmir Census 1931.

Part II.—Kathua District—(concluded).

Religion.	Age.	Population.			Unmarried.			Married.			Widowed.		
		Persons.	Males.	Females.	Persons.	Males.	Females.	Persons.	Males.	Females.	Persons.	Males.	Females.
1	2	3	4	5	6	7	8	9	10	11	12	13	14
Muslim.	*Total*	*39,647*	*21,619*	*18,028*	*18,074*	*10,808*	*7,266*	*18,207*	*9,291*	*8,916*	*3,366*	*1,520*	*1,846*
	0—1	1,298	611	687	1,298	611	687	....	....	....	....	....	....
	1—2	1,242	645	597	1,242	645	597	....	....	....	....	....	....
	2—3	1,294	666	628	1,294	666	628	....	....	....	....	....	....
	3—4	1,233	625	608	1,233	625	608	....	....	....	....	....	....
	4—5	1,145	596	549	1 136	587	549	9	9	....	....	....	....
	Total 0—5	*6,212*	*3,143*	*3,069*	*6,203*	*3,134*	*3,069*	*9*	*9*	....	....	....	....
	5—10	5,346	2,819	2,527	4,884	2,673	2,211	446	140	306	16	6	10
	10—15	5,173	2,751	2,422	4,027	2,411	1,616	1,099	324	775	47	16	31
	15—20	4,181	2,243	1,938	1,527	1,237	290	2,546	952	1,594	108	54	54
	20—30	7,229	3,963	3,266	1,048	979	69	5,827	2,764	3,063	354	220	134
	30—40	4,937	2,868	2,069	193	188	5	4,197	2,406	1,791	547	274	273
	40—50	2,997	1,744	1,253	137	134	3	2,211	1,337	874	649	273	376
	50—60	1,815	1,051	764	42	41	1	1,101	757	344	672	253	419
	60& over	1,757	1,037	720	13	11	2	771	602	169	973	424	549
Christian.	*Total*	*169*	*98*	*71*	*75*	*52*	*23*	*81*	*40*	*41*	*13*	*6*	*7*
	0—1	4	2	2	4	2	2	....	....	....	....	....	....
	1—2	1	1	....	1	1	....	....	....	....	....	....	....
	2—3	2	1	1	2	1	1	....	....	....	....	....	....
	3—4	3	1	2	3	1	2	....	....	....	....	....	....
	4—5	5	3	2	5	3	2	....	....	....	....	....	....
	Total 0—5	*15*	*8*	*7*	*15*	*8*	*7*	....	....	....	....	....	....
	5—10	18	10	8	18	10	8	....	....	....	....	....	....
	10—15	21	11	10	15	10	5	5	1	4	1	....	1
	15—20	31	18	13	11	9	2	18	7	11	2	2	....
	20—30	40	26	14	14	13	1	25	12	13	1	1	....
	30—40	23	13	10	2	2	....	18	10	8	3	1	2
	40—50	15	8	7	....	....	....	9	6	3	6	2	4
	50—60	5	3	2	....	....	....	5	3	2	....	....	....
	60& over	1	1	....	....	....	....	1	1	....	....	....	....

TABLE VII.—Age, Sex and Civil Condition.

Jammu and Kashmir Census 1931.

Part II.—Udhampur District.

Religion.	Age.	Population.			Unmarried.			Married.			Widowed.		
		Persons.	Males.	Females.	Persons.	Males.	Females.	Persons.	Males.	Females.	Persons.	Males.	Females.
1	2	3	4	5	6	7	8	9	10	11	12	13	14
All Religions.	*Total*	*273,668*	*143,514*	*130,154*	*123,060*	*74,452*	*48,608*	*122,708*	*59,959*	*62,749*	*27,900*	*9,103*	*18,797*
	0—1	8,645	4,396	4,249	8,645	4,396	4,249	—	—	—	—	—	—
	1—2	8,134	4,032	4,102	8,134	4,032	4,102	—	—	—	—	—	—
	2—3	8,244	4,012	4,232	8,244	4,012	4,232	—	—	—	—	—	—
	3—4	8,064	4,027	4,037	8,064	4,027	4,037	—	—	—	—	—	—
	4—5	7,467	3,773	3,694	7,467	3,773	3,694	—	—	—	—	—	—
	Total 0—5	*40,554*	*20,240*	*20,314*	*40,554*	*20,240*	*20,314*	—	—	—	—	—	—
	5—10	32,668	17,207	15,461	31,634	16,953	14,681	975	246	729	59	8	51
	10—15	30.156	15,819	14,337	25,757	15,092	10,665	4,216	702	3,514	183	25	158
	15—20	26,091	13.000	13,091	10,839	8,918	1,921	14,646	3,920	10,726	606	162	444
	20—30	51,090	26,008	25,082	9,722	9,008	714	38,836	16,018	22,818	2,532	982	1,550
	30—40	38,330	20,897	17,433	2,511	2,302	209	31,261	16,956	14.305	4,558	1,639	2,919
	40—50	24,324	13,430	10,894	982	938	44	17,563	10.737	6,826	5.779	1,755	4,024
	50—60	15,624	8,792	6,832	600	574	26	9,070	6,423	2,647	5,954	1,795	4,159
	60&over	14,831	8,121	6,710	461	427	34	6,141	4,957	1,184	8,229	2,737	5,492
Hindu (Brahmanic).	*Total*	*138,122*	*71,558*	*66,564*	*59,481*	*36,919*	*22,562*	*60,716*	*29,555*	*31.161*	*17,925*	*5,084*	*12,841*
	0—1	4,173	2,077	2,096	4,173	2,077	2,096	—	—	—	—	—	—
	1—2	3,750	1,833	1,917	3,750	1,833	1,917	—	—	—	—	—	—
	2—3	3,808	1,842	1,966	3,808	1,842	1,966	—	—	—	—	—	—
	3—4	3,691	1,833	1,858	3,691	1,833	1,858	—	—	—	—	—	—
	4—5	3,407	1,697	1,710	3,407	1,697	1,710	—	—	—	—	—	—
	Total 0—5	*18,829*	*9,282*	*9,547*	*18.829*	*9,282*	*9,547*	—	—	—	—	—	—
	5—10	15,338	7,976	7,362	14,766	7,853	6,913	548	120	428	24	3	21
	10—15	14,517	7,450	7,067	12,059	7,127	4,932	2,333	310	2,023	125	13	112
	15—20	12,961	6,344	6,617	5,207	4,517	690	7,331	1,750	5,581	423	77	346
	20—30	25,233	12,725	12,508	5,325	5,028	297	18,291	7,249	11,042	1,617	448	1,169
	30—40	19.778	10,560	9,218	1,742	1,598	144	15,080	8,097	6,983	2,956	865	2,091
	40—50	13,627	7,443	6,184	744	726	18	9,056	5,692	3,364	3,827	1,025	2,802
	50—60	9,217	5,144	4,073	450	442	8	4,844	3,612	1,232	3,923	1,090	2,833
	60&over	8,622	4,634	3,988	359	346	13	3,233	2,725	508	5,030	1,563	3,467
Hindu—(Arya).	*Total*	*17,641*	*9,151*	*8,490*	*7,518*	*4,662*	*2,856*	*8,115*	*3,832*	*4,283*	*2,008*	*657*	*1,351*
	0—1	485	247	238	485	247	238	—	—	—	—	—	—
	1—2	458	236	222	458	236	222	—	—	—	—	—	—
	2—3	500	253	247	500	253	247	—	—	—	—	—	—
	3—4	506	252	254	506	252	254	—	—	—	—	—	—
	4—5	457	242	215	457	242	215	—	—	—	—	—	—
	Total 0—5	*2,406*	*1,230*	*1,176*	*2,406*	*1,230*	*1,176*	—	—	—	—	—	—
	5—10	1,985	1,045	940	1,885	1,034	851	74	9	65	26	2	24
	10—15	1,894	957	937	1,527	914	613	336	38	298	31	5	26
	15—20	1,674	819	855	692	579	113	944	225	719	38	15	23
	20—30	3,372	1,707	1,665	717	617	100	2,495	1,023	1,472	160	67	93
	30—40	2,597	1,395	1,202	151	148	3	2,081	1,117	964	365	130	235
	40—50	1,675	860	815	54	54	—	1,205	694	511	416	112	304
	50—60	1,145	643	502	64	64	—	633	440	193	448	139	309
	60&over	893	495	398	22	22	—	347	286	61	524	187	387
Sikh.	*Total*	*328*	*178*	*150*	*153*	*87*	*66*	*161*	*80*	*71*	*24*	*11*	*13*
	0—1	10	5	5	10	5	5	—	—	—	—	—	—
	1—2	11	3	8	11	3	8	—	—	—	—	—	—
	2—3	9	5	4	9	5	4	—	—	—	—	—	—
	3—4	12	7	5	12	7	5	—	—	—	—	—	—
	4—5	10	5	5	10	5	5	—	—	—	—	—	—
	Total 0—5	*52*	*25*	*27*	*52*	*25*	*27*	—	—	—	—	—	—
	5—10	48	25	23	47	25	22	1	—	1	—	—	—
	10—15	44	23	21	36	21	15	8	2	6	—	—	—
	15—20	25	13	12	11	9	2	14	4	10	—	—	—
	20—30	42	16	26	2	2	—	38	13	25	2	1	1
	30—40	53	32	21	2	2	—	45	28	17	6	2	4
	40—50	35	28	7	1	1	—	26	19	7	8	8	—
	50—60	17	12	5	2	2	—	13	10	3	2	—	2
	60&over	12	4	8	—	—	—	6	4	2	6	—	6

TABLE VII.—Age, Sex and Civil Condition.

Jammu and Kashmir Census 1931.

Part II.—Udhampur District—(concluded).

Religion.	Age.	*Population.*			*Unmarried.*			*Married.*			*Widowed.*		
		Persons.	Males.	Females.	Persons.	Males.	Females.	Persons.	Males.	Females.	Persons.	Males.	Females.
1	2	3	4	5	6	7	8	9	10	11	12	13	14
Jain.	*Total*	*2*	*1*	*1*	....	....	....	*2*	*1*	*1*	....	....	....
	0—1	....	....	....	....	....	....	....	....	....	....	....	....
	1—2	....	....	....	....	....	....	....	....	....	....	....	....
	2—3	....	....	....	....	....	....	....	....	....	....	....	....
	3—4	....	....	....	....	....	....	....	....	....	....	....	....
	4—5	....	....	....	....	....	....	....	....	....	....	....	....
	Total 0—5	....	....	....	....	....	....	....	....	....	....	....	....
	5—10	....	....	....	....	....	....	....	....	....	....	....	....
	10—15	....	....	....	....	....	....	....	....	....	....	....	....
	15—20	....	....	....	....	....	....	....	....	....	....	....	....
	20—30	....	....	....	....	....	....	....	....	....	....	....	....
	30—50	....	....	....	....	....	....	....	....	....	....	....	....
	40—40	....	....	....	....	....	....	....	....	....	....	....	....
	50—60	2	1	1	....	....	....	2	1	1	....	....	....
	60& over	....	....	....	....	....	....	....	....	....	....	....	....
Buddhist.	*Total*	*492*	*245*	*247*	*207*	*111*	*96*	*243*	*119*	*124*	*42*	*15*	*27*
	0—1	13	8	5	13	8	5	....	....	....	....	....	....
	1—2	14	7	7	14	7	7	....	....	....	....	....	....
	2—3	11	5	6	11	5	6	....	....	....	....	....	....
	3—4	12	5	7	12	5	7	....	....	....	....	....	....
	4—5	10	5	5	10	5	5	....	....	....	....	....	....
	Total 0—5	*60*	*30*	*30*	*60*	*30*	*30*	....	....	....	....	....	....
	5—10	56	29	27	56	29	27	....	....	....	....	....	....
	10—15	57	29	28	54	29	25	2	....	2	1	....	1
	15—20	36	17	19	18	10	8	17	7	10	1	....	1
	20—30	95	44	51	12	8	4	78	33	45	5	3	2
	30—40	72	36	36	6	4	2	61	29	32	5	3	2
	40—50	53	25	28	....	....	....	42	21	21	11	4	7
	50—60	33	17	16	....	....	....	24	14	10	9	3	6
	60& over	30	18	12	1	1	....	19	15	4	10	2	8
Muslim.	*Total*	*117,051*	*62,361*	*54,690*	*55,689*	*32,667*	*23,022*	*53,464*	*26,360*	*27,104*	*7,898*	*3,334*	*4,564*
	0—1	3,963	2,059	1,904	3,963	2,059	1,904	....	....	....	....	....	....
	1—2	3,901	1,953	1,948	3,901	1,953	1,948	....	....	....	....	....	....
	2—3	3,916	1,907	2,009	3,916	1,907	2,009	....	....	....	....	....	....
	3—4	3,843	1,930	1,913	3,843	1,930	1,913	....	....	....	....	....	....
	4—5	3,583	1,824	1,759	3,583	1,824	1,759	....	....	....	....	....	....
	Total 0—5	*19,206*	*9,673*	*9,533*	*19,206*	*9,673*	*9,533*	....	....	....	....	....	....
	5—10	15,237	8,129	7,108	14,876	8,009	6,867	352	117	235	9	3	6
	10—15	13,639	7,357	6,282	12,077	6,999	5,078	1,536	351	1,185	26	7	19
	15—20	11,393	5,806	5,587	4,909	3,802	1,107	6,340	1,934	4,406	144	70	74
	20—30	22,338	11,511	10,827	3,665	3,353	312	17,926	7,695	10,231	747	463	284
	30—40	15,822	8,868	6,954	610	550	60	13,986	7,679	6,307	1,226	639	587
	40—50	8,934	5,074	3,860	183	157	26	7,234	4,311	2,923	1,517	606	911
	50—60	5,209	2,974	2,235	84	66	18	3,554	2,346	1,208	1,571	562	1,009
	60& over	5,273	2,969	2,304	79	58	21	2,536	1,927	609	2,658	984	1,674
Christian.	*Total*	*32*	*20*	*12*	*12*	*6*	*6*	*17*	*12*	*5*	*3*	*2*	*1*
	0—1	1	....	1	1	....	1	....	....	....	....	....	....
	1—2	....	....	....	....	....	....	....	....	....	....	....	....
	2—3	....	....	....	....	....	....	....	....	....	....	....	....
	3—4	....	....	....	....	....	....	....	....	....	....	....	....
	4—5	....	....	....	....	....	....	....	....	....	....	....	....
	Total 0—5	*1*	....	*1*	*1*	....	*1*	....	....	....	....	....	....
	5—10	4	3	1	4	3	1	....	....	....	....	....	....
	10—15	5	3	2	4	2	2	1	1	....	....	....	....
	15—20	2	1	1	2	1	1	....	....	....	....	....	....
	20—30	10	5	5	1	....	1	8	5	3	1	....	1
	30—40	8	6	2	....	....	....	8	6	2	....	....	....
	40—50	....	....	....	....	....	....	....	....	....	....	....	....
	50—60	1	1	....	....	....	....	....	....	....	1	1	....
	60 and over.	1	1	....	....	....	....	....	....	....	1	1	....

TABLE VII.—AGE, SEX AND CIVIL CONDITION.

Jammu and Kashmir Census 1931.

Part II.—Reasi District.

Religion.	Age.	Population. Persons.	Population. Males.	Population. Females.	Unmarried. Persons.	Unmarried. Males.	Unmarried. Females.	Married. Persons.	Married. Males.	Married. Females.	Widowed. Persons.	Widowed. Males	Widowed. Females.
1	2	3	4	5	6	7	8	9	10	11	12	13	14
All Religions.	*Total*	*235,245*	*124,210*	*111,035*	*110,434*	*66,916*	*43,518*	*103,234*	*50,149*	*53,085*	*21,577*	*7,145*	*14,432*
	0—1	7,683	3,849	3,834	7,683	3,849	3,834	....	....	....	....	....	....
	1—2	7,776	3,857	3,919	7,776	3,857	3,919	....	....	....	....	....	....
	2—3	7,760	3,844	3,916	7,760	3,844	3,916	....	....	....	....	....	....
	3—4	7,407	3,699	3,708	7,407	3,699	3,708	....	....	....	....	....	....
	4—5	7,049	3,552	3,497	6,979	3,519	3,460	62	32	30	8	1	7
	Total 0—5	*37,675*	*18,801*	*18,874*	*37,605*	*18,768*	*18,837*	*62*	*32*	*30*	*8*	*1*	*7*
	5—10	30,028	16,107	13,921	28,745	15,750	12,995	1,227	345	882	56	12	44
	10—15	27,716	14,960	12,756	23,409	14,161	9,248	4,178	775	3,403	129	24	105
	15—20	22,518	11,057	11,461	9,496	7,708	1,788	12,526	3,190	9,336	496	159	337
	20—30	42,882	21,435	21,447	7,518	7,048	470	33,200	13,568	19,632	2,164	819	1,345
	30—40	30,882	16,979	13,903	1,907	1,819	88	25,539	13,904	11,635	3,436	1,256	2,180
	40—50	19, 07	10,909	8,198	824	780	41	13,861	8,707	5,154	4,322	1,322	3,000
	50—60	12,245	7,079	5,166	508	480	28	7,296	5,247	2,049	4,441	1,352	3,089
	60 & over	12,292	6,983	5,309	422	402	20	5,345	4,381	964	6,525	2,200	4,325
Hindu—(Brahmanic).	*Total*	*71,401*	*37,537*	*33,864*	*29,788*	*19,273*	*10,515*	*31,360*	*15,249*	*16,111*	*10,253*	*3,015*	*7,238*
	0—1	2,021	1,019	1,002	2,021	1,019	1,002	....	....	....	....	....	....
	1—2	1,893	924	969	1,893	924	969	....	....	....	....	....	....
	2—3	1,902	935	967	1,902	935	967	....	....	....	....	....	....
	3—4	1,848	930	918	1,848	930	918	....	....	....	....	....	....
	4—5	1,784	882	902	1,729	864	865	47	17	30	8	1	7
	Total 0—5	*9,448*	*4,690*	*4,758*	*9,393*	*4,672*	*4,721*	*47*	*17*	*30*	*8*	*1*	*7*
	5—10	7,681	4,003	3,678	7,089	3,893	3,196	562	108	454	30	2	28
	10—15	7,185	3,747	3,438	5,686	3,520	2,166	1,435	219	1,216	64	8	56
	15—20	6,384	3,100	3,284	2,542	2,243	299	3,624	817	2,807	218	40	178
	20—30	12,944	6,435	6,509	2,776	2,715	61	9,160	3,481	5,679	1,008	239	769
	30—40	10,249	5,622	4,627	1,065	1,031	34	7,552	4,092	3,460	1,632	499	1,133
	40—50	7,242	4,036	3,146	529	511	18	4,553	2,972	1,581	2,160	613	1,547
	50—60	5,093	2,942	2,151	388	376	12	2,559	1,933	626	2,146	633	1,513
	60& over	5,175	2,902	2,273	320	312	8	1,868	1,610	258	2,987	980	2,007
Hindu—(Arya).	*Total*	*7,611*	*3,879*	*3,732*	*3,000*	*1,820*	*1,180*	*3,600*	*1,754*	*1,846*	*1,011*	*305*	*706*
	0—1	218	96	122	218	96	122	....	....	....	....	....	....
	1—2	192	90	102	192	90	102	....	....	....	....	....	....
	2—3	203	96	107	203	96	107	....	....	....	....	....	....
	3—4	200	98	102	200	98	102	....	....	....	....	....	....
	4—5	180	93	87	176	89	87	4	4	....	....	....	....
	Total 0—5	*993*	*473*	*520*	*989*	*469*	*520*	*4*	*4*	....	....	....	....
	5—10	788	406	382	732	390	342	51	13	38	5	3	2
	10—15	768	376	392	594	348	246	164	27	137	10	1	9
	15—20	692	321	371	256	213	43	413	104	309	23	4	19
	20—30	1,462	694	768	259	243	16	1,094	420	674	109	31	78
	30—40	1,179	648	531	98	89	9	896	499	397	185	60	125
	40—50	746	402	344	35	32	3	504	317	187	207	53	154
	50—60	470	271	199	16	16	....	264	198	66	190	57	133
	60& over	513	288	225	21	20	1	210	172	38	282	96	186
Sikh.	*Total*	*842*	*449*	*393*	*345*	*201*	*144*	*415*	*218*	*197*	*82*	*30*	*52*
	0—1	24	15	9	24	15	9	....	....	....	....	....	....
	1—2	29	16	13	26	16	13	....	....	....	....	....	....
	2—3	32	16	16	32	16	16	....	....	....	....	....	....
	3—4	24	12	12	24	12	12	....	....	....	....	....	....
	4—5	24	14	10	22	12	10	2	2	....	....	....	....
	Total 0—5	*133*	*73*	*60*	*131*	*71*	*60*	*2*	*2*	....	....	....	....
	5—10	99	54	45	93	49	44	5	5	....	1	....	1
	10—15	92	48	44	74	41	33	17	6	11	1	1	....
	15—20	81	32	49	21	15	6	59	17	42	1	....	1
	20—30	159	76	83	19	18	1	134	57	77	6	1	5
	30—40	127	75	52	5	5	....	104	62	42	18	8	10
	40—50	75	47	28	1	1	....	60	42	18	14	4	10
	50—60	47	26	21	1	1	....	26	19	7	20	6	14
	60& over	29	18	11	....	....	....	8	8	....	21	10	11

TABLE VII.—Age, Sex and Civil Condition.

Jammu and Kashmir Census 1931.

Part II.—Reasi District—(concluded).

Religion.	Age.	Population.			Unmarried.			Married.			Widowed.		
		Persons.	Males.	Females.	Persons.	Males.	Females.	Persons.	Males.	Females.	Persons.	Males.	Females.
1	2	3	4	5	6	7	8	9	10	11	12	13	14
Buddhist.	*Total*	*6*	*4*	*2*	*1*	*1*	....	*5*	*3*	*2*	....	....	....
	0—1	....	....	....	....	....	....	....	....	....	....	....	....
	1—2	....	....	....	....	....	....	....	....	....	....	....	....
	2—3	....	....	....	....	....	....	....	....	....	....	....	....
	3—4	....	....	....	....	....	....	....	....	....	....	....	....
	4—5	....	....	....	....	....	....	....	....	....	....	....	....
	Total 0—5	....	....	....	....	....	....	....	....	....	....	....	....
	5—10	1	1	....	....	....	....	1	1	....	....	....	....
	10—15	1	....	1	....	....	....	1	....	1	....	....	....
	15—20	2	2	....	1	1	....	1	1	....	....	....	....
	20—30	2	1	1	....	....	....	2	1	1	....	....	....
	30—40	....	....	....	....	....	....	....	....	....	....	....	....
	40—50	....	....	....	....	....	....	....	....	....	....	....	....
	50—60	....	....	....	....	....	....	....	....	....	....	....	....
	60 & over	....	....	....	....	....	....	....	....	....	....	....	....
Muslim.	*Total*	*155,353*	*82,322*	*73,031*	*77,284*	*45,613*	*31,671*	*67,841*	*32,917*	*34,924*	*10,228*	*3,792*	*6,436*
	0—1	5,418	2,718	2,700	5,418	2,718	2,700	....	....	....	....	....	....
	1—2	5,662	2,827	2,835	5,662	2,827	2,835	....	....	....	....	....	....
	2—3	5,621	2,797	2,824	5,621	2,797	2,824	....	....	....	....	....	....
	3—4	5,334	2,659	2,675	5,334	2,659	2,675	....	....	....	....	....	....
	4—5	5,061	2,563	2,498	5,052	2,554	2,498	9	9	....	....	....	....
	Total 0—5	*27,096*	*13,564*	*13,532*	*27,087*	*13,555*	*13,532*	*9*	*9*	....	....	....	....
	5—10	21,452	11,639	9,813	20,824	11,414	9,410	608	218	390	20	7	13
	10—15	19,667	10,787	8,880	17,052	10,250	6,802	2,561	523	2,038	54	14	40
	15—20	15,357	7,601	7,756	6,675	5,235	1,440	8,428	2,251	6,177	254	115	139
	20—30	28,310	14,227	14,083	4,464	4,072	392	22,805	9,607	13,198	1,041	548	493
	30—40	19,323	10,631	8,692	739	694	45	16,984	9,249	7,735	1,600	688	912
	40—50	10,939	6,259	4,680	259	236	23	8,741	5,373	3,368	1,939	650	1,289
	50—60	6,635	3,840	2,795	103	87	16	4,447	3,097	1,350	2,085	656	1,429
	60 & over	6,574	3,774	2,800	81	70	11	3,258	2,590	668	3,235	1,114	2,121
Christian.	*Total*	*32*	*19*	*13*	*16*	*8*	*8*	*13*	*8*	*5*	*3*	*3*	....
	0—1	2	1	1	2	1	1	....	....	....	....	....	....
	1—2	....	....	....	....	....	....	....	....	....	....	....	....
	2—5	2	....	2	2	....	2	....	....	....	....	....	....
	3—4	1	....	1	1	....	1	....	....	....	....	....	....
	4—5	....	....	....	....	....	....	....	....	....	....	....	....
	Total 0—5	*5*	*1*	*4*	*5*	*1*	*4*	....	....	....	....	....	....
	5—10	7	4	3	7	4	3	....	....	....	....	....	....
	10—15	3	2	1	3	2	1	....	....	....	....	....	....
	15—20	2	1	1	1	1	....	1	....	1	....	....	....
	20—30	5	2	3	....	....	....	5	2	3	....	....	....
	30—40	4	3	1	....	....	....	3	2	1	....	....	....
	40—50	5	5	....	....	....	....	3	3	....	1	1	....
	50—60	....	....	....	....	....	....	....	....	....	2	2	....
	60 & over	1	1	....	....	....	....	1	1	....	....	....	....

TABLE VII.—AGE, SEX AND CIVIL CONDITION.

Jammu and Kashmir Census 1931.

Part II.—Mirpur District.

Religion.	Age.	Population.			Unmarried.			Married.			Widowed.		
		Persons.	Males.	Females.	Persons.	Males.	Females.	Persons.	Males.	Females.	Persons.	Males.	Females.
1	2	3	4	5	6	7	8	9	10	11	12	13	14
All Religions.	*Total*	*344,747*	*178,831*	*165,916*	*163,551*	*97,311*	*66,240*	*147,680*	*69,629*	*78,051*	*33,516*	*11,891*	*21,625*
	0—1	11,828	6,025	5,803	11,828	6,025	5,803	—	—	—	—	—	—
	1—2	10,895	5,500	5,395	10,895	5,500	5,395	—	—	—	—	—	—
	2—3	11,337	5,715	5,622	11,337	5,715	5,622	—	—	—	—	—	—
	3—4	11,344	5,788	5,556	11,344	5,788	5,556	—	—	—	—	—	—
	4—5	10,785	5,545	5,240	10,784	5,544	5,240	1	1	—	—	—	—
	Total 0—5	*56,189*	*28,573*	*27,616*	*56,188*	*28,572*	*27,616*	*1*	*1*	—	—	—	—
	5—10	44,717	24,135	20,582	43,102	23,559	19,543	1,575	567	1,008	40	9	31
	10—15	40,235	21,955	18,380	34,999	20,715	14,284	5,226	1,217	4,009	110	23	87
	15—20	31,671	15,692	15,979	14,494	11,232	3,262	16,708	4,286	12,422	469	174	295
	20—30	60,531	29,224	31,307	10,863	9,817	1,046	46,674	17,936	28,738	2,994	1,471	1,523
	30—40	44,911	23,412	21,499	2,292	1,975	317	37,088	19,223	17,865	5,531	2,214	3,317
	40—50	28,967	15,396	13,571	837	746	91	21,078	12,566	8,512	7,032	2,084	4,968
	50—60	18,829	10,250	8,579	432	385	47	11,258	7,622	3,636	7,139	2,243	4,896
	60& over	18,597	10,194	8,403	344	310	34	8,072	6,211	1,861	10,181	3,673	6,508
Hindu—(Brahmanic).	*Total*	*50,102*	*26,416*	*23,686*	*23,531*	*14,282*	*9,249*	*21,288*	*10,423*	*10,865*	*5,283*	*1,711*	*3,572*
	0—1	1,735	857	878	1,735	857	878	—	—	—	—	—	—
	1—2	1,487	741	746	1,487	741	746	—	—	—	—	—	—
	2—3	1,545	810	735	1,545	810	735	—	—	—	—	—	—
	3—4	1,558	825	733	1,558	825	733	—	—	—	—	—	—
	4—5	1,435	748	687	1,435	748	687	—	—	—	—	—	—
	Total 0—5	*7,760*	*3,981*	*3,779*	*7,760*	*3,981*	*3,779*	—	—	—	—	—	—
	5—10	6,390	3,447	2,943	6,082	3,306	2,776	301	140	161	7	1	6
	10—15	5,916	3,169	2,747	4,999	2,922	2,077	896	243	653	21	4	17
	15—20	4,335	2,098	2,237	1,942	1,564	378	2,312	517	1,795	81	17	64
	20—30	8,086	3,933	4,153	1,661	1,530	131	6,003	2,269	3,734	422	134	288
	30—40	6,411	3,430	2,981	538	463	75	5,072	2,718	2,354	801	249	552
	40—50	4,651	2,579	2,072	244	229	15	3,300	2,014	1,286	1,107	336	771
	50—60	3,197	1,880	1,317	155	148	7	1,924	1,360	564	1,118	372	746
	60 &over	3,356	1,899	1,457	150	139	11	1,480	1,162	318	1,726	598	1,128
Hindu—(Arya).	*Total*	*7,492*	*3,804*	*3,688*	*3,398*	*1,956*	*1,442*	*3,351*	*1,614*	*1,737*	*743*	*234*	*509*
	0—1	256	144	112	256	144	112	—	—	—	—	—	—
	1—2	245	138	107	245	138	107	—	—	—	—	—	—
	2—3	247	125	122	247	125	122	—	—	—	—	—	—
	3—4	237	109	128	237	109	128	—	—	—	—	—	—
	4—5	231	113	118	231	113	118	—	—	—	—	—	—
	Total 0—5	*1,216*	*629*	*587*	*1,216*	*629*	*587*	—	—	—	—	—	—
	5—10	943	492	451	911	484	427	30	8	22	2	—	2
	10—15	851	436	415	740	414	326	107	22	85	4	—	4
	15—20	705	304	401	285	204	81	406	95	311	14	5	9
	20—30	1,365	644	721	197	180	17	1,102	439	663	66	25	41
	30—40	1,016	543	473	27	26	1	869	482	387	120	35	85
	40—50	623	338	285	13	12	1	448	277	171	162	49	113
	50—60	388	209	179	6	5	1	228	157	71	154	47	107
	60& over	385	209	176	3	2	1	161	134	27	221	73	148
Sikh.	*Total*	*9,432*	*4,848*	*4,584*	*4,543*	*2,657*	*1,886*	*4,167*	*1,954*	*2,213*	*722*	*237*	*485*
	0—1	393	215	178	393	215	178	—	—	—	—	—	—
	1—2	330	165	165	330	165	165	—	—	—	—	—	—
	2—3	317	148	169	317	148	169	—	—	—	—	—	—
	3—4	322	161	161	322	161	161	—	—	—	—	—	—
	4—5	349	167	182	348	166	182	1	1	—	—	—	—
	Total 0—5	*1,711*	*856*	*855*	*1,710*	*855*	*855*	*1*	*1*	—	—	—	—
	5—10	1,262	716	546	1,200	697	503	59	17	42	3	2	1
	10—15	1,147	606	541	952	573	379	193	32	161	2	1	1
	15—20	863	382	481	356	254	102	496	125	371	11	3	8
	20—30	1,504	668	836	210	188	22	1,239	460	779	55	20	35
	30—40	1,165	611	554	46	44	2	1,006	540	466	113	27	86
	40—50	783	454	329	35	23	12	620	385	235	128	46	82
	50—60	481	282	199	21	10	11	324	225	99	136	47	89
	60& over	516	273	243	13	13	—	229	169	60	274	91	183

TABLE VII.—AGE, SEX AND CIVIL CONDITION.

Jammu and Kashmir Census 1931.

Part II.—Mirpur District—(concluded).

Religion.	Age.	Population.			Unmarried			Married.			Widowed.		
		Persons.	Males.	Females.	Persons.	Males.	Females.	Persons.	Males.	Females.	Persons.	Males.	Females.
1	2	3	4	5	6	7	8	9	10	11	12	13	14
Jain.	*Total*	*8*	*3*	*5*	*5*	*2*	*3*	*3*	*1*	*2*	....	....	....
	0—1	....	....	....	....	....	....	....	....	....	....	....	....
	1—2	....	....	....	....	....	....	....	....	....	....	....	....
	2—3	....	....	....	....	....	....	....	....	....	....	....	....
	3—4	1	1	....	1	1	....	....	....	....	....	....	....
	4—5	....	....	....	....	....	....	....	....	....	....	....	....
	Total 0—5	*1*	*1*	....	*1*	*1*	....	....	....	....	....	....	....
	5—10	2	....	2	2	....	2	....	....	....	....	....	....
	10—15	2	1	1	2	1	1	....	....	....	....	....	....
	15—20	....	....	....	....	....	....	....	....	....	....	....	....
	20—30	1	....	1	....	....	....	1	....	1	....	....	....
	30—40	2	1	1	....	....	....	2	1	1	....	....	....
	40—50	....	....	....	....	....	....	....	....	....	....	....	....
	50—60	....	....	....	....	....	....	....	....	....	....	....	....
	60&over.	....	....	....	....	....	....	....	....	....	....	....	....
Muslim.	*Total*	*277,631*	*143,718*	*133,913*	*132,023*	*78,387*	*53,636*	*118,846*	*55,624*	*63,222*	*26,762*	*9,707*	*17,055*
	0—1	9,438	4,806	4,632	9,438	4,806	4,632	....	....	....	....	....	....
	1—2	8,830	4,454	4,376	8,830	4,454	4,376	....	....	....	....	....	....
	2—3	9,225	4,630	4,595	9,225	4,630	4,595	....	....	....	....	....	....
	3—4	9,219	4,686	4,533	9,219	4,686	4,533	....	....	....	....	....	....
	4—5	8,764	4,513	4,251	8,764	4,513	4,251	....	....	....	....	....	....
	Total 0—5	*45,476*	*23.089*	*22,387*	*45,476*	*23,089*	*22,387*	....	....	....	....	....	....
	5—10	36,106	19,474	16,632	34,893	19,066	15,827	1,185	402	783	28	6	22
	10—15	32,410	17,740	14,670	28,299	16,802	11,497	4,029	920	3,109	82	18	64
	15—20	25,761	12,906	12,855	11,909	9,210	2,699	13,489	3,547	9,942	363	149	214
	20—30	49,562	23,975	25,587	8,793	7,918	875	38,319	14,765	23,554	2,450	1,292	1,158
	30—40	36,307	18,819	17,488	1,680	1,442	238	30,131	15,475	14,656	4,496	1,902	2,594
	40—50	22,909	12,024	10,885	545	482	63	16,709	9,889	6,820	5,655	1,653	4,002
	50—60	14,760	7,878	6,882	250	222	28	8,782	5,880	2,902	5,728	1,776	3,952
	60&over.	14,340	7,813	6,527	178	156	22	6,202	4,746	1,456	7,960	2,911	5,049
Christian.	*Total*	*82*	*42*	*40*	*51*	*27*	*24*	*25*	*13*	*12*	*6*	*2*	*4*
	0—1	6	3	3	6	3	3	....	....	....	....	....	....
	1—2	3	2	1	3	2	1	....	....	....	....	....	....
	2—3	3	2	1	3	2	1	....	....	....	....	....	....
	3—4	7	6	1	7	6	1	....	....	....	....	....	....
	4—5	6	4	2	6	4	2	....	....	....	....	....	....
	Total 0—5	*25*	*17*	*8*	*25*	*17*	*8*	....	....	....	....	....	....
	5—10	14	6	8	14	6	8	....	....	....	....	....	....
	10—15	9	3	6	7	3	4	1	....	1	1	....	1
	15—20	7	2	5	2	....	2	5	2	3	....	....	....
	20—30	13	4	9	2	1	1	10	3	7	1	....	1
	30—40	10	8	2	1	....	1	8	7	1	1	1	....
	40—50	1	1	....	....	....	....	1	1	....	....	....	....
	50—60	3	1	2	....	....	....	....	....	....	3	1	2
	60&over.	....	....	....	....	....	....	....	....	....	....	....	....

TABLE VII.—Age, Sex and Civil Condition.

Jammu and Kashmr Census 1931.

Part II.—Chenani Jagir.

Religion.	Age.	Population.			Unmarried.			Married.			Widowed.		
		Persons.	Males.	Females.	Persons.	Males.	Females.	Persons.	Males.	Females.	Persons.	Males.	Females.
1	2	3	4	5	6	7	8	9	10	11	12	13	14
All Religions.	*Total*	*10,925*	*5,930*	*4,995*	*4,505*	*2,939*	*1,566*	*5,007*	*2,529*	*2,478*	*1,413*	*462*	*951*
	0—1	285	137	148	285	137	148	....	....	....	....	....	....
	1—2	269	123	146	269	123	146	....	....	....	....	....	....
	2—3	274	135	139	274	135	139	....	....	....	....	....	....
	3—4	287	153	134	287	153	134	....	....	....	....	....	....
	4—5	268	147	121	268	147	121	....	....	....	....	....	....
	Total 0—5	*1,383*	*695*	*688*	*1,383*	*695*	*688*	....	....	....	....	....	....
	5—10	1,163	640	523	1,116	626	490	46	14	32	1	....	1
	10—15	1,109	581	528	882	544	338	220	37	183	7	....	7
	15—20	1,032	503	529	368	332	36	634	166	468	30	5	25
	20—30	2,116	1,112	1,004	414	405	9	1,565	668	897	137	39	98
	30—40	1,690	974	716	163	159	4	1,264	723	541	263	92	171
	40—50	1,030	603	427	84	83	1	657	430	227	289	90	199
	50—60	732	446	286	56	56	....	381	294	87	295	96	199
	60&over	670	376	294	39	39	....	240	197	43	391	140	251
Hindu—(Brahmanic).	*Total*	*9,042*	*4,868*	*4,174*	*3,773*	*2,487*	*1,286*	*4,019*	*1,984*	*2,035*	*1,250*	*397*	*853*
	0—1	235	115	120	235	115	120	....	....	....	....	....	....
	1—2	220	104	116	220	104	116	....	....	....	....	....	....
	2—3	226	112	114	226	112	114	....	....	....	....	....	....
	3—4	238	125	113	238	125	113	....	....	....	....	....	....
	4—5	223	121	102	223	121	102	....	....	....	....	....	....
	Total 0—5	*1,142*	*577*	*565*	*1,142*	*577*	*565*	....	....	....	....	....	....
	5—10	966	534	432	934	527	407	31	7	24	1	....	1
	10—15	913	485	428	737	461	276	170	24	146	6	....	6
	15—20	826	393	433	301	274	27	503	118	385	22	1	23
	20-30	1,716	870	846	349	341	8	1,245	500	745	122	29	93
	30—40	1,407	799	608	145	142	3	1,018	578	440	244	79	165
	40—50	863	499	364	72	72	....	531	344	187	260	83	177
	50—60	629	382	247	54	54	....	315	243	72	260	85	175
	60&over	580	329	251	39	39	....	206	170	36	335	120	215
Hindu.—(Arya)	*Total*	*367*	*166*	*201*	*122*	*64*	*58*	*200*	*96*	*104*	*45*	*6*	*39*
	0—1	6	2	4	6	2	4	....	....	....	....	....	....
	1—2	6	1	5	6	1	5	....	....	....	....	....	....
	2—3	11	3	8	11	3	8	....	....	....	....	....	....
	3—4	11	4	7	11	4	7	....	....	....	....	....	....
	4—5	8	4	4	8	4	4	....	....	....	....	....	....
	Total 0—5	*42*	*14*	*28*	*42*	*14*	*28*	....	....	....	....	....	....
	5—10	33	15	18	31	14	17	2	1	1	....	....	....
	10—15	31	11	20	22	10	12	8	1	7	1	....	1
	15—20	38	17	21	8	8	....	27	8	19	3	1	2
	20—30	86	44	42	13	13	....	70	30	40	3	1	2
	30—40	56	31	25	3	3	....	51	28	23	2	....	2
	40—50	36	16	20	3	2	1	24	14	10	9	....	9
	50—60	20	12	8	....	....	....	12	10	2	8	2	6
	60&over	25	6	19	....	....	....	6	4	2	19	2	17
Sikh.	*Total*	*4*	*4*	....	*1*	*1*	....	*3*	*3*	....	....	....	....
	0—1	....	....	....	....	....	....	....	....	....	....	....	....
	1—2	....	....	....	....	....	....	....	....	....	....	....	....
	2—3	....	....	....	....	....	....	....	....	....	....	....	....
	3—4	....	....	....	....	....	....	....	....	....	....	....	....
	4—5	....	....	....	....	....	....	....	....	....	....	....	....
	Total 0—5	....	....	....	....	....	....	....	....	....	....	....	....
	5—10	*1*	*1*	....	*1*	*1*	....	....	....	....	....	....	....
	10—15	....	....	....	....	....	....	....	....	....	....	....	....
	15—20	....	....	....	....	....	....	....	....	....	....	....	....
	20—30	1	1	....	....	....	....	1	1	....	....	....	....
	30—40	2	2	....	....	....	....	2	2	....	....	....	....
	40—50	....	....	....	....	....	....	....	....	....	....	....	....
	50—60	....	....	....	....	....	....	....	....	....	....	....	....
	60&over	....	....	....	....	....	....	....	....	....	....	....	....

TABLE VII.—Age, Sex and Civil Condition.

Jammu and Kashmir Census 1931.

Part II.—Chenani Jagir—(concluded).

Religion.	Age.	Population.			Unmarried.			Married.			Widowed.		
		Persons.	Males.	Females.	Persons.	Males.	Females.	Persons.	Males.	Females.	Persons.	Males.	Females.
1	2	3	4	5	6	7	8	9	10	11	12	13	14
Muslim.	*Total*	*1,512*	*892*	*620*	*609*	*387*	*222*	*785*	*446*	*339*	*118*	*59*	*59*
	0—1	44	20	24	44	20	24	..	...	...	...	...	...
	1—2	43	18	25	43	18	25	...	...	...	...	...	...
	2—3	37	20	17	37	20	17	...	...	...	...	...	...
	3—4	38	24	14	38	24	14	...	...	...	...	...	...
	4—5	37	22	15	37	22	15	...	...	...	...	...	...
	Total 0—5	*199*	*104*	*95*	*199*	*104*	*95*	...	...	...	...	...	...
	5—10	163	90	73	150	84	66	13	6	7	...	...	...
	10—15	165	85	80	123	73	50	42	12	30	...	...	...
	15—20	168	93	75	59	50	9	104	40	64	5	3	2
	20—30	313	197	116	52	51	1	249	137	112	12	9	3
	30—40	225	142	83	15	14	1	193	115	78	17	13	4
	40—50	131	88	43	9	9	...	102	72	30	20	7	13
	50—60	83	52	31	2	2	...	54	41	13	27	9	18
	60&over	65	41	24	....	...	....	28	23	5	37	18	19

TABLE VII.—Age, Sex and Civil Condition.

Jammu and Kashmir Census 1931.

Part II.—Poonch Jagir.

Religion.	Age.	Population.			Unmarried.			Married.			Widowed.		
		Persons.	Males.	Females.	Persons.	Males.	Females.	Persons.	Males.	Females.	Persons.	Males.	°Females.
1	2	3	4	5	6	7	8	9	10	11	12	13	14
All Religions.	*Total*	*387,384*	*198,618*	*188,766*	*194,320*	*113,184*	*81,136*	*166,749*	*77,632*	*89,217*	*26,315*	*7,902*	*18,413*
	0—1	13,704	6,727	6,977	13,704	6,727	6,977	....	....	....	....	....	....
	1—2	13,788	6,777	7,011	13,788	6,777	7,011	....	....	....	....	....	....
	2—3	13,444	6,636	6,808	13,444	6,636	6,808	....	....	....	....	....	....
	3—4	13,254	6,598	6,656	13,253	6,598	6,655	1	....	1	....	....	....
	4—5	13,205	6,684	6,521	13,170	6,664	6,506	34	20	14	1	....	1
	Total 0—5	*67,395*	*33,422*	*33,973*	*67,359*	*33,402*	*33,957*	*35*	*20*	*15*	*1*	....	*1*
	5—10	54,867	29,591	25,276	53,579	29,250	24,329	1,250	332	918	38	9	29
	10—15	49,277	27,109	22,168	43,442	25,748	17,694	5,694	1,332	4,362	141	29	112
	15—20	36,226	17,839	18,387	16,435	12,591	3,844	19,266	5,064	14,202	525	184	341
	20—30	68,567	31,989	36,578	10,989	10,014	975	55,090	20,949	34,141	2,488	1,026	1,462
	30—40	51,149	26,044	25,105	1,537	1,376	161	45,094	23,258	21,836	4,518	1,410	3,108
	40—50	28,398	15,187	13,211	514	430	84	22,272	13,392	8,880	5,612	1,365	4,247
	50—60	16,138	8,807	7,331	222	181	41	10,528	7,262	3,266	5,388	1,364	4,024
	60& over	15,367	8,630	6,737	243	192	51	7,520	5,923	1,597	7,604	2,515	5,089
Hindu—(Brahmanic).	*Total*	*25,190*	*13,060*	*12,130*	*12,733*	*7,703*	*5,030*	*10,048*	*4,659*	*5,389*	*2,409*	*698*	*1,711*
	0—1	885	451	434	885	451	434	....	....	....	....	....	....
	1—2	891	444	447	891	444	447	....	....	....	....	....	....
	2—3	877	434	443	877	434	443	....	....	....	....	....	....
	3—4	847	434	413	847	434	413	....	....	....	....	....	....
	4—5	843	442	401	840	442	398	3̇	....	3	....	....	....
	Total 0—5	*4,343*	*2,205*	*2,138*	*4,340*	*2,205*	*2,135*	*3*	....	*3*	....	....	....
	5—10	3,464	1,834	1,630	3,377	1,822	1,555	83	11	72	4	1	3
	10—15	3,029	1,623	1,406	2,696	1,591	1,105	321	31	290	12	1	11
	15—20	2,276	1,126	1,150	1,073	890	183	1,161	227	934	42	9	33
	20—30	4,359	2,063	2,296	877	836	41	3,245	1,154	2,091	237	73	164
	30—40	3,182	1,691	1,491	200	194	6	2,547	1,380	1,167	435	117	318
	40—50	2,056	1,147	909	86	82	4	1,448	913	535	522	152	370
	50—60	1,258	695	563	42	42	....	717	511	206	499	142	357
	60& over	1,223	676	547	42	41	1	523	432	91	658	203	455
Hindu—(Arya).	*Total*	*280*	*156*	*124*	*130*	*85*	*45*	*133*	*65*	*68*	*17*	*6*	*11*
	0—1	6	2	4	6	2	4	....	....	....	....	....	....
	1—2	11	6	5	11	6	5	....	....	....	....	....	....
	2—3	12	8	4	12	8	4	....	....	....	....	....	....
	3—4	7	4	3	7	4	3	....	....	....	....	....	....
	4—5	9	4	5	9	4	5	....	....	....	....	....	....
	Total 0—5	*45*	*24*	*21*	*45*	*24*	*21*	....	....	....	....	....	....
	5—10	29	16	13	28	16	12	1	....	1	....	....	....
	10—15	35	19	16	27	17	10	8	2	6	....	....	....
	15—20	32	13	19	13	11	2	19	2	17	....	....	....
	20—30	75	40	35	15	15	....	55	23	32	5	2	3
	30—40	41	31	10	2	2	....	34	26	8	5	3	2
	40—50	14	8	6	....	....	....	9	7	2	5	1	4
	50—60	7	4	3	....	....	....	5	4	1	2	....	2
	60& over	2	1	1	....	....	....	2	1	1	....	....	....
Sikh.	*Total*	*11,344*	*5,773*	*5,571*	*5,771*	*3,371*	*2,400*	*4,632*	*2,131*	*2,501*	*941*	*271*	*670*
	0—1	464	247	217	464	247	217	....	....	....	....	....	....
	1—2	425	209	216	425	209	216	....	....	....	....	....	....
	2—3	416	200	216	416	200	216	....	....	....	....	....	....
	3—4	419	210	209	418	210	208	1	....	1	....	....	....
	4—5	402	204	198	399	204	195	2	....	2	1	....	1
	Total 0—5	*2,126*	*1,070*	*1,056*	*2,122*	*1,070*	*1,052*	*3*	....	*3*	*1*	....	*1*
	5—10	1,654	896	758	1,618	885	733	34	11	23	2	....	2
	10—15	1,453	788	665	1,273	762	511	177	26	151	3	....	3
	15—20	1,032	479	553	426	346	80	593	131	462	13	2	11
	20—30	1,940	867	1,073	268	254	14	1,587	589	998	85	24	61
	30—40	1,440	760	680	43	38	5	1,207	664	543	190	58	132
	40—50	839	438	401	15	10	5	599	369	230	225	59	166
	50—60	477	268	209	4	4	....	276	206	70	197	58	139
	60& over	383	207	176	2	2	....	156	135	21	225	70	155

TABLE VII.—Age, Sex and Civil Condition.

Jammu and Kashmir Census 1931.

Part II.—Poonch Jagir—(concluded).

Religion.	Age.	Population.			Unmarried.			Married.			Widowed.		
		Persons.	Males.	Females.	Persons.	Males.	Females.	Persons.	Males.	Females.	Persons.	Males.	Females.
1	2	3	4	5	6	7	8	9	10	11	12	13	14
Jain.	*Total*	*3*	*1*	*2*	*1*	....	*1*	*2*	*1*	*1*	....	....	....
	0—1	1	....	1	1	....	1	....	....	....	....	....	....
	1—2	....	....	....	....	....	....	....	....	....	....	....	....
	2—3	....	....	....	....	....	....	....	....	....	....	....	....
	3—4	....	....	....	....	....	....	....	....	....	....	....	....
	4—5	....	....	....	....	....	....	....	....	....	....	....	....
	Total 0—5	*1*	....	*1*	*1*	....	*1*	....	....	....	....	....	....
	5—10	....	....	....	....	....	....	....	....	....	....	....	....
	10—15	....	....	....	....	....	....	....	....	....	....	....	....
	15—20	1	....	1	....	....	....	1	....	1	....	....	....
	20—30	1	1	....	....	....	....	1	1	....	....	....	....
	30—40	....	....	....	....	....	....	....	....	....	....	....	....
	40—50	....	....	....	....	....	....	....	....	....	....	....	....
	50—60	....	....	....	....	....	....	....	....	....	....	....	....
	6 .& over	....	....	....	....	....	....	....	....	....	....	....	....
Muslim.	*Total*	*350,491*	*179,585*	*170,906*	*175,643*	*102,000*	*73,643*	*151,904*	*70,660*	*81,244*	*22,944*	*6,925*	*16,019*
	0—1	12,342	6,024	6,318	12,342	6,024	6,318	....	....	....	....	....	....
	1—2	12,459	6,116	6,343	12,459	6,116	6,343	....	....	....	....	....	....
	2—3	12,137	5,994	6,143	12,137	5,994	6,143	....	....	....	....	....	....
	3—4	11,977	5,948	6,029	11,977	5,948	6,029	....	....	....	....	....	....
	4—5	11,950	6,034	5,916	11,921	6,014	5,907	29	20	9	....	....	....
	Total 0—5	*60,865*	*30,116*	*30,749*	*60,836*	*30,096*	*30,740*	*29*	*20*	*9*	....	....	....
	5—10	49,709	26,839	22,870	48,546	26,521	22,025	1,131	310	821	32	8	24
	10—15	44,745	24,669	20,076	39,434	23,369	16,065	5,185	1,272	3,913	126	28	98
	15—20	32,877	16,216	16,661	14,919	11,341	3,578	17,489	4,703	12,786	469	172	297
	20—30	62,183	29,012	33,171	9,829	8,909	920	50,194	19,176	31,018	2,160	927	1,233
	30—40	46,480	23,558	22,922	1,291	1,142	149	41,301	21,184	20,117	3,888	1,232	2,656
	40—50	25,483	13,591	11,892	413	338	75	20,211	12,101	8,110	4,859	1,152	3,707
	50—60	14,394	7,839	6,555	176	135	41	9,528	6,540	2,988	4,690	1,164	3,526
	60& over	13,755	7,745	6,010	199	149	50	6,836	5,354	1,482	6,720	2,242	4,478
Christian.	*Total*	*76*	*43*	*33*	*42*	*25*	*17*	*30*	*16*	*14*	*4*	*2*	*2*
	0—1	6	3	3	6	3	3	....	....	....	....	....	....
	1—2	2	2	....	2	2	....	....	....	....	....	....	....
	2—3	2	....	2	2	....	2	....	....	....	....	....	....
	3—4	4	2	2	4	2	2	....	....	....	....	....	....
	4—5	1	....	1	1	....	1	....	....	....	....	....	....
	Total 0—5	*15*	*7*	*8*	*15*	*7*	*8*	....	....	....	....	....	....
	5—10	11	6	5	10	6	4	1	....	1	....	....	....
	10—15	15	10	5	12	9	3	3	1	2	....	....	....
	15—20	8	5	3	4	3	1	3	1	2	1	1	....
	20—30	9	6	3	....	....	....	8	6	2	1	....	1
	30—40	6	4	2	1	....	1	5	4	1	....	....	....
	40—50	6	3	3	....	....	....	5	2	3	1	1	....
	50—60	2	1	1	....	....	....	2	1	1	....	....	....
	60 & over	4	1	3	....	....	....	3	1	2	1	....	1

TABLE VII.—Age, Sex and Civil Condition.

Jammu and Kashmir Census 1931.

Part II.—Kashmir South (Srinagar).

Religion.	Age.	Population.			Unmarried.			Married.			Widowed.		
		Persons.	Males.	Females.	Persons.	Males.	Females.	Persons.	Males.	Females.	Persons.	Males.	Females.
1	1	3	4	5	6	7	8	9	10	11	12	13	14
All Religions.	*Total*	*771,943*	*419,190*	*352,753*	*359,779*	*218,511*	*141,268*	*355,660*	*174,516*	*181,145*	*56,504*	*26,164*	*30,340*
	0—1	21,056	10,574	10,482	21,056	10,574	10,482	—	—	—	—	—	—
	1—2	24,867	12,590	12,277	24,867	12,590	12,277	—	—	—	—	—	—
	2—3	24,901	12,653	12,248	24,901	12,653	12,248	—	—	—	—	—	—
	3—4	24,416	12,511	11,905	24,407	12,509	11,898	9	2	7	—	—	—
	4—5	22,684	11,808	10,876	22,668	11,804	10,864	16	4	12	—	—	—
	Total 0—5	*117,924*	*60,136*	*57,788*	*117,899*	*60,130*	*57,769*	*25*	*6*	*19*	—	—	—
	5—10	100,281	54,388	45,893	98,300	53,752	44,548	1,952	627	1,325	29	9	20
	10—15	92,254	50,258	41,996	80,518	47,929	32,589	11,548	2,263	9,285	188	66	122
	15—20	77,866	40,269	37,597	31,278	26,270	5,008	45,532	13,482	32,050	1,056	517	539
	20—30	154,032	80,606	73,426	24,694	23,707	987	123,859	53,358	70,501	5,479	3,541	1,938
	30—40	111,055	64,081	46,974	4,689	4,456	233	96,330	53,725	42,605	10,036	5,900	4,136
	40—50	62,606	36,608	25,998	1,545	1,474	71	47,858	29,599	18,259	13,203	5,535	7,668
	50—60	32,959	19,411	13,548	568	537	31	19,394	13,933	5,461	12,997	4,941	8,056
	60 & over	22,966	13,433	9,533	288	256	32	9,162	7,522	1,640	13,516	5,655	7,861
Hindu—(Brahmanic).	*Total*	*53,759*	*29,660*	*24,099*	*26,339*	*17,211*	*9,128*	*20,687*	*10,129*	*10,558*	*6,733*	*2,320*	*4,413*
	0—1	1,093	566	527	1,093	566	527	—	—	—	—	—	—
	1—2	1,337	667	670	1,337	667	670	—	—	—	—	—	—
	2—3	1,438	729	709	1,438	729	709	—	—	—	—	—	—
	3—4	1,453	751	702	1,453	751	702	—	—	—	—	—	—
	4—5	1,394	723	671	1,394	723	671	—	—	—	—	—	—
	Total 0—5	*6,715*	*3,436*	*3,279*	*6,715*	*3,436*	*3,279*	—	—	—	—	—	—
	5—10	6,489	3,346	3,143	6,453	3,340	3,113	35	6	29	1	—	1
	10—15	5,988	3,192	2,796	5,534	3,144	2,390	442	45	397	12	3	9
	15—20	5,303	3,018	2,285	2,701	2,389	312	2,493	600	1,893	109	29	80
	20—30	10,526	5,909	4,617	2,965	2,937	28	6,918	2,775	4,143	643	197	446
	30—40	7,802	4,559	3,243	1,024	1,019	5	5,567	3,119	2,448	1,211	421	790
	40—50	5,504	3,166	2,338	523	522	1	3,234	2,051	1,183	1,747	593	1,154
	50—60	3,530	1,982	1,548	286	286	....	1,489	1,097	392	1,755	599	1,156
	60 & over	1,902	1,052	850	138	138	....	509	436	73	1,255	478	777
Hindu—(Arya.	*Total*	*340*	*210*	*130*	*181*	*111*	*70*	*141*	*89*	*52*	*18*	*10*	*8*
	0—1	9	4	5	9	4	5	....	....	....	....	....	....
	1—2	11	5	6	11	5	6	....	....	....	....	....	....
	2—3	7	5	2	7	5	2	....	....	....	....	....	....
	3—4	9	5	4	9	5	4	....	....	....	....	....	....
	4—5	12	5	7	12	5	7	....	....	....	....	....	....
	Total 0—5	*48*	*24*	*24*	*48*	*24*	*24*	....	....	....	....	....	....
	5—10	52	28	24	51	28	23	1	....	1	....	....	....
	10—15	47	26	21	44	26	18	3	....	3	....	....	....
	15—20	34	23	11	21	17	4	13	6	7	....	....	....
	20—30	66	41	25	16	15	1	49	25	24	1	1	....
	30—40	50	37	13	1	1	....	46	34	12	3	2	1
	40—50	32	25	7	....	....	....	24	20	4	8	5	3
	50—60	8	5	3	....	....	....	4	4	....	4	1	3
	60 & over	3	1	2	....	....	....	1	....	1	2	1	1
Sikh.	*Total*	*3,997*	*2,303*	*1,694*	*1,933*	*1,225*	*708*	*1,847*	*974*	*873*	*217*	*104*	*113*
	0—1	131	75	56	131	75	56	....	....	....	....	....	....
	1—2	141	82	59	141	82	59	....	....	....	....	....	....
	2—3	142	72	70	142	72	70	....	....	....	....	....	....
	3—4	150	80	70	150	80	70	....	....	....	....	....	....
	4—5	130	69	61	130	69	61	....	....	....	....	....	....
	Total 0—5	*694*	*378*	*316*	*694*	*378*	*316*	....	....	....	....	....	....
	5—10	524	285	239	498	283	215	26	2	24	....	....	....
	10—15	453	248	205	386	240	146	67	8	59	....	....	....
	15—20	423	249	174	190	166	24	228	80	148	5	3	2
	20—30	835	502	333	144	138	6	669	349	320	22	15	7
	30—40	516	302	214	15	14	1	471	272	199	30	16	14
	40—50	282	167	115	5	5	....	237	148	89	40	14	26
	50—60	150	95	55	....	....	....	96	70	26	54	25	29
	60 & over	120	77	43	1	1	....	53	45	8	66	31	35

TABLE VII—Age, Sex and Civil Condition.

Jammu and Kashmir Census 1931.

Part II.—Kashmir South (Srinagar)—(concluded).

Religion.	Age.	Population.			Unmarried.			Married.			Widowed.		
		Persons.	Males.	Females.	Persons.	Males.	Females.	Persons.	Males.	Females.	Persons.	Males.	Females.
1	2	3	4	5	6	7	8	9	10	11	12	13	14
Muslim.	*Total*	*713,531*	*386,863*	*326,668*	*331,175*	*199,897*	*131,278*	*332,833*	*163,241*	*169,592*	*49.523*	*23,725*	*25,798*
	0—1	19,818	9,928	9,890	19,818	9,928	9,890	—	—	—	—	—	—
	1—2	23,374	11,833	11,541	23,374	11,833	11,541	—	—	—	—	—	—
	2—3	23,311	11,845	11,466	23,311	11,845	11,466	—	—	—	—	—	—
	3—4	22,802	11,675	11,127	22,793	11,673	11,120	9	2	7	—	—	—
	4—5	21,142	11,008	10,134	21,126	11,004	10,122	16	4	12	—	—	—
	Total 0—5	*110,447*	*56.289*	*54,158*	*110,422*	*56,283*	*54,139*	*25*	*6*	*19*	—	—	—
	5—10	93,195	50,719	42,476	91,277	50,091	41.186	1,890	619	1,271	28	9	19
	10—15	85,747	46,782	38,965	74,535	44,509	30,026	11,036	2,210	8,826	176	63	113
	15—20	72,084	36,968	35,116	28,349	23,689	4,660	42,793	12,794	29,999	942	485	457
	20—30	142,546	74,125	68,421	21,534	20,600	934	116,199	50,197	66,002	4,813	3,328	1,485
	30—40	102,629	59,154	43,475	3,634	3,414	220	90,204	50,280	39,924	8,791	5,460	3,331
	40—50	56,740	33,224	23,516	1,009	944	65	44,328	27,360	16,968	11,403	4,920	6,483
	50—60	29,229	17,309	11,920	274	250	24	17,774	12,744	5,030	11,181	4,315	6,866
	60& over	20,914	12,293	8,621	141	117	24	8,584	7,031	1,553	12,189	5,145	7,044
Christian.	*Total*	*268*	*122*	*146*	*123*	*49*	*74*	*134*	*70*	*64*	*11*	*3*	*8*
	0—1	3	—	3	3	—	3	—	—	—	—	—	—
	1—2	3	2	1	3	2	1	—	—	—	—	—	—
	2—3	2	2	—	2	2	—	—	—	—	—	—	—
	3—4	1	—	1	1	—	1	—	—	—	—	—	—
	4—5	4	2	2	4	2	2	—	—	—	—	—	—
	Total 0—5	*13*	*6*	*7*	*13*	*6*	*7*	—	—	—	—	—	—
	5—10	15	7	8	15	7	8	—	—	—	—	—	—
	10—15	13	6	7	13	6	7	—	—	—	—	—	—
	15—20	15	6	9	14	6	8	1	—	1	—	—	—
	20—30	49	21	28	30	13	17	19	8	11	—	—	—
	30—40	51	25	26	14	7	7	36	17	19	1	1	—
	40—50	46	24	22	8	3	5	34	19	15	4	2	2
	50—60	39	17	22	8	1	7	29	16	13	2	—	2
	60& over	27	10	17	8	—	8	15	10	5	4	—	4

TABLE VII.—Age, Sex and Civil Condition.

Jammu and Kashmir Census 1931.

Part II.—Kashmir North (Baramulla including Langet).

Religion.	Age.	*Population.*			*Unmarried.*			*Married.*			*Widowed.*		
		Persons.	Males.	Females.	Persons.	Males.	Females.	Persons.	Males.	Females.	Persons.	Males.	Females.
1	2	3	4	5	6	7	8	9	10	11	12	13	14
All Religions.	*Total*	*559,828*	*301,397*	*258,431*	*262,209*	*155,189*	*107,020*	*264,123*	*130,061*	*134,062*	*33,496*	*16,147*	*17,349*
	0—1	16,853	8,603	8,250	16,853	8,603	8,250	....	....	....	....	....	....
	1—2	19,130	9,648	9,482	19,130	9,648	9,482	....	....	....	....	....	....
	2—3	18,788	9,516	9,272	18,788	9,516	9,272	....	....	....	....	....	....
	3—4	18,139	9,335	8,804	18,139	9,335	8,804	....	....	....	....	....	....
	4—5	18,058	9,330	8,728	18,058	9,330	8,728	....	....	....	....	....	....
	Total 0—5	*90,968*	*46,432*	*44,536*	*90,968*	*46,432*	*44,536*	....	....	....	....	....	....
	5—10	71,269	38,846	32,423	70,114	38,496	31,618	1,142	346	796	13	4	9
	10—15	67,021	36,583	30,438	59,528	35,032	24,496	7,401	1,522	5,879	92	29	63
	15—20	57,372	29,439	27,933	23,347	18,308	5,039	33,352	10,794	22,558	673	337	336
	20—30	114,027	58,671	55,356	15,404	14,351	1,053	95,176	42,077	53,099	3,447	2,243	1,204
	30—40	80,061	44,557	35,504	1,921	1,751	170	72,245	39,441	32,804	5,895	3,365	2,530
	40—50	41,615	23,893	17,722	557	482	75	33,825	20,462	13,363	7,233	2,949	4,284
	50—60	21,001	12,510	8,491	208	186	22	13,518	9,436	4,082	7,275	2,888	4,387
	60& over	16,494	10,466	6,028	162	151	11	7,464	5,983	1,481	8,868	4,332	4,536
Hindu—(Brahmanic).	*Total*	*10,639*	*6,243*	*4,396*	*5,380*	*3,525*	*1,855*	*4,058*	*2,237*	*1,821*	*1,201*	*481*	*720*
	0—1	272	135	137	272	135	137	....	....	....	....	....	....
	1—2	286	143	143	286	143	143	....	....	....	....	....	....
	2—3	294	142	152	294	142	152	....	....	....	....	....	....
	3—4	294	146	148	294	146	148	....	....	....	....	....	....
	4—5	292	146	146	292	146	146	....	....	....	....	....	....
	Total 0—5	*1,438*	*712*	*726*	*1,438*	*712*	*726*	....	....	....	....	....	....
	5—10	1,264	671	593	1,255	671	584	8	....	8	1	....	1
	10—15	1,141	610	531	1,056	600	456	82	8	74	3	2	1
	15—20	960	569	391	537	460	77	405	104	301	18	5	13
	20—30	2,068	1,258	810	623	612	11	1,330	602	728	115	44	71
	30—40	1,660	1,076	584	229	228	1	1,192	750	442	239	98	141
	40—50	1,050	680	370	111	111	....	653	456	197	286	113	173
	50—60	628	397	231	68	68	....	267	213	54	293	116	177
	60& over	430	270	160	63	63	....	121	104	17	246	103	143
Sikh.	*Total*	*6,260*	*3,248*	*3.012*	*3,121*	*1,794*	*1,327*	*2,780*	*1,315*	*1,465*	*359*	*139*	*220*
	0—1	215	99	116	215	99	116	....	....	....	....	....	....
	1—2	228	115	113	228	115	113	....	....	....	....	....	....
	2—3	246	127	119	246	127	119	....	....	....	....	....	....
	3—4	237	115	122	237	115	122	....	....	....	....	....	....
	4—5	231	100	131	231	100	131	....	....	....	....	....	....
	Total 0—5	*1,157*	*556*	*601*	*1,157*	*556*	*601*	....	....	....	....	....	....
	5—10	878	478	400	872	475	397	6	3	3	....	....	....
	10—15	780	433	347	704	421	283	75	12	64	....	....	....
	15—20	655	320	335	247	206	41	403	112	291	5	2	3
	20—30	1,159	561	598	128	123	5	1,006	420	586	25	18	7
	30—40	753	402	351	6	6	....	686	370	316	61	26	35
	40—50	442	235	207	3	3	....	352	207	145	87	25	62
	50—60	238	133	105	2	2	....	158	111	47	78	20	58
	60& over	198	130	68	2	2	....	93	80	13	103	48	55
Muslim.	*Total*	*542,743*	*291,786*	*250,957*	*253,592*	*149,790*	*103,802*	*257,224*	*126,474*	*130,750*	*31,927*	*15,522*	*16,405*
	0—1	16,360	8,364	7,996	16,360	8,364	7,996	....	....	....	....	....	....
	1—2	18,612	9,387	9,225	18,612	9,387	9,225	....	....	....	....	....	....
	2—3	18,241	9,243	8,998	18,241	9,243	8,998	....	....	....	....	....	....
	3—4	17,603	9,069	8,534	17,603	9,069	8,534	....	....	....	....	....	....
	4—5	17,531	9,081	8,450	17,531	9,081	8,450	....	....	....	....	....	....
	Total 0—5	*88,347*	*45,144*	*43,203*	*88,347*	*45,144*	*43,203*	....	....	....	....	....	....
	5—10	69,107	37,683	31,424	67,967	37,336	30,631	1,128	343	785	12	4	8
	10—15	65,077	35,523	29,554	57,746	33,994	23,752	7,242	1,502	5,740	89	27	62
	15—20	55,739	28,542	27,197	22,551	17,634	4,917	32,538	10,578	21,960	650	330	320
	20—30	110,760	56,823	53,937	14,637	13,602	1,035	92,818	41,042	51,776	3,305	2,179	1,126
	30—40	77,621	43,067	34,554	1,675	1,514	161	70,353	38,313	32,040	5,593	3,240	2,353
	40—50	40,106	22,968	17,138	436	365	71	32,811	19,792	13,019	6,859	2,811	4,048
	50—60	20,126	11,974	8,152	137	116	21	13,088	9,107	3,981	6,901	2,751	4,150
	60&over	15,860	10,062	5,798	96	85	11	7,246	5,797	1,449	8,518	4,180	4,338

TABLE VII.—Age, Sex and Civil Condition.

Jammu and Kashmir Census 1931.

Part II.—Muzaffarabad District.

Religion.	Age.	Population.			Unmarried.			Married.			Widowed.		
		Persons.	Males.	Females.	Persons.	Males.	Females.	Persons.	Males.	Females.	Persons.	Males.	Females.
1	2	3	4	5	6	7	8	9	10	11	12	13	14
All Religions.	*Total*	*237,447*	*126,435*	*111,012*	*120,552*	*70,987*	*49,565*	*102,523*	*49,993*	*52,530*	*14,372*	*5,465*	*8,917*
	0—1	8,041	4,087	3,954	8,041	4,087	3,954	....	....	....	....	....	....
	1—2	8,803	4,424	4,379	8,803	4,424	4,379	....	....	....	....	....	....
	2—3	8,755	4,414	4,341	8,755	4,414	4,341	....	....	....	....	....	....
	3—4	8,378	4,242	4,136	8,374	4,242	4,132	4	....	4	....	....	....
	4—5	8,110	4,158	3,952	8,089	4,156	3,933	21	2	19	....	....	....
	Total 0—5	*42,087*	*21,325*	*20,762*	*42,062*	*21,323*	*20,739*	*25*	*2*	*23*	....	....	....
	5—10	33,403	18,184	15,219	32,916	17,973	14,943	473	208	265	14	3	11
	10—15	28,833	16,207	12,626	26,607	15,757	10,850	2,170	442	1,728	56	8	48
	15—20	20,919	10,623	10,296	10,110	7,868	2,242	10,525	2,663	7,862	284	92	192
	20—30	44,130	21,961	22,169	7,289	6,698	591	35,328	14,494	20,834	1,513	769	744
	30—40	32,297	17,646	14,651	1,062	943	119	28,838	15,613	13,225	2,397	1,090	1,307
	40—50	17,011	9,653	7,358	295	262	33	13,942	8,483	5,459	2,774	908	1,866
	50—60	9,436	5,296	4,140	107	85	22	6,515	4,370	2,145	2,814	841	1,973
	60& over	9,331	5,540	3,791	104	78	26	4,707	3,718	989	4,520	1,744	2,776
Hindu—(Brahmanic.)	*Total*	*4,429*	*2,648*	*1,781*	*2,221*	*1,452*	*769*	*1,799*	*1,069*	*730*	*409*	*127*	*282*
	0—1	137	76	61	137	76	61	....	....	....	....	....	....
	1—2	142	74	68	142	74	68	....	....	....	....	....	....
	2—3	131	67	64	131	67	64	....	....	....	....	....	....
	3—4	159	96	63	159	96	63	....	....	....	....	....	....
	4—5	209	146	63	208	146	62	1	....	1	....	....	....
	Total 0—5	*778*	*459*	*319*	*777*	*459*	*318*	*1*	....	*1*	....	....	....
	5—10	488	234	254	477	229	248	10	5	5	1	....	1
	10—15	443	231	212	394	221	173	47	10	37	2	....	2
	15—20	410	237	173	204	179	25	199	56	143	7	2	5
	20—30	939	590	349	225	220	5	666	355	311	48	15	33
	30—40	684	484	200	86	86	....	511	362	149	87	36	51
	40—50	358	231	127	38	38	....	227	164	63	93	29	64
	50—60	173	99	74	7	7	....	89	71	18	77	21	56
	60 & over	156	83	73	13	13	....	49	46	3	94	24	70
Sikh.	*Total*	*10,933*	*5,584*	*5,349*	*5,669*	*3,227*	*2,442*	*4,446*	*2,034*	*2,412*	*818*	*323*	*495*
	0—1	412	205	207	412	205	207	....	....	....	....	....	....
	1—2	420	203	217	420	203	217	....	....	....	....	....	....
	2—3	429	220	209	429	220	209	....	....	....	....	....	....
	3—4	408	213	195	408	213	195	....	....	....	....	....	....
	4—5	399	202	197	398	201	197	1	1	....	....	....	....
	Total 0—5	*2,068*	*1,043*	*1,025*	*2,067*	*1,042*	*1,025*	*1*	*1*	....	....	....	....
	5—10	1,624	867	757	1,611	864	747	13	3	10	....	....	....
	10—15	1,375	736	640	1,265	726	539	110	10	100	1	....	1
	15—20	957	411	546	409	309	100	538	98	440	10	4	6
	20—30	1,884	863	1,021	241	223	18	1,575	602	973	68	38	30
	30—40	1,318	705	613	49	37	12	1,146	608	538	123	60	63
	40—50	811	454	357	15	14	1	609	372	237	187	68	119
	50—60	473	265	208	5	5	....	281	197	84	187	63	124
	60& over	422	240	182	7	7	....	173	143	30	242	90	152
Muslim.	*Total*	*222,013*	*118,153*	*103,860*	*112,630*	*66,283*	*46,347*	*96,243*	*46,867*	*49,376*	*13,140*	*5,003*	*8,137*
	0—1	7,492	3,806	3,686	7,492	3,806	3,686	....	....	....	....	....	....
	1—2	8,240	4,146	4,094	8,240	4,146	4,094	....	....	....	....	....	....
	2—3	8,194	4,126	4,068	8,194	4,126	4,068	....	....	....	....	....	....
	3—4	7,810	3,932	3,878	7,806	3,932	3,874	4	....	4	....	....	....
	4—5	7,499	3,808	3,691	7,480	3,807	3,673	19	1	18	....	....	....
	Total 0—5	*39,235*	*19,818*	*19,417*	*39,212*	*19,817*	*19,395*	*23*	*1*	*22*	....	....	....
	5—10	31,284	17,078	14,206	30,821	16,875	13,946	450	200	250	13	3	10
	10—15	27,006	15,235	11,771	24,940	14,805	10,135	2,013	422	1,591	53	8	45
	15—20	19,513	9,970	9,573	9,492	7,376	2,116	9,784	2,508	7,276	267	86	181
	20—30	41,289	20,495	20,794	6,818	6,250	568	33,074	13,529	19,545	1,397	716	681
	30—40	30,284	16,448	13,836	926	819	107	27,171	14,635	12,536	2,187	994	1,193
	40—50	15,836	8,966	6,870	242	210	32	13,103	7,946	5,157	2,491	810	1,681
	50—60	8,790	4,932	3,858	95	73	22	6,145	4,102	2,043	2,550	757	1,793
	60& over	8,746	5,211	3,535	84	58	26	4,480	3,524	956	4,182	1,629	2,553

TABLE VII.—Age, Sex and Civil Condition.

Jammu and Kashmir Census 1931.

Part II.—Ladakh District.—(continued).

Religion.	Age.	Population.			Unmarried.			Married.			Widowed.		
		Persons.	Males.	Females.	Persons.	Males.	Females.	Persons.	Males.	Females.	Persons.	Males.	Females.
1	2	3	4	5	6	7	8	9	10	11	12	13	14
All Religions.	*Total*	*192,138*	*96,259*	*95,879*	*88,289*	*47,873*	*40,416*	*88,805*	*43,644*	*45,161*	*15,044*	*4,742*	*10,302*
	0—1	6,436	3,176	3,260	6,436	3,176	3,260	—	—	—	—	—	—
	1—2	5,773	2,829	2,944	5,773	2,829	2,944	—	—	—	—	—	—
	2—3	5,872	2,820	3,052	5,872	2,820	3,052	—	—	—	—	—	—
	3—4	5,638	2,752	2,886	5,638	2,752	2,886	—	—	—	—	—	—
	4—5	5,074	2,532	2,542	5,074	2,532	2,542	—	—	—	—	—	—
	Total 0—5	*28,793*	*14,109*	*14,684*	*28,793*	*14,109*	*14,684*	—	—	—	—	—	—
	5—10	21,987	11,409	10,578	21,872	11,378	10,494	110	30	80	5	1	4
	10—15	19,464	10,245	9,219	18,608	10,048	8,560	819	190	629	37	7	30
	15—20	15,029	7,681	7,348	8,504	5,242	3,262	6,216	2,318	3,898	309	121	188
	20—30	35,797	17,368	18,429	7,611	5,273	2,338	26,773	11,456	15,317	1,413	639	774
	30—40	27,962	13,876	14,086	1,520	961	559	24,473	12,162	12,311	1,969	753	1,216
	40—50	14,922	7,494	7,428	639	391	248	12,199	6,511	5,688	2,084	592	1,492
	50—60	15,693	7,888	7,805	410	257	153	11,625	6,720	4,905	3,658	911	2,747
	60&over	12,491	6,189	6,302	332	214	118	6,590	4,257	2,333	5,569	1,718	3,831
Hindu—(Brahmanic.)	*Total*	*292*	*245*	*47*	*109*	*86*	*23*	*175*	*161*	*24*	*8*	*8*	
	0—1	6	2	4	6	2	4	—	—	—	—	—	—
	1—2	3	3	—	3	3	—	—	—	—	—	—	—
	2—3	5	2	3	5	2	3	—	—	—	—	—	—
	3—4	3	1	2	3	1	2	—	—	—	—	—	—
	4—5	4	2	2	4	2	2	—	—	—	—	—	—
	Total 0—5	21	10	11	21	10	11	—	—	—	—	—	—
	5—10	13	7	6	13	7	6	—	—	—	—	—	—
	10—15	10	5	5	10	5	5	—	—	—	—	—	—
	15—20	23	17	6	12	11	1	11	6	5	—	—	—
	20—30	108	95	13	33	33	—	73	60	13	2	2	—
	30—40	95	90	5	16	16	—	74	69	5	5	5	—
	40—50	20	19	1	3	3	—	17	16	1	—	—	—
	50—60	2	2	—	1	1	—	—	—	—	1	1	—
	60&over	—	—	—	—	—	—	—	—	—	—	—	—
Buddhist.	*Total*	*38,212*	*19,029*	*19,183*	*17,388*	*8,654*	*8,734*	*17,405*	*9,133*	*8,272*	*3,419*	*1,242*	*2,177*
	0—1	934	472	462	934	472	462	—	—	—	—	—	—
	1—2	786	393	393	786	393	393	—	—	—	—	—	—
	2—3	864	400	464	864	400	464	—	—	—	—	—	—
	3—4	916	424	492	916	424	492	—	—	—	—	—	—
	4—5	815	393	422	815	393	422	—	—	—	—	—	—
	Total 0—5	*4,315*	*2,082*	*2,233*	*4,315*	*2,082*	*2,233*	—	—	—	—	—	—
	5—10	3,979	1,983	1,996	3,976	1,983	1,993	3	—	3	—	—	—
	10—15	3,688	1,823	1,865	3,613	1,798	1,815	70	24	46	5	1	4
	15—20	3,067	1,503	1,564	1,869	873	996	1,138	608	530	60	22	38
	20—30	6,298	3,126	3,172	1,865	876	989	4,201	2,159	2,042	232	91	141
	30—40	5,342	2,703	2,639	686	374	312	4,300	2,203	2,097	356	126	230
	40—50	4,409	2,244	2165	478	289	189	3,376	1,770	1,606	555	185	370
	50—60	3,555	1,775	1,780	311	197	114	2,493	1,324	1,169	751	254	497
	60&over	3,559	1,790	1,769	275	182	93	1,824	1,045	779	1,460	563	897
Muslim.	*Total*	*153,388*	*76,849*	*76,539*	*70,670*	*39,070*	*31,600*	*71,111*	*34,291*	*36,820*	*11,607*	*3,488*	*8,119*
	0—1	5,483	2,695	2,788	5,483	2,695	2,788	—	—	—	—	—	—
	1—2	4,975	2,428	2,547	4,975	2,428	2,547	—	—	—	—	—	—
	2—3	4,994	2,415	2,579	4,994	2,415	2,579	—	—	—	—	—	—
	3—4	4,712	2,324	2,388	4,712	2,324	2,388	—	—	—	—	—	—
	4—5	4,247	2,134	2,113	4,247	2,134	2,113	—	—	—	—	—	—
	Total 0—5	*24,411*	*11,996*	*12,415*	*24,411*	*11,996*	*12,415*	—	—	—	—	—	—
	5—10	17,964	9,403	8,561	17,853	9,372	8,481	106	30	76	5	1	4
	10—15	15,746	8,406	7,340	14,965	8,234	6,731	749	166	583	32	6	26
	15—20	11,918	6,147	5,771	6,613	4,350	2,263	5,057	1,699	3,358	248	98	150
	20—30	29,343	14,123	15,220	5,700	4,357	1,343	22,465	9,220	13,245	1,178	546	632
	30—40	22,485	11,057	11,428	815	571	244	20,063	9,864	10,199	1,607	622	985
	40—50	10,473	5,218	5,255	158	99	59	8,788	4,714	4,074	1,527	405	1,122
	50—60	12,123	6,106	6,017	98	59	39	9,122	5,391	3,731	2,903	656	2,247
	60& over	8,925	4,393	4,532	57	32	25	4,761	3,207	1,554	4,107	1,154	2,953

TABLE VII.—AGE, SEX AND CIVIL CONDITION.

Jammu and Kashmir Census 1931.

Part II—Ladakh District—(concluded).

Religion.	Age.	Population.			Unmarried.			Married.			Widowed.		
		Persons.	Males.	Females.	Persons.	Males.	Females.	Persons.	Males.	Females.	Persons.	Males.	Females.
1	2	3	4	5	6	7	8	9	10	11	12	13	14
Christian.	*Total*	*122*	*57*	*65*	*63*	*29*	*34*	*54*	*27*	*27*	*5*	*1*	*4*
	0—1	5	2	3	5	2	3	....	....	....	....	....	....
	1—2	6	3	3	6	3	3	....	....	....	....	....	....
	2—3	4	1	3	4	1	3	....	....	....	....	....	....
	3—4	4	2	2	4	2	2	....	....	....	....	....	....
	4—5	4	2	2	4	2	2	....	....	....	....	....	....
	Total 0—5	*23*	*10*	*13*	*23*	*10*	*13*	....	....	....	....	....	....
	5—10	16	8	8	16	8	8	....	....	....	....	....	....
	10—15	11	5	6	11	5	6	....	....	....	....	....	....
	15—20	7	4	3	5	3	2	2	1	1	....	....	....
	20—30	20	8	12	7	3	4	12	5	7	1	....	1
	30—40	18	8	10	1	....	1	16	8	8	1	....	1
	40—50	11	5	6	....	....	....	11	5	6	....	....	....
	50—60	11	3	6	....	....	....	10	5	5	1	....	1
	60&over	5	4	1	....	....	....	3	3	....	2	1	1

TABLE VII.—Age, Sex and Civil Condition.

Jammu and Kashmir Census 1931.

Part II—Gilgit District.

Religion.	Age.	Population.			Unmarried.			Married.			Widowed.		
		Persons.	Males.	Females.	Persons.	Males.	Females.	Persons.	Males.	Females.	Persons.	Males.	Females.
1	2	3	4	5	6	7	8	9	10	11	12	13	14
All Religions.	*Total*	*31,902*	*17,752*	*14,150*	*16,288*	*9,607*	*6,681*	*13,822*	*7,424*	*6,398*	*1,792*	*721*	*1,071*
	0—1	1,169	588	581	1,169	588	581	....	....	....	....	....	....
	1—2	946	461	485	946	461	485	....	....	....	....	....	....
	2—3	906	440	466	906	440	466	....	....	....	....	....	....
	3—4	992	502	490	992	502	490	....	....	....	....	....	....
	4—5	977	503	474	977	503	474	....	....	....	....	....	....
	Total 0—5	*4,990*	*2,494*	*2,496*	*4,990*	*2,494*	*2,496*	....	....	....	....	....	....
	5—10	4,230	2,276	1,954	4,195	2,266	1,929	33	9	24	2	1	1
	10—15	3,889	2,109	1,780	3,606	2,066	1,540	274	42	232	9	1	8
	15—20	3,252	1,778	1,474	1,764	1,284	480	1,422	468	954	66	26	40
	20—30	6,368	3,603	2,765	1,432	1,232	200	4,692	2,236	2,456	244	135	109
	30—40	4,507	2,669	1,838	235	213	22	3,947	2,309	1,638	325	147	178
	40—50	2,089	1,220	869	39	32	7	1,735	1,083	652	315	105	210
	50—60	1,420	855	565	14	12	2	1,038	731	307	368	112	256
	60 & over	1,157	748	409	13	8	5	681	546	135	463	194	269
Hindu—(Brahmanic).	*Total*	*974*	*900*	*74*	*396*	*363*	*33*	*533*	*496*	*37*	*45*	*41*	*4*
	0—1	7	6	1	7	6	1	....	....	....	....	....	....
	1—2	8	6	2	8	6	2	....	....	....	....	....	....
	2—3	9	5	4	9	5	4	....	....	....	....	....	....
	3—4	6	3	3	6	3	3	....	....	....	....	....	....
	4—5	5	2	3	5	2	3	....	....	....	....	....	....
	Total 0—5	*35*	*22*	*13*	*35*	*22*	*13*	....	....	....	....	....	....
	5—10	28	16	12	28	16	12	....	....	....	....	....	....
	10—15	24	16	8	24	16	8	....	....	....	....	....	....
	15—20	158	154	4	95	95	....	61	57	4	2	2	....
	20—30	424	402	22	174	174	....	233	212	21	17	16	1
	30—40	236	226	10	38	38	....	185	177	8	13	11	2
	40—50	54	51	3	2	2	....	45	43	2	7	6	1
	50—60	11	9	2	....	....	....	7	5	2	4	4	....
	60 & over	4	4	....	....	....	....	2	2	....	2	2	....
Muslim.	*Total*	*30,741*	*16,727*	*14,014*	*15,790*	*9,180*	*6,610*	*13,206*	*6,868*	*6,338*	*1,745*	*679*	*1,066*
	0—1	1,156	578	578	1,156	578	578	....	....	....	....	....	....
	1—2	929	450	479	929	450	479	....	....	....	....	....	....
	2—3	888	432	456	888	432	456	....	....	....	....	....	....
	3—4	980	496	484	980	496	484	....	....	....	....	....	....
	4—5	968	499	469	968	499	469	....	....	....	....	....	....
	Total 0—5	*4,921*	*2,455*	*2466*	*4,921*	*2,455*	*2,466*	....	....	....	....	....	....
	5—10	4,178	2,247	1,931	4,143	2,237	1,906	33	9	24	2	1	1
	10—15	3,849	2, 83	1,766	3,566	2,040	1,526	274	42	232	9	1	8
	15—20	3,084	1,616	1,468	1,663	1,183	480	1,357	409	948	64	24	40
	20—30	5,899	3,169	2,730	1,245	1,045	200	4,427	2,005	2,422	227	119	108
	30—40	4,236	2,416	1,820	190	170	20	3,736	2,111	1,625	310	135	175
	40—50	2,018	1,156	862	36	30	6	1,674	1,027	647	308	99	209
	50—60	1,404	841	563	14	12	2	1,026	721	305	364	108	256
	60 & over	1,152	744	408	12	8	4	679	544	135	461	192	269

TABLE VII.—AGE, SEX AND CIVIL CONDITION.

Jammu and Kashmir Census 1931.

Part II.—Frontier Ilaqas.

Religion.	Age.	Population.			Un-married.			Married.			Widowed.		
		Persons.	Males.	Females.	Persons.	Males.	Females.	Persons.	Males.	Females.	Persons.	Males.	Females.
1	2	3	4	5	6	7	8	9	10	11	12	13	14
All Religions.	*Total*	*64,544*	*34,490*	*30,054*	*30,024*	*18,064*	*11,960*	*30,662*	*15,082*	*15,580*	*3,858*	*1,344*	*2,514*
	0—1	1,958	1,066	892	1,958	1,066	892	....	....	....	....	....	....
	1—2	2,040	1,008	1,032	2,040	1,008	1,032	....	....	....	....	....	....
	2—3	2,072	974	1,098	2,071	974	1,097	1	....	1	....	....	....
	3—4	2,168	1,066	1,102	2,166	1,066	1,100	2	....	2	....	....	....
	4—5	2,175	1,103	1,072	2,173	1,102	1,071	2	1	1	....	....	....
	Total 0—5	*10,413*	*5,217*	*5,196*	*10,408*	*5,216*	*5,192*	*5*	*1*	*4*	....	....	....
	5—10	9,380	5,110	4,270	8,823	5,042	3,781	543	59	484	14	9	5
	10—15	8,495	4,787	3,708	6,852	4,414	2,438	1,606	349	1,257	37	24	13
	15—20	6,359	3,260	3,099	2,166	1,824	342	4,083	1,386	2,697	110	50	60
	20—30	11,084	5,513	5,571	1,379	1,241	138	9,310	4,079	5,231	395	193	202
	30—40	8,413	4,522	3,891	288	243	45	7,463	4,029	3,434	662	250	412
	40—50	4,961	2,841	2,120	75	63	12	4,129	2,554	1,575	757	224	533
	50—60	2,934	1,744	1,190	18	12	6	2,131	1,527	604	785	205	580
	60 & over	2,505	1,496	1,009	15	9	6	1,392	1,098	294	1,098	389	709
Hindu—(Brahmanic).	*Total*	*310*	*289*	*21*	*121*	*113*	*8*	*171*	*159*	*12*	*18*	*17*	*1*
	0—1	1	1	....	1	1	....	....	....	....	....	....	....
	1—2	1	1	....	1	1	....	....	....	....	....	....	....
	2—3	2	1	1	2	1	1	....	....	....	....	....	....
	3—4	3	2	1	3	2	1	....	....	....	....	....	....
	4—5	3	2	1	3	2	1	....	....	....	....	....	....
	Total 0—5	*10*	*7*	*3*	*10*	*7*	*3*	....	....	....	....	....	....
	5—10	8	5	3	8	5	3	....	....	....	....	....	....
	10—15	4	2	2	4	2	2	....	....	....	....	....	....
	15—20	36	33	3	24	24	....	11	8	3	1	1	....
	20—30	120	117	3	55	55	....	60	57	3	5	5	....
	30—40	103	96	7	18	18	....	75	60	6	10	9	1
	40—50	26	26	....	2	2	....	22	22	....	2	2	....
	50—60	3	3	....	....	....	....	3	3	....	....	....	....
	60 & over	....	....	....	....	....	....	....	....	....	....	....	....
Muslim.	*Total*	*64,199*	*34,175*	*30,024*	*29,885*	*17,937*	*11,948*	*30,477*	*14,914*	*15,563*	*3,837*	*1,324*	*2,513*
	0—1	1,956	1,064	892	1,956	1,064	892	....	....	....	....	....	....
	1—2	2,039	1,007	1,032	2,039	1,007	1,032	....	....	....	....	....	....
	2—3	2,068	973	1,095	2,067	973	1,094	1	....	1	....	....	....
	3—4	2,165	1,064	1,101	2,163	1,064	1,099	2	....	2	....	....	....
	4—5	2,171	1,100	1,071	2,169	1,099	1,070	2	1	1	....	....	....
	Total 0—5	*10,399*	*5,208*	*5,191*	*10,394*	*5,207*	*5,187*	*5*	*1*	*4*	....	....	....
	5—10	9,368	5,102	4,266	8,811	5,034	3,777	543	59	484	14	9	5
	10—15	8,491	4,785	3,706	6,848	4,412	2,436	1,606	349	1,257	37	24	13
	15—20	6,320	3,225	3 095	2,140	1,799	341	4,071	1,377	2,694	109	49	60
	20—30	10,953	5,389	5,564	1,322	1,184	138	9,243	4,019	5,224	388	186	202
	30—40	8,299	4,416	3,883	266	221	45	7,382	3,955	3,427	651	240	411
	40—50	4,933	2,813	2,120	71	59	12	4,107	2,532	1,575	755	222	533
	50—60	2,931	1,741	1,190	18	12	6	2,128	1,524	604	785	205	580
	60 & over	2,505	1,496	1,009	15	9	6	1,392	1,098	294	1,098	389	709

TABLE VII.—Age, Sex and Civil Condition.

Jammu and Kashmir Census 1931.

Part III.—Jammu City.

Religion.	Age.	*Population.* Persons.	Males.	Females.	*Unmarried.* Persons.	Males.	Females.	*Married.* Persons.	Males.	Females.	*Widowed.* Persons.	Males.	Females.
1	2	3	4	5	6	7	8	9	10	11	12	13	14
All Religions.	*Total*	*38,608*	*23,361*	*15,247*	*16,155*	*10,326*	*5,829*	*18,354*	*11,417*	*6,937*	*4,099*	*1,618*	*2,481*
	0—1	1,025	499	526	1,025	499	526	....	....	....	....	....	....
	1—2	856	413	443	856	413	443	....	....	....	....	....	....
	2—3	849	426	423	849	426	423	....	....	....	....	....	....
	3—4	881	457	424	881	457	424	....	....	....	....	....	....
	4—5	874	461	413	874	461	413	....	....	....	....	....	....
	Total 0—5	*4,485*	*2,256*	*2,229*	*4,485*	*2,256*	*2,229*	....	....	....	....	....	....
	5—10	3,908	2,111	1,797	3,157	1,417	1,740	748	694	54	3	....	3
	10—15	3,819	2,164	1,655	2,762	1,404	1,358	1,040	758	282	17	2	15
	15—20	4,381	2,770	1,611	2,306	1,986	320	1,989	751	1,238	86	33	53
	20—30	8,570	5,579	2,991	2,441	2,333	108	5,725	3,027	2,698	404	219	185
	30—40	5,779	3,772	2,007	606	578	28	4,388	2,842	1,546	785	352	433
	40—50	3,902	2,445	1,456	237	218	19	2,618	1,850	768	1,047	378	669
	50—60	2,198	1,348	850	89	73	16	1,212	959	253	897	316	581
	60& over	1,566	915	651	72	61	11	634	536	98	860	318	542
Hindu—(Brahmanic).	*Total*	*20,714*	*12,481*	*8,233*	*7,715*	*4,889*	*2,826*	*10,523*	*6,712*	*3,811*	*2,476*	*880*	*1,596*
	0—1	521	258	263	521	258	263	....	....	....	....	....	....
	1—2	453	227	225	453	227	226	....	....	....	....	....	....
	2—3	434	222	212	434	222	212	....	....	....	....	....	....
	3—4	426	222	204	426	222	204	....	....	....	....	....	....
	4—5	407	213	194	407	213	194	....	....	....	....	....	....
	Total 0—5	*2,241*	*1,142*	*1,099*	*2,241*	*1,142*	*1,099*	....	....	....	....	....	....
	5—10	1,942	1,068	874	1,238	394	844	703	674	29	1	....	1
	10—15	1,987	1,160	827	1,116	451	665	867	708	159	4	1	3
	15—20	2,406	1,546	860	1,273	1,128	145	1,089	400	689	44	18	26
	20—30	4,597	2,946	1,651	1,315	1,273	42	3,060	1,582	1,478	222	91	131
	30—40	3,090	1,959	1,131	307	296	11	2,307	1,477	830	476	186	290
	40—50	2,232	1,372	860	128	122	6	1,456	1,035	421	648	215	433
	50—60	1,304	773	531	56	46	10	686	541	145	562	186	376
	60 & over	915	515	400	41	37	4	355	295	60	519	183	336
Hindu—(Arya).	*Total*	*3,384*	*1,870*	*1,514*	*1,425*	*866*	*559*	*1,632*	*871*	*761*	*327*	*133*	*194*
	0—1	91	38	53	91	38	53	....	....	....	....	....	....
	1—2	72	30	42	72	30	42	....	....	....	....	....	....
	2—3	75	32	43	75	32	43	....	....	....	....	....	....
	3—4	84	40	44	84	40	44	....	....	....	....	....	....
	4—5	81	42	39	81	42	39	....	....	....	....	....	....
	Total 0—5	*403*	*182*	*221*	*403*	*182*	*221*	....	....	....	....	....	....
	5—10	389	204	185	371	200	171	18	4	14	....	....	....
	10—15	355	189	166	303	174	129	50	14	36	2	1	1
	15—20	354	188	166	151	127	24	195	58	137	8	3	5
	20—30	722	401	321	151	141	10	528	233	295	43	27	16
	30—40	516	307	209	29	28	1	419	247	172	68	32	36
	40—50	349	212	137	10	8	2	259	177	82	80	27	53
	50—60	172	112	60	1	....	1	105	87	18	66	25	41
	60& over	124	75	49	6	6	....	58	51	7	60	18	42
Hindu—(Brahmo).	*Total*	*4*	*3*	*1*	*2*	*2*	....	*2*	*1*	*1*	....	....	....
	0—1	....	....	....	....	....	....	....	....	....	....	....	....
	1—2	....	....	....	....	....	....	....	....	....	....	....	....
	2—3	....	....	....	....	....	....	....	....	....	....	....	....
	3—4	....	....	....	....	....	....	....	....	....	....	....	....
	4—5	....	....	....	....	....	....	....	....	....	....	....	....
	Total 0—5	....	....	....	....	....	....	....	....	....	....	....	....
	5—10	....	....	....	....	....	....	....	....	....	....	....	....
	10—15	....	....	....	....	....	....	....	....	....	....	....	....
	15—20	1	1	....	1	1	....	....	....	....	....	....	....
	20—30	1	1	....	1	1	....	....	....	....	....	....	....
	30—40	2	1	1	....	....	....	2	1	1	....	....	....
	40—50	....	....	....	....	....	....	....	....	....	....	....	....
	50—60	....	....	....	....	....	....	....	....	....	....	....	....
	60& over	....	....	....	....	....	....	....	....	....	....	....	....

TABLE VII—AGE, SEX AND CIVIL CONDITION.

Jammu and Kashmir Census 1931.

Part III.—Jammu City—(continued).

Religion.	Age.	Population.			Unmarried			Married.			Widowed.		
		Persons.	Males.	Females.	Persons.	Males.	Females.	Persons.	Males.	Females.	Persons	Males.	Females.
1	2	3	4	5	6	7	8	9	10	11	12	13	14
Jain.	*Total*	*563*	*297*	*266*	*307*	*178*	*129*	*197*	*92*	*105*	*59*	*27*	*32*
	0—1	12	9	3	12	9	3	--	--	--	--	--	--
	1—2	14	9	5	14	9	5	--	--	--	--	--	--
	2—3	19	10	9	19	10	9	--	--	--	--	--	--
	3—4	16	8	8	16	8	8	--	--	--	--	--	--
	4—5	12	6	6	12	6	6	--	--	--	--	--	--
	Total 0—5	*73*	*42*	*31*	*73*	*42*	*31*	--	--	--	--	--	--
	5—10	68	30	38	68	30	38	--	--	--	--	--	--
	10—15	70	31	39	67	31	36	3	....	3	--	--	--
	15—20	55	27	28	34	22	12	19	4	15	2	1	1
	20—30	103	58	45	37	29	8	62	26	36	4	3	1
	30—40	71	38	33	14	13	1	47	23	24	10	2	8
	40—50	65	34	31	9	8	1	37	19	18	19	7	12
	50—60	40	25	15	4	3	1	23	15	8	13	7	6
	60& over	18	12	6	1	....	1	6	5	1	11	7	4
Buddhist.	*Total*	*9*	*4*	*5*	*5*	*2*	*3*	*4*	*2*	*2*	--	--	--
	0—1	1	....	1	1	....	1	....	....	--	--	--	--
	1—2	....	....	....	....	....	....	....	....	--	--	--	--
	2—3	1	....	1	1	....	1	....	....	--	--	--	--
	3—4	....	....	....	....	....	....	....	....	--	--	--	--
	4—5	....	....	....	....	....	....	....	....	--	--	--	--
	Total 0—5	*2*	....	*2*	*2*	....	*2*	--	--	--	--	--	--
	5—10	2	1	1	2	1	1	....	--	--	--	--	--
	10—15	....	....	....	....	....	....	....	....	--	--	--	--
	15—20	2	1	1	1	1	....	1	....	1	--	--	--
	20—30	2	1	1	....	....	....	2	1	1	--	--	--
	30—40	....	....	....	....	....	....	....	....	--	--	--	--
	40—50	1	1	....	....	....	....	1	1	--	--	--	--
	50—60	....	....	....	....	....	....	....	....	--	--	--	--
	60& over	....	....	....	....	....	....	....	....	--	--	--	--
Sikh.	*Total*	*1,296*	*757*	*539*	*640*	*410*	*230*	*538*	*305*	*233*	*118*	*42*	*76*
	0—1	44	27	17	44	27	17	....	....	--	--	--	--
	1—2	37	20	17	37	20	17	....	....	....	--	--	--
	2—3	34	19	15	34	19	15	....	....	--	--	--	--
	3—4	32	17	15	32	17	15	....	....	--	--	--	--
	4—5	37	20	17	37	20	17	....	....	--	--	--	--
	Total 0—5	*184*	*103*	*81*	*184*	*103*	*81*	....	....	--	--	--	--
	5—10	175	97	78	169	97	72	4	....	4	2	--	2
	10—15	156	87	69	142	86	56	3	1	2	11	--	11
	15—20	125	71	54	60	46	14	54	24	30	11	1	10
	20—30	243	143	100	56	52	4	178	84	94	9	7	2
	30—40	189	119	70	13	13	....	159	99	60	17	7	10
	40—50	101	60	41	4	3	1	77	50	27	20	7	13
	50—60	69	43	26	7	6	1	41	29	12	21	8	13
	60& over	54	34	20	5	4	1	22	18	4	27	12	15
Muslim.	*Total*	*12,036*	*7,621*	*4,415*	*5,788*	*3,818*	*1,970*	*5,191*	*3,297*	*1,894*	*1,057*	*506*	*551*
	0—1	322	148	174	322	148	174	....	....	--	--	--	--
	1—2	257	116	141	257	116	141	....	....	--	--	--	--
	2—3	265	131	134	265	131	134	....	....	--	--	--	--
	3—4	301	155	146	301	155	146	....	....	--	--	--	--
	4—5	298	148	150	298	148	150	....	....	--	--	--	--
	Total 0—5	*1,443*	*698*	*745*	*1,443*	*698*	*745*	....	--	--	--	--	--
	5—10	1,267	674	593	1,246	660	586	21	14	7	--	--	....
	10—15	1,202	676	526	1,093	643	450	109	33	76	--	--	....
	15—20	1,382	915	467	770	652	118	594	255	339	18	8	10
	20—30	2,779	1,973	806	874	833	41	1,788	1,055	733	117	85	32
	30—40	1,821	1,290	531	239	225	14	1,387	949	438	195	116	79
	40—50	1,110	742	368	83	75	8	760	549	211	267	118	149
	50—60	592	384	208	21	18	3	344	280	64	227	86	141
	60& over	440	269	171	19	14	5	188	162	26	233	93	140

TABLE VII—Age, Sex and Civil Condition.

Jammu and Kashmir Census 1931.

Part III.—Jammu City—(concluded).

Religion.	Age.	Population.			Unmarried.			Married.			Widowed.		
		Persons.	Males.	Females.	Persons.	Males.	Females.	Persons.	Males.	Females.	Persons.	Males.	Females.
1	2	3	4	5	6	7	8	9	10	11	12	13	14
Christian.	*Total*	*602*	*328*	*274*	*273*	*161*	*112*	*267*	*137*	*130*	*62*	*30*	*32*
	0—1	34	19	15	34	19	15	....	....	....	....	....	....
	1—2	23	11	12	23	11	12	....	....	....	....	....	....
	2—3	21	12	9	21	12	9	....	....	....	....	....	....
	3—4	22	15	7	22	15	7	....	....	....	....	....	....
	4—5	39	32	7	39	32	7	....	....	....	....	....	....
	Total 0—5	*139*	*89*	*50*	*139*	*89*	*50*	....	....	....	....	....	....
	5—10	65	37	28	63	35	28	2	2	....	....	....	....
	10—15	49	21	28	41	19	22	8	2	6	....	....	....
	15—20	56	21	35	16	9	7	37	10	27	3	2	1
	20—30	123	56	67	7	4	3	107	46	61	9	6	3
	30—40	90	58	32	4	3	1	67	46	21	19	9	10
	40—50	44	25	19	3	2	1	28	19	9	13	4	9
	50—60	21	11	10	....	....	....	13	7	6	8	4	4
	60 & over	15	10	5	....	....	....	5	5	....	10	5	5

TABLE VII.—AGE, SEX AND CIVIL CONDITION.

Jammu and Kashmir Census 1931.

Part III.—Srinagar City.

Religion.	Age.	Population.			Unmarried.			Married.			Widowed.		
		Persons.	Males.	Females.	Persons.	Males.	Females.	Persons.	Males.	Females.	Persons.	Males.	Females.
1	2	3	4	5	6	7	8	9	10	11	12	13	14
All Religions.	*Total*	*173,573*	*94,793*	*78,780*	*83,265*	*51,630*	*31,635*	*75,568*	*37,529*	*38,039*	*14,740*	*5,634*	*9,106*
	0—1	3,578	1,842	1,736	3,578	1,842	1,736	....	— —	— —	— —	— —	— —
	1—2	4,393	2,200	2,193	4,393	2,200	2,193	....	....	....	....	....	— —
	2—3	4,940	2,481	2,459	4,940	2,481	2,459	....	....	....	....	....	— —
	3—4	5,098	2,580	2,518	5,098	2,580	2,518	....	....	— —	....	....	— —
	4—5	4,869	2,466	2,403	4,869	2,466	2,403	....	....	— —	— —	— —	— —
	Total 0—5	*22,878*	*11,569*	*11,309*	*22,878*	*11,569*	*11,309*	....	— —	— —	— —	— —	— —
	5—10	22,147	11,502	10,645	22,008	11,485	10,523	132	17	115	7	— —	7
	10—15	20,688	11,021	9,667	18,837	10,811	8,026	1,808	200	1,608	43	10	33
	15—20	18,656	10,114	8,542	8,858	7,519	1,339	9,484	2,492	6,992	314	103	211
	20—30	35,289	19,177	16,112	7,929	7,605	324	25,918	10,866	15,052	1,442	706	736
	30—40	25,055	14,690	10,365	1,783	1,706	77	20,676	11,801	8,875	2,596	1,183	1,413
	40—50	15,683	9,063	6,620	635	615	20	11,174	7,161	4,013	3,874	1,287	2,587
	50—60	8,380	4,866	3,514	240	231	9	4,572	3,436	1,136	3,568	1,199	2,369
	60& over	4,797	2,791	2,006	97	89	8	1,804	1,556	248	2,896	1,146	1,750
Hindu—(Brahmanic).	*Total*	*33 345*	*18,247*	*15,098*	*16,239*	*10,647*	*5,592*	*12,866*	*6,176*	*6,690*	*4,240*	*1,424*	*2,816*
	0—1	577	306	271	577	306	271	....	— —	— —	— —	— —	— —
	1—2	752	367	385	752	367	385	....	....	— —	— —	— —	— —
	2—3	885	439	446	885	439	446	....	....	— —	....	....	— —
	3—4	917	474	443	917	474	443	....	....	— —	— —	....	....
	4—5	888	455	433	888	455	433	....	— —	— —	— —	— —	— —
	Total 0—5	*4,019*	*2,041*	*1,978*	*4,019*	*2,041*	*1,978*	....	— —	— —	— —	— —	— —
	5—10	4,023	2,062	1,961	4,017	2,062	1,955	5	— —	5	1	— —	1
	10—15	3,692	2,000	1,692	3,430	1,971	1,459	256	27	229	6	2	4
	15—20	3,492	2,036	1,456	1,785	1,610	175	1,631	407	1,224	76	19	57
	20—30	6,645	3,702	2,943	1,858	1,836	22	4,373	1,740	2,633	414	126	288
	30—40	4,730	2,714	2,016	626	623	3	3,370	1,836	1,534	734	255	479
	40—50	3,403	1,906	1,497	288	288	....	1,999	1,248	751	1,116	370	746
	50—60	2,230	1,202	1,028	155	155	....	943	675	268	1,132	372	760
	60& over	1,111	584	527	61	61	....	289	243	46	761	280	481
Hindu—(Arya).	*Total*	*324*	*199*	*125*	*166*	*101*	*65*	*140*	*88*	*52*	*18*	*10*	*8*
	0—1	9	4	5	9	4	5	....	— —	— —	— —	— —	— —
	1—2	11	5	6	11	5	6	....	— —	....	— —	— —	— —
	2—3	7	5	2	7	5	2	....	— —	....	— —	— —	....
	3—4	8	4	4	8	4	4	....	....	....	— —	....	....
	4—5	10	4	6	10	4	6	....	....	— —	— —	— —	— —
	Total 0—5	*45*	*22*	*23*	*45*	*22*	*23*	....	....	— —	— —	— —	— —
	5—10	46	24	22	45	24	21	1	....	1	— —	— —	— —
	10—15	41	22	19	38	22	16	3	....	3	— —	....	....
	15—20	33	22	11	21	17	4	12	5	7	....	....	....
	20—30	64	40	24	16	15	1	47	24	23	1	1	— —
	30—40	53	39	14	1	1	....	49	36	13	3	2	1
	40—50	31	24	7	....	....	....	23	19	4	8	5	3
	50—60	8	5	3	....	....	....	4	4	— —	4	1	3
	60& over	3	1	2	....	....	....	1	— —	1	2	1	1
Sikh.	*Total*	*870*	*634*	*236*	*374*	*269*	*105*	*444*	*333*	*111*	*52*	*32*	*20*
	0—1	18	9	9	18	9	9	— —	— —	— —	— —	— —	— —
	1—2	14	5	9	14	5	9	— —	— —	— —	— —	— —	— —
	2—3	18	6	12	18	6	12	— —	— —	— —	— —	— —	— —
	3—4	28	19	9	28	19	9	— —	— —	— —	— —	— —	— —
	4—5	17	10	7	17	10	7	— —	— —	— —	— —	— —	— —
	Total 0—5	*95*	*49*	*46*	*95*	*49*	*46*	— —	— —	— —	— —	— —	— —
	5—10	78	49	29	77	49	28	1	— —	1	— —	— —	— —
	10—15	67	43	24	61	40	21	6	3	3	— —	— —	— —
	15—20	108	85	23	63	56	7	44	28	16	1	1	....
	20—30	252	198	54	67	64	3	178	129	49	7	5	2
	30—40	145	114	31	8	8	....	126	99	27	11	7	4
	40—50	69	53	16	2	2	....	59	48	11	8	3	5
	50—60	41	31	10	— —	— —	— —	24	20	4	17	11	6
	60& over	15	12	3	1	1	— —	6	6	— —	8	5	3

TABLE VII.—Age, Sex and Civil Condition.

Jammu and Kashmir Census 1931.

Part III.—City Srinagar—(concluded).

Religion.	Age.	Population.			Unmarried.			Married.			Widowed.		
		Persons.	Males.	Females.	Persons.	Males	Females.	Persons.	Males.	Females.	Persons.	Males.	Females.
1	2	3	4	5	6	7	8	9	10	11	12	13	14
Muslim.	*Total*	*138,764*	*75,583*	*63,181*	*66,362*	*40,558*	*25,804*	*61,984*	*30,861*	*31,123*	*10,418*	*4,164*	*6,254*
	0—1	2,972	1,523	1,449	2,972	1,523	1,449	....	....	....	....	....	....
	1—2	3,612	1,820	1,792	3,612	1,820	1,792	....	....	....	....	....	....
	2—3	4,028	2,029	1,999	4,028	2,029	1,999	....	....	....	....	....	....
	3—4	4,144	2,083	2,061	4,144	2,083	2,061	....	....	....	....	....	....
	4—5	3,950	1,995	1,955	3,950	1,995	1,955	....	....	....	....	....	....
	Total 0—5	*18,706*	*9,450*	*9,256*	*18,706*	*9,450*	*9,256*	....	....	....	....	....	....
	5—10	17,985	9,360	8,625	17,854	9,343	8,511	125	17	108	6	....	6
	10—15	16,874	8,949	7,925	15,294	8,771	6,523	1,543	170	1,373	37	8	29
	15—20	15,005	7,963	7,042	6,974	5,829	1,145	7,794	2,051	5,743	237	83	154
	20—30	28,277	15,212	13,065	5,955	5,674	281	21,302	8,964	12,338	1,020	574	446
	30—40	20,076	11,798	8,278	1,134	1,067	67	17,095	9,813	7,282	1,847	918	929
	40—50	12,137	7,058	5,079	338	322	16	9,061	5,829	3,232	2,738	907	1,831
	50—60	6,062	3,609	2,453	79	75	4	3,571	2,720	851	2,412	814	1,598
	60&over	3,642	2,184	1,458	28	27	1	1,493	1,297	196	2,121	860	1,261
Christian.	*Total*	*257*	*118*	*139*	*118*	*49*	*69*	*128*	*66*	*62*	*11*	*3*	*8*
	0—1	2	....	2	2	....	2	....	....	....	....	....	....
	1—2	3	2	1	3	2	1	....	....	....	....	....	....
	2—3	2	2	....	2	2	....	....	....	....	....	....	....
	3—4	1	....	1	1	....	1	....	....	....	....	....	....
	4—5	4	2	2	4	2	2	....	....	....	....	....	....
	Total 0—5	*12*	*6*	*6*	*12*	*6*	*6*	....	....	....	....	....	....
	5—10	15	7	8	15	7	8	....	....	....	....	....	....
	10—15	13	6	7	13	6	7	....	....	....	....	....	....
	15—20	15	6	9	14	6	8	1	....	1	....	....	....
	20—30	46	20	26	30	13	17	16	7	9	....	....	....
	30—40	50	24	26	14	7	7	35	16	19	1	1	....
	40—50	43	22	21	7	3	4	32	17	15	4	2	2
	50—60	37	17	20	6	1	5	29	16	13	2	....	2
	60&over.	26	10	16	7	....	7	15	10	5	4	....	4

TABLE VIII.

Civil condition by age for selected castes.

Jammu and Kashmir Census 1931.

1. This table contains statistics of Civil condition by age for selected castes and tribes, whereas Table VII deals with the total population.

2. Figures for Christians and Sikhs do not appear in this Table as their Civil condition has been dealt with in table VII.

3. This table is the same as the corresponding table in 1921 Census with the exception that there is a slight difference in age-groups.

4. The figures of Brahmans by sex given in column 3 of this table do not include Mohyal Brahmans numbering 5120 persons as details of their Civil condition were not sorted for.

TABLE

Civil condition by age

Jammu and

Serial No.	Caste, tribe or race.	Sex.	Population dealt with.	Unmarried						
				Total.	0 to 6.	7 to 13.	14 to 16.	17 to 23.	24 to 43.	44 and over.
1.	2	3	4	5	6	7	8	9	10	11
	Hindus.									
1	Arora ..	Males ..	1,032	469	164	77	52	89	62	25
		Females ..	776	317	148	139	18	9	3	....
2	Brahman (excluding Mohyals numbering 5,120 persons).	Males ..	94,931	50,990	16,556	13,680	5,758	7,278	5,889	1,829
		Females ..	90,390	32,352	15,926	12,431	2,520	1,073	290	112
3	Basith ..	Males ..	3,071	1,646	532	419	154	190	320	31
		Females ..	3,142	1,268	640	353	128	83	37	27
4	Batwal ..	Males ..	3,045	1,585	581	530	154	146	100	74
		Females ..	2,600	1,103	627	355	75	21	11	14
5	Chamar ..	Males ..	21,672	10,808	4,109	3,393	1,192	1,242	628	244
		Females ..	19,517	7,501	4,112	2,660	569	125	31	4
6	Gaddi ..	Males ..	5,599	2,678	942	819	267	347	235	68
		Females ..	5,742	1,634	912	666	49	4	3	....
7	Jat ..	Males ..	12.287	6,380	2,379	2,067	674	685	458	117
		Females ..	11,084	4,304	2,305	1,652	249	66	23	9
8	Kashmiri Pandit ..	Males ..	35,060	19,954	5,274	5,223	1,030	3,520	3,081	926
		Females ..	28,028	10,828	5,117	4,908	706	78	17	2
9	Khatri ..	Males ..	11,254	5,771	1,908	1,429	619	961	655	199
		Females ..	9,302	3,731	1,881	1,456	273	87	26	8
10	Megh ..	Males ..	37,062	18,267	6,096	5,529	1,870	2,455	1,808	569
		Females ..	32,968	11,389	6,135	4,311	700	125	93	25
11	Rajput ..	Males ..	87,339	47,984	13,963	12,786	.727	7,187	7,587	1,734
		Females ..	71,118	23,873	12,054	9,054	1,734	478	468	85
12	Saryara ..	Males ..	1,243	573	229	159	62	76	36	11
		Females ..	1,111	394	188	145	16	39	6	...—
	Muslims.									
13	Arain ..	Males ..	12,727	6,680	2,366	2,233	691	828	456	106
		Females ..	10,195	4,188	2,278	1,559	240	82	24	5
14	Bafinda ..	Males ..	17,679	9,403	3,567	3,138	1,099	1,034	465	100
		Females ..	16,193	6,643	3,525	2,418	454	138	54	54
15	Bakarwal ..	Males ..	2,[illegible]88	1,678	715	600	148	138	72	5
		Females ..	2,461	993	592	320	55	23	3	....
16	Balti ..	Males ..	23,274	11,858	4,881	4,070	1,243	1,153	460	51
		Females ..	24,052	10,519	4,977	3,801	988	652	91	10
17	Gujjar ..	Males ..	216,958	114,989	46,546	38,292	12,691	11,507	5,455	498
		Females ..	185,823	78,033	42,239	28,203	5,154	1,886	437	114
18	Jat ..	Males ..	62,227	33,857	12,794	10,967	3,917	3,701	2,187	291
		Females ..	57,856	23,309	12,684	8,057	1,720	645	179	24
19	Kashmiri ..	Males ..	730,769	378,449	137,775	127,506	42,546	48,112	19,981	2,529
		Females ..	622,053	253,623	131,230	97,638	19,009	4,135	1,378	233

VIII.

FOR SELECTED CASTES.

Kashmir Census 1931.

Married.							*Widowed.*						
Total.	0 to 6	7 to 13.	14 to 16.	17 to 23.	24 to 43.	44 and over.	Total.	0 to 6.	7 to 13.	14 to 16.	17 to 23.	24 to 43.	44 and over.
12	13	14	15	16	17	18	19	20	21	22	23	24	'25
475	....	87	4	34	214	136	88	....	....	....	2	25	61
340	....	6	17	68	190	59	119	....	1	....	....	51	67
36,311	....	874	827	4.017	18,419	12,174	7,630	....	15	80	334	2,422	4,779
39,693	....	1,339	4,670	10,482	18,098	5,104	18,345	....	44	231	759	6,420	10,891
1,176	2	9	16	99	609	441	249	....	2	....	1	73	173
1,380	....	12	98	334	676	260	494	....	11	3	38	135	307
1,177	....	10	45	170	663	289	283	....	....	2	23	98	160
1,127	1	44	120	292	540	130	370	....	2	2	16	143	207
9,365	6	138	255	1,243	5,075	2,648	1,499	....	20	14	67	452	946
9,411	1	369	1,061	2,173	4,328	1,479	2,605	....	9	53	96	876	1,571
2,367	....	8	43	363	1,178	775	554	....	....	52	54	167	291
3,071	....	52	298	768	1,353	600	1,037	....	3	11	30	368	625
5,052	....	127	147	444	2,557	1,777	855	....	....	3	25	229	598
5,339	....	258	744	1,124	2,461	752	1,441	....	7	14	28	429	963
12,213	....	63	81	1,245	7,555	3,269	2,893	....	....	5	78	979	1,831
12,133	....	65	847	3,510	6,440	1,271	5,067	....	2	19	161	1,712	3,173
4,671	....	301	75	383	2,557	1,355	812	....	1	10	14	309	478
4,036	....	61	320	1,001	2,145	509	1,535	....	2	31	99	521	882
15,560	3	93	317	1,762	8,621	4,764	3,235	....	8	27	160	1,007	2,033
16,139	2	468	1,646	4,013	8,014	1,996	5,440	....	11	90	256	1,686	3,397
33,041	....	421	366	3,134	17,667	11,453	6,314	....	4	22	229	2,128	3,931
33,218	....	1,162	3,059	8,781	15,765	4,451	14,027	....	327	182	1,043	4,094	8,381
558	1	8	18	81	289	161	112	....	....	....	12	36	64
519	....	15	62	144	243	55	198	....	....	6	16	57	119
5,008	....	76	121	622	2,835	1,354	1,039	....	6	4	28	342	659
4,901	....	145	425	1,118	2,480	733	1,106	....	2	14	24	317	749
7,274	....	116	220	919	4,125	1,894	1,002	....	3	17	40	325	617
7,824	....	249	729	2,055	3,791	1,000	1,726	....	22	15	32	503	1,154
1,133	....	9	33	142	642	307	77	....	....	....	3	24	50
1,318	2	61	248	320	526	161	150	....	1	....	17	31	101
10,276	....	36	128	1,134	5,629	3,349	1,140	1	6	13	69	401	650
10,941	1	37	375	1,784	6,526	2,218	2,592	....	2	8	113	597	1,872
89,918	3	1,374	2,157	10,903	50,968	24,213	12,051	....	18	105	611	4,307	7,010
92,290	28	3,035	8,804	22,121	46,640	11,662	15,500	....	44	188	867	4,233	10,168
23,711	....	350	779	3,627	12,022	6,933	4,659	....	5	19	174	1,794	2,667
27,307	....	683	2,001	6,912	14,027	3,684	7,240	....	16	44	178	1,865	5,137
311,009	10	2,181	5,869	43,437	191,529	67,983	41,311	....	22	167	1,630	16,761	22,731
320,856	38	5,136	26,179	83,478	174,613	31,412	47,574	....	54	384	1,533	12,446	33,157

TABLE

CIVIL CONDITION BY AGE

Jammu and

Serial No.	Caste, tribe or race.	Sex.	Population dealt with.	Unmarried. Total.	0 to 6.	7 to 13.	14 to 16.	17 to 23.	24 to 43.	44 and over
1	2	3	4	5	6	7	8	9	10	11
	Muslims.—(*concluded*).									
20	Mughal ..	Males ..	15,820	8.641	3,226	2,805	1,035	955	505	115
		Females ..	14.378	6.507	3,600	2,145	452	125	137	48
21	Pathan ..	Males ..	10,554	5,851	1,985	1.928	605	740	527	66
		Females ..	8,734	3,924	1.994	1,383	341	178	18	10
22	Rajput ..	Males ..	101,875	56,817	22.069	18,443	6,540	6,596	2,772	397
		Females ..	93,574	40,737	21.237	14,500	3,315	1,136	397	152
23	Sayed ..	Males ..	20,675	11,481	4,257	3.805	1,370	1,340	612	97
		Females ..	19,051	8.453	4,480	2,981	699	212	62	19
24	Sheikh ..	Males ..	15.623	8.667	3,406	2.585	938	1,103	540	95
		Females ..	13,361	5.824	2,886	2,053	583	214	70	18
25	Tarkhan ..	Males ..	7,616	3,993	1,526	1,202	410	500	247	108
		Females ..	6,789	2,914	1,589	947	233	118	24	3
26	Shin ..	Males ..	7,126	3,849	1,399	1,438	493	355	155	9
		Females ..	7,013	3,004	1,600	1,075	214	76	29	10
27	Yashkun ..	Males ..	19,091	10,278	3,673	3,567	1,345	1,231	454	8
		Females ..	17,069	7,378	3,729	2,839	526	230	51	3
8	Brokpa ..	Males ..	6,691	3,386	1,440	1,145	315	312	151	23
		Females ..	6,413	2,698	1,437	888	221	93	52	7
	Buddhist.									
29	Mangrik ..	Males ..	16,943	7,733	2,377	2,510	722	848	742	534
		Females ..	17,164	7,878	2,537	2,435	796	1,008	801	301
	Tribal.									
30	Sansi ..	Males ..	78	42	17	9	5	5	6	....
		Females ..	56	4	6	11	2	4	1	....

VIII.

FOR SELECTED CASTES.

Kashmir Census 1931.

Married.							Widowed.						
Total.	0 to 6.	7 to 13.	14 to 16.	17 to 23.	24 to 43.	44 and over.	Total.	0 to 6.	7 to 13.	14 to 16.	17 to 23.	24 to 43	44 and over.
12	13	14	15	16	17	18	19	20	21	22	23	24	25
6,344	2	43	107	747	3,522	1,923	835	.. —	....	7	29	291	508
6,508	....	92	555	1,719	3,230	912	1,363	....	2	5	56	295	1,005
4,177	1	44	113	479	2,405	1,135	526	....	3	1	17	201	304
4,038	3	104	292	957	2,155	527	772	....	....	42	28	219	483
40,228	....	710	968	4,801	22,988	10,761	4,830	....	11	24	160	1,638	2,997
43,064	4	812	3,599	10,553	22,994	5,102	9,773	....	64	63	262	2,796	6,588
8,252	1	69	134	1,012	4,871	2,165	942	....	....	10	30	328	574
8,730	1	103	568	2,247	4,945	866	1,868	.. —	2	16	64	558	1,228
6,139	2	97	185	1,092	3,328	1,435	817	— —	1	2	34	315	465
6,285	3	140	589	1,627	3,202	724	1,252	— ..	2	12	46	354	838
3,150	1	29	75	368	1,896	781	473	— ..	2	1	19	162	289
3,149	— —	89	267	747	1,595	451	726	....	2	6	25	201	492
3,061	.. —	28	114	428	1,750	741	216	....	1	3	10	90	112
3,433	1	209	291	760	1,743	429	576	.. —	1	5	20	199	351
7,935	— —	22	149	1,020	4,790	1,954	878	— —	2	3	54	284	535
8,391	— ..	232	752	2,189	4,435	783	1,300	— —	5	7	57	426	805
3,030	— —	3	21	367	1,767	872	275	— —	....	— —	8	62	205
3,189	1	6	139	567	1,868	608	526	1	.. —	1	16	103	405
8,113	— —	4	36	1,055	3,927	3,091	1,097	— —	1	1	38	212	845
7,341	— —	— —	— —	874	3,903	2,564	1,945	— —	.. —	— —	61	386	1,498
28	— —	— —	1	1	13	13	8	— —	— —	— —	2	4	2
22	— —	— —	5	4	12	1	10	— —	— —	— —	— —	1	9

TABLE IX.

INFIRMITIES.

Part I.—Distribution by age.

Jammu and Kashmir Census 1931.

1. The return of infirmity was not registered in the Frontier Illaqas and consequently no figures for this area have been shown in the Table.

2. Persons with more than one infirmity have been treated as single persons for columns 2, 3 and 4 of this table, but for columns 5 to 16 they have been treated as if separate individuals and consequently the total obtained by adding the figures of columns 5 to 16 exceeds the total of columns 2, 3, and 4 by one unit for each individual with 2 infirmities and so on.

3. Details of persons suffering from more than one infirmity are recorded on this page by way of additional information.

Particulars of persons suffering from more than one infirmity :—

Infirmity.	Persons.	Males.	Females.
Insanity and Deaf-muteness ..	44	34	10
„ „ Blindness ..	10	8	2
„ „ Leprosy ..	4	1	3
Deaf-muteness and Blindness ..	46	28	18
„ „ Leprosy ..	25	16	9
Blindness and Leprosy ..	26	15	11
Total ..	155	102	35

TABLE IX—INFIRMITIES.

PART I.—DISTRIBUTION BY AGE.

Jammu and Kashmir Census 1931.

Age.	Population afflicted.			Insane.			Deaf-mutes.			Blind.			Lepers.		
	Persons.	Males.	Females.	Persons.	Males.	Females.	Persons.	Males.	Females.	Persons.	Males.	Females.	Persons.	Males.	Females.
1	2	3	4	5	6	7	8	9	10	11	12	13	14	15	16
0—1 ..	20	11	9	..	..	..	9	4	5	9	6	3	2	1	1
1—2 ..	46	24	22	1	1	..	21	10	11	18	10	8	6	3	3
2—3 ..	108	61	47	5	4	1	65	36	29	27	15	12	11	6	5
3—4 ..	166	97	69	10	7	3	119	68	51	30	18	12	10	5	5
4—5 ..	206	115	91	17	9	8	146	84	62	36	19	17	12	6	6
Total 0—5 ..	**546**	**308**	**238**	**33**	**21**	**12**	**360**	**202**	**158**	**120**	**68**	**52**	**41**	**21**	**20**
5—10 ..	1,212	697	515	104	58	46	842	495	347	217	119	98	64	34	30
10—15 ..	1,393	797	596	129	77	52	931	534	397	263	144	119	87	53	34
15—20 ..	1,365	771	594	173	113	60	797	448	349	284	147	137	125	74	51
20—25 ..	1,406	821	585	191	127	64	742	439	303	328	169	159	161	97	64
25—30 ..	1,236	772	464	175	124	51	531	333	198	330	181	149	214	143	71
30—35 ..	1,140	721	419	163	117	46	423	271	152	334	183	151	234	160	74
35—40 ..	1,030	626	404	123	86	37	316	205	111	369	183	186	232	159	73
40—45 ..	841	515	326	100	67	33	237	158	79	316	158	158	193	136	57
45—50 ..	772	469	303	76	54	22	167	110	57	364	182	182	171	127	44
50—55 ..	664	390	274	56	42	14	122	78	44	352	172	180	137	101	36
55—60 ..	697	379	318	33	22	11	94	57	37	461	214	247	115	89	26
60—65 ..	671	364	307	29	19	10	80	49	31	466	223	243	103	78	25
65—70 ..	439	239	200	13	8	5	35	23	12	353	179	174	43	31	12
70 and over ..	1,369	731	638	26	17	9	110	79	31	1,142	566	576	106	78	28
Total all ages ..	**14,781**	**8,600**	**6,181**	**1,424**	**952**	**472**	**5,787**	**3,481**	**2,306**	**5,699**	**2,888**	**2,811**	**2,026**	**1,381**	**645**

PART II.—DISTRIBUTION BY DISTRICTS.

District or State.	Population afflicted			Insane.			Deaf-mutes.			Blind.			Lepers.		
	Persons.	Males.	Females.	Persons.	Males.	Females.	Persons.	Males.	Females.	Persons.	Males.	Females.	Persons.	Males.	Females.
1	2	3	4	5	6	7	8	9	10	11	12	13	14	15	16
Jammu and Kashmir State ..	**14,781**	**8,600**	**6,181**	**1,424**	**952**	**472**	**5,787**	**3,481**	**2,306**	**5,699**	**2,888**	**2,811**	**2,026**	**1,381**	**645**
I. Jammu Province ..	**7,296**	**4,178**	**3,118**	**542**	**339**	**203**	**2,728**	**1,619**	**1,109**	**2,968**	**1,470**	**1,498**	**1,118**	**792**	**826**
(a) Total Districts ..	*6,009*	*3,413*	*2,596*	*393*	*259*	*134*	*2,334*	*1,403*	*931*	*2,592*	*1,274*	*1,318*	*736*	*507*	*229*
1. Jammu District ..	1,161	705	456	67	48	19	504	323	181	517	306	241	44	29	15
2. Kathua	693	408	285	39	24	15	245	173	72	362	178	184	50	35	15
3. Udhampur District (including Bhadrawah) ..	1,819	1,005	814	121	79	42	790	447	343	592	253	339	345	243	102
4. Riasi District ..	962	552	410	62	34	28	300	179	121	389	194	195	217	149	68
5. Mirpur	1,374	743	631	104	74	30	495	281	214	702	343	359	80	51	29
(b) Total Jagirs ..	*1,287*	*765*	*522*	*149*	*80*	*69*	*394*	*216*	*178*	*376*	*196*	*180*	*382*	*285*	*97*
6. Chenani Jagir ..	69	40	29	9	7	2	16	8	8	24	13	11	23	15	8
7. Poonch	1,218	725	493	140	73	67	378	208	170	352	183	169	359	270	89
II. Kashmir Province ..	**5,500**	**3,474**	**2,026**	**810**	**575**	**235**	**1,999**	**1,308**	**691**	**2,022**	**1,134**	**888**	**732**	**500**	**232**
8. Baramulla (including Langet) or Kashmir North ..	1,886	1,157	729	273	180	93	636	402	234	759	419	340	238	169	69
9. Srinagar (including city) or Kashmir South ..	2,897	1,860	1,037	419	312	107	1,113	733	380	1,066	627	439	333	212	121
10. Muzaffarabad ..	717	457	260	118	83	35	250	173	77	197	88	109	161	119	42
III. Frontier Districts ..	**1,985**	**948**	**1,037**	**72**	**38**	**34**	**1,060**	**554**	**506**	**709**	**284**	**425**	**176**	**89**	**87**
11. Ladakh District ..	1,565	714	851	54	28	26	720	364	356	662	260	402	157	77	80
12. Gilgit .. —	420	234	186	18	10	8	310	190	150	47	24	23	19	12	7

TABLE X.

Occupation or Means of Livelihood.

Jammu and Kashmir Census 1931.

Note 1.—The arrangement of this Table is based on the scheme of classification of occupations prescribed by the Census Commissioner for India.

Note 2.—This Table gives the figures of Earners and Working dependants for each occupational group. It also shows for each occupational group the number of persons who follow it as a subsidiary occupation to some other principal occupation.

Note 3.—The following groups in which no entries have been recorded do not appear in this Table:—

Groups 3, 9, 10, 12, 13, 14, 15, 19, 20, 26, 30, 32, 35, 40, 41, 92, 93, 109, 120, 155, 156 and 179.

Note 4.—Prisoners undergoing rigorous imprisonment have been treated as Working Dependants and those undergoing simple imprisonment as Non-working Dependants, in accordance with the instructions received from the Census Commissioner for India.

TABLE X.

OCCUPATION.

Jammu and Kashmir Census 1931.

District, Ilaqa, Jagir or City.	Total population.	TOTAL OF ALL CLASSES. Total population. Total earners (principal occupation). Males.	Females.	Total working dependents. Males.	Females.	Total non-working dependent population. Males.	Females.	Total earners with subsidiary occupation. Males.	Females.	CLASS A. Production of raw materials. TOTAL OF CLASS A. Total earners (principal occupation). Males.	Females.	Total working dependents. Males.	Females.	Total following occupation as subsidiary to others. Males.	Females.
Jammu and Kashmir State ..	**3,646,243**	**752,104**	**56,045**	**221,997**	**895,159**	**984,237**	**756,701**	**194,795**	**21,397**	**569,068**	**21,701**	**203,024**	**24,660**	**153,669**	**13,726**
I. Jammu Province ..	**1,788,441**	**395,957**	**38,746**	**95,656**	**411,040**	**451,202**	**395,840**	**98,177**	**15,697**	**314,783**	**13,645**	**87,006**	**17,888**	**73,703**	**10,497**
1. Jammu District (*including City*) ..	375,240	97,501	4,774	13,171	77,007	95,047	87,740	23,330	2,758	58,480	1,641	10,995	232	12,595	1,375
2. Kathua District ..	161,232	42,495	3,815	4,860	39,377	38,638	32,047	9,769	1,849	31,723	1,529	4,232	1,926	6,686	858
3. Udhampur " ..	273,668	51,983	2,899	17,088	69,896	74,443	57,359	18,967	2,117	44,430	1,994	15,356	2,470	15,837	1,503
4. Reasi " ..	235,245	57,317	9,455	13,902	54,643	52,991	46,937	11,968	4,355	52,063	5,833	12,975	5,945	9,941	3,625
5. Mirpur " ..	344,747	65,677	2,790	18,394	83,394	94,760	79,732	20,818	3,252	52,867	1,455	17,347	6,494	16,973	2,025
6. Poonch Jagir ..	387,384	78,666	14,751	27,120	86,077	92,832	87,938	12,722	1,347	73,368	1,305	25,082	691	11,148	1,095
7. Chenani " ..	10,925	2,318	262	1,121	646	2,491	4,087	594	19	1,852	188	1,019	130	523	16
II. Kashmir Province ..	**1,569,218**	**297,536**	**11,179**	**109,639**	**411,083**	**439,797**	**299,954**	**87,637**	**4,153**	**201,860**	**3,047**	**104,012**	**3,706**	**72,173**	**1,897**
8. Kashmir North ..	559,828	100,566	6,429	42,724	134,300	158,107	117,702	33,433	1,116	79,068	789	41,241	947	28,532	611
9. Kashmir South (*including City*) ..	771,943	150,852	3,323	47,137	217,764	221,201	131,666	43,639	2,600	81,693	1,221	44,070	682	34,139	999
10. Muzaffarabad ..	237,447	46,118	1,427	19,828	58,999	60,489	50,586	10,615	437	41,099	1,037	18,701	2,077	9,502	287
III. Frontier Districts ..	**288,584**	**58,611**	**6,120**	**16,652**	**73,056**	**73,238**	**60,907**	**8,931**	**1,547**	**52,425**	**5,009**	**12,006**	**3,066**	**7,793**	**1,332**
11. Ladakh ..	192,138	42,570	5,511	12,491	59,481	41,198	30,887	5,246	1,449	38,508	4,458	8,718	285	4,788	1,261
12. Gilgit ..	31,902	7,587	118	729	7,281	9,436	6,751	2,082	60	6,026	78	439	8	1,492	35
13. Frontier Ilaqas ..	64,544	8,454	491	3,432	6,294	22,604	23,269	1,603	38	7,891	473	2,849	2,773	1,513	36
IV. Cities :—															
14. Srinagar[1] ..	173,573	46,965	1,485	1,394	1,478	46,434	75,817	2,303	438	3,202	266	125	303	455	284
15. Jammu (*excludes Railway population*) ..	38,474	12,724	1,020	504	4,549	10,000	9,677	2,136	117	575	24	14	5	355	4

TABLE X.

OCCUPATION.

Jammu and Kashmir Census 1931.

District, Ilaqa, Jagir or City.	Sub-Class I. Exploitation of animals and vegetation. Total earners (principal occupation). Males.	Females.	Total working dependents. Males.	Females.	Total following occupation as subsidiary to others. Males.	Females.	Order I. Pasture and Agriculture. Total earners (principal occupation). Males.	Females.	Total working dependents. Males.	Females.	Total following occupation as subsidiary to others. Males.	Females.	Sub-Order I (a). Cultivation. Total earners (principal occupation). Males.	Females.	Total working dependents. Males.	Females.	Total following occupation as subsidiary to others. Males.	Females.
Jammu and Kashmir State ..	563,245	21,667	203,009	24,439	153,612	13,700	566,946	21,620	202,961	24,322	153,391	13,627	539,064	19,802	174,358	18,163	149,712	12,536
I. Jammu Province ..	314,737	13,643	87,006	17,888	73,698	10,495	314,630	13,640	86,994	17,887	73,683	10,495	295,963	12,214	71,159	13,922	71,562	9,756
1. Jammu District (*including city*) ..	58,470	1,641	10,995	232	12,595	1,375	58,451	1,639	10,987	232	12,591	1,375	56,602	1,519	8,753	142	12,337	1,319
2. Kathua " ..	31,692	1,528	4,232	1,926	6,685	857	31,684	1,528	4,232	1,926	6,683	857	26,915	1,146	3,120	778	5,810	650
3. Udhampur " ..	44,423	1,994	15,356	2,470	15,834	1,503	44,423	1,994	15,356	2,470	15,834	1,503	42,761	1,824	13,671	940	15,479	1,401
4. Reasi " ..	52,062	5,532	12,975	5,945	9,941	3,624	52,045	5,532	12,974	5,945	9,941	3,624	44,264	4,865	10,891	5,412	9,467	3,263
5. Mirpur " ..	52,861	1,455	17,347	6,494	16,072	2,025	52,861	1,455	17,344	6,493	16,963	2,025	52,339	1,450	14,765	6,318	16,916	2,024
6. Poonch Jagir ..	73,368	1,305	25,082	691	11,148	1,095	73,364	1,304	25,082	691	11,148	1,095	71,275	1,243	18,955	204	11,030	1,084
7. Chenani Jagir ..	1,852	188	1,019	130	523	16	1,852	188	1,019	130	523	16	1,807	167	1,004	128	523	15
II. Kashmir Province ..	201,102	3,020	104,004	3,497	72,139	1,874	199,861	2,976	103,968	3,381	71,933	1,801	191,286	2,672	92,061	1,227	70,403	1,455
8. Kashmir North ..	79,054	789	41,233	947	28,521	611	78,364	752	41,231	947	28,416	541	74,203	668	38,331	808	27,687	372
9. Kashmir South (*including city*) ..	80,950	1,194	44,070	473	34,116	976	80,409	1,187	44,036	357	34,015	973	76,517	998	40,501	269	33,280	804
10. Muzaffarabad ..	41,098	1,037	18,701	2,077	9,502	287	41,097	1,037	18,701	2,077	9,502	287	40,566	1,006	13,229	150	9,436	279
II. Frontier Districts ..	52,406	5,004	11,999	3,054	7,775	1,331	52,405	5,004	11,999	3,054	7,775	1,331	51,815	4,916	11,138	3,014	7,747	1,325
11. Ladakh ..	38,508	4,458	8,718	285	4,788	1,261	38,507	4,458	8,718	285	4,788	1,261	38,150	4,371	8,643	266	4,764	1,255
12. Gilgit ..	6,019	75	439	3	1,485	34	6,019	75	439	3	1,485	34	5,864	74	33	....	1,483	34
13. Frontier Ilaqas ..	7,879	471	2,842	2,766	1,502	36	7,879	471	2,842	2,766	1,502	36	7,801	471	2,462	2,748	1,500	36
IV. Cities :—																		
14. Srinagar ..	2,483	239	125	94	435	261	2,361	233	124	94	421	260	1,372	103	116	71	223	127
15. Jammu (*excludes Ry. population*) ..	574	24	14	5	355	4	504	24	13	5	355	4	489	11	13	5	342	1

TABLE X.

OCCUPATION.

Jammu and Kashmir Census 1931.

District, Ilaqa, Jagir or City.	GROUP 1. Non-cultivating proprietors taking rent in money or kind.						GROUP 2. Estate agents and managers of owners.					
	Total earners (principal occupation).		Total working dependents.		Total following occupation as subsidiary to others.		Total earners (principal occupation).		Total working dependents.		Total following occupation as subsidiary to others.	
	Males.	Females.	Males.	Females.	Males.	Females.	Males.	Females.	Males.	Females.	Males.	Females.
Jammu and Kashmir State ..	**24,688**	**4,411**	**10,368**	**4,570**	**5,693**	**2,515**	**7**	**2**	....	**15**	**1**	**11**
I. Jammu Province ..	**13,549**	**3,427**	**7,261**	**2,244**	**2,283**	**1,870**	**7**	**2**	....	**15**	**1**	**11**
1. Jammu District (*including city*) ..	1,751	594	244	52	701	339	7	....	....	....	....	....
2. Kathua " ..	4,826	456	140	71	400	313	....	....	....	....	....	....
3. Udhampur " ..	571	261	134	87	343	278	....	....	....	....	1	....
4. Reasi " ..	4,965	1,422	288	16	221	145	....	2	....	15	....	11
5. Mirpur " ..	869	473	628	2,002	384	627	....	....	....	....	....	....
6. Poonch Jagir ..	525	211	5,808	12	184	166	....	....	....	....	....	....
7. Chenani Jagir ..	42	10	19	4	50	2	....	....	....	....	....	....
II. Kashmir Province ..	**3,826**	**447**	**768**	**80**	**2,035**	**587**	....	....	....	....	....	....
8. Kashmir North ..	1,089	144	265	16	589	154	....	....	....	....	....	....
9. Kashmir South (*including city*) ..	2,475	223	471	52	1,323	351	....	....	....	....	....	....
10. Muzaffarabad ..	262	80	32	12	123	82	....	....	....	....	....	....
III. Frontier Districts ..	**7,313**	**537**	**2,339**	**2,246**	**1,375**	**58**	....	....	....	....	....	....
11. Ladakh ..	71	97	2	....	26	21	....	....	....	....	....	....
12. Gilgit ..	73	6	5	....	6	4	....	....	....	....	....	....
13. Frontier Ilaqas ..	7,169	434	2,332	2,246	1,343	33	....	....	....	....	....	....
IV. Cities:—												
14. Srinagar ..	258	11	26	25	52	9	....	....	....	....	....	....
15. Jammu (*excludes Ry. population*) ..	102	4	12	5	72	1	....	....	....	....	....	....

TABLE X.

OCCUPATION.

Jammu and Kashmir Census 1931.

District, Ilaqa, Jagir or City.	Group 4. Rent collectors, clerks etc. Total earners (principal occupation). Males.	Females.	Total working dependents. Males.	Females.	Total following occupation as subsidiary to others. Males.	Females.	Group 5. Cultivating owners. Total earners (principal occupation.) Males.	Females.	Total working dependents. Males.	Females.	Total following occupation as subsidiary to others. Males.	Females.	Group 6. Tenant cultivators. Total earners (principal occupation). Males.	Females.	Total working dependents. Males.	Females.	Total following occupation as subsidiary to others. Males.	Females.
Jammu and Kashmir State	192	....	1	....	15	....	315,471	8,580	102,032	4,375	87,636	4,278	187,233	6,024	61,503	8,000	54,642	4,671
I. Jammu Province	....	....	....	....	....	....	142,932	3,305	28,547	3,280	32,940	2,586	129,872	4,882	34,963	7,642	34,797	4,284
1. Jammu District (*including city*)	....	....	....	....	....	....	14,291	212	2,148	9	2,707	105	35,420	421	6,189	73	8,220	210
2. Kathua "	....	....	....	....	....	....	8,768	180	1,719	16	2,942	99	12,098	387	1,189	12	2,251	127
3. Udhampur "	....	....	....	....	....	....	28,020	1,073	9,381	530	9,556	407	13,452	403	4,140	319	5,523	563
4. Reasi "	....	....	....	....	....	....	12,273	572	3,090	1,629	2,702	684	25,708	2,801	7,466	3,752	6,266	2,390
5. Mirpur "	....	....	....	....	....	....	11,087	188	2,884	930	4,909	392	39,670	766	11,244	3,378	11,563	964
6. Poonch Jagir	....	....	....	....	....	....	67,872	981	8,979	113	9,906	895	2,391	46	4,096	37	719	21
7. Chenani "	....	....	....	....	....	....	621	99	346	53	218	4	1,133	58	639	71	255	9
II. Kashmir Province	192	....	1	....	15	....	133,709	1,592	65,789	826	49,100	599	51,997	618	25,445	321	19,094	332
8. Kashmir North	189	....	1	....	15	....	52,500	378	27,707	571	19,500	157	20,419	146	10,358	221	7,583	61
9. Kashmir South (*including city*)	....	....	....	....	....	....	52,451	554	28,793	157	22,017	301	20,396	215	11,197	60	8,911	117
10. Muzaffarabad	3	....	....	....	....	....	28,752	660	9,289	98	6,683	141	11,182	257	3,890	40	2,600	54
III. Frontier Districts	....	....	....	....	....	....	38,830	3,683	7,696	269	5,596	1,093	5,364	524	1,095	37	751	155
11. Ladakh	....	....	....	....	....	....	33,070	3,590	7,560	233	4,129	1,063	4,724	513	1,080	33	589	152
12. Gilgit	....	....	....	....	....	....	5,193	61	23	....	1,326	27	577	7	3	....	147	3
13. Frontier Ilaqas	....	....	....	....	....	....	567	32	113	36	141	3	63	4	12	4	15	....
IV. Cities :—																		
14. Srinagar	....	....	....	....	....	....	802	65	64	33	123	84	312	27	26	13	48	34
15. Jammu (*excludes Ry. population*)	....	....	....	....	....	....	330	2	....	....	244	....	31	....	1	....	25	....

TABLE X.

Occupation.

Jammu and Kashmir Census 1931.

District, Ilaqa, Jagir or City.	Group 7. Agricultural Labourers. Total earners (principal occupation). Males.	Females.	Total working dependents. Males.	Females.	Total following occupation as subsidiary to others. Males.	Females.	Group 8. [Cultivators of jhum, taungya and shifting areas. Total earners (principal occupation). Males.	Females.	Total working dependents. Males.	Females.	Total following occupation as subsidiary to others. Males.	Females.	Order I (b). Cultivation of special crops, fruits etc. (planters, managers, clerks and labourers.) Total of Order I (b). Total earners (principal occupation). Males.	Females.	Total working dependents. Males.	Females.	Total following occupation as subsidiary to others. Males.	Females.
Jammu and Kashmir State ..	11,066	780	452	1,161	1,522	1,059	407	5	2	42	203	2	886	176	35	45	357	246
I. Jammu Province ..	9,196	593	386	699	1,338	1,003	407	5	2	42	203	2	195	73	3	21	91	82
1. Jammu District (*including city*) ..	5,133	292	172	8	709	665	....	....	....	....	....	....	111	57	3	17	24	38
2 Kathua „ ..	1,223	123	72	679	217	111	....	....	....	....	....	....	53	7	....	1	57	34
3. Udhampur „ ..	718	87	16	4	56	153	....	....	....	....	....	....	9	....	....	....	4	1
4. Reasi „ ..	1,318	68	47	....	278	33	....	....	....	....	....	....	20	8	....	....	5	7
5. Mirpur „ ..	713	23	9	8	60	41	....	....	....	....	....	....	....	....	....	3	....	1
6. Poonch Jagir ..	80	....	70	....	18	....	407	5	2	42	203	2	2	....	....	....	1	1
7. Chenani „ ..	11	....	....	....	....	....	....	....	....	....	....	....	....	1	....	....	....	....
II. Kashmir Province ..	1,562	15	58	....	159	37	....	....	....	....	....	....	684	103	32	24	266	164
8. Kashmir North ..	463	5	15	....	50	35	....	....	....	....	....	....	63	7	12	1	18	30
9. Kashmir South (*including city*) ..	732	1	25	....	79	....	....	....	....	....	....	....	620	96	20	23	248	134
10. Muzaffarabad ..	367	9	18	....	30	2	....	....	....	....	....	....	1	....	....	....	....	....
III. Frontier Districts ..	308	172	8	462	25	19	....	....	....	....	....	....	7	....	....	....	....	....
11. Ladakh ..	285	171	1	....	20	19	....	....	....	....	....	....	....	....	....	....	....	....
12. Gilgit ..	21	....	2	....	4	....	....	....	....	....	....	....	7	....	....	....	....	....
13. Frontier Ilaqas ..	2	1	5	462	1	....	....	....	....	....	....	....	....	....	....	....	....	....
IV. Cities.—																		
14. Srinagar ..	....	....	....	....	....	....	....	....	....	....	....	....	367	96	6	23	176	133
15. Jammu (*excludes Ry. population*) ..	26	5	....	....	1	....	....	....	....	....	....	....	58	13	....	....	6	2

TABLE X.

OCCUPATION.

Jammu and Kashmir Census 1931.

District, Ilaqa, Jagir or City.	Group 11. Coffee. Total earners (principal occupation). Males.	Females.	Total working dependents. Males.	Females.	Total following occupation as subsidiary to others. Males.	Females.	Group 16. Market gardeners, flowers and fruit growers. Total earners (principal occupation). Males.	Females.	Total working dependents. Males.	Females.	Total following occupation as subsidiary to others. Males.	Females.	Order I (c). Forestry. Total of Order I (c). Total earners (principal occupation). Males.	Females.	Total working dependents. Males.	Females.	Total following occupation as subsidiary to others. Males.	Females.
Jammu and Kashmir State	....	....	....	3	....	1	886	176	35	42	357	245	1,489	3	26	4	359	3
I. Jammu Province	....	....	....	3	....	1	195	73	3	18	91	81	474	2	5	....	206	1
1. Jammu District (*including city*)	....	....	....	....	....	....	111	57	3	17	24	38	123	....	3	....	36	1
2. Kathua „	....	....	....	....	....	....	53	7	....	1	57	34	8	....	....	....	8	....
3. Udhampur „	....	....	....	....	....	....	9	....	....	....	4	1	245	2	2	....	111	....
4. Reasi „	....	....	....	....	....	....	20	8	....	....	5	7	47	....	....	....	22	....
5. Mirpur „	....	....	....	3	....	1	....	....	....	....	....	....	26	....	....	....	15	....
6. Poonch Jagir	....	....	....	....	....	....	2	....	....	....	1	1	25	....	....	....	14	....
7. Chenani „	....	....	....	....	....	....	....	1	....	....	....	....	....	....	....	....	....	....
II. Kashmir Province	....	....	....	....	....	....	684	103	32	24	266	164	1,014	1	21	4	158	2
8. Kashmir North	....	....	....	....	....	....	63	7	12	1	18	30	375	....	9	....	48	2
9. Kashmir South (*including city*)	....	....	....	....	....	....	620	96	20	23	248	134	451	1	3	....	75	....
10. Muzaffarabad	....	....	....	....	....	....	1	....	....	....	....	....	188	....	9	4	30	....
III. Frontier Districts	....	....	....	....	....	....	7	....	....	....	....	....	1	....	....	....	....	....
11. Ladakh	....	....	....	....	....	....	....	....	....	....	....	....	1	....	....	....	....	....
12. Gilgit	....	....	....	....	....	....	7	....	....	....	....	....	....	....	....	....	....	....
13. Frontier Ilaqas	....	....	....	....	....	....	....	....	....	....	....	....	....	....	....	....	....	....
IV. Cities.—																		
14. Srinagar	....	....	....	....	....	....	367	96	6	23	176	133	250	....	....	....	7	....
15. Jammu (*excludes Ry. population*)	....	....	....	....	....	....	58	13	....	....	6	2	7	....	....	....	7	....

TABLE X.

Occupation.

Jammu and Kashmir Census 1931.

District, Ilaqa, Jagir or City.	Group 17. Forest officers, rangers, guards etc.						Group 18. Wood cutter and charcoal burners.						Order I (d). Stock raising. Total of Order I (d).					
	Total earners (principal occupation).		Total working dependents.		Total following occupation as subsidiary to others.		Total earners (principal occupation).		Total working dependents.		Total following occupation as subsidiary to others.		Total earners (principal occupation).		Total working dependents.		Total following occupation as subsidiary to others.	
	Males.	Females.	Males.	Females.	Males.	Females.	Males.	Females.	Males.	Females.	Males.	Females.	Males.	Females.	Males.	Females.	Males.	Females.
Jammu and Kashmir State ..	1,171	2	7	....	315	1	318	1	19	4	44	2	25,408	1,629	28,518	6,109	2,885	841
I. Jammu Province ..	368	1	5	....	190	1	106	1	....	....	16	....	18,046	1,341	15,827	3,944	1,824	656
1. Jammu District (*including city*) ..	68	....	3	....	27	1	55	....	....	....	9	....	1,613	63	2,228	73	194	17
2. Kathua „ ..	8	....	....	....	8	....	....	....	....	....	....	....	4,708	375	1,112	1,147	808	173
3. Udhampur „ ..	201	1	2	....	107	....	44	1	....	....	4	....	1,408	168	1,683	1,530	240	101
4. Reasi „ ..	47	....	....	....	22	....	....	....	....	....	....	....	7,714	649	2,083	633	447	354
5. Mirpur „ ..	26	....	....	....	15	....	....	....	....	....	....	....	496	5	2,579	172	32	....
6. Poonch Jagir ..	18	....	....	....	11	....	7	....	....	....	3	....	2,062	61	6,127	487	103	10
7. Chenani „ ..	....	....	....	....	....	....	....	....	....	....	....	....	45	20	15	2	....	1
II. Kashmir Province ..	803	1	2	....	125	....	211	....	19	4	28	2	6,780	200	11,830	2,125	1,031	179
8. Kashmir North ..	252	....	2	....	40	....	123	....	7	....	8	2	3,681	77	2,863	138	605	137
9. Kashmir South (*including city*) ..	397	1	....	....	65	....	54	....	3	....	10	....	2,757	92	3,504	64	390	34
10. Muzaffarabad ..	154	....	....	....	20	....	34	....	9	4	10	....	342	31	5,463	1,923	36	8
III. Frontier Districts ..	....	....	....	....	....	....	1	....	....	....	....	....	582	88	881	40	28	6
11. Ladakh ..	....	....	....	....	....	....	1	....	....	....	....	....	356	87	75	19	24	6
12. Gilgit ..	....	....	....	....	....	....	....	....	....	....	....	....	148	1	406	3	2	....
13. Frontier Ilaqas ..	....	....	....	....	....	....	....	....	....	....	....	....	78	......	380	18	2	....
IV. Cities.—																		
14. Srinagar ..	250	....	....	....	7	....	....	....	....	....	....	....	372	34	2	......	15	....
15. Jammu (*excludes Ry. population*) ..	7	....	....	....	7	....	....	....	....	....	....	....	8	......	......	......	....	1

TABLE X.

OCCUPATION.

Jammu and Kashmir Census 1931.

District, Ilaqa, Jagir or City.	Group 21. Cattle and buffalo breeders and keepers.						Group 22. Breeders of Transport animals.						Group 23. Herdsmen, shepherds and breeders of other animals.					
	Total earners (principal occupation).		Total working dependents.		Total following occupation as subsidiary to others.		Total earners (principal occupation).		Total working dependents.		Total following occupation as subsidiary to others.		Total earners (principal occupation).		Total working dependents.		Total following occupation as subsidiary to others.	
	Males.	Females.	Males.	Females.	Males.	Females.	Males.	Females.	Males.	Females.	Males.	Females.	Males.	Females.	Males.	Females.	Males.	Females.
Jammu and Kashmir State ..	6,389	428	6,972	647	1,203	240	279	1	15	....	71	16	18,740	1,200	21,531	5,462	1,609	585
I. Jammu Province. ..	2,812	267	3,069	509	615	103	197	1	12	....	65	16	15,037	1,073	12,746	3,435	1,144	537
1. Jammu District (*including city*) ..	299	3	430	9	24	1	....	....	....	....	....	....	1,314	60	1,798	64	170	16
2. Kathua " ..	369	161	183	96	373	84	173	1	2	....	61	16	4,166	213	927	1,051	374	73
3. Udhampur " ..	237	46	234	116	64	8	4	....	....	....	1	....	1,167	122	1,449	1,414	175	93
4. Riasi " ..	835	15	10	2	100	3	2	....	....	....	3	....	6,877	634	2,073	531	344	351
5. Mirpur " ..	9	....	60	....	....	....	6	....	4	....	....	....	481	5	2,515	172	32	....
6 Poonch Jagir ..	1,063	42	2,152	286	54	7	12	....	6	....	....	....	987	19	3,969	201	49	3
7. Chenani " ..	....	....	....	....	....	....	....	....	....	....	....	....	45	20	15	2	....	1
II. Kashmir Province ..	3,482	160	3,842	138	575	137	74	....	2	....	5	....	3,224	40	7,986	1,987	451	42
8. Kashmir North ..	1,917	71	1,631	89	356	131	....	....	....	....	....	....	1,764	6	1,232	40	249	6
9. Kashmir South (*including City*) ..	1,537	88	1927	34	217	6	74	....	2	....	5	....	1,146	4	1,575	30	168	28
10. Muzaffarabad ..	28	1	284	15	2	....	....	....	....	....	....	....	314	30	5,179	1,908	34	8
III. Frontier Districts. ..	95	1	61	....	13	....	8	....	1	....	1	....	479	87	799	40	14	6
11. Ladakh ..	87	1	60	....	12	....	....	....	....	....	....	....	269	86	15	19	12	6
12. Gilgit ..	8	....	1	....	1	....	8	....	1	....	1	....	132	1	404	3	....	....
13. Frontier Ilaqas ..	....	....	....	....	....	....	....	....	....	....	....	....	78	....	380	18	2	....
IV. Cities.—																		
14. Srinagar ..	298	34	....	....	10	....	74	....	2	....	5	....	 8	....	....	....	....	....
15. Jammu (*excludes By. population*) ..	....	....	....	....	....	....	....	....	....	....	....	....	....	....	....	....	....	1

TABLE X.

OCCUPATION.

Jammu and Kashmir Census 1931.

District, Ilaqa, Jagir or City.	Order I. (e). Raising of small animals and insects. Total of Order I. (e).						Group 24. Birds, Bees, etc.						Group 25. Silk-Worms.					
	Total earners (principal occupation).		Total working dependents.		Total following occupation as subsidiary to others.		Total earners (principal occupation).		Total working dependents.		Total following occupation as subsidiary to others.		Total earners (principal occupation).		Total working dependents.		Total following occupation as subsidiary to others.	
	Males.	Females.	Males.	Females.	Males.	Females.	Males.	Females.	Males.	Females.	Males.	Females.	Males.	Females.	Males.	Females.	Males.	Females.
Jammu and Kashmir State ..	99	10	24	1	80	1	....	10	....	....	....	....	99	....	24	1	80	1
I. Jammu Province ..	2	10	....	....	....	....	....	10	....	....	....	....	2	....	....	....	....	....
1. Jammu District (*including city*) ..	2	....	....	....	....	....	....	....	....	....	....	....	2	....	....	....	....	....
2. Kathua " ..	....	....	....	....	....	....	....	....	....	....	....	....	....	....	....	....	....	....
3. Udhampur " ..	....	....	....	....	....	....	....	....	....	....	....	....	....	....	....	....	....	....
4. Reasi " ..	....	10	....	....	....	....	....	10	....	....	....	....	....	....	....	....	....	....
5. Mirpur " ..	....	....	....	....	....	....	....	....	....	....	....	....	....	....	....	....	....	....
6. Poonch Jagir ..	....	....	....	....	....	....	....	....	....	....	....	....	....	....	....	....	....	....
7. Chenani " ..	....	....	....	....	....	....	....	....	....	....	....	....	....	....	....	....	....	....
II. Kashmir Province ..	97	....	24	1	80	1	....	....	....	....	....	....	97	....	24	1	80	1
8. Kashmir North ..	42	....	16	....	58	....	....	....	....	....	....	....	42	....	16	....	58	....
9. Kashmir South (*including City*) ..	55	....	8	1	22	1	....	....	....	....	....	....	55	....	8	1	22	1
10. Muzaffarabad ..	....	....	....	....	....	....	....	....	....	....	....	....	....	....	....	....	....	....
III. Frontier Districts ..	....	....	....	....	....	....	....	....	....	....	....	....	....	....	....	....	....	....
11. Ladakh ..	....	....	....	....	....	....	....	....	....	....	....	....	....	....	....	....	....	....
12. Gilgit ..	....	....	....	....	....	....	....	....	....	....	....	....	....	....	....	....	....	....
13. Frontier Ilaqas ..	....	....	....	....	....	....	....	....	....	....			....	....	....	....	....	....
IV. Cities.—																		
14. Srinagar ..	....	....	....	....	....	....	....	....	....	....	....	....	....	....	....	....	....	....
15. Jammu (*excludes Ry. population*) ..	2	....	....	....	....	....	....	....	....	....	....	....	2	....	....	....	....	....

TABLE X.

OCCUPATION.

Jammu and Kashmir Census 1931.

District, Ilaqa, Jagir or City.	ORDER 2. Fishing and hunting. TOTAL OF ORDER 2.						GROUP 27. Fishing and pearling.						GROUP 28. Hunting.					
	Total earners (principal occupation).		Total working dependents.		Total following occupation as subsidiary to others.		Total earners (principal occupation).		Total working dependents.		Total following occupation as subsidiary to others.		Total earners (principal occupation).		Total working dependents.		Total following occupation as subsidiary to others.	
	Males.	Females.	Males.	Females.	Males.	Females.	Males.	Females.	Males.	Females.	Males.	Females.	Males.	Females.	Males.	Females.	Males.	Females.
Jammu and Kashmir State ..	1,299	47	48	117	221	73	1,241	47	48	117	199	73	58	....	....	....	22	....
I. Jammu Province ..	57	3	12	1	15	....	47	3	12	1	15	....	10	....	....	....	....	....
1. Jammu District (*including City*) ..	28	2	8	....	4	....	18	2	8	....	4	....	10	....	....	....	....	....
2. Kathua „ ..	8	....	....	....	2	....	8	....	....	....	2	....	....	....	....	....	....	....
3. Udhampur „ ..	....	....	....	....	....	....	....	....	....	....	....	....	....	....	....	....	....	....
4. Reasi „ ..	17	....	1	....	....	....	17	....	1	....	....	....	....	....	....	....	....	....
5. Mirpur „ ..	....	....	3	1	9	....	....	....	3	1	9	....	....	....	....	....	....	....
6. Poonch Jagir ..	4	1	....	....	....	....	4	1	....	....	....	....	....	....	....	....	....	....
7. Chenani „ ..	....	....	....	....	....	....	....	....	....	....	....	....	....	....	....	....	....	....
II. Kashmir Province ..	1,241	44	36	116	206	73	1,194	44	36	116	184	73	47	....	....	....	22	....
8. Kashmir North ..	690	37	2	....	105	70	660	37	2	....	85	70	30	....	....	....	20	....
9. Kashmir South (*including City*) ..	550	7	34	116	101	3	534	7	34	116	99	3	16	....	....	....	2	....
10. Muzaffarabad ..	1	....	....	....	....	....	....	....	....	....	....	....	1	....	....	....	....	....
III. Frontier Districts ..	1	....	....	....	....	....	....	....	....	....	....	....	1	....	....	....	....	....
11. Ladakh ..	1	....	....	....	....	....	....	....	....	....	....	....	1	....	....	....	....	....
12. Gilgit ..	....	....	....	....	....	....	....	....	....	....	....	....	....	....	....	....	....	....
13. Frontier Ilaqas ..	....	....	....	....	....	....	....	....	....	....	....	....	....	....	....	....	....	....
IV. Cities.—																		
14. Srinagar ..	122	6	1	....	14	1	122	6	1	....	14	1	....	....	....	....	....	....
15. Jammu (excludes Ry. Population)	10	....	1	....	....	....	8	....	1	....	....	....	2	....	....	....	....	....

TABLE X.

OCCUPATION.

Jammu and Kashmir Census 1931.

District, Ilaqa, Jagir or City.	Sub-Class II. Exploitation of minerals. Total of Sub-Class II.						Order 3. Metallic minerals. Total of Order 3.						Group 29. Gold.					
	Total earners (principal occupation).		Total working dependents.		Total following occupation as subsidiary to others.		Total earners (principal occupation).		Total working dependents.		Total following occupation as subsidiary to others.		Total earners (principal occupation).		Total working dependents.		Total following occupation as subsidiary to others.	
	Males.	Females.	Males.	Females.	Males.	Females.	Males.	Females.	Males.	Females.	Males.	Females.	Males.	Females.	Males.	Females.	Males.	Females.
Jammu and Kashmir State ..	823	34	15	221	57	26	36	5	12	12	28	1	19	5	4	12	17	1
I. Jammu Province ..	46	2	....	....	5	2	3	....	....	....	....	....	....	....	....	....	....	....
1. Jammu District (*including city*) ..	1	....	....	....	....	....	....	....	....	....	....	....	....	....	....	....	....	....
2. Kathua „ ..	31	1	....	....	1	1	2	....	....	....	....	....	....	....	....	....	....	....
3. Udhampur	7	....	....	....	3	....	....	....	....	....	....	....	....	....	....	....	....	....
4. Reasi „ ..	1	1	....	....	....	1	1	....	....	....	....	....	....	....	....	....	....	....
5. Mirpur „ ..	6	....	....	....	1	....	....	....	....	....	....	....	....	....	....	....	....	....
6. Poonch Jagir ..	....	....	....	....	....	....	....	....	....	....	....	....	....	....	....	....	....	....
7. Chenani „ ..	....	....	....	....	....	....	....	....	....	....	....	....	....	....	....	....	....	....
II. Kashmir Province ..	758	27	8	209	34	23	14	....	8	....	11	....	....	....	....	....	....	....
8. Kashmir North ..	14	....	8	....	11	....	11	....	8	....	11	....	....	....	....	....	....	....
9. Kashmir South (*including City*) ..	743	27	....	209	23	23	3	....	....	....	....	....	....	....	....	....	....	....
10. Muzaffarabad ..	1	....	....	....	....	....	....	....	....	....	....	....	....	....	....	....	....	....
III. Frontier Districts ..	19	5	7	12	18	1	19	5	4	12	17	1	19	5	4	12	17	1
11. Ladakh ..	....	....	....	....	....	....	....	....	....	....	....	....	....	....	....	....	....	....
12. Gilgit ..	7	3	....	5	7	1	7	3	....	5	7	1	7	3	....	5	7	1
13. Frontier Ilaqas ..	12	2	7	7	11	....	12	2	4	7	10	....	12	2	4	7	10	....
IV. Cities.—																		
14. Srinagar ...	719	27	....	209	20	23	....	....	....	....	....	....	....	....	....	....	....	....
15. Jammu (*excludes Ry. population*)	1	....	....	....	....	....	....	....	....	....	....	....	....	....	....	....	....	....

TABLE X.

OCCUPATION.

Jammu and Kashmir Census 1931.

District, Ilaqa, Jagir or City.	Group 31. Lead, silver and zinc. Total earners (principal occupation).		Total working dependents.		Total following occupation as subsidiary to others.		Group 33. Tin and wolfram. Total earners (principal occupation).		Total working dependents.		Total following occupation as subsidiary to others.		Group 34. Other metallic minerals. Total earners (principal occupation).		Total working dependents.		Total following occupation as subsidiary to others.	
	Males.	Females.	Males.	Females.	Males.	Females.	Males.	Females.	Males.	Females.	Males.	Females.	Males	Females.	Males.	Females.	Males.	Females.
Jammu and Kashmir State ..	11	....	8	....	11	....	4	....	....	....	....	....	2	....	....	....	....	....
I. Jammu Province ..	....	....	....	....	....	....	1	....	....	....	....	....	2	....	....	....	....	....
1. Jammu District (*including city*) ..	....	....	....	....	....	....	....	....	....	....	....	....	....	....	....	....	....	....
2. Kathua " ..	....	....	....	....	....	....	....	....	....	....	....	....	2	....	....	....	....	....
3. Udhampur District ..	....	....	....	....	....	....	....	....	....	....	....	....	....	....	....	....	....	....
4. Riasi " ..	....	....	....	....	....	....	1	....	....	....	....	....	....	....	....	....	....	....
5. Mirpur " ..	....	....	....	....	....	....	....	....	....	....	....	....	....	....	....	....	....	....
6. Poonch Jagir ..	....	....	....	....	....	....	....	....	....	....	....	....	....	....	....	....	....	....
7. Chenani " ..	....	....	....	....	....	....	....	....	....	....	....	....	....	....	....	....	....	....
II. Kashmir Province ..	11	....	8	....	11	....	3	....	....	....	....	....	....	....	....	....	....	....
8. Kashmir North ..	11	....	8	....	11	....	....	....	....	....	....	....	....	....	....	....	....	....
9. Kashmir South (*including City*) ..	....	....	....	....	....	....	3	....	....	....	....	....	....	....	....	....	....	....
10. Muzaffarabad ..	....	....	....	....	....	....	....	....	....	....	....	....	....	....	....	....	....	....
III. Frontier Districts ..	....	....	....	....	....	....	....	....	....	....	....	....	....	....	....	....	....	....
11. Ladakh ..	....	....	....	....	....	....	....	....	....	....	....	....	....	....	....	....	....	....
12. Gilgit ..	....	....	....	....	....	....	....	....	....	....	....	....	....	....	....	....	....	....
13. Frontier Ilaqas ..	....	....	....	....	....	....	....	....	....	....	....	....	....	....	....	....	....	....
IV. Cities.																		
14. Srinagar ..	....	....	....	....	....	....	....	....	....	....	....	....	....	....	....	....	....	....
15. Jammu (*excludes Ry. population*)	....	....	....	....	....	....	....	....	....	....	....	....	....	....	....	....	....	....

TABLE X.

OCCUPATION.

Jammu and Kashmir Census 1931.

District, Ilaqa, Jagir or City.	Order 4. Non-metallic minerals. Total of Order 4.						Group 36. Petroleum.						Group 37. Building materials (including stone materials for cement-manufacture and clays).					
	Total earners (principal occupation).		Total working dependents.		Total following occupation as subsidiary to others.		Total earners (principal occupation).		Total working dependents.		Total following occupation as subsidiary to others.		Total earners (principal occupation).		Total working dependents.		Total following occupation as subsidiary to others.	
	Males.	Females.	Males.	Females.	Males.	Females.	Males.	Females.	Males.	Females.	Males.	Females.	Males.	Females.	Males.	Females.	Males.	Females.
Jammu and Kashmir State ..	787	29	3	209	29	25	1	....	....	....	....	....	752	29	3	209	25	25
I. Jammu Province ..	43	2	....	....	5	2	1	....	....	....	....	....	8	2	....	....	1	2
1. Jammu District (*including City*) ..	1	....	....	....	....	....	1	....	....	....	....	....	....	....	....	....	....	....
2. Kathua „ ..	29	1	....	....	1	1	....	....	....	....	....	....	....	1	....	....	....	1
3. Udhampur „ ..	7	....	....	....	3	....	....	....	....	....	....	....	2	....	....	....	....	....
4. Reasi „ ..	....	1	....	....	....	1	....	....	....	....	....	....	....	1	....	....	....	1
5. Mirpur „ ..	6	....	....	....	1	....	....	....	....	....	....	....	6	....	....	....	1	....
6. Poonch Jagir ..	....	....	....	....	....	....	....	....	....	....	....	....	....	....	....	....	....	....
7. Chenani „ ..	....	....	....	....	....	....	....	....	....	....	....	....	....	....	....	....	....	....
II. Kashmir Province ..	744	27	....	209	23	23	....	....	....	....	....	....	744	27	....	209	23	23
8. Kashmir North ..	3	....	....	....	....	....	....	....	....	....	....	....	3	....	....	....	....	....
9. Kashmir South (*including City*) ..	740	27	....	209	23	23	....	....	....	....	....	....	740	27	....	209	23	23
10. Muzaffarabad ..	1	....	....	....	....	....	....	....	....	....	....	....	1	....	....	....	....	....
III. Frontier Districts ..	....	....	3	....	1	....	....	....	....	....	....	....	....	....	3	....	1	....
11. Ladakh ..	....	....	....	....	....	....	....	....	....	....	....	....	....	....	....	....	....	....
12. Gilgit ..	....	....	....	....	....	....	....	....	....	....	....	....	....	....	....	....	....	....
13. Frontier Ilaqas ..	....	....	3	....	1	....	....	....	....	....	....	....	....	....	3	....		....
IV. Cities.—																		
14. Srinagar ..	719	27	....	209	20	23	....	....	....	....	....	....	719	27	....	209	20	23
15. Jammu (excludes Ry. Population)	1	....	....	....	....	....	1	....	....	....	....	....	....	....	....	....	....	....

TABLE X.

OCCUPATION.

Jammu and Kashmir Census 1931.

District, Ilaqa, Jagir or City.	Group 38. Mica.						Group 39. Precious and semi-precious stones.						Class B. Preparation and supply of material substances. Total of Class B.					
	Total earners (principal occupation).		Total working dependents.		Total following occupation as subsidiary to others.		Total earners (principal occupation).		Total working dependents.		Total following occupation as subsidiary to others.		Total earners (principal occupation).		Total working dependents.		Total following occupation as subsidiary to others.	
	Males.	Females.	Males.	Females.	Males.	Females.	Males.	Females.	Males.	Females.	Males.	Females.	Males.	Females.	Males.	Females.	Males.	Females.
Jammu and Kashmir State ..	5	....	....	....	3	....	29	....	....	....	1	....	103,978	10,584	3,221	6,394	25,101	5,941
I. Jammu Province ..	5	....	....	....	3	....	29	....	....	....	1	....	43,848	8,527	989	3,470	15,020	3,776
1. Jammu District (*including City*) ..	....	....	....	....	....	....	....	....	....	....	....	....	20,684	1,545	424	500	6,424	818
2. Kathua " ..	....	....	....	....	....	....	20	....	....	....	1	....	6,551	1,926	154	1,476	2,121	835
3. Udhampur " ..	5	....	....	....	3	....	....	....	....	....	....	....	4,074	555	163	270	1,954	461
4. Reasi " ..	....	....	....	....	....	....	....	....	....	....	....	....	2,286	3,512	104	101	1,047	613
5. Mirpur " ..	....	....	....	....	....	....	....	....	....	....	....	....	8,075	710	98	321	2,632	884
6. Poonch Jagir ..	....	....	....	....	....	....	....	....	....	....	....	....	1,960	245	40	794	795	164
7. Chenani " ..	....	....	....	....	....	....	....	....	....	....	....	....	218	34	6	8	47	1
II. Kashmir Province ..	....	....	....	....	....	....	....	....	....	....	....	....	58,867	1,773	2,070	2,907	9,900	2,054
8. Kashmir North ..	....	....	....	....	....	....	....	....	....	....	....	....	13,117	313	612	626	3,199	424
9. Kashmir South (*including City*)	....	....	....	....	....	....	....	....	....	....	....	....	43,682	1,399	1,367	1,948	6,135	1,531
10. Muzaffarabad ..	....	....	....	....	....	....	....	....	....	....	....	....	2,068	61	91	333	566	99
III. Frontier Districts ..	....	....	....	....	....	....	....	....	....	....	....	....	1,263	284	162	17	181	111
11. Ladakh ..	....	....	....	....	....	....	....	....	....	....	....	....	808	278	1	1	111	87
12. Gilgit ..	....	....	....	....	....	....	....	....	....	....	....	....	365	5	....	15	44	23
13. Frontier Ilaqas ..	....	....	....	....	....	....	....	....	....	....	....	....	90	1	161	1	26	1
IV. Cities—																		
14. Srinagar ..	....	....	....	....	....	....	....	....	....	....	....	....	26,335	613	506	1,079	990	109
15. Jammu (*excludes Ry. population*)	....	....	....	....	....	....	....	....	....	....	....	....	5,296	235	81	114	351	46

TABLE X.

OCCUPATION.

Jammu and Kashmir Census 1931.

District, Ilaqa, Jagir or City.	SUB-CLASS III Industry. TOTAL OF SUB-CLASS III.						ORDER 5. Textiles. TOTAL OF ORDER 5.						GROUP 42. Cotton ginning, cleaning and pressing.					
	Total earners (principal occupation).		Total working dependents.		Total following occupation as subsidiary to others.		Total earners (principal occupation).		Total working dependents.		Total following occupation as subsidiary to others.		Total earners (principal occupation).		Total working dependents.		Total following occupation as subsidiary to others.	
	Males.	Females.	Males.	Females.	Males.	Females.	Males.	Females.	Males.	Females.	Males.	Females.	Males.	Females.	Males.	Females.	Males.	Females.
Jammu and Kashmir State ..	69,411	6,435	2,250	5,449	15,963	4,589	10,052	2,177	618	3,460	2,639	2,326	293	97	13	10	101	4
I. Jammu Province ..	28,064	4,839	680	2,714	9,263	3,026	5,076	1,506	136	940	1,982	1,461	132	97	7	10	55	4
1. Jammu District (*including City*) ..	12,501	1,063	342	473	3,554	583	2,402	335	31	119	917	244	29	....	....	....	17	....
2. Kathua „ ..	4,503	1,395	98	846	1,433	705	861	429	78	447	344	501	12	....	....	....	4	1
3. Udhampur „ ..	2,206	410	57	216	1,171	317	176	223	2	102	86	133	....	....	....	....	....	....
4. Reasi „ ..	1,271	1,110	56	100	581	464	189	200	2	76	99	214	3	87	....	10	2	2
5. Mirpur „ ..	6,281	623	88	318	2,003	796	1,295	263	18	111	484	337	50	10	5	....	13	1
6. Poonch Jagir ..	1,184	223	33	757	496	160	149	52	5	84	51	32	38	....	2	....	19	....
7. Chenani „ ..	118	15	6	4	25	1	4	4	....	1	1	....	....	....	....	....	....	....
II. Kashmir Province ..	41,003	1,340	1,440	2,719	6,631	1,481	4,940	425	453	2,516	650	785	161	....	6	....	46	....
8. Kashmir North ..	8,118	217	500	539	2,093	277	746	73	199	480	107	166	66	....	4	....	21	....
9. Kashmir South (*including City*) ..	31,765	1,066	856	1,850	4,199	1,108	3,958	336	200	1,772	441	596	76	....	....	....	20	....
10. Muzaffarabad ..	1,120	57	84	330	339	96	236	16	54	255	42	23	19	....	2	....	5	....
III. Frontier Districts ..	344	256	130	16	69	82	36	246	29	4	7	80	....	....	....	....	....	....
11. Ladakh ..	148	250	....	1	33	81	28	245	....	1	6	80	....	....	....	....	....	....
12. Gilgit ..	149	5	....	15	24	....	6	1	....	3	....	....	....	....	....	....	....	....
13. Frontier Ilaqas ..	47	1	130	....	12	1	2	....	29	....	1	....	....	....	....	....	....	....
IV. Cities—																		
14. Srinagar ..	20,286	425	343	994	608	65	2,985	205	47	933	134	6	....	....	....	....	....	....
15. Jammu (*excludes Ry. population*) ..	2,543	211	64	104	128	39	191	11	2	5	18	2	6	....	....	....	....	....

TABLE X.

OCCUPATION.

Jammu and Kashmir Census 1931.

District, Ilaqa, Jagir or city.	Group 43. Cotton spinning, sizing and weaving. Total earners (principal occupation).		Total working dependents.		Total following occupation as subsidiary to others.		Group 44. Jute pressing, spinning and weaving. Total earners (principal occupation).		Total working dependents.		Total following occupation as subsidiary to others.		Group 45. Rope, twine, string and other fibers. Total earners (principal occupation).		Total working dependents.		Total following occupation as subsidiary to others.	
	Males.	Females.	Males.	Females.	Males.	Females.	Males.	Females.	Males.	Females.	Males.	Females.	Males.	Females.	Males.	Females.	Males.	Females.
Jammu and Kashmir State ..	4,911	1,512	222	1,050	1,953	1,451	8	4	....	1	2	2	83	1	....	....	20	....
I. Jammu Province ..	4,417	1,225	123	896	1,792	1,336	8	4	....	1	2	2	12	....	....	....	7	....
1. Jammu District (*including City*) ..	2,083	329	29	117	866	239	8	....	....	....	2	....	7	....	....	....	5	....
2. Kathua " ..	814	414	78	436	320	482	....	4	....	1	....	2	4	....	....	....	2	....
3. Udhampur " ..	158	214	2	102	86	125	....	....	....	....	....	....	1	....	....	....	....	....
4. Reasi " ..	136	63	1	64	46	211	....	....	....	....	....	....	....	....	....	....	....	....
5. Mirpur " ..	1,162	160	12	111	455	251	....	....	....	....	....	....	....	....	....	....	....	....
6. Poonch Jagir ..	62	42	....	65	18	28	....	....	....	....	....	....	....	....	....	....	....	....
7. Chenani " ..	2	3	....	1	1	....	....	....	....	....	....	....	....	....	....	....	....	....
II. Kashmir Province ..	464	45	71	153	154	37	....	....	....	....	....	....	71	1	....	....	18	....
8. Kashmir North ..	48	5	13	75	27	9	....	....	....	....	....	....	5	....	....	....	1	....
9. Kashmir South (*including City*) ..	233	29	6	54	97	10	....	....	....	....	....	....	66	1	....	....	12	....
10. Muzaffarabad	183	11	52	24	30	18	....	....	....	....	....	....	....	....	....	....	....	....
III. Frontier Districts ..	30	242	29	1	7	78	....	....	....	....	....	....	....	....	....	....	....	....
11. Ladakh ..	28	242	....	1	6	78	....	....	....	....	....	....	....	....	....	....	....	....
12. Gilgit ..	....	....	....	....	....	....	....	....	....	....	....	....	....	....	....	....	....	....
13. Frontier Ilaqas ..	2	....	29	....	1	....	....	....	....	....	....	....	....	....	....	....	....	....
IV. Cities—																		
14. Srinagar ..	....	....	....	....	....	....	....	....	....	....	....	....	....	....	....	....	....	....
15. Jammu (*excludes Ry. population*) ..	....	5	....	3	....	1	5	....	....	....	2	....	....	....	....	....	....	....

TABLE X.

OCCUPATION.

Jammu and Kashmir Census 1931.

District, Ilaqa, Jagir or City.	Group 46. Wool carding, spinning and weaving. Total earners (principal occupation).		Total working dependents.		Total following occupation as subsidiary to others.		Group 47. Silk spinning and weaving. Total earners (principal occupation).		Total working dependents.		Total following occupation as subsidiary to others.		Group 48. Hair (horse hair) etc. Total earners (principal occupation).		Total working dependents.		Total following occupation as subsidiary to others.	
	Males.	Females.	Males.	Females.	Males.	Females.	Males.	Females.	Males.	Females.	Males	Females	Males.	Females.	Males.	Females	Males.	Females.
Jammu and Kashmir State	745	194	147	1,443	182	752	322	4	152	1	49	1	7	....	1	....	1	....
I. Jammu Province ..	55	17	....	10	18	13	79	4	1	1	2	....	3	....	....	....	....	....
1. Jammu District (*includig city*) ..	....	....	....	....	....	....	78	4	1	1	2	....	3	....	....	....	....	....
2. Kathua " ..	23	6	....	10	18	4	....	....	....	....	....	....	....	....	....	....	....	....
3. Udhampur " ..	11	9	....	....	....	8	....	....	....	....	....	....	....	....	....	....	....	....
4. Reasi " ..	....	1	....	....	....	1	....	....	....	....	....	....	....	....	....	....	....	....
5. Mirpur " ..	1	....	....	....	....	....	....	....	....	....	....	....	....	....	....	....	....	....
6. Poonch Jagir ..	20	....	....	....	....	....	1	....	....	....	....	....	....	....	....	....	....	....
7. Chenani " ..	....	1	....	....	....	....	....	....	....	....	....	....	....	....	....	....	....	....
II. Kashmir Province ..	690	173	147	1,430	164	737	243	....	151	....	47	1	4	....	1	....	1	....
8. Kashmir North ..	129	67	2	414	11	156	242	....	151	....	47	1	....	....	....	....	....	....
9. Kashmir South (*including city*) ..	534	101	145	785	146	580	....	....	....	....	....	....	4	....	1	....	1	....
10. Muzaffarabad ..	27	5	....	231	7	1	1	....	....	....	....	....	....	....	....	....	....	....
III. Frontier Districts ..	....	4	....	3	....	2	....	....	....	....	....	....	....	....	....	....	....	....
11. Ladakh ..	....	3	....	....	....	2	....	....	....	....	....	....	....	....	....	....	....	....
12. Gilgit ..	....	1	....	3	....	....	....	....	....	....	....	....	....	....	....	....	....	....
13. Frontier Ilaqas ..	....	....	....	....	....	....	....	....	....	....	....	....	....	....	....	....	....	....
IV. Cities.—																		
14. Srinagar ..	....	....	....	....	....	....	....	....	....	....	....	....	....	....	....	....	....	....
15. Jammu (*excludes Ry. popuation*) ..	....	....	....	....	....	....	46	4	1	1	2	..	....	....	....	....	....	....

TABLE X.

OCCUPATION.

Jammu and Kashmir Census 1931.

District, Ilaqa, Jagir or City.	Group 49. Dyeing, bleaching, printing, preparation and sponging of textiles. Total earners (principal occupation).		Total working dependents.		Total following occupation as subsidiary to others.		Group 50. Lace, Crepe, embroideries, fringes etc. and insufficiently described textile industries. Total earners (principal (occupation).		Total working dependents.		Total following occupation as subsidiary to others.		Order 6. Hides, skins and hard materials from the animal kingdom. Total of Order 6. Total earners (principal occupation).		Total working dependents.		Total following occupation as subsidiary to others	
	Males.	Females.	Males.	Females.	Males.	Females.	Males.	Females.	Males.	Females.	Males.	Females.	Males.	Females.	Males.	Females.	Males.	Females.
Jammu and Kashmir State ..	396	19	27	....	85	14	3,287	340	56	955	246	102	4,616	306	76	120	1,497	377
I. Jammu Province ..	263	19	3	....	44	13	107	140	3	22	62	93	2,210	278	26	116	869	362
1. Jammu District (*including city*) ..	157	....	....	....	22	4	37	2	1	1	3	1	989	43	9	9	369	14
2. Kathua „ ..	7	....	....	....	....	1	1	5	....	....	....	11	298	79	....	59	58	57
3. Udhampur „ ..	6	....	....	....	....	....	....	....	....	....	....	....	214	38	10	43	112	43
4. Reasi „ ..	9	....	....	....	3	....	41	49	1	2	48	....	30	39	2	....	26	113
5. Mirpur „ ..	82	18	1	....	16	8	....	75	....	....	....	77	424	8	3	....	147	72
6. Poonch Jagir ..	1	1	2	....	3	....	27	9	1	19	11	4	253	71	2	5	156	63
7. Chenani ..	1	....	....	....	....	....	1	....	....	....	....	....	2	....	....	....	1	....
II. Kashmir Province ..	133	....	24	....	41	1	3,174	206	53	933	184	9	2,406	28	50	4	628	15
8. Kashmir North ..	72	....	23	....	10	....	184	1	6	....	50	....	808	20	20	3	135	9
9. Kashmir South (*including City*) ..	57	....	1	....	31	....	2,988	205	47	933	134	6	1,588	8	30	1	491	6
10. Muzaffarabad ..	4	....	....	....	....	1	2	....	....	....	....	3	10	....	....	....	2	....
III. Frontier Districts ..	....	....	....	....	....	....	6	....	....	....	....	....	....	....	....	....	....	....
11. Ladakh ..	....	....	....	....	....	....	....	....	....	....	....	....	....	....	....	....	....	....
12. Gilgit ..	....	....	....	....	....	....	6	....	....	....	....	....	....	....	....	....	....	....
13. Frontier Ilaqas ..	....	....	....	....	....	....	....	....	....	....	....	....	....	....	....	....	....	....
IV. Cities— ..																		
14. Srinagar ..	....	....	....	....	....	....	2,985	205	47	933	134	6	417	3	6	1	34	6
15. Jammu (*excludes Ry. population*) ..	102	....	....	....	11	....	32	2	1	1	3	1	57	....	....	....	4	....

TABLE X.

OCCUPATION.

Jammu and Kashmir Census 1931.

District, Ilaqa, Jagir or City.	Group 51. Working in leather. Total earners (principal occupation).		Total working dependents.		Total following occupation as subsidiary to others.		Group 52. Furriers and persons occupied with feathers and bristles; brush-makers. Total earners (principal occupation).		Total working dependents.		Total following occupation as subsidiary to others.		Group 53. Bone, ivory, horn, shell etc. workers (except buttons). Total earners (principal occupation).		Total working dependents.		Total following occupation as subsidiary to others.	
	Males.	Females.	Males.	Females.	Males.	Females.	Males	Females.	Males.	Females.	Males.	Females.	Males.	Females.	Males.	Females.	Males.	Females.
Jammu and Kashmir State ..	4,533	304	76	107	1,483	377	66	2	....	13	7	....	17	....	....	....	7	....
I. Jammu Province ..	2,127	276	26	103	855	362	66	2	....	13	7	....	17	....	....	....	7	....
1. Jammu District (*including City*) ..	960	43	9	9	308	14	23	....	....	....	1	....	6	....	....	....	....	....
2. Kathua „ ..	274	70	....	46	58	57	24	....	....	13	....	....	....	....	....	....	....	....
3. Udhampur „ ..	199	38	10	43	105	43	4	....	....	....	....	....	11	....	....	....	7	....
4. Reasi „ ..	30	30	2	....	26	113	....	....	....	....	....	....	....	....	....	....	....	....
5. Mirpur „ ..	424	8	3	....	147	72	....	....	....	....	....	....	....	....	....	....	....	....
6. Poonch Jagir ..	238	69	2	5	150	63	15	2	....	....	6	....	....	....	....	....	....	....
7. Chenani Jagir ..	2	....	....	....	1	....	....	....	....	....	....	....	....	....	....	....	....	....
II. Kashmir Province ..	2,406	28	50	4	628	15	....	....	....	....	....	....	....	....	....	....	....	....
8. Kashmir North ..	808	20	20	3	135	9	....	....	....	....	....	....	....	....	....	....	....	....
9. Kashmir South (*including City*) ..	1,588	8	30	1	491	6	....	....	....	....	....	....	....	....	....	....	....	....
10. Muzaffarabad ..	10	....	....	....	2	....	....	....	....	....	....	....	....	....	....	....	....	....
III. Frontier Districts ..	....	....	....	....	....	....	....	....	....	....	....	....	....	....	....	....	....	....
11. Ladakh ..	....	....	....	....	....	....	....	....	....	....	....	....	....	....	....	....	....	....
12. Gilgit ..	....	....	....	....	....	....	....	....	....	....	....	....	....	....	....	....	....	....
13. Frontier Ilaqas ..	....	....	....	....	....	....	....	....	....	....	....	....	....	....	....	....	....	....
IV. Cities—																		
14. Srinagar ..	417	3	6	1	....	6	....	....	....	....	....	....	....	....	....	....	....	....
15. Jammu (*excluding Ry. population*)	57	....	....	....	4	....	....	....	....	....	....	....	....	....	....	....	....	....

TABLE X.

OCCUPATION.

Jammu and Kashmir Census 1931.

District, Ilaqa, Jagir or City.	ORDER 7. Wood. TOTAL OF ORDER 7.						GROUP 54. Sawyers.						GROUP 55. Carpenters, turners and joiners, etc.					
	Total earners (principal occupation).		Total working dependents.		Total following occupation as subsidiary to others.		Total earners (principal occupation).		Total working dependents.		Total following occupation as subsidiary to others.		Total earners (principal occupation).		Total working dependents.		Total following occupation as subsidiary to others.	
	Males.	Females.	Males.	Females.	Males.	Females.	Males.	Females.	Males.	Females.	Males.	Females.	Males.	Females.	Males.	Females.	Males.	Females.
Jammu and Kashmir State ..	9,399	525	277	37	2,910	337	1,691	24	27	2	374	4	5,678	31	207	2	1,830	5
I. Jammu Province ..	4,203	139	86	34	1,415	70	430	17	10	2	177	4	2,610	15	49	....	931	4
1. Jammu District (*including City*) ..	1,715	28	52	12	696	17	90	5	3	....	21	....	1,158	3	36	....	516	1
2. Kathua „ ..	924	9	3	20	207	2	72	....	....	....	21	....	338	....	....	....	116	....
3. Udhampur „ ..	362	23	3	....	151	27	204	11	....	....	76	4	78	1	1	....	41	....
4. Reasi „ ..	107	77	1	....	77	21	13	1	....	....	13	....	63	9	1	....	43	....
5. Mirpur „ ..	1,001	2	12	....	252	3	11	....	1	....	43	....	935	2	9	....	191	3
6. Poonch Jagir ..	92	....	9	....	32	....	39	....	6	....	3	....	38	....	2	....	24	....
7. Chenani „ ..	2	....	6	2	....	....	1	....	....	2	....	....	....	....	....	....	....	....
II. Kashmir Province ..	5,156	386	143	2	1,486	267	1,248	7	15	....	197	....	3,041	16	112	1	890	1
8. Kashmir North ..	1,491	5	49	....	575	2	289	....	7	....	97	....	897	4	32	....	386	....
9. Kashmir South (*including City*) ..	3,484	369	85	1	854	256	876	1	4	....	80	....	2,080	12	76	1	479	1
10. Muzaffarabad ..	181	12	9	1	57	9	83	6	4	....	20	....	64	....	4	....	25	....
III. Frontier Districts ..	40	....	48	1	9	....	13	....	2	....	....	....	27	....	46	1	9	....
11. Ladakh ..	14	....	....	....	....	....	1	....	....	....	....	....	13	....	....	....	....	....
12. Gilgit ..	18	....	....	1	7	....	8	....	....	....	....	....	10	....	....	1	7	....
13. Frontier Ilaqas ..	8	....	48	....	2	....	4	....	2	....	....	....	4	....	46	....	2	....
IV. Cities.—																		
14. Srinagar ..	1,827	11	24	....	42	1	752	1	3	....	18	....	1,075	10	21	....	24	1
15. Jammu (*excludes Ry. population*) ..	272	9	1	....	8	2	41	1	....	....	....	....	202	....	1	....	7	....

TABLE X.

OCCUPATION.

Jammu and Kashmir Census 1931.

District, Ilaqa, Jagir or City.	Group 56. Basket-makers and other industries of woody materials, including leaves and thatchers and builders working with bamboo reeds or similar materials.						Order 8. Metals. Total of Order 8.						Group 57. Smelting, forging and rolling of iron and other metals.					
	Total earners (principal occupation).		Total working dependents.		Total following occupation as subsidiary to others.		Total earners (principal occupation).		Total working dependents.		Total following occupation as subsidiary to others.		Total earners (principal occupation).		Total working dependents.		Total following occupation as subsidiary to others.	
	Males.	Females.	Males.	Females.	Males.	Females.	Males	Females.	Males.	Females.	Males.	Females.	Males.	Females.	Males.	Females.	Males.	Females.
Jammu and Kashmir State ..	**2,030**	**470**	**43**	**33**	**706**	**328**	**4,013**	**33**	**192**	**3**	**1,319**	**10**	**910**	**2**	**21**	....	**285**	**1**
I. Jammu Province ..	**1,163**	**107**	**27**	**32**	**307**	**62**	**1,804**	**15**	**105**	....	**779**	**5**	**428**	....	**8**	....	**275**	....
1. Jammu District (*including city*) ..	467	20	13	12	159	16	844	6	77	....	197	4	20	....	....	....	....	....
2. Kathua " ..	514	9	3	20	70	2	283	....	2	....	118	....	164	....	2	....	97	....
3. Udhampur " ..	80	11	2	....	34	23	146	....	2	....	145	1	34	....	1	....	58	....
4. Reasi " ..	31	67	....	....	21	21	130	1	13	....	103	....	37	....	5	....	20	....
5. Mirpur " ..	55	....	2	....	18	....	294	1	4	....	163	....	166	....	....	....	96	....
6. Poonch Jagir ..	15	....	1	....	5	....	80	7	7	....	49	....	....	....	....	....	2	....
7. Chenani " ..	1	....	6	....	....	....	18	....	....	....	4	....	7	....	....	....	2	....
II. Kashmir Province ..	**867**	**363**	**16**	**1**	**399**	**266**	**2,141**	**18**	**69**	**3**	**514**	**5**	**482**	**2**	**13**	....	**10**	**1**
8. Kashmir North ..	305	1	10	....	92	2	528	14	22	1	161	1	....	....	....	....	....	....
9. Kashmir South (*including City*) ..	528	356	5	....	295	255	1,566	4	43	1	308	4	482	2	13	....	10	1
10. Muzaffarabad ..	34	6	1	1	12	9	47	....	4	1	45	....	....	....	....	....	....	....
III. Frontier Districts ..	....	....	....	....	....	....	**68**	....	**18**	....	**26**	....	....	....	....	....	....	....
11. Ladakh ..	....	....	....	....	....	....	46	....	....	....	13	....	....	....	....	....	....	....
12. Gilgit ..	....	....	....	....	....	....	15	....	....	....	5	....	....	....	....	....	....	....
13. Frontier Ilaqas ..	....	....	....	....	....	....	7	....	18	....	8	....	....	....	....	....	....	....
IV. Cities— ..																		
14. Srinagar ..	....	....	....	....	....	....	887	3	23	1	23	1	482	2	13	....	10	1
15. Jammu (*excludes Ry. population*) ..	29	8	....	....	1	2	216	....	10	....	2	....	17	....	....	....	....	....

TABLE X.

OCCUPATION.

Jammu and Kashmir Census 1931.

District, Ilaqa, Jagir or City.	Group 58. Makers of arms, guns, etc.						Group 59. Blacksmiths, other workers in iron, makers of implements.						Group 60. Workers in brass, copper, and bell metal.					
	Total earners (principal occupation).		Total working dependents.		Total following occupation as subsidiary to others.		Total earners (principal occupation.)		Total working dependents.		Total following occupation as subsidiary to others.		Total earners (principal occupation).		Total working dependents.		Total following occupation as subsidiary to others.	
	Males.	Females.	Males.	Females.	Males.	Females.	Males.	Females.	Males.	Females.	Males.	Females.	Males.	Females.	Males.	Females.	Males.	Females.
Jammu and Kashmir State ..	30	....	3	....	2	....	2,356	12	155	1	1,000	8	706	5	13	1	30	....
I. Jammu Province ..	30	....	3	....	2	....	1,258	11	91	....	500	5	88	4	3	....	2	....
1. Jammu District (*including City*) ..	16	....	....	....	2	....	726	6	74	....	195	4	82	....	3	....	....	....
2. Kathua „ ..	....	....	....	....	....	....	117	....	....	....	20	....	2	....	....	....	1	....
3. Udhampur „ ..	....	....	....	....	....	....	112	....	1	....	87	1	....	....	....	....	....	....
4. Reasi „ ..	....	....	....	....	....	....	93	1	8	....	83	....	....	....	....	....	....	....
5. Mirpur „ ..	....	....	....	....	....	....	128	1	4	....	67	....	....	....	....	....	....	....
6. Poonch Jagir ..	13	....	3	....	....	....	72	3	4	....	46	....	4	4	....	....	1	....
7. Chenani „ ..	1	....	....	....	....	....	10	....	....	....	2	....	....	....	....	....	....	....
II. Kashmir Province ..	....	....	....	....	....	....	1,030	1	46	1	474	3	618	1	10	1	28	....
8. Kashmir North ..	....	....	....	....	....	....	471	....	22	....	154	....	55	....	....	....	7	....
9. Kashmir South (*including City*)	....	....	....	....	....	....	516	1	20	....	276	3	563	1	10	1	21	....
10. Muzaffarabad ..	....	....	....	....	....	....	43	....	4	1	44	....	....	....	....	....	....	....
III. Frontier Districts ..	....	....	....	....	....	....	68	....	18	....	26	....	....	....	....	....	....	....
11. Ladakh ..	....	....	....	....	....	....	46	....	....	....	13	....	....	....	....	....	....	....
12. Gilgit ..	....	....	....	....	....	....	15	....	....	....	5	....	....	....	....	....	....	....
13. Frontier Ilaqas ..	....	....	....	....	....	....	7	....	18	....	8	....	....	....	....	....	....	....
IV. Cities—																		
14. Srinagar ..	....	....	....	....	....	....	....	....	....	....	....	....	405	1	10	1	13	....
15. Jammu (*excludes Ry. population*)	2	....	....	....	....	....	126	....	7	....	2	....	71	....	3	....	....	....

TABLE X.

OCCUPATION.

Jammu and Kashmir Census 1931.

District, Ilaqa, Jagir or city.	Group 61. Workers in other metals except precious metals.						Group 62. Workers in mints, die-sinkers, etc.						Order 9. Ceramics. Total of Order 9.					
	Total earners (principal occupation).		Total working dependents.		Total following occupation as subsidiary to others.		Total earners (principal occupation).		Total working dependents.		Total following occupation as subsidiary to others.		Total earners (principal occupation).		Total working dependents.		Total following occupation as subsidiary to others.	
	Males.	Females.	Males.	Females.	Males.	Females.	Males.	Females.	Males.	Females.	Males.	Females.	Males.	Females.	Males.	Females.	Males.	Females.
Jammu and Kashmir State	9	....	....	....	2	....	2	14	....	1	....	1	3,705	473	67	133	1,269	622
I. Jammu Province ..	....	....	....	....	....	....	....	....	....	....	....	....	1,933	261	18	112	641	353
1. Jammu District (*includig city*) ..	....	....	....	....	....	....	....	....	....	....	....	....	778	34	7	8	116	31
2. Kathua ,, ..	....	....	....	....	....	....	....	....	....	....	....	....	303	46	....	58	134	34
3. Udhampur ,, ..	....	....	....	....	....	....	....	....	....	....	....	....	155	19	4	....	127	20
4. Reasi ,, ..	....	....	....	....	....	....	....	....	....	....	....	....	32	20	....	....	11	28
5. Mirpur ,, ..	....	....	....	....	....	....	....	....	....	....	....	....	576	101	4	46	202	203
6. Poonch Jagir ..	....	....	....	....	....	....	....	....	....	....	....	....	85	41	3	....	49	37
7. Chenani ,, ..	....	....	....	....	....	....	....	....	....	....	....	....	4	....	....	....	2	....
II. Kashmir Province ..	9	....	....	....	2	....	2	14	....	1	....	1	1,771	212	49	21	647	269
8. Kashmir North ..	....	....	....	....	....	....	2	14	....	1	....	1	764	22	38	1	242	35
9. Kashmir South (*including city*) ..	5	....	....	....	1	....	....	....	....	....	....	....	959	184	11	20	383	193
10. Muzaffarabad ..	4	....	....	....	1	....	....	....	....	....	....	....	48	6	....	....	22	41
III. Frontier Districts ..	....	....	....	....	....	....	....	....	....	....	....	....	1	....	....	....	1	....
11. Ladakh :	....	....	....	....	....	....	....	....	....	....	....	....	1	....	....	....	1	....
12. Gilgit ..	....	....	....	....	....	....	....	....	....	....	....	....	....	....	....	....	....	....
13. Frontier Ilaqas ..	....	....	....	....	....	....	....	....	....	....	....	....	....	....	....	....	....	....
IV. Cities.—																		
14. Srinagar ..	....	....	....	....	....	....	....	....	....	....	....	....	114	56	3	9	1	5
15. Jammu (*excludes Ry. popuation*) ..	....	....	....	....	....	....	....	....	....	....	....	....	85	9	1	4	2	2

TABLE X.

Occupation.

Jammu and Kashmir Census 1931.

District, Ilaqa, Jagir or City.	Group 63. Potters and makers of earthen-ware. Total earners (principal occupation). Males.	Females.	Total working dependents. Males.	Females.	Total following occupation as subsidiary to others. Males.	Females.	Group 64. Brick and tile makers. Total earners (principal occupation). Males.	Females.	Total working dependents. Males.	Females.	Total following occupation as subsidiary to others. Males.	Females.	Group 65. Other workers in ceramics. Total earners (principal occupation). Males.	Females.	Total working dependents. Males.	Females.	Total following occupation as subsidiary to others. Males.	Females.
Jammu and Kashmir State ..	3,485	470	65	131	1,275	620	201	....	2	....	13	2	19	3	....	2	1	....
I. Jammu Province ..	1,715	258	16	110	628	351	199	....	2	....	12	2	19	3	....	2	1	....
1. Jammu District (*including City*) ..	593	31	5	6	113	29	170	....	2	....	2	2	15	3	....	2	1	....
2. Kathua " ..	276	46	....	58	124	34	27	....	....	....	10	....	....	....	....	....	....	....
3. Udhampur " ..	149	19	4	....	127	20	2	....	....	....	....	....	4	....	....	....	....	....
4. Reasi " ..	32	20	....	....	11	28	....	....	....	....	....	....	....	....	....	....	....	....
5. Mirpur " ..	576	101	4	46	202	203	....	....	....	....	....	....	....	....	....	....	....	....
6. Poonch Jagir ..	85	41	3	....	49	37	....	....	....	....	....	....	....	....	....	....	....	....
7. Chenani " ..	4	....	....	....	2	....	....	....	....	....	....	....	....	....	....	....	....	....
II. Kashmir Province ..	1,769	212	49	21	646	269	2	....	....	....	1	....	....	....	....	....	....	....
8. Kashmir North ..	762	22	38	1	242	35	2	....	....	....	....	....	....	....	....	....	....	....
9. Kashmir South (*including City*) ..	959	184	11	20	383	193	....	....	....	....	....	....	....	....	....	....	....	....
10. Muzaffarabad	48	6	....	....	21	41	....	....	....	....	1	....	....	....	....	....	....	....
III. Frontier Districts ..	1	....	....	....	1	....	....	....	....	....	....	....	....	....	....	....	....	....
11. Ladakh ..	1	....	....	....	1	....	....	....	....	....	....	....	....	....	....	....	....	....
12. Gilgit ..	....	....	....	....	....	....	....	....	....	....	....	....	....	....	....	....	....	....
13. Frontier Ilaqas ..	....	....	....	....	....	....	....	....	....	....	....	....	....	....	....	....	....	....
IV. Cities—																		
14. Srinagar ..	114	56	3	9	1	5	....	....	....	....	....	....	....	....	....	....	....	....
15. Jammu (*excludes Ry. population*) ..	53	9	....	4	....	....	32	....	1	....	2	2	....	....	....	....	....	....

TABLE X.

OCCUPATION.

Jammu and Kashmir Census 1931.

District, Ilaqa, Jagir or City.	ORDER 10. Chemical products properly so-called and analogous. TOTAL OF ORDER 10.						GROUP 66. Manufacture of matches, fire-works and other explosives.						GROUP 67. Manufacture of aerated and mineral waters and ice.					
	Total earners (principal occupation).		Total working dependents.		Total following occupation as subsidiary to others.		Total earners (principal occupation).		Total working dependents.		Total following occupation as subsidiary to others.		Total earners (principal occupation).		Total working dependents.		Total following occupation as subsidiary to others.	
	Males.	Females.	Males.	Females.	Males.	Females.	Males.	Females.	Males.	Females.	Males.	Females.	Males.	Females.	Males.	Females.	Males.	Females.
Jammu and Kashmir State ..	2,414	113	87	40	1,013	87	81	2	1	....	15	2	7	....	....	....	....	....
I. Jammu Province ..	942	109	36	40	374	81	55	2	1	....	11	....	7	....	....	....	....	....
1. Jammu District (*including city*) ..	400	67	31	12	166	27	24	....	....	....	6	....	7	....	....	....	....	....
2. Kathua „ ..	194	7	....	18	42	7	15	....	....	....	....	....	....	....	....	....	....	....
3. Udhampur „ ..	59	7	1	....	47	4	3	....	....	....	....	....	....	....	....	....	....	....
4. Reasi „ ..	30	13	....	....	34	22	....	....	....	....	....	....	....	....	....	....	....	....
5. Mirpur „ ..	232	12	3	10	74	18	13	2	1	....	5	....	....	....	....	....	....	....
6. Poonch Jagir ..	23	....	1	....	10	2	....	....	....	....	....	....	....	....	....	....	....	....
7. Chenani „ ..	4	3	....	....	1	1	....	....	....	....	....	....	....	....	....	....	....	....
II. Kashmir Province ..	1,472	4	51	....	639	6	26	....	....	....	4	2	....	....	....	....	....	....
8. Kashmir North ..	554	2	30	....	272	....	23	....	....	....	2	....	....	....	....	....	....	....
9. Kashmir South (*including city*) ..	890	1	21	....	356	4	....	....	....	....	1	....	....	....	....	....	....	....
10. Muzaffarabad ..	28	1	....	....	11	2	3	....	....	....	1	2	....	....	....	....	....	....
III. Frontier Districts ..	....	....	....	....	....	....	....	....	....	....	....	....	....	....	....	....	....	....
11. Ladakh ..	....	....	....	....	....	....	....	....	....	....	....	....	....	....	....	....	....	....
12. Gilgit ..	....	....	....	....	....	....	....	....	....	....	....	....	....	....	....	....	....	....
13. Frontier Ilaqas ..	....	....	....	....	....	....	....	....	....	....	....	....	....	....	....	....	....	....
IV. Cities.—																		
14. Srinagar ..	162	....	....	....	8	....	....	....	....	....	....	....	....	....	....	....	....	....
15. Jammu (*excludes Ry. population*) ..	45	....	....	....	6	....	23	....	....	....	6	....	7	....	....	....	....	....

TABLE X.

OCCUPATION.

Jammu and Kashmir Census 1931.

District, Ilaqa, Jagir or city.	Group 68. Manufacture and refining of vegetable oils.						Group 69. Manufacture and refining of mineral oils.						Group 70. Others.					
	Total earners (principal occupation).		Total working dependents.		Total following occupation as subsidiary to others.		Total earners (principal occupation).		Total working dependents.		Total following occupation as subsidiary to others.		Total earners (principal occupation).		Total working dependents.		Total following occupation as subsidiary to others.	
	Males.	Females.	Males.	Females.	Males.	Females.	Males.	Females.	Males.	Females.	Males.	Females.	Males.	Females.	Males.	Females.	Males.	Females.
Jammu and Kashmir State ..	2,316	100	86	30	998	77	2	11	....	10	....	8	8	....	....	....	....	....
I. Jammu Province ..	870	96	35	30	383	73	2	11	....	10	....	8	8	....	....	....	....	....
1. Jammu District (*including City*) ..	360	67	31	12	160	27	....	....	....	....	....	....	....	....	....	....	....	....
2. Kathua „ ..	179	7	....	18	42	7	....		....	....	....	....	....	....	....	....	....	....
3. Udhampur „ ..	46	7	1	....	47	4	2	....	....	....	....	....	8	....	....	....	....	....
4. Reasi „ ..	30	7	....	....	34	15	....	6	....	....	....	7	....	....	....	....	....	....
5. Mirpur „ ..	219	8	2	....	69	18	....	2	....	10	....	....	....	....	....	....	....	....
6. Poonch Jagir ..	23	....	1	....	10	2	....	....	....	....	....	....	....	....	....	....	....	....
7. Chenani „ ..	4	....	....	....	1	....	....	3	....	....	....	1	....	....	....	....	....	....
II. Kashmir Province ..	1,446	4	51	....	685	4	....	....	....	....	....	....	....	....	....	....	....	....
8. Kashmir North ..	531	2	30	....	270	....	....	....	....	....	....	....	....	....	....	....	....	....
9. Kashmir South (*including City*) ..	890	1	21	....	355	4	....	....	....	....	....	....	....	....	....	....	....	....
10. Muzaffarabad ..	25	1	....	....	10	....	....	....	....	....	....	....	....	....	....	....	....	....
III. Frontier Districts ..	....	....	....	....	....	....	....	....	....	....	....	....	....	....	....	....	....	....
11. Ladakh ..	....	....	....	....	....	....	....	....	....	....	....	....	....	....	....	....	....	....
12. Gilgit ..	....	....	....	....	....	....	....	....	....	....	....	....	....	....	....	....	....	....
13. Frontier Ilaqas ..	....	....	....	....	....	....	....	....	....	....	....	....	....	....	....	....	....	....
IV. Cities.—																		
14. Srinagar ..	162	....	....	....	8	....	....	....	....	....	....	....	....	....	....	....	....	....
15. Jammu (*excludes Ry. population*) ..	15	....	....	....	....	....	....	....	....	....	....	....	....	....	....	....	....	....

TABLE X.

OCCUPATION.

Jammu and Kashmir Census 1931.

District, Ilaqa, Jagir or City.	ORDER 11. Food Industries. TOTAL OF ORDER 11.						GROUP 71. Rice-pounders and huskers and flour grinders.						GROUP 72. Grain parchers, etc.					
	Total earners (principal occupation).		Total working dependents.		Total following occupation as subsidiary to others.		Total earners (principal occupation).		Total working dependents.		Total following occupation as subsidiary to others.		Total earners (principal occupation).		Total working dependents.		Total following occupation as subsidiary to others.	
	Males.	Females.	Males.	Females.	Males.	Females.	Males.	Females.	Males.	Females.	Males.	Females.	Males.	Females.	Males.	Females.	Males.	Females.
Jammu and Kashmir State ..	**4,639**	**219**	**109**	**35**	**748**	**132**	**1,582**	**148**	**45**	**7**	**423**	**54**	**91**	**35**	**2**	**15**	**13**	**58**
I. Jammu Province ..	**2,419**	**192**	**58**	**26**	**534**	**105**	**1,350**	**144**	**26**	**4**	**373**	**48**	**82**	**29**	....	**15**	**13**	**50**
. Jammu District (*including City*) ..	1,245	73	28	8	224	65	527	51	10	....	135	21	78	10	....	5	13	39
2. Kathua ,, ..	344	40	12	10	87	26	193	31	2	1	67	16	....	11	....	9	....	8
3. Udhampur ,, ..	332	24	10	5	94	5	243	23	10	2	72	5	4	....	....	....	....	....
4. Reasi ,, ..	212	12	3	1	41	5	172	12	1	....	26	5	....	....	....	....	....	....
5. Mirpur ,, ..	201	25	5	....	65	3	154	17	3	....	59	1	....	8	....	....	....	2
6. Poonch Jagir ..	58	9	....	1	20	1	38	7	....	....	11	....	....	....	....	1	....	1
7. Chenani ,, ..	27	3	....	1	3	....	23	3	....	1	3	....	....	....	....	....	....	....
II. Kashmir Province ..	**2,201**	**25**	**50**	**9**	**213**	**26**	**231**	**4**	**18**	**3**	**50**	**6**	**9**	**6**	**2**	....	....	**8**
8. Kashmir North ..	949	18	11	1	92	21	43	2	6	1	12	5	9	6	2	....	....	8
9. Kashmir South (*including City*) ..	1,121	5	38	6	83	5	172	1	11	....	31	1	....	....	....	....	....	....
10. Muzaffarabad ..	131	2	1	2	38	....	16	1	1	2	7	....	....	....	....	....	....	....
III. Frontier Districts ..	**19**	**2**	**1**	....	**1**	**1**	**1**	....	**1**	....	....	....	....	....	....	....	....	....
11. Ladakh ..	13	2	....	....	1	1	....	....	....	....	....	....	....	....	....	....	....	....
12. Gigit ..	5	....	....	....	....	....	....	....	....	....	....	....	....	....	....	....	....	....
13. Frontier Ilaqas ..	1	....	1	....	....	....	1	....	1	....	....	....	....	....	....	....	....	....
IV. Cities.—																		
14. Srinagar ..	549	....	2	3	7	4	51	....	....	....	....	....	....	....	....	....	....	....
15. Jammu (*excludes Ry. population*) ..	382	6	9	1	24	2	67	1	2	....	10	1	25	4	....	1	....	1

TABLE X.

OCCUPATION.

Jammu and Kashmir Census 1931.

District, Ilaqa, Jagir or City.	Group 73. Butchers.						Group 74. Makers of sugar molasses and gur.						Group 75. Sweetmeat and condiment makers.					
	Total earners (principal occupation).		Total working dependents.		Total following occupation as subsidiary to others.		Total earners (principal occupation.)		Total working dependents.		Total following occupation as subsidiary to others.		Total earners (principal occupation).		Total working dependents.		Total following occupation as subsidiary to others.	
	Males.	Females.	Males.	Females.	Males.	Females.	Males.	Females.	Males.	Females	Males.	Females.	Males.	Females.	Males.	Females.	Males.	Females.
Jammu and Kashmir State ..	1,330	5	24	7	103	6	2	....	....	....	....	....	577	11	22	3	95	2
I. Jammu Province ..	305	5	8	4	41	6	2	....	....	....	....	....	546	9	22	3	92	1
1. Jammu District (*including city*) ..	136	1	6	....	8	4	2	....	....	....	....	....	439	6	12	3	63	1
2. Kathua " ..	59	1	....	....	3	2	....	....	....	....	....	....	31	3	10	....	9	....
3. Udhampur " ..	49	1	....	3	8	....	....	....	....	....	....	....	36	....	....	....	14	....
4. Reasi " ..	10	....	....	1	9	....	....	....	....	....	....	....	20	....	....	....	4	....
5. Mirpur " ..	27	....	2	....	6	....	....	....	....	....	....	....	20	....	....	....	....	....
6. Poonch Jagir ..	20	2	....	....	7	....	....	....	....	....	....	....	....	....	....	....	2	....
7. Chenani ..	4	....	....	....	....	....	....	....	....	....	....	....	....	....	....	....	....	....
II. Kashmir Province ..	1,017	....	16	3	61	....	....	....	....	....	....	....	31	2	....	....	3	1
8. Kashmir North ..	215	....	....	....	28	....	....	....	....	....	....	....	31	2	....	....	3	1
9. Kashmir South (*including City*) ..	747	....	16	3	20	....	....	....	....	....	....	....	....	....	....	....	....	....
10. Muzaffarabad ..	55	....	....	....	13	....	....	....	....	....	....	....	....	....	....	....	....	....
III. Frontier Districts ..	8	....		....	1	....	....	....	....	....	....	....	....	....	....	....	....	....
11. Ladakh ..	3	....	....	....	1	....	....	....	....	....	....	....	....	....	....	....	....	....
12. Gilgit ..	5	....	....	....	....	....	....	....	....	....	....	....	....	....	....	....	....	....
13. Frontier Ilaqas ..	....	....	....	....	....	....	....	....	....	....	....	....	....	....	....	....	....	....
IV. Cities— ..																		
14. Srinagar ..	498	....	2	3	7	....	....	....	....	....	....	....	....	....	....	....	....	....
15. Jammu (*excludes Ry. population*) ..	79	....	6	....	5	....	....	....	....	....	....	....	211	1	1	....	9	....

TABLE X.

OCCUPATION.

Jammu and Kashmir Census 1931.

District, Ilaqa, Jagir or City.	Group 76. Toddy drawers. Total earners (principal occupation). Males.	Females.	Total working dependents. Males.	Females.	Total following occupation as subsidiary to others. Males.	Females.	Group 77. Brewers and distillers. Total earners (principal occupation). Males.	Females.	Total working dependents. Males.	Females.	Total following occupation as subsidiary to others. Males.	Females.	Group 78. Manufacturers of tobacco. Total earners (principal occupation). Males.	Females.	Total working dependents. Males.	Females.	Total following occupation as subsidiary to others. Males.	Females.
Jammu and Kashmir State ..	60	....	....	....	7	....	10	....	2	....	2	....	51	....	....	....	6	....
I. Jammu Province ..	60	....	....	....	7	....	8	....	2	....	2	....	48	....	....	....	6	....
1. Jammu District (*including city*) ..	39	....	....	....	5	....	....	....	....	....	....	....	6	....	....	....	....	....
2. Kathua " ..	21	....	....	....	2	....	....	....	....	....	1	....	40	....	....	....	5	....
3. Udhampur " ..	....	....	....	....	....	....	....	....	....	....	....	....	....	....	....	....	....	....
4. Reasi " ..	....	....	....	....	....	....	8	....	2	....	1	....	2	....	....	....	1	....
5. Mirpur " ..	....	....	....	....	....	....	....	....	....	....	....	....	....	....	....	....	....	....
6. Poonch Jagir ..	....	....	....	....	....	....	....	....	....	....	....	....	....	....	....	....	....	....
7. Chenani " ..	....	....	....	....	....	....	....	....	....	....	....	....	....	....	....	....	....	....
II. Kashmir Province ..	....	....	....	....	....	....	2	....	....	....	....	....	3	....	....	....	....	....
8. Kashmir North ..	....	....	....	....	....	....	....	....	....	....	....	....	....	....	....	....	....	....
9. Kashmir South (*including city*) ..	....	....	....	....	....	....	....	....	....	....	....	....	....	....	....	....	....	....
10. Muzaffarabad ..	....	....	....	....	....	....	2	....	....	....	....	....	3	....	....	....	....	....
III. Frontier Districts ..	....	....	....	....	....	....	....	....	....	....	....	....	....	....	....	....	....	....
11. Ladakh ..	....	....	....	....	....	....	....	....	....	....	....	....	....	....	....	....	....	....
12. Gilgit ..	....	....	....	....	....	....	....	....	....	....	....	....	....	....	....	....	....	....
13. Frontier Ilaqas ..	....	....	....	....	....	....	....	....	....	....	....	....	....	....	....	....	....	....
IV. Cities :—																		
14. Srinagar ..	....	....	....	....	....	....	....	....	....	....	....	....	....	....	....	....	....	....
15. Jammu (*excludes Ry. population*)	....	....	....	....	....	....	....	....	....	....	....	....	....	....	....	....	....	....

TABLE X.

OCCUPATION.

Jammu and Kashmir Census 1931.

District, Ilaqa, Jagir or City.	Group 79. Manufacturers of Opium. Total earners (principal occupation).		Total working dependents.		Total following occupation as subsidiary to others.		Group 80. Manufacturers of Ganja. Total earners (principal (occupation).		Total working dependents.		Total following occupation as subsidiary to others.		Group 81. Others. Total earners (principal occupation).		Total working dependents.		Total following occupation as subsidiary to others.	
	Males.	Females.	Males.	Females.	Males.	Females.	Males.	Females.	Males.	Females.	Males.	Females.	Males.	Females.	Males.	Females.	Males.	Females.
Jammu and Kashmir State ..	18	....	....	....	....	....	....	5	....	....	....	....	918	15	14	3	99	12
I. Jammu Province ..	18	....	....	....	....	....	....	5	....	....	....	....	....	....	....	....	....	....
1. Jammu District (*including city*) ..	18	....	....	....	....	....	....	5	....	....	....	....	....	....	....	....	....	....
2. Kathua " ..	....	....	....	....	....	....	....	....	....	....	....	....	....	....	....	....	....	....
3. Udhampur " ..	....	....	....	....	....	....	....	....	....	....	....	....	....	....	....	....	....	....
4. Reasi " ..	....	....	....	....	....	....	....	....	....	....	....	....	....	....	....	....	....	....
5. Mirpur " ..	....	....	....	....	....	....	....	....	....	....	....	....	....	....	....	....	....	....
6. Poonch Jagir ..	....	....	....	....	....	....	....	....	....	....	....	....	....	....	....	....	....	....
7. Chenani " ..	....	....	....	....	....	....	....	....	....	....	....	....	....	....	....	....	....	....
II. Kashmir Province ..	....	....	....	....	....	....	....	....	....	....	....	....	908	13	14	3	99	11
8. Kashmir North ..	....	....	....	....	....	....	....	....	....	....	....	....	651	8	3	....	49	7
9. Kashmir South (*including city*) ..	....	....	....	....	....	....	....	....	....	....	....	....	202	4	11	3	32	4
10. Muzaffarabad ..	....	....	....	....	....	....	....	....	....	....	....	....	55	1	....	....	18	....
III. Frontier Districts ..	....	....	....	....	....	....	....	....	....	....	....	....	10	2	....	....	....	1
11. Ladakh ..	....	....	....	....	....	....	....	....	....	....	....	....	10	2	....	....	....	1
12. Gilgit ..	....	....	....	....	....	....	....	....	....	....	....	....	....	....	....	....	....	....
13. Frontier Ilaqas ..	....	....	....	....	....	....	....	....	....	....	....	....	....	....	....	....	....	....
IV. Cities:—																		
14. Srinagar ..	....	....	....	....	....	....	....	....	....	....	....	....	....	....	....	....	....	4
15. Jammu (*excludes Ry. population*)	....	....	....	....	....	....	....	....	....	....	....	....	....	....	....	....	....	....

TABLE X.

OCCUPATION.

Jammu and Kashmir Census 1931.

District, Ilaqa, Jagir or City.	ORDER 12. Industries of dress and the toilet. TOTAL OF ORDER 12. Total earners (principal occupation). Males.	Females.	Total working dependents. Males.	Females.	Total following occupation as subsidiary to others. Males.	Females.	GROUP 82. Boot, shoe, sandal and clog makers. Total earners (principal occupation). Males.	Females.	Total working dependents. Males.	Females.	Total following occupation as subsidiary to others. Males.	Females.	GROUP 83. Tailors, milliners, dress-makers and darners. Total earners (principal occupation). Males.	Females.	Total working dependents. Males.	Females.	Total following occupation as subsidiary to others. Males.	Females.
Jammu and Kashmir State ..	25,953	2,320	732	1,571	3,928	610	2,637	188	92	197	953	229	16,514	1,877	444	1,097	1,428	287
I. Jammu Province ..	6,995	2,086	179	1,400	2,289	510	2,517	180	90	179	915	221	1,854	1,765	59	1,022	521	213
1. Jammu District (*including city*) ..	2,943	333	81	302	781	156	831	28	28	62	270	50	697	216	32	74	79	[illegible]
2. Kathua " ..	965	738	2	214	411	68	424	41	....	27	269	32	114	691	....	185	44	[illegible]
3. Udhampur " ..	549	50	21	66	279	64	167	2	....	5	104	24	258	45	18	32	117	[illegible]
4. Reasi " ..	357	738	31	22	166	57	120	64	26	15	52	38	156	672	2	6	53	[illegible]
5. Mirpur " ..	1,822	187	30	129	538	152	922	28	31	64	186	68	435	124	7	65	194	[illegible]
6. Poonch Jagir ..	332	36	5	667	104	13	43	15	5	6	30	9	188	15	....	060	32	[illegible]
7. Chenani " ..	27	4	....	....	10	....	10	2	....	....	4	....	6	2	....	....	2	....
II. Kashmir Province ..	18,814	228	519	160	1,617	99	104	7	....	18	34	7	14,548	109	353	64	892	24
8. Kashmir North ..	1,804	60	120	42	371	34	....	....	....	....	....	....	1,020	44	73	11	149	[illegible]
9. Kashmir South (*including City*) ..	16,660	148	387	47	1,152	44	....	....	....	....	....	....	13,400	60	277	42	712	[illegible]
10. Muzaffarabad ..	350	20	12	71	94	21	104	7	....	18	34	7	128	5	3	11	31	[illegible]
III. Frontier Districts ..	144	6	34	11	22	1	16	1	2	....	4	1	112	8	32	11	15	....
11. Ladakh ..	31	3	....	....	10	....	9	....	....	....	3	....	18	2	....	....	5	....
12. Gilgit ..	84	2	....	11	11	....	6	....	....	....	1	....	66	1	....	11	10	....
13. Frontier Ilaqas ..	29	1	34	....	1	1	1	1	2	....	....	1	28	....	32	....	....	....
IV. Cities.—																		
14. Srinagar ..	12,420	139	228	46	350	42	....	....	....	....	....	....	10,163	5	169	41	296	[illegible]
15. Jammu (*excludes Ry. population*)	780	86	22	94	34	27	168	13	....	3	9	9	393	13	21	....	13	....

TABLE X.

OCCUPATION.

Jammu and Kashmir Census 1931.

District, Ilaqa, Jagir or City.	Group 84. Embroiderers, hat makers and makers of other articles of wear.						Group 85. Washing and cleaning.						Group 86. Barbers, hair-dressers and wig-makers.					
	Total earners (principal occupation).		Total working dependents.		Total following occupation as subsidiary to others.		Total earners (principal occupation).		Total working dependents.		Total following occupation as subsidiary to others.		Total earners (principal occupation).		Total working dependents.		Total following occupation as subsidiary to others.	
	Males.	Females.	Males.	Females.	Males.	Females.	Males.	Females.	Males.	Females.	Males.	Females.	Males.	Females.	Males.	Females.	Males.	Females.
Jammu and Kashmir State ..	1,856	106	53	219	65	21	1,177	124	12	22	236	102	3,733	13	125	29	1,243	5
I. Jammu Province ..	12	95	....	162	4	20	726	25	6	1	217	36	1,851	9	18	29	629	4
1. Jammu District (*including City*) ..	4	66	....	158	2	19	470	8	5	1	148	23	915	4	15	....	281	1
2. Kathua " ..	....	....	....	2	....	....	124	2	1	....	30	8	303	4	1	....	67	2
3. Udhampur " ..	....	....	....	....	....	....	40	2	....	....	5	1	78	....	....	20	53	....
4. Reasi " ..	....	1	....	1	....	....	20	....	....	....	11	....	59	1	1	....	49	....
5. Mirpur " ..	6	23	....	....	2	....	45	12	....	....	23	2	412	....	1	....	133	1
6. Poonch Jagir ..	2	5	....	1	....	1	21	1	....	....	....	2	78	....	....	....	42	....
7. Chenani " ..	....	....	....	....	....	....	....	....	....	....	....	....	6	....	....	....	4	....
II. Kashmir Province ..	1,844	11	53	57	61	1	445	98	6	21	18	66	1,872	3	107	....	612	1
8. Kashmir North ..	31	3	1	13	2	....	154	13	4	18	16	29	599	....	42	....	204	....
9. Kashmir South (*including City*) ..	1,771	7	50	2	56	....	282	78	2	3	....	33	1,206	3	58	....	384	....
10. Muzaffarabad ..	42	1	2	42	3	1	9	7	....	....	2	4	67	....	7	....	24	1
III. Frontier Districts ..	....	....	....	....	....	....	6	1	....	....	1	....	10	1	....	....	2	....
11. Ladakh ..	....	....	....	....	....	....	....	1	....	....	1	....	4	....	....	....	1	....
12. Gilgit ..	....	....	....	....	....	....	6	....	....	....	....	....	6	1	....	....	....	....
13. Frontier Ilaqas ..	....	....	....	....	....	....	....	....	....	....	....	....	....	....	....	....	1	....
IV. Cities.—																		
14. Srinagar ..	1,501	7	50	2	44	....	282	78	2	3	....	33	474	1	7	....	10	....
15. Jammu (*excludes Ry. population*) ..	2	54	....	91	....	18	82	5	....	....	1	....	133	1	1	....	11	....

TABLE X.

OCCUPATION.

Jammu and Kashmir Census 1931.

District, Ilaqa, Jagir or City.	Group 87. Other industries connected with the toilet.						Order 13. Furniture Industries. Total of Order 13.						Group 88. Cabinet makers, carriage painters, etc.					
	Total earners (principal occupation).		Total working dependents.		Total following occupation as subsidiary to others.		Total earners (principal occupation).		Total working dependents.		Total following occupation as subsidiary to others.		Total earners (principal occupation).		Total working dependents.		Total following occupation as subsidiary to others.	
	Males.	Females.	Males.	Females.	Males.	Females.	Males.	Females.	Males.	Females.	Males.	Females.	Males.	Females.	Males.	Females.	Males.	Females.
Jammu and Kashmir State ..	36	12	6	7	3	16	64	11	....	4	7	7	62	10	....	4	7	7
I. Jammu Province ..	35	12	6	7	3	16	52	11	....	4	6	7	50	10	....	4	6	7
1. Jammu District (*including city*) ..	20	11	1	7	1	13	19	3	....	....	4	....	17	2	....	....	4	....
2. Kathua „ ..	....	....	....	....	1	....	8	....	....	....	....	....	8	....	....	....	....	....
3. Udhampur „ ..	6	1	3	....	....	....	5	....	....	....	1	....	5	....	....	....	1	....
4. Reasi „ ..	2	....	2	....	1	3	....	....	....	....	....	....	....	....	....	....	....	....
5. Mirpur „ ..	2	....	....	....	....	....	18	8	....	4	....	7	18	8	....	4	....	7
6. Poonch Jagir ..	....	....	....	....	....	....	2	....	....	....	1	....	2	....	....	....	1	....
7. Chenani „ ..	5	....	....	....	....	....	....	....	....	....	....	....	....	....	....	....	....	....
II. Kashmir Province ..	1	....	....	....	....	....	8	....	....	....	....	....	8	....	....	....	....	....
8. Kashmir North ..	....	....	....	....	....	....	....	....	....	....	....	....	....	....	....	....	....	....
9. Kashmir South (*including City*) ..	1	....	....	....	....	....	....	....	....	....	....	....	....	....	....	....	....	....
10. Muzaffarabad ..	....	....	....	....	....	....	8	....	....	....	....	....	8	....	....	....	....	....
III. Frontier Districts ..	....	....	....	....	....	....	4	....	....	....	1	....	4	....	....	....	1	....
11. Ladakh ..	....	....	....	....	....	....	4	....	....	....	1	....	4	....	....	....	1	....
12. Gilgit ..	....	....	....	....	....	....	....	....	....	....	....	....	....	....	....	....	....	....
13. Frontier Ilaqas ..	....	....	....	....	....	....	....	....	....	....	....	....	....	....	....	....	....	....
IV. Cities— ..																		
14. Srinagar ..	....	....	....	....	....	....	....	....	....	....	....	....	....	....	....	....	....	....
15. Jammu (*excludes Ry. population*) ..	2	....	....	....	....	....	17	1	....	....	2	....	15	....	....	....	2	....

TABLE X.

OCCUPATION.

Jammu and Kashmir Census 1931.

District, Ilaqa, Jagir or City.	Group 89. Upholsterers, tent-makers, etc.						Order 14. Building Industries. Total of Order 14.						Group 90. Lime burners, cement workers; excavators and well sinkers; stone cutters and dressers; brick layers and masons; builders (other than buildings made of bamboo or similar materials), painters, decorators of houses, tilers, plumbers, etc.					
	Total earners (principal occupation).		Total working dependents.		Total following occupation as subsidiary to others.		Total earners (principal occupation).		Total working dependents.		Total following occupation as subsidiary to others.		Total earners (principal occupation).		Total working dependents.		Total following occupation as subsidiary to others.	
	Males.	Females.	Males.	Females.	Males.	Females.	Males.	Females.	Males.	Females.	Males.	Females.	Males.	Females.	Males.	Females.	Males.	Females.
Jammu and Kashmir State ..	2	1	....	....	....	....	610	25	25	2	83	4	610	25	25	2	83	4
I. Jammu Province ..	2	1	....	....	....	....	464	25	4	....	41	4	464	25	4	....	41	4
1. Jammu District (*including city*) ..	2	1	....	....	....	....	243	24	1	....	10	4	243	24	1	....	10	4
2. Kathua " ..	....	....	....	....	....	....	75	....	....	....	10	....	75	....	....	....	10	....
3. Udhampur " ..	....	....	....	....	....	....	38	....	2	....	8	....	38	....	2	....	8	....
4. Reasi " ..	....	....	....	....	....	....	61	....	....	....	6	....	61	....	....	....	6	....
5. Mirpur " ..	....	....	....	....	....	....	24	1	....	....	5	....	24	1	....	....	5	....
6. Poonch Jagir ..	....	....	....	....	....	....	18	....	1	....	2	....	18	....	1	....	2	....
7. Chenani " ..	....	....	....	....	....	....	5	....	....	....	....	....	5	....	....	....	....	....
II. Kashmir Province ..	....	....	....	....	....	....	143	....	21	2	41	....	143	....	21	2	41	....
8. Kashmir North ..	....	....	....	....	....	....	63	....	....	1	16	....	63	....	....	1	16	....
9. Kashmir South (*including City*) ..	....	....	....	....	....	....	51	....	19	1	15	....	51	....	19	1	15	....
10. Muzaffarabad ..	....	....	....	....	....	....	29	....	2	....	10	....	29	....	2	....	10	....
III. Frontier Districts ..	....	....	....	....	....	....	3	....	....	....	1	....	3	....	....	....	1	....
11. Ladakh ..	....	....	....	....	....	....	3	....	....	....	1	....	3	....	....	....	1	....
12. Gilgit ..	....	....	....	....	....	....	....	....	....	....	....	....	....	....	....	....	....	....
13. Frontier Ilaqas ..	....	....	....	....	....	....	....	....	....	....	....	....	....	....	....	....	....	....
IV. Cities— ..																		
14. Srinagar ..	....	....	....	....	....	....	....	....	....	....	....	....	....	....	....	....	....	....
15. Jammu (*excludes Ry. population*) ..	2	1	....	....	....	....	117	23	1	....	6	4	117	23	1	....	6	4

TABLE X.

Occupation.

Jammu and Kashmir Census 1931.

District, Ilaqa, Jagir or City.	Order 15. Construction of means of transport. Total of Order 15.						Group 91. Persons engaged in making, assembling or repairing motor vehicles or cycles.						Order 16. Production and transmission of physical force. Total of Order 16.					
	Total earners (principal occupation).		Total working dependents.		Total following occupation as subsidiary to others.		Total earners (principal occupation).		Total working dependents.		Total following occupation as subsidiary to others.		Total earners (principal occupation).		Total working dependents.		Total following occupation as subsidiary to others.	
	Males.	Females.	Males.	Females.	Males.	Females.	Males.	Females.	Males.	Females.	Males.	Females.	Males.	Females.	Males.	Females.	Males.	Females.
Jammu and Kashmir State ..	8	....	....	....	....	....	8	....	....	....	....	....	53	....	....	....	8	....
I. Jammu Province ..	8	....	....	....	....	....	8	....	....	....	....	....	51	....	....	....	7	....
1. Jammu District (*including city*) ..	5	....	....	....	....	....	5	....	....	....	....	....	51	....	....	....	7	....
2. Kathua „ ..	....	....	....	....	....	....	....	....	....	....	....	....	....	....	....	....	....	....
3. Udhampur „ ..	1	....	....	....	....	....	1	....	....	....	....	....	....	....	....	....	....	....
4. Reasi „ ..	....	....	....	....	....	....	....	....	....	....	....	....	....	....	....	....	....	....
5. Mirpur „ ..	2	....	....	....	....	....	2	....	....	....	....	....	....	....	....	....	....	....
6. Poonch Jagir ..	....	....	....	....	....	....	....	....	....	....	....	....	....	....	....	....	....	....
7. Chenani „ ..	....	....	....	....	....	....	....	....	....	....	....	....	....	....	....	....	....	....
II. Kashmir Province ..	....	....	....	....	....	....	....	....	....	....	....	....	2	....	....	....	1	....
8. Kashmir North ..	....	....	....	....	....	....	....	....	....	....	....	....	....	....	....	....	....	....
9. Kashmir South (*including City*) ..	....	....	....	....	....	....	....	....	....	....	....	....	....	....	....	....	....	....
10. Muzaffarabad ..	....	....	....	....	....	....	....	....	....	....	....	....	2	....	....	....	1	....
III. Frontier Districts ..	....	....	....	....	....	....	....	....	....	....	....	....	....	....	....	....	....	....
11. Ladakh ..	....	....	....	....	....	....	....	....	....	....	....	....	....	....	....	....	....	....
12. Gilgit ..	....	....	....	....	....	....	....	....	....	....	....	....	....	....	....	....	....	....
13. Frontier Ilaqas ..	....	....	....	....	....	....	....	....	....	....	....	....	....	....	....	....	....	....
IV. Cities.—																		
14. Srinagar ..	....	....	....	....	....	....	....	....	....	....	....	....	....	....	....	....	....	....
15. Jammu (*excludes Ry. population*)	5	....	....	....	....	....	5	....	....	....	....	....	51	....	....	....	7	....

TABLE X.

OCCUPATION.

Jammu and Kashmir Census 1931.

District, Ilaqa, Jagir or City.	Group 94. Heat, light, electricity, motive power, etc. Gas works and electric light and power. Total earners (principal occupation).		Total working dependents.		Total following occupation as subsidiary to others.		Order 17. Miscellaneous and undefined industries. Total of Order 17. Total earners (principal) (occupation).		Total working dependents.		Total following occupation as subsidiary to others.		Group 95. Printers, engravers, book-binders. Total earners (principal occupation).		Total working dependents.		Total following occupation as subsidiary to others.	
	Males.	Females.	Males.	Females.	Males.	Females.	Males.	Females.	Males.	Females.	Males.	Females.	Males.	Females.	Males.	Females.	Males.	Females.
Jammu and Kashmir State ..	53	....	....	....	8	....	3,885	233	67	44	522	77	26	....	....	....	1	....
I. Jammu Province ..	51	....	....	....	7	....	1,907	217	32	42	326	68	25	....	....	....	1	....
1. Jammu District (*including city*) ..	51	....	....	....	7	....	867	117	25	3	67	21	20	....	....	....	1	....
2. Kathua „ ..	....	....	....	....	....	....	248	41	1	20	22	10	....	....	....	....	....	....
3. Udhampur „ ..	....	....	....	....	....	....	169	26	2	....	121	20	....	....	....	....	....	....
4. Reasi „ ..	....	....	....	....	....	....	123	10	4	1	18	4	....	....	....	....	....	....
5. Mirpur „ ..	....	....	....	....	....	....	392	15	....	18	73	1	....	....	....	....	....	....
6. Poonch Jagir ..	....	....	....	....	....	....	83	7	....	....	22	12	5	....	....	....	....	....
7. Chenani „ ..	....	....	....	....	....	....	25	1	....	....	3	....	....	....	....	....	....	....
II. Kashmir Province ..	2	....	....	....	1	....	1,949	14	35	2	195	9	1	....	....	....	....	....
8. Kashmir North ..	....	....	....	....	....	....	409	3	11	1	61	9	....	....	....	....	....	....
9. Kashmir South (*including city*) ..	....	....	....	....	....	....	1,488	11	22	1	116	....	....	....	....	....	....	....
10. Muzaffarabad ..	2	....	....	....	1	....	52	....	2	....	18	....	1	....	....	....	....	....
III. Frontier Districts ..	....	....	....	....	....	....	29	2	....	....	1	....	....	....	....	....	....	....
11. Ladakh ..	....	....	....	....	....	....	8	....	....	....	....	....	....	....	....	....	....	....
12. Gilgit ..	....	....	....	....	....	....	21	2	....	....	1	....	....	....	....	....	....	....
13. Frontier Ilaqas ..	....	....	....	....	....	....	....	....	....	....	....	....	....	....	....	....	....	....
IV. Cities :—																		
14. Srinagar ..	....	....	....	....	....	....	925	8	10	1	9	....	....	....	....	....	....	....
15. Jammu (*excludes Ry. population*)	51	....	....	....	7		325	66	18	....	15	....	9	....	....	....	1	....

TABLE X.

Occupation.

Jammu and Kashmir Census 1931.

District, Ilaqa, Jagir or City.	Group 96. Makers of musical instruments. Total earners (principal occupation). Males.	Females.	Total working dependents. Males.	Females.	Total following occupation as subsidiary to others. Males.	Females.	Group 97. Makers of clocks and surgical or scientific instruments, etc. Total earners (principal occupation). Males.	Females.	Total working dependents. Males.	Females.	Total following occupation as subsidiary to others. Males.	Females.	Group 98. Makers of jewellary and ornaments. Total earners (principal occupation). Males.	Females.	Total working dependents. Males.	Females.	Total following occupation as subsidiary to others. Males.	Females.
Jammu and Kashmir State ..	4	....	....	....	....	....	61	....	....	....	4	....	3,350	19	42	3	453	....
I. Jammu Province ..	3	....	....	....	....	....	23	....	....	....	....	....	1,545	9	9	1	288	....
1. Jammu District (*including City*) ..	3	....	....	....	....	....	20	....	....	....	....	....	714	2	7	....	54	....
2. Kathua ,, ..	....	....	....	....	....	....	....	....	....	....	....	....	162	....	1	....	20	....
3. Udhampur ,, ..	....	....	....	....	....	....	1	....	....	....	....	....	152	3	1	....	117	....
4. Reasi ,, ..	....	....	....	....	....	....	....	....	....	....	....	....	90	3	....	1	15	....
5. Mirpur ,, ..	....	....	....	....	....	....	....	....	....	....	....	....	338	....	....	....	59	....
6. Poonch Jagir ..	....	....	....	....	....	....	2	....	....	....	....	....	67	....	....	....	20	....
7. Chenani ,, ..	....	....	....	....	....	....	....	....	....	....	....	....	22	1	....	....	3	....
II. Kashmir Province ..	1	....	....	....	....	....	38	....	....	....	4	....	1,792	10	33	2	165	....
8. Kashmir North ..	....	....	....	....	....	....	3	....	....	....	....	....	383	1	11	1	54	....
9. Kashmir South (*including City*) ..	....	....	....	....	....	....	35	....	....	....	4	....	1,366	9	20	1	97	....
10. Muzaffarabad ..	1	....	....	....	....	....	....	....	....	....	....	....	43	....	2	....	14	....
III. Frontier Districts ..	....	....	....	....	....	....	....	....	....	....	....	....	13	....	....	....	....	....
11. Ladakh ..	....	....	....	....	....	....	....	....	....	....	....	....	8	....	....	....	....	....
12. Gilgit ..	....	....	....	....	....	....	....	....	....	....	....	....	5	....	....	....	....	....
13. Frontier Ilaqas ..	....	....	....	....	....	....	....	....	....	....	....	....	....	....	....	....	....	....
IV. Cities.—																		
14. Srinagar ..	....	....	....	....	....	....	35	....	....	....	4	....	890	8	10	1	5	....
15. Jammu (*excludes Ry. population*) ..	3	....	....	....	....	....	16	....	....	....	....	....	221	....	1	....	8	....

TABLE X.

OCCUPATION.

Jammu and Kashmir Census 1931.

District, Ilaqa, Jagir or City.	Group 99. Other miscellaneous and undefined industries (toy-making taxidermy, etc). Total earners (principal occupation). Males.	Females.	Total working dependents. Males.	Females.	Total following occupation as subsidiary to others. Males.	Females.	Group 100. Scavenging. Total earners (principal occupation). Males.	Females.	Total working dependents. Males.	Females.	Total following occupation as subsidiary to others. Males.	Females.	Sub-class IV. Transport. Total Sub-class IV. Total earners (principal occupation). Males.	Females.	Total working dependents. Males.	Females.	Total following occupation as subsidiary to others. Males.	Females.
Jammu and Kashmir State ..	43	21	....	....	12	19	396	193	25	41	52	58	8,468	455	388	74	1,817	60
I. Jammu Province ..	22	21	....	....	9	19	289	187	23	41	28	49	3,420	273	88	3	578	17
1. Jammu District (*including City*) ..	18	....	....	....	7	....	92	115	18	3	5	21	2,502	244	28	....	330	5
2. Kathua " ..	....	....	....	....	....	....	86	41	....	20	2	10	215	4	52	....	29	....
3. Udhampur " ..	....	21	....	....	....	19	16	2	1	....	4	1	224	2	1	2	95	1
4. Reasi " ..	2	....	....	....	1	....	31	7	4	....	2	4	145	13	7	1	32	....
5. Mirpur " ..	....	....	....	....	....	....	54	15	....	18	14	1	311	9	....	....	88	11
6. Poonch Jagir ..	2	....	....	....	1	....	7	7	....	....	1	12	16	....	....	....	2	....
7. Chenani " ..	....	....	....	....	....	....	3	....	....	....	....	....	7	1	....	....	2	....
II. Kashmir Province ..	26	....	....	....	3	....	91	4	2	....	23	9	4,935	182	300	71	1,210	43
8. Kashmir North ..	....	....	....	....	....	....	23	2	....	....	7	9	1,084	25	43	....	493	4
9. Kashmir South (*including City*) ..	26	....	....	....	3	....	61	2	2	....	12	....	3,774	156	256	71	679	39
10. Muzaffarabad ..	....	....	....	....	....	....	7	....	....	....	4	....	77	1	1	....	38	....
III. Frontier Districts ..	....	....	....	....	....	....	16	2	....	....	1	....	118	....	....	....	29	....
11. Ladakh ..	....	....	....	....	....	....	....	....	....	....	....	....	55	....	....	....	11	....
12. Gilgit ..	....	....	....	....	....	....	16	2	....	....	1	....	52	....	....	....	18	....
13. Frontier Ilaqas ..	....	....	....	....	....	....	....	....	....	....	....	....	6	....	....	....	....	....
IV. Cities—																		
14. Srinagar ..	....	....	....	....	....	....	....	....	....	....	....	....	2,126	42	124	60	231	8
15. Jammu (*excludes Ry. population*) ..	13	....	....	....	6	....	63	66	17	....	....	....	710	....	....	....	32	....

TABLE X.

OCCUPATION.

Jammu and Kashmr Census 1931.

District, Ilaqa, Jagir or City.	Order 18. Transport by air. Total of Order 18.						Group 101. Persons concerned with aerodromes and aeroplanes.						Order 19. Transport by water. Total of Order 19.					
	Total earners (principal occupation).		Total working dependents.		Total following occupation as subsidiary to others.		Total earners (principal occupation).		Total working dependents.		Total following occupation as subsidiary to others.		Total earners (principal occupation).		Total working dependents.		Total following occupation as subsidiary to others.	
	Males.	Females.	Males.	Females.	Males.	Females.	Males.	Females.	Males.	Females.	Males.	Females.	Males.	Females.	Males.	Females.	Males.	Females.
Jammu and Kashmir State ..	4	....	....	....	....	....	4	....	....	....	....	....	3,743	184	221	71	1,152	42
I. Jammu Province ..	4	....	....	....	....	....	4	....	....	....	....	....	508	4	7	....	136	....
1. Jammu District (*including city*) ..	4	....	....	....	....	....	4	....	....	....	....	....	311	....	....	....	33	....
2. Kathua ,, ..	....	....	....	....	....	....	....	....	....	....	....	....	35	4	....	....	16	....
3. Udhampur ,, ..	....	....	....	....	....	....	....	....	....	....	....	....	38	....	....	....	31	....
4. Reasi ,, ..	....	....	....	....	....	....	....	....	....	....	....	....	17	....	7	....	3	....
5. Mirpur ,, ..	....	....	....	....	....	....	....	....	....	....	....	....	106	....	....	....	51	....
6. Poonch Jagir ..	....	....	....	....	....	....	....	....	....	....	....	....	1	....	....	....	2	....
7. Chenani ,, ..	....	....	....	....	....	....	....	....	....	....	....	....	....	....	....	....	....	....
II. Kashmir Province ..	....	....	....	....	....	....	....	....	....	....	....	....	3,235	180	214	71	1,016	42
8. Kashmir North ..	....	....	....	....	....	....	....	....	....	....	....	....	735	25	28	....	433	4
9. Kashmir South (*including city*) ..	....	....	....	....	....	....	....	....	....	....	....	....	2,500	155	186	71	583	38
10. Muzaffarabad ..	....	....	....	....	....	....	....	....	....	....	....	....	....	....	....	....	....	....
III. Frontier Districts ..	....	....	....	....	....	....	....	....	....	....	....	....	....	....	....	....	....	....
11. Ladakh ..	....	....	....	....	....	....	....	....	....	....	....	....	....	....	....	....	....	....
12. Gilgit ..	....	....	....	....	....	....	....	....	....	....	....	....	....	....	....	....	....	....
13. Frontier Ilaqas ..	....	....	....	....	....	....	....	....	....	....	....	....	....	....	....	....	....	....
IV. Cities.—																		
14. Srinagar ..	....	....	....	....	....	....	....	....	....	....	....	....	1,301	41	122	60	218	7
15. Jammu (*excludes Ry. population*) ..	....	....	....	....	....	....	....	....	....	....	....	....	2	....	....	....	....	....

TABLE X.

OCCUPATION.

Jammu and Kashmir Census 1931.

District, Ilaqa, Jagir or City.	Group 102. Ship-owners, Boat-owners and their employees, officers, mariners, etc., ship brokers, boatmen and towmen. Total earners (principal occupation). Males.	Females.	Total working dependents. Males.	Females.	Total following occupation as subsidiary to others. Males.	Females.	Group 103. Persons (other than labourers) employed in harbours, docks, rivers and canals, including pilots. Total earners (principal occupation). Males.	Females.	Total working dependents. Males.	Females.	Total following occupation as subsidiary to others. Males.	Females.	Group 104. Labourers employed on harbours, docks, rivers and canals. Total earners (principal occupation). Males.	Females.	Total working dependents. Males.	Females.	Total following occupation as subsidiary to others. Males.	Females.
Jammu and Kashmir State ..	3,098	180	208	71	1,024	42	236	....	....	....	75	....	409	4	13	....	53	....
I. Jammu Province ..	125	....	7	....	11	....	233	....	....	....	75	....	150	4	....	....	50	....
1. Jammu District (*including City*) ..	100	....	....	....	6	....	94	....	....	....	15	....	117	....	....	....	12	....
2. Kathua " ..	4	....	....	....	4	....	18	....	....	....	4	....	13	4	....	....	8	....
3. Udhampur " ..	5	....	....	....	....	....	13	....	....	....	1	....	20	....	....	....	30	....
4. Reasi " ..	11	....	7	....	....	....	6	....	....	....	3	....	....	....	....	....	....	....
5. Mirpur "	5	....	....	....	1	....	101	....	....	....	50	....	....	....	....	....	....	....
6. Poonch Jagir ..	....	....	....	....	....	....	1	....	....	....	2	....	....	....	....	....	....	....
7. Chenani " ..	....	....	....	....	....	....	....	....	....	....	....	....	....	....	....	....	....	....
II. Kashmir Province ..	2,973	180	201	71	1,013	42	3	....	....	....	....	....	259	....	13	....	3	....
8. Kashmir North ..	474	25	15	....	430	4	....	....	....	....	....	....	....	....	....	....	....	....
9. Kashmir South (*including City*) ..	2,499	155	186	71	583	38	1	....	....	....	....	....	....	....	....	....	....	....
10. Muzaffarabad ..	....	....	....	....	....	....	2	....	....	....	....	....	259	....	13	....	3	....
III. Frontier Districts ..	....	....	....	....	....	....	....	....	....	....	....	....	....	....	....	....	....	....
11. Ladakh ..	....	....	....	....	....	....	....	....	....	....	....	....	....	....	....	....	....	....
12. Gilgit ..	....	....	....	....	....	....	....	....	....	....	....	....	....	....	....	....	....	....
13. Frontier Ilaqas ..	....	....	....	....	....	....	....	....	....	....	....	....	....	....	....	....	....	....
IV. Cities.—																		
14. Srinagar ..	1,301	41	122	60	218	7	....	....	....	....	....	....	....	....	....	....	....	....
15. Jammu (*excludes Ry. population*) ..	2	....	....	....	....	....	....	....	....	....	....	....	....	....	....	....	....	....

TABLE X.

Occupation.

Jammu and Kashmir Census 1931.

District, Ilaqa, Jagir or City.	Order 20. Transport by Road. Total of Order 20.						Group 105. Persons (other than labourers) employed on the construction and maintenance of roads and bridges.						Group 106. Labourers employed on roads and bridges.					
	Total earners (principal occupation).		Total working dependents.		Total following occupation as subsidiary to others.		Total earners (principal occupation.)		Total working dependents.		Total following occupation as subsidiary to others.		Total earners (principal occupation).		Total working dependents.		Total following occupation as subsidiary to others.	
	Males.	Females.	Males.	Females.	Males.	Females.	Males.	Females.	Males.	Females.	Males.	Females.	Males.	Females.	Males.	Females.	Males.	Females.
Jammu and Kashmir State ..	3,828	270	162	1	528	18	571	2	....	....	38	....	1,419	242	82	....	186	4
I. Jammu Province ..	2,637	268	80	1	391	17	571	2	....	....	38	....	633	240	1	....	58	4
1. Jammu District (*including City*) ..	2,027	244	27	....	276	5	555	....	....	....	38	....	524	238	....	....	30	4
2. Kathua " ..	140	....	52	....	11	....	....	....	....	....	....	....	6	....	....	....	4	....
3. Udhampur " ..	131	1	1	....	37	1	....	....	....	....	....	....	97	....	1	....	24	....
4. Reasi " ..	128	13	....	1	29	....	1	2	....	....	....	....	6	1	....	....	....	....
5. Mirpur " ..	190	9	....	....	36	11	1	....	....	....	....	....	....	....	....	....	....	....
6. Poonch Jagir ..	14	....	....	....	....	....	12	....	....	....	....	....	....	....	....	....	....	....
7. Chenani " ..	7	1	....	....	2	....	2	....	....	....	....	....	....	1	....	....	....	....
II. Kashmir Province ..	1,191	2	82	....	137	1	....	....	....	....	....	....	786	2	81	....	128	....
8. Kashmir North ..	238	....	12	....	35	....	....	....	....	....	....	....	238	....	12	....	35	....
9. Kashmir South (*including City*)	908	1	69	....	82	1	....	....	....	....	....	....	505	1	68	....	73	....
10. Muzaffarabad ..	45	1	1	....	20	....	....	....	....	....	....	....	43	1	1	....	20	....
III. Frontier Districts ..	....	....	....	....	....	....	....	....	....	....	....	....	....	....	....	....	....	....
11. Ladakh ..	....	....	....	....	....	....	....	....	....	....	....	....	....	....	....	....	....	....
12. Gilgit ..	....	....	....	....	....	....	....	....	....	....	....	....	....	....	....	....	....	....
13. Frontier Ilaqas ..	....	....	....	....	....	....	....	....	....	....	....	....	....	....	....	....	....	....
IV. Cities—																		
14. Srinagar ..	528	1	2	....	10	1	....	....	....	....	....	....	125	1	1	....	1	....
15. Jammu (*excludes Ry. population*)	641	....	....	....	23	....	174	....	....	....	6	....	174	....	....	....	2	....

TABLE X.

OCCUPATION.

Jammu and Kashmir Census 1931.

District, Ilaqa, Jagir or City.	GROUP 107. Owners, managers and employees (excluding personal servants) connected with mechanically driven vehicles (including trams).						GROUP 108. Owners, managers and employees (excluding personal servants) connected with other vehicles.						GROUP 110. Pack elephant, camel, mules, ass and bullock owners and drivers.					
	Total earners (principal occupation).		Total working dependents.		Total following occupation as subsidiary to others.		Total earners (principal occupation).		Total working dependents.		Total following occupation as subsidiary to others.		Total earners (principal occupation).		Total working dependents.		Total following occupation as subsidiary to others.	
	Males.	Females.	Males.	Females.	Males.	Females.	Males.	Females.	Males.	Females.	Males.	Females.	Males.	Females.	Males.	Females.	Males.	Females.
Jammu and Kashmir State ..	2	....	....	....	....	....	578	....	1	....	23	1	1,257	26	79	1	280	13
I. Jammu Province ..	....	....	....	....	....	....	175	....	....	....	14	....	1,257	26	79	1	280	13
1. Jammu District (*including City*) ..	....	....	....	....	....	....	175	....	....	....	14	....	772	6	27	....	193	1
2. Kathua „ ..	....	....	....	....	....	....	....	....	....	....	....	....	134	....	52	....	7	....
3. Udhampur „ ..	....	....	....	....	....	....	....	....	....	....	....	....	34	1	....	....	13	1
4. Reasi „ ..	....	....	....	....	....	....	....	....	....	....	....	....	121	10	....	1	29	....
5. Mirpur „ ..	....	....	....	....	....	....	....	....	....	....	....	....	189	9	....	....	36	11
6. Poonch Jagir ..	....	....	....	....	....	....	....	....	....	....	....	....	2	....	....	....	....	....
7. Chenani „ ..	....	....	....	....	....	....	....	....	....	....	....	....	5	....	....	....	2	....
II. Kashmir Province ..	2	....	....	....	....	....	403	....	1	....	9	1	....	....	....	....	....	....
8. Kashmir North ..	....	....	....	....	....	....	....	....	....	....	....	....	....	....	....	....	....	....
9. Kashmir South (*including City*)	....	....	....	....	....	....	403	....	1	....	9	1	....	....	....	....	....	....
10. Muzaffarabad ..	2	....	....	....	....	....	....	....	....	....	....	....	....	....	....	....	....	....
III. Frontier Districts ..	....	....	....	....	....	....	....	....	....	....	....	....	....	....	....	....	....	....
11. Ladakh ..	....	....	....	....	....	....	....	....	....	....	....	....	....	....	....	....	....	....
12. Gilgit ..	....	....	....	....	....	....	....	....	....	....	....	....	....	....	....	....	....	....
13. Frontier Ilaqas ..	....	....	....	....	....	....	....	....	....	....	....	....	....	....	....	....	....	....
IV. Cities—																		
14. Srinagar ..	....	....	....	....	....	....	403	....	1	....	9	1	....	....	....	....	....	....
15. Jammu (*excludes Ry. population*)	....	....	....	....	....	....	175	....	....	....	14	....	118	....	....	....	....	....

TABLE X.

OCCUPATION.

Jammu and Kashmir Census 1931.

District, Ilaqa, Jagir or city.	Group 111.						Order 21.						Group 112.					
	Porters and messengers.						Transport by rail. Total of Order 21.						Railway employees of all kinds other than coolies.					
	Total earners (principal occupation).		Total working dependents.		Total following occupation as subsidiary to others.		Total earners (principal occupation).		Total working dependents.		Total following occupation as subsidiary to others.		Total earners (principal occupation).		Total working dependents.		Total following occupation as subsidiary to others.	
	Males.	Females.	Males.	Females.	Males.	Females.	Males.	Females.	Males.	Females.	Males.	Females.	Males.	Females.	Males.	Females.	Males.	Females.
Jammu and Kashmir State	1	....	....	....	1	....	52	1	1	2	25	....	31	1	1	2	21	....
I. Jammu Province ..	1	....	....	....	1	....	51	1	1	2	9	....	30	1	1	2	5	....
1. Jammu District (*including city*) ..	1	....	....	....	1	....	44	....	1	....	8	....	27	....	1	....	4	....
2. Kathua „ ..	....	....	....	....	....	....	2	....	....	....	....	....	2	....	....	....	....	....
3. Udhampur „ ..	....	....	....	....	....	....	....	1	....	2	....	....	....	1	....	2	....	....
4. Reasi „ ..	....	....	....	....	....	....	....	....	....	....	....	....	....	....	....	....	....	....
5. Mirpur „ ..	....	....	....	....	....	....	4	....	....	....	1	....	....	....	....	....	1	....
6. Poonch Jagir ..	....	....	....	....	....	....	1	....	....	....	....	....	1	....	....	....	....	....
7. Chenani „ ..	....	....	....	....	....	....	....	....	....	....	....	....	....	....	....	....	....	....
II. Kashmir Province ..	....	....	....	....	....	....	1	....	....	....	16	....	1	....	....	....	16	....
8. Kashmir North ..	....	....	....	....	....	....	....	....	....	....	....	....	....	....	....	....	....	....
9. Kashmir South (*including city*) ..	....	....	....	....	....	....	....	....	....	....	....	....	....	....	....	....	....	....
10. Muzaffarabad ..	....	....	....	....	....	....	1	....	....	....	16	....	1	....	....	....	16	....
III. Frontier Districts ..	....	....	....	....	....	....	....	....	....	....	....	....	....	....	....	....	....	....
11. Ladakh ..	....	....	....	....	....	....	....	....	....	....	....	....	....	....	....	....	....	....
12. Gilgit ..	....	....	....	....	....	....	....	....	....	....	....	....	....	....	....	....	....	....
13. Frontier Ilaqas ..	....	....	....	....	....	....	....	....	....	....	....	....	....	....	....	....	....	....
IV. Cities.—																		
14. Srinagar ..	....	....	....	....	....	....	....	....	....	....	....	....	....	....	....	....	....	....
15. Jammu (*excludes Ry. population*) ..	....	....	....	....	1	....	3	....	....	....	....	....	3	....	....	....	....	....

TABLE X.

OCCUPATION.

Jammu and Kashmir Census 1931.

District, Ilaqa, Jagir or City.	GROUP 113. Labourers employed on railway construction and maintenance and coolies and porters employed on railway premises.						ORDER 22. Post Office, Telegraph and Telephone services. TOTAL OF ORDER 22.						GROUP 114. Post-office, Telegraph and Telephone services.					
	Total earners (principal occupation).		Total working dependents.		Total following occupation as subsidiary to others.		Total earners (principal occupation).		Total working dependents.		Total following occupation as subsidiary to others.		Total earners (principal occupation).		Total working dependents.		Total following occupation as subsidiary to others.	
	Males.	Females.	Males.	Females.	Males.	Females.	Males.	Females.	Males.	Females.	Males.	Females.	Males.	Females.	Males.	Females.	Males.	Females.
Jammu and Kashmir State ..	21	....	....	....	4	....	841	....	4	....	112	....	841	....	4	....	112	....
I. Jammu Province ..	21	....	....	....	4	....	220	....	....	....	42	....	220	....	....	....	42	....
1. Jammu District (*including City*) ..	17	....	....	....	4	....	116	....	....	....	13	....	116	....	....	....	13	....
2. Kathua ,, ..		....	....	....	....	....	38	....	....	....	2	....	38	....	....	....	2	....
3. Udhampur ,, ..	....	....	....	....	....	....	55	....	....	....	27	....	55	....	....	....	27	....
4. Reasi ,, ..	....	....	....	....	....	....	....	....	....	....	....	....	....	....	....	....	....	....
5. Mirpur ,, ..	4	....	....	....	....	....	11	....	....	....	....	....	11	....	....	....	....	....
6. Poonch Jagir ..	....	....	....	....	....	....	....	....	....	....	....	....	....	....	....	....	....	....
7. Chenani ,, ..	....	....	....	....	....	....	....	....	....	....	....	....	....	....	....	....	....	....
II. Kashmir Province ..	....	....	....	....	....	....	508	....	4	....	41	....	508	....	4	....	41	....
8. Kashmir North ..	....	....	....	....	....	....	111	....	3	....	25	....	111	....	3	....	25	....
9. Kashmir South (*including City*) ..	....	....	....	....	....	....	366	....	1	....	14	....	366	....	1	....	14	....
10. Muzaffarabad ..	....	....	....	....	....	....	31	....	....	....	2	....	31	....	....	....	2	....
III. Frontier Districts ..	....	....	....	....	....	....	118	....	....	....	29	....	118	....	....	....	29	....
11. Ladakh ..	....	....	....	....	....	....	55	....	....	....	11	....	55	....	....	....	11	....
12. Gilgit ..	....	....	....	....	....	....	52	....	....	....	18	....	52	....	....	....	18	....
13. Frontier Ilaqas ..	....	....	....	....	....	....	6	....	....	....	....	....	6	....	....	....	....	....
IV. Cities—																		
14. Srinagar ..	....	....	....	....	....	....	297	....	....	....	3	....	297	....	....	....	3	....
15. Jammu (*excludes Ry. population*) ..	....	....	....	....	....	....	64	....	....	....	9	....	64	....	....	....	9	....

TABLE X.

OCCUPATION.

Jammu and Kashmir Census 1931.

District, Ilaqa, Jagir or City.	Sub-class V. Trade. Total of Sub-class V. Total earners (principal occupation). Males.	Females.	Total working dependents. Males.	Females.	Total following occupation as subsidiary to others. Males.	Females.	Order 23. Banks, establishments of credit, exchange and insurance. Total of Order 23. Total earners (principal occupation). Males.	Females.	Total working dependents. Males.	Females.	Total following occupation as subsidiary to others. Males.	Females.	Group 115. Bank managers, money lenders, exchange and insurance agents, money changers and brokers and their employees. Total earners (principal occupation). Males.	Females.	Total working dependents. Males.	Females.	Total following occupation as subsidiary to others. Males.	Females.
Jammu and Kashmir State ..	26,099	3,694	583	871	7,321	1,292	2,026	128	39	....	1,039	70	2,026	128	39	....	1,039	70
I. Jammu Province ..	12,364	3,415	221	753	5,179	733	1,911	127	37	....	1,003	59	1,911	127	37	....	1,003	59
1. Jammu District (*including City*) ..	5,081	238	54	27	2,540	230	538	13	7	....	187	8	538	13	7	....	187	8
2. Kathua " ..	1,833	527	4	630	659	130	241	9	1	....	187	7	241	9	1	....	187	7
3. Udhampur " ..	1,644	143	105	52	688	143	420	21	13	....	206	8	420	21	13	....	206	8
4. Reasi " ..	870	2,389	41	....	434	149	303	73	12	....	192	22	303	73	12	....	192	22
5. Mirpur " ..	1,483	78	10	3	541	77	207	9	4	....	197	13	207	9	4	....	197	13
6. Poonch Jagir ..	760	22	7	37	297	4	199	2	....	....	34	1	199	2	....	....	34	1
7. Chenani " ..	93	18	....	4	20	....	3	....	....	....	....	....	3	....	....	....	....	....
II. Kashmir Province ..	12,929	251	330	117	2,059	530	115	1	2	....	36	11	115	1	2	....	36	11
8. Kashmir North ..	3,915	71	69	87	613	143	14	....	....	....	2	....	14	....	....	....	2	....
9. Kashmir South (*including City*) ..	8,143	177	255	27	1,257	384	101	1	2	....	34	11	101	1	2	....	34	11
10. Muzaffarabad	871	3	6	3	189	3	....	....	....	....	....	....	....	....	....	....	....	....
III. Frontier Districts ..	806	28	32	1	83	29	....	....	....	....	....	....	....	....	....	....	....	....
11. Ladakh ..	605	28	1	....	67	6	....	....	....	....	....	....	....	....	....	....	....	....
12. Gilgit ..	164	....	....	....	2	23	....	....	....	....	....	....	....	....	....	....	....	....
13. Frontier Ilaqas ..	37	....	31	1	14	....	....	....	....	....	....	....	....	....	....	....	....	....
IV. Cities—																		
14. Srinagar ..	3,923	146	39	25	151	36	....	....	....	....	....	....	....	....	....	....	....	....
15. Jammu (*excludes Ry. population*) ..	2,043	24	17	10	191	7	175	7	1	....	31	4	175	7	1	....	31	4

TABLE X.

OCCUPATION.

Jammu and Kashmir Census 1931.

District, Ilaqa, Jagir or City.	Order 24.						Group 116.						Order 25.					
	Brokerage Commission and Export.						*Brokers, commission agents, commercial travellers, warehouse owners and employees.*						*Trade in Textiles.*					
	TOTAL OF ORDER 24.												TOTAL OF ORDER 25.					
	Total earners (principal occupation).		Total working dependents.		Total following occupation as subsidiary to others.		Total earners (principal occupation).		Total working dependents.		Total following occupation as subsidiary to others.		Total earners (principal occupation).		Total working dependents.		Total following occupation as subsidiary to others.	
	Males.	Females.	Males.	Females.	Males.	Females.	Males.	Females.	Males.	Females.	Males.	Females.	Males.	Females.	Males.	Females.	Males.	Females.
Jammu and Kashmir State ..	81	1	....	....	10	....	81	1	....	....	10	....	2,046	21	25	....	396	10
I. Jammu Province ..	42	1	....	....	4	....	42	1	....	....	4	....	899	8	16	....	280	6
1. Jammu District (*including city*) ..	23	1	....	....	1	....	23	1	....	....	1	....	453	....	6	....	76	....
2. Kathua " ..	2	....	....	....	1	....	2	....	....	....	1	....	40	....	....	....	28	....
3. Udhampur " ..	16	....	....	....	2	....	16	....	....	....	2	....	204	1	3	....	121	....
4. Reasi " ..	....	....	....	....	....	....	....	....	....	....	....	....	41	5	7	....	18	....
5. Mirpur " ..	1	....	....	....	....	....	1	....	....	....	....	....	114	1	....	....	17	6
6. Poonch Jagir ..	....	....	....	....	....	....	....	....	....	....	....	....	26	1	....	....	19	....
7. Chenani " ..	....	....	....	....	....	....	....	....	....	....	....	....	12	....	....	....	1	....
II. Kashmir Province ..	39	....	....	....	6	....	39	....	....	....	6	....	1,122	12	8	....	91	4
8. Kashmir North ..	27	....	....	....	4	....	27	....	....	....	4	....	165	6	1	....	11	3
9. Kashmir South (*including city*) ..	4	....	....	....	....	....	4	....	....	....	....	....	775	5	7	....	57	1
10. Muzaffarabad ..	8	....	....	....	2	....	8	....	....	....	2	....	182	1	....	....	23	....
III. Frontier Districts ..	....	....	....	....	....	....	....	....	....	....	....	....	24	1	1	....	25	....
11. Ladakh ..	....	....	....	....	....	....	....	....	....	....	....	....	24	1	1	....	25	....
12. Gilgit ..	....	....	....	....	....	....	....	....	....	....	....	....	....	....	....	....	....	....
13. Frontier Ilaqas ..	....	....	....	....	....	....	....	....	....	....	....	....	....	....	....	....	....	....
IV. Cities :—																		
14. Srinagar ..	....	....	....	....	....	....	....	....	....	....	....	....	478	5	7	....	27	1
15. Jammu (*excludes Ry. population*)	19	1	....	....	1	....	19	1	....	....	1	....	182	....	....	....	19	....

TABLE X.

OCCUPATION.

Jammu and Kashmir Census 1931.

District, Ilaqa, Jagir or City.	Group 117. Trade in piece-goods, wool, cotton, silk, hair and other textiles.						Order 26. Trade in skins, leather and furs. Total of Order 26.						Group 118. Trade in skins, leather, furs, feathers, horn etc. and the articles made from these.					
	Total earners (principal occupation).		Total working dependents.		Total following occupation as subsidiary to others.		Total earners (principal occupation).		Total working dependents.		Total following occupation as subsidiary to others.		Total earners (principal occupation).		Total working dependents.		Total following occupation as subsidiary to others.	
	Males.	Females.	Males.	Females.	Males.	Females.	Males.	Females.	Males.	Females.	Males.	Females.	Males.	Females.	Males.	Females.	Males.	Females.
Jammu and Kashmir State ..	2,045	21	25	....	396	10	417	5	....	....	55	1	417	5	....	....	55	1
I. Jammu Province ..	899	8	16	....	280	6	25	5	....	....	28	....	25	5	....	....	28	....
1. Jammu District (*including city*) ..	453	....	6	....	76	....	4	5	....	....	1	....	4	5	....	....	1	....
2. Kathua " ..	49	....	....	....	28	....	15	....	....	....	25	....	15	....	....	....	25	....
3. Udhampur " ..	204	1	3	....	121	....	3	....	....	....	....	....	3	....	....	....	....	....
4. Reasi " ..	41	5	7	....	18	....	....	....	....	....	2	....	....	....	....	....	2	....
5. Mirpur " ..	114	1	....	....	17	6	2	....	....	....	....	....	2	....	....	....	....	....
6. Poonch Jagir ..	26	1	....	....	19	....	....	....	....	....	....	....	....	....	....	....	....	....
7. Chenani " ..	12	....	....	....	1	....	1	....	....	....	....	....	1	....	....	....	....	....
II. Kashmir Province ..	1,122	12	8	....	91	4	33	....	....	....	9	....	33	....	....	....	9	....
8. Kashmir North ..	165	6	1	....	11	3	4	....	....	....	4	....	4	....	....	....	4	....
9. Kashmir South (*including City*) ..	775	5	7	....	57	1	29	....	....	....	5	....	29	....	....	....	5	....
10. Muzaffarabad ..	182	1	....	....	23	....	....	....	....	....	....	....	....	....	....	....	....	....
III. Frontier Districts ..	24	1	1	....	25	....	359	....	....	....	18	1	359	....	....	....	18	1
11. Ladakh ..	24	1	1	....	25	....	355	....	....	....	18	1	355	....	....	....	18	1
12. Gilgit ..	....	....	....	....	....	....	4	....	....	....	....	....	4	....	....	....	....	....
13. Frontier Ilaqas ..	....	....	....	....	....	....	....	....	....	....	....	....	....	....	....	....	....	....
IV. Cities— ..																		
14. Srinagar ..	478	5	7	....	27	1	....	....	....	....	....	....	....	....	....	....	....	....
15. Jammu (*excludes Ry. population*) ..	182	....	....	....	19	....	....	....	....	....	....	....	....	....	....	....	....	....

TABLE X.

OCCUPATION.

Jammu and Kashmir Census 1931.

District, Ilaqa, Jagir or City.	Order 27. Trade in wood. Total of Order 27.						Group 119. Trade in wood (not in fire wood).						Group 121. Trade in bamboos and canes.					
	Total earners (principal occupation).		Total working dependents.		Total following occupation as subsidiary to others.		Total earners (principal occupation).		Total working dependents.		Total following occupation as subsidiary to others.		Total earners (principal occupation).		Total working dependents.		Total following occupation as subsidiary to others.	
	Males.	Females.	Males.	Females.	Males.	Females.	Males.	Females.	Males.	Females.	Males.	Females.	Males.	Females.	Males.	Females.	Males.	Females.
Jammu and Kashmir State ..	662	89	3	8	149	96	505	65	3	4	89	40	....	1	....	....	....	1
I. Jammu Province ..	287	87	1	8	98	89	132	63	1	4	38	33	....	1	....	....	....	1
1. Jammu District (*including city*) ..	156	2	....	....	53	....	28	1	....	....	4	....	....	....	....	....	....	....
2. Kathua " ..	40	44	....	4	9	31	38	44	....	4	4	29	....	....	....	....	....	....
3. Udhampur " ..	17	1	1	....	10	1	17	....	1	....	10	....	....	1	....	....	....	1
4. Reasi " ..	72	28	....	....	22	57	47	18	....	....	16	4	....	....	....	....	....	....
5. Mirpur " ..	1	....	....	....	3	....	1	....	....	....	3	....	....	....	....	....	....	....
6. Poonch Jagir ..	....	....	....	....	1	....	....	....	....	....	1	....	....	....	....	....	....	....
7. Chenani " ..	1	12	....	4	....	....	1	....	....	....	....	....	....	....	....	....	....	....
II. Kashmir Province ..	375	2	2	....	51	7	373	2	2	....	51	7	....	....	....	....	....	....
8. Kashmir North ..	2	....	....	....	....	....	....	....	....	....	....	....	....	....	....	....	....	....
9. Kashmir South (*including city*) ..	371	2	2	....	50	7	371	2	2	....	50	7	....	....	....	....	....	....
10. Muzaffarabad ..	2	....	....	....	1	....	2	....	....	....	1	....	....	....	....	....	....	....
III. Frontier Districts ..	....	....	....	....	....	....	....	....	....	....	....	....	....	....	....	....	....	....
11. Ladakh ..	....	....	....	....	....	....	....	....	....	....	....	....	....	....	....	....	....	....
12. Gilgit ..	....	....	....	....	....	....	....	....	....	....	....	....	....	....	....	....	....	....
13. Frontier Ilaqas ..	....	....	....	....	....	....	....	....	....	....	....	....	....	....	....	....	....	....
IV. Cities—																		
14. Srinagar ..	283	2	2	....	6	....	283	2	2	....	6	....	....	....	....	....	....	....
15. Jammu (*excludes Ry. population*) ..	22	1	....	....	2	....	17	1	....	....	2	....	....	....	....	....	....	....

TABLE X.

OCCUPATION.

Jammu and Kashmir Census 1931.

District, Ilaqa, Jagir or City.	Group 122. Trade in thatchers and other forest produce. Total earners (principal occupation). Males.	Females.	Total working dependents. Males.	Females.	Total following occupation as subsidiary to others. Males.	Females.	Order 28. Trade in metals. Total of Order 28. Total earners (principal occupation). Males.	Females.	Total working dependents. Males.	Females.	Total following occupation as subsidiary to others. Males.	Females.	Group 98. Trade in metals, machinery, knives, tools, etc. Total earners (principal occupation). Males.	Females	Total working dependents. Males.	Females.	Total following occupation as subsidiary to others. Males.	Females.
Jammu and Kashmir State ..	157	23	....	4	60	55	19	....	....	....	....	....	19	....	....	....	....	....
I. Jammu Province ..	155	23	....	4	60	55	17	....	....	....	....	....	17	....	....	....	....	....
1. Jammu District (*including City*) ..	128	1	....	....	49	....	17	....	....	....	....	....	17	....	....	....	....	....
2. Kathua „ ..	2	....	....	....	5	2	....	....	....	....	....	....	....	....	....	....	....	....
3. Udhampur „ ..	....	....	....	....	....	....	....	....	....	....	....	....	....	....	....	....	....	....
4. Reasi „ ..	25	10	....	....	6	53	....	....	....	....	....	....	....	....	....	....	....	....
5. Mirpur „ ..	....	....	....	....	....	....	....	....	....	....	....	....	....	....	....	....	....	....
6. Poonch Jagir ..	....	....	....	....	....	....	....	....	....	....	....	....	....	....	....	....	....	....
7. Chenani „ ..	....	12	....	4	....	....	....	....	....	....	....	....	....	....	....	....	....	....
II. Kashmir Province ..	2	....	....	....	....	....	2	....	....	....	....	....	2	....	....	....	....	....
8. Kashmir North ..	2	....	....	....	....	....	1	....	....	....	....	....	1	....	....	....	....	....
9. Kashmir South (*including City*) ..	....	....	....	....	....	....	....	....	....	....	....	....	....	....	....	....	....	....
10. Muzaffarabad ..	....	....	....	....	....	....	1	....	....	....	....	....	1	....	....	....	....	....
III. Frontier Districts ..	....	....	....	....	....	....	....	....	....	....	....	....	....	....	....	....	....	....
11. Ladakh ..	....	....	....	....	....	....	....	....	....	....	....	....	....	....	....	....	....	....
12. Gilgit ..	....	....	....	....	....	....	....	....	....	....	....	....	....	....	....	....	....	....
13. Frontier Ilaqas ..	....	....	....	....	....	....	....	....	....	....	....	....	....	....	....	....	....	....
IV. Cities—																		
14. Srinagar ..	....	....	....	....	....	....	....	....	....	....	....	....	....	....	....	....	....	....
15. Jammu (*excludes Ry. population*) ..	5	....	....	....	....	....	17	....	....	....	....	....	17	....	....	....	....	....

TABLE X.

Occupation.

Jammu and Kashmir Census 1931.

District, Ilaqa, Jagir or City.	Group 125. Drugs, dyes, paints, petroleum, explosives, etc.						Order 31. Hotels, cafes, restaurants, etc. Total of Order 31.						Group 126. Venders of wine, liquors, aerated waters and ice.					
	Total earners (principal occupation).		Total working dependents.		Total following occupation as subsidiary to others.		Total earners (principal occupation).		Total working dependents.		Total following occupation as subsidiary to others.		Total earners (principal occupation).		Total working dependents.		Total following occupation as subsidiary to others.	
	Males.	Females.	Males.	Females.	Males.	Females.	Males.	Females.	Males.	Females.	Males.	Females.	Males.	Females.	Males.	Females.	Males.	Females.
Jammu and Kashmir State ..	29	2	....	....	20	3	1,494	112	15	57	86	25	86	....	....	1	6	....
I. Jammu Province ..	26	2	....	....	20	3	611	24	5	39	57	4	42	....	....	....	4	....
1. Jammu District (*including City*) ..	7	....	....	....	....	2	411	7	1	3	22	1	22	....	....	....	2	....
2. Kathua „ ..	12	....	....	....	12	....	108	2	....	....	17	1	....	....	....	....	....	....
3. Udhampur „ ..	7	....	....	....	8	1	58	2	....	....	15	....	14	....	....	....	2	....
4. Reasi „ ..	....	2	....	....	....	....	19	6	....	....	1	2	1	....	....	....	....	....
5. Mirpur „ ..	....	....	....	....	....	....	6	3	....	....	....	....	....	....	....	....	....	....
6. Poonch Jagir ..	....	....	....	....	....	....	4	4	4	36	2	....	....	....	....	....	....	....
7. Chenani „ ..	....	....	....	....	....	....	5	....	....	....	....	....	5	....	....	....	....	....
II. Kashmir Province ..	3	....	....	....	....	....	872	88	10	18	29	21	36	....	....	1	2	....
8. Kashmir North ..	1	....	....	....	....	....	16	1	....	....	1	....	1	....	....	....	1	....
9. Kashmir South (*including City*) ..	1	....	....	....	....	....	834	87	10	18	21	21	33	....	....	1	....	....
10. Muzaffarabad ..	1	....	....	....	....	....	22	....	....	....	7	....	2	....	....	....	1	....
III. Frontier Districts ..	....	....	....	....	....	....	11	....	....	....	....	....	8	....	....	....	....	....
11. Ladakh ..	....	....	....	....	....	....	8	....	....	....	....	....	8	....	....	....	....	....
12. Gilgit ..	....	....	....	....	....	....	3	....	....	....	....	....	....	....	....	....	....	....
13. Frontier Ilaqas ..	....	....	....	....	....	....	....	....	....	....	....	....	....	....	....	....	....	....
IV. Cities— ..																		
14. Srinagar ..	....	....	....	....	....	....	734	87	10	18	21	21	33	....	....	1	....	....
15. Jammu (*excludes Ry. population*) ..	7	....	....	....	....	....	301	4	1	3	14	....	21	....	....	....	2	....

TABLE X.

OCCUPATION.

Jammu and Kashmir Census 1931.

District, Ilaqa, Jagir or City.	Group 127. Owners and managers of hostels, cook shops, sarais etc., (and employees).						Group 128. Hawkers of drink and food stuffs.						Order 32. Other trade in food stuffs. Total of Order 32.					
	Total earners (principal occupation).		Total working dependents.		Total following occupation as subsidiary to others.		Total earners (principal occupation).		Total working dependents.		Total following occupation as subsidiary to others.		Total earners (principal occupation).		Total working dependents.		Total following occupation as subsidiary to others.	
	Males.	Females.	Males.	Females.	Males.	Females.	Males.	Females.	Males.	Females.	Males.	Females.	Males.	Females.	Males.	Females.	Males.	Females.
Jammu and Kashmir State ..	1,175	106	14	56	58	23	233	6	1	....	22	2	8,510	2,837	284	120	2,064	414
I. Jammu Province ..	355	18	4	39	35	2	214	6	1	....	18	2	4,377	2,724	49	30	1,125	208
1. Jammu District (*including city*) ..	201	7	....	3	7	1	188	....	1	....	13	....	1,789	78	26	6	352	111
2. Kathua ,, ..	93	2	....	....	12	1	15	....	....	....	5	....	1,034	320	2	21	265	62
3. Udhampur ,, ..	37	2	....	....	13	....	7	....	....	....	....	....	301	33	4	3	61	16
4. Reasi ,, ..	14	3	....	....	1	....	4	3	....	....	....	2	386	2,256	13	....	189	8
5. Mirpur ,, ..	6	....	....	....	....	....	....	3	....	....	....	....	675	21	4	....	137	11
6. Poonch Jagir ..	4	4	4	36	2	....	....	....	....	....	....	....	181	11	....	....	119	....
7. Chenani ,, ..	....	....	....	....	....	....	....	....	....	....	....	....	11	5	....	....	2	....
II. Kashmir Province ..	817	88	10	17	23	21	19	....	....	....	4	....	3,971	87	230	89	915	201
8. Kashmir North ..	12	1	....	....	....	....	3	....	....	....	....	....	1,26[illegible]	30	29	85	251	6
9. Kashmir South (*including city*) ..	801	87	10	17	21	21	....	....	....	....	....	....	2,233	55	197	4	532	192
10. Muzaffarabad ..	4	....	....	....	2	....	16	....	....	....	4	....	476	2	4	....	132	3
III. Frontier Districts ..	8	....	....	....	....	....	....	....	....	....	....	....	162	26	5	1	24	5
11. Ladakh ..	....	....	....	....	....	....	....	....	....	....	....	....	158	26	....	....	23	5
12. Gilgit ..	3	....	....	....	....	....	....	....	....	....	....	....	2	....	....	....	....	....
13. Frontier Ilaqas ..	....	....	....	....	....	....	....	....	....	....	....	....	2	....	5	1	1	....
IV. Cities.—																		
14. Srinagar ..	701	87	10	17	21	21	....	....	....	....	....	....	710	28	8	2	46	11
15. Jammu (*excludes Ry. population*) ..	153	4	....	3	6	....	127	....	1	....	6	....	841	5	9	1	88	1

TABLE X.

Occupation.

Jammu and Kashmir Census 1931.

District, Ilaqa, Jagir or City.	Order 29. Trade in pottery, bricks and tiles. Total of Order 29. Total earners (principal occupation). Males.	Females.	Total working dependents. Males.	Females.	Total following occupation as subsidiary to others. Males.	Females.	Group 124. Trade in pottery, bricks and tiles. Total earners (principal occupation). Males.	Females.	Total working dependents. Males.	Females.	Total following occupation as subsidiary to others. Males.	Females.	Order 30. Trade in chemical products. Total of Order 30. Total earners (principal occupation). Males.	Females.	Total working dependents. Males.	Females.	Total following occupation as subsidiary to others. Males.	Females.
Jammu and Kashmir State ..	38	2	....	....	3	....	38	2	....	....	3	....	29	2	....	....	20	3
I. Jammu Province ..	8	2	....	....	3	....	8	2	....	....	3	....	26	2	....	....	20	3
1. Jammu District (*including city*) ..	....	....	....	....	....	....	....	....	....	....	....	....	7	....	....	....	....	2
2. Kathua " ..	3	....	....	....	2	....	3	....	....	....	2	....	12	....	....	....	12	....
3. Udhampur " ..	1	2	....	....	1	....	1	2	....	....	1	....	7	....	....	....	8	1
4. Reasi " ..	....	....	....	....	....	....	....	....	....	....	....	....	....	2	....	....	....	....
5. Mirpur " ..	....	....	....	....	....	....	....	....	....	....	....	....	....	....	....	....	....	....
6. Poonch Jagir ..	4	....	....	....	....	....	4	....	....	....	....	....	....	....	....	....	....	....
7. Chenani " ..	....	....	....	....	....	....	....	....	....	....	....	....	....	....	....	....	....	....
II. Kashmir Province ..	30	....	....	....	....	....	30	....	....	....	....	....	3	....	....	....	....	....
8. Kashmir North ..	30	....	....	....	....	....	30	....	....	....	....	....	1	....	....	....	....	....
9. Kashmir South (*including city*) ..	....	....	....	....	....	....	....	....	....	....	....	....	1	....	....	....	....	....
10. Muzaffarabad ..	....	....	....	....	....	....	....	....	....	....	....	....	1	....	....	....	....	....
III. Frontier Districts ..	....	....	....	....	....	....	....	....	....	....	....	....	....	....	....	....	....	....
11. Ladakh ..	....	....	....	....	....	....	....	....	....	....	....	....	....	....	....	....	....	....
12. Gilgit ..	....	....	....	....	....	....	....	....	....	....	....	....	....	....	....	....	....	....
13. Frontier Ilaqas ..	....	....	....	....	....	....	....	....	....	....	....	....	....	....	....	....	....	....
IV. Cities— ..																		
14. Srinagar ..	....	....	....	....	....	....	....	....	....	....	....	....	....	....	....	....	....	....
15. Jammu (*excludes Ry. population*) ..	....	....	....	....	....	....	....	....	....	....	....	....	7	....	....	....	....	....

TABLE X.

OCCUPATION.

Jammu and Kashmir Census 1931.

District, Ilaqa, Jagir or City.	Group 129. Grain and pulse dealers.						Group 130. Dealers in sweetmeats, sugar and spices.						Group 131. Dealers in dairy products, eggs and poultry.					
	Total earners (principal occupation).		Total working dependents.		Total following occupation as subsidiary to others.		Total earners (principal occupation).		Total working dependents.		Total following occupation as subsidiary to others.		Total earners (principal occupation).		Total working dependents.		Total following occupation as subsidiary to others.	
	Males.	Females.	Males.	Females.	Males.	Females.	Males.	Females.	Males.	Females.	Males.	Females.	Males.	Females.	Males.	Females.	Males.	Females.
Jammu and Kashmir State ..	**3,161**	**2,516**	**34**	**2**	**918**	**17**	**1,266**	**32**	**13**	**1**	**283**	**6**	**671**	**117**	**17**	**9**	**156**	**267**
I. Jammu Province ..	**2,565**	**2,494**	**24**	....	**775**	**7**	**350**	**2**	....	....	**35**	....	**273**	**103**	**4**	**8**	**109**	**106**
1. Jammu District (*including city*) ..	821	6	8	....	227	1	82	....	....	....	5	....	78	18	2	....	32	41
2. Kathua " ..	544	232	....	....	135	1	104	....	....	....	13	....	152	68	2	7	53	54
3. Udhampur " ..	122	3	1	....	22	3	34	....	....	....	9	....	34	9	....	1	23	5
4. Reasi " ..	251	2,242	11	....	143	2	13	2	....	....	4	....	9	8	....	....	....	6
5. Mirpur " ..	674	....	4	....	136	....	....	....	....	....	1	....	....	....	....	....	....	....
6. Poonch Jagir ..	151	11	....	....	112	....	18	....	....	....	2	....	....	....	....	....	....	....
7. Chenani " ..	2	....	....	....	....	....	9	....	....	....	1	....	....	....	....	....	1	....
II. Kashmir Province ..	**542**	**21**	**10**	**2**	**127**	**10**	**815**	**7**	**13**	**1**	**242**	**1**	**397**	**14**	**8**	**1**	**47**	**161**
8. Kashmir North ..	107	....	....	....	6	....	....	....	....	....	....	....	20	....	....	....	4	....
9. Kashmir South (*including city*) ..	420	21	10	2	111	10	813	7	13	1	241	1	349	14	8	1	38	161
10. Muzaffarabad ..	15	....	....	....	10	....	2	....	....	....	1	....	28	....	....	....	5	....
III. Frontier Districts ..	**54**	**1**	....	....	**16**	....	**101**	**23**	....	....	**6**	**5**	**1**	....	**5**	....	....	....
11. Ladakh ..	54	1	....	....	16	....	101	23	....	....	6	5	....	....	....	....	....	....
12. Gilgit ..	....	....	....	....	....	....	....	....	....	....	....	....	....	....	....	....	....	....
13. Frontier Ilaqas ..	....	....	....	....	....	....	....	....	....	....	....	....	1	....	5	....	....	....
IV. Cities—																		
14. Srinagar ..	**273**	**20**	**6**	**2**	**18**	**10**	**366**	**6**	**2**	....	**22**	....	....	....	....	....	....	....
15. Jammu (*excludes Ry. population*) ..	**259**	....	**5**	....	**20**	....	**20**	....	....	....	....	....	**64**	....	**2**	....	**12**	....

TABLE X.

OCCUPATION.

Jammu and Kashmir Census 1931.

District, Ilaqa, Jagir or City.	Group 132. Dealers in animals for food. Total earners (principal occupation).		Total working dependents.		Total following occupation as subsidiary to others.		Group 133. Dealers in fodder for animals. Total earners (principal occupation).		Total working dependents.		Total following occupation as subsidiary to others.		Group 134. Dealers in other food stuffs. Total earners (principal occupation).		Total working dependents.		Total following occupation as subsidiary to others.	
	Males.	Females.	Males.	Females.	Males.	Females.	Males.	Females.	Males.	Females.	Males.	Females.	Males.	Females.	Males.	Females.	Males.	Females.
Jammu and Kashmir State ..	106	....	3	....	12	1	286	74	13	13	27	62	2,802	96	204	95	640	60
I. Jammu Province ..	104	....	3	....	12	1	256	71	12	7	23	54	696	54	6	15	151	40
1. Jammu District (*including city*) ..	21	....	2	....	6	1	244	47	10	5	23	46	447	7	4	1	54	22
2. Kathua " ..	....	....	....	....	....	....	....	....	....	....	....	....	118	20	....	14	51	7
3. Udhampur " ..	82	....	1	....	4	....	12	21	2	2	....	8	16	....	....	....	2	....
4. Reasi " ..	....	....	....	....	....	....	....	....	....	....	....	....	108	4	2	....	42	....
5. Mirpur " ..	....	....	....	....	....	....	....	....	....	....	....	....	....	21	....	....	....	11
6. Poonch Jagir ..	1	....	....	....	2	....	....	....	....	....	....	....	7	....	....	....	2	....
7. Chenani " ..	....	....	....	....	....	....	....	3	....	....	....	....	....	2	....	....	....	....
II. Kashmir Province ..	2	....	....	....	....	....	30	3	1	6	4	8	2,101	40	193	79	487	20
8. Kashmir North ..	1	....	....	....	....	....	5	....	1	6	1	....	1,119	30	28	79	239	6
9. Kashmir South (*including city*) ..	....	....	....	....	....	....	22	3	....	....	3	8	869	8	166	....	132	11
10. Muzaffarabad ..	1	....	....	....	....	....	3	....	....	....	....	....	413	2	4	....	116	3
III. Frontier Districts ..	....	....	....	....	....	....	....	....	....	....	....	....	5	2	....	1	2	....
11. Ladakh ..	....	....	....	....	....	....	....	....	....	....	....	....	2	2	....	....	1	....
12. Gilgit ..	....	....	....	....	....	....	....	....	....	....	....	....	2	....	....	....	....	....
13. Frontier Ilaqas ..	....	....	....	....	....	....	....	....	....	....	....	....	1	....	....	1	1	....
IV. Cities.—																		
14. Srinagar ..	....	....	....	....	....	....	18	....	....	....	....	....	....	....	....	....	....	....
15. Jammu (*excludes Ry. population*) ..	....	....	....	....	....	....	3	2	....	....	....	1	421	3	2	1	51	1

TABLE X.

OCCUPATION.

Jammu and Kashmir Census 1931.

District, Ilaqa, Jagir or City.	Group 135. Dealers in tobacco.						Group 136. Dealers in opium.						Group 137. Dealers in ganja.					
	Total earners (principal occupation).		Total working dependents.		Total following occupation as subsidiary to others.		Total earners (principal occupation).		Total working dependents.		Total following occupation as subsidiary to others.		Total earners (principal occupation).		Total working dependents.		Total following occupation as subsidiary to others.	
	Males.	Females.	Males.	Females.	Males.	Females.	Males.	Females.	Males.	Females.	Males.	Females.	Males.	Females.	Males.	Females.	Males.	Females.
Jammu and Kashmir State ..	213	2	....	....	27	1	3	....	....	....	1	....	2	....	....	....	....	....
I. Jammu Province ..	129	....	....	....	19	....	3	....	....	....	1	....	1	....	....	....	....	....
1. Jammu District (*including city*) ..	93	....	....	....	5	....	3	....	....	....	....	....	....	....	....	....	....	....
2. Kathua „ ..	26	....	....	....	13	....	....	....	....	....	....	....	....	....	....	....	....	....
3. Udhampur „ ..	1	....	....	....	1	....	....	....	....	....	....	....	....	....	....	....	....	....
4. Reasi „ ..	5	....	....	....	....	....	....	....	....	....	....	....	....	....	....	....	....	....
5. Mirpur „ ..	....	....	....	....	....	....	....	....	....	....	....	....	1	....	....	....	....	....
6. Poonch Jagir ..	4	....	....	....	....	....	....	....	....	....	1	....	....	....	....	....	....	....
7. Chenani „ ..	....	....	....	....	....	....	....	....	....	....	....	....	....	....	....	....	....	....
II. Kashmir Province ..	83	2	....	....	8	1	....	....	....	....	....	....	1	....	....	....	....	....
8. Kashmir North ..	9	....	....	....	1	....	....	....	....	....	....	....	1	....	....	....	....	....
9. Kashmir South (*including city*) ..	60	2	....	....	7	1	....	....	....	....	....	....	....	....	....	....	....	....
10. Muzaffarabad ..	14	....	....	....	....	....	....	....	....	....	....	....	....	....	....	....	....	....
III. Frontier Districts ..	1	....	....	....	....	....	....	....	....	....	....	....	....	....	....	....	....	....
11. Ladakh ..	1	....	....	....	....	....	....	....	....	....	....	....	....	....	....	....	....	....
12. Gilgit ..	....	....	....	....	....	....	....	....	....	....	....	....	....	....	....	....	....	....
13. Frontier Ilaqas ..	....	....	....	....	....	....	....	....	....	....	....	....	....	....	....	....	....	....
IV. Cities—																		
14. Srinagar ..	53	2	....	....	6	1	....	....	....	....	....	....	....	....	....	....	....	....
15. Jammu (*excludes Ry. population*) ..	71	....	....	....	5	....	3	....	....	....	....	....	....	....	....	....	....	....

TABLE X.

OCCUPATION.

Jammu and Kashmir Census 1931.

District, Ilaqa, Jagir or City.	Order 33. Trade in clothing and toilet articles. Total of Order 33. Total earners (principal occupation). Males.	Females.	Total working dependents. Males.	Females.	Total following occupation as subsidiary to others. Males.	Females.	Group 138. Trade in ready-made clothing and other articles of dress and the toilet (hats, umbrellas, socks, ready-made shoes, perfumes etc.) Total earners (principal occupation). Males.	Females.	Total working dependents. Males.	Females.	Total following occupation as subsidiary to others. Males.	Females.	Order 34. Trade in furniture. Total of Order 34. Total earners (principal occupation). Males.	Females.	Total working dependents. Males.	Females.	Total following occupation as subsidiary to others. Males.	Females.
Jammu and Kashmir State	875	7	1	....	67	1	875	7	1	....	67	1	305	3	1	....	28	4
I. Jammu Province	198	5	....	....	44	1	198	5	....	....	44	1	134	....	1	....	23	....
1. Jammu District (*including City*)	110	5	....	....	24	....	110	5	....	....	24	....	94	....	....	....	2	....
2. Kathua "	55	....	....	....	14	1	55	....	....	....	14	1	....	....	....	....	1	....
3. Udhampur "	15	....	....	....	4	....	15	....	....	....	4	....	35	....	1	....	17	....
4. Reasi "	15	....	....	....	....	....	15	....	....	....	....	....	....	....	....	....	....	....
5. Mirpur "	3	....	....	....	2	....	3	....	....	....	2	....	....	....	....	....	....	....
6. Poonch Jagir	....	....	....	....	....	....	....	....	....	....	....	....	4	....	....	....	2	....
7. Chenani "	....	....	....	....	....	....	....	....	....	....	....	....	1	....	....	....	1	....
II. Kashmir Province	677	2	1	....	23	....	677	2	1	....	23	....	171	3	....	....	5	4
8. Kashmir North	26	....	....	....	4	....	26	....	....	....	4	....	8	....	....	....	1	....
9. Kashmir South (*including City*)	649	2	1	....	19	....	649	2	1	....	19	....	155	3	....	....	4	4
10. Muzaffarabad	2	....	....	....	....	....	2	....	....	....	....	....	8	....	....	....	....	....
III. Frontier Districts	....	....	....	....	....	....	....	....	....	....	....	....	....	....	....	....	....	....
11. Ladakh	....	....	....	....	....	....	....	....	....	....	....	....	....	....	....	....	....	....
12. Gilgit	....	....	....	....	....	....	....	....	....	....	....	....	....	....	....	....	....	....
13. Frontier Ilaqas	....	....	....	....	....	....	....	....	....	....	....	....	....	....	....	....	....	....
IV. Cities:—																		
14. Srinagar	649	2	1	....	19	....	649	2	1	....	19	....	106	....	....	....	....	....
15. Jammu (*excludes Ry. population*)	58	....	....	....	8	....	58	....	....	....	8	....	63	....	....	....	1	....

TABLE X.

Occupation.

Jammu and Kashmir Census 1931.

District, Ilaqa, Jagir or City.	Group 139. Trade in furniture, carpets, curtains and bedding. Total earners (principal occupation).		Total working dependents.		Total following occupation as subsidiary to others.		Group 140. Hardware, cooking utensils, porcelain, crockery, glassware, bottles, articles for gardening. Total earners (principal occupation).		Total working dependents.		Total following occupation as subsidiary to others.		Order 35. Trade in building materials. Total of Order 35. Total earners (principal occupation).		Total working dependents.		Total following occupation as subsidiary to others.	
	Males.	Females.	Males.	Females.	Males.	Females.	Males.	Females.	Males.	Females.	Males.	Females.	Males.	Females.	Males.	Females.	Males.	Females.
Jammu and Kashmir State ..	233	....	1	....	25	....	72	3	....	....	3	4	16	....	....	....	2	....
I. Jammu Province ..	79	....	1	....	21	....	55	....	....	....	2	....	15	....	....	....	2	....
1. Jammu District (*including city*) ..	47	....	....	....	1	....	47	....	....	....	1	....	4	....	....	....	1	....
2. Kathua „ ..	....	....	....	....	1	....	....	....	....	....	....	....	....	....	....	....	....	....
3. Udhampur „ ..	31	....	1	....	17	....	4	....	....	....	....	....	....	....	....	....	....	....
4. Reasi „ ..	....	....	....	....	....	....	....	....	....	....	....	....	....	....	....	....	....	....
5. Mirpur „ ..	....	....	....	....	....	....	....	....	....	....	....	....	11	....	....	....	1	....
6. Poonch Jagir	1	....	....	....	2	....	3	....	....	....	....	....	....	....	....	....	....	....
7. Chenani „ ..	....	....	....	....	....	....	1	....	....	....	1	....	....	....	....	....	....	....
II. Kashmir Province ..	154	....	....	....	4	....	17	3	....	....	1	4	1	....	....	....	....	....
8. Kashmir North ..	8	....	....	....	1	....	....	....	....	....	....	....	....	....	....	....	....	....
9. Kashmir South (*including city*) ..	146	....	....	....	3	....	9	3	....	....	1	4	....	....	....	....	....	....
10. Muzaffarabad ..	....	....	....	....	....	....	8	....	....	....	....	....	1	....	....	....	....	....
III. Frontier Districts ..	....	....	....	....	....	....	....	....	....	....	....	....	....	....	....	....	....	....
11. Ladakh ..	....	....	....	....	....	....	....	....	....	....	....	....	....	....	....	....	....	....
12. Gilgit ..	....	....	....	....	....	....	....	....	....	....	....	....	....	....	....	....	....	....
13. Frontier Ilaqas ..	....	....	....	....	....	....	....	....	....	....	....	....	....	....	....	....	....	....
IV. Cities :—																		
14. Srinagar ..	106	....	....	....	....	....	....	....	....	....	....	....	....	....	....	....	....	....
15. Jammu (*excludes Ry. population*)	45	....	....	....	....	....	18	....	....	....	1	....	4	....	....	....	1	....

TABLE X.

Occupation.

Jammu and Kashmir Census 1931.

District, Ilaqa, Jagir or City.	Order 36. Group 141. Trade in building materials (other than bricks, tiles and woody materials). Total earners (principal occupation). Males.	Females.	Total working dependents. Males.	Females.	Total following occupation as subsidiary to others. Males.	Females.	Trade in means of transport. Total of Order 36. Total earners (principal occupation). Males.	Females.	Total working dependents. Males.	Females.	Total following occupation as subsidiary to others. Males.	Females.	Group 142. Dealers and hirers in mechanical transport motors, cycles etc. Total earners (principal occupation). Males.	Females.	Total working dependents. Males.	Females.	Total following occupation as subsidiary to others. Males.	Females.
Jammu and Kashmir State ..	16	....	....	....	2	....	2,294	31	54	3	354	4	523	....	10	....	80	....
I. Jammu Province ..	15	....	....	....	2	....	442	1	1	....	121	1	18	....	....	....	6	....
1. Jammu District (*including City*) ..	4	....	....	....	1	....	146	1	....	....	29	1	4	....	....	....	....	....
2. Kathua ,, ..	....	....	....	....	....	....	184	....	1	....	60	....	....	....	....	....	....	....
3. Udhampur ,, ..	....	....	....	....	....	....	49	....	....	....	11	....	14	....	....	....	5	....
4. Reasi ,, ..	....	....	....	....	....	....	....	....	....	....	1	....	....	....	....	....	1	....
5. Mirpur ,, ..	11	....	....	....	1	....	54	....	....	....	15	....	....	....	....	....	....	....
6. Poonch Jagir ..	....	....	....	....	....	....	9	....	....	....	5	....	....	....	....	....	....	....
7. Chenani ,, ..	....	....	....	....	....	....	....	....	....	....	....	....	....	....	....	....	....	....
II. Kashmir Province ..	1	....	....	....	....	....	1,790	30	51	3	232	3	459	....	10	....	74	....
8. Kashmir North ..	....	....	....	....	....	....	706	29	27	....	81	3	....	....	....	....	....	....
9. Kashmir South (*including City*) ..	....	....	....	....	....	....	898	1	22	....	136	....	459	....	10	....	74	....
10. Muzaffarabad ..	1	....	....	....	....	....	96	....	2	3	15	....	....	....	....	....	....	....
III. Frontier Districts ..	....	....	....	....	....	....	62	....	2	....	1	....	46	....	....	....	....	....
11. Ladakh ..	....	....	....	....	....	....	59	....	....	....	1	....	46	....	....	....	....	....
12. Gilgit ..	....	....	....	....	....	....	....	....	....	....	....	....	....	....	....	....	....	....
13. Frontier Ilaqas ..	....	....	....	....	....	....	3	....	2	....	....	....	....	....	....	....	....	....
IV. Cities.—																		
14. Srinagar ..	....	....	....	....	....	....	16	1	....	....	....	....	....	....	....	....	....	....
15. Jammu (*excludes Ry. population*) ..	4	....	....	....	1	....	17	....	....	....	3	....	4	....	....	....	....	....

TABLE X.

OCCUPATION.

Jammu and Kashmir Census 1931.

District, Ilaqa, Jagir or City.	Group 143. Dealers and hirers in other carriages, carts, boats, etc.						Group 144. Dealers and hirers of elephants, camels, horses, cattle, asses, mules etc.						Order 37. Trade in Fuel. Total of Order 37.					
	Total earners (principal occupation).		Total working dependents.		Total following occupation as subsidiary to others.		Total earners (principal occupation).		Total working dependents.		Total following occupation as subsidiary to others.		Total earners (principal occupation).		Total working dependents.		Total following occupation as subsidiary to others.	
	Males.	Females.	Males.	Females.	Males.	Females.	Males.	Females.	Males.	Females.	Males.	Females.	Males.	Females.	Males.	Females.	Males.	Females.
Jammu and Kashmir State ..	615	1	1	....	34	....	1,156	30	43	3	240	4	256	361	16	667	71	568
I. Jammu Province ..	6	....	....	....	....	....	418	1	1	....	115	1	240	358	16	665	38	295
1. Jammu District (*including city*) ..	5	....	....	....	....	....	137	1	....	....	29	1	137	117	5	15	9	103
2. Kathua „ ..	....	....	....	....	....	....	184	....	1	....	60	....	66	152	....	605	7	28
3. Udhampur „ ..	1	....	....	....	....	....	34	....	....	....	6	....	28	70	1	45	18	104
4. Reasi „ ..	....	....	....	....	....	....	....	....	....	....	....	....	6	19	8	....	3	60
5. Mirpur „ ..	....	....	....	....	....	....	54	....	....	....	15	....	....	....	....	....	....	....
6. Poonch Jagir ..	....	....	....	....	....	....	9	....	....	....	5	....	2	....	2	....	1	....
7. Chenani „ ..	....	....	....	....	....	....	....	....	....	....	....	....	1	....	....	....	....	....
II. Kashmir Province ..	607	1	1	....	34	....	724	29	40	3	124	3	16	3	....	2	33	273
8. Kashmir North ..	457	....	....	....	18	....	339	29	27	....	63	3	3	3	....	2	....	128
9. Kashmir South (*including city*) ..	64	1	....	....	7	....	375	....	12	....	53	....	2	....	....	....	33	145
10. Muzaffarabad ..	86	....	1	....	9	....	10	....	1	3	6	....	11	....	....	....	....	....
III. Frontier Districts ..	2	....	....	....	....	....	14	....	2	....	1	....	....	....	....	....	....	....
11. Ladakh ..	....	....	....	....	....	....	13	....	....	....	1	....	....	....	....	....	....	....
12. Gilgit ..	....	....	....	....	....	....	....	....	....	....	....	....	....	....	....	....	....	....
13. Frontier Ilaqas ..	2	....	....	....	....	....	1	....	2	....	....	....	....	....	....	....	....	....
IV. Cities.—																		
14. Srinagar ..	16	1	....	....	....	....	....	....	....	....	....	....	....	....	....	....	....	....
15. Jammu (*excludes Ry. population*) ..	5	....	....	....	....	....	8	....	....	....	3	....	28	6	....	6	5	2

TABLE X.

OCCUPATION.

Jammu and Kashmir Census 1931.

District, Ilaqa, Jagir or City.	Group 145. Dealers in firewood, charcoal, coal, cowdung, etc.						Order 38. Trade in articles of luxury and those pertaining to letters and arts and sciences. Total of Order 38.						Group 146. Dealers in precious stones, jewellery (real and imitation), clocks, optical instruments, etc.					
	Total earners (principal occupation).		Total working dependents.		Total following occupation as subsidiary to others.		Total earners (principal occupation).		Total working dependents.		Total following occupation as subsidiary to others.		Total earners (principal occupation).		Total working dependents.		Total following occupation as subsidiary to others.	
	Males.	Females.	Males.	Females.	Males.	Females.	Males.	Females.	Males.	Females.	Males.	Females.	Males.	Females.	Males.	Females.	Males.	Females.
Jammu and Kashmir State ..	256	361	16	667	71	568	152	6	2	1	14	9	69	....	....	....	5	....
I. Jammu Province ..	240	358	16	665	38	295	102	6	1	1	9	9	62	....	....	....	3	....
1. Jammu District (*including city*) ..	137	117	5	15	9	103	87	....	....	....	8	....	59	....	....	....	3	....
2. Kathua " ..	66	152	....	605	7	28	4	....	....	....	....	....	....	....	....	....	....	....
3. Udhampur " ..	28	70	1	45	18	104	2	....	....	....	....	....	1	....	....	....	....	....
4. Reasi " ..	6	19	8	....	3	60	5	....	1	....	1	....	....	....	....	....	....	....
5. Mirpur " ..	....	....	....	....	....	....	4	6	....	1	....	9	2	....	....	....	....	....
6. Poonch Jagir ..	2	....	2	....	1	....	....	....	....	....	....	....	....	....	....	....	....	....
7. Chenani " ..	1	....	....	....	....	....	....	....	....	....	....	....	....	....	....	....	....	....
II. Kashmir Province ..	16	3	....	2	33	273	49	....	1	....	5	....	7	....	....	....	2	....
8. Kashmir North ..	3	3	....	2	....	128	22	....	1	....	1	....	....	....	....	....	....	....
9. Kashmir South (*including city*) ..	2	....	....	....	33	145	11	....	....	....	2	....	7	....	....	....	2	....
10. Muzaffarabad ..	11	....	....	....	....	....	16	....	....	....	2	....	....	....	....	....	....	....
III. Frontier Districts ..	....	....	....	....	....	....	1	....	....	....	....	....	....	....	....	....	....	....
11. Ladakh ..	....	....	....	....	....	....	1	....	....	....	....	....	....	....	....	....	....	....
12. Gilgit ..	....	....	....	....	....	....	....	....	....	....	....	....	....	....	....	....	....	....
13. Frontier Ilaqas ..	....	....	....	....	....	....	....	....	....	....	....	....	....	....	....	....	....	....
IV. Cities :—																		
14. Srinagar ..	....	....	....	....	....	....	....	....	....	....	....	....	....	....	....	....	....	....
15. Jammu (*excludes Ry. population*)	28	6	....	6	5	2	78	....	....	....	7	....	59	....	....	....	3	....

TABLE X.

OCCUPATION.

Jammu and Kashmir Census 1931.

District, Ilaqa, Jagir or City.	Group 147. Dealers in common bangles, bead necklaces, fans, small articles, toys, hunting and fishing tackle, flowers, etc. — Total earners (principal occupation). Males.	Females.	Total working dependents. Males.	Females.	Total following occupation as subsidiary to others. Males.	Females.	Group 148. Publishers, booksellers, stationers, dealers in music, pictures, musical instruments and curiosities. — Total earners (principal occupation). Males.	Females.	Total working dependents. Males.	Females.	Total following occupation as subsidiary to others. Males.	Females.	Order 39. Trade of other sorts. Total of Order 39. — Total earners (principal occupation). Males.	Females.	Total working dependents. Males.	Females.	Total following occupation as subsidiary to others. Males.	Females.
Jammu and Kashmir State	59	6	2	1	4	9	24	....	....	....	5	....	6,880	89	143	15	2,963	87
I. Jammu Province	18	6	1	1	1	9	22	....	....	....	5	....	3,030	65	94	10	2,324	58
1. Jammu District (*including city*)	9	....	....	....	....	....	19	....	....	....	5	....	1,705	9	9	3	1,775	4
2. Kathua „	3	....	....	....	....	....	1	....	....	....	....	....	20	....	....	....	31	....
3. Udhampur „	....	....	....	....	....	....	1	....	....	....	....	....	488	13	82	4	214	13
4. Reasi „	4	....	1	....	1	....	1	....	....	....	....	....	23	....	....	....	5	....
5. Mirpur „	2	6	....	1	....	9	....	....	....	....	....	....	405	38	2	2	169	38
6. Poonch Jagir	....	....	....	....	....	....	....	....	....	....	....	....	331	4	1	1	114	3
7. Chenani „	....	....	....	....	....	....	....	....	....	....	....	....	58	1	....	....	16	....
II. Kashmir Province	40	....	1	....	3	....	2	....	....	....	....	....	3,663	23	25	5	624	6
8. Kashmir North	22	....	1	....	1	....	....	....	....	....	....	....	1,538	2	11	....	253	3
9. Kashmir South (*including city*)	4	....	....	....	....	....	....	....	....	....	....	....	2,080	21	14	5	364	3
10. Muzaffarabad	14	....	....	....	2	....	2	....	....	....	....	....	45	....	....	....	7	....
III. Frontier Districts	1	....	....	....	....	....	....	....	....	....	....	....	187	1	24	....	15	23
11. Ladakh	1	....	....	....	....	....	....	....	....	....	....	....	....	1	....	....	....	....
12. Gilgit	....	....	....	....	....	....	....	....	....	....	....	....	155	....	....	....	2	23
13. Frontier Ilaqas	....	....	....	....	....	....	....	....	....	....	....	....	32	....	24	....	13	....
IV. Cities—																		
14. Srinagar	....	....	....	....	....	....	....	....	....	....	....	....	947	21	11	5	32	3
15. Jammu (*excludes Ry. population*)	....	....	....	....	....	....	19	....	....	....	4	....	231	....	6	....	11	....

TABLE X.

OCCUPATION.

Jammu and Kashmir Census 1931.

District, Ilaqa, Jagir or City.	Group 149. Dealers in rags, stable refuse, etc.						Group 150. General store-keepers and shop-keepers, otherwise unspecified.						Group 151. Itinerant traders, pedlars and hawkers (of other than food), etc.					
	Total earners (principal occupation).		Total working dependents.		Total following occupation as subsidiary to others.		Total earners (principal (occupation).		Total working dependents.		Total following occupation as subsidiary to others.		Total earners (principal occupation).		Total working dependents.		Total following occupation as subsidiary to others.	
	Males.	Females.	Males.	Females.	Males.	Females.	Males.	Females.	Males.	Females.	Males.	Females.	Males.	Females.	Males.	Females.	Males.	Females.
Jammu and Kashmir State ..	12	1	....	....	26	....	6,042	88	110	15	1,305	87	36	....	....	....	4	....
I. Jammu Province ..	12	....	....	....	26	....	2,288	65	83	10	706	58	36	....	....	....	4	....
1. Jammu District (*including city*) ..	5	....	....	....	....	....	1,038	9	4	3	199	4	8	....	....	....	....	....
2. Kathua „ ..	7	....	....	....	26	....	3	....	....	....	1	....	5	....	....	....	....	....
3. Udhampur „ ..	....	....	....	....	....	....	466	13	76	4	210	13	14	....	....	....	4	....
4. Reasi „ ..	....	....	....	....	....	....	23	....	....	....	5	....	....	....	....	....	....	....
5. Mirpur „ ..	....	....	....	....	....	....	388	38	2	2	162	38	1	....	....	....	....	....
6. Poonch Jagir ..	....	....	....	....	....	....	314	4	1	1	114	3	8	....	....	....	....	....
7. Chenani „ ..	....	....	....	....	....	....	56	1	....	....	15	....	....	....	....	....	....	....
II. Kashmir Province ..	....	....	....	....	....	....	3,617	23	25	5	599	6	....	....	....	....	....	....
8. Kashmir North ..	....	....	....	....	....	....	1,504	2	11	....	242	3	....	....	....	....	....	....
9. Kashmir South (*including city*) ..	....	....	....	....	....	....	2,079	21	14	5	352	3	....	....	....	....	....	....
10. Muzaffarabad ..	....	....	....	....	....	....	34	....	....	....	5	....	....	....	....	....	....	....
III. Frontier Districts ..	....	1	....	....	....	....	137	....	2	....	....	23	....	....	....	....	....	....
11. Ladakh ..	....	1	....	....	....	....	....	....	....	....	....	....	....	....	....	....	....	....
12. Gilgit ..	....	....	....	....	....	....	132	....	....	....	....	23	....	....	....	....	....	....
13. Frontier Ilaqas ..	....	....	....	....	....	....	5	....	2	....	....	....	....	....	....	....	....	....
IV. Cities.—																		
14. Srinagar ..	....	....	....	....	....	....	947	21	11	5	32	3	....	....	....	....	....	....
15. Jammu (*excludes Ry. population*) ..	5	....	....	....	....	....	107	....	1	....	6	....	2	....	....	....	....	....

TABLE X.

OCCUPATION.

Jammu and Kashmir Census 1931.

District, Ilaqa, Jagir or City.	GROUP 152. Other trades (including farmers of pounds, tolls and markets).						CLASS C. Public Administration and Liberal Arts. TOTAL OF CLASS C.						SUB-CLASS VI. Public Force. TOTAL OF SUB-CLASS VI.					
	Total earners (principal occupation).		Total working dependents.		Total following occupation as subsidiary to others.		Total earners (principal occupation).		Total working dependents.		Total following occupation as subsidiary to others.		Total earners (principal occupation).		Total working dependents.		Total following occupation as subsidiary to others.	
	Males.	Females.	Males.	Females.	Males.	Females.	Males.	Females.	Males.	Females.	Males.	Females.	Males.	Females.	Males.	Females.	Males.	Females.
Jammu and Kashmir State ..	790	....	33	....	1,628	....	34,270	1,205	381	89	9,571	377	9,087	12	33	2	2,915	2
I. Jammu Province ..	694	....	11	....	1,583	....	16,960	717	172	39	5,471	279	5,786	3	8	....	2,111	1
1. Jammu District (*including city*) ..	654	....	5	....	1,576	....	10,314	593	58	26	2,720	114	4,599	2	3	....	1,477	....
2. Kathua " ..	5	....	....	....	4	....	1,444	133	16	5	479	67	275	1	....	....	32	....
3. Udhampur " ..	8	....	6	....	....	....	1,621	42	29	4	795	34	260	....	2	....	136	1
4. Reasi " ..	....	....	....	....	....	....	667	41	19	2	391	14	120	....	....	....	159	....
5. Mirpur " ..	16	....	....	....	7	....	1,767	86	23	1	644	42	272	....	....	....	175	....
6. Poonch Jagir ..	9	....	....	....	....	....	927	19	27	1	426	8	241	....	3	....	123	....
7. Chenani " ..	2	....	....	....	1	....	120	3	....	....	16	....	19	....	....	....	9	....
II. Kashmir Province ..	46	....	....	....	25	....	15,021	298	149	41	3,267	77	2,765	9	10	2	380	1
8. Kashmir North ..	34	....	....	....	11	....	2,818	23	44	3	750	23	339	....	6	....	71	....
9. Kashmir South (*including city*) ..	1	....	....	....	12	....	11,302	256	67	37	2,225	40	2,283	9	4	2	258	1
10. Muzaffarabad ..	11	....	....	....	2	....	901	19	38	1	292	14	143	....	....	....	51	....
III. Frontier Districts ..	50	....	22	....	15	....	2,389	190	60	9	833	21	536	....	15	....	424	....
11. Ladakh	....	....	....	....	....	....	1,462	184	2	8	301	20	78	....	....	....	....	....
12. Gilgit ..	23	....	....	....	2	....	753	5	13	....	506	1	457	....	....	....	424	....
13. Frontier Ilaqas ..	27	....	22	....	13	....	174	1	45	1	26	....	1	....	15	....	....	....
IV. Cities.—																		
14. Srinagar ..	....	....	....	....	....	....	7,495	211	22	35	418	33	1,261	....	....	2	103	....
15. Jammu (*excludes Ry. population*) ..	117	....	5	....	5	....	3,744	216	24	11	893	31	723	....	....	....	475	....

TABLE X.

OCCUPATION.

Jammu and Kashmir Census 1931.

District, Ilaqa, Jagir or City.	Order 40. Army. Total of Order 40.						Group 153. Army (Imperial).						Group 154. Army (Indian States).					
	Total earners (principal occupation).		Total working dependents.		Total following occupation as subsidiary to others.		Total earners (principal occupation).		Total working dependents.		Total following occupation as subsidiary to others.		Total earners (principal occupation).		Total working dependents.		Total following occupation as subsidiary to others.	
	Males.	Females.	Males.	Females.	Males.	Females.	Males.	Females.	Males.	Females.	Males.	Females.	Males.	Females.	Males.	Females.	Males.	Females.
Jammu and Kashmir State ..	5,599	9	15	....	1,731	1	829	....	....	....	1,006	1	4,770	9	15	....	725	....
I. Jammu Province ..	4,308	....	....	....	1,268	1	826	....	....	....	1,006	1	3,482	....	....	....	262	....
1. Jammu District (*including city*) ..	3,721	....	....	....	979	....	512	....	....	....	849	....	3,209	....	....	....	130	....
2. Kathua " ..	124	....	....	....	13	....	124	....	....	....	13	....	....	....	....	....	....	....
3. Udhampur " ..	54	....	....	....	15	1	22	....	....	....	9	1	32	....	....	....	6	....
4. Reasi " ..	68	....	....	....	84	....	51	....	....	....	68	....	17	....	....	....	16	....
5. Mirpur " ..	140	....	....	....	97	....	3	....	....	....	3	....	146	....	....	....	94	....
6. Poonch Jagir ..	176	....	....	....	72	....	98	....	....	....	56	....	78	....	....	....	16	....
7. Chenani " ..	16	....	....	....	8	....	16	....	....	....	8	....	....	....	....	....	....	....
II. Kashmir Province ..	783	9	....	....	42	....	....	....	....	....	....	....	783	9	....	....	42	....
8. Kashmir North ..	56	....	....	....	32	....	....	....	....	....	....	....	56	....	....	....	2	....
9. Kashmir South (*including city*) ..	714	9	....	....	38	....	....	....	....	....	....	....	714	9	....	....	38	....
10. Muzaffarabad ..	13	....	....	....	2	....	....	....	....	....	....	....	13	....	....	....	2	....
III. Frontier Districts ..	508	....	15	....	421	....	3	....	....	....	....	....	505	....	15	....	421	....
11. Ladakh ..	69	....	....	....	....	....	....	....	....	....	....	....	69	....	....	....	....	....
12. Gilgit ..	438	....	....	....	421	....	3	....	....	....	....	....	435	....	....	....	421	....
13. Frontier Ilaqas ..	1	....	15	....	....	....	....	....	....	....	....	....	1	....	15	....	....	....
IV. Cities:—																		
14. Srinagar ..	81	....	....	....	34	....	....	....	....	....	....	....	81	....	....	....	34	....
15. Jammu (*excludes Ry. population*)	257	....	....	....	105	....	....	....	....	....	....	....	257	....	....	....	105	....

TABLE X.

OCCUPATION.

Jammu and Kashmr Census 1931.

District, Ilaqa, Jagir or City.	Order 43. Police. Total of Order 43. Total earners (principal occupation).		Total working dependents.		Total following occupation as subsidiary to others.		Group 157. Police. Total earners (principal occupation).		Total working dependents.		Total following occupation as subsidiary to others.		Group 158. Village watchmen. Total earners (principal occupation).		Total working dependents.		Total following occupation as subsidiary to others.	
	Males.	Females.	Males.	Females.	Males.	Females.	Males.	Females.	Males.	Females.	Males.	Females.	Males.	Females.	Males.	Females.	Males.	Females.
Jammu and Kashmir State ..	3,488	3	13	2	1,134	1	2,568	....	6	2	814	....	920	3	12	....	370	1
I. Jammu Province ..	1,478	3	8	....	843	....	896	....	2	....	622	....	582	3	6	....	221	....
1. Jammu District (*including city*) ..	878	2	3	....	498	....	555	....	1	....	415	....	323	2	2	....	83	....
2. Kathua " ..	151	1	....	....	19	....	58	....	....	....	3	....	93	1	....	....	16	....
3. Udhampur " ..	206	....	2	....	121	....	157	....	1	....	67	....	49	....	1	....	54	....
4. Reasi " ..	52	....	....	....	75	....	32	....	....	....	47	....	20	....	....	....	28	....
5. Mirpur " ..	123	....	....	....	78	....	39	....	....	....	47	....	84	....	....	....	31	....
6. Poonch Jagir ..	65	....	3	....	51	....	55	....	....	....	42	....	10	....	3	....	9	....
7. Chenani " ..	3	....	....	....	1	....	....	....	....	....	1	....	3	....	....	....	....	....
II. Kashmir Province ..	1,982	....	10	2	338	1	1,647	....	4	2	190	....	335	....	6	....	148	1
8. Kashmir North ..	283	....	6	....	69	....	146	....	3	....	15	....	137	....	3	....	54	....
9. Kashmir South (*including city*) ..	1,569	....	4	2	220	1	1,388	....	1	2	134	....	181	....	3	....	86	1
10. Muzaffarabad ..	130	....	....	....	49	....	113	....	....	....	41	....	17	....	....	....	8	....
III. Frontier Districts ..	28	....	....	....	3	....	25	....	....	....	2	....	3	....	....	....	1	....
11. Ladakh ..	9	....	....	....	....	....	8	....	....	....	....	....	1	....	....	....	....	....
12. Gilgit ..	19	....	....	....	3	....	17	....	....	....	2	....	2	....	....	....	1	....
13. Frontier Ilaqas ..	....	....	....	....	....	....	....	....	....	....	....	....	....	....	....	....	....	....
IV. Cities :—																		
14. Srinagar ..	1,180	....	....	2	69	....	1,180	....	....	2	69	....	....	....	....	....	....	....
15. Jammu (*excludes Ry. population*)	465	....	....	....	370	....	365	....	....	....	369	....	100	....	....	....	11	....

TABLE X.

OCCUPATION.

Jammu and Kashmir Census 1931.

District, Ilaqa, Jagir or City.	Sub-Class VII. Public Administration. Total of Sub-Class VII.						Order 44. Public Administration. Total of Order 44.						Group 159. Service of the State.					
	Total earners (principal occupation).		Total working dependents.		Total following occupation as subsidiary to others.		Total earners (principal occupation.)		Total working dependents.		Total following occupation as subsidiary to others.		Total earners (principal occupation).		Total working dependents.		Total following occupation as subsidiary to others.	
	Males.	Females.	Males.	Females.	Males.	Females.	Males.	Females.	Males.	Females.	Males.	Females.	Males.	Females.	Males.	Females.	Males.	Females.
Jammu and Kashmir State ..	12,611	389	94	39	2,981	91	12,611	389	94	39	2,981	91	11,837	310	80	38	2,735	73
I. Jammu Province ..	5,731	197	31	9	1,532	50	5,731	197	31	9	1,532	50	5,404	131	27	8	1,442	45
1. Jammu District (*including city*) ..	3,206	124	12	3	600	20	3,206	121	12	3	600	20	2,901	60	11	2	532	16
2. Kathua " ..	445	5	1	....	157	3	445	5	1	....	157	3	440	5	1	....	151	3
3. Udhampur " ..	511	10	11	3	205	6	511	10	11	3	205	6	493	9	8	3	191	5
4. Reasi " ..	250	14	....	2	93	1	250	14	....	2	93	1	250	14	....	2	93	1
5. Mirpur " ..	816	31	7	....	249	16	816	31	7	....	249	16	812	31	7	....	247	16
6. Poonch Jagir ..	439	10	....	1	221	4	439	10	....	1	221	4	439	9	....	1	221	4
7. Chenani " ..	64	3	....	....	7	....	64	3	....	....	7	....	64	3	....	....	7	....
II. Kashmir Province ..	6,290	190	41	30	1,297	38	6,290	190	41	30	1,297	38	5,848	177	31	30	1,173	25
8. Kashmir North ..	905	14	16	....	187	14	905	14	16	....	187	14	821	7	7	....	158	1
9. Kashmir South (*including city*)	4,991	168	11	30	972	20	4,991	168	11	30	972	20	4,658	166	10	30	893	20
10. Muzaffarabad ..	394	8	14	....	138	4	394	8	14	....	138	4	369	4	14	....	122	4
III. Frontier Districts ..	590	2	22	....	132	3	590	2	22	....	132	3	585	2	22	....	120	3
11. Ladakh ..	225	2	....	....	61	2	225	2	....	....	61	2	223	2	....	....	49	2
12. Gilgit ..	217	....	....	....	66	1	217	....	....	....	66	1	214	....	....	....	66	1
13. Frontier Ilaqas ..	148	....	22	....	5	....	148	....	22	....	5	....	148	....	22	....	5	....
IV. Cities—																		
14. Srinagar ..	4,099	160	7	30	186	20	4,099	160	7	30	186	20	3,867	158	7	30	186	20
15. Jammu (*excludes Ry. population*)	2,126	91	11	2	291	10	2,126	91	11	2	291	10	1,976	36	10	2	286	10

TABLE X.

OCCUPATION.

Jammu and Kashmir Census 1931.

District, Ilaqa, Jagir or City.	Group 160. Service of Indian and Foreign States.						Group 161. Municipal and other local (not village) service.						Group 162. Village officials and servants other than watchmen.					
	Total earners (principal occupation).		Total working dependents.		Total following occupation as subsidiary to others.		Total earners (principal occupation.)		Total working dependents.		Total following occupation as subsidiary to others.		Total earners (principal occupation).		Total working dependents.		Total following occupation as subsidiary to others.	
	Males.	Females.	Males.	Females.	Males.	Females.	Males.	Females.	Males.	Females.	Males.	Females.	Males.	Females.	Males.	Females.	Males.	Females
Jammu and Kashmir State ..	127	10	....	1	34	2	438	68	1	....	16	14	214	1	13	....	176	2
I. **Jammu Province** ..	119	9	....	1	34	2	159	56	1	....	10	1	49	1	3	....	46	2
1. Jammu District (*including city*) ..	116	9	....	1	34	2	152	55	1	....	5	....	37	....	....	....	29	2
2. Kathua " ..	....	....	....	....	....	....	5	....	....	....	5	....	....	....	....	....	1	....
3. Udhampur " ..	3	....	....	....	....	....	2	1	....	....	....	1	8	....	3	....	14	....
4. Reasi " ..	....	....	....	....	....	....	....	....	....	....	....	....	....	....	....	....	....	....
5. Mirpur " ..	....	....	....	....	....	....	....	....	....	....	....	....	4	....	....	....	2	....
6. Poonch Jagir ..	....	....	....	....	....	....	....	....	....	....	....	....	....	1	....	....	....	....
7. Chenani " ..	....	....	....	....	....	....	....	....	....	....	....	....	....	....	....	....	....	....
II. **Kashmir Province** ..	8	1	....	....	....	....	273	12	....	....	6	13	161	....	10	....	118	....
8. Kashmir North ..	8	1	....	....	....	....	17	6	....	....	1	13	59	....	9	....	28	....
9. Kashmir South (*including city*)	....	....	....	....	....	....	240	2	....	....	....	....	93	....	1	....	79	....
10. Muzaffarabad ..	....	....	....	....	....	....	16	4	....	....	5	....	9	....	....	....	11	....
III. **Frontier Districts** ..	....	....	....	....	....	....	1	....	....	....	....	....	4	....	....	....	12	....
11. Ladakh ..	....	....	....	....	....	....	....	....	....	....	....	....	2	....	....	....	12	....
12. Gilgit ..	....	....	....	....	....	....	1	....	....	....	....	....	2	....	....	....	....	....
13. Frontier Ilaqas ..	....	....	....	....	....	....	....	....	....	....	....	....	....	....	....	....	....	....
IV. **Cities—**																		
14. Srinagar ..	....	....	....	....	....	....	232	2	....	....	....	....	....	....	....	....	....	....
15. Jammu (*excludes Ry. population*) ..	....	....	....	....	....	....	146	55	1	....	5	....	4	....	....	....	....	....

TABLE X.

OCCUPATION.

Jammu and Kashmir Census 1931.

District, Ilaqa, Jagir or City.	Sub-Class VIII. Professions and liberal arts. Total of Sub-class VIII. Total earners (principal occupation). Males.	Females.	Total working dependents. Males.	Females.	Total following occupation as subsidiary to others. Males.	Females.	Order 45. Religion. Total of Order 45. Total earners (principal occupation). Males.	Females.	Total working dependents. Males.	Females.	Total following occupation as subsidiary to others. Males.	Females.	Group 163. Priests, Ministers, etc. Total earners (principal occupation). Males.	Females.	Total working dependents. Males.	Females.	Total following occupation as subsidiary to others. Males.	Females.
Jammu and Kashmir State ..	12,572	804	234	48	3,695	234	7,962	473	154	33	2,535	164	3,994	173	105	12	1,025	45
I. Jammu Province ..	5,343	517	133	30	1,823	223	3,162	235	69	24	1,229	144	1,238	90	36	3	514	39
1. Jammu District (*including city*) ..	2,509	267	43	23	643	94	1,401	105	28	20	477	56	380	14	9	....	95	6
2. Kathua „ ..	724	127	15	5	280	64	569	113	14	3	284	46	332	87	10	3	66	23
3. Udhampur „ ..	850	32	16	1	454	27	387	17	8	....	213	15	197	1	2	....	130	....
4. Reasi „ ..	297	27	19	....	139	13	103	23	1	....	98	8	154	11	1	....	96	5
5. Mirpur „ ..	670	53	16	1	220	26	449	23	16	1	149	17	136	7	14	....	87	5
6. Poonch Jagir ..	247	9	24	....	82	4	98	4	2	....	38	2	82	....	....	....	31	....
7. Chenani „ ..	37	....	....	....	....	....	35	....	....	....	....	....	7	....	....	....	....	....
II. Kashmir Province ..	5,966	99	98	9	1,590	38	3,695	7	76	1	1,046	7	2,371	4	63	1	498	6
8. Kashmir North ..	1,574	9	22	3	492	9	1,058	....	17	1	247	4	640	....	14	1	146	3
9. Kashmir South (*including city*) ..	4,028	79	52	5	995	19	2,452	7	40	....	751	....	1,543	4	30	....	305	....
10. Muzaffarabad ..	364	11	24	1	103	10	185	....	19	....	48	3	179	....	19	....	47	3
III. Frontier Districts ..	1,233	188	23	9	277	18	1,105	131	9	8	260	13	335	79	6	8	13	....
11. Ladakh ..	1,159	182	2	8	240	18	1,039	179	2	8	232	13	283	77	2	8	....	....
12. Gilgit ..	79	5	13	....	16	....	42	1	....	....	12	....	42	1	....	....	12	....
13. Frontier Ilaqas ..	25	1	8	1	21	....	24	1	7	....	16	....	10	1	4	....	1	....
IV. Cities:—																		
14. Srinagar ..	2,135	51	15	3	129	13	935	2	8	....	59	....	995	2	8	....	59	....
15. Jammu (*excludes Ry. population*)	896	124	13	9	127	21	366	42	8	9	74	15	322	....	8	....	68	....

TABLE X.

Occupation.

Jammu and Kashmir Census 1931.

District, Ilaqa, Jagir or City.	Group 164. Monks, nuns and religious mendicants. Total earners (principal occupation). Males.	Females.	Total working dependents. Males.	Females.	Total following occupation as subsidiary to others. Males.	Females.	Group 165. Other religious workers. Total earners (principal occupation). Males.	Females.	Total working dependents. Males.	Females.	Total following occupation as subsidiary to others. Males.	Females.	Group 166. Servants in religious edifices, burial and burning grounds, pilgrim conductors and circumcisers, etc. Total earners (principal occupation). Males.	Females.	Total working dependents. Males.	Females.	Total following occupation as subsidiary to others. Males.	Females.
Jammu and Kashmir State ..	1,005	106	18	11	345	60	2,282	188	24	9	898	56	681	6	7	1	267	3
I. Jammu Province ..	804	106	18	11	277	60	986	85	15	9	418	42	84	4	....	1	20	3
1. Jammu District (*including city*) ..	557	27	11	11	175	29	443	60	8	8	188	20	81	4	....	1	19	1
2. Kathua „ ..	124	55	....	....	61	23	115	1	4	....	127	....	....	....	....	....	....	....
3. Udhampur „ ..	34	1	4	....	26	....	154	15	2	....	47	15	2	....	....	....	1	....
4. Reasi „ ..	....	12	....	....	....	3	9	....	....	....	2	....	....	....	....	....	....	....
5. Mirpur „ ..	48	11	2	....	14	4	264	5	....	1	48	6	1	....	....	....	....	2
6. Poonch Jagir ..	13	....	1	....	1	1	3	4	1	....	6	1	....	....	....	....	....	....
7. Chenani „ ..	28	....	....	....	....	....	....	....	....	....	....	....	....	....	....	....	....	....
II. Kashmir Province ..	184	....	....	....	59	....	553	1	9	....	258	1	587	2	4	....	231	....
8. Kashmir North ..	....	....	....	....	....	....	405	....	3	....	100	1	4	....	....	....	1	....
9. Kashmir South (*including city*) ..	183	....	....	....	59	....	148	1	6	....	158	....	578	2	4	....	229	....
10. Muzaffarabad ..	1	....	....	....	....	....	....	....	....	....	....	....	5	....	....	....	1	....
III. Frontier Districts ..	17	....	....	....	9	....	743	102	....	....	222	13	10	....	3	....	16	....
11. Ladakh ..	17	....	....	....	9	....	739	102	....	....	222	13	....	....	....	....	1	....
12. Gilgit ..	....	....	....	....	....	....	....	....	....	....	....	....	....	....	....	....	....	....
13. Frontier Ilaqas ..	....	....	....	....	....	....	4	....	....	....	....	....	10	....	3	....	15	....
IV. Cities.—																		
14. Srinagar ..	....	....	....	....	....	....	....	....	....	....	....	....	....	....	....	....	....	....
15. Jammu (*excludes Ry. population*) ..	7	....	....	....	1	....	5	38	....	8	....	14	32	4	....	1	5	1

TABLE X.

OCCUPATION.

Jammu and Kashmir Census 1931.

District, Ilaqa, Jagir or City.	Order 46. Law. Total of Order 46. Total earners (principal occupation).		Total working dependents.		Total following occupation as subsidiary to others.		Group 167. Lawyers of all kinds, including Qazis, law agents and mukhtiars. Total earners (principal occupation).		Total working dependents.		Total following occupation as subsidiary to others.		Group 168. Lawyers, clerks, petition-writers, etc. Total earners (principal occupation).		Total working dependents.		Total following occupation as subsidiary to others.	
	Males.	Females.	Males.	Females.	Males.	Females.	Males.	Females.	Males.	Females.	Males.	Females.	Males.	Females.	Males.	Females.	Males.	Females.
Jammu and Kashmir State ..	586	1	12	....	139	....	121	1	2	....	38	....	445	....	10	....	101	....
I. Jammu Province ..	296	....	9	....	88	....	49	....	....	....	22	....	247	....	9	....	66	....
1. Jammu District (*including city*) ..	181	....	9	....	37	....	37	....	....	....	7	....	144	....	9	....	30	....
2. Kathua „ ..	18	....	....	....	4	....	5	....	....	....	....	....	13	....	....	....	4	....
3. Udhampur „ ..	49	....	....	....	19	....	5	....	....	....	12	....	44	....	....	....	7	....
4. Reasi „ ..	4	....	....	....	....	....	....	....	....	....	....	....	4	....	....	....	....	....
5. Mirpur „ ..	29	....	....	....	20	....	....	....	....	....	....	....	29	....	....	....	20	....
6. Poonch Jagir ..	15	....	....	....	8	....	2	....	....	....	3	....	13	....	....	....	5	....
7. Chenani „ ..	....	....	....	....	....	....	....	....	....	....	....	....	....	....	....	....	....	....
II. Kashmir Province ..	267	1	3	....	51	....	72	1	2	....	16	....	195	....	1	....	35	....
8. Kashmir North ..	13	....	....	....	5	....	....	....	....	....	1	....	13	....	....	....	4	....
9. Kashmir South (*including city*) ..	247	1	3	....	43	....	72	1	2	....	15	....	175	....	1	....	28	....
10. Muzaffarabad ..	7	....	....	....	3	....	....	....	....	....	....	....	7	....	....	....	3	....
III. Frontier Districts ..	3	....	....	....	....	....	....	....	....	....	....	....	3	....	....	....	....	....
11. Ladakh ..	....	....	....	....	....	....	....	....	....	....	....	....	....	....	....	....	....	....
12. Gilgit ..	3	....	....	....	....	....	....	....	....	....	....	....	3	....	....	....	....	....
13. Frontier Ilaqas ..	....	....	....	....	....	....	....	....	....	....	....	....	....	....	....	....	....	....
IV. Cities :—																		
14. Srinagar ..	218	1	3	....	22	....	63	1	2	....	12	....	155	....	1	....	10	....
15. Jammu (*excludes Ry. population*)	78	....	....	....	11	....	34	....	....	....	7	....	44	....	....	....	4	....

TABLE X.

Occupation.

Jammu and Kashmr Census 1931.

District, Ilaqa, Jagir or City.	Order 47. Medicine. Total of Order 47.						Group 169. Registered medical practitioners including oculists.						Group 170. Other persons practising the healing arts without being registered.					
	Total earners (principal occupation).		Total working dependents.		Total following occupation as subsidiary to others.		Total earners (principal occupation).		Total working dependents.		Total following occupation as subsidiary to others.		Total earners (principal occupation).		Total working dependents.		Total following occupation as subsidiary to others.	
	Males.	Females.	Males.	Females.	Males.	Females.	Males.	Females.	Males.	Females.	Males.	Females.	Males.	Females.	Males.	Females.	Males.	Females.
Jammu and Kashmir State ..	997	116	6	8	160	35	267	9	3	1	48	1	382	14	2	1	82	5
I. Jammu Province ..	435	89	5	6	85	28	104	5	3	....	23	....	227	10	1	....	48	3
1. Jammu District (*including city*) ..	226	59	5	3	31	14	70	4	3	....	8	....	68	2	1	....	11	1
Kathua " ..	41	11	....	2	19	7	7	....	....	....	2	....	30	....	....	....	16	....
3. Udhampur " ..	109	2	....	1	13	2	7	1	....	....	1	....	101	1	....	....	6	....
4. Reasi " ..	10	3	....	....	11	3	7	....	....	....	8	....	1	....	....	....	3	1
5. Mirpur " ..	32	13	....	....	6	1	3	....	....	....	1	....	25	7	....	....	5	1
6. Poonch Jagir ..	17	1	....	....	5	1	10	....	....	....	3	....	2	....	....	....	2	....
7. Chenani " ..	....	....	....	....	....	....	....	....	....	....	....	....	....	....	....	....	....	....
II. Kashmir Province ..	513	23	1	2	72	7	159	4	....	1	24	1	135	4	1	1	37	2
8. Kashmir North ..	124	4	1	1	30	2	23	....	....	....	7	....	91	4	1	1	21	2
9. Kashmir South (*including city*) ..	352	14	....	1	35	3	123	4	....	1	17	1	39	....	....	....	12	....
10. Muzaffarabad ..	37	5	....	....	7	2	13	....	....	....	....	....	5	....	....	....	4	....
III. Frontier Districts ..	49	4	....	....	3	....	4	....	....	....	1	....	20	....	....	....	2	....
11. Ladakh ..	45	....	....	....	3	....	4	....	....	....	1	....	20	....	....	....	2	....
12. Gilgit ..	4	4	....	....	....	....	....	....	....	....	....	....	....	....	....	....	....	....
13. Frontier Ilaqas ..	....	....	....	....	....	....	....	....	....	....	....	....	....	....	....	....	....	....
IV. Cities.—																		
14. Srinagar ..	271	14	....	....	7	2	82	4	....	....	1	1	....	....	....	....	....	....
15. Jammu (*excludes Ry. population*) ..	125	20	4	....	8	4	56	4	3	....	5	....	25	1	....	....	....	....

TABLE X.

OCCUPATION.

Jammu and Kashmir Census 1931.

District, Ilaqa, Jagir or City.	Group 171. Dentists. Total earners (principal occupation). Males.	Females.	Total working dependents. Males.	Females.	Total following occupation as subsidiary to others. Males.	Females.	Group 172. Midwives, vaccinators, compounders, nurses, masseurs, etc. Total earners (principal occupation). Males.	Females.	Total working dependents. Males.	Females.	Total following occupation as subsidiary to others. Males.	Females.	Group 173. Veterinary Surgeons. Total earners (principal occupation). Males.	Females.	Total working dependents. Males.	Females.	Total following occupation as subsidiary to others. Males.	Females.
Jammu and Kashmir State ..	19	1	....	....	2	....	313	89	....	5	25	24	16	3	1	1	3	5
I. Jammu Province ..	19	1	....	....	2	....	83	70	....	5	16	20	2	3	1	1	1	5
1. Jammu District (*including city*) ..	17	1	....	....	2	....	70	49	....	2	10	9	1	3	1	1	....	4
2. Kathua " ..	....	....	....	....	....	....	4	11	....	2	1	7	....	....	....	....	....	....
3. Udhampur " ..	....	....	....	....	....	....	....	....	....	1	5	1	1	....	....	....	1	1
4. Reasi " ..	....	....	....	....	....	....	2	3	....	....	....	2	....	....	....	....	....	....
5. Mirpur " ..	....	....	....	....	....	....	4	6	....	....	....	....	....	....	....	....	....	....
6. Poonch Jagir ..	2	....	....	....	....	....	3	1	....	....	....	1	....	....	....	....	....	....
7. Chenani " ..	....	....	....	....	....	....	....	....	....	....	....	....	....	....	....	....	....	....
II. Kashmir Province ..	....	....	....	....	....	....	206	15	....	....	9	4	13	....	....	....	2	....
8. Kashmir North ..	....	....	....	....	....	....	10	....	....	....	2	....	....	....	....	....	....	....
9. Kashmir South (*including city*) ..	....	....	....	....	....	....	177	10	....	....	4	2	13	....	....	....	2	....
10. Muzaffarabad ..	....	....	....	....	....	....	19	5	....	....	3	2	....	....	....	....	....	....
III. Frontier Districts ..	....	....	....	....	....	....	24	4	....	....	....	....	1	....	....	....	....	....
11. Ladakh	....	....	....	....	....	....	30	....	....	....	....	....	1	....	....	....	....	....
12. Gilgit ..	....	....	....	....	....	....	4	4	....	....	....	....	....	....	....	....	....	....
13. Frontier Ilaqas ..	....	....	....	....	....	....	....	....	....	....	....	....	....	....	....	....	....	....
IV. Cities.—																		
14. Srinagar ..	....	....	....	....	....	....	177	10	....	....	4	1	12	....	....	....	2	....
15. Jammu (*excludes Ry. population*) ..	3	....	....	....	....	....	40	15	....	....	3	4	1	....	1	....	....	....

TABLE X.

OCCUPATION.

Jammu and Kashmir Census 1931.

District, Ilaqa, Jagir or City.	Order 48. Instruction. Total of Order 48.						Group 174. Professors and teachers of all kinds.						Group 175. Clerks and servants connected with education.					
	Total earners (principal occupation).		Total working dependents.		Total following occupation as subsidiary to others.		Total earners (principal occupation).		Total working dependents.		Total following occupation as subsidiary to others.		Total earners (principal occupation).		Total working dependents.		Total following occupation as subsidiary to others.	
	Males.	Females.	Males.	Females.	Males.	Females.	Males.	Females.	Males.	Females.	Males.	Females.	Males.	Females.	Males.	Females.	Males.	Females.
Jammu and Kashmir State ..	1,887	175	44	4	331	43	1,450	121	19	4	213	25	437	54	25	....	118	18
I. Jammu Province ..	732	111	28	....	144	27	463	64	2	....	67	13	269	47	24	....	77	14
1. Jammu District (*including city*) ..	418	74	....	....	59	4	295	47	....	....	31	2	123	27	....	....	28	2
2. Kathua " ..	36	3	....	....	3	9	28	....	....	....	1	1	8	3	....	....	2	8
3. Udhampur " ..	95	12	5	....	37	7	35	7	....	....	19	3	60	5	5	....	18	4
4. Reasi " ..	77	1	....	....	28	2	24	1	....	....	....	2	53	....	....	....	28	....
5. Mirpur " ..	56	19	....	....	3	5	37	7	....	....	3	5	19	12	....	....	....	....
6. Poonch Jagir ..	50	2	21	....	14	....	44	2	2	....	13	....	6	....	19	....	1	....
7. Chenani " ..	....	....	....	....	....	....	....	....	....	....	....	....	....	....	....	....	....	....
II. Kashmir Province ..	1,105	64	5	4	181	16	937	57	4	4	140	12	168	7	1	....	41	4
8. Kashmir North ..	204	5	1	....	45	3	36	....	....	....	4	....	168	5	1	....	41	3
9. Kashmir South (*including city*) ..	836	54	4	3	121	10	836	52	4	3	121	9	....	2	....	....	....	1
10. Muzaffarabad ..	65	5	....	1	15	3	65	5	....	1	15	3	....	....	....	....	....	....
III. Frontier Districts ..	50	....	13	....	6	....	50	....	13	....	6	....	....	....	....	....	....	....
11. Ladakh	33	....	....	....	4	....	33	....	....	....	4	....	....	....	....	....	....	....
12. Gilgit ..	16	....	13	....	2	....	16	....	13	....	2	....	....	....	....	....	....	....
13. Frontier Ilaqas ..	1	....	....	....	....	....	1	....	....	....	....	....	....	....	....	....	....	....
IV. Cities.—																		
14. Srinagar ..	569	31	1	2	37	5	569	31	1	2	37	5	....	....	....	....	....	....
15. Jammu (*excludes Ry. population*) ..	276	61	....	....	26	2	212	41	....	....	21	1	64	20	....	....	5	1

TABLE X.

OCCUPATION.

Jammu and Kashmir Census 1931.

District, Ilaqa, Jagir or City.	ORDER 49. Letters, arts and sciences (other than 44) — TOTAL OF ORDER 49.						GROUP 176. Public scribes, stenographers, etc.						GROUP 177. Architects, surveyors, engineers, and their employees (not being State servants).					
	Total earners (principal occupation).		Total working dependents.		Total following occupation as subsidiary to others.		Total earners (principal occupation).		Total working dependents.		Total following occupation as subsidiary to others.		Total earners (principal occupation).		Total working dependents.		Total following occupation as subsidiary to others.	
	Males.	Females.	Males.	Females.	Males.	Females.	Males.	Females.	Males.	Females.	Males.	Females.	Males.	Females.	Males.	Females.	Males.	Females.
Jammu and Kashmir State ..	1,160	39	38	3	530	42	19	4	1	....	2	1	25	....	....	....	7	....
I. Jammu Province ..	718	32	24	....	282	29	18	4	....	....	2	1	9	....	....	....	5	....
1. Jammu District (*including city*) ..	223	29	1	....	39	20	18	4	....	....	2	1	9	....	....	....	3	....
2. Kathua " ..	60	....	1	....	10	2	....	....	....	....	....	....	....	....	....	....	....	....
3. Udhampur " ..	210	1	3	....	172	3	....	....	....	....	....	....	....	....	....	....	2	....
4. Reasi " ..	43	....	18	....	2	....	....	....	....	....	....	....	....	....	....	....	....	....
5. Mirpur " ..	113	....	....	....	42	3	....	....	....	....	....	....	....	....	....	....	....	....
6. Poonch Jagir ..	67	2	1	....	17	1	....	....	....	....	....	....	....	....	....	....	....	....
7. Chenani " ..	2	....	....	....	....	....	....	....	....	....	....	....	....	....	....	....	....	....
II. Kashmir Province ..	386	4	13	2	240	8	1	....	....	....	....	....	3	....	....	....	....	....
8. Kashmir North ..	175	....	3	1	165	....	....	....	....	....	....	....	....	....	....	....	....	....
9. Kashmir South (*including city*) ..	141	3	5	1	45	6	1	....	....	....	....	....	....	....	....	....	....	....
10. Muzaffarabad ..	70	1	5	....	30	2	....	....	....	....	....	....	3	....	....	....	....	....
III. Frontier Districts ..	56	3	1	1	8	5	....	....	1	....	....	....	13	....	....	....	2	....
11. Ladakh ..	42	3	....	....	1	5	....	....	....	....	....	....	....	....	....	....	....	....
12. Gilgit ..	14	....	....	....	2	....	....	....	....	....	....	....	13	....	....	....	2	....
13. Frontier Ilaqas ..	....	....	1	1	5	....	....	....	1	....	....	....	....	....	....	....	....	....
IV. Cities.—																		
14. Srinagar ..	82	3	3	1	4	6	....	....	....	....	....	....	....	....	....	....	....	....
15. Jammu (*excludes Ry. population*) ..	51	1	1	....	8	....	6	1	....	....	....	....	9	....	....	....	3	....

TABLE X.

OCCUPATION.

Jammu and Kashmr Census 1931.

District, Ilaqa, Jagir or City.	Order 178. Authors, editors, journalists and photographers.						Group 180. Scientists, astronomers, botanists, etc.						Group 181. Horoscope casters, astrologers, fortune tellers, wizards, witches and mediums.					
	Total earners (principal occupation).		Total working dependents.		Total following occupation as subsidiary to others.		Total earners (principal occupation).		Total working dependents.		Total following occupation as subsidiary to others.		Total earners (principal occupation).		Total working dependents.		Total following occupation as subsidiary to others.	
	Males.	Females.	Males.	Females.	Males.	Females.	Males.	Females.	Males.	Females.	Males.	Females.	Males.	Females.	Males.	Females.	Males.	Females.
Jammu and Kashmir State ..	29	....	2	....	1	....	3	....	....	....	....	....	16	....	1	....	1	....
I. Jammu Province ..	2	....	....	....	....	....	3	....	....	....	....	....	11	....	....	....	1	....
1. Jammu District (*including city*) ..	1	....	....	....	....	....	1	....	....	....	....	....	10	....	....	....	1	....
Kathua " ..	....	....	....	....	....	....	....	....	....	....	....	....	....	....	....	....	....	....
3. Udhampur " ..	1	....	....	....	....	....	....	....	....	....	....	....	....	....	....	....	....	....
4. Reasi " ..	....	....	....	....	....	....	....	....	....	....	....	....	1	....	....	....	....	....
5. Mirpur " ..	....	....	....	....	....	....	....	....	....	....	....	....	....	....	....	....	....	....
6. Poonch Jagir ..	....	....	....	....	....	....	2	....	....	....	....	....	....	....	....	....	....	....
7. Chenani " ..	....	....	....	....	....	....	....	....	....	....	....	....	....	....	....	....	....	....
II. Kashmir Province ..	27	....	2	....	1	....	....	....	....	....	....	....	5	....	1	....	....	....
8. Kashmir North ..	....	....	....	....	....	....	....	....	....	....	....	....	2	....	....	....	....	....
9. Kashmir South (*including city*) ..	27	....	2	....	1	....	....	....	....	....	....	....	....	....	....	....	....	....
10. Muzaffarabad ..	....	....	....	....	....	....	....	....	....	....	....	....	3	....	1	....	....	....
III. Frontier Districts ..	....	....	....	....	....	....	....	....	....	....	....	....	....	....	....	....	....	....
11. Ladakh :	....	....	....	....	....	....	....	....	....	....	....	....	....	....	....	....	....	....
12. Gilgit ..	....	....	....	....	....	....	....	....	....	....	....	....	....	....	....	....	....	....
13. Frontier Ilaqas ..	....	....	....	....	....	....	....	....	....	....	....	....	....	....	....	....	....	....
IV. Cities.—																		
14. Srinagar ..	27	....	2	....	1	....	....	....	....	....	....	....	....	....	....	....	....	....
15. Jammu (*excludes Ry. popuation*) ..	1	....	....	....	....	....	1	....	....	....	....	....	10	....	....	....	1	....

TABLE X.

OCCUPATION.

Jammu and Kashmir Census 1931.

District, Ilaqa, Jagir or City.	Group 182. Musicians (composers and performers other than military) actors, dancers, etc.						Group 183. Managers and employees of places of public entertainment, race courses, societies, clubs, etc.						Group 184. Conjurors, acrobats, reciters, exhibitors of curiosities and wild animals, etc.					
	Total earners (principal occupation).		Total working dependents.		Total following occupation as subsidiary to others.		Total earners (principal occupation.)		Total working dependents.		Total following occupation as subsidiary to others.		Total earners (principal occupation).		Total working dependents.		Total following occupation as subsidiary to others.	
	Males.	Females.	Males.	Females.	Males.	Females.	Males.	Females.	Males.	Females.	Males.	Females.	Males.	Females.	Males.	Females.	Males.	Females.
Jammu and Kashmir State ..	757	23	14	3	334	19	41	10	....	....	7	19	270	2	20	....	178	3
I. Jammu Province ..	366	16	4	....	94	7	41	10	....	....	7	19	268	2	20	....	173	2
1. Jammu District (*including city*) ..	118	13	1	....	26	....	39	10	....	....	7	18	27	2	....	....	....	1
2. Kathua " ..	39	....	1	....	7	....	....	....	....	....	....	1	21	....	....	....	3	1
3. Udhampur " ..	26	1	1	....	10	3	....	....	....	....	....	....	183	....	2	....	160	....
4. Reasi " ..	33	....	....	....	2	....	....	....	....	....	....	....	9	....	18	....	....	....
5. Mirpur " ..	85	....	....	....	32	3	....	....	....	....	....	....	28	....	....	....	10	....
6. Poonch Jagir ..	63	2	1	....	17	1	2	....	....	....	....	....	....	....	....	....	....	....
7. Chenani " ..	2	....	....	....	....	....	....	....	....	....	....	....	....	....	....	....	....	....
II. Kashmir Province ..	348	4	10	2	234	7	....	....	....	....	....	....	2	....	....	....	5	1
8. Kashmir North ..	173	....	3	1	165	....	....	....	....	....	....	....	....	....	....	....	....	....
9. Kashmir South (*including city*)	113	3	3	1	44	6	....	....	....	....	....	....	....	....	....	....	....	....
10. Muzaffarabad ..	62	1	4	....	25	1	....	....	....	....	....	....	2	....	....	....	5	1
III. Frontier Districts ..	43	3	....	1	6	5	....	....	....	....	....	....	....	....	....	....	....	....
11. Ladakh ..	42	3	....	....	1	5	....	....	....	....	....	....	....	....	....	....	....	....
12. Gilgit ..	1	....	....	....	....	....	....	....	....	....	....	....	....	....	....	....	....	....
13. Frontier Ilaqas ..	....	....	....	1	5	....	....	....	....	....	....	....	....	....	....	....	....	....
IV. Cities—																		
14. Srinagar ..	55	3	1	1	3	6	....	....	....	....	....	....	....	....	....	....	....	....
15. Jammu (*excludes Ry. population*)	15	....	1	....	4	....	9	....	....	....	....	....	....	....	....	....	....	....

TABLE X.

OCCUPATION.

Jammu and Kashmir Census 1931.

District, Ilaqa, Jagir or City.	Class D. Miscellaneous. Total of Class D.						Sub-Class IX. Persons living on their income. Total of Sub-Class IX.						Group 50. Persons living principally on their income. Total of Order 50.					
	Total earners (principal occupation).		Total working dependents.		Total following occupation as subsidiary to others.		Total earners (principal occupation.)		Total working dependents.		Total following occupation as subsidiary to others.		Total earners (principal occupation).		Total working dependents.		Total following occupation as subsidiary to others.	
	Males.	Females.	Males.	Females.	Males.	Females.	Males.	Females.	Males.	Females.	Males.	Females.	Males.	Females.	Males.	Females.	Males.	Females.
Jammu and Kashmir State ..	**44,788**	**22,555**	**15,371**	**864,016**	**6,454**	**1,353**	**1,967**	**100**	**110**	**495**	**787**	**56**	**1,967**	**100**	**110**	**495**	**787**	**56**
I. Jammu Province ..	20,466	**15,857**	**7,489**	**389,643**	**3,983**	**1,145**	**935**	**91**	**88**	**494**	**674**	**54**	**935**	**91**	**88**	**494**	**674**	**54**
1. Jammu District (*including City*) ..	8,023	1,195	1,694	76,249	1,600	451	616	55	83	479	441	19	616	55	83	479	441	19
2. Kathua " ..	2,777	227	458	35,970	483	89	40	2	....	....	62	5	40	2	....	....	62	5
3. Udhampur " ..	1,858	308	1,540	67,152	381	119	22	1	1	....	22	4	22	1	1	....	22	4
4. Reasi " ..	2,301	369	804	48,595	589	103	34	7	....	1	44	4	34	7	....	1	44	4
5. Mirpur " ..	2,968	539	926	76,578	569	301	93	7	3	5	66	13	93	7	3	5	66	13
6. Poonch Jagir ..	2,411	13,182	1,971	84,591	353	80	125	19	1	9	39	9	125	19	1	9	39	9
7. Chenani " ..	128	37	96	508	8	2	5	....	....	....	....	....	5	....	....	....	....	....
II. Kashmir Province ..	**21,788**	**6,961**	**3,458**	**404,409**	**2,347**	125	**1,023**	**9**	**22**	**1**	**113**	**2**	**1,023**	**9**	**22**	**1**	**113**	**2**
8. Kashmir North ..	5,563	5,304	827	132,724	952	58	10	....	....	....	2	....	10	....	....	....	2	....
9. Kashmir South (*including City*)	14,175	447	1,633	215,097	1,140	30	995	8	19	1	57	2	995	8	19	1	57	2
10. Muzaffarabad ..	2,050	310	998	56,588	255	37	18	1	3	....	54	....	18	1	3	....	54	....
III. Frontier Districts ..	**2,534**	**637**	**4,424**	**69,964**	**124**	**83**	**9**	....	....	....	....	....	9	....	....	....	....	....
11. Ladakh ..	1,792	591	3,770	59,187	46	81	2	....	....	....	....	....	2	....	....	....	....	....
12. Gilgit ..	443	30	277	7,258	40	1	7	....	....	....	....	....	7	....	....	....	....	....
13. Frontier Ilaqas ..	299	16	377	3,519	38	1	....	....	....	....	....	....	....	....	....	....	....	....
IV. Cities—																		
14. Srinagar ..	9,933	395	741	61	440	12	942	6	13	....	43	....	942	6	13	....	43	....
15. Jammu (*excludes Ry. population*)	3,109	546	385	4,419	537	36	300	47	52	7	116	8	300	47	52	7	116	8

TABLE X.

OCCUPATION.

Jammu and Kashmir Census 1931.

District, Ilaqa, Jagir or City.	Group 185. Proprietors (other than of agricultural land), fund and scholarship holders and pensioners.						Sub-Class X. Domestic service. Total of Sub-Class X.						Order 51. Domestic service. Total of Order 51.					
	Total earners (principal occupation).		Total working dependents.		Total following occupation as subsidiary to others.		Total earners (principal occupation).		Total working dependents.		Total following occupation as subsidiary to others.		Total earners (principal occupation).		Total working dependents.		Total following occupation as subsidiary to others.	
	Males.	Females.	Males.	Females.	Males.	Females.	Males.	Females.	Males.	Females.	Males.	Females.	Males.	Females.	Males.	Females.	Males.	Females.
Jammu and Kashmir State ..	1,967	100	110	495	787	56	20,403	13,314	8,413	531,770	2,320	258	20,403	13,314	8,413	531,770	2,329	258
I. Jammu Province ..	935	91	88	494	674	54	8,261	7,343	1,405	63,742	1,442	170	8,261	7,343	1,405	63,742	1,442	170
1. Jammu District (*including city*) ..	616	55	83	479	441	19	2,508	205	162	3,525	371	90	2,508	205	162	3,525	371	90
2. Kathua " ..	40	2	....	....	62	5	1,315	57	64	5	95	4	1,315	57	64	5	95	4
3. Udhampur " ..	22	1	1	....	22	4	900	69	386	31	188	13	900	69	386	31	188	13
4. Reasi " ..	34	7	....	1	44	4	1,260	32	463	7	390	4	1,260	32	463	7	390	4
5. Mirpur " ..	93	7	3	5	66	13	965	53	122	1,302	166	45	965	53	122	1,302	166	45
6. Poonch Jagir ..	125	19	1	9	39	9	1,261	6,802	208	58,872	224	12	1,261	6,802	208	58,872	224	12
7. Chenani " ..	5	....	....	....	....	....	52	35	....	....	8	2	52	35	....	....	8	2
II. Kashmir Province ..	1,023	9	22	1	113	2	10,079	5,536	2,761	404,312	804	48	10,079	5,536	2,761	404,312	804	48
8. Kashmir North ..	10	....	....	....	2	....	2,439	5,229	649	132,701	268	40	2,439	5,229	649	132,701	268	40
9. Kashmir South (*including city*) ..	995	8	19	1	57	2	6,400	157	1,177	215,052	429	5	6,400	157	1,177	215,052	429	5
10. Muzaffarabad ..	18	1	3	....	54	....	1,240	150	935	56,559	107	3	1,240	150	935	56,559	107	3
III. Frontier Districts ..	9	....	....	....	....	....	2,063	435	4,247	63,716	83	40	2,063	435	4,247	63,716	83	40
11. Ladakh ..	2	....	....	....	....	....	1,608	410	3,770	52,958	34	40	1,608	410	3,770	52,958	34	40
12. Gilgit ..	7	....	....	....	....	....	309	9	231	7,255	30	....	309	9	231	7,255	30	....
13. Frontier Ilaqas ..	....	....	....	....	....	....	146	16	246	3,503	19	....	146	16	246	3,503	19	....
IV. Cities :—																		
14. Srinagar ..	942	6	13	....	43	....	4,104	138	394	25	147	4	4,104	138	394	25	147	4
15. Jammu (*excludes Ry. population*)	300	47	52	7	116	8	1,458	226	3	1	136	15	1,458	226	3	1	136	15

TABLE X.

OCCUPATION.

Jammu and Kashmir Census 1931.

District, Ilaqa, Jagir or City.	Group 186. Private motor drivers and cleaners.						Group 187. Other domestic service.						Sub-Class XI. Insufficiently described occupation. Total of Sub-class XI.					
	Total earners (principal occupation).		Total working dependents.		Total following occupation as subsidiary to others.		Total earners (principal occupation).		Total working dependents.		Total following occupation as subsidiary to others.		Total earners (principal occupation).		Total working dependents.		Total following occupation as subsidiary to others.	
	Males.	Females.	Males.	Females.	Males.	Females.	Males.	Females.	Males.	Females.	Males.	Females.	Males.	Females.	Males.	Females.	Males.	Females.
Jammu and Kashmir State ..	**2,144**	**42**	**363**	**3,526**	**183**	**65**	**18,259**	**13,272**	**8,050**	**528,244**	**2,146**	**193**	**13,684**	**6,592**	**5,361**	**331,182**	**2,128**	**698**
I. Jammu Province ..	**2,017**	**42**	**362**	**3,526**	**146**	**65**	**6,244**	**7,301**	**1,043**	**60,216**	**1,296**	**105**	**5,917**	**6,500**	**5,319**	**324,923**	**1,163**	**681**
1. Jammu District (*including city*) ..	457	12	....	3,524	19	59	2,051	283	162	1	352	31	2,876	624	1,008	72,209	554	317
2. Kathua „ ..	75	1	49	1	5	1	1,240	56	15	4	90	3	918	76	379	35,858	203	55
3. Udhampur „ ..	72	1	....	....	16	....	828	68	386	31	172	13	445	177	1,068	67,112	87	89
4. Reasi „ ..	814	17	310	1	44	4	446	15	153	6	346	....	264	179	327	48,579	107	51
5. Mirpur „ ..	17	....	....	....	3	....	948	53	122	1,302	163	45	921	172	767	74,980	152	139
6. Poonch Jagir ..	581	11	3	....	59	1	680	6,791	205	58,872	165	11	442	5,272	1,674	25,678	60	30
7. Chenani „ ..	1	....	....	....	....	....	51	35	....	....	8	2	51	....	96	507	....	....
II. Kashmir Province ..	**127**	....	**1**	....	**37**	....	**9,952**	**5,536**	**2,760**	**404,312**	**767**	**48**	**7,597**	**79**	**179**	**30**	**939**	**12**
8. Kashmir North ..	36	....	....	....	10	....	2,403	5,229	640	132,701	258	40	2,027	11	73	2	514	5
9. Kashmir South (*including city*) ..	4	....	....	....	1	....	6,396	157	1,177	215,052	428	5	5,316	49	102	27	378	6
10. Muzaffarabad ..	87	....	1	....	26	....	1,153	150	934	56,559	81	3	254	19	4	1	47	1
III. Frontier Districts ..	....	....	....	....	....	....	**2,063**	**435**	**4,247**	**63,716**	**83**	**40**	**170**	**13**	**63**	**6,229**	**26**	**5**
11. Ladakh ..	....	....	....	....	....	....	1,608	410	3,770	52,958	34	40	38	10	....	6,229	5	3
12. Gilgit ..	....	....	....	....	....	....	309	9	231	7,255	30	....	25	3	1	....	5	1
13. Frontier Ilaqas ..	....	....	....	....	....	....	146	16	246	3,503	19	....	107	....	62	....	16	1
IV. Cities— ..																		
14. Srinagar ..	....	....	....	....	....	....	4,104	138	394	25	147	4	4,522	46	55	27	241	6
15. Jammu (*excludes Ry. population*) ..	299	....	....	....	13	....	1,159	226	3	1	123	15	1,151	213	65	4,401	277	13

TABLE X.

OCCUPATION.

Jammu and Kashmir Census 1931.

District, Ilaqa, Jagir or City.	Order 52. General terms which do not indicate a definite occupation. Total of Order 52. Total earners (principal occupation).		Total working dependents.		Total following occupation as subsidiary to others.		Group 188. Manufacturers, business-men and contractors otherwise unspecified. Total earners (principal occupation).		Total working dependents.		Total following occupation as subsidiary to others.		Group 189. Cashiers, Accountants, Book keepers, Clerks and other employees in unspecified offices and ware-houses of shops. Total earners (principal occupation).		Total working dependents.		Total following occupation as subsidiary to others.	
	Males.	Females.	Males.	Females.	Males.	Females.	Males.	Females.	Males.	Females.	Males.	Females.	Males.	Females.	Males.	Females.	Males.	Females.
Jammu and Kashmir State ..	13,684	6,592	5,561	331,182	2,128	698	1,738	15	16	5	578	5	497	7	302	....	83	....
I. Jammu Province ..	5,917	6,500	5,319	324,923	1,163	681	727	7	8	....	284	4	183	....	294	....	34	....
1. Jammu District (*including city*) ..	2,876	624	1,008	72,209	554	317	279	5	4	....	52	4	72	....	2	....	7	....
2. Kathua ,, ..	918	76	379	35,858	203	55	80	....	....	....	79	....	....	....	....	....	....	....
3. Udhampur ,, ..	445	177	1,068	67,112	87	89	37	....	....	....	8	....	1	....	....	....	1	....
4. Reasi ,, ..	264	179	327	48,579	107	51	66	1	....	....	51	....	90	....	14	....	21	....
5. Mirpur ,, ..	921	172	767	74,980	152	139	254	1	4	....	86	....	....	....	....	....	....	....
6. Poonch Jagir ..	442	5,272	1,674	25,678	60	30	10	....	....	....	8	....	20	....	278	....	5	....
7. Chenani ,, ..	51	....	96	507	....	....	1	....	....	....	....	....	....	....	....	....	....	....
II. Kashmir Province ..	7,597	79	179	30	939	12	1,010	8	8	5	291	1	314	7	8	....	49	....
8. Kashmir North ..	2,027	11	73	2	514	5	116	....	2	....	172	....	283	....	8	....	48	....
9. Kashmir South (*including city*) ..	5,316	49	102	27	378	6	825	8	5	5	96	1	....	....	....	....	....	....
10. Muzaffarabad ..	254	19	4	1	47	1	69	....	1	....	23	....	31	7	....	....	1	....
III. Frontier Districts ..	170	13	63	6,229	26	5	1	....	....	....	3	....	....	....	....	....	....	....
11. Ladakh ..	38	10	....	6.229	5	3	1	....	....	....	3	....	....	....	....	....	....	....
12. Gilgit ..	25	3	1	....	5	1	....	....	....	....	....	....	....	....	....	....	....	....
13. Frontier Ilaqas ..	107	....	62	....	16	1	....	....	....	....	....	....	....	....	....	....	....	....
IV. Cities— ..																		
14. Srinagar ..	4,522	46	55	27	241	6	753	7	4	5	71	1	....	....	....	....	....	....
15. Jammu (*excludes Ry. population*) ..	1,151	213	65	4,401	277	13	158	....	3	....	22	....	34	....	1	....	1	....

TABLE X.

OCCUPATION.

Jammu and Kashmir Census 1931.

District, Ilaqa, Jagir or City.	GROUP 190. Mechanics otherwise unspecified. Total earners (principal occupation).		Total working dependents.		Total following occupation as subsidiary to others.		GROUP 191. Labourers and workmen otherwise unspecified. Total earners (principal occupation).		Total working dependents.		Total following occupation as subsidiary to others.		SUB-CLASS XII. Unproductive. TOTAL OF SUB-CLASS XII. Total earners (principal occupation).		Total working dependents.		Total following occupation as subsidiary to others.	
	Males.	Females.	Males.	Females.	Males.	Females.	Males.	Females.	Males.	Females.	Males.	Females.	Males.	Females.	Males.	Females.	Males.	Females.
Jammu and Kashmir State ..	120	....	199	....	35	9	11,329	6,570	5,044	331,177	1,432	684	8,734	2,549	1,287	569	1,210	341
I. Jammu Province ..	118	....	199	....	35	9	4,889	6,493	4,818	324,923	810	668	5,353	1,923	677	484	704	240
1. Jammu District (*including city*) ..	15	....	1	....	2	....	2,510	619	1,001	72,209	493	313	2,023	221	441	36	234	25
2. Kathua „ ..	79	....	....	....	33	....	759	76	379	35,858	91	55	504	92	15	107	123	25
3. Udhampur „ ..	....	....	....	....	....	....	407	177	1,068	67,112	78	89	491	61	85	9	84	13
4. Reasi „ ..	24	....	....	....	....	....	84	178	313	48,579	35	51	743	151	14	8	48	44
5. Mirpur „ ..	....	....	....	....	....	....	667	171	763	74,980	66	139	989	307	34	291	185	104
6. Poonch Jagir ..	....	....	198	....	....	9	412	5,272	1,198	25,678	47	21	583	1,089	88	32	30	29
7. Chenani „ ..	....	....	....	....	....	....	50	....	96	507	....	....	20	2	....	1	....	....
II. Kashmir Province ..	2	....	....	....	....	....	6,271	64	163	25	599	11	3,089	437	496	66	491	63
8. Kashmir North ..	2	....	....	....	....	....	1,626	11	63	2	294	5	1,087	64	105	21	168	13
9. Kashmir South (*including city*) ..	....	....	....	....	....	....	4,491	41	97	22	282	5	1,464	233	335	17	276	17
10. Muzaffarabad ..	....	....	....	....	....	....	154	12	3	1	23	1	538	140	56	28	47	33
III. Frontier Districts ..	....	....	....	....	....	....	169	13	63	6,229	23	5	292	189	114	19	15	38
11. Ladakh ..	....	....	....	....	....	....	37	10	....	6,229	2	3	144	171	....	....	7	38
12. Gilgit ..	....	....	....	....	....	....	25	3	1	....	5	1	102	18	45	3	5	....
13. Frontier Ilaqas ..	....	....	....	....	....	....	107	....	62	....	16	1	46	....	69	16	3	....
IV. Cities.—																		
14. Srinagar ..	....	....	....	....	....	....	3,769	39	51	22	170	5	365	205	279	9	9	2
15. Jammu (*excludes Ry. population*) ..	12	....	1	....	2	....	947	213	60	4,401	252	13	200	60	265	10	8	....

TABLE X.

OCCUPATION.

Jammu and Kashmir Census 1931.

District, Ilaqa, Jagir or City.	Order 53. Inmates of Jails, asylums and alms houses. Total of Order 53. Total earners (principal occupation).		Total working dependents.		Total following occupation as subsidiary to others.		Group 192. Inmates of jails, asylums and alms houses. Total earners (principal occupation).		Total working dependents.		Total following occupation as subsidiary to others.		Order 54. Beggars, vagrants, prostitutes. Total of Order 54. Total earners (principal occupation).		Total working dependents.		Total following occupation as subsidiary to others.	
	Males.	Females.	Males.	Females.	Males.	Females.	Males.	Females.	Males.	Females.	Males.	Females.	Males.	Females.	Males.	Females.	Males.	Females.
Jammu and Kashmir State ..	9	789	782	12	1	....	9	789	782	12	1	....	8,716	1,758	504	557	1,208	341
I. Jammu Province ..	2	789	451	10	....	....	2	789	451	10	....	....	5,342	1,132	225	474	708	240
1. Jammu District (*including city*) ..	....	....	396	10	....	....	....	....	396	10	....	....	2,015	219	44	26	234	25
2. Kathua " ..	....	1	....	....	....	....	....	1	....	....	....	....	503	91	15	107	122	25
3. Udhampur " ..	....	....	2	....	....	....	....	....	2	....	....	....	491	61	83	9	84	13
4. Reasi " ..	2	....	1	....	....	....	2	....	1	....	....	....	741	151	13	8	48	44
5. Mirpur " ..	....	....	6	....	....	....	....	....	6	....	....	....	989	307	28	291	185	104
6. Poonch Jagir	....	788	46	....	....	....	....	788	46	....	....	....	583	301	42	32	30	29
7. Chenani " ..	....	....	....	....	....	....	....	....	....	....	....	....	20	2	....	1	....	....
II. Kashmir Province ..	3	....	292	2	1	....	3	....	292	2	1	....	3,086	437	204	64	490	63
8. Kashmir North ..	....	....	....	....	....	....	....	....	....	....	....	....	1,087	64	105	21	168	13
9. Kashmir South (*including city*) ..	3	....	266	2	1	....	3	....	266	2	1	....	1,461	233	69	15	275	17
10. Muzaffarabad ..	....	....	26	....	....	....	....	....	26	....	....	....	538	140	30	28	47	33
III. Frontier Districts ..	4	....	39	....	....	....	4	....	39	....	....	....	288	189	75	19	15	38
11. Ladakh ..	2	....	....	....	....	....	2	....	....	....	....	....	142	171	....	....	7	38
12. Gilgit ..	2	....	39	....	....	....	2	....	39	....	....	....	100	18	6	3	5	....
13. Frontier Ilaqas ..	....	....	....	....	....	....	....	....	....	....	....	....	46	....	69	16	3	....
IV. Cities :—																		
14. Srinagar ..	....	....	266	2	....	....	....	....	266	2	....	....	365	205	13	7	9	2
15. Jammu (*excludes Ry. population*)	....	....	252	10	....	....	....	....	252	10	....	....	192	58	12	....	8	....

TABLE X.

OCCUPATION.

Jammu and Kashmir Census 1931.

District, Ilaqa, Jagir or City.	Group 193. Beggars and vagrants.						Group 194. Procurers and prostitutes.						Order 55. Other unclassified non-productive industries. Total of Order 55.					
	Total earners (principal occupation).		Total working dependents.		Total following occupation as subsidiary to others.		Total earners (principal occupation).		Total working dependents.		Total following occupation as subsidiary to others.		Total earners (principal occupation).		Total working dependents.		Total following occupation as subsidiary to others.	
	Males.	Females.	Males.	Females.	Males.	Females.	Males.	Females.	Males.	Females.	Males.	Females.	Males.	Females.	Males.	Females.	Males.	Females.
Jammu and Kashmir State ..	8,529	1,485	501	557	1,207	338	187	273	3	....	1	3	9	2	1	....	1	....
I. Jammu Province ..	5,329	1,101	222	474	702	239	13	31	3	....	1	1	9	2	1	....	1	....
1. Jammu District (*including city*) ..	2,013	193	44	26	234	25	2	26	....	....	....	....	8	2	1	....	....	....
2. Kathua " ..	503	91	15	107	122	25	....	....	....	....	....	....	1	....	....	....	1	....
3. Udhampur " ..	491	60	83	9	84	13	....	1	....	....	....	....	....	....	....	....	....	....
4. Reasi " ..	730	147	10	8	47	43	11	4	3	....	1	1	....	....	....	....	....	....
5. Mirpur " ..	989	307	28	291	185	104	....	....	....	....	....	....	....	....	....	....	....	....
6. Poonch Jagir	583	301	42	32	30	29	....	....	....	....	....	....	....	....	....	....	....	....
7. Chenani " ..	20	2	....	1	....	....	....	....	....	....	....	....	....	....	....	....	....	....
II. Kashmir Province ..	2,912	223	204	64	490	63	174	214	....	....	....	....	....	....	....	....	....	....
8. Kashmir North ..	1,082	48	105	21	168	13	5	16	....	....	....	....	....	....	....	....	....	....
9. Kashmir South (*including city*) ..	1,292	35	69	15	275	17	169	198	....	....	....	....	....	....	....	....	....	....
10. Muzaffarabad ..	538	140	30	28	47	33	....	....	....	....	....	....	....	....	....	....	....	....
III. Frontier Districts ..	288	161	75	19	15	36	....	28	....	....	....	2	....	....	....	....	....	....
11. Ladakh ..	142	143	....	....	7	36	....	28	....	....	....	2	....	....	....	....	....	....
12. Gilgit ..	100	18	6	3	5	....	....	....	....	....	....	....	....	....	....	....	....	....
13. Frontier Ilaqas ..	46	....	69	16	3	....	....	....	....	....	....	....	....	....	....	....	....	....
IV. Cities :—																		
14. Srinagar ..	206	18	13	7	9	2	159	187	....	....	....	....	....	....	....	....	....	....
15. Jammu (*excludes Ry. population*)	190	32	12	....	8	....	2	26	....	....	....	....	8	2	1	....	....	....

TABLE X.

OCCUPATION.

Jammu and Kashmir Census 1931.

District, Ilaqa, Jagir or City.	Group 195. Other unclassified non-productive industries.						Remarks.
	Total earners (principal occupation).		Total working dependents.		Total following occupation as subsidiary to others.		
	Males.	Females.	Males.	Females.	Males.	Females.	
Jammu and Kashmir State ..	9	2	1	....	1	....	
I. Jammu Province ..	9	2	1	....	1	....	
1. Jammu District (*including city*) ..	8	2	1	....	....	....	
2. Kathua ,, ..	1	....	....	....	1	....	
3. Udhampur ,, ..	....	....	....	....	....	....	
4. Reasi ,, ..	....	....	....	....	....	....	
5. Mirpur ,, ..	....	....	....	....	....	....	
6. Poonch Jagir ..	....	....	....	....	....	....	
7. Chenani ,, ..	....	....	....	....	....	....	
II. Kashmir Province ..	....	....	....	....	....	....	
8. Kashmir North ..	....	....	....	....	....	....	
9. Kashmir South (*including city*) ..	....	....	....	....	....	....	
10. Muzaffarabad ..	....	....	....	....	....	....	
III. Frontier Districts ..	....	....	....	....	....	....	
11. Ladakh ..	....	....	....	....	....	....	
12. Gilgit ..	....	....	....	....	....	....	
13. Frontier Ilaqas ..	....	....	....	....	....	....	
IV. Cities.—							
14. Srinagar ..	....	....	....	....	....	....	
15. Jammu (*excludes Ry. population*) ..	8	2	1	....	....	1	

TABLE XI.

Occupation by Caste, Tribe and Race.

Jammu and Kashmir Census 1931.

1. Prisoners (378 males and 10 females) have been treated as Non-working Dependants.

2. The figures against Kashmiri Pandits include 1,521 Attars who are really Kashmiri Khatris.

3. Columns 3 and 4 give combined figures for Earners and Working dependants, though columns 12 and onwards give details for Earners only. The separate details for Earners and Working dependants for columns 3 and 4 are given below :—

Caste, Tribe or Race.	Earners.		Working Dependants.	
	Males.	Females.	Males.	Females.
Brahmans (excluding Mohyals) ..	54,538	4,059	9,871	46,079
Chumar ..	8,762	920	5,388	10,997
Chuhra ..	419	31	53	322
Hajjam ..	1,245	88	328	1,047
Jat ..	5,485	185	2,076	6,137
Jhiwar ..	3,030	551	410	2,235
Kashmiri Pandit ..	17,536	238	2,371	12,282
Khatri ..	5,104	297	1,460	4,134
Lohar ..	3,065	289	947	2,769
Mahajan ..	5,419	314	1,327	5,361
Rajput ..	42,394	2,769	16,248	40,175
Tarkhan ..	2,784	157	819	2,397
Zargar ..	943	52	136	851
Batwal ..	1,563	106	299	1,306
Doom ..	10,734	1,142	1,591	7,855
Mangrik ..	9,719	3,910	944	7,689
Anglo-Indian ..	40	26	2	6
European ..	71	54	....	....
Bafinda ..	8,809	505	2,552	8,462
Darzi ..	623	78	173	578
Gujjar ..	90,576	2,780	45,778	97,894
Kumhiar ..	3,279	342	916	2,951
Lohar ..	3,113	220	1,080	3,833
Rajput ..	39,327	1,425	23,629	50,011
Tarkhan ..	3,621	168	1,045	3,568
Teli ..	4,403	250	893	3,953
Chuhra ..	793	139	227	635
Yashkun ..	7,387	183	3,266	7,347
Mochi ..	2,544	150	1,174	2,436

TABLE XI.

Occupation by Selected Caste, Tribe and Race.

Jammu and Kashmir Census 1931.

	Caste Tribe or Race.	Traditional Occupation.	Population dealt with. Earners and working dependants. Males.	Population dealt with. Earners and working dependants. Females.	Population dealt with. Non-working dependants. Both Sexes	Number of actual workers whose traditional caste occupation was returned as their.— Principal means of livelihood. Males.	Principal means of livelihood. Females.	Subsidiary means of livelihood. Males.	Subsidiary means of livelihood. Females.	No. of actual workers returning their traditional occupation as their principal means of livelihood who had some subsidiary occupation. Males.	Females.	Recorded principal occupation of atual workers other than traditional caste occupation. 1. Exploitation of animals and vegetation. Income from rent of Land. Males.	Income from rent of Land. Females.	Cultivators of all kinds. Males.	Cultivators of all kinds. Females.	Agents and Managers of landed estates, planters, Forest officers and their clerks, rent collectors etc. Males.	Agents and Managers etc. Females.
	1	2	3	4	5	6	7	8	9	10	11	12	13	14	15	16	17
Hindu.	Brahmans (excluding Mohyals) ..	Priest ..	64,409	50,138	70,774	2,522	91	1,528	100	1,006	44	1,372	777	39,810	2,155	170	— —
	Chumar ..	Cobbler ..	14,150	11,917	15,122	1,091	72	2,586	68	360	28	217	24	6,371	415	25	— —
	Chuhra ..	Scavenging ..	472	353	782	64	20	2	1	7	10	1	1	276	4	2	— —
	Hajjam ..	Barber ..	1,573	1,135	1,527	773	6	195	....	214	4	15	17	343	26	2	— —
	Jat ..	Agriculture ..	7,561	6,322	9,488	5,028	47	22	....	620	52	57	88	....	....	— —	....
	Jhiwar ..	Water carrier ..	3,440	2,786	3,931	1,040	292	132	1	127	153	28	4	232	19	6	— —
	Kashmiri Pandit ..	State service ..	19,907	12,520	30,661	5,399	37	1,119	19	465	12	2,151	70	2,776	51	64	— —
	Khatri ..	Trade and State service ..	6,564	4,431	9,561	2,595	39	204	1	678	30	233	34	715	31	34	— —
	Lohar ..	Black smith ..	4,012	3,058	3,718	814	4	607	23	432	2	70	22	1,791	202	50	— —
	Mahajan ..	Trade and money lending ..	6,746	5,675	8,588	3,801	68	305	2	1,012	47	120	29	455	16	30	....
	Rajput ..	State service ..	58,642	42,944	56,871	25,838	1,513	794	29	6,949	866	2,060	413	10,063	248	119	....
	Tarkhan ..	Carpenter ..	3,603	2,554	3,822	1,484	16	388	....	507	11	36	14	913	85	7	....
	Zargar ..	Gold and silver smith ..	1,079	903	1,298	727	6	25	....	94	6	8	....	64	7	— —	....
	Batwal ..	Labour ..	1,862	1,412	2,371	992	27	13	25	161	55	9	3	....	....	....	— —
	Doom ..	Labour ..	12,325	8,997	13,007	1,839	270	600	61	336	236	116	15	5,600	368	72	— —
	Mangrik (Buddhists)	Agriculture ..	10,663	11,599	11,845	6,847	1,868	....	....	147	11	....	....	1,536	1,431	— —	— —
Christian.	Anglo-Indian ..	....	42	32	49	....	....	....	....	....	....	....	....	....	....	— —	— —
	European ..	....	71	54	73	....	....	....	....	....	....	....	....	....	....	1	— —
Muslim.	Bafinda ..	Weaving ..	11,361	8,967	13,544	1,874	184	1,984	9	614	339	64	21	5,893	165	— —	— —
	Darzi ..	Tailoring ..	796	650	941	252	61	200	4	55	23	3	2	328	9	— —	— —
	Gujjar ..	Agriculture and cattle breeding	136,354	100,674	165,753	81,891	1,640	2,788	869	15,561	1,806	219	183	864	1	97	— —
	Kumhar ..	Potters and carriers ..	4,195	3,293	4,795	945	107	898	11	314	245	22	18	1,944	71	11	— —
	Lohar ..	Blacksmith ..	4,193	4,053	7,885	606	4	1,398	7	226	2	29	16	2,122	160	7	— —
	Rajput ..	State Service and Agriculture ..	62,956	51,436	81,057	35,153	788	2,891	15	10,478	720	427	293	199	10	28	— —
	Tarkhan ..	Carpentry ..	4,666	3,736	6,003	637	17	1,138	6	237	2	23	10	2,669	80	2	— —
	Toli ..	Oil pressing ..	5,296	4,203	6,335	825	84	526	4	288	7	199	13	1,852	62	17	— —
	Chuhra ..	Sweeping ..	1,020	774	1,585	140	29	33	1	53	9	33	3	386	31	1	— —
	Yashkun ..	Agriculture ..	10,653	7,530	17,977	6,707	155	18	2	1,035	25	....	....	....	....	— —	— —
	Mochi ..	Cobbler ..	3,718	2,586	4,748	719	53	962	6	176	19	8	1	1,638	42	— —	— —

TABLE XI.

Occupation by Selected Caste, Tribe and Race.

Jammu and Kashmir Census 1931.

	Caste Tribe or Race.	Traditional Occupation.	Recorded Principal occupation of actual workers other than traditional caste occupation.																			
			1. Exploitation of animals and vegetation.						2. Extraction of minerals.				3. Industries.				4. Transport.				5. Trade.	
			Field Labourers, wood cutters etc.		*Raisers of live-stock, milkmen and herdsmen.*		*Fishing and hunting.*		*Owners Managers, Clerks etc.*		*Labourers.*		*Owners Managers, Clerks etc.*		*Artisans and other workmen.*		*Owners, Managers Ships-officers etc.*		*Labourers Boatmen, Carters, Palki bearers etc.*			
			Males.	Females.	Males.	Females.	Males.	Females.	Males.	Females.	Males.	Females.	Males.	Females.	Males.	Females.	Males.	Females.	Males.	Females.	Males.	Females.
			18	19	20	21	22	23	24	25	26	27	28	29	30	31	32	33	34	35	36	37
Hindu.	Brahmans (excluding Mohyals) ..	Priest ..	248	32	494	69	12	....	..	..	8	5	6	6	419	300	34	1	396	21	2,948	34
	Chamar ..	Cobbler ..	250	196	188	44	....	3	..	..	41	1	..	..	42	69	1	1	98	11	68	6
	Chubra ..	Scavenging ..	5	....	1	....	....	....	..	..	..	..	..	..	17	..	..	..	..	..	5	..
	Hajjam ..	Barber ..	19	11	6	8	....	....	..	..	..	1	..	..	19	9	2	6	3	..	6	..
	Jat ..	Agriculture ..	36	7	29	2	....	....	..	..	4	..	..	..	20	20	..	..	27	..	21	1
	Jhiwar ..	Water carrier ..	92	13	7	....	16	....	..	..	15	..	..	..	463	32	..	..	98	25	236	5
	Kashmiri Pandit ..	State Service ..	3	....	1	....	....	....	..	..	1	..	2	..	299	29	2	..	80	3	2,659	5
	Khatri ..	Trade and State service ..	27	5	34	5	1	....	7	..	3	..	19	..	504	74	3	..	103	3	83	1
	Lohar ..	Blacksmith ..	50	6	63	13	3	....	4	..	6	1	7	1	52	21	2	..	9	..	9	..
	Mahajan ..	Trade and money lending ..	8	3	18	1	....	....	2	..	3	1	1	6	132	86	2	..	36	1	5	..
	Rajput ..	State service ..	471	13	715	149	7	2	..	13	29	5	3	..	114	55	..	1	122	47	266	3
	Tarkhan ..	Carpenter ..	153	3	20	8	1	....	..	1	10	1	..	..	39	14	3	..	3	2	16	..
	Zargar ..	Gold and silver smith ..	5	1	....	....	....	....	..	..	1	1	..	..	46	17	..	..	5	..	38	..
	Batwal ..	Labour ..	251	52	81	....	....	....	..	..	3	..	..	..	26	7	..	..	2	..	..	1
	Doom ..	Labour ..	652	85	217	66	17	....	...	..	50	5	41	2	674	80	—	..	50	9	103	124
	Mangrik (Buddhists)	Agriculture ..	132	....	154	72	....	....	..	..	..	..	..	..	34	50	—	..	119	—	438	31
Christian.	Anglo-Indian ..	....	....	....	....	....	....	....	..	..	..	..	..	..	1	4	..	..	..	..	..	1
	European ..	....	....	....	....	....	1	....	..	..	..	..	..	..	6	7	—	..	..	..	10	2
Muslim.	Bafinda —	Weaving ..	98	5	163	....	2	....	..	..	24	..	1	—	116	20	4	..	30	1	70	1
	Darzi —	Tailoring ..	4	....	11	....	....	....	..	..	..	..	..	1	5	1	—	..	2	—	..	..
	Gujjar —	Agriculture and cattle breeding	1,027	56	1,408	190	....	4	..	..	10	5	9	2	436	144	8	20	273	8	286	145
	Kumhar —	Potters and carriers ..	22	4	32	16	....	....	..	..	..	..	—	—	25	8	6	..	83	—	27	5
	Lohar —	Blacksmith ..	89	2	42	5	4	....	13	..	..	2	1	—	66	2	—	..	18	—	4	—
	Rajput —	State Service and Agriculture ..	312	19	505	14	1	15	1	..	17	1	—	3	766	57	7	..	260	2	146	3
	Tarkhan —	Carpentry ..	64	....	35	7	....	....	1	..	1	..	..	..	77	12	..	..	5	—	4	1
	Teli —	Oil pressing ..	126	5	46	7	....	....	1	—	4	1	—	—	130	36	58	—	801	10	80	2
	Chuhra —	Sweeping ..	15	6	13	4	....	....	..	—	1	..	—	—	75	19	—	—	1	—	—	—
	Yashkun —	Agriculture ..	27	....	105	—..	....	....	—	—	3	—	—	—	50	2	21	—	16	—	22	1
	Mochi —	Cobbler ..	18	....	29	2	....	....	—	—	1	—	—	—	26	13	1	—	10	—	4	1

TABLE XI.

Occupation by Selected Caste, Tribe and Race.

Jammu and Kashmir Census 1931.

Religion	Caste Tribe or Race.	Traditional Occupation.	Recorded principal occupation of actual workers other than traditional caste occupation.																							
			6. Public Force.				7. Public Administration.				8 Arts and Professions.						9.		10.		11. Insufficiently described.				12.	
			Commissioned and Gazetted Officers.		Others.		Gazetted Officers.		Others.		Religion.		Lawyers, Doctors and Teachers.		Others.		Persons living on their income.		Domestic service.		Contractors, Clerks, Cashiers etc., otherwise unspecified.		Labourers unspecified.		Beggars and Prostitutes.	
			Males.	Females.	Males.	Females.	Males.	Females.	Males.	Females.	Males.	Females.	Males.	Females.	Males.	Females.	Males.	Females.	Males.	Females.	Males.	Females.	Males.	Females.	Males.	Females.
			38	39	40	41	42	43	44	45	46	47	48	49	50	51	52	53	54	55	56	57	58	59	60	61
Hindu.	Brahmans (excluding Mohyals) ..	Priest ..	47	..	826		45	1	1,751	26	233	1	358	37	351	51	398	14	1,338	249	135	43	268	86	349	60
	Chamar ..	Cobbler ..	..	..	23	..	..	..	77	1	1	..	..	1	1	1	23	..	136	21	8	3	87	26	14	23
	Chuhra ..	Scavenging	..	..	..	2	1	..	4	1	..	2	..	..	8	..	24	..	4	..	..	..	..	..	7	3
	Hajjam ..	Barber ..	..	..	11	..	..	..	22	..	..	..	1	1	3	..	3	..	10	1	..	..	5	2	2	..
	Jat ..	Agriculture ..	5	..	45	..	1	..	23	2	..	1	4	..	6	1	42	4	70	5	8	..	14	2	45	5
	Jhiwar ..	Water carrier ..	..	..	65	..	1	1	48	2	2	..	5	2	107	10	44	4	409	99	40	28	71	11	5	4
	Kashmiri Pandit ..	State service ..	2	..	337	..	..	..	14	12	987	4	265	2	41	2	352	6	1,741	13	283	1	31	1	46	2
	Khatri ..	Trade and State Service ..	3	..	1	..	..	..	5	..	14	..	114	21	44	17	162	14	315	36	50	12	8	..	27	5
	Lohar ..	Blacksmith ..	2	..	55	..	1	..	5	1	..	..	1	..	3	2	6	1	43	11	13	..	3	1	3	3
	Mahajan ..	Trade and money lending ..	..	..	47	..	14	..	223	4	15	21	102	20	55	3	28	8	268	17	28	25	15	4	11	1
	Rajput ..	State Service ..	5	..	708	..	2	..	274	5	33	3	60	6	55	9	399	15	697	145	38	48	80	4	43	13
	Tarkhan ..	Carpenter ..	..	..	12	..	..	..	11	..	1	2	1	1	5	..	5	..	32	7	2	..	24	2	6	1
	Zargar ..	Gold and silver smith ..	2	..	2	..	1	..	5	3	2	1	3	3	6	..	..	..	16	10	2	..	8	1	2	2
	Batwal ..	Labour ..	..	..	..	..	..	..	19	..	1	..	5	5	1	..	24	..	124	5	6	..	16	5	3	1
	Doom ..	Labour ..	..	..	100	..	..	..	250	5	5	..	6	9	35	16	35	..	478	43	19	16	58	14	227	15
	Mangrik (Buddhists)	Agriculture ..	..	..	1	..	..	..	48	1	183	160	7	..	..	..	2	..	136	75	..	10	7	127	75	76
Christian.	Anglo-Indian ..	......	4	..	1	..	..	..	12	6	2	1	2	7	..	6	..	1	18	..	..	..	..	..	..	..
	European ..	......	1	..	3	..	3	..	11	7	7	6	1	18	1	4	11	7	13	3	2	..	..	..	..	..
Muslim.	Bafinda ..	Weaving ..	3	..	9	..	..	..	48	1	11	..	22	3	..	4	12	7	193	23	15	..	52	17	105	53
	Darzi ..	Tailoring ..	..	..	1	..	..	..	1	..	..	..	..	..	..	..	1	1	6	..	1	..	2	..	6	3
	Gujjar ..	Agriculture and cattle breeding	4	..	328	..	..	..	309	4	94	4	73	..	62	1	126	4	1,829	109	44	4	416	35	763	221
	Kumhar ..	Potters and carriers ..	..	..	1	..	..	..	4	..	..	..	7	..	..	..	65	..	32	5	1	..	24	3	26	15
	Lohar ..	Blacksmith ..	1	..	11	..	..	..	8	5	4	..	3	..	5	..	10	1	30	4	..	..	13	3	27	19
	Rajput ..	State Service and Agriculture ..	..	..	32	..	..	..	52	..	23	..	49	3	45	3	156	10	666	45	80	1	159	50	304	108
	Tarkhan ..	Carpentry ..	..	..	17	..	..	..	7	..	3	..	2	3	..	..	8	..	29	5	2	..	27	6	8	17
	Teli ..	Oil pressing ..	..	..	14	..	..	..	12	1	1	..	3	2	16	2	15	..	63	5	7	..	78	6	55	14
	Chuhra ..	Sweeping ..	..	..	33	1	..	..	29	5	..	..	..	..	12	..	4	..	25	3	3	..	8	26	18	8
	Yashkun ..	Agriculture ..	..	..	11	..	..	..	80	..	17	..	8	..	1	..	3	..	173	19	11	..	98	1	34	5
	Mochi ..	Cobbler ..	2	..	..	..	..	..	7	..	2	..	..	1	1	2	5	..	29	7	..	..	21	1	23	27

TABLE XII.—(I) & (II).

EDUCATED UNEMPLOYMENT.

Jammu and Kashmir Census 1931.

1. The number of unemployed given in the Imperial table excludes Undermatrics, particulars about whom are given in the table below :—

2. Column 2 of parts I and II of the main tables excludes the number of unemployed under 20 and above 40 years of age.

EDUCATED UNEMPLOYMENT BY CLASS (UNDERMATRICS).

Class.	Total Un-employed.	Aged 20—24.		Aged 25—29.		Aged 30—34.		Aged 35—39.	
		Under one year.	Over one year.	Under one year.	Over one year.	Under one year.	Over one year.	Under one year.	Over one year.
Brahmans ..	184	19	124	2	23	—	10	1	5
Depressed Hindus ..	....	....	....	....	—	—	—	—	—
Other Hindus ..	15	1	7	....	2	1	3	1	—
Muslims ..	52	5	40	....	6	—	1	—	—
Anglo Indians ..	....	....	....	....	....	....	—	—	—
All other Classes ..	....	....	....	....	....	—	—	—	—
Total ..	251	25	171	2	31	1	14	2	5

Total of English knowing unemployed under 20 years	75
Do. do. do. who are 40 years and over	2
Total number of Educated unemployed whose fathers are Soldiers	1
Do. do. do. do. Cultivators	23
Do. do. do. do. Artisans	12
Do. do. do. do. menials or servants	13
Do. do. do. who though not totally unemployed failed to obtain employment with which they are satisfied	30

TABLE XII—(I).

EDUCATED UNEMPLOYMENT BY CLASS.

Class.	Total Unemployed.	Aged 20—24. Unemployed for less than one year.	Aged 20—24. Unemployed for one year or more.	Aged 25—29. Unemployed for less than one year.	Aged 25—29. Unemployed for one year or more.	Aged 30—34. Unemployed for less than one year.	Aged 30—34. Unemployed for one year or more.	Aged 35—39. Unemployed for less than one year.	Aged 35—39. Unemployed for one year or more.
Brahmans ..	226	25	169	6	21	....	4	....	1
Depressed Hindus ..	....	....	....	....	....	....	....	....	....
Other Hindus ..	26	2	15	....	8	....	....	....	1
Muslims ..	37	6	27	....	2	....	2	....	....
Anglo Indians ..	....	....	....	....	....	....	....	....	....
All other classes ..	....	....	....	....	....	....	....	....	....
Total ..	289	33	211	6	31	....	6	....	2

Total of English knowing unemployed under 20 years .. 73

Do. do. do. who are forty years and over .. Nil.

Total number of educated unemployed whose fathers are :—

Soldiers .. Nil.

Cultivators .. 35

Artisans .. 16

Menials or servants .. 25

Total number of educated unemployed (Matric or S. L. C.) who though not totally unemployed failed to obtain employment with which they are satisfied .. 26

TABLE XII—(II).

Educated Unemployment by Degree.

Degree.	Total-Unemployed.	*Aged 20—24.* Unemployed for less than one year.	*Aged 20—24.* Unemployed for one year or more.	*Aged 25—29.* Unemployed for less than one year.	*Aged 25—29.* Unemployed for one year or more.	*Aged 30—34.* Unemployed for less than one year.	*Aged 30—34.* Unemployed for one year or more.	*Aged 35—39.* Unemployed for less than one year.	*Aged 35—39.* Unemployed for one year or more.
British Degrees	1	....	1	....	....	....	....	....	....
Continental Degrees	....	....	....	....	....	....	....	....	....
Other Foreign Degrees	....	....	....	....	....	....	....	....	....
Indian Degrees :—	....	....	....	....	....	....	....	....	....
Medical	....	....	....	....	....	....	....	....	....
Legal	1	1	....	....	....	....	....	....	....
Agricultural	....	....	....	....	....	....	....	....	....
Commerce	....	....	....	....	....	....	....	....	....
M. A.	3	1	1	....	1	....	....	....	....
M. Sc.	1	....	....	....	1	....	....	....	....
B. A.	28	6	16	....	6	....	....	....	....
B. Sc.	2	....	1	....	1	....	....	....	....
B. Eng. or L. C. E.	3	1	1	....	....	....	....	....	1
B. T. or L. T.	....	....	....	....	....	....	....	....	....
S. L. C. or Matric	250	24	191	6	22	....	6	....	1
Total	289	33	211	6	31	....	6	....	2

TABLE XIII.

LITERACY BY RELIGION AND AGE.

Jammu and Kashmir Census 1931.

NOTES.

1. This table like table VII is divided into three parts.

Part I contains statistics for the entire State and the different Provinces comprising it and for every religion returned.

Part II gives the figures separately for each district and

Part III shows the details for the two cities (Jammu and Srinagar

2. The "Frontier Ilaqas" have been included in this table at the current Census though excluded during 1921 Census.

3. This table is the same as the corresponding one in 1921 Census with the exception that the lowest age-group 0-10 has been divided into two groups 0-5 and 5-10.

4. 134 Sansis (78 males and 56 females) falling under no prevailing religion have been shown under the head "Others."

5. Persons literate in English are included in the figures for the total literates.

6. Literacy figures for Hindi are inclusive of those for Sanskrit as well.

7. The following statement shows literacy among Christians by race:—

Christian.	*Total.*			*0—5*			*5—10*			*10—15*			*15—20*			*20 and over.*		
	P.	M.	F.	P.	M.	F.	P.	M.	F.	P.	M.	F.	P.	M.	F.	P.	M.	F.
Total Literates ..	568	305	263	3	1	2	37	22	15	45	27	18	53	26	27	430	229	201
Europeans and Anglo-Indians ..	260	117	143	3	1	2	12	9	3	6	4	2	15	5	10	224	98	126
Indian Christian ..	308	188	120	..	..	..	25	13	12	39	23	16	38	21	17	206	131	75
Literates in English	392	193	199	2	1	1	20	12	8	20	13	7	34	16	18	316	151	165
Europeans and Anglo-Indians ..	251	109	142	2	1	1	12	8	4	6	4	2	14	5	9	217	91	126
Indian Christians ..	141	84	57	..	..	..	8	4	4	14	9	5	20	11	9	99	60	39

TABLE

LITERACY BY RELIGION

Jammu and Kashmir

District or Province.	Age.	POPULATION.								
		Total.			*Literate.*			*Illiterate.*		
		Persons.	Males.	Females.	Persons.	Males.	Females.	Persons.	Males.	Females.
1	2	3	4	5	6	7	8	9	10	11
Jammu and Kashmir State.	**All religions.**									
	0—5 ..	579,542	291,931	287,611	....	....	....	579,542	291,931	287,611
	5—10 ..	469,120	253,182	215,938	5,573	4,523	1,050	463,547	248,659	214,888
	10—15 ..	429,988	234,021	195,967	10,459	8,908	1,551	419,529	225,113	194,416
	15—20 ..	350,597	178,694	171,903	17,489	15,837	1,652	333,108	162,857	170,251
	20 and over ..	1,816,996	980,510	836,486	90,364	85,539	4,825	1,726,632	894,971	831,661
	Total ..	*3,646,243*	*1,938,338*	*1,707,905*	*123,885*	*114,807*	*9,078*	*3,522,358*	*1,823,531*	*1,698,827*
	Brahmanic (Hindu.)									
	0—5 ..	91,182	45,341	45,841	....	....	....	91,182	45,341	45,841
	5—10 ..	73,797	39,362	34,435	2,818	2,233	585	70,979	37,129	33,850
	10—15 ..	69,020	36,973	32,047	5,189	4,353	836	63,831	32,620	31,211
	15—20 ..	60,138	30,954	29,184	8,813	7,951	862	51,325	23,003	28,322
	20 and over ..	348,136	190,719	157,417	47,795	45,304	2,491	300,341	145,415	154,926
	Total ..	*642,273*	*343,349*	*298,924*	*64,615*	*59,841*	*4,774*	*577,658*	*283,508*	*294,150*
	Arya.									
	0—5 ..	14,281	7,277	7,004	....	....	....	14,281	7,277	7,004
	5—10 ..	11,428	6,173	5,255	313	212	101	11,115	5,961	5,154
	10—15 ..	10,775	5,722	5,053	564	408	156	10,211	5,314	4,897
	15—20 ..	9,156	4,585	4,571	777	608	169	8,379	3,977	4,402
	20 and over ..	48,304	26,589	21,715	3,033	2,609	424	45,271	23,980	21,291
	Total ..	*93,944*	*50,346*	*43,598*	*4,687*	*3,837*	*850*	*89,257*	*46,509*	*42,748*
	Brahmo.									
	0—5 ..	....	....	....	....	....	....	....	....	....
	5—10 ..	....	....	....	....	....	....	....	....	....
	10—15 ..	1	1	....	1	1	....	....	....	....
	15—20 ..	1	1	....	1	1	....	....	....	....
	20 and over ..	3	2	1	2	1	1	1	1	....
	Total ..	*5*	*4*	*1*	*4*	*3*	*1*	*1*	*1*	....
	Buddhist.									
	0—5 ..	4,377	2,112	2,265	....	....	....	4,377	2,112	2,265
	5—10 ..	4,038	2,014	2,024	16	15	1	4,022	1,999	2,023
	10—15 ..	3,746	1,852	1,894	32	31	1	3,714	1,821	1,893
	15—20 ..	3,108	1,524	1,584	95	94	1	3,013	1,430	1,583
	20 and over ..	23,455	11,785	11,670	1,476	1,451	25	21,979	10,334	11,645
	Total ..	*38,724*	*19,287*	*19,437*	*1,619*	*1,591*	*28*	*37,105*	*17,696*	*19,409*
	Jain.									
	0—5 ..	78	46	32	....	....	....	78	46	32
	5—10 ..	73	32	41	37	18	19	36	14	22
	10—15 ..	74	34	40	52	31	21	22	3	19
	15—20 ..	59	30	29	42	25	17	17	5	12
	20 and over ..	313	177	136	183	145	38	130	32	98
	Total ..	*597*	*319*	*278*	*314*	*219*	*95*	*283*	*100*	*183*
	Muslim.									
	0—5 ..	459,985	232,278	227,707	....	....	....	459,985	232,278	227,707
	5—10 ..	372,408	201,588	170,820	2,002	1,765	237	370,406	199,823	170,583
	10—15 ..	339,907	185,953	153,954	3,951	3,575	376	335,956	182,378	153,578
	15—20 ..	273,180	139,253	133,927	6,791	6,381	410	266,389	132,872	133,517
	20 and over ..	1,372,156	738,180	633,976	32,875	31,733	1,142	1,339,281	706,447	632,834
	Total ..	*2,817,636*	*1,497,252*	*1,320,384*	*45,619*	*43,454*	*2,165*	*2,772,017*	*1,453,798*	*1,318,219*

XIII.

AND AGE.

Census 1931.

Literate in											
English.			*Urdu.*			*Hindi.*			*Other Vernaculars.*		
Persons.	Males.	Females.	Persons.	Males.	Females.	Persons	Males.	Females.	Persons.	Males.	Females.
12	13	14	15	16	17	18	19	20	21	22	23
....	....	....	....	....	....	....	....	....	....	....	....
658	601	57	3,178	2,981	197	776	244	532	961	697	264
1,642	1,533	109	5,802	5,493	309	1,204	469	735	1,811	1,413	398
3,901	3,735	166	8,469	8,138	331	1,681	983	698	3,438	2,981	457
13,268	12,791	477	38,749	37,863	886	10,325	8,413	1,912	28,022	26,472	1,550
19,469	*18,660*	*809*	*56,198*	*54,475*	*1,723*	*13,986*	*10,109*	*3,877*	*34,232*	*31,563*	*2,669*
....	....	....	....	....	....	....	....	....	....	....	....
446	417	29	1,446	1,373	73	605	196	409	321	247	74
1,083	1,021	62	2,540	2,447	93	941	373	568	625	512	113
2,439	2,357	82	3,631	3,538	93	1,385	842	543	1,358	1,214	144
9,200	8,991	209	17,674	17,423	251	9,098	7,554	1,544	11,823	11,336	487
13,168	*12,786*	*352*	*25,291*	*24,781*	*510*	*12,029*	*8,965*	*3,064*	*14,127*	*13,309*	*818*
....	....	....	....	....	....	....	....	....	....	....	....
35	30	5	130	123	7	122	38	84	26	21	5
90	78	12	224	214	10	202	80	122	48	36	12
199	183	16	287	269	18	228	109	119	63	47	16
708	675	33	1,070	1,016	54	791	505	286	464	413	51
1,032	*966*	*66*	*1,711*	*1,622*	*89*	*1,343*	*732*	*611*	*601*	*517*	*84*
....	....	....	....	....	....	....	....	....	....	....	....
....	....	....	....	....	....	....	....	....	....	....	....
....	....	....	1	1	....	....	....	....	....	....	....
1	1	....	....	....	....	....	....	....	....	....	....
1	1	....	....	....	....	1	....	1	....	....	....
2	*2*	....	*1*	*1*	....	*1*	....	*1*	....	....	....
....	....	....	....	....	....	....	....	....	....	....	....
....	....	....	4	4	....	....	....	....	12	11	1
1	1	....	8	8	....	....	....	....	23	22	1
2	2	....	14	14	....	....	....	....	79	78	1
5	5	....	58	57	1	1	1	....	1,412	1,388	24
8	*8*	....	*84*	*83*	*1*	*1*	*1*	....	*1,526*	*1,499*	*27*
....	....	....	....	....	....	....	....	....	....	....	....
2	2	....	11	11	....	20	2	18	4	3	1
7	7	....	15	15	....	21	3	18	9	6	3
13	13	....	12	12	....	13	....	13	4	....	4
15	14	1	31	31	....	64	33	31	73	67	6
37	*36*	*1*	*69*	*69*	....	*118*	*38*	*80*	*90*	*76*	*14*
....	....	....	....	....	....	....	....	....	....	....	....
134	122	12	1,417	1,308	109	1	1	....	450	334	116
376	355	21	2,736	2,545	191	....	....	....	839	675	164
1 ,064	1,026	38	4,181	3,980	201	3	3	....	1,543	1,372	171
2,594	2,542	52	18,529	17,996	533	54	52	2	11,698	11,143	555
4,168	*4,015*	*123*	*26,863*	*25,829*	*1,034*	*58*	*56*	*2*	*14,530*	*13,524*	*1,006*

TABLE

Literacy by Reli-

Jammu and Kashmir

District or Province.	Age.	Population.								
		Total.			Literate.			Illiterate.		
		Persons.	Males.	Females.	Persons.	Males.	Females.	Persons.	Males.	Females.
1	2	3	4	5	6	7	8	9	10	11
Jammu and Kashmir State.	**Sikh.**									
	0—5 ..	9,239	4,651	4,588	....	....	....	9,239	4,651	4,588
	5—10 ..	7,087	3,856	3,231	350	258	92	6,737	3,598	3,139
	10—15 ..	6,224	3,359	2,865	625	482	143	5,599	2,877	2,722
	15—20 ..	4,730	2,236	2,494	917	751	166	3,813	1,485	2,328
	20 and over ..	23,382	12,355	11,027	4,566	4,064	502	18,816	8,291	10,525
	Total ..	*50,662*	*26,457*	*24,205*	*6,458*	*5,555*	*903*	*44,204*	*20,902*	*23,302*
	Christian.									
	0—5 ..	373	209	164	....	....	....	373	209	164
	5—10 ..	273	150	123	37	22	15	236	128	108
	10—15 ..	223	117	106	45	27	18	178	90	88
	15—20 ..	208	103	105	53	26	27	155	77	78
	20 and over ..	1,186	664	522	430	229	201	756	435	321
	Total ..	*2,263*	*1,243*	*1,020*	*565*	*304*	*261*	*1,698*	*939*	*759*
	Zoroastrian.									
	0—5 ..	1	1	....	....	....	....	1	1	....
	5—10 ..	....	....	....	....	....	....	....	....	....
	10—15 ..	....	....	....	....	....	....	....	....	....
	15—20 ..	1	....	1	....	....	....	1	....	1
	20 and over ..	3	2	1	3	2	1	....	....	....
	Total ..	*5*	*3*	*2*	*3*	*2*	*1*	*2*	*1*	*1*
	Tribal.									
	0—5 ..	26	16	10	....	....	....	26	16	10
	5—10 ..	16	7	9	....	....	....	16	7	9
	10—15 ..	18	10	8	....	....	....	18	10	8
	15—20 ..	16	8	8	....	....	....	16	8	8
	20 and over ..	58	37	21	1	1	....	57	36	21
	Total ..	*134*	*78*	*56*	*1*	*1*	....	*133*	*77*	*56*
Jammu Province.	**All Religions.**									
	0—5 ..	284,367	142,218	142,149	....	....	....	284,367	142,218	142,149
	5—10 ..	228,570	122,969	105,601	3,527	2,763	764	225,043	120,206	104,837
	10—15 ..	210,032	113,832	96,200	6,529	5,366	1,163	203,503	108,466	95,037
	15—20 ..	169,800	85,644	84,156	10,362	9,101	1,261	159,438	76,543	82,895
	20 and over ..	895,672	478,152	417,520	52,590	48,823	3,767	843,082	429,329	413,753
	Total ..	*1,788,441*	*942,815*	*845,626*	*73,008*	*66,053*	*6,955*	*1,715,433*	*876,762*	*838,671*
	Brahmanic.									
	0—5 ..	82,185	40,695	41,490	....	....	....	82,185	40,695	41,490
	5—10 ..	65,507	35,083	30,424	1,938	1,506	432	63,569	33,577	29,992
	10—15 ..	61,410	32,917	28,493	3,570	2,918	652	57,840	29,999	27,841
	15—20 ..	53,248	26,926	26,322	5,868	5,153	715	47,380	21,773	25,607
	20 and over ..	309,520	167,743	141,777	31,535	29,387	2,148	277,985	138,356	139,629
	Total ..	*571,870*	*303,364*	*268,506*	*42,911*	*38,964*	*3,947*	*528,959*	*264,400*	*264,559*
	Arya.									
	0—5 ..	14,200	7,234	6,966	....	....	....	14,200	7,234	6,966
	5—10 ..	11,348	6,128	5,220	278	191	87	11,070	5,937	5,133
	10—15 ..	10,706	5,682	5,024	526	384	142	10,180	5,298	4,882
	15—20 ..	9,097	4,549	4,548	734	579	155	8,363	3,970	4,393
	20 and over ..	48,021	26,388	21,633	2,829	2,442	387	45,192	23,946	21,246
	Total ..	*93,372*	*49,981*	*43,391*	*4,367*	*3,596*	*771*	*89,005*	*46,385*	*42,620*

XIII.

GION AND AGE.

Census 1931.

Literate in											
English.			*Urdu.*			*Hindi.*			*Other Vernaculars.*		
Persons.	Males.	Females.	Persons.	Males.	Females.	Persons.	Males.	Females.	Persons.	Males.	Females.
12	13	14	15	16	17	18	19	20	21	22	23
....	....	....	....	....	....	....	....	....	....	....	....
21	18	3	160	154	6	28	7	21	141	79	62
65	58	7	262	252	10	40	13	27	258	159	99
149	137	12	331	317	14	51	29	22	386	268	118
425	409	16	1,337	1,296	41	312	267	45	2,492	2,092	400
660	*622*	*38*	*2,090*	*2,019*	*71*	*431*	*316*	*115*	*3,277*	*2,598*	*679*
....	....	....	....	....	....	....	....	....	....	....	....
20	12	8	10	8	2	....	....	....	7	2	5
20	13	7	16	11	5	....	....	....	9	3	6
34	16	18	13	8	5	1	....	1	5	2	3
316	151	165	50	44	6	4	1	3	60	33	27
390	*192*	*198*	*89*	*71*	*18*	*5*	*1*	*4*	*81*	*40*	*41*
....	....	....	....	....	....	....	....	....	....	....	....
....	....	....	....	....	....	....	....	....	....	....	....
....	....	....	....	....	....	....	....	....	....	....	....
....	....	....	....	....	....	....	....	....	....	....	....
3	2	1	....	....	....	....	....	....	....	....	....
3	*2*	*1*	....	....	....	....	....	....	....	....	....
....	....	....	....	....	....	....	....	....	....	....	....
....	....	....	....	....	....	....	....	....	....	....	....
....	....	....	....	....	....	....	....	....	....	....	....
....	....	....	....	....	....	....	....	....	....	....	....
1	1	....	....	....	....	....	....	....	....	....	....
1	*1*	....	....	....	....	....	....	....	....	....	....
....	....	....	....	....	....	....	....	....	....	....	....
293	265	28	1,973	1,856	117	653	220	433	608	422	186
653	587	66	3,702	3,510	192	1,051	431	620	1,123	838	285
1,431	1,320	111	5,541	5,320	221	1,439	826	613	1,951	1,635	316
4,952	4,704	248	24,473	23,800	673	8,929	7,214	1,715	14,236	13,105	1,131
7,329	*6,876*	*453*	*35,689*	*34,486*	*1,203*	*12,072*	*8,691*	*3,381*	*17,918*	*16,000*	*1,918*
....	....	....	....	....	....	....	....	....	....	....	....
194	178	16	994	960	34	498	177	321	252	191	61
406	363	43	1,855	1,803	52	807	342	465	502	410	92
830	762	68	2,780	2,716	64	1,159	693	466	1,099	982	117
3,192	3,024	168	11,845	11,653	192	7,789	6,413	1,376	8,709	8,297	412
4,622	*4,327*	*295*	*17,474*	*17,132*	*342*	*10,253*	*7,625*	*2,628*	*10,562*	*9,880*	*682*
....	....	....	....	....	....	....	....	....	....	....	....
28	25	3	118	112	6	109	34	75	23	20	3
75	67	8	216	207	9	188	75	113	47	35	12
173	161	12	280	264	16	220	108	112	61	46	15
585	560	25	1,039	989	50	756	492	264	449	401	48
861	*813*	*48*	*1,653*	*1,572*	*81*	*1,273*	*709*	*564*	*580*	*502*	*78*

TABLE

LITERACY BY RELI-

Jammu and Kashmir

District or Province.	Age.	Population. Total. Persons.	Total. Males.	Total. Females.	Literate. Persons.	Literate. Males.	Literate. Females.	Illiterate. Persons.	Illiterate. Males.	Illiterate. Females.
1	2	3	4	5	6	7	8	9	10	11
Jammu Province.	**Brahmo.**									
	0—5 ..	...	....	....	....	....	....	....	....	....
	5—10 ..	....	....	....	....	....	....	....	....	....
	10—15 ..	1	1	....	1	1	....	....	....	....
	15—20 ..	1	1	....	1	1	....	....	....	....
	20 and over ..	2	1	1	2	1	1	....	....	....
	Total ..	*4*	*3*	*1*	*4*	*3*	*1*	....	....	....
	Sikh.									
	0—5 ..	5,284	2,655	2,629	....	....	....	5,284	2,655	2,629
	5—10 ..	4,037	2,213	1,824	233	161	72	3,804	2,052	1,752
	10—15 ..	3,598	1,931	1,667	389	286	103	3,209	1,645	1,564
	15—20 ..	2,680	1,244	1,436	525	415	110	2,155	829	1,326
	20 and over ..	13,683	7,154	6,529	2,677	2,335	342	11,006	4,819	6,187
	Total ..	*29,282*	*15,197*	*14,085*	*3,824*	*3,197*	*627*	*25,458*	*12,000*	*13,458*
	Jain.									
	0—5 ..	77	45	32	....	....	....	77	45	32
	5—10 ..	73	32	41	37	18	19	36	14	22
	10—15 ..	73	33	40	51	30	21	22	3	19
	15—20 ..	58	29	29	41	24	17	17	5	12
	20 and over ..	310	175	135	181	143	38	129	32	97
	Total ..	*591*	*314*	*277*	*310*	*215*	*95*	*281*	*99*	*182*
	Buddhist.									
	0—5 ..	62	30	32	....	....	....	62	30	32
	5—10 ..	59	31	28	....	....	....	59	31	28
	10—15 ..	58	29	29	....	....	....	58	29	29
	15—20 ..	40	20	20	....	....	....	40	20	20
	20 and over ..	288	143	145	10	10	....	278	133	145
	Total ..	*507*	*253*	*254*	*10*	*10*	....	*497*	*243*	*254*
	Muslim.									
	0—5 ..	182,225	91,368	90,857	....	....	....	182,225	91,368	90,857
	5—10 ..	147,312	79,356	67,956	1,024	877	147	146,288	78,479	67,809
	10—15 ..	133,991	73,139	60,852	1,968	1,730	238	132,023	71,409	60,614
	15—20 ..	104,492	52,785	51,707	3,167	2,916	251	101,325	49,869	51,456
	20 and over ..	523,001	276,051	246,950	15,240	14,429	811	507,761	261,622	246,139
	Total ..	*1,091,021*	*572,699*	*518,322*	*21,399*	*19,952*	*1,447*	*1,069,622*	*552,747*	*516,875*
	Christian.									
	0—5 ..	328	190	138	....	....	....	328	190	138
	5—10 ..	228	124	104	17	10	7	211	114	97
	10—15 ..	187	96	91	24	17	7	163	79	84
	15—20 ..	177	87	90	26	13	13	151	74	77
	20 and over ..	833	490	343	115	75	40	718	415	303
	Total ..	*1,753*	*987*	*766*	*182*	*115*	*67*	*1,571*	*872*	*699*
	Tribal.									
	0—5 ..	6	1	5	....	....	....	6	1	5
	5—10 ..	6	2	4	....	....	....	6	2	4
	10—15 ..	8	4	4	....	....	....	8	4	4
	15—20 ..	7	3	4	....	....	....	7	3	4
	20 and over ..	14	7	7	1	1	....	13	6	7
	Total ..	*41*	*17*	*24*	*1*	*1*	....	*40*	*16*	*24*

XIII.

GION AND AGE.

Census 1931.

Literate in											
English.			*Urdu.*			*Hindi.*			*Other Vernaculars.*		
Persons.	Males.	Females.	Persons.	Males.	Females.	Persons.	Males.	Females.	Persons.	Males.	Females.
12	13	14	15	16	17	18	19	20	21	22	23
....	....	....	....	....	....	....	....	....	....	....	....
....	....	....	....	....	....	....	....	....	....	....	....
....	....	....	1	1	....	....	....	....	....	....	....
1	1	....	....	....	....	....	....	....	....	....	....
1	1	....	....	....	....	1	....	1	....	....	....
2	*2*	....	*1*	*1*	....	*1*	....	*1*	....	....	....
....	....	....	....	....	....	....	....	....	....	....	....
9	6	3	107	102	5	25	6	19	92	47	45
28	24	4	171	163	8	35	11	24	155	88	67
74	67	7	209	199	10	45	24	21	197	125	72
215	202	13	883	856	27	273	235	38	1,306	1,042	264
326	*299*	*27*	*1,370*	*1,320*	*50*	*378*	*276*	*102*	*1,750*	*1,302*	*448*
....	....	....	....	....	....	....	....	....	....	....	....
2	2	....	11	11	....	20	2	18	4	3	1
6	6	....	15	15	....	21	3	18	9	6	3
12	12	....	12	12	....	13	....	13	4	....	4
13	12	1	31	31	....	64	33	31	73	67	6
33	*32*	*1*	*69*	*69*	....	*118*	*38*	*80*	*90*	*76*	*14*
....	....	....	....	....	....	....	....	....	....	....	....
....	....	....	....	....	....	....	....	....	....	....	....
....	....	....	....	....	....	....	....	....	....	....	....
....	....	....	....	....	....	....	....	....	....	....	....
1	1	....	1	1	....	....	....	....	8	8	....
1	*1*	....	*1*	*1*	....	....	....	....	*8*	*8*	....
....	....	....	....	....	....	....	....	....	....	....	....
56	51	5	735	665	70	1	1	....	232	160	72
133	123	10	1,430	1,311	119	....	....	....	405	296	109
328	311	17	2,250	2,123	127	1	1	....	588	481	107
893	872	21	10,643	10,245	398	42	40	2	3,662	3,272	390
1,410	*1,357*	*53*	*15,058*	*14,344*	*714*	*44*	*42*	*2*	*4,887*	*4,209*	*678*
....	....	....	....	....	....	....	....	....	....	....	....
4	3	1	8	6	2	....	....	....	5	1	4
5	4	1	14	10	4	....	....	....	5	3	2
13	6	7	10	6	4	1	....	1	2	1	1
51	31	20	31	25	6	4	1	3	29	18	11
73	*44*	*29*	*63*	*47*	*16*	*5*	*1*	*4*	*41*	*23*	*18*
....	....	....	....	....	....	....	....	....	....	....	....
....	....	....	....	....	....	....	....	....	....	....	....
....	....	....	....	....	....	....	....	....	....	....	....
....	....	....	....	....	....	....	....	....	....	....	....
1	1	....	....	....	....	....	....	....	....	....	....
1	*1*	....	....	....	....	....	....	....	....	....	....

TABLE

Literacy by Reli-

Jammu and Kashmir

District or Province.	Age.	Population.								
		Total.			*Literate.*			*Illiterate.*		
		Persons.	Males.	Females.	Persons.	Males.	Females.	Persons.	Males.	Females.
1	2	3	4	5	6	7	8	9	10	11
Kashmir Province.	**All Religions.**									
	0—5 ..	250,979	127,893	123,086	....	....	....	250,979	127,893	123,086
	5—10 ..	204,953	111,418	93,535	1,903	1,637	266	203,050	109,781	93,269
	10—15 ..	188,108	103,048	85,060	3,699	3,328	371	184,409	99,720	84,689
	15—20 ..	156,157	80,331	75,826	6,579	6,215	364	149,578	74,116	75,462
	20 and over ..	769,021	424,332	344,689	33,390	32,450	940	735,631	391,882	343,749
	Total ..	*1,569,218*	*847,022*	*722,196*	*45,571*	*43,630*	*1,941*	*1,523,647*	*803,392*	*720,255*
	Brahmanic.									
	0—5 ..	8,931	4,607	4,324	....	....	....	8,931	4,607	4,324
	5—10 ..	8,241	4,251	3,990	858	713	145	7,383	3,538	3,845
	10—15 ..	7,572	4,033	3,539	1,600	1,419	181	5,972	2,614	3,358
	15—20 ..	6,673	3,824	2,849	2,824	2,682	142	3,849	1,142	2,707
	20 and over ..	37,410	21,836	15,574	15,546	15,217	329	21,864	6,619	15,245
	Total ..	*68,827*	*38,551*	*30,276*	*20,828*	*20,031*	*797*	*47,999*	*18,520*	*29,479*
	Arya.									
	0—5 ..	63	34	29	....	....	....	63	34	29
	5—10 ..	65	36	29	30	19	11	35	17	18
	10—15 ..	63	36	27	36	22	14	27	14	13
	15—20 ..	50	31	19	38	26	12	12	5	7
	20 and over ..	227	158	69	161	132	29	66	26	40
	Total ..	*468*	*295*	*173*	*265*	*199*	*66*	*203*	*96*	*107*
	Brahmo.									
	0—5 ..	....	....	....	....	....	....	....	....	....
	5—10 ..	....	....	....	....	....	....	....	....	....
	10—15 ..	....	....	....	....	....	....	....	....	....
	15—20 ..	....	....	....	....	....	....	....	....	....
	20 and over ..	1	1	....	....	....	....	1	1	....
	Total ..	*1*	*1*	....	....	....	....	*1*	*1*	....
	Sikh.									
	0—5 ..	3,919	1,977	1,942	....	....	....	3,919	1,977	1,942
	5—10 ..	3,026	1,630	1,396	111	94	17	2,915	1,536	1,379
	10—15 ..	2,609	1,417	1,192	231	192	39	2,378	1,225	1,153
	15—20 ..	2,035	980	1,055	380	327	53	1,655	653	1,002
	20 and over ..	9,601	5,131	4,470	1,817	1,670	147	7,784	3,461	4,323
	Total ..	*21,190*	*11,135*	*10,055*	*2,539*	*2,283*	*256*	*18,651*	*8,852*	*9,799*
	Jain.									
	0—5 ..	....	....	....	....	....	....	....	....	....
	5—10 ..	....	....	....	....	....	....	....	....	....
	10—15 ..	1	1	....	1	1	....	....	....	....
	15—20 ..	1	1	....	1	1	....	....	....	....
	20 and over ..	1	1	....	1	1	....	....	....	....
	Total ..	*3*	*3*	....	*3*	*3*	....	....	....	....
	Buddhist.									
	0—5 ..	....	....	....	....	....	....	....	....	....
	5—10 ..	....	....	....	....	....	....	....	....	....
	10—15 ..	....	....	....	....	....	....	....	....	....
	15—20 ..	1	1	....	1	1	....	....	....	....
	20 and over ..	4	4	....	....	....	....	4	4	....
	Total ..	*5*	*5*	....	*1*	*1*	....	*4*	*4*	....

XIII.

GION AND AGE.

Census 1931.

Literate in											
English.			*Urdu.*			*Hindi.*			*Other Vernaculars.*		
Persons.	Males.	Females.	Persons.	Males.	Females.	Persons.	Males.	Females.	Persons.	Males.	Females.
12	13	14	15	16	17	18	19	20	21	22	23
....	....	....	....	....	....	....	....	....	....	....	70
361	332	29	1,103	1,030	73	117	23	94	322	252	107
975	932	43	1,941	1,832	109	148	36	112	635	528	130
2,423	2,371	52	2,669	2,569	100	177	95	82	1,310	1,180	357
8,025	7,816	209	12,938	12,750	188	1,119	933	186	11,308	10,951	....
11,784	*11,451*	*333*	*18,651*	*18,181*	*470*	*1,561*	*1,087*	*474*	*13,575*	*12,911*	*664*
....	....	....	....	....	....	....	....	....	....	....	12
250	237	13	440	404	36	102	18	84	66	54	20
672	653	19	677	636	41	130	29	101	121	101	26
1,596	1,583	13	825	797	28	162	87	75	241	215	74
5,890	5,851	39	5,662	5,606	56	1043	883	160	2,951	2,877	....
8,408	*8,324*	*84*	*7,604*	*7,443*	*161*	*1,437*	*1,017*	*420*	*3,379*	*3,247*	*132*
....	....	....	....	....	....	....	....	....	....	....	....
7	5	2	9	9	....	13	4	9	1	1	....
15	11	4	6	5	1	14	5	9	1	1	....
24	21	3	5	3	2	7	1	6	2	1	1
102	95	7	21	18	3	30	11	19	8	8	....
148	*132*	*16*	*41*	*35*	*6*	*64*	*21*	*43*	*12*	*11*	*1*
....	....	....	....	....	....	....	....	....	....	....	....
....	....	....	....	....	....	....	....	....	....	....	....
....	....	....	....	....	....	....	....	....	....	....	....
....	....	....	....	....	....	....	....	....	....	....	....
....	....	....	....	....	....	....	....	....	....	....	....
....	....	....	....	....	....	....	....	....	....	....	....
....	....	....	....	....	....	....	....	....	....	....	15
12	12	....	50	49	1	2	1	1	47	32	32
36	33	3	88	86	2	4	2	2	103	71	44
71	66	5	117	114	3	6	5	1	186	142	126
201	198	3	421	410	11	38	31	7	1,157	1,031	....
320	*309*	*11*	*676*	*659*	*17*	*50*	*39*	*11*	*1,493*	*1,276*	*217*
....	....	....	....	....	....	....	....	....	....	....	....
....	....	....	....	....	....	....	....	....	....	....	....
1	1	....	....	....	....	....	....	....	....	....	....
1	1	....	....	....	....	....	....	....	....	....	....
1	1	....	....	....	....	....	....	....	....	....	....
3	*3*	....	....	....	....	....	....	....	....	....	....
....	....	....	....	....	....	....	....	....	....	....	....
....	....	....	....	....	....	....	....	....	....	....	....
....	....	....	....	....	....	....	....	....	....	....	....
1	1	....	....	....	....	....	....	....	....	....	....
....	....	....	....	....	....	....	....	....	....	....	....
1	*1*	....	....	....	....	....	....	....	....	....	....

TABLE

LITERACY BY RELI-

Jammu and Kashmir

District or Province.	Age.	Population. Total. Persons.	Total. Males.	Total. Females.	Literate. Persons.	Literate. Males.	Literate. Females.	Illiterate. Persons.	Illiterate. Males.	Illiterate. Females.
1	2	3	4	5	6	7	8	9	10	11
Kashmir Province.	**Zoroastrian.**									
	0—5 ..	1	1	....	....	....	—	1	1	—
	5—10 ..	....	....	....	....	....	—	....	....	....
	10—15 ..	....	....	....	....	....	—	....	....	....
	15—20 ..	1	....	1	....	....	—	1	....	1
	20 and over ..	3	2	1	3	2	1	—	....	—
	Total ..	*5*	*3*	*2*	*3*	*2*	*1*	*2*	*1*	*1*
	Muslim.									
	0—5 ..	238,029	121,251	116,778	....	....	....	238,029	121,251	116,778
	5—10 ..	193,586	105,480	88,106	889	803	86	192,697	104,677	88,020
	10—15 ..	177,830	97,540	80,290	1,815	1,686	129	176,015	95,854	80,161
	15—20 ..	147,366	75,480	71,886	3,314	3,169	145	144,052	72,311	71,741
	20 and over ..	721,476	397,051	324,425	15,615	15,313	302	705,861	381,738	324,123
	Total ..	*1,478,287*	*796,802*	*681,485*	*21,633*	*20,971*	*662*	*1,456,654*	*775,831*	*680,823*
	Christian.									
	0—5 ..	16	8	8	—	—	—	16	8	8
	5—10 ..	25	16	9	15	8	7	10	8	2
	10—15 ..	23	15	8	16	8	8	7	7	—
	15—20 ..	21	9	12	21	9	12	—	—	—
	20 and over ..	254	118	136	247	115	132	7	3	4
	Total ..	*339*	*166*	*173*	*299*	*140*	*159*	*40*	*26*	*14*
	Tribal.									
	0—5 ..	20	15	5	....	—	—	20	15	5
	5—10 ..	10	5	5	....	—	—	10	5	5
	10—15 ..	10	6	4	....	—	—	10	6	4
	15—20 ..	9	5	4	....	—	—	9	5	4
	20 and over ..	44	30	14	—	—	—	44	30	14
	Total ..	*93*	*61*	*32*	—	—	—	*93*	*61*	*32*
Frontier Districts.	**All Religions.**									
	0—5 ..	44,196	21,820	22,376	—	—	—	44,196	21,820	22,376
	5—10 ..	35,597	18,795	16,802	143	123	20	35,454	18,672	16,782
	10—15 ..	31,848	17,141	14,707	231	214	17	31,617	16,927	14,690
	15—20 ..	24,640	12,719	11,921	548	521	27	24,092	12,198	11,894
	20 and over ..	152,303	78,026	74,277	4,384	4,266	118	147,919	73,760	74,159
	Total ..	*288,584*	*148,501*	*140,083*	*5,306*	*5,124*	*182*	*283,278*	*143,377*	*139,901*
	Brahmanic.									
	0—5 ..	66	39	27	....	—	—	66	39	27
	5—10 ..	49	28	21	22	14	8	27	14	13
	10—15 ..	38	23	15	19	16	3	19	7	12
	15—20 ..	217	204	13	121	116	5	96	88	8
	20 and over ..	1,206	1,140	66	714	700	14	492	440	52
	Total ..	*1,576*	*1,434*	*142*	*876*	*846*	*30*	*700*	*588*	*112*
	Arya.									
	0—5 ..	18	9	9	....	—	....	18	9	9
	5—10 ..	15	9	6	5	2	3	10	7	3
	10—15 ..	6	4	2	2	2	—	4	2	2
	15—20 ..	9	5	4	5	3	2	4	2	2
	20 and over ..	56	43	13	43	35	8	13	8	5
	Total ..	*104*	*70*	*34*	*55*	*42*	*13*	*49*	*28*	*21*

XIII.

GION AND AGE.

Census 1931.

Literate in											
English.			*Urdu.*			*Hindi.*			*Other Vernaculars.*		
Persons.	Males.	Females.	Persons.	Males.	Females.	Persons.	Males.	Females.	Persons.	Males.	Females.
12	13	14	15	16	17	18	19	20	21	22	23
...	...	...	...	...	...	...	...	...	...	...	...
...	...	...	...	...	...	...	...	...	...	...	...
...	...	...	...	...	...	...	...	...	...	...	...
...	...	...	...	...	...	...	...	...	...	...	...
3	2	1	...	...	...	...	...	...	...	...	...
3	*2*	*1*	...	...	...	...	...	...	...	...	...
...	...	...	...	...	...	...	...	...	...	...	...
77	70	7	604	568	36	...	...	...	208	165	43
237	226	11	1,170	1,105	65	...	...	...	408	355	53
711	691	20	1,720	1,654	66	2	2	...	881	822	59
1,603	1,573	30	6,819	6,701	118	8	8	...	7,185	7,031	154
2,628	*2,560*	*68*	*10,313*	*10,028*	*285*	*10*	*10*	...	*8,682*	*8,373*	*309*
...	...	...	...	...	...	...	...	...	...	...	...
15	8	7	...	...	...	...	...	...	...	...	...
14	8	6	...	...	...	...	...	...	2	...	2
19	8	11	2	1	1	...	...	...	...	...	...
225	96	129	15	15	...	...	...	...	7	4	3
273	*120*	*153*	*17*	*16*	*1*	...	...	...	*9*	*4*	*5*
...	...	...	...	...	...	...	...	...	...	...	...
...	...	...	...	...	...	...	...	...	...	...	...
...	...	...	...	...	...	...	...	...	...	...	...
...	...	...	...	...	...	...	...	...	...	...	...
...	...	...	...	...	...	...	...	...	...	...	...
...	...	...	...	...	...	...	...	...	...	...	...
...	...	...	...	...	...	...	...	...	...	...	...
4	4	...	102	95	7	6	1	5	31	23	8
14	14	...	159	151	8	5	2	3	53	47	6
47	44	3	259	249	10	65	62	3	177	166	11
291	271	20	1,338	1,313	25	277	266	11	2,478	2,416	62
356	*334*	*23*	*1,858*	*1,808*	*50*	*353*	*331*	*22*	*2,739*	*2,652*	*87*
...	...	...	...	...	...	...	...	...	...	...	...
2	2	...	12	9	3	5	1	4	3	2	1
5	5	...	8	8	...	4	2	2	2	1	1
13	12	1	26	25	1	64	62	2	18	17	1
118	116	2	167	164	3	266	258	8	163	162	1
138	*135*	*3*	*213*	*206*	*7*	*339*	*323*	*16*	*186*	*182*	*4*
...	...	...	...	...	...	...	...	...	...	...	...
...	...	...	3	2	1	...	...	...	2	...	2
...	...	...	2	2	...	...	...	...	...	...	...
2	1	1	2	2	...	1	...	1	...	...	...
21	20	1	10	9	1	5	2	3	7	4	3
23	*21*	*2*	*17*	*15*	*2*	*6*	*2*	*4*	*9*	*4*	*5*

TABLE

Literacy by Reli-

Jammu and Kashmir

District or Province.	Age.	Population. Total. Persons.	Total. Males.	Total. Females.	Literate. Persons.	Literate. Males.	Literate. Females.	Illiterate. Persons.	Illiterate. Males.	Illiterate. Females.
1	2	3	4	5	6	7	8	9	10	11
Frontier Districts.	**Sikh.**									
	0—5 —	36	19	17	—	—	—	36	19	17
	5—10 —	24	13	11	6	3	3	18	10	8
	10—15 —	17	11	6	5	4	1	12	7	5
	15—20 —	15	12	3	12	9	3	3	3	—
	20 and over —	98	70	28	72	59	13	26	11	15
	Total —	*190*	*125*	*65*	*95*	*75*	*20*	*95*	*50*	*45*
	Jain.									
	0—5 ..	1	1	....	....	—	—	1	1	—
	5—10 ..	....	....	....	....	....	....	—	—	—
	10—15 ..	....	....	....	....	....	....	....	....	—
	15—20 ..	....	....	....	....	....	....	....	....	....
	20 and over ..	2	1	1	1	1	....	1	....	1
	Total ..	*3*	*2*	*1*	*1*	*1*	....	*2*	*1*	*1*
	Buddhist.									
	0—5 ..	4,315	2,082	2,233	....	....	....	4,315	2,082	2,233
	5—10 ..	3,979	1,983	1,996	16	15	1	3,963	1,968	1,995
	10—15 ..	3,688	1,823	1,865	32	31	1	3,656	1,792	1,864
	15—20 ..	3,057	1,503	1,564	94	93	1	2,973	1,410	1,563
	20 and over ..	23,163	11,638	11,525	1,466	1,441	25	21,697	10,197	11,500
	Total ..	*38,212*	*19,029*	*19,183*	*1,608*	*1,580*	*28*	*36,604*	*17,449*	*19,155*
	Muslim.									
	0—5 ..	39,731	19,659	20,072	....	....	....	39,731	19,659	20,072
	5—10 ..	31,510	16,752	14,758	89	85	4	31,421	16,667	14,754
	10—15 ..	28,086	15,274	12,812	168	159	9	27,918	15,115	12,803
	15—20 ..	21,322	10,988	10,334	310	296	14	21,012	10,692	10,320
	20 and over ..	127,679	65,078	62,601	2,020	1,991	29	125,659	63,087	62,572
	Total ..	*248,328*	*127,751*	*120,577*	*2,587*	*2,531*	*56*	*245,741*	*125,220*	*120,521*
	Christian.									
	0—5 —	29	11	18	—	—	—	29	11	18
	5—10 —	20	10	10	5	4	1	15	6	9
	10—15 ..	13	6	7	5	2	3	8	4	4
	15—20 ..	10	7	3	6	4	2	4	3	1
	20 and over ..	99	56	43	68	39	29	31	17	14
	Total ..	*171*	*90*	*81*	*84*	*49*	*35*	*87*	*41*	*46*
Jammu District.	**All Religions.**									
	0—5 ..	57,933	28,575	29,358	....	....	....	57,933	28,575	29,358
	5—10 ..	45,551	24,887	20,664	1,521	1,079	442	44,030	23,808	20,222
	10—15 ..	42,525	23,465	19,060	2,726	2,072	654	39,799	21,393	18,406
	15—20 ..	36,137	19,328	16,809	4,506	3,806	700	31,631	15,522	16,109
	20 and over ..	193,094	109,464	83,630	19,689	17,586	2,103	173,405	91,878	81,527
	Total ..	*375,240*	*205,719*	*169,521*	*28,442*	*24,543*	*3,899*	*346,798*	*181,176*	*165,622*
	Brahmanic									
	0—5 ..	26,210	12,501	13,709	....	....	....	26,210	12,501	13,709
	5—10 ..	19,522	10,830	8,692	929	666	263	18,593	10,164	8,429
	10—15 ..	18,132	10,326	7,806	1,706	1,333	373	16,426	8,993	7,433
	15—20 ..	16,358	8,819	7,539	3,002	2,581	421	13,356	6,238	7,118
	20 and over ..	93,124	52,207	40,917	13,687	12,385	1,302	79,437	39,822	39,615
	Total ..	*173,346*	*94,683*	*78.663*	*19.324*	*16,965*	*2,359*	*154,022*	*77,718*	*76,304*

Part

XIII.

.GION AND AGE.

Census 1931.

Literate in											
English.			*Urdu.*			*Hindi.*			*Other Vernaculars.*		
Persons.	Males.	Females.	Persons.	Males.	Females.	Persons.	Males.	Females.	Persons.	Males.	Females.
12	13	14	15	16	17	18	19	20	21	22	23
—	....	....	....	....	....	—	—	—	....	—	—
—	....	....	3	3	—	1	—	1	2	—	2
1	1	....	3	3	....	1	....	1	—	....	—
4	4	....	5	4	1	....	....	....	3	1	2
9	9	....	33	30	3	1	1	....	29	19	10
14	*14*	....	*44*	*40*	*4*	*3*	*1*	*2*	*34*	*20*	*14*
....	....	....	....	....	....	....	....	....	....	....	—
....	....	....	....	....	....	....	....	....	....	....	—
....	....	....	....	....	....	....	....	....	....	....	—
....	....	....	....	....	....	....	....	....	....	....	—
1	1	....	....	....	....	....	....	....	....	....	—
1	*1*	....	....	....	....	....	—	....	....	....	—
—	—	....	—	—	—	—	—	—	—	—	—
—	—	....	4	4	—	—	—	—	12	11	1
1	1	....	8	8	—	—	—	—	23	22	1
1	1	....	14	14	—	—	—	—	79	78	1
4	4	—	57	56	1	1	1	—	1,404	1,380	24
6	*6*	—	*83*	*82*	*1*	*1*	*1*	—	*1,518*	*1,491*	*27*
—	....	....	....	....	—	—	—	....	....	—	—
1	1	....	78	75	3	—	—	....	10	9	1
6	6	....	136	129	7	....	....	....	26	24	2
25	24	1	211	203	8	....	....	....	74	69	5
98	97	1	1,067	1,050	17	4	4	—	851	840	11
130	*128*	*2*	*1,492*	*1,457*	*35*	*4*	*4*	—	*961*	*942*	*19*
—	—	—	....	....	—	—	—	—	—	—	—
1	1	—	2	2	—	—	—	—	2	1	1
1	1	....	2	1	1	—	—	—	2	—	2
2	2	....	1	1	—	—	—	—	3	1	2
40	24	16	4	4	—	—	—	—	24	11	13
44	*28*	*16*	*9*	*8*	*1*	—	—	—	*31*	*13*	*18*
II.											
—	....	....	....	....	....	....	....	....	....	....	—
150	125	25	747	667	80	325	85	240	299	202	97
347	289	58	1,347	1,213	134	477	170	307	555	400	155
792	699	93	2,076	1,939	137	635	322	313	1,003	846	157
2,834	2,623	211	8,303	7,905	398	3,541	2,573	968	5,011	4,485	526
4,123	*3,736*	*387*	*12,473*	*11,724*	*749*	*4,978*	*3,150*	*1,828*	*6,868*	*5,933*	*935*
....	....	....	....	....	....	....	....	....	....	....	....
101	86	15	424	401	23	245	64	181	159	115	44
218	179	39	797	763	34	368	131	237	323	260	63
472	409	63	1,316	1,280	36	529	276	253	685	616	69
1,892	1,738	154	5,381	5,269	112	3,103	2,306	797	3,311	3,072	239
2,683	*2,412*	*271*	*7,918*	*7,713*	*205*	*4,245*	*2,777*	*1,468*	*4,478*	*4,063*	*415*

TABLE

LITERACY BY RELI-

Jammu and Kashmir

District or Province.	Age.	POPULATION.								
		Total.			*Literate.*			*Illiterate.*		
		Persons.	Males.	Females.	Persons.	Males.	Females.	Persons.	Males.	Females.
1	2	3	4	5	6	7	8	9	10	11
Jammu District.	**Arya.**									
	0—5 ..	7,019	3,593	3,426	—	—	—	7,019	3,593	3,426
	5—10 ..	5,571	3,077	2,494	119	84	35	5,452	2,993	2,459
	10—15 ..	5,184	2,852	2,332	214	162	52	4,970	2,690	2,280
	15—20 ..	4,202	2,183	2,019	314	254	60	3,888	1,929	1,959
	20 and over ..	21,734	12,354	9,380	1,201	1,017	184	20,533	11,337	9,196
	Total ..	*43,710*	*24,059*	*19,651*	*1,848*	*1,517*	*331*	*41,862*	*22,542*	*19,320*
	Brahmo.									
	0—5 ..	....	....	....	—	....	....	....	....	....
	5—10 ..	....	....	....	....	....	....	....	....	....
	10—15 ..	1	1	....	1	1	....	....	....	....
	15—20 ..	1	1	....	1	1	....	....	....	....
	20 and over ..	2	1	1	2	1	1	....	....	....
	Total ..	*4*	*3*	*1*	*4*	*3*	*1*	....	....	....
	Sikh.									
	0—5 ..	1,183	600	583	—	—	—	1,183	600	583
	5—10 ..	906	484	422	62	33	29	844	451	393
	10—15 ..	803	433	370	116	75	41	687	358	329
	15—20 ..	628	312	316	160	123	37	468	189	279
	20 and over ..	3,334	1,848	1,486	702	585	117	2,632	1,263	1,369
	Total ..	*6,854*	*3,677*	*3,177*	*1,040*	*816*	*224*	*5,814*	*2,861*	*2,953*
	Muslim.									
	0—5 ..	23,171	11,679	11,492	....	....	....	23,171	11,679	11,492
	5—10 ..	19,299	10,366	8,933	363	272	91	18,936	10,094	8,842
	10—15 ..	18,192	9,750	8,442	620	458	162	17,572	9,292	8,290
	15—20 ..	14,755	7,920	6,835	971	812	159	13,784	7,108	6,676
	20 and over ..	73,919	42,487	31,432	3,834	3,400	434	70,085	39,087	30,998
	Total ..	*149,336*	*82,202*	*67,134*	*5,758*	*4,942*	*846*	*143,548*	*77,260*	*66,288*
Kathua District.	**All Religions.**									
	0—5 ..	23,238	11,912	11,326	....	....	....	23,238	11,912	11,326
	5—10 ..	19,576	10,402	9,174	277	245	32	19,299	10,157	9,142
	10—15 ..	18,914	9,943	8,971	524	465	59	18,390	9,478	8,912
	15—20 ..	16,125	8,225	7,900	769	701	68	15,356	7,524	7,832
	20 and over ..	83,379	45,511	37,868	4,360	4,180	180	79,019	41,331	37,688
	Total ..	*161,232*	*85,993*	*75,239*	*5,930*	*5,591*	*339*	*155,302*	*80,402*	*74,900*
	Brahmanic.									
	0—5 ..	14,453	7,459	6,994	....	—	—	14,453	7,459	6,994
	5—10 ..	12,146	6,459	5,687	230	207	23	11,916	6,252	5,664
	10—15 ..	11,718	6,117	5,601	429	388	41	11,289	5,729	5,560
	15—20 ..	10,108	5,046	5,062	611	567	44	9,497	4,479	5,018
	20 and over ..	56,242	30,161	26,081	3,645	3,522	123	52,597	26,639	25,958
	Total ..	*104,667*	*55,242*	*49,425*	*4,915*	*4,684*	*231*	*99,752*	*50,558*	*49,194*
	Arya.									
	0—5 ..	2,479	1,271	1,208	—	—	—	2,479	1,271	1,208
	5—10 ..	1,999	1,077	922	14	11	3	1,985	1,066	919
	10—15 ..	1,943	1,031	912	25	15	10	1,918	1,016	902
	15—20 ..	1,754	892	862	34	22	12	1,720	870	850
	20 and over ..	8,096	4,495	3,601	193	166	27	7,903	4,329	3,574
	Total ..	*16,271*	*8,766*	*7,505*	*266*	*214*	*52*	*16,005*	*8,552*	*7,453*

XIII.

GION AND AGE.

Census 1931.

Literate in											
English.			*Urdu.*			*Hindi.*			*Other Vernaculars.*		
Persons.	Males.	Females.	Persons.	Males.	Females.	Persons.	Males.	Females.	Persons.	Males.	Females.
12	13	14	15	16	17	18	19	20	21	22	23
....	....	....	....	....	....	....	....	....	....	....	....
13	10	3	44	41	3	46	17	29	16	16	....
33	28	5	86	82	4	69	31	38	26	21	5
82	74	8	127	120	7	75	38	37	30	22	8
276	256	20	417	389	28	294	180	114	214	192	22
404	*368*	*36*	*674*	*632*	*42*	*484*	*266*	*218*	*286*	*251*	*35*
....	....	....	....	....	....	....	....	....	....	....	....
....	....	....	....	....	....	....	....	....	....	....	....
....	....	....	1	1	....	....	....	....	....	....	....
1	1	....	....	....	....	....	....	....	....	....	....
1	1	....	....	....	....	1	....	1	....	....	....
2	*2*	....	*1*	*1*	....	*1*	....	*1*	....	....	....
....	....	....	....	....	....	....	....	....	....	....	....
6	3	3	28	24	4	14	2	12	14	4	10
18	14	4	47	40	7	19	5	14	32	16	16
38	32	6	55	49	6	18	7	11	49	35	14
130	121	9	215	202	13	67	42	25	290	220	70
192	*170*	*22*	*345*	*315*	*30*	*118*	*56*	*62*	*385*	*275*	*110*
....	....	....	....	....	....	....	....	....	....	....	....
27	24	3	233	185	48	....	....	....	103	63	40
70	61	9	390	303	87	....	....	....	160	94	66
180	166	14	557	473	84	1	1	....	233	172	61
490	475	15	2,234	1,993	241	12	12	....	1,098	920	178
767	*726*	*41*	*3,414*	*2,954*	*460*	*13*	*13*	....	*1,594*	*1,249*	*345*
....	....	....	....	....	....	....	....	....	....	....	....
38	37	1	165	162	3	56	32	24	18	14	4
64	62	2	335	330	5	97	50	47	28	23	5
88	86	2	439	425	14	153	104	49	89	86	3
351	348	3	1,479	1,451	28	1,351	1,236	115	1,179	1,145	34
541	*533*	*8*	*2,418*	*2,368*	*50*	*1,657*	*1,422*	*235*	*1,314*	*1,268*	*46*
....	....	....	....	....	....	....	....	....	....	....	....
35	35	....	136	135	1	52	31	21	7	6	1
59	58	1	274	272	2	85	48	37	11	10	1
70	69	1	336	331	5	136	100	36	69	67	2
293	291	2	1,073	1,064	9	1,280	1,184	96	999	983	16
457	*453*	*4*	*1,819*	*1,802*	*17*	*1,553*	*1,363*	190	*1,086*	*1,066*	*20*
....	....	....	....	....	....	....	....	....	....	....	....
1	1	....	8	8	....	4	1	3	1	1	....
....	....	....	12	12	....	12	2	10	1	1	....
3	2	1	14	14	....	15	4	11	2	2	....
20	20	....	65	60	5	66	48	18	42	38	4
24	*23*	*1*	*99*	*94*	*5*	*97*	*55*	*42*	*46*	*42*	*4*

TABLE

LITERACY BY RELI-

Jammu and Kashmir

District or Province.	Age.	Population.								
		Total.			*Illiterate.*			*Literate.*		
		Persons.	Males.	Females.	Persons.	Males.	Females.	Persons.	Males.	Females.
1	2	3	4	5	6	7	8	9	10	11
Kathua District.	**Sikh.**									
	0—5 ..	79	31	48	....	....	....	79	31	48
	5—10 ..	67	37	30	5	3	2	62	34	28
	10—15 ..	59	33	26	7	6	1	52	27	25
	15—20 ..	51	26	25	10	7	3	41	19	22
	20 and over ..	222	141	81	47	42	5	175	99	76
	Total ..	*478*	*268*	*210*	*69*	*58*	*11*	*409*	*210*	*199*
	Muslim.									
	0—5 ..	6,212	3,143	3,069	....	....	....	6,212	3,143	3,069
	5—10 ..	5,346	2,819	2,527	28	24	4	5,318	2,795	2,523
	10—15 ..	5 173	2,751	2,422	63	56	7	5,110	2,695	2,415
	15—20 ..	4,181	2,243	1,938	114	105	9	4,067	2,138	1,929
	20 and over ..	18,735	10,663	8,072	474	449	25	18,261	10,214	8,047
	Total ..	*39,647*	*21,619*	*18,028*	*679*	*634*	*45*	*38,968*	*20,985*	*17,983*
Udhampur District.	**All Religions.**									
	0—5 ..	40,554	20,240	20,314	....	....	....	40,554	20,240	20,314
	5—10 ..	32,668	17,207	15,461	410	358	52	32,258	16,849	15,409
	10—15 ..	30,156	15,819	14,337	783	707	76	29,373	15,112	14,261
	15—20 ..	26,091	13,000	13,091	1,364	1,278	86	24,727	11,722	13,005
	20 and over ..	144,199	77,248	66,951	8,151	7,881	270	136,048	69,367	66,681
	Total ..	*273,668*	*143,514*	*130,154*	*10,708*	*10,224*	*484*	*262,960*	*133,290*	*129,670*
	Brahmanic.									
	0—5 ..	18,829	9,282	9,547	....	....	....	18,829	9,282	9,547
	5—10 ..	15,338	7,976	7,362	279	243	36	15,059	7,733	7,326
	10—15 ..	14,517	7,450	7,067	507	456	51	14,010	6,994	7,016
	15—20 ..	12,961	6,344	6,617	901	842	59	12,060	5,502	6,558
	20 and over ..	76,477	40,506	35,971	6,029	5,837	192	70,448	34,669	35,779
	Total ..	*138,122*	*71,558*	*66,564*	*7,716*	*7,378*	*338*	*130,406*	*64,180*	*66,226*
	Arya.									
	0—5 ..	2,406	1,230	1,176	....	....	....	2,406	1,230	1,176
	5—10 ..	1,985	1,045	940	48	39	9	1,937	1,006	931
	10—15 ..	1,894	957	937	113	97	16	1,781	860	921
	15—20 ..	1,674	819	855	160	147	13	1,514	672	842
	20 and over ..	9,682	5,100	4,582	442	415	27	9,240	4,685	4,555
	Total ..	*17,641*	*9,151*	*8,490*	*763*	*698*	*65*	*16,878*	*8,453*	*8,425*
	Sikh.									
	0—5 ..	52	25	27	....	....	....	52	25	27
	5—10 ..	48	25	23	5	4	1	43	21	22
	10—15 ..	44	23	21	8	7	1	36	16	20
	15—20 ..	25	13	12	10	9	1	15	4	11
	20 and over ..	159	92	67	61	56	5	98	36	62
	Total ..	*328*	*178*	*150*	*84*	*76*	*8*	*244*	*102*	*142*
	Muslim.									
	0—5 ..	19,206	9,673	9,533	....	....	....	19,206	9,673	9,533
	5—10 ..	15,237	8,129	7,108	78	72	6	15,159	8,057	7,102
	10—15 ..	13,639	7,357	6,282	154	146	8	13,485	7,211	6,274
	15—20 ..	11,393	5,806	5,587	291	278	13	11,102	5,528	5,574
	20 and over ..	57,576	31,396	26,180	1,601	1,559	42	55,975	29,837	26,138
	Total ..	*117,051*	*62,361*	*54,690*	*2,124*	*2,055*	*69*	*114,927*	*60,306*	*54,621*

XIII.

GION AND AGE.

Census 1931.

Literate in											
English.			*Urdu.*			*Hindi.*			*Other Vernaculars.*		
Persons.	Males.	Females.	Persons.	Males.	Females.	Persons.	Males.	Females.	Persons.	Males.	Females.
12	13	14	15	16	17	18	19	20	21	22	23
....	....	....	....	....	....	....	....	....	....	....	....
....	....	....	4	3	1	....	....	....	1	....	1
....	....	....	5	5	....	....	....	....	2	1	1
2	2	....	6	5	1	2	....	2	....	....	....
6	6	....	25	24	1	4	3	1	12	9	3
8	*8*	....	*40*	*37*	*3*	*6*	*3*	*3*	*15*	*10*	*5*
....	....	....	....	....	....	....	....	....	....	....	....
2	1	1	17	16	1	....	....	....	9	7	2
5	4	1	44	41	3	....	....	....	14	11	3
13	13	....	83	75	8	....	....	....	18	17	1
31	30	1	316	303	13	1	1	....	126	115	11
51	*48*	*3*	*460*	*435*	*25*	*1*	*1*	....	*167*	*150*	*17*
....	....	....	....	....	....	....	....	....	....	....	....
27	27	....	249	240	9	88	52	36	46	39	7
89	85	4	449	441	8	164	110	54	81	71	10
190	185	5	715	700	15	256	202	54	203	191	12
577	570	7	3,061	3,015	46	1,452	1,279	173	3,061	3,017	44
883	*867*	*16*	*4,474*	*4,396*	*78*	*1,960*	*1,643*	*317*	*3,391*	*3,318*	*73*
....	....	....	....	....	....	....	....	....	....	....	....
20	20	....	166	159	7	69	41	28	24	23	1
56	55	1	273	269	4	126	83	43	52	49	3
118	115	3	425	419	6	206	160	46	152	148	4
394	393	1	1,902	1,882	20	1,324	1,174	150	2,409	2,388	21
588	*583*	*5*	*2,766*	*2,729*	*37*	*1,725*	*1,458*	*267*	*2,637*	*2,608*	*29*
....	....	....	....	....	....	....	....	....	....	....	....
3	3	....	23	23	....	19	11	8	3	2	1
19	16	3	53	52	1	38	27	11	3	2	1
35	34	1	69	66	3	49	41	8	7	6	1
81	79	2	167	164	3	117	96	21	77	76	1
138	*132*	*6*	*312*	*305*	*7*	*223*	*175*	*48*	*90*	*86*	*4*
....	....	....	....	....	....	....	....	....	....	....	....
....	....	....	3	3	....	....	....	....	2	1	1
....	....	....	5	5	....	....	....	....	3	2	1
3	3	....	6	5	1	1	1	....	....	....	....
12	11	1	28	28	....	1	1	....	20	16	4
15	*14*	*1*	*42*	*41*	*1*	*2*	*2*	....	*25*	*19*	*6*
....	....	....	....	....	....	....	....	....	....	....	....
4	4	....	57	55	2	....	....	....	17	13	4
13	13	....	118	115	3	....	....	....	23	18	5
33	32	1	214	209	5	....	....	....	44	37	7
87	85	2	960	938	22	8	8	....	546	528	18
137	*134*	*3*	*1,349*	*1,317*	*32*	*8*	*8*	....	*630*	*596*	*34*

TABLE

Literacy by Reli-

Jammu and Kashmir

District or Province.	Age.	Population. Total. Persons.	Total. Males.	Total. Females.	Literate. Persons.	Literate. Males.	Literate. Females.	Illiterate. Persons.	Illiterate. Males.	Illiterate. Females.
1	2	3	4	5	6	7	8	9	10	11
Riasi District.	**All Religions.**									
	0—5 ..	37,675	18,801	18,874	....	....	....	37,675	18,801	18,874
	5—10 ..	30,028	16,107	13,921	170	140	30	29,858	15,967	13,891
	10—15 ..	27,716	14,960	12,756	308	268	40	27,408	14,692	12,716
	15—20 ..	22,518	11,057	11,461	538	483	55	21,980	10,574	11,406
	20 and over ..	117,308	63,285	54,023	3,789	3,617	172	113,519	59,668	53,851
	Total ..	*235,245*	*124,210*	*111,035*	*4,805*	*4,508*	*297*	*230,440*	*119,702*	*110,738*
	Brahmanic.									
	0—5 ..	9,448	4,690	4,758	....	....	....	9,448	4,690	4,758
	5—10 ..	7,681	4,003	3,678	110	89	21	7,571	3,914	3,657
	10—15 ..	7,185	3,747	3,438	190	157	33	6,995	3,590	3,405
	15—20 ..	6,384	3,100	3,284	315	279	36	6,069	2,821	3,248
	20 and over ..	40,703	21,997	18,706	2,369	2,262	107	38,334	19,735	18,599
	Total ..	*71,401*	*37,537*	*33,864*	*2,984*	*2,787*	*197*	*68,417*	*34,750*	*33,667*
	Arya.									
	0—5 ..	993	473	520	....	....	....	993	473	520
	5—10 ..	788	406	382	6	4	2	782	402	380
	10—15 ..	768	376	392	5	5	....	763	371	392
	15—20 ..	692	321	371	21	14	7	671	307	364
	20 and over ..	4,370	2,303	2,067	89	73	16	4,281	2,230	2,051
	Total ..	*7,611*	*3,879*	*3,732*	*121*	*96*	*25*	*7,490*	*3,783*	*3,707*
	Sikh.									
	0—5 ..	133	73	60	....	....	....	133	73	60
	5—10 ..	99	54	45	10	5	5	89	49	40
	10—15 ..	92	48	44	12	8	4	80	40	40
	15—20 ..	81	32	49	22	16	6	59	16	43
	20 and over ..	437	242	195	144	129	15	293	113	180
	Total ..	*842*	*419*	*393*	*188*	*158*	*30*	*654*	*291*	*363*
	Muslim.									
	0—5 ..	27,096	13,564	13,532	....	....	....	27,096	13,564	13,532
	5—10 ..	21,452	11,639	9,813	44	42	2	21,408	11,597	9,811
	10—15 ..	19,667	10,787	8,880	101	98	3	19,566	10,689	8,877
	15—20 ..	15,357	7,601	7,756	180	174	6	15,177	7,427	7,750
	20 and over ..	71,781	38,731	33,050	1,186	1,152	34	70,595	37,579	33,016
	Total ..	*155,353*	*82,322*	*73,031*	*1,511*	*1,466*	*45*	*153,842*	*80,856*	*72,986*
Mirpur District.	**All Religions.**									
	0—5 ..	56,189	28,573	27,616	....	....	....	56,189	28,573	27,616
	5—10 ..	44,717	24,135	20,582	698	544	154	44,019	23,591	20,428
	10—15 ..	40,335	21,955	18,380	1,251	997	254	39,084	20,958	18,126
	15—20 ..	31,671	15,692	15,979	1,708	1,453	255	29,963	14,239	15,724
	20 and over ..	171,835	88,476	83,359	9,059	8,345	714	162,776	80,131	82,645
	Total ..	*344,747*	*178,831*	*165,916*	*12,716*	*11,339*	*1,377*	*332,031*	*167,492*	*164,539*
	Brahmanic.									
	0—5 ..	7,760	3,981	3,779	....	....	....	7,760	3,981	3,779
	5—10 ..	6,390	3,447	2,943	274	205	69	6,116	3,242	2,874
	10—15 ..	5,916	3,169	2,747	479	356	123	5,437	2,813	2,624
	15—20 ..	4,335	2,098	2,237	632	514	118	3,703	1,584	2,119
	20 and over ..	25,701	13,721	11,980	3,551	3,241	310	22,150	10,480	11,670
	Total ..	*50,102*	*26,416*	*23,686*	*4,936*	*4,316*	*620*	*45,166*	*22,100*	*23,066*

Literate in											
English.			*Urdu.*			*Hindi.*			*Other Vernaculars.*		
Persons.	Males.	Females.	Persons.	Males.	Females.	Persons.	Males.	Females.	Persons.	Males.	Females.
13	14	15	16	17	18	19	20	21	22	23	24
....	....	....	....	....	....	....	....	....	....	....	....
3	3	....	113	111	2	30	10	20	24	16	8
3	3	....	212	206	6	51	23	28	42	36	6
29	29	....	316	306	10	101	67	34	92	81	11
118	114	4	1,791	1,766	25	801	718	83	1,079	1,019	60
153	*149*	*4*	*2,432*	*2,389*	*43*	*983*	*818*	*165*	*1,237*	*1,152*	*85*
....	....	—	....	....	....	....	....	....	....	....	....
2	2	—	71	71	....	29	10	19	8	6	2
3	3	—	123	119	4	49	21	28	15	14	1
21	21	—	164	159	5	90	62	28	40	37	3
88	86	2	862	852	10	732	654	78	687	670	17
114	*112*	*2*	*1,220*	*1,201*	*19*	*900*	*747*	*153*	*750*	*727*	*23*
—	....	—	—	—	—	—	—	—	—	—	—
—	....	—	4	3	1	1	—	1	1	1	—
—	—	—	3	3	—	2	2	—	—	—	—
3	3	—	8	6	2	8	3	5	2	2	—
8	6	2	42	37	5	23	18	5	16	12	4
11	*9*	*2*	*57*	*49*	*8*	*34*	*23*	*11*	*19*	*15*	*4*
—	—	—	—	—	—	—	—	—	—	—	—
—	—	—	4	4	—	—	—	—	6	1	5
—	—	—	6	6	—	—	—	—	6	2	4
1	1	—	8	8	—	3	2	1	10	5	5
3	3	—	51	51	—	35	35	—	55	40	15
4	*4*	—	*69*	*69*	—	*38*	*37*	*1*	*77*	*48*	*29*
—	—	....	....	....	....	—	....	....	—	—	—
1	1	....	34	33	1	....	....	....	9	8	1
—	—	....	80	78	2	....	....	....	21	20	1
4	4	....	136	133	3	....	....	....	40	37	3
18	18	—	836	826	10	11	11	—	321	297	24
23	*23*	—	*1,086*	*1,070*	*16*	*11*	*11*	—	*391*	*362*	*29*
....	....	....	....	....	....	....	....	....	....	....	....
50	50	....	411	399	12	133	30	103	104	65	39
86	85	1	755	730	25	220	54	166	190	128	62
204	200	4	1,031	1,004	27	239	101	138	234	148	86
635	625	10	5,532	5,428	104	1,317	1,014	303	1,575	1,278	297
975	*960*	*15*	*7,729*	*7,561*	*168*	*1,909*	*1,199*	*710*	*2,103*	*1,619*	*484*
....	....	....	....	....	....	....	....	....	....	....	....
26	26	....	144	142	2	87	22	65	17	15	2
35	34	1	260	254	6	145	39	106	39	29	10
87	87	....	327	319	8	155	70	85	63	38	25
264	262	2	1,759	1,732	27	960	760	200	568	487	81
412	*409*	*3*	*2,490*	*2,447*	*43*	*1,347*	*891*	*456*	*687*	*569*	*118*

TABLE

Literacy by Reli-

Jammu and Kashmir

District or Province.	Age.	Population. Total. Persons.	Total. Males.	Total. Females.	Literate. Persons.	Literate. Males.	Literate. Females.	Illiterate. Persons.	Illiterate. Males.	Illiterate. Females.
1	2	3	4	5	6	7	8	9	10	11
Mirpur District.	**Arya.**									
	0—5 ..	1,216	629	587	....	....	....	1,216	629	587
	5—10 ..	943	492	451	85	49	36	858	443	415
	10—15 ..	851	436	415	156	96	60	695	340	355
	15—20 ..	705	304	401	185	129	56	520	175	345
	20 and over ..	3,777	1,943	1,834	806	693	113	2,971	1,250	1,721
	Total ..	*7,492*	*3,804*	*3,688*	*1,232*	*967*	*265*	*6,260*	*2,837*	*3,423*
	Sikh.									
	0—5 ..	1,711	856	855	....	....	....	1,711	856	855
	5—10 ..	1,262	716	546	110	79	31	1,152	637	515
	10—15 ..	1,147	606	541	169	122	47	978	484	494
	15—20 ..	863	382	481	195	145	50	668	237	431
	20 and over ..	4,449	2,288	2,161	1,003	844	159	3,446	1,444	2,002
	Total ..	*9,432*	*4,848*	*4,584*	*1,477*	*1,190*	*287*	*7,955*	*3,658*	*4,297*
	Muslim.									
	0—5 ..	45,476	23,089	22,387	....	....	....	45,476	23,089	22,387
	5—10 ..	36,106	19,474	16,632	225	209	16	35,881	19,265	16,616
	10—15 ..	32,410	17,740	14,670	445	422	23	31,965	17,318	14,647
	15—20 ..	25,761	12,906	12,855	694	665	29	25,067	12,241	12,826
	20 and over ..	137,878	70,509	67,369	3,689	3,562	127	134,189	66,947	67,242
	Total ..	*277,631*	*143,718*	*133,913*	*5,053*	*4,858*	*195*	*272,578*	*138,860*	*133,718*
Chenani Jagir.	**All Religions.**									
	0—5 ..	1,383	695	688	....	....	....	1,383	695	688
	5—10 ..	1,163	640	523	16	15	1	1,147	625	522
	10—15 ..	1,109	581	528	29	27	2	1,080	554	526
	15—20 ..	1,032	503	529	50	43	7	982	460	522
	20 and over ..	6,238	3,511	2,727	507	481	26	5,731	3,030	2,701
	Total ..	*10,925*	*5,930*	*4,995*	*602*	*566*	*36*	*10,323*	*5,364*	*4,959*
	Brahmanic.									
	0—5 ..	1,142	577	565	....	....	....	1,142	577	565
	5—10 ..	966	534	432	11	11	....	955	523	432
	10—15 ..	913	485	428	20	19	1	893	466	427
	15—20 ..	826	393	433	41	35	6	785	358	427
	20 and over ..	5,195	2,879	2,316	454	433	21	4,741	2,446	2,295
	Total ..	*9,042*	*4,868*	*4,174*	*526*	*498*	*28*	*8,516*	*4,370*	*4,146*
	Arya.									
	0—5 ..	42	14	28	....	....	....	42	14	28
	5—10 ..	33	15	18	....	....	....	33	15	18
	10—15 ..	31	11	20	....	....	....	31	11	20
	15—20 ..	38	17	21	1	1	....	37	16	21
	20 and over ..	223	109	114	2	1	1	221	108	113
	Total ..	*367*	*166*	*201*	*3*	*2*	*1*	*364*	*164*	*200*
	Sikh.									
	0—5 ..	....	....	....	....	....	....	....	....	....
	5—10 ..	1	1	....	....	....	....	1	1	....
	10—15 ..	....	....	....	....	....	....	....	....	....
	15—20 ..	....	....	....	....	....	....	....	....	....
	20 and over ..	3	3	....	1	1	....	2	2	....
	Total ..	*4*	*4*	....	*1*	*1*	....	*3*	*3*	....

XIII.

GION AND AGE.

Census 1931.

Literate in.											
English.			*Urdu.*			*Hindi.*			*Other Vernaculars.*		
Persons.	Males.	Females.	Persons.	Males.	Females.	Persons.	Males.	Females.	Persons.	Males.	Females.
12	13	14	15	16	17	18	19	20	21	22	23
....	....	....	....	....	....	....	....	....	....	....	....
10	10	....	36	34	2	37	5	32	2	....	2
22	22	....	57	53	4	63	12	51	14	9	5
46	45	1	55	52	3	68	21	47	16	11	5
185	184	1	309	302	7	230	138	92	82	69	13
263	*261*	*2*	*457*	*441*	*16*	*398*	*176*	*222*	*114*	*89*	*25*
....	....	....	....	....	....	....	....	....	....	....	....
2	2	....	48	48	....	8	2	6	52	27	25
6	6	....	72	71	1	12	3	9	79	42	37
18	17	1	77	75	2	15	10	5	85	43	42
40	38	2	338	331	7	118	109	9	507	366	141
66	*63*	*3*	*535*	*525*	*10*	*153*	*124*	*29*	*723*	*478*	*245*
....	....	....	....	....	....	....	....	....	....	....	....
10	10	....	183	175	8	1	1	....	31	23	8
22	22	....	365	352	13	....	....	....	58	48	10
52	51	1	572	558	14	....	....	....	70	56	14
139	137	2	3,124	3,062	62	8	7	1	418	356	62
223	*220*	*3*	*4,244*	*4,147*	*97*	*9*	*8*	*1*	*577*	*483*	*94*
....	....	....	....	....	....	....	....	....	....	....	....
1	1	....	10	10	....	1	1	....	4	3	1
2	2	....	17	17	....	4	3	1	6	5	1
3	3	....	19	19	....	9	5	4	19	16	3
19	19	....	112	107	5	80	68	12	296	287	9
25	*25*	....	*158*	*153*	*5*	*94*	*77*	*17*	*325*	*311*	*14*
....	....	....	....	....	....	....	....	....	....	....	....
....	....	....	8	8	....	1	1	....	2	2	....
1	1	....	12	12	....	4	3	1	3	3	....
3	3	....	14	14	....	8	4	4	16	14	2
18	18	....	83	79	4	79	68	11	274	268	6
22	*22*	....	*117*	*113*	*4*	*92*	*76*	*16*	*295*	*287*	*8*
....	....	....	....	....	....	....	....	....	....	....	....
....	....	....	....	....	....	....	....	....	....	....	....
....	....	....	....	....	....	....	....	....	....	....	....
....	....	....	....	....	....	1	1	....	....	....	....
1	1	....	....	....	....	1	....	1	....	....	....
1	*1*	....	....	....	....	*2*	*1*	*1*	....	....	....
....	....	....	....	....	....	....	....	....	....	....	....
....	....	....	....	....	....	....	....	....	....	....	....
....	....	....	....	....	....	....	....	....	....	....	....
....	....	....	....	....	....	....	....	....	....	....	....
....	....	....	1	1	....	....	....	....	....	....	....
....	....	....	*1*	*1*	....	....	....	....	....	....	....

TABLE

Literacy by Reli-

Jammu and Kashmir

District or Province.	Age.	Population. Total. Persons.	Total. Males.	Total. Females.	Literate. Persons.	Literate. Males.	Literate. Females.	Illiterate. Persons.	Illiterate. Males.	Illiterate. Females.
1	2	3	4	5	6	7	8	9	10	11
Chenani Jagir.	**Muslim.**									
	0—5 ..	199	104	95	--	--	--	199	104	95
	5—10 ..	163	90	73	5	4	1	158	86	72
	10—15 ..	165	85	80	9	8	1	156	77	79
	15—20 ..	168	93	75	8	7	1	160	86	74
	20 and over ..	817	520	297	50	46	4	767	474	293
	Total ..	*1,512*	*892*	*620*	*72*	*65*	*7*	*1,440*	*827*	*613*
Poonch Jagir.	**All Religions.**									
	0—5 ..	67,395	33,422	33,973	....	....	--	67,395	33,422	33,973
	5—10 ..	54,867	29,591	25,276	435	382	53	54,432	29,209	25,223
	10—15 ..	49,277	27,109	22,168	908	830	78	48,369	26,279	22,090
	15—20 ..	36,226	17,839	18,387	1,427	1,337	90	34,799	16,502	18,297
	20 and over ..	179,619	90,657	88,962	7,035	6,733	302	172,584	83,924	88,660
	Total ..	*387,384*	*198,618*	*188,766*	*9,805*	*9,282*	*523*	*377,579*	*189,336*	*188,243*
	Brahmanic.									
	0—5 ..	4,343	2,205	2,138	--	--	--	4,343	2,205	2,138
	5—10 ..	3,464	1,834	1,630	105	85	20	3,359	1,749	1,610
	10—15 ..	3,029	1,623	1,406	239	209	30	2,790	1,414	1,376
	15—20 ..	2,276	1,126	1,150	366	335	31	1,910	791	1,119
	20 and over ..	12,078	6,272	5,806	1,800	1,707	93	10,278	4,565	5,713
	Total ..	*25,190*	*13,060*	*12,130*	*2,510*	*2,336*	*174*	*22,680*	*10,724*	*11,956*
	Arya.									
	0—5 ..	45	24	21	--	--	--	45	24	21
	5—10 ..	29	16	13	6	4	2	23	12	11
	10—15 ..	35	19	16	13	9	4	22	10	12
	15—20 ..	32	13	19	19	12	7	13	1	12
	20 and over ..	139	84	55	96	77	19	43	7	36
	Total ..	*280*	*156*	*124*	*134*	*102*	*32*	*146*	*54*	*92*
	Sikh.									
	0—5 ..	2,126	1,070	1,056	--	--	--	2,126	1,070	1,056
	5—10 ..	1,654	896	758	41	37	4	1,613	859	754
	10—15 ..	1,453	738	665	77	68	9	1,376	720	656
	15—20 ..	1,032	479	553	128	115	13	904	364	540
	20 and over ..	5,079	2,540	2,539	719	678	41	4,360	1,862	2,498
	Total ..	*11,344*	*5,773*	*5,571*	*965*	*898*	*67*	*10,379*	*4,875*	*5,504*
	Muslim.									
	0—5 ..	60,865	30,116	30,749	--	--	--	60,865	30,116	30,749
	5—10 ..	49,709	26,839	22,870	281	254	27	49,428	26,585	22,843
	10—15 ..	44,745	24,669	20,076	576	542	34	44,169	24,127	20,042
	15—20 ..	32,877	16,216	16,661	909	875	34	31,968	15,341	16,627
	20 and over ..	162,295	81,745	80,550	4,406	4,261	145	157,889	77,484	80,405
	Total ..	*350,491*	*179,585*	*170,906*	*6,172*	*5,932*	*240*	*344,319*	*173,653*	*170,666*
Baramulla (including Langet) or Kashmir North.	**All Religions.**									
	0—5 ..	90,968	46,432	44,536	--	--	--	90,968	46,432	44,536
	5—10 ..	71,269	38,846	32,423	310	287	23	70,959	38,559	32,400
	10—15 ..	67,021	36,583	30,438	676	638	38	66,345	35,945	30,400
	15—20 ..	57,372	29,439	27,933	1,431	1,384	47	55,941	28,055	27,886
	20 and over ..	273,198	150,097	123,101	7,684	7,543	141	265,514	142,554	122,960
	Total ..	*559,828*	*301,397*	*258,431*	*10,101*	*9,852*	*249*	*549,727*	*291,545*	*258,182*

XIII.

GION AND AGE.

Census 1931.

Literate in											
English.			*Urdu.*			*Hindi.*			*Other Vernaculars.*		
Persons.	Males.	Females.	Persons.	Males.	Females.	Persons.	Males.	Females.	Persons.	Males.	Females.
12	13	14	15	16	17	18	19	20	21	22	23
....	....	....	....	....	....	....	....	....	....	....	....
1	1	....	2	2	....	....	....	....	2	1	1
1	1	....	5	5	....	....	....	....	3	2	1
....	....	....	5	5	....	....	....	....	3	2	1
....	....	....	28	27	1	....	....	....	22	19	3
2	*2*	....	*40*	*39*	*1*	....	....	....	*30*	*24*	*6*
....	....	....	....	....	....	....	....	....	....	....	....
24	22	2	278	267	11	20	10	10	113	83	30
62	61	1	587	573	14	38	21	17	221	175	46
125	118	7	945	927	18	46	25	21	311	267	44
418	405	13	4,195	4,128	67	387	326	61	2,035	1,874	161
629	*606*	*23*	*6,005*	*5,895*	*110*	*491*	*382*	*109*	*2,680*	*2,399*	*281*
....	....	....	....	....	....	....	....	....	....	....	....
10	9	1	45	44	1	15	8	7	35	24	11
34	33	1	116	114	2	30	17	13	59	45	14
59	58	1	198	194	4	35	21	14	74	62	12
243	236	7	785	775	10	311	267	44	461	429	32
346	*336*	*10*	*1,144*	*1,127*	*17*	*391*	*313*	*78*	*629*	*560*	*69*
....	....	....	....	....	....	....	....	....	....	....	....
1	1	....	3	3	....	2	....	2	....	....	....
1	1	....	5	5	....	4	1	3	3	2	1
4	3	1	7	6	1	4	....	4	4	3	1
14	14	....	39	37	2	25	12	13	18	14	4
20	*19*	*1*	*54*	*51*	*3*	*35*	*13*	*22*	*25*	*19*	*6*
....	....	....	....	....	....	....	....	....	....	....	....
1	1	....	29	20	....	3	2	1	17	14	3
4	4	....	36	36	....	4	3	1	33	25	8
12	12	....	57	57	....	6	4	2	53	42	11
24	23	1	225	219	6	48	45	3	422	391	31
41	*40*	*1*	*338*	*332*	*6*	*61*	*54*	*7*	*525*	*472*	*53*
....	....	....	....	....	....	....	....	....	....	....	....
11	10	1	209	199	10	....	....	....	61	45	16
22	22	....	428	417	11	....	....	....	126	103	23
46	45	1	683	670	13	....	....	....	180	160	20
128	127	1	3,145	3,096	49	2	1	1	1,131	1,037	94
207	*204*	*3*	*4,465*	*4,382*	*83*	*2*	*1*	*1*	*1,498*	*1,345*	*153*
....	....	....	....	....	....	....	....	....	....	....	....
24	21	3	185	181	4	4	....	4	97	85	12
84	82	2	377	368	9	4	1	3	211	187	24
293	287	6	659	649	10	14	9	5	465	439	26
1,092	1,069	23	2,702	2,683	19	107	95	12	3,783	3,696	87
1,493	*1,459*	*34*	*3,923*	*3,881*	*42*	*129*	*105*	*24*	*4,556*	*4,407*	*149*

TABLE

Literacy by Reli-

Jammu and Kashmir

District or Province.	Age.	Population. Total. Persons.	Total. Males.	Total. Females.	Literate. Persons.	Literate. Males.	Literate. Females.	Illiterate. Persons.	Illiterate. Males.	Illiterate. Females.
1	2	3	4	5	6	7	8	9	10	11
Baramulla (including Langet) or Kashmir North.	**Brahmanic.**									
	0—5 ..	1,438	712	726	—	—	—	1,438	712	726
	5—10 ..	1,264	671	593	57	49	8	1,207	622	585
	10—15 ..	1,141	610	531	134	127	7	1,007	483	524
	15—20 ..	960	569	391	346	338	8	614	231	383
	20 and over ..	5,836	3,681	2,155	2,362	2,330	32	3,474	1,351	2,123
	Total ..	*10,639*	*6,243*	*4,396*	*2,899*	*2,844*	*55*	*7,740*	*3,399*	*4,341*
	Arya.									
	0—5 ..	11	7	4	....	....	....	11	7	4
	5—10 ..	6	3	3	3	2	1	3	1	2
	10—15 ..	8	5	3	6	4	2	2	1	1
	15—20 ..	8	3	5	5	3	2	3	....	3
	20 and over ..	34	25	9	24	21	3	10	4	6
	Total ..	*67*	*43*	*24*	*38*	*30*	*8*	*29*	*13*	*16*
	Sikh.									
	0—5 ..	1,157	556	601	—	—	—	1,157	556	601
	5—10 ..	878	478	400	39	32	7	839	446	393
	10—15 ..	780	433	347	83	67	16	697	366	331
	15—20 ..	655	320	335	135	119	16	520	201	319
	20 and over ..	2,790	1,461	1,329	550	519	31	2,240	942	1,298
	Total ..	*6,260*	*3,248*	*3,012*	*807*	*737*	*70*	*5,453*	*2,511*	*2,942*
	Muslim.									
	0—5 ..	88,347	45,144	43,203	....	....	....	88,347	45,144	43,203
	5—10 ..	69,107	37,683	31,424	206	200	6	68,901	37,483	31,418
	10—15 ..	65,077	35,523	29,554	447	435	12	64,630	35,088	29,542
	15—20 ..	55,739	28,542	27,197	940	921	19	54,799	27,621	27,178
	20 and over ..	264,473	144,894	119,579	4,714	4,658	56	259,759	140,236	119,523
	Total ..	*542,743*	*291,786*	*250,957*	*6,307*	*6,214*	*93*	*536,436*	*285,572*	*250,864*
	Christian.									
	0—5 ..	1	....	1	—	—	—	1	....	1
	5—10 ..	10	9	1	5	4	1	5	5	....
	10—15 ..	10	9	1	6	5	1	4	4	—
	15—20 ..	5	3	2	5	3	2	....	—	....
	20 and over ..	35	15	20	34	15	19	1	—	1
	Total ..	*61*	*36*	*25*	*50*	*27*	*23*	*11*	*9*	*2*
	Tribal.									
	0—5 ..	14	13	1	—	—	....	14	13	1
	5—10 ..	4	2	2	....	—	....	4	2	2
	10—15 ..	5	3	2	....	—	....	5	3	2
	15—20 ..	5	2	3	....	....	—	5	2	3
	20 and over ..	30	21	9	—	—	—	30	21	9
	Total ..	*58*	*41*	*17*	—	—	—	*58*	*41*	*17*
Srinagar (including City) or Kashmir South.	**All Religions.**									
	0—5 ..	117,924	60,136	57,788	—	—	—	117,924	60,136	57,788
	5—10 ..	100,281	54,388	45,893	1,348	1,143	205	98,933	53,245	45,688
	10—15 ..	92,254	50,258	41,996	2,564	2,291	273	89,690	47,967	41,723
	15—20 ..	77,866	40,269	37,597	4,413	4,176	237	73,453	36,093	37,360
	20 and over ..	383,618	214,139	169,479	21,459	20,887	572	362,159	193,252	168,907
	Total ..	*771,943*	*419,190*	*352,753*	*29,784*	*28,497*	*1,287*	*742,159*	*390,693*	*351,466*

XIII.

GION AND AGE.

Census 1931.

Literate in											
English.			*Urdu.*			*Hindi.*			*Other Vernaculars.*		
Persons.	Males.	Females.	Persons.	Males.	Females.	Persons.	Males.	Females.	Persons.	Males.	Females.
12	13	14	15	16	17	18	19	20	21	22	23
....	....	....	....	....	....	....	....	....	....	....	....
7	6	1	36	33	3	3	....	3	11	10	1
34	34	....	77	73	4	2	....	2	21	20	1
124	123	1	159	158	1	11	7	4	52	50	2
701	696	5	859	854	5	97	86	11	705	694	11
866	*859*	*7*	*1,131*	*1,118*	*13*	*113*	*93*	*20*	*789*	*774*	*15*
....	....	....	....	....	....	....	....	....	....	....	....
....	....	....	2	2	....	1	....	1	....	....	....
4	3	1	1	1	....	1	....	1	....	....	....
4	3	1	....	....	....	1	....	1	....	....	....
15	15	....	7	5	2	1	....	1	1	1	....
23	*21*	*2*	*10*	*8*	*2*	*4*	....	*4*	*1*	*1*	....
....	....	....	....	....	....	....	....	....	....	....	....
3	3	....	17	17	....	....	....	....	19	13	7
8	8	....	30	30	....	1	1	....	44	28	16
21	20	1	42	42	....	2	2	....	70	55	15
70	70	....	127	126	1	4	4	....	349	319	30
102	*101*	*1*	*216*	*215*	*1*	*7*	*7*	....	*482*	*414*	*68*
....	....	....	....	....	....	....	....	....	....	....	....
9	8	1	130	129	1	....	....	....	67	63	4
33	32	1	269	264	5	....	....	....	145	139	6
140	138	2	457	449	8	....	....	....	343	334	9
275	274	1	1,708	1,697	11	5	5	....	2,726	2,682	44
457	*452*	*5*	*2.564*	*2,539*	*25*	*5*	*5*	....	*3,281*	*3,218*	*63*
....	....	....	....	....	....	....	....	....	....	....	....
5	4	1	....	....	....	....	....	....	....	....	....
5	5	....	....	....	....	....	....	....	1	....	1
4	3	1	1	....	1	....	....	....	....	....	....
31	14	17	1	1	....	....	....	....	2	....	2
45	*26*	*19*	*2*	*1*	*1*	....	....	....	*3*	....	*3*
....	....	....	....	....	....	....	....	....	....	....	....
....	....	....	....	....	....	....	....	....	....	....	....
....	....	....	....	....	....	....	....	....	....	....	....
....	....	....	....	....	....	....	....	....	....	....	....
....	....	....	....	....	....	....	....	....	....	....	....
....	....	....	....	....	....	....	....	....	....	....	....
....	....	....	....	....	....	....	....	....	....	....	....
327	301	26	750	691	59	97	20	77	174	131	43
859	820	39	1,260	1,173	87	123	33	90	322	265	57
2,044	2,002	42	1,589	1,512	77	136	77	59	644	585	59
6,469	6,288	181	8,147	8,007	140	823	699	124	6,020	5,893	127
9,699	*9,411*	*288*	*11,746*	*11,383*	*363*	*1,179*	*829*	*350*	*7,160*	*6,874*	*286*

TABLE

Literacy by Reli-

Jammu and Kashmir

District or Province.	Age.	Population. Total. Persons.	Total. Males.	Total. Females.	Literate. Persons.	Literate. Males.	Literate. Females.	Illiterate. Persons.	Illiterate. Males.	Illiterate. Females.
1	2	3	4	5	6	7	8	9	10	11
Srinagar (including City) or Kashmir South.	**Brahmanic.**									
	0—5 ..	6,715	3,436	3,279	....	....	....	6,715	3,436	3,279
	5—10 ..	6,489	3,346	3,143	723	611	112	5,766	2,735	3,031
	10—15 ..	5,988	3,192	2,796	1,352	1,212	140	4,636	1,980	2,656
	15—20 ..	5,303	3,018	2,285	2,298	2,202	96	3,005	816	2,189
	20 and over ..	29,264	16,668	12,596	12,057	11,863	194	17,207	4,805	12,402
	Total ..	*53,759*	*29,660*	*24,099*	*16,430*	*15,888*	*542*	*37,329*	*13,772*	*23,557*
	Arya.									
	0—5 ..	48	24	24	....	....	....	48	24	24
	5—10 ..	52	28	24	26	16	10	26	12	14
	10—15 ..	47	26	21	29	17	12	18	9	9
	15—20 ..	34	23	11	31	22	9	3	1	2
	20 and over ..	159	109	50	127	101	26	32	8	24
	Total ..	*340*	*210*	*130*	*213*	*156*	*57*	*127*	*54*	*73*
	Brahmo.									
	0—5 ..	....	....	....	....	....	....	....	....	....
	5—10 ..	....	....	....	....	....	....	....	....	....
	10—15 ..	....	....	....	....	....	....	....	....	....
	15—20 ..	....	....	....	....	....	....	....	....	....
	20 and over ..	1	1	....	....	....	....	1	1	....
	Total ..	*1*	*1*	....	....	....	....	*1*	*1*	....
	Sikh.									
	0—5 ..	694	378	316	....	....	....	694	378	316
	5—10 ..	524	285	239	28	25	3	496	260	236
	10—15 ..	453	248	205	53	48	5	400	200	200
	15—20 ..	423	249	174	104	95	9	319	154	165
	20 and over ..	1,903	1,143	760	402	374	28	1,501	769	732
	Total ..	*3,997*	*2,303*	*1,694*	*587*	*542*	*45*	*3,410*	*1,761*	*1,649*
	Jain.									
	0—5 ..	....	....	....	....	....	....	....	....	....
	5—10 ..	....	....	....	....	....	....	....	....	....
	10—15 ..	1	1	....	1	1	....	....	....	....
	15—20 ..	1	1	....	1	1	....	....	....	....
	20 and over ..	1	1	....	1	1	....	....	....	....
	Total ..	*3*	*3*	....	*3*	*3*	....	....	....	....
	Buddhist.									
	0—5 ..	....	....	....	....	....	....	....	....	....
	5—10 ..	....	....	....	....	....	....	....	....	....
	10—15 ..	....	....	....	....	....	....	....	....	....
	15—20 ..	1	1	....	1	1	....	....	....	....
	20 and over ..	4	4	....	....	....	....	4	4	....
	Total ..	*5*	*5*	....	*1*	*1*	....	*4*	*4*	....
	Muslim.									
	0—5 ..	110,447	56,289	54,158	....	....	....	110,447	56,289	54,158
	5—10 ..	93,195	50,719	42,476	501	487	74	92,634	50,232	42,4 2
	10—15 ..	85,747	46,782	38,965	1,119	1,010	109	84,628	45,772	38,856
	15—20 ..	72,084	36,968	35,116	1,963	1,849	114	70,121	35,119	35,002
	20 and over ..	352,058	196,105	155,953	8,664	8,452	212	343,394	187,653	155,741
	Total ..	*713,531*	*386,863*	*326,668*	*12,307*	*11,798*	*509*	*701,224*	*375,065*	*326,159*

XIII.

GION AND AGE.

Census 1931.

Literate in											
English.			*Urdu.*			*Hindi.*			*Other Vernaculars.*		
Persons.	Males.	Females.	Persons.	Males.	Females.	Persons.	Males.	Females.	Persons.	Males.	Females.
12	13	14	15	16	17	18	19	20	21	22	23
....	....	....	....	....	....	....	....	....	....	....	....
236	224	12	360	332	28	84	16	68	43	39	4
623	605	18	539	506	33	109	28	81	81	73	8
1,431	1,420	11	590	567	23	126	73	53	151	142	9
4,882	4,850	32	4,428	4,387	41	777	677	100	1,970	1,949	21
7,172	7,099	*73*	*5,917*	*5,792*	*125*	*1,096*	*794*	*302*	*2,245*	*2,203*	*42*
....	....	....	....	....	....	....	....	....	....	....	....
7	5	2	6	6	....	12	4	8	1	1	....
11	8	3	4	3	1	13	5	8	1	1	....
19	17	2	5	3	2	6	1	5	1	1	....
80	73	7	11	10	1	29	11	18	7	7	....
117	*103*	*14*	*26*	*22*	*4*	*60*	*21*	*39*	*10*	*10*	....
....	....	....	....	....	....	....	....	....	....	....	....
....	....	....	....	....	....	....	....	....	....	....	....
....	....	....	....	....	....	....	....	....	....	....	....
....	....	....	....	....	....	....	....	....	....	....	....
....	....	....	....	....	....	....	....	....	....	....	....
....	....	....	....	....	....	....	....	....	....	....	....
....	....	....	....	....	....	....	....	....	....	....	....
8	8	....	11	11	....	1	....	1	8	6	2
19	17	2	18	18	....	1	....	1	15	13	2
33	31	2	28	26	2	2	1	1	41	37	4
82	80	2	106	98	8	16	10	6	198	186	12
142	*136*	*6*	*163*	*153*	*10*	*20*	*11*	*9*	*262*	*242*	*20*
....	....	....	....	....	....	....	....	....	....	....	....
....		....	....	....	....	....	....	....	....	....	....
1	1	....	....	....	....	....	....	....	....	....	....
1	1	....	....	....	....	....	....	....	....	....	....
1	1	....	....	....	....	....	....	....	....	....	....
3	*3*	....	....	....	....	....	....	....	....	....	....
....	....	....	....	....	....	....	....	....	....	....	....
....	....	....	....	....	....	....	....	....	....	....	....
....	....	....	....	....	....	....	....	....	....	....	....
1	1	....	....	....	....	....	....	....	....	....	....
....	....	....	....	....	....	....	....	....	....	....	....
1	*1*	....	....	....	....	....	....	....	....	....	....
....	....	....	....	....	....	....	....	....	....	....	....
66	60	6	373	342	31	....	....	....	122	85	37
196	186	10	699	646	53	....	....	....	224	178	46
545	527	18	965	915	50	2	2	....	451	405	46
1,235	1,206	29	3,588	3,498	90	1	1	....	3,840	3,747	93
2,042	*1,979*	*63*	*5,625*	*5,401*	*224*	*3*	*3*	....	*4,637*	*4,415*	*222*

TABLE

Literacy by Reli-

Jammu and Kashmir

District or Province.	Age.	Population. Total. Persons.	Total. Males.	Total. Females.	Literate. Persons.	Literate. Males.	Literate. Females.	Illiterate. Persons.	Illiterate. Males.	Illiterate. Females.
1	2	3	4	5	6	7	8	9	10	11
Srinagar (including City) or Kashmir South.	**Christian.**									
	0—5 ..	13	6	7	....	....	....	13	6	7
	5—10 ..	15	7	8	10	4	6	5	3	2
	10—15 ..	13	6	7	10	3	7	3	3	....
	15—20 ..	15	6	9	15	6	9	....	....	....
	20 and over ..	212	97	115	206	94	112	6	3	3
	Total ..	*268*	*122*	*146*	*241*	*107*	*134*	*27*	*15*	*12*
	Tribal.									
	0—5 ..	6	2	4	....	....	....	6	2	4
	5—10 ..	6	3	3	....	....	....	6	3	3
	10—15 ..	5	3	2	....	....	....	5	3	2
	15—20 ..	4	3	1	....	....	....	4	3	1
	20 and over ..	14	9	5	....	....	....	14	9	5
	Total ..	*35*	*20*	*15*	....	....	....	*35*	*20*	*15*
Muzaffarabad District.	**All Religions.**									
	0—5 ..	42,087	21,325	20,762	....	....	....	42,087	21,325	20,762
	5—10 ..	33,403	18,184	15,219	245	207	38	33,158	17,977	15,181
	10—15 ..	28,833	16,207	12,626	459	399	60	28,374	15,808	12,566
	15—20 ..	20,919	10,623	10,296	735	655	80	20,184	9,968	10,216
	20 and over ..	112,205	60,096	52,109	4,247	4,020	227	107,958	56,076	51,882
	Total ..	*237,447*	*126,435*	*111,012*	*5,686*	*5,281*	*405*	*231,761*	*121,154*	*110,607*
	Brahmanic.									
	0—5 ..	778	459	319	....	....	....	778	459	319
	5—10 ..	488	234	254	78	53	25	410	181	229
	10—15 ..	443	231	212	114	80	34	329	151	178
	15—20 ..	410	237	173	180	142	38	230	95	135
	20 and over ..	2,310	1,487	823	1,127	1,024	103	1,183	463	720
	Total ..	*4,429*	*2,648*	*1,781*	*1,499*	*1,299*	*200*	*2,930*	*1,349*	*1,581*
	Arya.									
	0—5 ..	4	3	1	....	....	....	4	3	1
	5—10 ..	7	5	2	1	1	....	6	4	2
	10—15 ..	8	5	3	1	1	....	7	4	3
	15—20 ..	8	5	3	2	1	1	6	4	2
	20 and over ..	34	24	10	10	10	....	24	14	10
	Total ..	*61*	*42*	*19*	*14*	*13*	*1*	*47*	*29*	*18*
	Sikh.									
	0—5 ..	2,068	1,043	1,025	....	....	....	2,068	1,043	1,025
	5—10 ..	1,624	867	757	44	37	7	1,580	830	750
	10—15 ..	1,376	736	640	95	77	18	1,281	659	622
	15—20 ..	957	411	546	141	113	28	816	298	518
	20 and over ..	4,908	2,527	2,381	865	777	88	4,043	1,750	2,293
	Total ..	*10,933*	*5,584*	*5,349*	*1,145*	*1,004*	*141*	*9,788*	*4,580*	*5,208*
	Muslim.									
	0—5 ..	39,235	19,818	19,417	....	....	....	39,235	19,818	19,417
	5—10 ..	31,284	17,078	14,206	122	116	6	31,162	16,962	14,200
	10—15 ..	27,006	15,235	11,771	249	241	8	26,757	14,994	11,763
	15—20 ..	19,543	9,970	9,573	411	399	12	19,132	9,571	9,561
	20 and over ..	104,945	56,052	48,893	2,237	2,203	34	102,708	53,849	48,859
	Total ..	*222,013*	*118,153*	*103,860*	*3,019*	*2,959*	*60*	*218,994*	*115,194*	*103,800*

XIII.

GION AND AGE.

Census 1931.

Literate in											
English.			*Urdu.*			*Hindi.*			*Other Vernaculars.*		
Persons.	Males.	Females.	Persons.	Males.	Females.	Persons.	Males.	Females.	Persons.	Males.	Females.
12	13	14	15	16	17	18	19	20	21	22	23
....	....	....	....	....	....	....	....	....	....	....	....
10	4	6	....	....	....	....	....	....	....	....	....
9	3	6	....	....	....	....	....	....	1	....	1
14	5	9	1	1	....	....	....	....	....	....	....
187	76	111	14	14	....	....	....	....	5	4	1
220	*88*	*132*	*15*	*15*	....	....	....	....	*6*	*4*	*2*
....	....	....	....	....	....	....	....	....	....	....	....
....	....	....	....	....	....	....	....	....	....	....	....
....	....	....	....	....	....	....	....	....	....	....	....
....	....	....	....	....	....	....	....	....	....	....	....
....	....	....	....	....	....	....	....	....	....	....	....
....	....	....	....	....	....	....	....	....	....	....	....
....	....	....	....	....	....	....	....	....	....	....	....
10	10	....	168	158	10	16	3	13	51	36	15
32	30	2	304	291	13	21	2	19	102	76	26
86	82	4	421	408	13	27	9	18	201	156	45
464	459	5	2,089	2,060	29	189	139	50	1,505	1,362	143
592	*581*	*11*	*2,982*	*2,917*	*65*	*253*	*153*	*100*	*1,859*	*1,630*	*229*
....	....	....	....	....	....	....	....	....	....	....	....
7	7	....	44	39	5	15	2	13	12	5	7
15	14	1	61	57	4	19	1	18	19	8	11
41	40	1	76	72	4	25	7	18	38	23	15
307	305	2	375	365	10	169	120	49	276	234	42
370	*366*	*4*	*556*	*533*	*23*	*228*	*130*	*98*	*345*	*270*	*75*
....	....	....	....	....	....	....	....	....	....	....	....
....	....	....	1	1	....	....	....	....	....	....	....
....	....	....	1	1	....	....	....	....	....	....	....
1	1	....	....	....	....	....	....	....	1	....	1
7	7	....	3	3	....	....	....	....	....	....	....
8	*8*	....	*5*	*5*	....	....	....	....	*1*	....	*1*
....	....	....	....	....	....	....	....	....	....	....	....
1	1	....	22	21	1	1	1	....	20	14	6
9	8	1	40	38	2	2	1	1	44	30	14
17	15	2	47	46	1	2	2	....	75	50	25
49	48	1	188	186	2	18	17	1	610	526	84
76	*72*	*4*	*297*	*291*	*6*	*23*	*21*	*2*	*749*	*620*	*129*
....	....	....	....	....	....	....	....	....	....	....	....
2	2	....	101	97	4	....	....	....	19	17	2
8	8	....	202	195	7	....	....	....	39	38	1
26	26	....	298	290	8	....	....	....	87	83	4
93	93	....	1,523	1,506	17	2	2	....	619	602	17
129	*129*	....	*2,124*	*2,088*	*36*	*2*	*2*	....	*764*	*740*	*24*

TABLE

Literacy by Reli-

Jammu and Kashmir

District or Province.	Age.	Population. Total. Persons.	Total. Males.	Total. Females.	Literate. Persons.	Literate. Males.	Literate. Females.	Illiterate. Persons.	Illiterate. Males.	Illiterate. Females.
1	2	3	4	5	6	7	8	9	10	11
Muzaffarabad District	**Christian.**									
	0—5 ..	2	2	....	....	....	....	2	2	....
	5—10 ..	....	....	....	....	....	....	....	....	....
	10—15 ..	....	....	....	....	....	....	....	....	....
	15—20 ..	1	....	1	1	....	1	....	....	....
	20 and over ..	7	6	1	7	6	1	....	....	....
	Total ..	*10*	*8*	*2*	*8*	*6*	*2*	*2*	*2*	....
Ladakh District.	**All Religions.**									
	0—5 ..	28,793	14,109	14,684	....	....	....	28,793	14,109	14,684
	5—10 ..	21,987	11,409	10,578	78	66	12	21,909	11,343	10,566
	10—15 ..	19,464	10,245	9,219	126	116	10	19,338	10,129	9,209
	15—20 ..	15,029	7,681	7,348	292	278	14	14,737	7,403	7,334
	20 and over ..	106,865	52,815	54,050	2,961	2,883	78	103,904	49,932	53,972
	Total ..	*192,138*	*96,259*	*95,879*	*3,457*	*3,343*	*114*	*188,681*	*92,916*	*95,765*
	Brahmanic.									
	0—5 ..	21	10	11	....	....	....	21	10	11
	5—10 ..	13	7	6	6	2	4	7	5	2
	10—15 ..	10	5	5	5	3	2	5	2	3
	15—20 ..	23	17	6	12	11	1	11	6	5
	20 and over ..	225	206	19	131	127	4	94	79	15
	Total ..	*292*	*246*	*47*	*154*	*143*	*11*	*138*	*102*	*36*
	Arya.									
	0—5 ..	4	——	4	——	——	——	4	——	4
	5—10 ..	4	2	2	1	——	1	3	2	1
	10—15 ..	2	1	1	——	——	——	2	1	1
	15—20 ..	3	2	1	3	2	1	——	——	——
	20 and over ..	14	11	3	11	10	1	3	1	2
	Total ..	*27*	*16*	*11*	*15*	*12*	*3*	*12*	*4*	*8*
	Sikh.									
	0—5 ..	19	11	8	....	....	....	19	11	8
	5—10 ..	11	6	5	5	2	3	6	4	2
	10—15 ..	7	5	2	3	2	1	4	3	1
	15—20 ..	11	8	3	11	8	3	....	....	....
	20 and over ..	49	33	16	42	31	11	7	2	5
	Total ..	*97*	*63*	*34*	*61*	*43*	*18*	*36*	*20*	*16*
	Buddhist.									
	0—5 ..	4,315	2,082	2,233	....	....	....	4,315	2,082	2,233
	5—10 ..	3,979	1,983	1,996	16	15	1	3,963	1,968	1,995
	10—15 ..	3,688	1,823	1,865	32	31	1	3,656	1,792	1,864
	15—20 ..	3,067	1,503	1,564	94	93	1	2,973	1,410	1,563
	20 and over ..	23,163	11,638	11,525	1,466	1,441	25	21,697	10,197	11,500
	Total ..	*38,212*	*19,029*	*19,183*	*1,608*	*1,580*	*28*	*36,604*	*17,449*	*19,155*
	Muslim.									
	0—5 ..	24,411	11,996	12,415	....	....	....	24,411	11,996	12,415
	5—10 ..	17,964	9,403	8,561	45	43	2	17,919	9,360	8,559
	10—15 ..	15,746	8,406	7,340	81	78	3	15,665	8,328	7,337
	15—20 ..	11,918	6,147	5,771	166	160	6	11,752	5,987	5,765
	20 and over ..	83,349	40,897	42,452	1,264	1,248	16	82,085	39,649	42,436
	Total ..	*153,388*	*76,849*	*76,639*	*1,556*	*1,529*	*27*	*151,832*	*75,320*	*76.512*

XIII.

GION AND AGE.

Census 1931.

Literate in											
English.			*Urdu.*			*Hindi.*			*Other Vernaculars.*		
Persons.	Males.	Females.	Persons.	Males.	Females.	Persons.	Males.	Females.	Persons.	Males.	Females.
12	13	14	15	16	17	18	19	20	21	22	23
....	....	....	....	....	....	....	....	....	....	....	....
....	....	....	....	....	....	....	....	....	....	....	....
....	....	....	....	....	....	....	....	....	....	....	....
1	....	1	....	....	....	....	....	....	....	....	....
7	6	1	....	....	....	....	....	....	....	....	....
8	*6*	*2*	....	....	..	....	....	....	....	....	....
....	....	....	....	....	....	....	....	....	....	....	....
2	2	....	52	48	4	3	....	3	21	16	5
10	10	....	77	73	4	3	1	2	36	32	4
27	24	3	140	136	4	1	1	....	124	117	7
152	142	10	815	801	14	12	10	2	1,982	1,930	52
191	*178*	*13*	*1,084*	*1,058*	*26*	*19*	*12*	*7*	*2,163*	*2,095*	*68*
....	....	....	....	....	....	....	....	....	....	....	....
....	....	....	4	2	2	2	....	2	....	....	....
2	2	....	....	....	....	2	1	1	1	....	1
5	4	1	6	6	....	1	1	....	....	....	....
58	57	1	52	50	2	10	9	1	11	11	....
65	*63*	*2*	*62*	*58*	*4*	*15*	*11*	*4*	*12*	*11*	*1*
....	....	....	....	....	....	....	....	....	....	....	....
....	....	....	1	....	1	....	....	....	....	....	....
....	....	....	....	....	....	....	....	....	....	....	....
2	1	1	1	1	....	....	....	....	....	....	....
7	7	....	3	3	....	1	....	1	....	....	....
9	*8*	*1*	*5*	*4*	*1*	*1*	....	*1*	....	....	....
....	....	....	....	....	....	....	....	....	....	....	....
....	....	....	2	2	....	1	....	1	2	....	2
1	1	....	1	1	....	1	....	1	....	....	....
4	4	....	4	3	1	....	....	....	3	1	2
8	8	....	20	17	3	....	....	....	14	6	8
13	*13*	....	*27*	*23*	*4*	*2*	....	*2*	*19*	*7*	*12*
....	....	....	....	....	....	....	....	....	....	....	....
....	....	....	4	4	....	....	....	....	13	11	1
1	1	....	8	8	....	....	....	....	23	22	1
1	1	....	14	14	....	....	....	....	79	78	1
4	4	....	57	56	1	1	1	....	1,404	1,380	24
6	*6*	....	*83*	*82*	*1*	*1*	*1*	....	*1,518*	*1,491*	*27*
....	....	....	....	....	....	....	....	....	....	....	....
1	1	....	39	38	1	....	....	....	5	4	1
5	5	....	66	63	3	....	....	....	10	10	....
13	12	1	114	111	3	....	....	....	39	37	2
54	53	1	680	672	8	....	....	....	530	523	7
73	*71*	*2*	*899*	*884*	*15*	....	...	....	*584*	*574*	*10*

TABLE

Literacy by Reli-

Jammu and Kashmir

District or Province.	Age.	Population. Total. Persons.	Total. Males.	Total. Females.	Literate. Persons.	Literate. Males.	Literate. Females.	Illiterate. Persons.	Illiterate. Males.	Illiterate. Females.
1	2	3	4	5	6	7	8	9	10	11
Ladakh District.	**Christians.**									
	0—5 ..	23	10	13	....	....	....	23	10	13
	5—10 ..	16	8	8	5	4	1	11	4	7
	10—15 ..	11	5	6	5	2	3	6	3	3
	15—20 ..	7	4	3	6	4	2	1	....	1
	20 and over ..	65	30	35	47	26	21	18	4	14
	Total ..	*122*	*57*	*65*	*63*	*36*	*27*	*59*	*21*	*38*
Gilgit District.	**All Religions.**									
	0—5 ..	4,990	2,494	2,496	....	....	....	4,990	2,494	2,496
	5—10 ..	4,230	2,276	1,954	50	44	6	4,180	2,232	1,948
	10—15 ..	3,889	2,109	1,780	83	77	6	3,806	2,032	1,774
	15—20 ..	3,252	1,778	1,474	200	191	9	3,052	1,587	1,465
	20 and over ..	15,541	9,095	6,446	1,017	983	34	14,524	8,112	6,412
	Total ..	*31,902*	*17,752*	*14,150*	*1,350*	*1,295*	*55*	*30,552*	*16,457*	*14,095*
	Brahmanic.									
	0—5 ..	35	22	13	....	....	....	35	22	13
	5—10 ..	28	16	12	13	10	3	15	6	9
	10—15 ..	24	16	8	13	12	1	11	4	7
	15—20 ..	158	154	4	93	90	3	65	64	1
	20 and over ..	729	692	37	487	477	10	242	215	27
	Total ..	*974*	*900*	*74*	*606*	*589*	*17*	*368*	*311*	*57*
	Arya.									
	0—5 ..	11	7	4	....	....	....	11	7	4
	5—10 ..	7	4	3	3	2	1	4	2	2
	10—15 ..	4	3	1	2	2	....	2	1	1
	15—20 ..	5	3	2	2	1	1	3	2	1
	20 and over ..	34	25	9	27	21	6	7	4	3
	Total ..	*61*	*42*	*19*	*34*	*26*	*8*	*27*	*16*	*11*
	Sikh.									
	0—5 ..	16	8	8	....	....	....	16	8	8
	5—10 ..	13	7	6	1	1	....	12	6	6
	10—15 ..	10	6	4	2	2	....	8	4	4
	15—20 ..	2	2	....	....	....	....	2	2	....
	20 and over ..	44	33	11	27	25	2	17	8	9
	Total ..	*85*	*56*	*29*	*30*	*28*	*2*	*55*	*28*	*27*
	Jain.									
	0—5 ..	1	1	....	....	....	....	1	1	....
	5—10 ..	....	....	....	....	....	....	....	....	....
	10—15 ..	....	....	....	....	....	....	....	....	....
	15—20 ..	....	....	....	....	....	....	....	....	....
	20 and over ..	2	1	1	1	1	....	1	....	1
	Total ..	*3*	*2*	*1*	*1*	*1*	....	*2*	*1*	*1*
	Muslim.									
	0—5 ..	4,921	2,455	2,466	....	....	....	4,921	2,455	2,466
	5—10 ..	4,178	2,247	1,931	33	31	2	4,145	2,216	1,929
	10—15 ..	3,849	2,083	1,766	66	61	5	3,783	2,022	1,761
	15—20 ..	3,084	1,616	1,468	105	100	5	2,979	1,516	1,463
	20 and over ..	14,709	8,326	6,383	464	453	11	14,245	7,873	6,372
	Total ..	*30,741*	*16,727*	*14,014*	*668*	*645*	*23*	*30,073*	*16,082*	*13,991*

XIII.

GION AND AGE.

Census 1931.

Literate in											
English.			*Urdu.*			*Hindi.*			*Other Vernaculars.*		
Persons.	Males.	Females.	Persons.	Males.	Females.	Persons.	Males.	Females.	Persons.	Males.	Females.
12	13	14	15	16	17	18	19	20	21	22	23
....	....	....	....	....	....	....	....	....	....	....	....
1	1	....	2	2	....	....	....	....	2	1	1
1	1	....	2	1	1	....	....	....	2	....	2
2	2	....	1	1	....	....	....	....	3	1	2
21	13	8	3	3	....	....	....	....	23	10	13
25	*17*	*8*	*8*	*7*	*1*	....	....	....	*30*	*12*	*18*
....	....	....	....	....	....	....	....	....	....	....	....
2	2	....	42	39	3	3	1	2	3	2	1
4	4	....	69	65	4	2	1	1	8	7	1
19	19	....	102	97	5	63	61	2	16	14	2
126	119	7	436	425	11	264	255	9	191	184	7
151	*144*	*7*	*649*	*626*	*23*	*332*	*318*	*14*	*218*	*207*	*11*
....	....	....	....	....	....	....	....	....	....	....	....
2	2	....	8	7	1	3	1	2	....	....	....
3	3	....	8	8	....	2	1	1	....	....	....
8	8	....	19	18	1	62	61	1	4	3	1
59	58	1	105	104	1	255	248	7	68	67	1
72	*71*	*1*	*140*	*137*	*3*	*322*	*311*	*11*	*72*	*70*	*2*
....	....	....	....	....	....	....	....	....	....	....	....
....	....	....	2	2	....	....	....	....	1	....	1
....	....	....	2	2	....	....	....	....	....	....	....
....	....	....	1	1	....	1	....	1	....	....	....
14	13	1	6	5	1	4	2	2	3	1	2
14	*13*	*1*	*11*	*10*	*1*	*5*	*2*	*3*	*4*	*1*	*3*
....	....	....	....	....	....	....	....	....	....	....	....
....	....	....	1	1	....	....	....	....	....	....	....
....	....	....	2	2	....	....	....	....	....	....	....
....	....	....	....	....	....	....	....	....	....	....	....
1	1	....	11	11	....	1	1	....	14	12	2
1	*1*	....	*14*	*14*	....	*1*	*1*	....	*14*	*12*	*2*
....	....	....	....	....	....	....	....	....	....	....	....
....	....	....	....	....	....	....	....	....	....	....	....
....	....	....	....	....	....	....	....	....	....	....	....
....	....	....	....	....	....	....	....	....	....	....	....
1	1	....	....	....	....	....	....	....	....	....	....
1	*1*	....	....	....	....	....	....	....	....	....	....
....	....	....	....	....	....	....	....	....	....	....	....
....	....	....	31	29	2	....	....	....	2	2	....
1	1	....	57	53	4	....	....	....	8	7	1
11	11	....	82	78	4	....	....	....	12	11	1
42	42	....	313	304	9	4	4	....	105	103	2
54	*54*	....	*453*	*464*	*19*	*4*	*4*	....	*127*	*123*	*4*

TABLE

Literacy by Reli-

Jammu and Kashmir

District or Province.	Age.	Population. Total. Persons.	Total. Males.	Total. Females.	Literate. Persons.	Literate. Males.	Literate. Females.	Illiterate. Persons.	Illiterate. Males.	Illiterate. Females.
1	2	3	4	5	6	7	8	9	10	11
Gilgit District.	**Christian.**									
	0—5 ..	6	1	5	....	....	....	6	1	5
	5—10 ..	4	2	2	....	....	....	4	2	2
	10—15 ..	2	1	1	....	....	....	2	1	1
	15—20 ..	3	3	....	....	....	....	3	3	....
	20 and over ..	23	18	5	11	6	5	12	12	....
	Total ..	*38*	*25*	*13*	*11*	*6*	*5*	*27*	*19*	*8*
Frontier Ilaqas.	**All Religions.**									
	0—5 ..	10,413	5,217	5,196	....	....	....	10,413	5,217	5,196
	5—10 ..	9,380	5,110	4,270	15	13	2	9,365	5,097	4,268
	10—15 ..	8,495	4,787	3,708	22	21	1	8,473	4,766	3,707
	15—20 ..	6,359	3,260	3,099	56	52	4	6,303	3,208	3,095
	20 and over ..	29,897	16,116	13,781	406	400	6	29,491	15,716	13,775
	Total ..	*64,544*	*34,490*	*30,054*	*499*	*486*	*13*	*64,045*	*34,004*	*30,041*
	Brahmanic.									
	0—5 ..	10	7	3	....	....	....	10	7	3
	5—10 ..	8	5	3	3	2	1	5	3	2
	10—15 ..	4	2	2	1	1	....	3	1	2
	15—20 ..	36	33	3	16	15	1	20	18	2
	20 and over ..	252	242	10	96	96	....	156	146	10
	Total ..	*310*	*289*	*21*	*116*	*114*	*2*	*194*	*175*	*19*
	Arya.									
	0—5 ..	3	2	1	....	....	....	3	2	1
	5—10 ..	4	3	1	1	....	1	3	3	....
	10—15 ..	....	....	....	....	....	....	....	....	....
	15—20 ..	1	....	1	....	....	....	1	....	1
	20 and over ..	8	7	1	5	4	1	3	3	....
	Total ..	*16*	*12*	*4*	*6*	*4*	*2*	*10*	*8*	*2*
	Sikh.									
	0—5 ..	1	....	1	....	....	....	1	....	1
	5—10 ..	....	....	....	....	....	....	....	....	....
	10—15 ..	....	....	....	....	....	....	....	....	....
	15—20 ..	2	2	....	1	1	....	1	1	....
	20 and over ..	5	4	1	3	3	....	2	1	1
	Total ..	*8*	*6*	*2*	*4*	*4*	....	*4*	*2*	*2*
	Muslim.									
	0—5 ..	10,399	5,208	5,191	....	....	....	10,399	5,208	5,191
	5—10 ..	9,368	5,102	4,266	11	11	....	9,357	5,091	4,266
	10—15 ..	8,491	4,785	3,706	21	20	1	8,470	4,765	3,705
	15—20 ..	6,320	3,225	3,095	39	36	3	6,281	3,189	3,092
	20 and over ..	29,821	15,855	13,766	292	290	2	29,329	15,565	13,764
	Total ..	*64,199*	*34,175*	*30,024*	*363*	*357*	*6*	*63,836*	*33,818*	*30,018*
	Christian.									
	0—5 ..	....	....	....	....	....	....	....	....	....
	5—10 ..	....	....	....	....	....	....	....	....	....
	10—15 ..	....	....	....	....	....	....	....	....	....
	15—20 ..	....	....	....	....	....	....	....	....	....
	20 and over ..	11	8	3	10	7	3	1	1	....
	Total ..	*11*	*8*	*3*	*10*	*7*	*3*	*1*	*1*	—

XIII.

GION AND AGE.

Census 1931.

Literate in											
English.			*Urdu.*			*Hindi.*			*Other Vernaculars.*		
Persons.	Males.	Females.	Persons.	Males.	Females.	Persons.	Males.	Females.	Persons.	Males.	Females.
12	13	14	15	16	17	18	19	20	21	22	23
....	....	....	....	....	....	....	....	....	....	....	....
....	....	....	....	....	....	....	....	....	....	....	....
....	....	....	....	....	....	....	....	....	....	....	....
....	....	....	....	....	....	....	....	....	....	....	....
9	4	5	1	1	....	....	....	....	1	1	....
9	*4*	*5*	*1*	*1*	....	....	....	....	*1*	*1*	....
....	....	....	....	....	....	....	....	....	....	....	....
....	....	....	8	8	....	....	....	....	7	5	2
....	....	....	13	13	....	....	....	....	9	8	1
1	1	....	17	16	1	1	....	1	37	35	2
13	10	3	87	87	....	1	1	....	305	302	3
14	*11*	*3*	*125*	*124*	*1*	*2*	*1*	*1*	*358*	*350*	*8*
....	....	....	....	....	....	....	....	....	....	....	....
....	....	....	....	....	....	....	....	....	3	2	1
....	....	....	....	....	....	....	....	....	1	1	....
....	....	....	1	1	....	1	....	1	14	14	....
1	1	....	10	10	....	1	1	....	84	84	....
1	*1*	....	*11*	*11*	....	*2*	*1*	*1*	*102*	*101*	*1*
....	....	....	....	....	....	....	....	....	....	....	....
....	....	....	....	....	....	....	....	....	1	....	1
....	....	....	....	....	....	....	....	....	....	....	....
....	....	....	....	....	....	....	....	....	....	....	....
....	....	....	1	1	....	....	....	....	4	3	1
....	....	....	*1*	*1*	....	....	....	....	*5*	*3*	*2*
....	....	....	....	....	....	....	....	....	....	....	....
....	....	....	....	....	....	....	....	....	....	....	....
....	....	....	....	....	....	....	....	....	....	....	....
....	....	....	1	1	....	....	....	....	....	....	....
....	....	....	2	2	....	....	....	....	1	1	....
....	....	....	3	3	....	....	....	....	*1*	*1*	....
....	....	....	....	....	....	....	....	....	....	....	....
....	....	....	8	8	....	....	....	....	3	3	....
....	....	....	13	13	....	....	....	....	8	7	1
1	1	....	15	14	1	....	....	....	23	21	2
2	2	....	74	74	....	....	....	....	216	214	2
3	*3*	....	*110*	*109*	*1*	....	....	....	*250*	*245*	*5*
....	....	....	....	....	....	....	....	....	....	....	....
....	....	....	....	....	....	....	....	....	....	....	....
....	....	....	....	....	....	....	....	....	....	....	....
....	....	....	....	....	....	....	....	....	....	....	....
10	7	3	....	....	....	....	....	....	....	....	....
10	*7*	*3*	....	....	....	....	....	....	....	....	....

TABLE

LITERACY BY RELI-

Jammu and Kashmir

District or Province.	Age.	POPULATION. Total. Persons.	Total. Males.	Total. Females.	Literate. Persons.	Literate. Males	Literate. Females.	Illiterate. Persons.	Illiterate. Males.	Illiterate. Females
1	2	3	4	5	6	7	8	9	10	11
										Part
Srinagar City.	**All Religions.**									
	0—5 ..	22,878	11,569	11,309	....	..	....	22,878	11,569	11,309
	5—10 ..	22,147	11,502	10,645	952	775	177	21,195	10,727	10,468
	10—15 ..	20,688	11,021	9,667	1,714	1,475	239	18,974	9,546	9,428
	15—20 ..	18,656	10,114	8,542	2,723	2,533	190	15,933	7,581	8,352
	20 and over ..	89,204	50,587	38,617	12,186	11,697	489	77,018	38,890	38,128
	Total ..	*173,573*	*94,793*	*78,780*	*17,575*	*16,480*	*1,095*	*155,998*	*78,313*	*77,685*
	Brahmanic.									
	0—5 ..	4,019	2,041	1,978	....	....	....	4,019	2,041	1,978
	5—10 ..	4,023	2,062	1,961	572	469	103	3,451	1,593	1,858
	10—15 ..	3,692	2,000	1,692	1,061	925	136	2,631	1,075	1,556
	15—20 ..	3,492	2,036	1,456	1,712	1,623	89	1,780	413	1,367
	20 and over ..	18,119	10,108	8,011	8,131	7,965	166	9,988	2,143	7,845
	Total ..	*33,345*	*18,247*	*15,098*	*11,476*	*10,982*	*494*	*21,869*	*7,265*	*14,604*
	Arya.									
	0—5 ..	45	22	23	....	....	....	45	22	23
	5—10 ..	46	24	22	22	13	9	24	11	13
	10—15 ..	41	22	19	28	16	12	13	6	7
	15—20 ..	33	22	11	28	20	8	5	2	3
	20 and over ..	159	109	50	123	97	26	36	12	24
	Total ..	*324*	*199*	*125*	*201*	*146*	*55*	*123*	*53*	*70*
	Sikh.									
	0—5 ..	95	49	46	....	....	....	95	49	46
	5—10 ..	78	49	29	16	13	3	62	36	26
	10—15 ..	67	43	24	24	20	4	43	23	20
	15—20 ..	108	85	23	51	44	7	57	41	16
	20 and over ..	522	408	114	218	193	25	304	215	89
	Total	*870*	*634*	*236*	*309*	*270*	*39*	*561*	*364*	*197*
	Jain.									
	0—5 ..	....	....	....	....	....	....	....	....	....
	5—10 ..	....	....	....	....	....	....	....	....	....
	10—15 ..	1	1	....	1	1	....	....	....	....
	15—20 ..	1	1	....	1	1	....	....	....	....
	20 and over ..	1	1	....	1	1	....	....	....	....
	Total	*3*	*3*	....	*3*	*3*	....	....	....	....
	Buddhist.									
	0—5 ..	....	....	....	....	....	....	....	....	....
	5—10 ..	....	....	....	....	....	....	....	....	....
	10—15 ..	....	....	....	....	....	....	....	....	....
	15—20 ..	1	1	....	1	1	....	....	....	....
	20 and over ..	4	4	....	....	....	....	4	4	....
	Total ..	*5*	*5*	....	*1*	*1*	....	4	*4*	....
	Zoroastrian.									
	0—5 ..	1	1	....	....	....	....	1	1	....
	5—10 ..	....	....	....	....	....	....	....	....	....
	10—15 ..	....	....	....	....	....	....	....	....	....
	15—20 ..	1	....	1	....	....	....	1	....	1
	20 and over ..	2	2	....	2	2	....	....	....	....
	Total ..	*4*	*3*	*1*	*2*	*2*	....	*2*	*1*	*1*

XIII.

GION AND AGE.

Census 1931.

Literate in											
English.			*Urdu.*			*Hindi.*			*Other Vernaculars.*		
Persons.	Males.	Females.	Persons.	Males.	Females.	Persons.	Males.	Females.	Persons.	Males.	Females.
12	13	14	15	16	17	18	19	20	21	22	23
III.											
....	....	....	....	....	....	....	....	....	....	....	....
295	269	26	483	433	50	85	15	70	89	58	31
759	722	37	713	642	71	108	22	86	134	89	45
1,728	1,690	38	724	666	58	95	42	53	176	135	41
5,481	5,308	173	4,696	4,584	112	501	395	106	1,508	1,410	98
8,263	*7,789*	*274*	*6,616*	*6,325*	*291*	*789*	*474*	*315*	*1,907*	*1,692*	*215*
....	....	....	....	....	....	....	....	....	....	....	....
215	203	12	262	237	25	73	11	62	22	18	4
563	545	18	360	327	33	95	18	77	43	35	8
1,247	1,236	11	311	290	21	89	41	48	65	56	9
4,169	4,139	30	2,792	2,757	35	460	378	82	710	691	19
6,194	*6,123*	*71*	*3,725*	*3,611*	*114*	*717*	*448*	*269*	*840*	*800*	*40*
....	....	....	....	....	....	....	....	....	....	....	....
6	4	2	4	4	....	11	4	7	1	1	....
11	8	3	4	3	1	12	4	8	1	1	....
18	16	2	5	3	2	4	....	4	1	1	....
79	72	7	10	9	1	27	9	18	7	7	....
114	*100*	*14*	*23*	*19*	*4*	*54*	*17*	*37*	*10*	*10*	....
....	....	....	....	....	....	....	....	....	....	....	....
5	5	....	5	5	....	1	....	1	5	3	2
13	12	1	5	5	....	1	....	1	5	3	2
23	22	1	11	9	2	1	....	1	16	13	3
68	6[illegible]	2	65	58	7	13	7	6	72	62	10
109	*105*	*4*	*86*	*77*	*9*	16	7	9	*98*	*81*	*17*
....	....	....	....	....	....	....	....	....	....	....	....
....	....	....	....	....	....	....	....	....	....	....	....
1	1	....	....	....	....	....	....	....	....	....	....
1	1	....	....	....	....	....	....	....	....	....	....
1	1	....	....	....	....	....	....	....	....	....	....
3	*3*	....	....	....	....	....	....	....	....	....	....
....	....	....	....	....	....	....	....	....	....	....	....
....	....	....	....	....	....	....	....	....	....	....	....
1	1	....	....	....	....	....	....	....	....	....	....
....	....	....	....	....	....	....	....	....	....	....	....
1	1	....	....	....	....	....	....	....	....	....	....
....	....	....	....	....	....	....	....	....	....	....	....
....	....	....	....	....	....	....	....	....	....	....	....
....	....	....	....	....	....	....	....	....	....	....	....
2	2	....	....	....	....	....	....	....	....	....	....
2	*2*	....	....	....	....	....	....	....	....	....	....

TABLE

Literacy by Reli-

Jammu and Kashmir

District or Province.	Age.	Population.								
		Total.			Literate.			Illiterate.		
		Persons.	Males.	Females.	Persons.	Males.	Females.	Persons.	Males.	Females.
1	2	3	4	5	6	7	8	9	10	11
Srinagar City.	**Muslim.**									
	0—5 ..	18,706	9,450	9,256	....	....	....	18,706	9,450	9,256
	5—10 ..	17,985	9,360	8,625	332	276	56	17,653	9,084	8,569
	10—15 ..	16,874	8,949	7,925	590	510	80	16,284	8,439	7,845
	15—20 ..	15,005	7,963	7,042	915	838	77	14,090	7,125	6,965
	20 and over ..	70,194	39,861	30,333	3,514	3,349	165	66,680	36,512	30,168
	Total ..	*138,764*	*75,583*	*63,181*	*5,351*	*4,973*	*378*	*133,413*	*70,610*	*62,803*
	Christian.									
	0—5 ..	12	6	6	....	....	....	12	6	6
	5—10 ..	15	7	8	10	4	6	5	3	2
	10—15 ..	13	6	7	10	3	7	3	3	....
	15—20 ..	15	6	9	15	6	9	....	....	....
	20 and over ..	202	93	109	197	90	107	5	3	2
	Total ..	*257*	*118*	*139*	*232*	*103*	*129*	*25*	*15*	*10*
Jammu City.	**All Religions.**									
	0—5 ..	4,485	2,256	2,229	....	....	....	4,485	2,256	2,229
	5—10 ..	3,908	2,111	1,797	1,058	697	361	2,850	1,414	1,436
	10—15 ..	3,822	2,164	1,658	1,748	1,213	535	2,074	951	1,123
	15—20 ..	4,381	2,770	1,611	2,770	2,205	565	1,611	565	1,046
	20 and over ..	22,017	14,060	7,957	11,077	9,381	1,696	10,940	4,679	6,261
	Total ..	*38,613*	*23,361*	*15,252*	*16,653*	*13,496*	*3,157*	*21,960*	*9,865*	*12,095*
	Brahmanic.									
	0—5 ..	2,241	1,142	1,099	....	....	....	2,241	1,142	1,099
	5—10 ..	1,942	1,068	874	638	423	215	1,304	645	659
	10—15 ..	1,986	1,159	827	1,073	764	309	913	395	518
	15—20 ..	2,406	1,546	860	1,857	1,507	350	549	39	510
	20 and over ..	12,139	7,566	4,573	7,774	6,688	1,086	4,365	878	3,487
	Total ..	*20,714*	*12,481*	*8,233*	*11,342*	*9,352*	*1,960*	*9,372*	*3,099*	*6,273*
	Arya.									
	0—5 ..	403	182	221	....	...	....	403	182	221
	5—10 ..	389	204	185	84	56	28	305	148	157
	10—15 ..	355	189	166	135	93	42	220	96	124
	15—20 ..	354	188	166	194	141	53	160	47	113
	20 and over ..	1,883	1,107	776	743	599	144	1,140	508	632
	Total ..	*3,384*	*1,870*	*1,514*	*1,156*	*889*	*267*	*2,228*	*981*	*1,247*
	Brahmo.									
	0—5 ..	....	....	....	....	....	....	....	....	....
	5—10 ..	....	....	....	....	....	....	....	....	....
	10—15 ..	1	1	....	1	1	....	....	....	....
	15—20 ..	1	1	....	1	1	....	....	....	....
	20 and over ..	2	1	1	2	1	1	....	....	....
	Total ..	*4*	*3*	*1*	*4*	*3*	*1*	....	....	....
	Sikh.									
	0—5 ..	184	103	81	....	....	....	184	103	81
	5—10 ..	175	97	78	52	26	26	123	71	52
	10—15 ..	156	87	69	95	60	35	61	27	34
	15—20 ..	145	91	54	121	89	32	24	2	22
	20 and over ..	636	379	257	470	375	95	166	4	162
	Total ..	*1,296*	*757*	*539*	*738*	*550*	*188*	*558*	*207*	*351*
	Muslim.									
	0—5 ..	1,443	698	745	....	....	....	1,443	698	745
	5—10 ..	1,267	674	593	238	169	69	1,029	505	524
	10—15 ..	1,202	676	526	377	254	123	825	422	403
	15—20 ..	1,382	915	467	544	437	107	838	478	360
	20 and over ..	6,742	4,658	2,084	1,836	1,528	308	4,906	3,130	1,776
	Total ..	*12,036*	*7,621*	*4,415*	*2,995*	*2,388*	*607*	*9,041*	*5,233*	*3,808*

XIII.

GION AND AGE.

Census 1931.

Literate in											
English.			*Urdu.*			*Hindi.*			*Other Vernaculars.*		
Persons.	Males.	Females.	Persons.	Males.	Females.	Persons	Males.	Females.	Persons.	Males.	Females.
12	13	14	15	16	17	18	19	20	21	22	23
....	....	....	....	....	....	....	....	....	....	....	....
59	53	6	212	187	25	....	....	....	61	36	25
162	153	9	344	307	37	....	....	....	84	50	34
424	409	15	396	363	33	1	1	....	94	65	29
983	955	28	1,815	1,746	69	1	1	....	715	647	68
1,628	*1,570*	*58*	*2,767*	*2,603*	*164*	*2*	*2*	....	954	798	*156*
....	....	....	....	....	....	....	....	....	....	....	....
10	4	6	....	....	....	....	....	....	1	....	1
9	3	6	....	....	....	....	....	....	....	....	....
14	5	9	1	1	....	....	....	....	....	....	....
179	73	106	14	14	....	....	....	....	4	3	1
212	*85*	*127*	*15*	*15*	....	....	....	....	*5*	3	*2*
....	....	....	....	....	....	....	....	....	....	....	....
130	108	22	479	419	60	260	59	201	189	111	78
274	220	54	747	640	107	355	98	257	372	255	117
560	471	89	1,027	920	107	473	201	272	710	613	97
2,144	1,947	197	3,998	3,692	306	2,174	1,347	827	2,761	2,395	366
3.108	*2,746*	*362*	*6,251*	*5,671*	*580*	*3,262*	*1,705*	*1,557*	*4,032*	*3,374*	*658*
....	....	....	....	....	....	....	....	....	....	....	....
87	75	12	257	243	14	194	43	151	100	62	38
164	129	35	415	388	27	268	73	195	226	174	52
308	248	60	639	610	29	391	174	217	519	475	44
1.423	1,275	148	2,663	2,582	81	1,862	1,173	689	1,826	1,658	168
1,982	*1,727*	*255*	*3,974*	*3,823*	*151*	*2,715*	*1,463*	*1,252*	*2,671*	*2,369*	*302*
....	....	....	....	....	....	....	....	....	....	....	....
12	9	3	28	27	1	36	12	24	8	8	....
24	19	5	47	45	2	51	18	33	13	11	2
58	59	8	69	64	5	53	20	33	14	7	7
198	180	18	258	236	22	205	115	90	82	68	14
292	*258*	*34*	*402*	*372*	*30*	*345*	*165*	*180*	*117*	*94*	*23*
....	....	....	....	....	....	....	....	....	....	....	....
....	....	....	....	....	....	....	....	....	....	....	....
....	....	....	1	1	....	....	....	....	....	....	....
1	1	....	....	....	....	....	....	....	....	....	....
1	1	....	....	....	....	1	....	1	....	....	....
2	*2*	....	*1*	*1*	...	*1*	....	*1*	....	....	....
....	....	....	....	....	....	....	....	....	....	....	....
5	2	3	24	20	4	11	2	9	12	2	10
17	13	4	34	29	5	15	4	11	29	14	15
32	26	6	35	30	5	16	6	10	38	27	11
108	102	6	141	129	12	41	25	16	180	119	61
162	*143*	*19*	*234*	*208*	*26*	*83*	*37*	*46*	*259*	*162*	*97*
....	....	....	....	....	....	....	....	....	....	....	....
23	20	3	153	114	39	....	....	....	62	35	27
61	52	9	226	155	71	....	....	....	90	47	43
145	132	13	264	199	65	1	1	....	134	105	29
374	360	14	883	695	188	4	4	....	575	469	106
603	*564*	*39*	*1,526*	*1,163*	*363*	*5*	*5*	....	*861*	*656*	*205*

TABLE XIV.

LITERACY BY SELECTED CASTES, ETC.

Jammu and Kashmir Census 1931.

1. This Table and Tables VIII and XI deal only with a few selected castes.

2. The figures of Christians and Sikhs do not appear in this Table as their Civil condition and literacy have been dealt with in Table VII and XIII respectively.

3. The totals of different castes in this table do not tally with the totals of those castes in Table XVII as the population of each caste below seven years has been omitted from this table.

TABLE XIV.

Literacy by selected Castes, Tribes or Races.

Jammu and Kashmir Census 1931.

Caste, Tribe or Race.	Population (seven years and over).											
	Total.			Literate.			Illiterate.			Literate in English.		
	Persons.	Males.	Females.	Persons.	Males.	Females.	Persons.	Males	Females.	Persons.	Males.	Females.
1	2	3	4	5	6	7	8	9	10	11	12	13
Hindu.												
Brahman ..	152,839	78,375	74,464	14,875	13,326	1,549	137,964	65,049	72,915	1,893	1,727	166
Basith ..	5,039	2,537	2,502	74	72	2	4,965	2,465	2,500	2	2	......
Chamar ..	32,961	17,557	15,404	152	143	9	32,809	17,414	15,395	4	4	......
Jat ..	18,687	9,908	8,779	286	276	10	18,401	9,632	8,769	15	15	......
Kashmiri Pandit ..	52,697	29,786	22,911	19,467	18,915	552	33, 30	10,871	22,359	8,369	8,306	63
Khatri ..	16,767	9,346	7,421	6,477	5,159	1,318	10,290	4,187	6,103	1,285	1,173	112
Megh ..	57,794	30,963	26,831	463	423	40	57,331	30,540	26,791	39	36	3
Rajput ..	132,440	73,376	59,064	8,538	8,127	411	123,902	65,249	58,653	826	811	15
Muslim.												
Arain ..	18,278	10,361	7,917	320	297	23	17,958	10,064	7,894	18	18	......
Balti ..	37,466	18,392	19,074	665	660	5	36,801	17,732	19,069	14	14	......
Bakkarwal ..	4,040	2,173	1,867	38	38	....	4,002	2,135	1,867	......	......	......
Gujjar ..	313,965	170,409	143,556	2,307	2,234	73	311,658	168,175	143,483	78	78	......
Jat ..	94,605	49,433	45,172	1,124	1,085	39	93,481	48,348	45,133	69	68	1
Kashmiri ..	1,083,769	592,984	490,785	21,639	20,914	725	1,062,130	572,070	490,060	2,696	2,636	60
Mughal ..	23,370	12,592	10,778	757	698	59	22,613	11,894	10,719	68	66	2
Pathan ..	15,305	8,568	6,737	778	690	88	14,527	7,878	6,649	83	79	4
Rajput ..	152,139	79,806	72,333	4,707	4,405	302	147,432	75,401	72,031	352	346	6
Sheikh ..	22,687	12,215	10,472	1,202	967	235	21,485	11,248	10,237	202	184	18
Shin ..	11,139	5,727	5,412	139	137	2	11,000	5,590	5,410	5	5	......
Yashkun ..	28,758	15,418	13,340	283	279	4	28,475	15,139	13,336	9	9	......
Buddhist.												
Mangrik ..	29,193	14,566	14,627	1,427	1,406	21	27,766	13,160	14,606	2	2	......
Tribal.												
Sansi ..	111	61	50	1	1	....	110	60	50	1	1	......

TABLE XV.

PART I.—LANGUAGE.

Jammu and Kashmir Census 1931.

NOTE 1.—This table is divided into two parts. Part I is again divided into four sub-parts and shows number of persons speaking.—

(*a*) the Vernaculars of the State,

(*b*) Vernaculars of India,

(*c*) Vernaculars of other Asiatic Countries,

(*d*) European languages.

Besides the above four divisions a small table showing number of persons returning unclassified languages and dialects has also been given at the end of part (d).

The different languages and dialects in the above four groups have been classified in accordance with the Revised Scheme.

PART II.—BILINGUALISM.

NOTE 2.—This part is sub-divided into two parts again and

PART A.—Bilingualism gives by tehsils the number of persons who speak one subsidiary language besides their mother-tongue.

PART B.—shows by tehsils the figures of Tri and Poly-lingualism *i. e.*, the number of persons speaking more than one subsidiary language besides their mother-tongue.

For Area of Bilingualism tehsil has been taken as the Unit in this State in accordance with the instructions of the Census Commissioner for India.

NOTE 3.—The trilinguals shown in Part II-B are not included with the bilinguals detailed in Part II-A.

NOTE 4.—In case of Kashmiri, Western Pahari and Punjabi languages, the principal dialect of a language has been taken as mother tongue in the Jammu Province, while in the Kashmir Province and Frontier Districts the aggregate of all dialects of these languages has been shown under the column of mother tongue. As such the details of these languages in Part I and Part II-A and B will not coincide. But in the case of 'Shina' which is generally spoken in the Frontier Districts the Principal dialect itself (*i. e.* Shina) has been taken as mother tongue in the Kashmir Province and Frontier Districts.

NOTE 5.—This table (Part II) is confined only to the following ten principal mother-tongues in the State, *viz.*,

(1) Dogri, (2) Kashmiri, (3) Gojari, (4) Pahari, (5) Punjabi, (6) Chabhali (Lehnda), (7) Pothwari, (8) Balti, (9) Ladakhi, (10) Shina.

NOTE 6.—The total population speaking one or other of the mother-tongues dealt with have been omitted in Part II-B in such Tehsils etc., where no person returned two or more subsidiary languages, but that the figures in columns 3—5 at the head of the table represent the total population of the State.

TABLE XV (Part I).

(a) Languages of the State.

Jammu and Kashmir Census 1931.

District, Jagir or Ilaqa.	Population.			Tibeto Chinese Family. Tibeto-Burman Sub-Family. Tibeto Himalayan Branch. Tibetan Group. Bhotia.														
				Total.			Bhotia.			Balti.			Ladakhi.			Tibetan.		
	Persons.	Males.	Females.	Persons.	Males.	Females.	Persons.	Males.	Females.	Persons.	Males.	Females.	Persons.	Males.	Females.	Persons.	Males.	Females.
Jammu and Kashmir State ..	3,646,243	1,938,336	1,707,905	179,480	89,100	90,380	42	40	2	137,914	68,467	69,447	41,418	20,546	20,872	12	7	5
I. Jammu Province ..	1,788,441	942,815	845,626	632	386	296	25	25	....	185	127	58	472	234	238	....	..	..
1. Jammu District ..	375,240	205,719	169,521	47	37	10	25	25	....	18	12	6	4	....	4	....	..	..
2. Kathua " ..	161,232	85,993	75,239	....	....	....	....	....	....	....	....	....	....	....	....	....	..	..
3. Udhampur " ..	273,668	143,514	130,154	554	280	274	....	....	....	120	68	52	434	212	222	....	..	..
4. Reasi " ..	235,245	124,210	111,035	34	22	12	....	....	....	....	....	....	34	22	12	....	..	..
5. Mirpur " ..	344,747	178,831	165,916	2	2	....	....	....	....	2	2	....	....	....	....	....	..	..
6. Poonch Jagir ..	387,384	198,618	188,766	45	45	....	....	....	....	45	45	....	....	....	....	....	..	..
7. Chenani " ..	10,925	5,930	4,995	....	....	....	....	....	....	....	....	....	....	....	....	....	..	..
II. Kashmir Province ..	1,569,218	847,022	722,196	682	424	258	2	2	....	623	379	244	45	36	9	12	7	5
8. Kashmir South (*including Municipality*) ..	771,943	419,190	352,753	621	387	234	2	2	....	566	346	220	41	32	9	12	7	5
9. Kashmir North ..	559,828	301,397	258,431	55	32	23	....	....	....	52	29	23	3	3	....	....	..	..
10. Muzaffarabad ..	237,447	126,435	111,012	6	5	1	....	....	....	5	4	1	1	1	....	....	..	..
III. Frontier Districts ..	288,584	148,501	140,083	178,116	88,290	89,826	15	13	2	137,106	67,961	69,145	40,901	20,276	20,625	....	..	..
11. Ladakh District ..	192,138	96,259	95,879	177,641	87,962	89,679	....	....	....	136,838	67,735	69,103	40,711	20,189	20,522	....	..	..
12. Gilgit " ..	31,902	17,752	14,150	237	215	22	15	13	2	215	195	20	7	7	....	....	..	..
13. Frontier Ilaqas ..	64,544	34,490	30,054	238	113	125	....	....	....	53	31	22	183	80	103	....	..	..

TABLE XV (PART I).

LANGUAGES OF THE STATE.

Jammu and Kashmir Census 1931.

District, Jagir or Ilaqa.	Tibeto-Chinese Family. Tibeto-Burman Sub-Family. Tibeto Himalayan Branch. Tibetan Group. BHOTIA.—concluded.									Indo-European Family. Aryan Sub-Family. Dardic Branch. KHOWAR GROUP.								
	Brukshas.			Kashgari.			Khapli.			Chitrali.			Yasni.			Punyali.		
	Persons.	Males.	Females.	Persons.	Males.	Females.	Persons.	Males.	Females.	Persons.	Males.	Females.	Persons.	Males.	Females.	Persons.	Males.	Females.
Jammu and Kashmir State ..	91	37	54	2	2	....	1	1	....	6,951	3,662	3,289	1	1	....	1	1	....
I. Jammu Province ..	....	....	....	....	....	....	....	....	....	....	....	....	....	....	....	....	....	....
1. Jammu District ..	....	....	....	....	....	....	....	....	....	....	....	....	....	....	....	....	....	....
2. Kathua ,, ..	....	....	....	....	....	....	....	....	....	....	....	....	....	....	....	....	....	....
3. Udhampur ,, ..	....	....	....	....	....	....	....	....	....	....	....	....	....	....	....	....	....	....
4. Reasi ,, ..	....	....	....	....	....	....	....	....	....	....	....	....	....	....	....	....	....	....
5. Mirpur ,, ..	....	....	....	....	....	....	....	....	....	....	....	....	....	....	....	....	....	....
6. Poonch Jagir ..	....	....	....	....	....	....	....	....	....	....	....	....	....	....	....	....	....	....
7. Chenani ,, ..	....	....	....	....	....	....	....	....	....	....	....	....	....	....	....	....	....	....
II. Kashmir Province.	....	....	....	....	....	....	....	....	....	48	41	7	1	1	....	....	....	....
8. Kashmir South (*including Municipality.*) ..	....	....	....	....	....	....	....	....	....	35	35	....	1	1	....	....	....	....
9. Kashmir North ..	....	....	....	....	....	....	....	....	....	9	4	5	....	....	....	....	....	....
10. Muzaffarabad ..	....	....	....	....	....	....	....	....	....	4	2	2	....	....	....	....	....	....
III. Frontier Districts.	91	37	54	2	2	....	1	1	....	6,903	3,621	3,232	....	....	....	1	1	....
11. Ladakh District ..	91	37	54	....	....	....	1	1	....	....	....	....	....	....	....	1	1	....
12. Gilgit ,, ..	....	....	....	....	....	....	....	....	....	163	139	24	....	....	....	....	....	....
13. Frontier Ilaqas ..	....	....	....	2	2	....	....	....	....	6,740	3,482	3,258	....	....	....	....	....	....

TABLE XV (Part I).

Languages of the State.

Jammu and Kashmir Census 1931.

District, Jagir or Ilaqa.	Indo-European Family. Aryan Sub-Family. Dardic Branch. Kafir Group. Bashgali.			Dardis-Tani.			Dard Group. Kohistani. Total.			Kaghani.			Kohistani.			Bambagi.		
	Persons.	Males.	Females.	Persons.	Males.	Females.	Persons.	Males.	Females.	Persons.	Males.	Females.	Persons.	Males.	Females.	Persons.	Males.	Females.
Jammu and Kashmir State ..	7	6	1	6,232	3,181	3,051	3,121	1,594	1,527	2,766	1,427	1,339	57	41	16	298	126	172
I. Jammu Province ..	....	....	....	....	....	....	1,249	610	639	1,077	551	526	....	....	....	172	59	113
1. Jammu District ..	....	....	....	....	....	....	353	210	143	353	210	143	....	....	....	....	....	....
2. Kathua „ ..	....	....	....	....	....	....	55	44	11	55	44	11	....	....	....	....	....	....
3. Udhampur „ ..	....	....	....	....	....	....	502	159	343	330	100	230	....	....	....	172	59	113
4. Reasi „ ..	....	....	....	....	....	....	338	196	142	338	196	142	....	....	....	....	....	....
5. Mirpur „ ..	....	....	....	....	....	....	....	....	....	....	....	....	....	....	....	....	....	....
6. Poonch Jagir ..	....	....	....	....	....	....	1	1	....	1	1	....	....	....	....	....	....	....
7. Chenani „ ..	....	....	....	....	....	....	....	....	....	....	....	....	....	....	....	....	....	....
II. Kashmir Province ..	....	....	....	6,232	3,181	3,051	1,872	984	888	1,689	876	813	57	41	16	126	67	59
8. Kashmir South (*including Municipality*) ..	....	....	....	256	140	116	1,568	792	776	1,567	791	776	1	1	....	....	....	....
9. Kashmir North ..	....	....	....	5,976	3,041	2,935	293	186	107	122	85	37	45	34	11	126	67	59
10. Muzaffarabad ..	....	....	....	....	....	....	11	6	5	....	....	....	11	6	5	....	....	....
III. Frontier Districts ..	7	6	1	....	....	....	....	....	....	....	....	....	....	....	....	....	....	....
11. Ladakh District ..	....	....	....	....	....	....	....	....	....	....	....	....	....	....	....	....	....	....
12. Gilgit „ ..	....	....	....	....	....	....	....	....	....	....	....	....	....	....	....	....	....	....
*13. Frontier Ilaqas ..	7	6	1	....	....	....	....	....	....	....	....	....	....	....	....	....	....	....

TABLE XV (PART I).

(a) LANGUAGES OF THE STATE.

Jammu and Kashmir Census 1931.

Indo-European Family. Aryan Sub-Family. Dardic Branch. Dard Group—(continued). KASHMIRI.

District, Jagir or Ilaqa.	Total. Persons.	Total. Males.	Total. Females.	Banjwahi. Persons.	Banjwahi. Males.	Banjwahi. Females.	Kashmiri. Persons.	Kashmiri. Males.	Kashmiri. Females.	Kishtwari. Persons.	Kishtwari. Males.	Kishtwari. Females.	Poguli. Persons.	Poguli. Males.	Poguli. Females.	Rambani. Persons.	Rambani. Males.	Rambani. Females.
Jammu and Kashmir State ..	1,413,166	764,133	649,033	672	337	335	1,370,673	741,954	628,719	12,577	6,596	5,981	9,751	5,147	4,604	1,919	976	943
I. Jammu Province ..	163,834	88,407	75,427	672	337	335	121,431	66,290	55,141	12,483	6,534	5,954	9,751	5,147	4,604	1,918	976	942
1. Jammu District ..	2,870	2,528	342	....	....	....	2,795	2,455	340	23	21	2	....	....	....	4	4	....
2. Kathua „ ..	1,951	1,171	780	....	....	....	1,947	1,167	780	4	4	....	....	....	....	....	....	....
3. Udhampur „ ..	118,559	63,218	55,341	672	337	335	76,494	41,367	35,127	12,460	6,508	5,952	9,691	5,107	4,584	1,914	972	942
4. Reasi „ ..	22,544	11,953	10,591	....	....	....	22,338	11,795	10,543	....	....	....	60	40	20	....	....	....
5. Mirpur „ ..	759	742	17	....	....	....	759	742	17	....	....	....	....	....	....	....	....	....
6. Poonch Jagir ..	16,739	8,504	8,235	....	....	....	16,739	8,504	8,235	....	....	....	....	....	....	....	....	....
7. Chenani „ ..	412	291	121	....	....	....	359	260	99	1	1	....	....	....	....	....	....	....
II. Kashmir Province ..	1,247,497	674,534	572,963	....	....	....	1,247,424	674,489	572,935	72	45	27	....	....	....	1	....	1
8. Kashmir South (*including Municipality*) ..	723,570	392,618	330,952	....	....	....	723,500	392,576	330,924	69	42	27	....	....	....	1	....	1
9. Kashmir North ..	502,583	270,275	232,308	....	....	....	502,581	270,273	232,308	2	2	....	....	....	....	....	....	....
10. Muzaffarabad ..	21,344	11,641	9,703	....	....	....	21,343	11,640	9,703	1	1	....	....	....	....	....	....	....
III. Frontier Districts ..	1,835	1,192	643	....	....	....	1,818	1,175	643	17	17	....	....	....	....	....	....	....
11. Ladakh District ..	1,535	939	596	....	....	....	1,519	923	596	16	16	....	....	....	....	....	....	....
12. Gilgit „ ..	246	207	39	....	....	....	245	206	39	1	1	....	....	....	....	....	....	....
13. Frontier Ilaqas ..	54	46	8	....	....	....	54	46	8	....	....	....	....	....	....	....	....	....

TABLE XV (Part I).

(a) Languages of the State.

Jammu and Kashmir Census 1931.

Indo-European Family. — Aryan Sub-Family. — Dardic Branch. — Dard Group.

District, Jagir or Illaqa.	Kashmiri.—(concluded). Siraji. Persons.	Males.	Females.	Shina. Total. Persons.	Males.	Females.	Shina. Persons.	Males.	Females.	Brukpa. Persons.	Males.	Females.	Gilgiti. Persons.	Males.	Females.	Astori. Persons.	Males.	Females.
Jammu and Kashmir State ..	17,574	9,123	8,451	67,453	35,349	32,104	63,918	33,379	30,539	1,554	782	772	23	17	6	4	4	....
I. Jammu Province ..	17,574	9,123	8,451	....	....	....	....	....	....	....	....	....	....	....	....	....	....	....
1. Jammu District ..	48	48	....	....	....	....	....	....	....	....	....	....	....	....	....	....	....	....
2. Kathua " ..	....	....	....	....	....	....	....	....	....	....	....	....	....	....	....	....	....	....
3. Udhampur " ..	17,328	8,927	8,401	....	....	....	....	....	....	....	....	....	....	....	....	....	....	....
4. Reasi " ..	146	118	28	....	....	....	....	....	....	....	....	....	....	....	....	....	....	....
5. Mirpur " ..	....	....	....	....	....	....	....	....	....	....	....	....	....	....	....	....	....	....
6. Poonch Jagir ..	....	....	....	....	....	....	....	....	....	....	....	....	....	....	....	....	....	....
7. Chenani " ..	52	30	22	....	....	....	....	....	....	....	....	....	....	....	....	....	....	....
II. Kashmir Province ..	....	....	....	162	103	59	33	26	7	....	....	....	23	17	6	1	1	....
8. Kashmir South (*including Municipality.*) ..	....	....	....	58	46	12	14	14	....	....	....	....	23	17	6	....	....	....
9. Kashmir North ..	....	....	....	91	50	41	9	5	4	....	....	....	....	....	....	1	1	....
10. Muzaffarabad ..	....	....	....	13	7	6	10	7	3	....	....	....	....	....	....	....	....	....
III. Frontier Districts ..	....	....	....	67,291	35,246	32,045	63,885	33,353	30,532	1,554	782	772	....	....	....	3	3	....
11. Ladakh District ..	....	....	....	12,367	6,925	5,442	10,813	6,143	4,670	1,554	782	772	....	....	....	....	....	....
12. Gilgit " ..	....	....	....	28,248	14,823	13,425	28,111	14,699	13,412	....	....	....	....	....	....	....	....	....
13. Frontier Ilaqas ..	....	....	....	26,676	13,498	13,178	24,961	12,511	12,450	....	....	....	....	....	....	3	3	....

TABLE XV.—Part I.

(a) Languages of the State.

Jammu and Kashmir Census 1931.

District, Jagir or Ilaqa.	Indo-European Family. Aryan Sub-Family. *Dardic Branch.* Dard Group. Shina—(*concluded*). *Chillasi.*			*Nagri.*			*Shikwar.*			*Outer Sub-Branch.* North Western Group. Sanskrit. *Sanskrit.*			*Lahnda (Chabhali).*			Indo-European Family. Aryan Sub-Family. *Inner Sub-Branch.* Central Group. Punjabi. *Dogri.*		
	Persons.	Males.	Females.	Persons.	Males.	Females.	Persons.	Males.	Females.	Persons.	Males.	Females.	Persons.	Males.	Females.	Persons.	Males.	Females.
Jammu and Kashmir State ..	**106**	**60**	**46**	**136**	**123**	**13**	**1,712**	**984**	**728**	**1**	**1**	....	**44,460**	**23,129**	**21,331**	**549,917**	**293,986**	**255,931**
I. Jammu Province ..	....	....	....	....	....	....	....	....	....	....	....	....	**44,460**	**23,129**	**21,331**	**547,534**	**292,139**	**255,395**
1. Jammu District ..	....	....	....	....	....	....	....	....	....	....	....	....	175	172	3	234,071	127,991	106,080
2. Kathua " ..	....	....	....	....	....	....	....	....	....	....	....	....	....	....	....	132,741	70,356	62,385
3. Udhampur " ..	....	....	....	....	....	....	....	....	....	....	....	....	....	....	....	87,665	45,084	42,581
4. Reasi " ..	....	....	....	....	....	....	....	....	....	....	....	....	9,970	5,237	4,733	56,413	29,451	26,962
5. Mirpur " ..	....	....	....	....	....	....	....	....	....	....	....	....	34,314	17,719	16,595	27,860	14,523	13,337
6. Poonch Jagir ..	....	....	....	....	....	....	....	....	....	....	....	....	....	....	....	855	511	344
7. Chenani " ..	....	....	....	....	....	....	....	....	....	....	....	....	1	1	....	7,929	4,223	3,706
II. Kashmir Province ..	**105**	**59**	**46**	....	....	....	....	....	....	**1**	**1**	....	....	....	....	**1,662**	**1,168**	**494**
8. Kashmir South (*including Municipality*) ..	21	15	6	....	....	....	....	....	....	1	1	....	....	....	....	1,402	1,003	399
9. Kashmir North ..	81	44	37	....	....	....	....	....	....	....	....	....	....	....	....	128	82	46
10. Muzaffarabad ..	3	....	3	....	....	....	....	....	....	....	....	....	....	....	....	132	83	49
III. Frontier Districts ..	**1**	**1**	....	**136**	**123**	**13**	**1,712**	**984**	**728**	....	....	....	....	....	....	**721**	**679**	**42**
11. Ladakh District ..	....	....	....	....	....	....	....	....	....	....	....	....	....	....	....	56	56	....
12. Gilgit ..	1	1	....	136	123	13	....	....	....	....	....	....	....	....	....	469	431	38
13. Frontier Ilaqas ..	....	....	....	....	....	....	1,712	984	728	....	....	....	....	....	....	196	192	4

TABLE XV.—PART I.

LANGUAGES OF THE STATE.

Jammu and Kashmir Census 1931.

District, Jagir or Illaqa.	Indo-European Family. Aryan Sub-Family. Inner Sub-Branch. Central Group. Punjabi—(concluded). Kandiali.			Central Group. Rajasthani. Gojari.			Pahari Group. Western Pahari. Total.			Western Pahari. Pahari.			Western Pahari. Bhadarwahi.		
	Persons.	Males.	Females.	Persons.	Males.	Females.	Persons.	Males.	Females.	Persons.	Males.	Females.	Persons.	Males.	Females.
Jammu and Kashmir State ..	**67**	**44**	**23**	**317,762**	**170,528**	**147,234**	**633,036**	**326,705**	**306,331**	**595,754**	**307,989**	**287,765**	**20,357**	**10,016**	**10,341**
I. Jammu Province ..	....	....	....	**208,933**	**111,482**	**97,451**	**454,616**	**232,166**	**222,450**	**417,363**	**213,471**	**203,892**	**20,328**	**9,995**	**10,333**
1. Jammu District ..	....	....	....	45,380	24,046	21,334	391	307	84	211	151	60	161	137	24
2. Kathua " ..	....	....	....	11,286	6,679	4,607	10,889	5,485	5,404	7,234	3,817	3,417	147	145	2
3. Udhampur " ..	....	....	....	22,895	11,411	11,484	39,689	20,180	19,509	6,520	3,481	3,039	19,899	9,606	10,293
4. Reasi " ..	....	....	....	70,686	37,512	33,174	72,630	38,245	34,385	72,556	38,176	34,380	74	69	5
5. Mirpur " ..	....	....	....	9,747	5,175	4,572	15,244	7,922	7,322	15,209	7,890	7,319	35	32	3
6. Poonch Jagir ..	....	....	....	48,426	26,402	22,024	313,915	159,037	154,878	313,912	159,037	154,875	3	....	3
7. Chenani " ..	....	....	....	513	257	256	1,858	990	868	1,721	919	802	9	6	3
II. Kashmir Province ..	**2**	**2**	....	**107,849**	**58,448**	**49,401**	**178,292**	**94,411**	**83,881**	**178,264**	**94,391**	**83,873**	**28**	**20**	**8**
8. Kashmir South (*including Municipality*) ..	2	2	....	31,458	16,891	14,567	4,178	2,210	1,968	4,167	2,201	1,966	11	9	2
9. Kashmir North ..	....	....	....	28,445	15,861	12,584	10,266	5,442	4,824	10,266	5,442	4,824	....	....	....
10. Muzaffarabad ..	....	....	....	47,946	25,696	22,250	163,848	86,759	77,089	163,831	86,748	77,083	17	11	6
III. Frontier Districts ..	**65**	**42**	**23**	**980**	**598**	**382**	**128**	**128**	....	**127**	**127**	....	**1**	**1**	....
11. Ladakh District ..	....	....	....	....	....	....	1	1	....	1	1	....	....	....	....
12. Gilgit " ..	....	....	....	445	247	198	127	127	....	126	126	....	1	1	....
13. Frontier Ilaqas ..	65	42	23	535	351	184	....	....	....	....	....	....	....	....	....

TABLE XV.—(Part I).

Languages of the State.

Jammu and Kashmir Census 1931.

District, Jagir or Ilaqa.	Indo-European Family. Aryan Sub-Family. Inner Sub-Branch. Pahari Group.									Dravidian Family.					
	Western Pahari (concluded).									Dravida Group.			Andhra Group.		
	Gaddi.			Padari.			Sarori.			Tamil.			Telegu.		
	Persons.	Males.	Females.	Persons.	Males.	Females.	Persons.	Males.	Females.	Persons.	Males.	Females.	Persons.	Males.	Females.
Jammu and Kashmir State ..	9,798	4,986	4,812	5,425	2,828	2,597	1,702	886	816	10	10	....	6	1	5
I. Jammu Province ..	9,798	4,986	4,812	5,425	2,828	2,597	1,702	886	816	....	....	....	6	1	5
1. Jammu District ..	19	19	....	....	....	....	....	....	....	....	....	....	....	....	....
2. Kathua „ ..	3,508	1,523	1,985	....	....	....	....	....	....	....	....	....	....	....	....
3. Udhampur „ ..	6,209	3,419	2,790	5,359	2,788	2,571	1,702	886	816	....	....	....	....	....	....
4. Reasi „ ..	....	....	....	....	....	....	....	....	....	....	....	....	....	....	....
5. Mirpur „ ..	....	....	....	....	....	....	....	....	....	....	....	....	1	....	1
6. Poonch Jagir ..	....	....	....	....	....	....	....	....	....	....	....	....	....	....	....
7. Chenani „ ..	62	25	37	66	40	26	....	....	....	....	....	....	5	1	4
II. Kashmir Province ..	....	....	....	....	....	....	....	....	....	9	9	....	....	....	....
8. Kashmir South (*including Municipality*) ..	....	....	....	....	....	....	....	....	....	8	8	....	....	....	....
9. Kashmir North ..	....	....	....	....	....	....	....	....	....	1	1	....	....	....	....
10. Muzaffarabad ..	....	....	....	....	....	....	....	....	....	....	....	....	....	....	....
III. Frontier Districts ..	....	....	....	....	....	....	....	....	....	1	1	....	....	....	....
11. Ladakh District ..	....	....	....	....	....	....	....	....	....	....	....	....	....	....	....
12. Gilgit „ ..	....	....	....	....	....	....	....	....	....	1	1	....	....	....	....
13. Frontier Ilaqas ..	....	....	....	....	....	....	....	....	....	....	....	....	....	....	....

TABLE XV.—PART I.

(b) LANGUAGES OF INDIA.

Jammu and Kashmir Census 1931.

District, Jagir or Ilaqa.	Tibeto-Chinese Family. Tibeto Burma Sub-family. Assam Burmese Branch. Burma Group. Burmese.			Sanskrit Sub-Branch. Sanskrit Group. Sanskrit.			Indo-European Family. Aryan Sub-family. Indo-Aryan Branch. OUTER SUB-BRANCH. North-Western Group. Lahnda. Total.			Pothwari			Hazara.			Punchi.		
	Persons.	Males.	Females.	Persons.	Males.	Females.	Persons.	Males.	Females.	Persons.	Males.	Females.	Persons.	Males.	Females.	Persons.	Males.	Females.
Jammu and Kashmir State ..	3	....	3	1	1	....	51,723	27,525	24,198	51,062	26,869	24,193	649	649	....	12	7	5
I. Jammu Province ..	3	....	3	1	1	....	51,035	26,843	24,192	51,035	26,843	24,192	....	....	....	....	....	....
1. Jammu District ..	....	....	....	1	1	....	67	56	11	67	56	11	....	....	....	....	....	....
2. Kathua District ..	....	....	....	....	....	....	12	10	2	12	10	2	....	....	....	....	....	....
3. Udhampur District ..	....	....	....	....	....	....	26	25	1	26	25	1	....	....	....	....	....	....
4. Reasi " ..	....	....	....	....	....	....	10	9	1	10	9	1	....	....	....	....	....	....
5. Mirpur " ..	2	....	2	....	....	....	50,881	26,719	24,162	50,881	26,719	24,162	....	....	....	....	....	....
6. Poonch Jagir ..	1	....	1	....	....	....	39	24	15	39	24	15	....	....	....	....	....	....
7. Chenani " ..	....	....	....	....	....	....	....	....	....	....	....	....	....	....	....	....	....	....
II. Kashmir Province ..	....	....	....	....	....	....	686	680	6	26	25	1	649	619	....	11	6	5
8. Kashmir South (*including Municipality*) ..	....	....	....	....	....	....	....	....	....	....	....	....	....	....	....	....	....	....
9. Kashmir North ..	....	....	....	....	....	....	649	649	....	....	....	....	649	649	....	....	....	....
10. Muzaffarabad ..	....	....	....	....	....	....	37	31	6	26	25	1	....	....	....	11	6	5
III. Frontier Districts ..	....	....	....	....	....	....	2	2	....	1	1	....	....	....	....	1	1	....
11. Ladakh District ..	....	....	....	....	....	....	1	1	....	1	1	....	....	....	....	....	....	....
12. Gilgit ..	....	....	....	....	....	....	....	....	....	....	....	....	....	....	....	....	....	....
13. Frontier Ilaqas ..	....	....	....	....	....	....	1	1	....	....	....	....	....	....	....	1	1	....

TABLE XV.—PART I.

(b) LANGUAGES OF INDIA.

Jammu and Kashmir Census 1931.

District, Jagir or Ilaqa.	Indo-European Family. Ayran Sub-Family. Indo Aryan Branch.																	
	OUTER SUB-BRANCH.												MEDIATE SUB-BRANCH.			INNER SUB-BRANCH.		
	North Western Group.			Southern Group.						Eastern Group.			Mediate Group.			Central Group.		
	SINDHI.			MARATHI.									EASTERN HINDI.			GUJRATI.		
	Sindhi.			Koli.			Marathi.			Bengali.			Purbi.			Gujrati.		
	Persons.	Males.	Females.	Persons.	Males.	Females.	Persons.	Males.	Females.	Persons.	Males.	Females.	Persons.	Males.	Females.	Persons.	Males.	Females.
Jammu and Kashmir State ..	9	8	1	13	13	....	12	8	4	66	41	25	3	1	2	289	235	54
I. Jammu Province ..	8	7	1	....	....	....	11	7	4	34	25	9	3	1	2	201	191	10
1. Jammu District ..	5	4	1	....	....	....	8	4	4	26	19	7	2	....	2	7	5	2
2. Kathua " ..	....	....	....	....	....	....	....	....	....	2	1	1	1	1	....	1	1	....
3. Udhampur " ..	....	....	....	....	....	....	2	2	....	2	2	....	....	....	....	181	181	....
4. Reasi " ..	....	....	....	....	....	....	....	....	....	....	....	....	....	....	....	1	1	....
5. Mirpur " ..	1	1	....	....	....	....	1	1	....	1	....	1	....	....	....	2	....	2
6. Poonch Jagir ..	2	2	....	....	....	....	....	....	....	2	2	....	....	....	....	9	3	6
7. Chenani " ..	....	....	....	....	....	....	....	....	....	1	1	....	....	....	....	....	....	....
II. Kashmir Province ..	....	....	....	13	13	....	1	1	....	32	16	16	....	....	....	81	44	37
8. Kashmir South (*including Municipality*) ..	....	....	....	13	13	....	1	1	....	27	11	16	....	....	....	63	27	36
9. Kashmir North ..	....	....	....	....	....	....	....	....	....	5	5	....	....	....	....	1	1	....
10. Muzaffarabad ..	....	....	....	....	....	....	....	....	....	....	....	....	....	....	....	17	16	1
III. Frontier Districts ..	1	1	....	....	....	....	....	....	....	....	....	....	....	....	....	7	....	7
11. Ladakh District ..	....	....	....	....	....	....	....	....	....	....	....	....	....	....	....	....	....	....
12. Gilgit ..	1	1	....	....	....	....	....	....	....	....	....	....	....	....	....	....	....	....
13. Frontier Ilaqas :	....	....	....	....	....	....	....	....	....	....	....	....	....	....	....	7	....	7

TABLE XV.—PART I.

(b) LANGUAGES OF INDIA.

Jammu and Kashmir Census 1931.

Indo-European Family. — Aryan Sub-Family. — Indo-Aryan Branch. — INNER SUB-BRANCH. — Central Group.

District, Jagir or Ilaqa.	PUNJABI. Total.			Kangri.			Powadhi.			Punjabi.			Gurmukhi.			RAJASTHANI. Total.		
	Persons.	Males.	Females.	Persons.	Males.	Females.	Persons.	Males.	Females.	Persons.	Males.	Females.	Persons.	Males.	Females.	Persons.	Males.	Females.
Jammu and Kashmir State ..	330,066	174,910	155,156	255	199	56	430	104	326	329,201	174,448	154,753	180	159	21	2,583	1,389	1,194
I. Jammu Province ..	307,468	162,625	144,843	203	147	56	430	104	326	306,835	162,374	144,461	....	....	....	2,583	1,389	1,194
1. Jammu District ..	87,217	47,701	39,516	15	1	14	93	4	89	87,109	47,696	39,413	....	....	....	2,358	1,259	1,099
2. Kathua „ ..	3,987	2,040	1,947	25	1	24	258	50	208	3,704	1,989	1,715	....	....	....	118	68	50
3. Udhampur „ ..	3,203	2,648	555	119	102	17	19	14	5	3,065	2,532	533	....	....	....	....	....	....
4. Reasi „ ..	1,985	1,346	639	....	....	....	60	36	24	1,925	1,310	615	....	....	....	15	9	6
5. Mirpur „ ..	203,810	104,827	98,983	....	....	....	....	....	....	203,810	104,827	98,983	....	....	....	33	19	14
6. Poonch Jagir ..	7,137	3,945	3,192	3	2	1	....	....	....	7,134	3,943	3,191	....	....	....	....	....	....
7. Chenani „ ..	129	118	11	41	41	....	....	....	....	88	77	11	....	....	....	59	34	25
II. Kashmir Province ..	20,056	10,796	9,260	49	49	....	....	....	....	19,844	10,605	9,239	163	142	21	....	....	....
8. Kashmir south (*including Municipality*) ..	6,256	3,734	2,522	....	....	....	....	....	....	6,120	3,603	2,517	136	131	5	....	....	....
9. Kashmir North ..	10,035	5,087	4,948	1	1	....	....	....	....	10,007	5,075	4,932	27	11	16	....	....	....
10. Muzaffarabad ..	3,765	1,975	1,790	48	48	....	....	....	....	3,717	1,927	1,700	....	....	....	....	....	....
III. Frontier Districts ..	2,542	1,469	1,053	3	3	....	....	....	....	2,522	1,469	1053	17	17	....	....	....	....
11. Ladakh District ..	162	112	50	3	3	....	....	....	--	159	109	50	....	--	--	--	--	--
12. Gilgit „ ..	393	295	98	....	--	--	--	--	--	376	278	98	17	17	--	--	--	--
13. Frontier Ilaqas ..	1,987	1,082	905	--	--	--	--	--	--	1,987	1,082	905	--	--	--	--	--	--

TABLE XV.—Part I.

(b) Languages of India.

Jammu and Kashmir Census 1931.

Indo-European Family. — Aryan Sub-Family. — Indo-Aryan Branch. — Inner Sub-Branch. — Central Group.

District, Jagir or Ilaqa.	Rajasthani—(concluded).						Western Hindi.											
	Labhani.			*Marwari.*			*Total.*			*Hindi.*			*Hindustani.*			*Urdu.*		
	Persons.	Males.	Females.	Persons.	Males.	Females.	Persons.	Males.	Females.	Persons.	Males.	Females.	Persons.	Males.	Females.	Persons.	Males.	Females.
Jammu and Kashmir State ..	2,357	1,272	1,085	226	117	109	6,257	3,499	2,758	3,071	1,580	1,491	1,827	1,116	711	1,319	783	536
I. Jammu Province ..	2,357	1,272	1,085	226	117	109	4,590	2,523	2,067	2,204	1,085	1,119	1,350	841	509	1,036	597	439
1. Jammu District ..	2,134	1,144	990	224	115	109	1,714	1,027	687	415	263	152	309	206	103	990	558	432
2. Kathua „ ..	118	68	50	....	....	....	70	38	32	1	1	....	68	36	32	1	1	....
3. Udhampur „ ..	....	....	....	....	....	....	112	93	19	....	....	....	106	87	19	6	6	....
4. Reasi „ ..	14	8	6	1	1	....	571	192	379	540	163	377	29	27	2	2	2	....
5. Mirpur „ ..	32	18	14	1	1	....	1,956	1,065	891	1,246	657	589	700	399	301	10	9	1
6. Poonch Jagir ..	....	....	....	....	....	....	161	102	59	2	1	1	132	80	52	27	21	6
7. Chenani „ ..	59	34	25	....	....	....	6	6	....	....	....	....	6	6	....	....	....	....
II. Kashmir Province ..	....	....	....	....	....	....	1,041	603	438	361	207	154	457	260	197	221	134	87
8. Kashmir South (*including Municipality*) ..	....	....	....	....	....	....	391	227	164	44	33	11	190	108	82	156	85	71
9. Kashmir North ..	....	....	....	....	....	....	582	321	261	303	165	138	240	129	111	38	26	12
10. Muzaffarabad ..	....	....	....	....	....	....	68	55	13	14	9	5	27	23	4	27	23	4
III. Frontier Districts ..	....	....	....	....	....	....	626	373	253	506	288	218	20	15	5	62	52	10
11. Ladakh District ..	....	....	....	....	....	....	96	83	13	85	76	9	6	2	4	5	5	....
12. Gilgit „ ..	....	....	....	....	....	....	36	26	10	14	6	8	14	13	1	8	7	1
13. Frontier Ilaqas ..	....	....	....	....	....	....	494	264	230	407	206	201	....	....	....	49	40	9

TABLE XV.—Part I.

(b) Languages of India.

Jammu and Kashmir Census 1931.

District, Jagir or Ilaqa.	Indo-European Family. Aryan Sub-Family. Indo Aryan Branch. Inner Sub-Branch.																	
	Central Group—(concld.)			Pahari Group.														
	Western Hindi—(concld.)			Western Pahari.														
	Goali.			Naipali (Gorkhali).			Bhuttani.			Total.			Mandeali.			Chambiali (Chameali).		
	Persons.	Males.	Females.	Persons.	Males.	Females.	Persons.	Males.	Females.	Persons.	Males.	Females.	Persons.	Males.	Females.	Persons.	Males.	Females.
Jammu and Kashmir State ..	40	20	20	1,120	810	310	6	5	1	283	224	59	97	97	....	168	120	48
I. Jammu Province ..	....	....	....	326	254	72	....	....	....	282	223	59	96	96	....	168	120	48
1. Jammu District ..	....	....	....	211	152	59	....	....	....	....	....	....	....	....	....	....	....	....
2. Kathua ,, ..	....	....	....	59	52	7	....	....	....	48	35	13	....	....	....	48	35	13
3. Udhampur ,, ..	....	....	....	22	21	1	....	....	....	234	188	46	96	96	....	120	85	35
4. Reasi ,, ..	....	....	....	28	24	4	....	....	....	....	....	....	....	....	....	....	....	....
5. Mirpur ,, ..	....	....	....	....	....	....	....	....	....	....	....	....	....	....	....	....	....	....
6. Poonch Jagir ..	....	....	....	5	4	1	....	....	....	....	....	....	....	....	....	....	....	....
7. Chenani ,, ..	....	....	....	1	1	....	....	....	....	....	....	....	....	....	....	....	....	....
II. Kashmir Province ..	2	2	....	424	186	238	6	5	1	1	1	....	1	1	....	....	....	....
8. Kashmir South (*including Municipality*) ..	1	1	....	422	184	238	6	5	1	....	....	....	....	....	....	....	....	....
9. Kashmir North ..	1	1	....	1	1	....	....	....	....	....	....	....	....	....	....	....	....	....
10. Muzaffarabad ..	....	....	....	1	1	....	....	....	....	1	1	....	1	1	....	....	....	....
III. Frontier Districts ..	38	18	20	370	370	....	....	....	....	....	....	....	....	....	....	....	....	....
11. Ladakh District ..	....	....	....	2	2	....	....	....	....	....	....	....	....	....	....	....	....	....
12. Gilgit ,, ..	....	....	....	320	320	....	....	....	....	....	....	....	....	....	....	....	....	....
13. Frontier Ilaqas ..	38	18	20	48	48	....	....	....	....	....	....	....	....	....	....	....	....	....

TABLE XV.—PART I.

(b) LANGUAGES OF INDIA.

Jammu and Kashmir Census 1931.

District, Jagir or Ilaqa.	Indo-European Family. Aryan Sub-Family. Indo-Aryan Branch. Inner Sub-Branch. PAHARI GROUP. (Western Pahari).			Eranian Branch. EASTERN GROUP. Afghanistan—Balochistan Sub-Group.																	
	Pangwali.			*Balochi.*			*Pashto.*			*Yagisthani.*			*Pathani.*			*Peshawari.*			*Afgani.*		
	Persons.	Males.	Females.	Persons.	Males.	Females.	Persons.	Males.	Females.	Persons.	Males.	Females.	Persons.	Males.	Females.	Persons.	Males.	Females.	Persons.	Males.	Females.
Jammu and Kashmir State ..	18	7	11	4	3	1	3,354	1,967	1,387	33	33	1	4	3	1	2	2	....	15	8	7
I. Jammu Province ..	18	7	11	3	2	1	406	309	97	....	....	....	....	....	....	....	....	....	....	....	....
1. Jammu District ..	....	....	....	....	....	....	198	126	72	....	....	....	....	....	....	....	....	....	....	....	....
2. Kathua „ ..	....	....	....	....	....	....	5	5	....	....	....	....	....	....	....	....	....	....	....	....	....
3. Udhampur „ ..	18	7	11	....	....	....	19	19	....	....	....	....	....	....	....	....	....	....	....	....	....
4. Reasi „ ..	....	....	....	3	2	1	16	10	6	....	....	....	....	....	....	....	....	....	....	....	....
5. Mirpur „ ..	....	....	....	....	....	....	117	109	8	....	....	....	....	....	....	....	....	....	....	....	....
6. Poonch Jagir ..	....	....	....	....	....	....	40	33	7	....	....	....	....	....	....	....	....	....	....	....	....
7. Chenani „ ..	....	....	....	....	....	....	11	7	4	....	....	....	....	....	....	....	....	....	....	....	....
II. Kashmir Province ..	....	....	....	1	1	....	2,100	1,123	977	33	33	1	4	3	1	2	2	....	7	3	4
8. Kashmir South (*including Municipality*) ..	....	....	....	....	....	....	1,306	697	609	29	29	....	4	3	1	2	2	....	3	2	1
9. Kashmir North ..	....	....	....	1	1	....	580	295	285	4	3	1	....	....	....	....	....	....	....	....	....
10. Muzaffarabad ..	....	....	....	....	....	....	214	131	83	....	....	....	....	....	....	....	....	....	4	1	3
III. Frontier Districts ..	....	....	....	....	....	....	848	535	313	....	....	....	....	....	....	....	....	....	8	5	3
11. Ladakh District ..	....	....	....	....	....	....	3	2	1	....	....	....	....	....	....	....	....	....	....	....	....
12. Gilgit „ ..	....	....	....	....	....	....	205	145	60	....	....	....	....	....	....	....	....	....	8	5	3
13. Frontier Ilaqas ..	....	....	....	....	....	....	640	388	252	....	....	....	....	....	....	....	....	....	....	....	....

TABLE XV.—Part I.

(c) Asiatic Languages.

Jammu and Kashmir Census 1931.

District, Jagir or Ilaqa.	Tibeto-Burman Sub-Family.						Assam-Burmese Branch.			Tibeto-Chinese Family. Tibeto-Burman Sub-Family. Tibeto-Himalayan Branch.		
	Eastern Sub-Group.			Western Branch.			Bara or Budo Group.			Tibetan Group.		
	Dumi.			*Lahuli.*			*Matrai.*			*Lhassi.*		
	Persons.	Males.	Females.	Persons.	Males.	Females.	Persons.	Males.	Females.	Persons.	Males.	Females.
Jammu and Kashmir State ..	179	118	61	1	....	1	2	1	1	196	109	87
I. Jammu Province ..	....	....	....	....	....	....	....	....	....	....	....	....
1. Jammu District ..	....	....	....	....	....	....	....	....	....	....	....	....
2. Kathua „ ..	....	....	....	....	....	....	....	....	....	....	....	....
3. Udhampur „ ..	....	....	....	....	....	....	....	....	....	....	....	....
4. Reasi „ ..	....	....	....	....	....	....	....	....	....	....	....	....
5. Mirpur „ ..	....	....	....	....	....	....	....	....	....	....	....	....
6. Poonch Jagir ..	....	....	....	....	....	....	....	....	....	....	....	....
7. Chenani „ ..	....	....	....	....	....	....	....	....	....	....	....	....
II. Kashmir Province ..	....	....	....	....	....	....	2	1	1	4	....	4
8. Kashmir South (*including Municipality*) ..	....	....	....	....	....	....	....	....	....	4	....	4
9. Kashmir North ..	....	....	....	....	....	....	1	1	....	....	....	....
10. Muzaffarabad ..	....	....	....	....	....	....	1	....	1	....	....	....
III. Frontier Districts ..	179	118	61	1	....	1	....	....	....	192	109	83
11. Ladakh District ..	....	....	....	1	....	1	....	....	....	192	109	83
12. Gilgit „ ..	....	....	....	....	....	....	....	....	....	....	....	....
13. Frontier Ilaqas ..	179	118	61	....	....	....	....	....	....	....	....	....

TABLE XV.—PART I.

(c) LANGUAGES OF ASIA.

Jammu and Kashmir Census 1931.

District, Jagir or Ilaqa.	Mongolian Family.						Semitic Family.			Indo-European Family.			Malayo-Polynesian Family.			Eranian Family.					
	URAL-ALATIC GROUP.			MONOSYLLABIC OR CHINESE GROUP.						ERANIAN GROUP.			MALAYAN GROUP.			EASTERN GROUP.			PERSIAN GROUP.		
	Yarkandi (Turkh).			*Chinese.*			*Arabic.*			*Persian.*			*Javanese.*			*Wokhoi.*			*Badakhashi.*		
	Persons.	Males.	Females.	Persons.	Males.	Females.	Persons.	Males.	Females.	Persons.	Males.	Females.	Persons.	Males.	Females.	Persons.	Males.	Females.	Persons.	Males.	Females.
Jammu and Kashmir State ..	86	80	6	3	2	1	11	7	4	146	91	55	4	....	4	574	328	246	150	105	45
I. Jammu Province ..	1	1	....	2	1	1	4	2	2	8	6	2	4	....	4	....	....	..	..	..	..
1. Jammu District ..	....	....	....	1	....	1	....	....	....	7	6	1	....	....	....	....	....	..	..	..	..
2. Kathua „ ..	....	....	....	....	....	....	....	....	....	....	....	....	....	....	....	....	....	..	..	..	..
3. Udhampur „ ..	1	1	....	1	1	....	....	....	....	....	....	....	....	....	....	....	....	..	..	..	..
4. Reasi „ ..	....	....	....	....	....	....	....	....	....	....	....	....	....	....	....	....	....	..	..	..	..
5. Mirpur „ ..	....	....	....	....	....	....	4	2	2	....	....	....	4	....	4	....	....	..	..	..	..
6. Poonch Jagir ..	....	....	....	....	....	....	....	....	....	1	....	1	....	....	....	....	....	..	..	..	..
7. Chenani „ ..	....	....	....	....	....	....	....	....	....	....	....	....	....	....	....	....	....	..	..	..	..
II. Kashmir Province ..	23	23	....	....	....	....	6	4	2	23	14	9	....	....	....	10	5	5	..	..	..
8. Kashmir South (*including Municipality*) ..	23	23	....	....	....	....	5	3	2	16	8	8	....	....	....	10	5	5	..	..	..
9. Kashmir North ..	....	....	....	....	....	....	....	....	....	2	1	1	....	....	....	....	....	..	..	..	..
10. Muzaffarabad ..	....	....	....	....	....	....	1	1	....	5	5	....	....	....	....	....	....	..	..	..	..
III. Frontier Districts ..	62	56	6	1	1	....	1	1	....	115	71	44	....	....	....	564	323	241	150	105	45
11. Ladakh District ..	60	55	5	1	1	....	1	1	....	2	....	2	....	....	....	....	....	..	..	..	..
12. Gilgit „ ..	2	1	1	....	....	....	....	....	....	36	27	9	....	....	....	2	2	..	..	..	..
13. Frontier Ilaqas ..	....	....	....	....	....	....	....	....	....	77	44	33	....	....	....	562	321	241	150	105	45

TABLE XV.—Part I.

(d) Languages of Europe.

Jammu and Kashmir Census 1931.

District, Jagir or Ilaqa	Indo-European Family.																																			
	Teutonic Group.												Romance Group.												Celtic Group.			Balto Slavonic Group.		
	English.			Dutch.			Danish.			German.			French.			Italian.			Portuguese.			Spanish.			Gaelic.			Russian.		
	Persons.	Males.	Females.	Persons.	Males.	Females.	Persons.	Males.	Females.	Persons.	Females.	Females.	Persons.	Males.	Females.	Persons.	Males.	Females.	Persons.	Males.	Females.	Persons.	Males.	Females.	Persons.	Males.	Females.	Persons.	Males.	Females.
Jammu and Kashmir State ..	300	131	169	1	1	..	2	1	1	8	5	3	11	6	5	5	..	5	1	..	1	2	..	2	1	1	..	3	2	1
I. Jammu Province ..	47	26	21	..	..	..	..	..	..	1	1	..	2	..	2	..	..	..	..	..	..	..	..	..	1	1	..	..	..	..
1. Jammu District ..	31	16	15	..	..	..	..	..	..	1	1	..	2	..	2	..	..	..	..	..	..	..	..	..	1	1	..	..	..	..
2. Kathua " ..	..	..	..	..	..	..	..	..	..	..	..	..	..	..	..	..	..	..	..	..	..	..	..	..	..	..	..	..	..	..
3. Udhampur " ..	1	1	..	..	..	..	..	..	..	..	..	..	..	..	..	..	..	..	..	..	..	..	..	..	..	..	..	..	..	..
4. Reasi " ..	1	1	..	..	..	..	..	..	..	..	..	..	..	..	..	..	..	..	..	..	..	..	..	..	..	..	..	..	..	..
5. Mirpur " ..	8	5	3	..	..	..	..	..	..	..	..	..	..	..	..	..	..	..	..	..	..	..	..	..	..	..	..	..	..	..
6. Poonch Jagir ..	6	3	3	..	..	..	..	..	..	..	..	..	..	..	..	..	..	..	..	..	..	..	..	..	..	..	..	..	..	..
7. Chenani " ..	..	..	..	..	..	..	..	..	..	..	..	..	..	..	..	..	..	..	..	..	..	..	..	..	..	..	..	..	..	..
II. Kashmir Province ..	224	92	132	1	1	..	1	1	..	3	1	2	3	2	1	5	..	5	1	..	1	2	..	2	..	..	..	3	2	1
8. Kashmir South (*including Municipality*) ..	196	75	121	..	..	..	..	..	..	1	1	..	2	2	..	..	..	..	..	..	..	..	..	..	..	..	..	3	2	1
9. Kashmir North ..	21	11	10	1	1	..	1	1	..	1	..	1	1	..	1	5	..	5	1	..	1	2	..	2	..	..	..	..	..	..
10. Muzaffarabad ..	7	6	1	..	..	..	..	..	..	1	..	1	..	..	..	..	..	..	..	..	..	..	..	..	..	..	..	..	..	..
III. Frontier Districts ..	29	13	16	..	..	..	1	..	1	4	3	1	6	4	2	..	..	..	..	..	..	..	..	..	..	..	..	..	..	..
11. Ladakh District ..	4	1	3	..	..	..	1	..	1	4	3	1	6	4	2	..	..	..	..	..	..	..	..	..	..	..	..	..	..	..
12. Gilgit " ..	15	5	10	..	..	..	..	..	..	..	..	..	..	..	..	..	..	..	..	..	..	..	..	..	..	..	..	..	..	..
13. Frontier Ilaqas ..	10	7	3	..	..	..	..	..	..	..	..	..	..	..	..	..	..	..	..	..	..	..	..	..	..	..	..	..	..	..

TABLE XV.

Unclassified Languages.

Jammu and Kashmir Census 1931.

District, Jagir or Ilaqa.	*Buroshaski.*			*Chohdi.*			*Goun.*			*Hespian.*		
	Persons.	Males.	Females.	Persons.	Males.	Females.	Persons.	Males.	Females.	Persons.	Males.	Females.
Jammu and Kashmir State ..	26,076	14,678	11,398	66	31	35	1	1	......	3	3	......
I. Jammu Province ..	......	......	......	......	......	......	......	......	......	......	......	......
1. Jammu District ..	......	......	......	......	......	......	......	......	......	......	......	......
2. Kathua „ ..	......	......	......	......	......	......	......	......	......	......	......	......
3. Udhampur „ ..	......	......	......	......	......	......	......	......	......	......	......	......
4. Reasi „ ..	......	......	......	......	......	......	......	......	......	......	......	......
5. Mirpur „ ..	......	......	......	......	......	......	......	......	......	......	......	......
6. Poonch Jagir ..	......	......	......	......	......	......	......	......	......	......	......	......
7. Chenani „ ..	......	......	......	......	......	......	......	......	......	......	......	......
II. Kashmir Province ..	1	1	......	66	31	35	......	......	......	3	3	......
8. Kashmir South (*including Municipality*) ..	......	......	......	......	......	......	......	......	......	......	......	......
9. Kashmir North ..	1	1	......	51	23	28	......	......	......	......	......	......
10. Muzaffarabad ..	......	......	......	15	8	7	......	......	......	3	3	......
III. Frontier Districts ..	26,075	14,677	11,398	......	......	......	1	1	......	......	......	......
11. Ladakh District ..	......	......	......	......	......	......	......	......	......	......	......	......
12. Gilgit „ ..	512	473	39	......	......	......	1	1	......	......	......	......
13. Frontier Ilaqas ..	25,563	14,204	11,359	......	......	......	......	......	......	......	......	......

TABLE XV.

UNCLASSIFIED LANGUAGES.

Jammu and Kashmir Census 1931.

District, Jagir or Ilaqa.	Hanzrek.			Kanjoli.			Karnatith.			Khadia.			Khilochi.		
	Persons.	Males.	Females.	Persons.	Males.	Females.	Persons.	Males.	Females.	Persons.	Males.	Females.	Persons.	Males.	Females.
Jammu and Kashmir State ..	305	180	125	9	9	....	1	1	....	71	34	37	238	142	96
I. Jammu Province ..	....	....	....	....	....	....	....	....	....	....	....	....	....	....	....
1. Jammu District ..	....	....	....	....	....	....	....	....	....	....	....	....	....	....	....
2. Kathua " ..	....	....	....	....	....	....	....	....	....	....	....	....	....	....	....
3. Udhampur " ..	....	....	....	....	....	....	....	....	....	....	....	....	....	....	....
4. Reasi " ..	....	....	....	....	....	....	....	....	....	....	....	....	....	....	....
5. Mirpur " ..	....	....	....	....	....	....	....	....	....	....	....	....	....	....	....
6. Poonch Jagir ..	....	....	....	....	....	....	....	....	....	....	....	....	....	....	....
7. Chenani " ..	....	....	....	....	....	....	....	....	....	....	....	....	....	....	....
II. Kashmir Province ..	....	....	....	....	....	....	1	1	....	....	....	....	....	....	....
8. Kashmir South (*including Municipality*) ..	....	....	....	....	....	....	....	....	....	....	....	....	....	....	....
9. Kashmir North ..	....	....	....	....	....	....	1	1	....	....	....	....	....	....	....
10. Muzaffarabad ..	....	....	....	....	....	....	....	....	....	....	....	....	....	....	....
III. Frontier Districts ..	305	180	125	9	9	....	....	....	....	71	34	37	238	142	96
11. Ladakh District ..	....	....	....	....	....	....	....	....	....	....	....	....	....	....	....
12. Gilgit " ..	300	175	125	9	9	....	....	....	....	....	....	....	117	71	46
13. Frontier Ilaqas ..	5	5	....	....	....	....	....	....	....	71	34	37	121	71	50

TABLE XV.

Unclassified Languages.

Jammu and Kashmir Census 1931.

District, Jagir or Ilaqa.	Khiwali.			Khokhri.			Mirpuri.			Mishkaan.			Moyali.		
	Persons.	Males.	Females.	Persons.	Males.	Males.	Persons.	Males.	Females.	Persons.	Males.	Females.	Persons.	Males.	Females.
Jammu and Kashmir State ..	122	72	50	34	20	14	3	2	1	1	1	....	2	2	....
I. Jammu Province ..	....	....	....	....	....	....	....	....	....	....	....	....	....	....	....
1. Jammu District ..	....	....	....	....	....	....	....	....	....	....	....	....	....	....	....
2. Kathua " ..	....	....	....	....	....	....	....	....	....	....	....	....	....	....	....
3. Udhampur " ..	....	....	....	....	....	....	....	....	....	....	....	....	....	....	....
4. Reasi " ..	....	....	....	....	....	....	....	....	....	....	....	....	....	....	....
5. Mirpur " ..	....	....	....	....	....	....	....	....	....	....	....	....	....	....	....
6. Poonch Jagir ..	....	....	....	....	....	....	....	....	....	....	....	....	....	....	....
7. Chenani " ..	....	....	....	....	....	....	....	....	....	....	....	....	....	....	....
II. Kashmir Province ..	....	....	....	34	20	14	3	2	1	....	....	....	....	....	....
8 Kashmir South (*including Municipality*) ..	....	....	....	....	....	....	....	....	....	....	....	....	....	....	....
9. Kashmir North ..	....	....	....	34	20	14	....	....	....	....	....	....	....	....	....
10. Muzaffrabad ..	....	....	....	....	....	....	3	2	1	....	....	....	....	....	....
III. Frontier Districts ..	122	72	50	....	....	....	....	....	....	1	1	....	2	2	....
11. Ladakh District ..	....	....	....	....	....	....	....	....	....	1	1	....	....	....	....
12. Gilgit " ..	4	4	....	....	....	....	....	....	....	....	....	....	2	2	....
13. Frontier Ilaqas ..	118	68	50	....	....	....	....	....	....	....	....	....	....	....	....

TABLE XV.

Unclassified Languages.

Jammu and Kashmir Census 1931.

District, Jagir or Ilaqa.	Moyani.			Normal.			Rooski.			Baziyari.			Perne.		
	Persons.	Males.	Females.	Persons.	Males.	Females.	Persons.	Males.	Females.	Persons.	Males.	Females.	Persons.	Males.	Females.
Jammu and Kashmir State ..	3	....	3	1	1	....	1	1	....	96	50	46	7	7	....
I. Jammu Province ..	....	....	....	....	....	....	....	....	....	96	50	46	7	7	....
1. Jammu District ..	....	....	....	....	....	....	....	....	....	96	50	46	....	....	....
2. Kathua " ..	....	....	....	....	....	....	....	....	....	....	....	....	7	7	....
3. Udhampur " ..	....	....	....	....	....	....	....	....	....	....	....	....	....	....	....
4. Riasi " ..	....	....	....	....	....	....	....	....	....	....	....	....	....	....	....
5. Mirpur " ..	....	....	....	....	....	....	....	....	....	....	....	....	....	....	....
6. Poonch Jagir ..	....	....	....	....	....	....	....	....	....	....	....	....	....	....	....
7. Chenani " ..	....	....	....	....	....	....	....	....	....	....	....	....	....	....	....
II. Kashmir Province ..	....	....	....	1	1	....	1	1	....	....	....	....	....	....	....
8. Kashmir South (*including Municipality*) ..	....	....	....	1	1	....	1	1	....	....	....	....	....	....	....
9. Kashmir North ..	....	....	....	....	....	....	....	....	....	....	....	....	....	....	....
10. Muzaffarabad ..	....	....	....	....	....	....	....	....	....	....	....	....	....	....	....
III. Frontier Districts ..	3	....	3	....	....	....	....	....	....	....	....	....	....	....	....
11. Ladakh District ..	....	....	....	....	....	....	....	....	....	....	....	....	....	....	....
12. Gilgit " ..	3	....	3	....	....	....	....	....	....	....	....	....	....	....	....
13. Frontier Ilaqas ..	....	....	....	....	....	....	....	....	....	....	....	....	....	....	....

TABLE XV.—Part II (A).

Bilingualism.

Jammu and Kashmir Census 1931.

Taluk.	Mother-tongue.	No. of Persons speaking Mother-tongue. Persons.	Males.	Females.	No. of Persons speaking Subsidiary Languages. Dogri. Persons.	Males.	Females.	Punjabi. Persons.	Males.	Females.	Kashmiri. Persons.	Males.	Females.	Remarks.
Jammu and Kashmir State.	Dogri ..	549,917	293,986	255,931	....	....	....	7,255	4,210	3,045	943	636	307	
	Kashmiri ..	1,370.763	742,016	628,747	3,573	2,426	1,147	5,302	3,525	1,777	....	....	....	
	Gojari ..	317,762	170,528	147,23	17,519	10,052	7,467	4,314	3,450	864	8,932	5,509	3,423	
	Pahari ..	595,783	308,010	287,773	4,213	2,709	1,504	2,015	1,114	901	5,941	3,342	2,599	
	Panjabi ..	329,433	174,659	154,774	3,584	2,012	1,572	—	....	....	6,943	3,976	2,967	
	Lahnda (Chabhali) ..	44,460	23,129	21,331	60	38	22	36	28	8	1	1	....	
	Pothwari ..	51,062	26,869	24,193	13	12	1	665	664	1	2	2	....	
	Balti ..	137,914	68,467	69,447	40	6	34	91	81	10	142	97	45	
	Ladakhi ..	41,418	20,546	20,872	....	....	....	6	6	....	11	7	4	
	Shina ..	63,918	33,379	30,539	4	4	—	381	367	14	28	20	8	
Jammu Province.	Dogri ..	547,534	292,139	255,395	....	—	....	7,057	4,072	2,985	624	408	216	
	Kashmiri ..	121,431	66,290	55,141	3,554	2,408	1,146	2,765	1,559	1,206	....	....	....	
	Gojari ..	208,933	111,482	97,451	17,519	10,052	7,467	1,882	1,102	780	712	550	162	
	Pahari ..	417,363	213,471	203,892	4,180	2,676	1,504	1,033	615	418	2,630	1,504	1,126	
	Panjabi ..	306,835	162,374	144,461	3,449	1,929	1,520	—	....	....	321	280	41	
	Lahnda (Chabhali) ..	44,460	23,129	21,331	60	38	22	36	28	8	1	1	....	
	Pothwari ..	51,035	26,843	24,192	13	12	1	665	664	1	2	2	....	
	Balti ..	185	127	58	39	5	34	3	1	2	2	2	—	
	Ladakhi ..	472	234	238	....	—	—	1	1	....	....	....	....	
	Dogri ..	88,143	49,730	38,413	—	—	—	2,655	1,926	729	177	162	15	
	Kashmiri ..	2,751	2,418	333	115	101	14	701	609	92	....	....	....	
	Gojari ..	17,426	9,405	8,021	6,335	3,444	2,891	563	355	208	13	8	5	

TABLE XV.—PART II (A).

BILINGUALISM.

Jammu and Kashmir Census 1931

Taluk.	Mother-tongue.	No. of Persons speaking Mother-tongue.			No. of Persons speaking Subsidiary Languages.									Remarks.
					Dogri.			Punjabi.			Kashmiri.			
		Persons.	Males.	Females.	Persons.	Males.	Females.	Persons.	Males.	Females.	Persons.	Males.	Females.	
Jammu District. Jammu Tehsil.	Pahari ..	111	100	11	10	5	5	15	15	....	....	....	....	
	Panjabi ..	21,293	12,405	8,888	1,051	642	409	....	....	....	109	85	24	
	Chabhali ..	168	166	2	1	1	....	7	7	....	1	1	....	
	Pothwari ..	63	53	10	3	2	1	4	3	1	....	....	....	
	Balti ..	18	12	6	2	1	1	1	....	1	2	2	....	
	Ladakhi ..	4	....	4	....	....	....	....	....	....	....	....	....	
Ranbirsinghpura Tehsil.	Dogri ..	33,726	18,672	15,054	....	....	....	350	205	145	2	2	....	
	Kashmiri ..	19	16	3	....	....	....	3	1	2	....	....	....	
	Gojari ..	364	216	148	2	2	....	236	116	120	....	....	....	
	Pahari ..	2	....	2	....	....	....	2	....	2	....	....	....	
	Panjabi ..	47,680	25,303	22,377	763	366	397	....	....	....	1	1	....	
	Chabhali ..	3	2	1	1	....	1	....	....	....	....	....	....	
	Pothwari ..	2	1	1	....	....	....	....	....	....	....	....	....	
	Balti ..	....	....	....	....	....	....	....	....	....	....	....	....	
	Ladakhi ..	....	....	....	....	....	....	....	....	....	....	....	....	
Samba Tehsil.	Dogri ..	54,804	29,045	25,759	....	....	....	356	148	208	7	7	....	
	Kashmiri ..	4	4	....	....	....	....	1	1	....	....	....	....	
	Gojari ..	11,915	6,074	5,841	3,191	1,654	1,537	38	35	3	....	....	....	
	Pahari ..	89	43	46	71	38	33	....	....	....	....	....	....	
	Panjabi ..	11,157	6,225	4,932	273	75	198	....	....	....	....	....	....	
	Chabhali ..	4	4	....	....	....	....	....	....	....	....	....	....	
	Pothwari ..	....	....	....	....	....	....	....	....	....	....	....	....	

District	Tahsil	Language												
		Balti	....	....	....	....	....	....	....	....	....	....	....	....
		Ladakhi	....	....	....	....	....	....	....	....	....	....	....	....
	Akhnoor Tahsil.	Dogri	57,398	30,544	26,854	....	....	....	439	277	162	2	1	1
		Kashmiri	21	17	4	2	1	1	....	....	....	....	....	....
		Gojari	15,675	8,351	7,324	257	179	78	75	53	22	....	....	....
		Pahari	9	8	1	....	....	....	....	....	....	....	....	....
		Panjabi	6,979	3,763	3,216	175	129	46	....	....	....	....	....	....
		Chabhali	....	....	....	....	....	....	....	....	....	....	....	....
		Pothwari	2	2	....	1	1	....	....	....	....	....	....	....
		Balti	....	....	....	....	....	....	....	....	....	....	....	....
		Ladakhi	....	....	....	....	....	....	....	....	....	....	....	....
Kathua District.	*Kathua Tahsil.*	Dogri	38,115	20,501	17,614	....	....	....	35	30	5	4	3	1
		Kashmiri	117	100	17	49	45	4	15	5	10	....	....	....
		Gojari	2,431	2,027	404	1,034	994	40	12	....	12	....	....	....
		Pahari	330	253	77	171	156	15	7	3	4	3	3	....
		Panjabi	1,896	1,002	894	223	99	124	....	....	....	....	....	....
		Chabhali	....	....	....	....	....	....	....	....	....	....	....	....
		Pothwari	4	2	2	....	....	....	....	....	....	....	....	....
		Balti	....	....	....	....	....	....	....	....	....	....	....	....
		Ladakhi	....	....	....	....	....	....	....	....	....	....	....	....
	Basohli Tahsil.	Dogri	49,293	25,711	23,582	....	....	....	36	9	27	54	32	22
		Kashmiri	1,818	1,058	760	179	115	64	....	....	....	....	....	....
		Gojari	3,909	1,981	1,928	498	481	17	....	....	....	....	....	....
		Pahari	6,878	3,540	3,338	209	160	49	....	....	....	....	....	....
		Panjabi	508	312	196	160	82	78	....	....	....	....	....	....
		Chabhali	....	....	....	....	....	....	....	....	....	....	....	....
		Pothwari	8	8	....	....	....	....	....	....	....	....	....	....
		Balti	....	....	....	....	....	....	....	....	....	....	....	....
		Ladakhi	....	....	....	....	....	....	....	....	....	....	....	....
		Dogri	45,333	24,144	21,189	....	....	....	37	29	8	....	....	....
		Kashmiri	12	9	3	3	3	....	....	....	....	....	....	....
		Gojari	4,946	2,671	2,275	3,106	1,652	1,454	16	14	2	....	....	....
		Pahari	26	24	2	6	4	2	....	....	....	....	....	....

TABLE XV.—PART II (A).

BILINGUALISM.

Jammu and Kashmir Census 1931.

Tahsil.	Mother-tongue.	No. of Persons speaking Mother-tongue.			No. of Persons speaking Subsidiary Languages. Dogri.			Panjabi.			Kashmiri.			Remarks.
		Persons.	Males.	Females.	Persons.	Males.	Females.	Persons.	Males.	Females.	Persons.	Males.	Females.	
Jasmergarh Tehsil.	Panjabi ...	1,300	675	625	84	71	13	....	....	....	....	....	....	
	Chabhali ...	....	....	....	....	....	....	....	....	....	....	....	....	
	Pothwari ...	....	....	....	....	....	....	....	....	....	....	....	....	
	Balti ...	....	....	....	....	....	....	....	....	....	....	....	....	
	Ladakhi ...	....	....	....	....	....	....	....	....	....	....	....	....	
Udhampur Tehsil.	Dogri ...	37,674	19,594	18,080	....	....	....	45	36	9	7	6	1	
	Kashmiri ...	2,590	1,684	906	468	266	202	50	46	4	....	....	....	
	Gojari ...	2,533	1,452	1,081	1,367	669	698	....	....	....	....	....	....	
	Pahari ...	3,913	2,073	1,840	753	396	357	1	1	....	17	15	2	
	Panjabi ...	593	344	249	175	98	77	....	....	....	16	10	6	
	Chabhali ...	....	....	....	....	....	....	....	....	....	....	....	....	
	Pothwari ...	17	17	....	7	7	....	....	....	....	....	....	....	
	Balti ...	117	67	50	36	4	32	1	1	....	....	....	....	
	Ladakhi ...	....	....	....	....	....	....	....	....	....	....	....	....	
Ramnagar Tehsil.	Dogri ...	46,181	23,144	23,037	....	....	....	411	99	312	146	94	52	
	Kashmiri ...	1,752	1,340	412	73	63	10	60	44	16	....	....	....	
	Gojari ...	1,762	254	1,508	....	....	....	....	....	....	....	....	....	
	Pahari ...	165	160	5	3	3	....	....	....	....	....	....	....	
	Panjabi ...	1,845	1,785	60	235	200	35	....	....	....	117	117	....	
	Chabhali ...	....	....	....	....	....	....	....	....	....	....	....	....	
	Pothwari ...	....	....	....	....	....	....	....	....	....	....	....	....	
	Balti ...	....	....	....	....	....	....	....	....	....	....	....	....	

District	Tehsil	Language	(cont.)											
		Ladakhi	....	....	....	....	....	....	....	....	....	....	....	....
UDHAMPUR DISTRICT.	Ramban Tehsil.	Dogri	339	552	287	....	....	....	45	43	2	14	14	....
		Kashmiri	31,036	17,151	14,785	588	543	45	278	275	3	....	....	....
		Gojari	7,864	4,106	3,758	112	90	22	4	4	....	555	450	105
		Pahari	2,114	1,092	1,022	42	38	4	10	7	3	1,833	953	880
		Panjabi	175	119	56	13	12	1	....	....	....	9	9	....
		Chabhali	....	....	....	....	....	....	....	....	....	....	....	....
		Pothwari	3	2	1	1	1	....	....	....	....	....	....	....
		Balti	3	1	2	1	....	1	1	....	1	....	....	....
		Ladakhi	....	....	....	....	....	....	....	....	....	....	....	....
	Kishtwar Tehsil.	Dogri	343	260	83	....	....	....	61	48	13	26	25	1
		Kashmiri	26,740	14,229	12,511	200	200	....	168	168	....	....	....	....
		Gojari	7,608	3,907	3,701	10	9	1	2	2	....	72	45	27
		Pahari	15	8	7	....	....	....	....	....	....	4	3	1
		Panjabi	166	105	61	1	1	....	....	....	....	1	1	....
		Chabhali	....	....	....	....	....	....	....	....	....	....	....	....
		Pothwari	....	....	....	....	....	....	....	....	....	....	....	....
		Balti	....	....	....	....	....	....	....	....	....	....	....	....
		Ladakhi	434	212	222	....	....	....	1	1	....	....	....	....
	Bhadarwah Tehsil.	Dogri	2,628	1,534	1,094	....	....	....	1,154	392	762	148	36	112
		Kashmiri	13,476	6,963	6,513	493	259	234	358	68	290	....	....	....
		Gojari	3,128	1,692	1,436	7	7	....	2	2	....	....	....	....
		Pahari	313	148	165	63	....	63	103	4	99	28	15	13
		Panjabi	288	179	107	122	42	80	....	....	....	....	....	....
		Chabhali	....	....	....	....	....	....	....	....	....	....	....	....
		Pothwari	6	6	....	....	....	....	....	....	....	....	....	....
		Balti	....	....	....	....	....	....	....	....	....	....	....	....
		Ladakhi	....	....	....	....	....	....	....	....	....	....	....	....
		Dogri	42,460	22,267	20,193	....	....	....	1,200	683	517	23	19	4
RIASI DISTRICT.	Riasi Tehsil.	Kashmiri	18,876	9,935	8,941	1,101	642	459	153	103	50	....	....	....
		Gojari	30,057	15,953	14,104	1,477	807	670	442	235	207	16	12	4
		Pahari	13,874	7,177	6,697	1,323	1,016	307	60	7	53	229	222	7
		Panjabi	931	584	347	119	76	43	....	....	....	26	21	5

TABLE XV.—PART II (A).

BILINGUALISM.

Jammu and Kashmir Census 1931.

Taluk.	Mother-tongue.	No. of Persons speaking Mother-tongue.			No. of Persons speaking Subsidiary Languages. Dogri.			Punjabi.			Kashmiri.			Remarks.
		Persons.	Males.	Females.	Persons.	Males.	Females.	Persons.	Males.	Females.	Persons.	Males.	Females.	
Riasi District.	Chabhali ..	20	17	3	4	4	....	2	2	....	....	....	....	
	Pothwari ..	5	5	....	....	....	....	....	....	....	....	....	....	
	Balti ..	....	....	....	....	....	....	....	....	....	....	....	....	
	Ladakhi ..	....	....	....	....	....	....	....	....	....	....	....	....	
Rampur Rajouri Tehsil.	Dogri ..	13,953	7,184	6,769	....	....	....	12	8	4	8	2	6	
	Kashmiri ..	3,462	1,860	1,602	106	62	44	78	46	32	....	....	....	
	Gojari ..	40,629	21,559	19,070	59	39	20	18	7	11	2	1	1	
	Pahari ..	58,682	30,999	27,683	129	108	21	87	63	24	135	84	51	
	Panjabi ..	994	726	268	1	1	....	....	....	....	4	3	1	
	Chabhali ..	9,950	5,220	4,730	25	9	16	....	....	....	....	....	....	
	Pothwari ..	5	4	1	....	....	....	1	1	....	1	1	....	
	Balti ..	....	....	....	....	....	....	....	....	....	....	....	....	
	Ladakhi ..	34	22	12	....	....	....	....	....	....	....	....	....	
Mirpur District. Mirpur Tehsil.	Dogri ..	174	138	36	....	....	....	40	31	9	....	....	....	
	Kashmiri ..	65	60	5	....	....	....	14	13	1	....	....	....	
	Gojari ..	8	5	3	....	....	....	....	....	....	....	....	....	
	Pahari ..	667	342	325	....	....	....	9	4	5	....	....	....	
	Panjabi ..	94,405	47,898	46,507	9	6	3	....	....	....	13	9	4	
	Chabhali ..	19	12	7	....	....	....	....	....	....	....	....	....	
	Pothwari ..	4,141	2,170	1,971	....	....	....	....	....	....	....	....	....	
	Balti ..	1	1	....	....	....	....	....	....	....	....	....	....	
	Ladakhi ..	....	....	....	....	....	....	....	....	....	....	....	....	

Mirpur District. *Kotli Tehsil.*	Dogri	20	7	13	...	...	...	7	5	2	...	...	...
	Kashmiri	653	647	6	3	3	...	27	27	...	...	...	...
	Gojari	9,446	5,033	4,413	...	...	...	20	19	1	1	1	...
	Pahari	14,309	7,447	6,862	...	...	...	5	5	...	2	...	2
	Panjabi	31,508	16,563	14,945	2	2	...	...	...	...	3	3	...
	Chabhali	111	62	49	...	...	...	...	...	...	...	...	...
	Pothwari	46,731	24,540	22,191	1	1	...	660	660	...	1	1	...
	Balti	1	1	...	...	...	...	...	...	...	...	...	...
	Ladakhi	...	...	...	...	...	...	...	...	...	...	...	...
Bhimber Tehsil.	Dogri	27,666	14,378	13,288	...	...	...	50	33	17	...	...	...
	Kashmiri	41	35	6	1	1	...	9	9	...	...	...	...
	Gojari	293	137	156	...	...	...	1	1	...	...	...	...
	Pahari	233	101	132	1	...	1	1	...	1	...	...	...
	Panjabi	77,897	40,366	37,531	15	4	11	...	...	...	8	7	1
	Chabhali	34,184	17,645	16,539	29	24	5	27	19	8	...	...	...
	Pothwari	9	9	...	...	...	...	...	...	...	...	...	...
	Balti	...	...	...	...	...	...	...	...	...	...	...	...
	Ladakhi	...	...	...	...	...	...	...	...	...	...	...	...
Poonch Jagir. *Bagh Tehsil.*	Dogri	1	1	...	...	...	...	1	1	...	...	...	...
	Kashmiri	136	93	43	...	...	...	...	...	...	...	...	...
	Gojari	1,878	1,312	566	...	...	...	...	...	...	...	...	...
	Pahari	91,702	46,100	45,602	...	...	...	36	32	4	2	...	2
	Panjabi	197	106	91	...	...	...	...	...	...	...	...	...
	Chabhali	...	...	...	...	...	...	...	...	...	...	...	...
	Pothwari	22	13	9	...	...	...	...	...	...	...	...	...
	Balti	...	...	...	...	...	...	...	...	...	...	...	...
	Ladakhi	...	...	...	...	...	...	...	...	...	...	...	...
Sadhnoti Tehsil.	Dogri	6	5	1	...	...	...	1	...	1	...	...	...
	Kashmiri	54	45	9	...	...	...	2	1	1	...	...	...
	Gojari	701	361	340	27	...	27	2	2	...	...	...	...
	Pahari	99,309	48,636	50,673	15	...	15	68	67	1	55	4	51
	Panjabi	351	263	88	1	1	...	...	...	...	1	1	...
	Chabhali	...	...	...	...	...	...	...	...	...	...	...	...

TABLE XV.—PART II (A).

BILINGUALISM.

Jammu and Kashmir Census 1931.

Taluk.	Mother-tongue.	No. of Persons speaking Mother-tongue.			No. of Persons speaking Subsidiary Languages. Dogri.			Panjabi.			Kashmiri.			Remarks.
		Persons.	Males.	Females.	Persons.	Males.	Females.	Persons.	Males.	Females.	Persons.	Males.	Females.	
Poonch Jagir.	Pothwari	1	1	....	....	....	....	....	....	....	....	....	....	
	Balti	26	26	....	....	....	....	....	....	....	....	....	....	
	Ladakhi	....	....	....	....	....	....	....	....	....	....	....	....	
Haveli Tehsil.	Dogri	748	419	329	....	....	....	118	66	52	....	....	....	
	Kashmiri	14,620	7,330	7,281	....	....	....	845	140	705	....	....	....	
	Gojari	26,395	14,088	12,307	....	....	....	35	29	6	43	28	15	
	Pahari	56,321	29,777	26,544	9	2	7	486	318	168	241	145	96	
	Panjabi	2,857	1,672	1,185	2	2	....	....	....	....	12	12	....	
	Chabhali	....	....	....	....	....	....	....	....	....	....	....	....	
	Pothwari	15	9	6	....	....	....	....	....	....	....	....	....	
	Balti	19	19	....	....	....	....	....	....	....	....	....	....	
	Ladakhi	....	....	....	....	....	....	....	....	....	....	....	....	
Mainder Tehsil.	Dogri	100	86	14	....	....	....	....	....	....	....	....	....	
	Kashmiri	1,929	1,027	902	....	....	....	3	3	....	....	....	....	
	Gojari	19,452	10,641	8,811	2	....	2	416	228	188	....	....	....	
	Pahari	66,580	34,524	32,056	1	1	....	143	89	54	77	56	21	
	Panjabi	3,729	1,902	1,827	2	2	....	....	....	....	1	1	....	
	Chabhali	....	....	....	....	....	....	....	....	....	....	....	....	
	Pothwari	1	1	....	....	....	....	....	....	....	....	....	....	
	Balti	....	....	....	....	....	....	....	....	....	....	....	....	
	Ladakhi	....	....	....	....	....	....	....	....	....	....	....	....	

District	Tehsil	Language	1	2	3	4	5	6	7	8	9	10	11	12
Chenani Jagir.	*Chenani.*	Dogri	7,929	4,223	3,706	....	....	....	4	3	1	6	5	1
		Kashmiri	359	260	99	173	104	69	....	....	....	....	....	....
		Gojari	513	257	256	35	25	10	....	....	....	10	5	5
		Pahari	1,721	919	802	1,374	749	625	....	....	....	4	4	....
		Panjabi	88	77	11	23	18	5	....	....	....	....	....	....
		Chabhali	1	1	....	....	....	....	....	....	....	....	....	....
		Pothwari	....	....	....	....	....	....	....	....	....	....	....	....
		Balti	....	....	....	....	....	....	....	....	....	....	....	....
		Ladakhi	....	....	....	....	....	....	....	....	....	....	....	....
Kashmir Province.		Dogri	1,662	1,168	494	....	....	....	127	74	53	314	223	91
		Kashmiri	1,247,497	674,534	572,963	17	16	1	2,487	1,921	566	....	....	....
		Gojari	107,849	58,448	49,401	....	....	....	2,430	2,346	84	8,220	4,959	3,261
		Western Pahari	178,292	94,411	83,881	....	....	....	958	475	483	3,311	1,838	1,473
		Panjabi	20,056	10,796	9,260	100	75	25	....	....	....	6,609	3,083	2,926
		Chabhali	....	....	....	....	....	....	....	....	....	....	....	....
		Pothwari	26	25	1	....	....	....	....	....	....	....	....	....
		Balti	623	379	244	1	1	....	24	18	6	91	48	43
		Ladakhi	45	36	9	....	....	....	5	5	....	....	....	....
		Shina	33	26	7	....	....	....	1	1	....	7	3	4
Kashmir South.	*Kulgam Tehsil.*	Dogri	593	371	222	....	....	....	15	3	12	288	207	81
		Kashmiri	141,967	75,163	66,804	4	4	....	130	97	33	....	....	....
		Gojari	3,099	1,604	1,495	....	....	....	6	....	6	362	223	139
		Western Pahari	348	187	161	....	....	....	2	....	2	113	54	59
		Panjabi	132	77	55	5	2	3	....	....	....	68	32	36
		Chabhali	....	....	....	....	....	....	....	....	....	....	....	....
		Pothwari	....	....	....	....	....	....	....	....	....	....	....	....
		Balti	3	2	1	1	1	....	1	1	....	....	....	....
		Ladakhi	....	....	....	....	....	....	....	....	....	....	....	....
		Shina	....	....	....	....	....	....	....	....	....	....	....	....
	Anantnag Tehsil.	Dogri	38	28	10	....	....	....	13	13	....	4	1	3
		Kashmiri	173,355	94,731	78,624	7	6	1	135	127	8	....	....	....
		Gojari	14,885	7,868	7,017	....	....	....	1	....	1	2,560	1,446	1,114
		Western Pahari	1,783	991	792	....	....	....	3	....	3	636	354	282

TABLE XV.—Part II (A)

Bilingualism.

Jammu and Kashmir Census 1931.

Taluk.		Mother-tongue.	No. of Persons speaking Mother-tongue.			No. of Persons speaking Subsidiary Languages.									Remarks.
						Dogri.			Panjabi.			Kashmiri.			
			Persons.	Males.	Females.	Persons.	Males.	Females.	Persons.	Males.	Females.	Persons.	Males.	Females.	
Kashmir South.	Anantnag Tehsil.	Panjabi ..	1,691	875	816	3	1	2	....	....	....	660	283	377	
		Chabhali ..	....	....	....	....	....	....	....	....	....	....	....	....	
		Pothwari ..	....	....	....	....	....	....	....	....	....	....	....	....	
		Balti ..	....	....	....	....	....	....	....	....	....	....	....	....	
		Ladakhi ..	1	1	....	....	....	....	....	....	....	....	....	....	
		Shina ..	....	....	....	....	....	....	....	....	....	....	....	....	
	Avantipura Tehsil.	Dogri ..	10	7	3	....	....	....	3	....	3	8	7	1	
		Kashmiri ..	141,037	77,366	63,671	....	....	....	161	153	8	....	....	....	
		Gojari ..	5,767	3,254	2,513	....	....	....	2,100	2,190	....	4,119	2,442	1,677	
		Western Pahari ..	1,349	613	736	....	....	....	627	242	385	715	242	473	
		Panjabi ..	1,580	909	671	54	54	....	....	....	....	1,462	895	567	
		Chabhali ..	....	....	....	....	....	....	....	....	....	....	....	....	
		Pothwari ..	....	....	....	....	....	....	....	....	....	....	....	....	
		Balti ..	40	20	20	....	....	....	....	....	....	20	4	16	
		Ladakhi ..	2	2	....	....	....	....	....	....	....	....	....	....	
		Shina ..	....	....	....	....	....	....	....	....	....	....	....	....	
	Srinagar Tehsil.	Dogri ..	429	367	62	....	....	....	2	1	1	6	1	5	
		Kashmiri ..	97,527	53,088	44,439	....	....	....	102	97	5	....	....	....	
		Gojari ..	7,688	4,146	3,542	....	....	....	20	12	8	60	56	4	
		Western Pahari ..	508	274	234	....	....	....	....	....	....	13	13	....	
		Panjabi ..	577	348	229	....	....	....	....	....	....	19	9	10	
		Chabhali ..	....	....	....	....	....	....	....	....	....	....	....	....	

District	Tehsil	Language												
KASHMIR SOUTH.	*Srinagar Tehsil.*	Pothwari	....	....	....	....	....	....	....	....	....	....	....	....
		Balti	405	247	158	....	....	....	2	2	....	45	30	15
		Ladakhi	....	....	....	....	....	....	....	....	....	....	....	....
		Shina	....	....	....	....	....	....	....	....	....	....	....	....
	Srinagar Municipality.	Dogri	332	230	102	....	....	....	35	24	11	4	3	1
		Kashmiri	169,684	92,270	77,414	5	5	....	98	....	98	....	....	....
		Gojari	19	19	....	....	....	....	....	....	....	1	1	....
		Western Pahari	190	145	45	....	....	....	12	10	2	10	....	10
		Panjabi	2,276	1,525	751	28	9	19	....	....	....	220	142	78
		Chabhali	....	....	....	....	....	....	....	....	....	....	....	....
		Pothwari	....	....	....	....	....	....	....	....	....	....	....	....
		Balti	118	77	41	....	....	....	13	10	3	19	13	6
		Ladakhi	38	29	9	....	....	....	4	4	....	....	....	....
		Shina	14	14	....	....	....	....	1	1	....	....	....	....
KASHMIR NORTH.	*Sripratapsinghpura Tehsil.*	Dogri	63	43	20	....	....	....	8	8	....	....	....	....
		Kashmiri	156,013	84,867	71,146	1	1	....	637	495	142	....	....	....
		Gojari	4,397	2,417	1,980	....	....	....	....	....	....	516	344	172
		Western Pahari	443	254	189	....	....	....	....	....	....	221	128	93
		Panjabi	1,899	994	905	....	....	....	....	....	....	1,272	655	617
		Chabhali	....	....	....	....	....	....	....	....	....	....	....	....
		Pothwari	....	....	....	....	....	....	....	....	....	....	....	....
		Balti	5	3	2	....	....	....	....	....	....	2	....	2
		Ladakhi	2	2	....	....	....	....	1	1	....	....	....	....
		Shina	3	3	....	....	....	....	....	....	....	1	1	....
	Baramulla Tehsil.	Dogri	52	30	22	....	....	....	35	19	16	2	2	....
		Kashmiri	142,178	76,776	65,402	....	....	....	431	384	47	....	....	....
		Gojari	2,482	1,507	975	....	....	....	16	16	....	43	27	16
		Western Pahari	815	447	368	....	....	....	3	3	....	71	48	23
		Panjabi	3,230	1,808	1,431	1	....	1	....	....	....	1,367	788	579
		Chabhali	....	....	....	....	....	....	....	....	....	....	....	....
		Pothwari	....	....	....	....	....	....	....	....	....	....	....	....
		Balti	9	5	4	....	....	....	6	4	2	2	....	2
		Ladakhi	....	....	....	....	....	....	....	....	....	....	....	....
		Shina	6	2	4	....	....	....	....	....	....	6	2	4

TABLE XV.—PART II (A).

BILINGUALISM.

Jammu and Kashmir Census 1931.

Taluk.	Tehsil	Mother-tongue.	No. of Persons speaking Mother-tongue.			No. of Persons speaking Subsidiary Languages. Dogri.			Punjabi.			Kashmiri.			Remarks.
			Persons.	Males.	Females.	Persons.	Males.	Females.	Persons.	Males.	Females.	Persons.	Males.	Females.	
Kashmir North.	Uttarmachipura Tehsil.	Dogri	13	9	4	....	....	....	5	5	....	2	2	....	
		Kashmiri	204,392	108,632	95,769	....	....	....	708	487	221	....	....	....	
		Gojari	21,566	11,937	9,629	....	....	....	195	126	69	536	407	129	
		Western Pahari	9,008	4,741	4,267	....	....	....	128	72	56	665	406	259	
		Panjabi	4,897	2,285	2,612	7	7	....	....	....	....	1,491	842	649	
		Chabhali	....	....	....	....	....	....	....	....	....	....	....	....	
		Pothwari	....	....	....	....	....	....	....	....	....	....	....	....	
		Balti	38	21	17	....	....	....	2	1	1	3	1	2	
		Ladakhi	1	1	....	....	....	....	....	....	....	....	....	....	
		Shina	....	....	....	....	....	....	....	....	....	....	....	....	
Muzaffarabad District.	Uri Tehsil.	Dogri	28	22	6	....	....	....	3	1	2	....	....	....	
		Kashmiri	13,255	7,242	6,013	....	....	....	60	58	2	....	....	....	
		Gojari	18,026	9,612	8,414	....	....	....	1	1	....	21	11	10	
		Western Pahari	39,086	20,717	18,369	....	....	....	66	50	16	621	379	242	
		Panjabi	986	542	444	....	....	....	....	....	....	26	15	11	
		Chabhali	....	....	....	....	....	....	....	....	....	....	....	....	
		Pothwari	14	14	....	....	....	....	....	....	....	....	....	....	
		Balti	1	1	....	....	....	....	....	....	....	....	....	....	
		Ladakhi	....	....	....	....	....	....	....	....	....	....	....	....	
		Shina	....	....	....	....	....	....	....	....	....	....	....	....	
		Dogri	100	58	42	....	....	....	8	....	8	....	....	....	
		Kashmiri	2,747	1,632	1,115	....	....	....	21	19	2	....	....	....	

District	Tehsil	Language												
Muzaffarabad District.	Muzaffarabad Tehsil.	Gojari	24,108	12,952	11,156	....	....	....	1	1	....	1	1	....
		Western Pahari	82,886	43,596	39,290	....	....	....	111	92	19	62	30	32
		Panjabi	2,762	1,421	1,341	2	2	....	....	....	....	23	21	2
		Chabhali	....	....	....	....	....	....	....	....	....	....	....	....
		Pothwari	12	11	1	....	....	....	....	....	....	....	....	....
		Balti	3	2	1	....	....	....	....	....	....	....	....	....
		Ladakh	1	1	....	....	....	....	....	....	....	....	....	....
		Shina	6	4	2	....	....	....	....	....	....	....	....	....
	Karnah Tehsil.	Dogri	4	3	1	....	....	....	....	....	....	....	....	....
		Kashmiri	5,342	2,767	2,575	....	....	....	4	4	....	....	....	....
		Gojari	5,812	3,132	2680	....	....	....	....	....	....	1	1	....
		Western Pahari	41,876	22,446	19,430	....	....	....	6	6	....	184	184	....
		Panjabi	17	12	5	....	....	....	....	....	....	1	1	....
		Chabhali	....	....	....	....	....	....	....	....	....	....	....	....
		Pothwari	....	....	....	....	....	....	....	....	....	....	....	....
		Balti	1	1	....	....	....	....	....	....	....	....	....	....
		Ladakhi	....	....	....	....	....	....	....	....	....	....	....	....
		Shina	4	3	1	....	....	....	....	....	....	....	....	....
Frontier Districts.		Dogri	721	679	42	....	....	....	71	64	7	5	5	....
		Kashmiri	1,835	1,192	643	2	2	....	50	45	5	....	....	....
		Gojari	980	598	382	....	....	....	2	2	....	....	....	....
		Western Pahari	128	128	....	33	33	....	24	24	....	....	....	....
		Panjabi	2,542	1,489	1,053	35	8	27	....	....	....	13	13	....
		Chabhali	....	....	....	....	....	....	....	....	....	....	....	....
		Pothwari	1	1	....	....	....	....	....	....	....	....	....	....
		Balti	137,106	67,961	69,145	....	....	....	64	62	2	49	47	2
		Ladakhi	40,901	20,276	20,625	....	....	....	....	....	....	11	7	4
		Shina	63,885	33,353	30,552	4	4	....	380	366	14	21	17	4
Ladakh District.	Kargil Tehsil.	Dogri	1	1	....	....	....	....	....	....	....	....	....	....
		Kashmiri	328	196	132	....	....	....	....	....	....	....	....	....
		Gojari	....	....	....	....	....	....	....	....	....	....	....	....
		Western Pahari	1	1	....	....	....	....	....	....	....	....	....	....
		Panjabi	30	23	7	....	....	....	....	....	....	....	....	....

TABLE XV.—Part II (A).

Bilingualism.

Jammu and Kashmir Census 1931.

Taluk.	Mother-tongue.	No. of Persons speaking Mother tongue.			No. of Persons speaking Subsidiary Languages.									Remarks.
					Dogri.			Panjabi.			Kashmiri.			
		Persons.	Males.	Females.	Persons.	Males.	Females.	Persons.	Males.	Females.	Persons.	Males.	Females.	
Ladakh District. Kargil Tehsil.	Chabbali ..	....	....	....	....	....	....	....	....	....	....	....	....	
	Pothwari ..	....	....	....	....	....	....	....	....	....	....	....	....	
	Balti ..	34,006	16,308	17,698	....	....	....	2	....	2	38	38	....	
	Ladakhi ..	7,323	3,487	3,836	....	....	....	....	....	....	....	....	....	
	Shina ..	7,540	3,904	3,642	....	....	....	....	....	....	1	1	....	
Ladakh Tehsil.	Dogri ..	51	51	....	....	....	....	....	....	....	1	1	....	
	Kashmiri ..	57	49	8	....	....	....	1	1	....	....	....	....	
	Gojari ..	....	....	....	....	....	....	....	....	....	....	....	....	
	Western Pahari ..	....	....	....	....	....	....	....	....	....	....	....	....	
	Panjabi ..	35	29	6	....	....	....	....	....	....	....	....	....	
	Chabbali ..	....	....	....	....	....	....	....	....	....	....	....	....	
	Pothwari ..	1	1	....	....	....	....	....	....	....	....	....	....	
	Balti ..	481	268	213	....	....	....	....	....	....	....	....	....	
	Ladakhi ..	33,353	16,667	16,686	....	....	....	....	....	....	11	7	4	
	Shina ..	....	....	....	....	....	....	....	....	....	....	....	....	
Skardu Tehsil.	Dogri ..	4	4	....	....	....	....	....	....	....	....	....	....	
	Kashmiri ..	1,150	694	456	....	....	....	10	10	....	....	....	....	
	Gojari ..	....	....	....	....	....	....	....	....	....	....	....	....	
	Western Pahari ..	....	....	....	....	....	....	....	....	....	....	....	....	
	Panjabi ..	97	60	37	....	....	....	....	....	....	1	1	....	
	Chabbali ..	....	....	....	....	....	....	....	....	....	....	....	....	
	Pothwari ..	....	....	....	....	....	....	....	....	....	....	....	....	

District	Tehsil / Ilaqa	Language													
		Balti	...	102,351	51,159	51,192	....	....	....	7	7	....	6	4	2
		Ladakhi	...	35	35	....	....	....	....	....	....	....	....	....	....
		Shina	...	3,267	2,239	1,028	....	....	....	....	....	....	....	....	....
Gilgit District.	Frontier Ilaqas.	Dogri	...	196	192	4	....	....	....	2	2	....	1	1	....
		Kashmiri	...	54	46	8	....	....	....	1	1	....	....	....	....
		Gojari	...	535	351	184	....	....	....	1	1	....	....	....	....
		Western Pahari	...	....	....	....	....	....	....	....	....	....	....	....	....
		Panjabi	...	1,987	1,082	905	25	....	25	....	....	....	5	5	....
		Chabhali	...	....	....	....	....	....	....	....	....	....	....	....	....
		Pothwari	...	....	....	....	....	....	....	....	....	....	....	....	....
		Balti	...	53	31	22	....	....	....	....	....	....	....	....	....
		Ladakhi	...	183	80	103	....	....	....	....	....	....	....	....	....
		Shina	...	24,961	12,511	12,450	....	....	....	6	6	....	....	....	....
	Gilgit Tehsil.	Dogri	...	469	431	38	....	....	....	69	62	7	3	3	....
		Kashmiri	...	246	207	39	2	2	....	38	33	5	....	....	....
		Gojari	...	445	247	198	....	....	....	1	1	....	....	....	....
		Western Pahari	...	127	127	....	33	33	....	24	24	....	....	....	....
		Panjabi	...	393	295	98	10	8	2	....	....	....	7	7	....
		Chabhali	...	....	....	....	....	....	....	....	....	....	....	....	....
		Pothwari	...	....	....	....	....	....	....	....	....	....	....	....	....
		Balti	...	215	195	20	....	....	....	55	55	....	5	5	....
		Ladakhi	...	7	7	....	....	....	....	....	....	....	....	....	....
		Shina	...	28,111	14,699	13,412	4	4	....	374	360	14	20	16	4

TABLE XV.—Part II (B).

Tri and Poly-lingualism.

Jammu and Kashmir Census 1931.

Taluk.	Mother-tongue.	No. of Persons speaking Mother-tongue.			No. of Persons speaking Subsidiary Languages. Dogri. (B)			Panjabi (C)			Kashmiri. (D)			Remarks.
		Persons.	Males.	Females.	Persons.	Males.	Females.	Persons.	Males.	Females.	Persons.	Males.	Females.	
Jammu and Kashmir State.	Dogri ..	549,917	293,986	255,931	....	....	....	287	180	107	287	180	107	180 males and 107 females speak three languages.
	Kashmiri ..	1,370,763	742,016	628,747	97	48	49	97	48	49	....	....	....	48 males and 49 females speak three languages.
	Gojari ..	317,762	170,528	147,234	16	11	5	2,207	2,198	9	2,219	2,207	12	2208 males and 13 females speak 3 languages. 1 male and 1 female speak Dogri and Panjabi, 10 males and 4 females Dogri and Kashmiri and 2197males and 8 females speak Panjabi and Kashmiri as their subsidiary languages.
	Pahari ..	595,783	308,010	287,773	133	73	60	758	287	471	705	292	413	326 males and 472 females speak 3 languages, 34 males and 59 females speak Dogri and Panjabi, 39 males and 1 female speak Dogri and Kashmiri and 253 males and 412 females speak Panjabi and Kashmiri as subsidiary languages.
	Panjabi ..	329,433	174,659	154,774	79	75	4	....	....	....	79	75	4	75 males and 4 females speak three languages.
	Chabhali ..	44,460	23,129	21,331	1	1	....	....	....	....	1	1	....	One male speaks 3 languages.
	Pothwari ..	51,062	26,869	24,193	3	2	1	4	3	1	1	1	....	3 males and 1 female speak three languages, 2 males and 1 female speak Dogri and Panjabi and 1 male speaks Panjabi and Kashmiri as their Subsidiary languages.
	Balti ..	137,914	68,467	69,447	....	....	....	7	3	4	7	3	4	3 males and 4 females speak three languages.
	Ladakhi ..	41,418	20,546	20,872	....	....	....	4	4	....	4	4	....	4 males speak 3 languages.
	Shina ..	63,918	33,379	30,539	....	....	....	2	2	....	2	2	....	2 males speak 3 languages.
Jammu Province ..	Dogri ..	547,534	292,139	255,395	....	....	....	239	143	96	239	143	96	143 males and 96 females speaking 3 languages.
	Kashmiri ..	121,431	66,290	55,141	91	46	45	91	46	45	....	....	....	46 males and 45 females speaking three languages.

	Jammu Province ..	Gojari ..	208,933	111,482	97,451	15	10	5	10	5	5	21	13	8	14 males (1 B+C, 9 B+D, 4 C+D speaking 3 languages) 9 females (1 B+C, 4 C+D 4 B+D speaking 3 languages.)
		Pahari ..	417,363	213,471	203,892	124	64	60	86	27	59	42	41	1	66 males (25 B+C, 39 B+D, 2 C+D speaking 3 languages) 60 females (59 B+C, and 1 B+D speaking 3 languages.)
		Panjabi ..	306,835	162,374	141,461	17	13	4	....	....	....	17	13	4	13 males and 4 females speaking 3 languages.
		Chabhali ..	44,460	23,129	21,331	1	1	....	....	....	....	1	1	....	One male speaking 3 languages.
		Pothwari ..	51,035	26,843	24,192	3	2	1	4	3	1	1	1	....	3 males (2 B+C and 1 C+D) and 1 female speaking 3 languages.
Jammu District.	*Jammu Tehsil.*	Dogri ..	88,143	49,730	38,413	....	....	....	105	104	1	105	104	1	104 males and 1 female speaking 3 languages.
		Kashmiri ..	2,751	2,418	333	22	18	4	22	18	4	....	....	....	18 males and 4 females speaking 3 languages.
		Gojari ..	17,426	9,405	8,021	6	5	1	2	1	1	4	4	....	5 males (1 B+C and 4 B+D) and 1 female speaking 3 languages).
		Panjabi ..	21,293	12,405	8,888	10	8	2	....	....	....	10	8	2	8 males and 2 females speaking 3 languages.
		Chabhali ..	168	166	2	1	1	....	....	....	....	1	1	....	One person speaking 3 languages.
		Pothwari ..	63	53	10	2	1	1	2	1	1	....	....	....	One male and one female speaking 3 languages.
	Ranbirsinghpura „ ..	Panjabi ..	47,680	25,303	22,377	1	1	....	....	....	....	1	1	....	One person speaking 3 languages.
	Samba „ ..	....	....	....	....	....	....	....	....	....	....	....	....	....	
	Akhnoor „ ..	....	....	....	....	....	....	....	....	....	....	....	....	....	
Kathua District.	*Kathua Tehsil* ..	Kashmiri ..	117	100	17	6	2	4	6	2	4	....	....	....	2 males and 4 females speaking three languages.
		Pahari ..	330	253	77	4	....	4	4	....	4	....	....	....	4 females speaking 3 languages.
	Basohli Tehsil ..	....	....	....	....	....	....	....	....	....	....	....	....	....	
	Jasmergarh Tehsil ..	....	....	....	....	....	....	....	....	....	....	....	....	....	
Udhampur District.	*Udhampur Tehsil* ..	Kashmiri ..	2,590	1,684	906	1	1	....	1	1	....	....	....	....	One Male speaking 3 languages.
		Pahari ..	3,913	2,073	1,840	12	11	1	1	1	....	11	10	1	11 males (10B+D and 1B+C) and 1 female speaking 3 languages.
	Ramnagar Tehsil ..	....	....	....	....	....	....	....	....	....	....	....	....	....	
	Ramban Tehsil ..	Dogri ..	839	552	287	....	....	....	1	1	....	1	1	....	1 male speaking 3 languages.
		Kashmiri ..	31,936	17,151	14,785	8	8	....	8	8	....	....	....	....	8 males „ „ „
		Gojari ..	7,864	4,106	3,758	....	....	....	4	4	....	4	4	....	4 „ „ „ „
		Panjabi ..	175	119	56	4	4	....	....	....	....	4	4	....	4 „ „ „ „
		Pahari ..	2,114	1,002	1,022	3	3	....	3	3	....	....	....	....	3 „ „ „ „

TABLE XV.—Part II (B).

Tri and Poly-lingualism.

Jammu and Kashmir Census 1931.

District	Taluk	Mother-tongue	No. of Persons speaking Mother-tongue: Persons	Males	Females	No. of Persons speaking Subsidiary Languages: Dogri (B): Persons	Males	Females	Panjabi (C): Persons	Males	Females	Kashmiri (D): Persons	Males	Females	Remarks
Udhampur District	Kishtwar Tehsil	Dogri	343	260	83	....	....	....	8	8	....	8	8	....	8 males speaking 3 languages.
		Kashmiri	26,740	14,229	12,511	1	1	....	1	1	....	....	....	....	1 male " " "
		Gojari	7,608	3,907	3,701	1	....	1	....	....	....	1	....	1	1 female " " "
	Bhalrawah Tehsil	Dogri	2,628	1,534	1,094	....	....	....	124	29	95	124	29	95	29 males and 95 females speaking three languages.
		Kashmiri	13,476	6,963	6,513	39	5	34	39	5	34	....	....	....	5 males and 34 females speaking three languages.
		Pahari	313	148	165	75	20	55	73	18	55	2	2	....	20 males (18B+C and 2B+D) and 55 females speaking three languages.
		Panjabi	286	179	107	2	....	2	....	....	....	2	....	2	2 females speaking 3 languages.
Riasi District	Riasi Tehsil	Dogri	42,460	22,267	20.193	....	....	....	1	1	....	1	1	....	1 male " " "
		Kashmiri	18,876	9,935	8,941	11	8	3	11	8	3	....	....	....	8 males and 3 females speaking 3 languages.
		Pahari	13,874	7,177	6,697	29	29	....	2	2	....	27	27	....	29 males (2B+C and 27B+D) speaking three languages.
	Rampur Rajouri Tehsil	Pothwari	5	4	1	....	....	....	1	1	....	1	1	....	1 male speaking three languages.
Mirpur District	Mirpur Tehsil	....	....	....	....	....	....	....	....	....	....	....	....	....	
	Kotli Tehsil	Kashmiri	653	647	6	3	3	....	3	3	....	....	....	....	3 males " " "
		Pothwari	46,731	24,540	22,191	1	1	....	1	1	....	....	....	....	1 male " " "
	Bhimber Tehsil	....	....	....	....	....	....	....	....	....	....	....	....	....	
Poonch Jagir	Bagh Tehsil	....	....	....	....	....	....	....	....	....	....	....	....	....	
	Sadhnoti Tehsil	Pahari	99,309	48,636	50,673	....	....	....	2	2	....	2	2	....	2 males " " "
	Haveli Tehsil	Gojari	26,395	14,088	12,307	....	....	....	4	....	4	4	....	4	4 females " " "
		Pahari	56,321	29,777	26,544	1	1	....	1	1	....	....	....	....	1 male " " "
	Mainder Tehsil	....	....	....	....	....	....	....	....	....	....	....	....	....	

Chenani Jagir—														
Chenani	Gojari	513	257	256	8	5	3	....	....	....	8	5	3	5 males and 3 females speaking three languages.
Kashmir Province	Dogri	1,662	1,168	494	....	....	....	42	37	5	42	37	5	37 males and 5 females speak 3 languages.
	Kashmiri	1,247,497	674,534	572,963	1	1	....	1	1	....	....	....	....	1 male speaks 3 languages.
	Gojari	107,849	58,448	49,401	1	1	....	2,197	2,193	4	2,198	2,194	4	2,194 males (1 B+D, 2,193 C+D) and 4 females (C+D) speak 3 languages.
	Western Pahari	178,292	94,411	83,881	....	....	....	663	251	412	663	251	412	251 males and 412 females speak 3 languages.
	Panjabi	20,056	10,796	9,260	62	62	....	....	....	....	62	62	....	62 males speak 3 languages.
	Chabhali	....	....	....	....	....	....	....	....	....	....	....	....	
	Pothwari	26	25	1	....	....	....	....	....	....	....	....	....	
	Balti	623	379	244	....	....	....	7	3	4	7	3	4	3 males and 4 females speak 3 languages.
	Ladakhi	45	36	9	....	....	....	4	4	....	4	4	....	4 males speak 3 languages.
	Shina	33	26	7	....	....	....	....	....	....	....	....	....	
Kashmir South. *Kulgam Tehsil*	Dogri	593	371	222	....	....	....	30	26	4	30	26	4	26 males and 4 females speak 3 languages.
	Kashmiri	141,967	75,163	66,804	....	....	....	....	....	....	....	....	....	
	Gojari	3,099	1,604	1,495	1	1	....	....	....	....	1	1	....	1 male speaks 3 languages.
	Western Pahari	348	187	161	....	....	....	2	....	2	2	....	2	2 females speak 3 languages.
	Panjabi	132	77	55	....	....	....	....	....	....	....	....	....	
	Chabhali	....	....	....	....	....	....	....	....	....	....	....	....	
	Pothwari	....	....	....	....	....	....	....	....	....	....	....	....	
	Balti	3	2	1	....	....	....	....	....	....	....	....	....	
	Ladakhi	....	....	....	....	....	....	....	....	....	....	....	....	
	Shina	....	....	....	....	....	....	....	....	....	....	....	....	
Anantnag Tehsil.	Dogri	38	28	10	....	....	....	....	....	....	....	....	....	
	Kashmiri	173,355	94,731	78,624	....	....	....	....	....	....	....	....	....	
	Gojari	14,885	7,868	7,017	....	....	....	1	....	1	1	....	1	1 female speaks three languages.
	Western Pahari	1,783	991	792	....	....	....	3	....	3	3	....	3	3 females speak 3 languages.
	Panjabi	1,691	875	816	1	1	....	....	....	....	1	1	....	1 male speaks 3 languages,
	Chabhali	....	....	....	....	....	....	....	....	....	....	....	....	
	Pothwari	....	....	....	....	....	....	....	....	....	....	....	....	
	Balti	....	....	....	....	....	....	....	....	....	....	....	....	
	Ladakhi	1	1	....	....	....	....	....	....	....	....	....	....	
	Shina	....	....	....	....	....	....	....	....	....	....	....	....	

TABLE XV.—Part II (B).

Tri and Poly-lingualism.

Jammu and Kashmir Census 1931.

Taluk.	Mother-tongue.	No. of Persons speaking Mother-tongue. Persons.	Males.	Females.	No. of Persons speaking Subsidiary Languages. Dogri. Persons.	Males.	Females.	Panjabi. Persons.	Males.	Females.	Kashmiri. Persons.	Males.	Females.	Remarks.
Kashmir South. Awantipura Tehsil	Dogri	10	7	3	....	....	....	8	7	1	8	7	1	7 males and 1 female speak 3 languages.
	Kashmiri	141,037	77,366	63,671	....	....	....	....	....	....	....	....	....	
	Gojari	5,767	3,254	2,513	....	....	....	2,189	2,189	....	2,189	2,180	....	2189 males speak 3 languages.
	Western Pahari	1,349	613	736	....	....	....	627	242	385	627	242	385	242 males and 385 females speak 3 languages.
	Panjabi	1,580	909	671	45	54	....	....	....	....	54	54	....	54 males speak 3 languages.
	Chabhali	....	....	....	....	....	....	....	....	....	....	....	....	
	Pothwari	....	....	....	....	....	....	....	....	....	....	....	....	
	Balti	40	20	20	....	....	....	....	....	....	....	....	....	
	Ladakhi	2	2	....	....	....	....	....	....	....	....	....	....	
	Shina	....	....	....	....	....	....	....	....	....	....	....	....	
Khas Tehsil / Srinagar Tehsil	Dogri	429	367	62	....	....	....	1	1	....	1	1	....	1 male speaks 3 languages.
	Kashmiri	97,527	53,088	44,439	....	....	....	....	....	....	....	....	....	
	Gojari	7,688	4,146	3,542	....	....	....	1	1	....	1	1	....	1 male speaks 3 languages.
	Western Pahari	508	274	234	....	....	....	....	....	....	....	....	....	
	Panjabi	577	318	229	....	....	....	....	....	....	....	....	....	
	Chabhali	....	....	....	....	....	....	....	....	....	....	....	....	
	Pothwari	....	....	....	....	....	....	....	....	....	....	....	....	
	Balti	405	247	158	....	....	....	....	....	....	....	....	....	
	Ladakhi	....	....	....	....	....	....	....	....	....	....	....	....	
	Shina	....	....	....	....	....	....	....	....	....	....	....	....	
Srinagar Municipality	Dogri	332	230	102	....	....	....	....	....	....	....	....	....	1 male speaks three languages.
	Kashmiri	169,684	92,270	77,414	1	1	....	1	1	....	....	....	....	

Kashmir South.	Srinagar Municipality	Gojari	19	19	....	....	....	....	....	....	....	....	....	....	
		Western Pahari	190	145	45	....	....	....	19	....	19	19	....	19	19 females speak 3 languages.
		Panjabi	2,276	1,525	751	....	....	....	....	....	....	....	....	....	
		Chabhali	....	....	....	....	....	....	....	....	....	....	....	....	
		Pothwari	....	....	....	....	....	....	....	....	....	....	....	....	
		Balti	118	77	41	....	....	....	5	3	2	5	3	2	3 males and 2 females speak 3 languages.
		Ladakhi	38	29	9	....	....	....	4	4	....	4	4	....	4 males speak 3 languages.
		Shina	14	14	....	....	....	....	....	....	....	....	....	....	
Kashmir North.	Sri Pratapsinghpura Tehsil	Dogri	63	43	20	....	....	....	....	....	....	....	....	....	
		Kashmiri	156,013	84,867	71,146	....	....	....	....	....	....	....	....	....	
		Gojari	4,397	2,417	1,980	....	....	....	....	....	....	....	....	....	
		Western Pahari	443	254	189	....	....	....	....	....	....	....	....	....	
		Panjabi	1,899	994	905	....	....	....	....	....	....	....	....	....	
		Chabhali	....	....	....	....	....	....	....	....	....	....	....	....	
		Pothwari	....	....	....	....	....	....	....	....	....	....	....	....	
		Balti	5	3	2	....	....	....	....	....	....	....	....	....	
		Ladakhi	2	2	....	....	....	....	....	....	....	....	....	....	
		Shina	3	3	....	....	....	....	....	....	....	....	....	....	
	Baramulla Tehsil	Dogri	52	30	22	....	....	....	....	....	....	....	....	....	
		Kashmiri	142,178	76,776	65,402	....	....	....	....	....	....	....	....	....	
		Gojari	....	....	....	....	....	....	....	....	....	....	....	....	
		Western Pahari	815	447	368	....	....	....	....	....	....	....	....	....	
		Panjabi	3,239	1,808	1,431	....	....	....	....	....	....	....	....	....	
		Chabhali	....	....	....	....	....	....	....	....	....	....	....	....	
		Pothwari	....	....	....	....	....	....	....	....	....	....	....	....	
		Balti	9	5	4	....	....	....	2	....	2	2	....	2	2 females speak 3 languages.
		Ladakhi	....	....	....	....	....	....	....	....	....	....	....	....	
		Shina	6	2	4	....	....	....	....	....	....	....	....	....	
	Uttarmachhipura Tehsil	Dogri	13	9	4	....	....	....	2	2	....	2	2	....	2 males speak 3 languages.
		Kashmiri	204,392	108,632	95,760	....	....	....	....	....	....	....	....	....	
		Gojari	21,566	11,937	9,629	....	....	....	6	3	3	6	3	3	3 males and 3 females speak 3 languages.
		Western Pahari	9,008	4,741	4,267	....	....	....	8	5	3	8	5	3	5 males and 3 females speak three languages.

TABLE XV.—PART II (B).

TRI AND POLY-LINGUALISM.

Jammu and Kashmir Census 1931.

District	Taluk.	Mother-tongue.	No. of Persons speaking Mother-tongue. Persons.	Males.	Females.	No. of Persons speaking Subsidiary Languages. Dogri. Persons.	Dogri. Males.	Dogri. Females.	Panjabi. Persons.	Panjabi. Males.	Panjabi. Females.	Kashmiri. Persons.	Kashmiri. Males.	Kashmiri. Females.	Remarks.
Kashmir North.	Uttarmachhipura Tehsil	Panjabi	4,897	2,285	2,612	5	5	....	....	....	....	5	5	....	5 males speak three languages.
		Chabhali	....	....	....	....	....	....	....	....	....	....	....	....	
		Pothwari	....	....	....	....	....	....	....	....	....	....	....	....	
		Balti	38	21	17	....	....	....	....	....	....	....	....	....	
		Ladakhi	1	1	....	....	....	....	....	....	....	....	....	....	
		Shina	....	....	....	....	....	....	....	....	....	....	....	....	
Muzaffarabad District.	Uri Tehsil	Dogri	28	22	6	....	....	....	....	....	....	....	....	....	
		Kashmiri	13,255	7,242	6,013	....	....	....	....	....	....	....	....	....	
		Gojari	18,026	9,612	8,414	....	....	....	....	....	....	....	....	....	
		Western Pahari	39,086	20,717	18,369	....	....	....	3	3	....	3	3	....	3 males speak 3 languages.
		Panjabi	986	542	444	....	....	....	....	....	....	....	....	....	
		Chabhali	....	....	....	....	....	....	....	....	....	....	....	....	
		Pothwari	14	14	....	....	....	....	....	....	....	....	....	....	
		Balti	1	1	....	....	....	....	....	....	....	....	....	....	
		Ladakhi	....	....	....	....	....	....	....	....	....	....	....	....	
		Shina	....	....	....	....	....	....	....	....	....	....	....	....	1 male speaks 3 languages.
	Muzaffarabad Tehsil	Dogri	100	58	42	....	....	....	1	1	....	1	1	....	
		Kashmiri	2,747	1,632	1,115	....	....	....	....	....	....	....	....	....	
		Gojari	24,108	12,952	11,156	....	....	....	....	....	....	....	....	....	
		Western Pahari	82,886	43,596	39,290	....	....	....	....	....	....	....	....	....	2 males speak 3 languages.
		Panjabi	2,762	1,421	1,341	2	2	....	....	....	....	2	2	....	
		Chabhali	....	....	....	....	....	....	....	....	....	....	....	....	

MUZAFFARABAD DISTRICT.	*Muzaffarabad Tehsil* ..	Pothwari ..	12	11	1	....	....	....	....	....	....	....	....	....	
		Balti ..	3	2	1	....	....	....	....	....	....	....	....	....	
		Ladakhi ..	1	1	....	....	....	....	....	....	....	....	....	....	
		Shina ..	6	4	2	....	....	....	....	....	....	....	....	....	
	Karnah Tehsil ..	Dogri ..	4	3	1	....	....	....	....	....	....	....	....	....	
		Kashmiri ..	5,342	2,767	2,575	....	....	....	....	....	....	....	....	....	
		Gojari ..	5,812	3,132	2,680	....	....	....	....	....	....	....	....	....	
		Western Pahari ..	41,876	22,446	19,430	....	....	....	1	1	....	1	1	....	1 male speaks 3 languages.
		Panjabi ..	17	12	5	....	....	....	....	....	....	....	....	....	
		Chabhali ..	....	....	....	....	....	....	....	....	....	....	....	....	
		Pothwari ..	....	....	....	....	....	....	....	....	....	....	....	....	
		Balti ..	1	1	....	....	....	....	....	....	....	....	....	....	
		Ladakhi ..	....	....	....	....	....	....	....	....	....	....	....	....	
		Shina ..	4	3	1	....	....	....	....	....	....	....	....	....	
	Frontier Districts ..	Dogri ..	721	679	42	....	....	....	6	....	6	6	....	6	6 females speak 3 languages.
		Kashmiri ..	1,835	1,192	643	5	1	4	5	1	4	....	....	....	1 male and 4 females speak 3 languages.
		Gojari ..	980	598	382	....	....	....	....	....	....	....	....	....	
		Western Pahari ..	128	128	....	9	9	....	9	9	....	....	....	....	9 males speak 3 languages.
		Panjabi ..	2,542	1,489	1,053	....	....	....	....	....	....	....	....	....	
		Chabhali ..	....	....	....	....	....	....	....	....	....	....	....	....	
		Pathwari ..	1	1	....	....	....	....	....	....	....	....	....	....	
		Balti ..	137,106	67,961	69,145	....	....	....	....	....	....	....	....	....	
		Ladakhi ..	40,901	20,276	20,625	....	....	....	....	....	....	....	....	....	
		Shina ..	63,885	33,353	30,532	....	....	....	2	2	....	2	2	....	2 males speak 3 languages.
LADAKH DISTRICT.	*Kargil Tehsil* ..	Dogri ..	1	1	....	....	....	....	....	....	....	....	....	....	
		Kashmiri ..	328	196	132	....	....	....	....	....	....	....	....	....	
		Gojari ..	....	....	....	....	....	....	....	....	....	....	....	....	
		Western Pahari ..	1	1	....	....	....	....	....	....	....	....	....	....	
		Panjabi ..	30	23	7	....	....	....	....	....	....	....	....	....	
		Chabhali ..	....	....	....	....	....	....	....	....	....	....	....	....	
		Pothwari ..	....	....	....	....	....	....	....	....	....	....	....	....	
		Balti ..	34,006	16,308	17,698	....	....	....	....	....	....	....	....	....	
		Ladakhi ..	7,323	3,487	3,836	....	....	....	....	....	....	....	....	....	
		Shina ..	7,546	3,904	3,642	....	....	....	....	....	....	....	....	....	

TABLE XV.—PART II (B).

TRI AND POLY-LINGUALISM.

Jammu and Kashmir Census 1931.

District	Taluk.	Mother-tongue.	No. of Persons speaking Mother-tongue. Persons.	Males.	Females.	Dogri. Persons.	Dogri. Males.	Dogri. Females.	Panjabi. Persons.	Panjabi. Males.	Panjabi. Females.	Kashmiri. Persons.	Kashmiri. Males.	Kashmiri. Females.	Remarks.
Ladakh District	Ladakh Tehsil	Dogri	51	51	....	....	....	....	....	....	....	....	....	....	
		Kashmiri	57	49	8	....	....	....	....	....	....	....	....	....	
		Gojari	....	....	....	....	....	....	....	....	....	....	....	....	
		Western Pahari	....	....	....	....	....	....	....	....	....	....	....	....	
		Panjabi	35	29	6	....	....	....	....	....	....	....	....	....	
		Chabhali	....	....	....	....	....	....	....	....	....	....	....	....	
		Pothwari	1	1	....	....	....	....	....	....	....	....	....	....	
		Balti	481	268	213	....	....	....	....	....	....	....	....	....	
		Ladakhi	33,353	16,667	16,686	....	....	....	....	....	....	....	....	....	
		Shina	....	....	....	....	....	....	....	....	....	....	....	....	
	Skardu Tehsil	Dogri	4	4	....	....	....	....	....	....	....	....	....	....	
		Kashmiri	1,150	694	456	....	....	....	....	....	....	....	....	....	
		Gojari	....	....	....	....	....	....	....	....	....	....	....	....	
		Western Pahari	....	....	....	....	....	....	....	....	....	....	....	....	
		Panjabi	97	60	37	....	....	....	....	....	....	....	....	....	
		Chabhali	....	....	....	....	....	....	....	....	....	....	....	....	
		Pothwari	....	....	....	....	....	....	....	....	....	....	....	....	
		Balti	102,351	51,159	51,192	....	....	....	....	....	....	....	....	....	
		Ladakhi	35	35	....	....	....	....	....	....	....	....	....	....	
		Shina	3,267	2,239	1,028	....	....	....	....	....	....	....	....	....	
	Frontier Ilaqas	Dogri	196	192	4	....	....	....	....	....	....	....	....	....	
		Kashmiri	54	46	8	....	....	....	....	....	....	....	....	....	

Gilgit District	Frontier Ilaqas	Gojari	535	351	184	....	....	....	....	....	....	....	....	....	
		Western Pahari	....	....	....	....	....	....	....	....	....	....	....	....	
		Panjabi	1,987	1,082	905	....	....	....	....	....	....	....	....	....	
		Chabhali	....	....	....	....	....	....	....	....	....	....	....	....	
		Pothwari	....	....	....	....	....	....	....	....	....	....	....	....	
		Balti	53	31	22	....	....	....	....	....	....	....	....	....	
		Ladakhi	183	80	103	....	....	....	....	....	....	....	....	....	
		Shina	21,961	12,511	12,450	....	....	....	....	....	....	....	....	....	
	Gilgit Tehsil	Dogri	469	431	38	....	....	....	6	....	6	6	....	6	6 females speak 3 languages.
		Kashmiri	246	207	39	5	1	4	5	1	4	....	....	....	1 male and 4 females speak 3 languages.
		Gojari	445	247	198	....	....	....	....	....	....	....	....	....	
		Western Pahari	127	127	....	9	9	....	9	9	....	....	....	....	9 males speak 3 languages.
		Panjabi	393	295	98	....	....	....	....	....	....	....	....	....	
		Chabhali	....	....	....	....	....	....	....	....	....	....	....	....	
		Pothwari	....	....	....	....	....	....	....	....	....	....	....	....	
		Balti	215	195	20	....	....	....	....	....	....	....	....	....	
		Ladakhi	7	7	....	....	....	....	....	....	....	....	....	....	
		Shina	28,111	14,699	13,112	....	....	....	2	2	....	2	2	..	2 males speak 3 languages.

TABLE XVI.

POPULATION BY RELIGION.

Jammu and Kashmir Census 1931.

1. The details of Christians by Sects have not been given on the fly-leaf as a separate Provincial Table of Christian Sects has been prepared (*vide* State Table VIII at the end of this volume).

TABLE

Population

Jammu and Kashmir

District, Ilaqa or Jagir.	Total Population.			Brahmanic.		
	Persons.	Males.	Females.	Persons.	Males.	Females.
1	2	3	4	5	6	7
Jammu & Kashmir State ..	**36,46,243**	**19,38,338**	**17,07,905**	**6,42,273**	**3,43,349**	**2,98,924**
I. Jammu Province ..	**17,88,441**	**9,42,815**	**8,45,626**	**5,71,870**	**3,03,364**	**2,68,506**
(a) *Total Districts* ..	*13,90,132*	*7,38,267*	*6,51,865*	*5,37,638*	*2,85,436*	*2,52,202*
1. Jammu (including City) ..	3,75,240	2,05,719	1,69,521	1,73,346	94,683	78,663
2. Kathua ..	1,61,232	85,993	75,239	1,04,667	55,242	49,425
3. Udhampur (including Bhadrawah) ..	2,73,668	1,43,514	1,30,154	1,38,122	71,558	66,564
4. Riasi ..	2,35,245	1,24,210	1,11,035	71,401	37,537	33,864
5. Mirpur ..	3,44,747	1,78,831	1,65,916	50,102	26,416	23,686
(b) *Total Jagirs* ..	*3,98,309*	*2,04,548*	*1,93,761*	*34,232*	*17,928*	*16,304*
6. Chenani Jagir ..	10,925	5,930	4,995	9.042	4,868	4,174
7. Poonch Jagir ..	3,87,384	1,98,618	1,88,766	25,190	13,060	12,130
II. Kashmir Province ..	**15,69,218**	**8,47,022**	**7,22,196**	**68,827**	**38,551**	**30,276**
8. Baramulla (including Langet) Kashmir North ..	5,59,828	3,01,397	2,58,431	10,639	6,243	4,396
9. Srinagar (including City) Kashmir South	7,71,943	4,19,190	3,52,753	53,759	29,660	24,099
10. Muzaffarabad ..	2,37,447	1,26,435	1,11,012	4,429	2,648	1,781
III. Frontier Districts ..	**2,88,584**	**1,48,501**	**1,40,083**	**1,576**	**1,434**	**142**
11. Ladakh ..	1,92,138	96,259	95,879	292	245	47
12. Gilgit ..	31,902	17,752	14,150	974	900	74
13. Frontier Ilaqas ..	64,544	34,490	30,054	310	289	21

XVI.

BY RELIGION.

Census 1931.

Hindu.						Total Hindu.			Sikh.		
Arya.			*Brahmo.*								
Persons.	Males.	Females.	Persons.	Males.	Females.	Persons.	Males.	Females.	Persons.	Males.	Females.
8	9	10	11	12	13	14	15	16	17	18	19
93,944	50,346	43,598	5	4	1	73,6,222	3,93,699	3,42,523	50,662	26,457	24,205
93,372	49,981	43,391	4	3	1	6,65,246	3,53,348	3,11,898	29,282	15,197	14,085
92,725	*49,659*	*43,066*	*4*	*3*	*1*	*6,30,367*	*3,35,098*	*2,95,269*	*17,934*	*9,420*	*8,514*
43,710	24,059	19,651	4	3	1	2,17,060	1,18,745	98,315	6,854	3,677	3,177
16,271	8,766	7,505	....	....	....	1,20,938	64,008	56,930	478	268	210
17,641	9,151	8,490	....	....	....	1,55,763	80,709	75,054	328	178	150
7,611	3,879	3,732	....	....	....	79,012	41,416	37,596	842	449	393
7,492	3,804	3,688	....	....	....	57,594	30,220	27,374	9,432	4,848	4,584
647	*322*	*325*	....	....	....	*34,879*	*18,250*	*16,629*	*11,348*	*5,777*	*5,571*
367	166	201	....	....	....	9,409	5,034	4,375	4	4	....
280	156	124	....	....	....	25,470	13,216	12,254	11,344	5,773	5,571
468	295	173	1	1	....	69,296	38,847	30,449	21,190	11,135	10,055
67	43	24	....	....	....	10,706	6,286	4,420	6,260	3,248	3,012
340	210	130	1	1	....	54,100	29,871	24,229	3,997	2,303	1,694
61	42	19	....	....	....	4,490	2,690	1,800	10,933	5,584	5,349
104	70	34	....	....	....	1,680	1,504	176	190	125	65
27	16	11	....	....	....	319	261	58	97	63	34
61	42	19	....	....	....	1,035	942	93	85	56	29
16	12	4	....	....	....	326	301	25	8	6	2

TABLE

POPULATION

Jammu and Kashmir

District, Ilaqa or Jagir.	Jain.			Buddhist.		
	Persons.	Males.	Females.	Persons.	Males.	Females.
	20	21	22	23	24	25
Jammu & Kashmir State ..	**597**	**319**	**278**	**38,724**	**19.287**	**19,437**
I. Jammu Province ..	**591**	**314**	**277**	**507**	**253**	**254**
(a) *Total Districts* ..	*588*	*313*	*275*	*507*	*253*	*254*
1. Jammu (including City) ..	578	309	269	9	4	5
2. Kathua ..	......	......	......	......	......	......
3. Udhampur (including Bhadrawah) ..	2	1	1	492	245	247
4. Riasi ..	......	......	......	6	4	2
5. Mirpur ..	8	3	5	......	......	......
(b) *Total Jagirs* ..	*3*	*1*	*2*	......	......	......
6. Chenani Jagir ..	......	......	......	......	......	......
7. Poonch Jagir ..	3	1	2	......	......	......
II. Kashmir Province ..	**3**	**3**	......	**5**	**5**	......
8. Baramulla (including Langet) Kashmir North ..	......	......	......	......	......	......
9. Srinagar (including City) Kashmir South	3	3	......	5	5	......
10. Muzaffarabad ..	......	......	......	......	......	......
III. Frontier Districts ..	**3**	**2**	**1**	**38,212**	**19,029**	**19,183**
11. Ladakh ..	......	......	......	38.212	19,029	19,183
12. Gilgit ..	3	2	1	......	......	......
13. Frontier Ilaqas ..	......	......	......	......	......	......

XVI.—(*concluded*).

BY RELIGION.

Census 1931.

Zoroastrian.			Muslim.			Christian.			Tribal.		
Persons.	Males.	Females.	Persons.	Males.	Females.	Persons.	Males.	Females.	Persons.	Males.	Females.
26	27	28	29	30	31	32	33	34	35	36	37
5	3	2	28,17,636	14,97,252	13,20,384	2,263	1,243	1,020	184	78	56
....	....	....	10,91,021	5,72,699	5,18,322	1,753	987	766	41	17	24
....	....	....	*7,39,018*	*3,92,222*	*3,46,796*	*1,677*	*944*	*733*	*41*	*17*	*24*
....	....	....	1,49,336	82,202	67,134	1,362	765	597	41	17	24
....	....	....	39,647	21,619	18,028	169	98	71	....	....	....
....	....	....	1,17,051	62,361	54,690	32	20	12	....	....	....
....	....	....	1,55,353	82,322	73,031	32	19	13	....	....	....
..	....	....	2,77,631	1,43,718	1,33,913	82	42	40	....	....	....
....	....	....	*3,52,003*	*1,80,477*	*1,71,526*	*76*	*43*	*33*	....	....	....
....	....	....	1,512	892	620	....	....	....	....	....	....
....	....	....	3,50,491	1,79,585	1,70,906	76	43	33	....	....	....
5	3	2	14,78,287	7,96,802	6,81,485	339	166	173	93	61	32
....	....	....	5,42,743	2,91,786	2,50,957	61	36	25	58	41	17
4	3	1	7,13,531	3,86,863	3,26,668	268	122	146	35	20	15
1	....	1	2,22,013	1,18,153	1,03,860	10	8	2	....	....	....
....	....	....	2,48,328	1,27,751	1,20,577	171	90	81	....	....	....
....	....	....	1,53,388	76,849	76,539	122	57	65	....	....	....
....	....	....	30,741	16,727	14,014	38	25	13	....	....	....
....	....	....	64,199	34,175	30,024	11	8	3	....	....	....

TABLE XVII.

RACE, TRIBE AND CASTE.

Jammu and Kashmir Census 1931.

TABLE XVII.

Race, Tribe and Caste.

Jammu and Kashmir Census 1931.

District, Jagir or Ilaqa.	Total.			Arain. Muslim.		Arghun. Muslim.		Arora. Hindu.		Arora. Muslim.		Arora. Sikh.		Bafinda. Muslim.		Bakkarwal. Muslim.		Balti. Muslim.	
	Persons.	Males.	Females.	Males.	Females.	Males.	Females.	Males.	Females.	Males.	Females.	Males.	Females.	Males.	Females.	Males.	Females.	Males.	Females.
1	2	3	4	5	6	7	8	9	10	11	12	13	14	15	16	17	18	19	20
Jammu and Kashmir State ..	**3,645,922**	**1,938,195**	**1,707,727**	**12,727**	**10,195**	**535**	**652**	**1,032**	**776**	**2**	**3**	**904**	**831**	**17,679**	**16,193**	**2,888**	**2,461**	**23,274**	**24,052**
I. Jammu Province, (*including Jagirs*) ..	**1,788,381**	**942,781**	**845,600**	**12,724**	**10,194**	....	....	**924**	**701**	**2**	**3**	**875**	**817**	**16,507**	**15,208**	**2,078**	**1,720**	**221**	**8**
(*a*) *Districts.*																			
1. Jammu District (*including City*) ..	375,198	205,697	169,501	8,094	6,076	....	....	701	541	2	....	182	173	572	487	216	146	19	5
2. Kathua ,, ..	161,232	85,993	75,239	1,168	925	....	....	....	....	....	....	11	7	3,487	2,814	71	38	....	....
3. Udhampur ,, (*including Bhadarwah*)	273,667	143,513	130,154	171	179	....	....	35	28	....	3	2	....	168	139	483	435	53	....
4. Riasi District ..	235,244	124,209	111,035	166	184	....	....	83	58	....	....	45	41	1,316	1,200	1,280	1,088	144	....
5. Mirpur ,, ..	344,738	178,826	165,912	3,032	2,744	....	....	75	54	....	....	601	567	5,179	4,779	20	9	....	....
(*b*) *Jagirs.*																			
6. Poonch Jagir ..	387,377	198,613	188,764	72	45	....	....	29	20	....	....	34	29	5,785	5,785	8	4	5	2
7. Chenani ,, ..	10,925	5,930	4,995	21	41	....	....	1	....	....	....	....	....	....	4	....	....	....	1
II. Kashmir Province ..	**1,568,993**	**846,934**	**722,064**	**3**	**1**	....	....	**104**	**71**	....	....	**26**	**11**	**1,172**	**985**	**810**	**741**	**156**	**142**
8. Srinagar (*including City*), (Kashmir South) ..	771,756	419,117	352,639	1	1	....	....	27	16	....	....	12	4	....	....	797	726	141	133
9. Baramulla (*including Langet*), (Kashmir North) ..	559,805	301,390	258,415	....	....	....	....	51	37	....	....	5	3	....	....	12	15	14	9
10. Muzaffarabad ..	237,437	126,427	111,010	2	....	....	....	26	18	....	....	9	4	1,172	985	1	....	1	....
III. Frontier Districts ..	**288,543**	**148,480**	**140,063**	....	....	**535**	**652**	**4**	**4**	....	....	**3**	**3**	....	....	....	....	**22,897**	**23,902**
11. Ladakh District ..	192,123	96,251	95,872	....	....	528	650	....	....	....	....	3	3	....	....	....	....	22,855	23,878
12. Gilgit ,, ..	31,886	17,746	14,140	....	....	7	2	1	....	....	....	....	....	....	....	....	....	27	10
13. Frontier Ilaqas ..	64,534	34,483	30,051	....	....	....	....	3	4	....	....	....	....	....	....	....	....	15	14

TABLE XVII.

Race, Tribe and Caste.

Jammu and Kashmir Census 1931.

District, Jagir or Ilaqa.	Banjara.		Barwala.		Basith.				Batwal.						Bawaria.		Bazigir.		Beda.	
	Muslim.		*Hindu.*		*Hindu.*		*Sikh.*		*Hindu.*		*Muslim.*		*Sikh.*		*Hindu.*		*Muslim.*		*Muslim.*	
	Males.	Females	Males.	Females.	Males.	Females.	Males.	Females.	Males.	Females.	Males.	Females.	Males.	Females.	Males.	Females.	Males.	Females.	Males.	Females.
	21	22	23	24	25	26	27	28	29	30	31	32	33	34	35	36	37	38	39	40
Jammu and Kashmir State ..	33	14	3,011	2,671	3,071	3,142	162	159	3,045	2,600	80	28	2	1	2	1	815	667	164	180
I. Jammu Province (*including Jagirs*) ..	33	14	3,011	2,671	3,071	3,142	162	159	3,045	2,600	80	28	2	1	2	1	805	659	....	....
(*a*) *Districts.*																				
1. Jammu District (*including City*) ..	17	14	2,365	2,108	109	116	....	....	2,897	2,479	37	28	2	1	2	1	223	200	....	....
2. Kathua " ..	13	....	10	5	....	....	....	....	73	57	....	....	....	....	....	....	272	200	....	....
3. Udhampur " (*including Bhadarwah*)	....	....	171	164	....	....	....	....	29	19	....	....	....	....	....	....	72	76	....	....
4. Riasi District ..	....	....	43	55	1,537	1,634	158	157	46	45	....	....	....	....	....	....	46	30	....	....
5. Mirpur " ..	3	....	392	303	1,425	1,392	4	2	....	....	....	....	....	....	....	....	192	153	....	....
(*b*) *Jagirs.*																				
6. Poonch Jagir ..	....	....	....	....	....	....	....	....	....	....	43	....	....	....	....	....	....	....	....	....
7. Chenani " ..	....	....	30	36	....	....	....	....	....	....	....	....	....	....	....	....	....	....	....	....
II. Kashmir Province ..	....	....	....	....	....	....	....	....	....	....	....	....	....	....	....	....	10	8	....	....
8. Srinagar (*including City*), (Kashmir South) ..	....	....	....	....	....	....	....	....	....	....	....	....	....	....	....	....	5	3	....	....
9. Baramulla (*including Langet*), (Kashmir North) ..	....	....	....	....	....	....	....	....	....	....	....	....	....	....	....	....	....	....	....	....
10. Muzaffarabad ..	....	....	....	....	....	....	....	....	....	....	....	....	....	....	....	....	5	5	....	....
III. Frontier Districts ..	....	....	....	....	....	....	....	....	....	....	....	....	....	....	....	....	....	....	164	180
11. Ladakh District ..	....	....	....	....	....	....	....	....	....	....	....	....	....	....	....	....	....	....	164	180
12. Gilgit " ..	....	....	....	....	....	....	....	....	....	....	....	....	....	....	....	....	....	....	....	....
13. Frontier Ilaqas ..	....	....	....	....	....	....	....	....	....	....	....	....	....	....	....	....	....	....	....	....

TABLE XVII.

Race, Tribe and Caste.

Jammu and Kashmir Census 1931.

District, Jagir or Ilaqa.	Beda.		Beldar.		Bhatti.		Bhiral.		Brahman.								Brukpa.		Budhan.	
	Buddhist.		*Muslim.*		*Muslim.*		*Muslim.*		*Kashmiri Pandit.*		*Mohyal.*		*Others.*		*Sikh.*		*Muslim.*		*Muslim.*	
	Males.	Females.	Males.	Females.	Males.	Females.	Males.	Females.	Males.	Females.	Males.	Females.	Males.	Females.	Males.	Females.	Males.	Females.	Males.	Females.
	41	42	43	44	45	46	47	48	49	50	51	52	53	54	55	56	57	58	59	60
Jammu and Kashmir State. ..	41	29	1,471	1,341	4,254	3,936	312	242	35,060	28,028	3,252	1,868	94,931	90,390	5,956	5,767	6,691	6,413	2,722	2,439
I. Jammu Province (*including Jagirs*) ..	....	....	1,471	1,341	4,254	3,986	312	242	1,281	830	3,061	1,735	94,344	89,954	5,458	5,362	....	....	2,878	2,140
(*a*) *Districts.*																				
1. Jammu District (*including City*) ..	....	....	868	800	693	662	93	102	686	322	315	271	30,626	27,199	12	10	....	....	4	3
2. Kathua " ..	....	....	600	540	....	....	189	109	6	....	354	2	16,632	18,923	1	....	....	....	....	....
3. Udhampur " (*including Bhadarwah*)	....	....	3	1	16	....	....	....	476	452	300	206	17,125	15,408	28	19	....	....	....	....
4. Riasi District ..	....	....	....	....	1,205	1,107	....	....	45	20	848	133	13,305	12,482	....	8	....	....	137	5
5. Mirpur " ..	....	....	....	....	791	873	30	31	31	4	840	725	5,973	5,677	22	46	....	....	232	300
(*b*) *Jagirs.*																				
6. Poonch Jagir ..	....	....	....	....	1,549	1,344	....	....	37	25	382	382	9,903	9,658	5,395	5,270	....	....	2,000	1,832
7. Chenani " ..	....	....	....	....	....	....	....	....	....	7	22	16	720	607	....	....	....	....	....	....
II. Kashmir Province ..	....	....	....	....	....	....	....	....	33,590	27,136	191	133	484	406	494	405	....	....	349	299
8. Srinagar (*including City*), (Kashmir South) ..	....	....	....	....	....	....	....	....	27,558	23,050	11	4	89	53	126	108	....	....	80	66
9. Baramulla (*including Langet*) (Kashmir North) ..	....	....	....	....	....	....	....	....	5,515	3,926	1	....	25	22	24	9	....	....	....	....
10. Muzaffarabad ..	....	....	....	....	....	....	....	....	517	151	179	129	370	331	344	288	....	....	269	233
III. Frontier Districts ..	41	29	....	....	....	....	....	....	189	63	....	....	103	30	4	....	6,691	6,413	....	....
11. Ladakh District ..	41	29	....	....	....	....	....	....	110	43	....	....	8	1	....	....	6,689	6,413	....	....
12. Gilgit " ..	....	....	....	....	....	....	....	....	62	19	....	....	95	29	4	....	2	....	....	....
13. Frontier Ilaqas ..	....	....	....	....	....	....	....	....	8	....	....	....	....	....	....	....	....	....	....	....

TABLE XVII.

Race, Tribe and Caste.

Jammu and Kashmir Census 1931.

District, Jagir or Ilaqa.	Chamar.				Changar.		Chhimba.				Chuhra.						Derwesh.		Darzi.	
	Hindu.		*Sikh.*		*Muslim.*		*Hindu.*		*Sikh.*		*Hindu.*		*Muslim.*		*Sikh.*		*Muslim.*		*Hindu.*	
	Males.	Females.	Males.	Females.	Males.	Females.	Males.	Females.	Males.	Females.	Males.	Females.	Males.	Females.	Males.	Females.	Males.	Females.	Males.	Females.
	61	62	63	64	65	66	67	68	69	70	71	72	73	74	75	76	77	78	79	80
Jammu and Kashmir State ..	21,672	19,517	20	11	103	72	122	123	1	....	846	761	1,761	1,618	....	....	1,096	889	14	14
I. Jammu Province (*including Jagirs*) ..	21,648	19,502	20	11	64	54	122	123	1	....	834	754	1,761	1,618	....	....	1,032	801	14	14
(*a*) *Districts.*																				
1. Jammu District (*including City*) ..	8,488	7,246	5	3	....	....	40	46	....	....	123	102	266	210	....	....	466	420	....	....
2. Kathua " ..	4,084	3,502	13	7	64	50	6	7	....	....	16	11	3	....	....	....	235	202	....	....
3. Udhampur " (*including Bhadarwah*)	3,225	3,001	....	....	....	....	32	13	....	....	2	1	35	....	....	....	25	35	14	14
4. Riasi District ..	2,628	2,461	....	....	....	4	8	2	....	....	14	12	632	701	....	....	176	24	....	....
5. Mirpur " ..	2,955	3,059	2	1	....	....	36	55	1	....	22	18	536	508	....	....	31	14	....	....
(*b*) *Jagirs.*																				
6. Poonch Jagir ..	98	87	....	....	....	....	....	....	....	....	655	609	250	164	....	....	99	106	....	....
7. Chenani " ..	170	146	....	....	....	....	....	....	....	....	2	1	39	35	....	....	....	....	....	....
II. Kashmir Province ..	24	15	....	....	39	18	....	....	....	....	12	7	....	....	....	....	....	....	....	....
8. Srinagar (*including City*), (Kashmir South) ..	24	15	....	....	....	....	....	....	....	....	12	7	....	....	....	....	....	....	....	....
9. Baramulla (*including Langet*), (Kashmir North) ..	....	....	....	....	....	....	....	....	....	....	....	....	....	....	....	....	....	....	....	....
10. Muzaffarabad ..	....	....	....	....	39	18	....	....	....	....	....	....	....	....	....	....	....	....	....	....
III. Frontier Districts ..	....	....	....	....	....	....	....	....	....	....	....	....	....	....	....	....	64	88	....	....
11. Ladakh District ..	....	....	....	....	....	....	....	....	....	....	....	....	....	....	....	....	64	88	....	....
12. Gilgit " ..	....	....	....	....	....	....	....	....	....	....	....	....	....	....	....	....	....	....	....	....
13. Frontier Ilaqas ..	....	....	....	....	....	....	....	....	....	....	....	....	....	....	....	....	....	....	....	....

TABLE XVII.

RACE, TRIBE AND CASTE.

Jammu and Kashmir Census 1931.

District, Jagir or Ilaqa.	DARZI.		DHIAR.		DHOBI.		DHUND.		DOMAL.		DOOM.				DOSALI.		GADDI.			
	Muslim.		*Hindu.*		*Muslim.*		*Muslim.*		*Muslim.*		*Hindu.*		*Sikh.*		*Hindu.*		*Hindu.*		*Muslim.*	
	Males.	Females.	Males.	Females.	Males.	Females.	Males.	Females.	Males.	Females.	Males.	Females.	Males.	Females.	Males.	Females.	Males.	Females.	Males.	Females.
	81	82	83	84	85	86	87	88	89	90	91	92	93	94	95	96	97	98	99	100
Jammu and Kashmir State ..	1,251	1,142	1,555	1,610	2,818	2,320	8,839	8,684	3,301	3,055	18,400	15,929	6	6	76	70	5,599	5,742	56	20
I. Jammu Province *(including Jagirs)* ..	1,235	1,130	1,555	1,610	2,697	2,165	6,015	6,139	3,301	3,055	18,400	15,929	6	6	76	70	5,599	5,742	56	17
(a) *Districts.*																				
1. Jammu District *(including City)* ..	99	76	....	....	1,499	1,265	3	2	27	5	5,865	4,850	5	6	44	88	23	....	1	....
2. Kathua " ..	57	33	....	....	528	386	....	....	....	....	4,886	4,065	....	....	10	14	1,978	2,061	25	2
3. Udhampur " *(including Bhadarwah)*	6	....	....	....	71	52	....	....	....	....	5,396	4,954	....	....	....	....	3,105	3,179	17	15
4. Riasi District ..	34	30	1,555	1,610	207	178	31	12	1,477	1,292	1,619	1,468	....	....	....	....	20	23	13	....
5. Mirpur " ..	956	933	....	....	338	251	1	....	56	41	82	69	....	....	....	....	3	1	....	....
(b) *Jagirs.*																				
6. Poonch Jagir ..	83	58	....	....	54	33	5,980	6,125	1,741	1,717	28	18	1	....	22	18	....	....	....	....
7. Chenani " ..	....	....	....	....	....	....	....	....	....	....	524	505	....	....	....	....	470	478	....	....
II. Kashmir Province ..	16	12	....	....	115	155	2,824	2,545	....	....	....	....	....	....	....	....	....	....	....	3
8. Srinagar *(including City)*, (Kashmir South) ..	1	....	....	....	1	....	....	....	....	....	....	....	....	....	....	....	....	....	....	....
9. Baramulla *(including Langet)*, (Kashmir North) ..	....	....	....	....	40	98	5	4	....	....	....	....	....	....	....	....	....	....	....	....
10. Muzaffarabad ..	15	12	....	....	68	57	2,819	2,541	....	....	....	....	....	....	....	....	....	....	....	3
III. Frontier Districts ..	....	....	....	....	6	....	....	....	....	....	....	....	....	....	....	....	....	....	....	....
11. Ladakh District ..	....	....	....	....	....	....	....	....	....	....	....	....	....	....	....	....	....	....	....	....
12. Gilgit " ..	....	....	....	....	4	....	....	....	....	....	....	....	....	....	....	....	....	....	....	....
13. Frontier Ilaqas ..	....	....	....	....	2	....	....	....	....	....	....	....	....	....	....	....	....	....	....	....

TABLE XVII.

Race, Tribe and Caste.

Jammu and Kashmir Census 1931.

District, Jagir or Ilaqa.	Galleban.		Gardi.		Ghirth.		Gorkha.				Gujjar.		Hajam.						Hanjis.	
	Muslim.		Hindu.		Hindu.		Hindu.		Muslim.		Muslim.		Hindu.		Muslim.		Sikh.		Muslim.	
	Males.	Females.	Males.	Females.	Males.	Females.	Males.	Females.	Males.	Females.	Males.	Females.	Males.	Females.	Males.	Females.	Males.	Females.	Males.	Females.
	101	102	103	104	105	106	107	108	109	110	111	112	113	114	115	116	117	118	119	120
Jammu and Kashmir State ..	5	6	76	97	75	50	883	190	....	3	216,958	185,823	2,251	1,984	7,578	6,926	5	4	7	3
I. Jammu Province (*including Jagirs*) ..	....	....	72	93	75	50	326	31	....	3	149,646	130,964	2,236	1,984	6,696	6,120	5	4	7	3
(a) *Districts.*																				
1. Jammu District (*including City*) ..	....	....	67	38	....	....	51	22	....	....	33,558	28,881	1,032	916	1,255	1,032	5	4	....	1
2. Kathua " ..	....	....	....	....	75	50	11	....	....	....	9,463	8,473	552	477	140	102	....	....	7	2
3. Udhampur " (*including Bhadarwah*),	....	....	....	....	....	....	1	3	....	....	13,057	11,814	285	241	217	203	....	....	....	....
4. Riasi District ..	....	....	5	4	....	....	28	6	....	3	38,232	33,493	292	269	1,242	1,277	....	....	....	....
5. Mirpur " ..	....	....	....	51	....	....	234	....	....	....	14,027	12,387	47	59	1,976	1,807	....	....	....	....
(b) *Jagirs.*																				
6. Poonch Jagir ..	....	....	....	....	....	....	1	....	....	....	41,031	35,616	3	1	1,861	1,696	....	....	....	....
7. Chenani " ..	....	....	....	....	....	....	....	....	....	....	278	300	25	21	5	3	....	....	....	....
II. Kashmir Province ..	2	3	4	4	....	....	277	159	....	....	65,554	53,519	9	....	815	736	....	....	....	....
8. Srinagar (*including City*), (Kashmir South) ..	....	....	4	4	....	....	277	159	....	....	15,605	14,137	9	....	33	39	....	....	....	....
9. Baramulla (*including Langet*), (Kashmir North) ..	2	3	....	....	....	....	....	....	....	....	18,048	15,934	....	....	....	....	....	....	....	....
10. Muzaffarabad ..	....	....	....	....	....	....	....	....	....	....	31,901	23,448	....	....	782	697	....	....	....	....
III. Frontier Districts ..	3	3	....	....	....	....	280	....	....	....	1,758	1,340	6	....	67	70	....	....	....	....
11. Ladakh District ..	3	3	....	....	....	....	....	....	....	....	....	....	....	....	....	....	....	....	....	....
12. Gilgit " ..	....	....	....	....	....	....	280	....	....	....	359	285	3	....	67	70	....	....	....	....
13. Frontier Ilaqas ..	....	....	....	....	....	....	....	....	....	....	1,399	1,055	3	....	....	....	....	....	....	....

TABLE XVII.

RACE, TRIBE AND CASTE.

Jammu and Kashmir Census 1931.

District, Jagir or Ilaqa.	HARNI.		JAT.						JHIWAR.		JHIWAR (MASHKI).		JHIWAR.		JOGI.				JOLAHA.	
	Muslim.		*Hindu.*		*Muslim.*		*Sikh.*		*Hindu.*		*Muslim.*		*Sikh.*		*Hindu.*		*Muslim.*		*Hindu.*	
	Males.	Females.	Males.	Females.	Males.	Females.	Males.	Females.	Males.	Females.	Males.	Females.	Males.	Females.	Males.	Females.	Males.	Females.	Males.	Females.
	121	122	123	124	125	126	127	128	129	130	131	132	133	134	135	136	137	138	139	140
Jammu and Kashmir State ..	2	....	12,287	11,084	62,227	57,856	2,852	2,767	5,338	4,819	1,080	940	15	9	1,783	1,303	1,498	1,393	20	20
I. Jammu Province (*including Jagirs*) ..	2	....	12,271	11,063	62,135	57,777	2,788	2,729	5,276	4,818	1,080	940	9	9	1,771	1,301	1,465	1,364	20	20
(*a*) *Districts.*																				
1. Jammu District (*including City*) ..	2	....	3,880	3,134	5,228	4,030	289	217	3,738	3,305	64	4	4	3	775	573	423	382	....	....
2. Kathua " ..	....	....	929	620	101	74	28	19	1,037	904	....	....	....	....	426	326	45	29	....	....
3. Udhampur " (*including Bhadarwah*)	....	....	95	57	66	34	....	....	194	136	....	....	....	....	312	208	11	2	....	....
4. Riasi District ..	....	....	24	3	1,272	1,171	10	2	98	89	52	50	....	....	120	118	142	86	20	20
5. Mirpur " ..	....	....	7,256	7,204	52,805	50,291	2,460	2.491	133	350	855	780	5	6	92	51	641	687	....	....
(*b*) *Jagirs.*																				
6. Poonch Jagir ..	....	....	38	26	2,631	2,177	1	....	45	34	109	106	....	....	1	....	203	178	....	....
7. Chenani " ..	....	....	49	39	32	....	....	....	31	....	....	....	....	....	45	25	....	....	....	....
II. Kashmir Province ..	....	....	15	1	76	69	64	38	24	1	....	....	6	....	12	2	33	29	....	....
8. Srinagar (*including City*), (Kashmir South) ..	....	....	4	....	73	68	9	8	12	....	....	....	6	....	6	....	....	....	....	....
9. Baramulla (*including Langet*), (Kashmir North) ..	....	....	....	....	....	....	3	....	5	1	....	....	....	....	2	....	....	....	....	....
10. Muzaffarabad ..	....	....	11	1	3	1	52	30	7	....	....	....	....	....	4	2	33	29	....	....
III. Frontier Districts ..	....	....	1	....	16	10	....	....	38	....	....	....	....	....	....	....	....	....	....	....
11. Ladakh District ..	....	....	....	....	....	....	....	....	....	....	....	....	....	....	....	....	....	....	....	....
12. Gilgit " ..	....	....	1	....	16	10	....	....	38	....	....	....	....	....	....	....	....	....	....	....
13. Frontier Ilaqas ..	....	....	....	....	....	....	....	....	....	....	....	....	....	....	....	....	....	....	....	....

TABLE XVII.

Race, Tribe and Caste.

Jammu and Kashmir Census 1931.

District, Jagir or Ilaqa.	Kalandar. Muslim.		Kumangar. Muslim.		Kanjar. Muslim.		Kashmiri Muslim Sub-castes. Aito.		Akhoon.		Bat.		Chaupan.		Dar.		Ganai.		Hajam.	
	Males.	Females.	Males.	Females.	Males.	Females.	Males.	Females.	Males.	Females.	Males.	Females.	Males.	Females.	Males.	Females.	Males.	Females.	Males.	Females.
	141	142	143	144	145	146	147	148	149	150	151	152	153	154	155	156	157	158	159	160
Jammu and Kashmir State ..	54	72	179	152	2	....	5,307	4,622	2,715	2,383	90,477	77,751	6,045	5,206	64,446	53,906	32,441	26,800	10,371	8,504
I. Jammu Province (*including Jagirs*) ..	54	72	147	118	....	....	373	341	107	172	9,933	8,429	289	171	2,880	2,395	1,094	833	326	325
(*a*) *Districts.*																				
1. Jammu District (*including City*) ..	37	56	....	....	....	....	4	1	....	....	877	549	....	....	162	109	47	1	2	3
2. Kathua „ ..	....	....	....	....	....	....	....	....	....	....	327	176	....	....	5	59	47	41	....	....
3. Udhampur „ (*including Bhadarwah*)	....	....	....	....	....	....	358	334	107	172	5,966	5,344	72	....	834	496	801	619	311	207
4. Riasi District ..	....	....	....	....	....	....	11	6	....	....	1,167	846	217	171	496	470	107	94	....	23
5. Mirpur „ ..	17	16	....	....	....	....	....	....	....	....	860	756	....	....	585	408	60	51	12	2
(*b*) *Jagirs.*																				
6. Poonch Jagir ..	....	....	147	118	....	....	....	....	....	....	667	746	....	....	798	848	32	27	....	....
7. Chenani „ ..	....	....	....	....	....	....	....	....	....	....	69	12	....	....	....	5	....	....	1	....
II. Kashmir Province ..	....	....	32	34	2	....	4,934	4,280	2,608	2,211	80,444	69,236	5,756	5,025	61,512	51,458	31,327	25,957	10,010	8,154
8. Srinagar (*including City*), (Kashmir South) ..	....	....	....	....	....	....	3,340	2,809	1,552	1,301	49,049	42,001	2,630	2,101	30,005	24,606	16,906	14,007	5,166	4,265
9. Baramulla (*including Langet*), (Kashmir North) ..	....	....	....	....	....	....	1,592	1,471	1,041	900	30,253	26,122	3,071	2,883	30,538	26,108	13,822	11,502	4,709	3,792
10. Muzaffarabad ..	....	....	32	34	2	....	2	....	15	10	1,142	1,113	55	41	969	744	599	448	135	97
III. Frontier Districts ..	....	....	....	....	....	....	....	1	....	....	100	86	....	12	54	53	20	10	35	25
11. Ladakh District ..	....	....	....	....	....	....	....	1	....	....	86	72	....	12	50	51	14	10	31	25
12. Gilgit „ ..	....	....	....	....	....	....	....	....	....	....	13	....	....	....	4	2	6	....	4	
13. Frontier Ilaqas ..	....	....	....	....	....	....	....	....	....	....	1	14	....	....	....	....	....	....	....	....

TABLE XVII.

RACE, TRIBE AND CASTE.

Jammu and Kashmir Census 1931.

District Jagir or Ilaqa.	Kashmiri Muslim Sub-castes.—(continued).																			
	Hanji.		*Khan.*		*Khauja.*		*Lon.*		*Magre.*		*Malik.*		*Mir.*		*Pandit.*		*Parai.*		*Pirzada.*	
	Males.	Females.	Males.	Females.	Males.	Females.	Males.	Females.	Males.	Females.	Males.	Females.	Males.	Females.	Males.	Females.	Males.	Females.	Males.	Females.
	161	162	163	164	165	166	167	168	169	170	171	172	173	174	175	176	177	178	179	180
Jammu and Kashmir State ..	2,334	1,780	18,195	15,770	3,236	2,669	34,312	300,55	4,523	4,145	31,211	26,743	55,092	47,155	1,911	1,673	8,317	7,180	4,452	3,995
I. Jammu Province (*including Jagirs*) ..	169	132	176	98	973	956	4,551	4,021	217	362	13,689	11,082	5,313	4,675	8	3	463	441	2	— —
(*a*) *Districts.*																				
1. Jammu District (*including City*) ..	5	....	41	7	6	....	121	62	15	26	264	125	302	245	3	....	47	36	2	— —
2. Kathua „ ..	....	....	14	3	....	43	....	5	....	....	71	17	19	23	....	....	3	1	— —	— —
3. Udhampur „ (*including Bhadarwah*)	164	131	77	48	....	2	2,704	2,156	114	145	4,007	2,683	1,639	1,283	....	....	236	201	— —	— —
4. Riasi District ..	....	....	42	40	....	....	440	395	69	101	2,934	2,746	880	742	....	....	112	141	....	....
5. Mirpur „ ..	....	1	1	....	7	6	444	233	19	22	3,956	3,556	852	799	5	3	40	36	....	....
(*b*) *Jagirs.*																				
6. Poonch Jagir ..	....	....	....	....	960	905	826	870	....	68	2,416	1,927	1,021	1,558	....	....	25	26	....	....
7. Chenani „ ..	....	....	1	....	....	....	16	....	....	....	41	28	14	25	....	....	....	....	....	....
II. Kashmir Province ..	2,165	1,648	18,017	15,672	2,227	1,679	29,593	25,370	4,306	3,733	17,458	15,604	49,586	42,285	1,902	1,670	7,852	6,739	4,444	3,995
8. Srinagar (*including City*), (Kashmir South) ..	1,247	841	9,401	8,265	256	246	10,736	9,161	2,271	1,974	9,038	8,130	22,526	19,243	960	802	3,513	2,971	1,012	970
9. Baramulla (*including Langet*, (Kashmir North) ..	918	807	8,595	7,399	583	496	17,671	15,686	2,009	1,776	7,646	6,856	24,258	20,786	877	801	4,173	3,607	3,309	2,940
10. Muzaffarabad ..	....	....	21	8	1,388	937	1,186	1,023	26	33	774	618	2,802	2,256	65	67	166	161	123	85
III. Frontier Districts ..	....	....	2	....	36	34	168	164	....	....	64	57	193	195	1	— —	2	....	6	....
11. Ladakh District ..	....	....	....	....	36	34	131	126	....	....	53	53	136	152	1	....	— —	— —	— —	....
12. Gilgit „ ..	....	....	2	....	....	....	17	....	....	....	7	....	19	2	....	....	2	— —	6	— —
13. Frontier Ilaqas ..	....	....	....	....	....	....	20	38	....	....	4	4	38	41	— —	— —	— —	— —	— —	— —

TABLE XVII.

Race, Tribe and Caste.

Jammu and Kashmir Census 1931.

District, Jagir or Ilaqa.	Kashmiri Muslim Sub-castes.—(concluded). Raina. Males.	Raina. Females.	Rather. Males.	Rather. Females.	Rishi. Males.	Rishi. Females.	Syed. Males.	Syed. Females.	Shah. Males.	Shah. Females.	Sheikh. Males.	Sheikh. Females.	Tantri. Males.	Tantri. Females.	Wain. Males.	Wain. Females.	Others. Males.	Others. Females.	Kayasth. Hindu. Males.	Kayasth. Hindu. Females
	181	182	183	184	185	186	187	188	189	190	191	192	193	194	195	196	197	198	199	200
Jammu and Kashmir State ..	2,111	1,762	21,765	17,960	5,672	4,626	6,756	5,821	10,333	9,027	40,264	34,711	6,158	6,095	39,670	32,443	222,655	189,269	29	14
I. Jammu Province (*including Jagirs*) ..	....	4	2,015	1,289	298	167	154	63	44	50	2,908	2,939	1,282	1,303	5,488	3,723	25,158	24,061	5	5
(a) *Districts.*																				
1. Jammu District (*including City*) ..	....	....	51	23	2	....	7	51	1	....	147	108	4	63	214	136	1,286	1,002	5	5
2. Kathua ,, ..	....	....	4	31	....	....	....	....	....	....	39	86	2	....	23	51	1,161	1,059	....	....
3. Udhampur ,, (*including Bhadarwah*)	....	....	1,491	823	233	114	31	....	43	50	1,947	1,886	619	625	4,072	2,199	13,354	14,233	....	....
4. Riasi District ..	....	4	184	186	39	9	114	....	....	....	605	626	38	....	941	951	3,749	3,012	....	....
5. Mirpur ,, ..	....	....	120	85	3	....	2	....	....	....	168	170	40	....	86	52	1,659	1,647	....	....
(b) *Jagirs.*																				
6. Poonch Jagir ..	....	....	165	141	21	44	....	12	....	....	....	62	579	616	152	334	3,883	3,098	....	....
7. Chenani ,, ..	....	....	....	....	....	....	....	....	....	....	2	1	....	....	....	....	66	10	....	....
II. Kashmir Province ..	2,105	1,755	19,643	16,572	5,374	4,459	6,059	5,298	10,289	8,977	37,320	31,737	4,875	4,790	34,080	28,622	196,956	164,936	24	9
8. Srinagar (*including City*), (Kashmir South) ..	1,262	1,038	10,776	8,993	3,224	2,624	2,938	2,528	7,087	6,032	20,602	17,098	2,159	2,369	20,631	17,318	127,321	106,041	23	9
9. Baramulla (*including Langet*), (Kashmir North) ..	338	283	8,714	7,435	2,123	1,815	2,930	2,594	3,174	2,923	15,068	13,190	2,619	2,355	13,284	11,208	66,626	55,958	1	....
10. Muzaffarabad ..	505	434	153	144	27	20	191	176	28	22	1,650	1,449	97	66	105	96	3,009	2,937	....	....
III. Frontier Districts ..	6	3	107	99	....	....	543	460	....	....	36	35	1	2	102	98	541	272	....	....
11. Ladakh District ..	5	3	103	99	....	....	7	2	....	....	....	....	....	2	100	98	343	129	....	....
12. Gilgit ,, ..	1	....	4	....	....	....	3	....	....	....	7	5	1	....	2	....	82	19	....	....
13. Frontier Ilaqas ..	....	....	....	....	....	....	533	458	....	....	29	30	....	....	....	....	116	124	....	....

TABLE XVII

Race, Tribe and Caste.

Jammu and Kashmir Census 1931.

District, Jagir or Ilaqa.	Khatik. Muslim. Males.	Khatik. Muslim. Females.	Khatri. Hindu. Males.	Khatri. Hindu. Females.	Khatri. Sikh. Males.	Khatri. Sikh. Females.	Khatri. Jain. Males.	Khatri. Jain. Females.	Khoja. Muslim. Males.	Khoja. Muslim. Females.	Khosha. Muslim. Males.	Khosha. Muslim. Females.	Khusra. Muslim. Males.	Khusra. Muslim. Females.	Kumhiar. Hindu. Males.	Kumhiar. Hindu. Females.	Kumhiar. Muslim. Males.	Kumhiar. Muslim. Females.	Kumhiar. Sikh. Males.	Kumhiar. Sikh. Females.
	201	202	203	204	205	206	207	208	209	210	211	212	213	214	215	216	217	218	219	220
Jammu and Kashmir State ..	295	284	11,254	9,302	1,147	922	310	271	1,894	1,877	5	30	2	....	3,020	2,376	6,550	5,733	18	26
I. Jammu Province (*including Jagirs*) ..	280	268	9,678	7,9.5	1,052	877	310	271	1,477	1,594	5	....	2	....	2,987	2,368	6,009	5,273	16	26
(*a*) *Districts.*																				
1. Jammu District (*including City*) ..	109	125	3,626	3,186	222	149	309	269	31	21	....	....	....	....	1,501	1,194	673	481	1	....
2. Kathua „ ..	121	95	570	465	18	21	....	....	7	17	5	....	....	....	953	771	92	66	....	....
3. Udhampur „ (*including Bhadarwah*)	....	4	1,097	942	16	22	....	....	13	15	....	....	....	....	95	68	428	476	....	....
4. Riasi District ..	....	....	1,034	889	27	20	....	....	915	898	....	....	....	....	233	209	549	526	....	....
5. Mirpur „ ..	50	44	1,998	1,643	551	494	....	....	49	82	....	....	2	....	128	111	2,411	2,082	15	26
(*b*) *Jagirs.*																				
6. Poonch Jagir ..	....	....	943	702	218	171	1	2	352	540	....	....	....	....	6	5	1,834	1,625	....	....
7. Chenani „ ..	....	....	110	88	....	....	....	....	111	21	....	....	....	....	11	10	22	17	....	....
II. Kashmir Province ..	15	16	1,781	1,345	70	34	....	....	379	280	....	....	....	....	18	8	489	408	....	....
8. Srinagar (*including City*), (Kashmir South) ..	2	....	383	243	50	13	....	....	6	....	....	....	....	....	15	8	....	....	....	....
9. Baramulla (*including Langet*), (Kashmir North) ..	13	16	480	331	10	9	....	....	....	....	....	....	....	....	....	....	....	....	....	....
10. **Muzaffarabad** ..	....	....	918	771	10	12	....	....	373	280	....	....	....	....	....	....	489	408	....	....
III. Frontier Districts ..	....	....	95	42	16	11	....	....	38	3	....	30	....	....	15	....	52	53	....	....
11. **Ladakh District** ..	....	....	14	7	....	....	....	....	....	....	....	....	....	....	13	....	....	....	....	....
12. **Gilgit** „ ..	....	....	54	24	16	11	....	....	3	....	....	....	....	....	2	....	52	53	....	....
13. **Frontier Ilaqas** ..	....	....	27	11	....	....	....	....	35	3	....	30	....	....	....	....	....	....	....	....

TABLE XVII.

Race, Tribe and Caste.

Jammu and Kashmir Census 1931.

District, Jagir or Ilaqa.	Lama.		Lobana.						Lohar.						Machhi.		Mahajan.			
	Buddhist.		*Hindu.*		*Muslim.*		*Sikh.*		*Hindu.*		*Muslim.*		*Sikh.*		*Muslim.*		*Hindu.*		*Sikh.*	
	Males.	Females.	Males.	Females.	Males.	Females.	Males.	Females.	Males.	Females.	Males.	Females.	Males.	Females.	Males.	Females.	Males.	Females.	Males.	Females.
	221	222	223	224	225	226	227	228	229	230	231	232	233	234	235	236	237	238	239	240
Jammu and Kashmir State ..	8	....	743	596	....	237	2,715	2,517	5,756	5,032	8,487	7,644	110	111	11	104	10,973	10,036	63	41
I. Jammu Province (*including Jagirs*) ..	8	....	691	577	....	237	2,294	2,064	5,727	5,032	7,410	6,739	110	111	11	104	10,878	9,971	63	41
(*a*) *Districts.*																				
1. Jammu District (*including City*) ..	....	....	186	110	....	8	2,104	1,913	1,686	1,151	737	558	106	108	11	59	4,850	4,139	34	26
2. Kathua „ ..	....	....	22	21	....	....	172	136	870	717	36	28	....	....	....	....	1,351	1,231	....	....
3. Udhampur „ (*including Bhadarwah*)	....	....	....	....	....	....	....	....	1,521	1,508	268	270	....	....	....	....	2,040	2,174	2	....
4. Riasi District ..	3	....	253	232	....	....	15	13	1,365	1,405	1,249	1,262	....	....	....	....	608	595	2	....
5. Mirpur „ ..	....	....	72	55	....	....	1	....	165	126	2,378	2,297	4	3	....	45	1,729	1,636	7	9
(*b*) *Jagirs.*																				
6. Poonch Jagir ..	....	....	158	159	....	229	2	2	35	42	2,742	2,324	....	....	....	....	179	113	17	6
7. Chenani „ ..	....	....	....	....	....	....	....	....	85	83	....	....	....	....	....	....	121	83	....	....
II. Kashmir Province ..	....	....	52	19	....	....	421	453	10	....	1,002	826	....	....	....	....	90	64	1	....
8. Srinagar (*including City*), (Kashmir South) ..	....	....	2	2	....	....	2	1	7	....	55	56	....	....	....	....	20	9	1	....
9. Baramulla (*including Langet*) (Kashmir North) ..	....	....	....	5	....	....	1	....	....	....	....	....	....	....	....	....	13	7	....	....
10. Muzaffarabad ..	....	....	50	12	....	....	418	452	3	....	947	770	....	....	....	....	57	48	....	....
III. Frontier Districts ..	5	....	....	....	....	....	....	....	19	....	75	79	....	....	....	....	5	1	....	....
11. Ladakh District ..	5	....	....	....	....	....	....	....	....	....	3	....	....	....	....	....	....	....	....	....
12. Gilgit „ ..	....	....	....	....	....	....	....	....	15	....	52	42	....	....	....	....	5	....	....	....
13. Frontier Ilaqas ..	....	....	....	....	....	....	....	....	4	....	20	37	....	....	....	....	....	1	....	....

TABLE XVII.

Race, Tribe and Caste.

Jammu and Kashmir Census 1931.

District, Jagir or Ilaqa.	Makhmi.		Malik.		Mangrik.				Masalli.		Mazahbi.		Megh.						Mehmar.	
	Muslim.		Muslim.		Budh.		Muslim.		Muslim.		Sikh.		Hindu.		Muslim.		Sikh.		Muslim.	
	Males.	Females.	Males.	Females.	Males.	Females.	Males.	Females.	Males.	Females.	Males.	Females.	Males.	Females.	Males.	Females.	Males.	Females.	Males.	Females.
	241	242	243	244	245	246	247	248	249	250	251	252	253	254	255	256	257	258	259	260
Jammu and Kashmir State ..	38,980	38,367	1,124	868	16,943	17,164	68	106	732	655	1	....	37,062	32,968	....	1	89	73	77	75
I. Jammu Province *(including Jagirs)* ..	....	....	40	....	11	21	2	....	732	655	....	....	37,051	32,959	....	1	89	73	77	75
(a) *Districts.*																				
1. Jammu District *(including City)* ..	....	....	....	....	....	....	....	....	....	....	....	....	15,692	13,099	....	....	42	34	37	26
2. Kathua ,, ..	....	....	40	....	....	....	....	....	....	....	....	....	3,295	2,858	....	....	2	1	40	47
3. Udhampur ,, *(including Bhadarwah)*	....	....	....	....	11	21	....	....	....	....	....	....	13,053	12,556	....	....	39	34	....	....
4. Riasi District ..	....	....	....	....	....	....	....	....	....	....	....	....	3,240	2,833	....	1	....	....	....	....
5. Mirpur ,, ..	....	....	....	....	....	....	....	....	560	464	....	....	814	759	....	....	6	4	....	2
(b) *Jagirs.*																				
6. Poonch Jagir ..	....	....	....	....	....	....	2	....	172	191	....	....	28	4	....	....	....	....	....	....
7. Chenani ,, ..	....	....	....	....	....	....	....	....	....	....	....	....	929	850	....	....	....	....	....	....
II. Kashmir Province ..	....	....	1,008	817	....	....	....	....	....	....	....	....	11	9	....	....	....	....	....	....
8. Srinagar *(including City)*, (Kashmir South) ..	....	....	6	3	....	....	....	....	....	....	....	....	11	9	....	....	....	....	....	....
9. Baramulla *(including Langet)*, (Kashmir North) ..	....	....	60	45	....	....	....	....	....	....	....	....	....	....	....	....	....	....	....	....
10. Muzaffarabad ..	....	....	942	769	....	....	....	....	....	....	....	....	....	....	....	....	....	....	....	....
III. Frontier Districts ..	38,980	38,367	76	51	16,932	17,143	68	106	....	....	1	....	....	....	....	....	....	....	....	....
11. Ladakh District ..	38,980	38,367	....	....	16,932	17,143	66	106	....	....	....	....	....	....	....	....	....	....	....	....
12. Gilgit ,, ..	....	....	76	51	....	....	....	....	....	....	1	....	....	....	....	....	....	....	....	....
13. Frontier Ilaqas ..	....	....	....	....	....	....	....	....	....	....	....	....	....	....	....	....	....	....	....	....

TABLE XVII.

Race, Tribe and Caste.

Jammu and Kashmir Census 1931.

District, Jagir or Ilaqa.	Mirasi.		Mirza Khani.		Machi.		Mon.		Moghal.		Nadaf.		Pathan.		Patoi.		Perna.			
	Muslim.		*Muslim.*		*Muslim.*		*Buddhist.*		*Muslim.*		*Muslim.*		*Muslim.*		*Muslim.*		*Hindu.*		*Muslim.*	
	Males.	Females.	Males.	Females.	Males.	Females.	Males.	Females.	Males.	Females.	Males.	Females.	Males.	Females.	Males.	Females.	Males.	Females.	Males.	Females.
	261	262	263	234	265	266	267	268	269	270	271	272	273	274	275	276	277	278	279	280
Jammu and Kashmir State ..	4,297	3,701	27	22	5,938	5,114	229	237	15,820	14,378	341	1	10,554	8,734	....	5	....	9	5	28
I. Jammu Province (*including Jagirs*) ..	3,700	3,233	....	....	5,503	4790	....	....	10,517	9,644	323	....	6,071	4,719	....	5	....	9	5	28
(*a*) *Districts.*																				
1. Jammu District (*including City*) ..	780	608	....	....	234	186	....	....	738	500	....	....	1,362	721	....	5	....	....	5	1
2. Kathua „ ..	102	99	....	....	13	5	....	....	49	23	....	....	104	105	....	....	....	9	....	27
3. Udhampur „ (*including Bhadarwah*)	31	29	....	....	113	94	....	....	135	174	....	....	495	487	....	....	....	....	....	....
4. Riasi District ..	471	418	....	....	515	463	....	....	1,817	1,702	....	....	535	454	....	....	....	....	....	....
5. Mirpur „ ..	664	571	....	....	2,439	2,112	....	....	3,467	3,000	....	....	726	513	....	....	....	....	....	....
(*b*) *Jagirs.*																				
6. Poonch Jagir ..	1,588	1,506	....	....	2,189	1,930	....	....	4,261	4,235	323	....	2,800	2,418	....	....	....	....	....	....
7. Chenani „ ..	4	2	....	....	....	....	....	....	....	10	....	....	49	21	....	....	....	....	....	....
II. Kashmir Province ..	571	443	....	....	434	324	....	....	5,195	4,663	18	1	3,808	3,478	....	....	....	....	....	....
8. Srinagar (*including City*), (Kashmir South) ..	1	....	....	....	12	5	....	....	121	36	....	....	558	488	....	....	....	....	....	....
9. Baramulla (*including Langet*), (Kashmir North) ..	....	....	....	....	....	....	....	....	110	202	....	....	696	620	....	....	....	....	....	....
10. Muzaffarabad ..	570	443	....	....	422	319	....	....	4,964	4,425	18	1	2,554	2,370	....	....	....	....	....	....
III. Frontier Districts ..	26	25	27	22	1	....	229	237	108	71	....	....	675	537	....	....	....	....	....	....
11. Ladakh District ..	26	25	....	....	....	....	229	237	25	10	....	....	1	3	....	....	....	....	....	....
12. Gilgit „ ..	....	....	1	....	....	....	....	....	82	61	....	....	292	209	....	....	....	....	....	....
13. Frontier Ilaqas ..	....	....	26	22	1	....	....	....	1	....	....	....	382	325	....	....	....	....	....	....

TABLE XVII.

RACE, TRIBE AND CASTE.

Jammu and Kashmir Census 1931.

District, Jagir or Ilaqa.	RAJPUT SUB-CASTES.																			
	AWAN.		BAIN.		BAMBA.		BHAU.				CHARAK.		CHAUHAN.				CHIB.			
	Muslim.		*Muslim.*		*Muslim.*		*Hindu.*		*Muslim.*		*Hindu.*		*Hindu.*		*Muslim.*		*Hindu.*		*Muslim.*	
	Males.	Females.	Males.	Females.	Males.	Females.	Males.	Females.	Males.	Females.	Males.	Females.	Males.	Females.	Males.	Females.	Males.	Females.	Males.	Females.
	281	282	283	284	285	286	287	288	289	290	291	292	293	294	295	296	297	298	299	300
Jammu and Kashmir State ..	17,820	15,780	378	300	1,836	1,773	1,713	1,425	369	392	1,975	1,399	86	41	2,264	1,683	4,304	3,201	4,565	4,468
I. Jammu Province (*including Jagirs*) ..	10,004	8,929	378	300	37	29	1,697	1,425	350	380	1,974	1,399	82	41	560	462	4,293	3,201	4,419	4,350
(*a*) *Districts.*																				
1. Jammu District (*including City*) ..	1,210	930	....	....	....	....	1,576	1,279	32	21	1,683	1,132	58	12	125	116	453	196	330	141
2. Kathua " ..	19	14	....	....	....	....	....	....	....	....	168	62	2	....	27	5	22	19	11	3
3. Udhampur " (*including Bhadarwah*)	4	13	....	....	....	....	90	83	4	....	62	79	5	14	106	101	169	254	31	32
4. Riasi District ..	312	250	....	....	29	19	19	57	50	33	15	101	....	....	37	32	80	116	197	255
5. Mirpur " ..	3,615	2,892	378	300	5	2	11	6	243	326	21	12	6	4	175	104	3,568	2,615	3,638	3,738
(*b*) *Jagirs.*																				
6. Poonch Jagir ..	4,844	4,830	....	....	3	8	....	....	21	....	9	4	10	11	89	104	1	1	211	181
7. Chenani " ..	....	....	....	....	....	....	1	....	....	....	16	9	1	....	1	....	....	....	1	....
II. Kashmir Province ..	7,816	6,808	....	....	1,795	1,741	10	....	19	12	1	....	4	....	1,704	1,216	....	....	140	118
8. Srinagar (*including City*), (Kashmir South) ..	751	691	....	....	428	415	10	....	1	....	1	....	4	....	837	681	....	....	....	....
9. Baramulla (*including Langet*), (Kashmir North) ..	387	314	....	....	177	189	....	....	18	12	....	....	....	....	804	471	....	....	5	....
10. Muzaffarabad ..	6,678	5,803	....	....	1,190	1,137	....	....	....	....	....	....	....	....	63	64	....	....	135	118
III. Frontier Districts ..	....	43	....	....	4	8	6	....	....	....	....	....	....	....	....	5	11	....	6	....
11. Ladakh District ..	....	....	....	....	....	....	....	....	....	....	....	....	....	....	....	....	....	....	....	....
12. Gilgit " ..	....	....	....	....	4	3	6	....	....	....	....	....	....	....	....	....	5	....	6	....
13. Frontier Ilaqas ..	....	43	....	....	....	....	....	....	....	....	....	....	....	....	....	5	6	....	....	....

TABLE XVII.

Race, Tribe and Caste.

Jammu and Kashmir Census 1931.

District, Jagir or Ilaqa.	RAJPUT SUB-CASTES—(continued).																			
	Duli.		Gakkhar.		Jarral.		Janjua.				Jaral.				Khakkha.		Khokhar.		Maldial.	
	Muslim.		Muslim.		Muslim.		Hindu.		Muslim.		Hindu.		Muslim.		Muslim.		Muslim.		Muslim.	
	Males.	Females.	Males.	Females.	Males.	Females.	Males.	Females.	Males.	Females.	Males.	Females.	Males.	Females.	Males	Females.	Males.	Females.	Males.	Females.
	301	302	303	304	305	306	307	308	309	310	311	312	313	314	315	316	317	318	319	320
Jammu and Kashmir State ..	15	12	8,631	8,095	59	19	32	4	3,237	2,785	459	399	6,141	5,486	4,231	3,503	3,545	3,155	8,310	7,380
I. Jammu Province (*including Jagirs*) ..	7	3	6,438	6,265	3	11	30	....	2,138	1,786	458	399	5,964	5,422	812	231	2,287	2,102	7,523	6,574
(*a*) *Districts.*																				
1. Jammu District (*including City*) ..	....	....	77	21	....	....	....	....	115	83	84	58	595	473	....	....	624	532	....	....
2. Kathua " ..	....	....	9	8	....	....	....	....	12	8	1	10	6	2	11	....	24	23	....	....
3. Udhampur " (*including Bhadarwah*)	....	....	70	32	....	....	....	....	4	6	329	303	74	78	....	11	43	5	....	....
4. Riasi District ..	....	....	408	368	....	....	30	....	727	637	38	26	3,181	2,913	....	....	617	545	8	104
5. Mirpur " ..	....	....	2,479	2,606	....	....	....	....	112	108	4	2	1,783	1,707	6	5	543	466	....	....
(*b*) *Jagirs.*																				
6. Poonch Jagir ..	7	3	3,395	3,213	3	11	....	....	1,168	944	2	....	321	245	795	215	401	520	7,516	6,470
7. Chenani " ..	....	....	....	17	....	....	....	....	....	....	....	....	4	4	....	....	35	11	....	....
II. Kashmir Province ..	8	9	2,175	1,815	56	8	2	4	1,096	998	1	....	139	64	3,419	3,277	1,250	1,051	787	746
8. Srinagar (*including City*), (Kashmir South) ..	8	7	33	25	....	....	....	....	113	86	1	....	40	....	33	26	109	53	....	....
9. Baramulla (*including Langet*), (Kashmir North) ..	....	2	114	94	2	....	....	....	82	104	....	....	19	....	4	6	....	....	78	65
10. Muzaffarabad ..	....	....	2,028	1,696	54	8	2	4	901	808	....	....	80	64	3,382	3,245	1,141	998	709	681
III. Frontier Districts ..	....	....	18	15	....	....	....	....	3	1	....	....	38	....	....	....	8	2	....	....
11. Ladakh District ..	....	....	....	....	....	....	....	....	....	....	....	....	....	....	....	....	....	....	....	....
12. Gilgit " ..	....	....	18	15	....	....	....	....	3	1	....	....	38	....	....	....	8	2	....	....
13. Frontier Ilaqas ..	....	....	....	....	....	....	....	....	....	....	....	....	....	....	....	....	....	....	....	....

TABLE XVII.

RACE, TRIBE AND CASTE.

Jammu and Kashmir Census 1931.

District, Jagir or Ilaqa.	RAJPUT SUB-CASTES—(continued).																			
	MANGRAL.		MANIHAS.				NARMAS.				SALEHRIA.				SAU.				OTHERS.	
	Muslim.		Hindu.		Muslim.		Hindu.		Muslim.		Hindu.		Muslim.		Hindu.		Muslim.		Hindu.	
	Males.	Females.	Males.	Females.	Males.	Females.	Males.	Females.	Males.	Females.	Males.	Females.	Males.	Females.	Males.	Females.	Males.	Females.	Males.	Females.
	321	322	323	324	325	326	327	328	329	330	331	332	333	334	335	336	337	338	339	340
Jammu and Kashmir State ..	4,925	4,584	5,900	4,160	4,415	4,267	51	68	3,407	3,450	1,093	742	4,709	3,452	62	....	465	429	71,664	59,679
I. **Jammu Province** (*including Jagirs*) ..	4,387	4,103	5,882	4,160	3,809	3,705	51	68	3,403	3,446	1,092	741	4,709	3,452	62	....	465	429	70,302	59,266
(a) *Districts.*																				
1. Jammu District (*including City*) ..	7	....	4,567	3,006	756	669	26	43	12	....	523	379	4,497	3,236	18	....	....	....	9,052	6,734
2. Kathua " ..	....	....	290	96	13	2	....	....	....	....	439	41	27	18	....	....	....	....	19,659	15,358
3. Udhampur " (*including Bhadarwah*)	....	10	688	760	60	49	....	....	....	....	27	175	4	33	....	....	....	....	28,792	26,354
4. Riasi District ..	301	244	98	94	455	588	1	....	56	19	84	136	106	97	44	....	....	....	10,221	10,056
5. Mirpur " ..	3,557	3,270	202	185	579	582	24	25	982	1,096	9	1	20	25	....	....	465	429	623	213
(b) *Jagirs.*																				
6. Poonch Jagir ..	522	579	3	1	1,945	1,815	....	....	2,353	2,331	8	8	55	43	....	....	....	....	356	288
7. Chenani " ..	....	....	34	18	1	....	....	....	....	....	2	1	....	....	....	....	....	....	1,599	1,323
II. **Kashmir Province** ..	537	481	11	....	606	562	....	....	4	4	1	1	....	....	....	....	....	....	905	394
8. Srinagar (*including City*), (Kashmir South) ..	15	10	11	....	7	2	....	....	4	4	1	1	....	....	....	....	....	....	740	351
9. Baramulla (*including Langet*), (Kashmir North) ..	21	16	....	....	....	....	....	....	....	....	....	....	....	....	....	....	....	....	77	21
10. Muzaffarabad ..	501	455	....	....	599	560	....	....	....	....	....	....	....	....	....	....	....	....	88	22
III. **Frontier Districts** ..	1	....	7	....	....	....	....	....	....	....	....	....	....	....	....	....	....	....	457	19
11. Ladakh District ..	....	....	....	....	....	....	....	....	....	....	....	....	....	....	....	....	....	....	68	....
12. Gilgit " ..	1	....	....	....	....	....	....	....	....	....	....	....	....	....	....	....	....	....	323	10
13. **Frontier Ilaqas** ..	....	....	7	....	....	....	....	....	....	....	....	....	....	....	....	....	....	....	66	9

TABLE XVII.

Race, Tribe and Caste.

Jammu and Kashmir Census 1931.

District, Jagir or Ilaqa.	Rajput Sub-Castes—(concld.). Others.		Rajput.		Rangrez.		Rattal.		Rigzong.		Sadhu.		Sapiada.		Saryara.				Sayed.	
	Muslim.		Sikh.		Muslim.		Hindu.		Buddhist.		Hindu.		Muslim.		Hindu.		Muslim.		Muslim.	
	Males.	Females.	Males.	Females.	Males.	Females.	Males.	Females.	Males.	Females.	Males.	Females.	Males.	Females.	Males.	Females.	Males.	Females.	Males.	Females.
	341	342	343	344	345	346	347	348	349	350	351	352	353	354	355	356	357	358	359	360
Jammu and Kashmir State ..	23,161	23,129	337	298	369	345	262	226	739	808	1,020	742	15	10	1,243	1,111	1	2	20,675	19,051
I. **Jammu Province** (*including Jagirs*) ..	22,470	22,545	319	282	369	345	262	226	8	7	1,009	742	15	10	1,243	1,111	1	2	13,448	12,501
(a) *Districts.*																				
1. Jammu District (*including City*) ..	1,181	1,082	255	232	66	60	....	7	....	....	450	372	1	9	548	515	1	2	1,496	1,219
2. Kathua " ..	140	88	1	1	9	....	44	48	....	....	181	184	....	....	345	264	....	....	44	21
3. Udhampur " (*including Bhadarwah*) ..	3,549	3,202	4	5	....	....	115	81	8	7	81	21	....	....	140	142	....	....	216	212
4. Riasi District ..	2,027	2,271	3	....	11	7	103	90	....	....	136	116	....	....	206	184	....	....	1,448	1,212
5. Mirpur " ..	7,225	7,551	50	43	263	251	....	....	....	....	122	35	8	1	....	....	....	....	2,653	2,421
(b) *Jagirs.*																				
6. Poonch Jagir ..	8,331	8,349	6	1	20	27	....	....	....	....	31	9	6	....	4	6	....	....	7,627	7,415
7. Chenani " ..	14	2	....	....	....	....	....	....	....	....	5	5	....	....	....	....	....	....	....	1
II. **Kashmir Province** ..	659	549	18	16	....	....	....	....	....	....	11	....	....	....	....	....	....	....	6,968	6,326
8. Srinagar (*including City*), (Kashmir South) ..	201	130	2	....	....	....	....	....	....	....	4	....	....	....	....	....	....	....	122	127
9. Baramulla (*including Langet*), (Kashmir North) ..	10	4	1	....	....	....	....	....	....	....	3	....	....	....	....	....	....	....	72	59
10. Muzaffarabad ..	445	418	15	16	....	....	....	....	....	....	4	....	....	....	....	....	....	....	6,774	6,140
III. **Frontier Districts** ..	32	35	....	....	....	....	....	....	731	801	....	....	....	....	....	....	....	....	223	224
11. Ladakh District ..	10	23	....	....	....	....	....	....	731	801	....	....	....	....	....	....	....	....	....	....
12. Gilgit " ..	14	8	....	....	....	....	....	....	....	....	....	....	....	....	....	....	....	....	223	224
13. Frontier Ilaqas ..	8	4	....	....	....	....	....	....	....	....	....	....	....	....	....	....	....	....	....	....

TABLE XVII.

Race, Tribe and Caste.

Jammu and Kashmir Census 1931.

District, Jagir or Ilaqa.	Sheikh.		Shin.		Sudhan.		Tharkhan.						Teli.				Thathayar.			
	Muslim.		Muslim.		Muslim.		Hindu.		Muslim.		Sikh.		Hindu.		Muslim.		Hindu.		Muslim.	
	Males.	Females.	Males.	Females.	Males.	Females.	Males.	Females.	Males.	Females.	Males.	Females.	Males.	Females.	Males.	Females.	Males.	Females.	Males.	Females.
	361	362	363	364	365	366	367	368	369	370	371	372	373	374	375	376	377	378	379	380
Jammu and Kashmir State ..	15,623	13,361	7,126	7,013	33,201	35,393	5,460	4,519	7,616	6,789	27	26	5	4	8,221	7,613	36	35	5	....
I. Jammu Province (*including Jagirs*) ..	11,395	9,777	....	....	32,929	35,124	5,460	4,518	7,338	6,567	27	25	5	4	8,014	7,470	36	35	....	....
(*a*) *Districts.*																				
1. Jammu District (*including City*) ..	1,358	1,217	....	....	26	1	3,005	2,380	1,103	847	6	5	2	1	3,445	3,106	18	18	....	....
2. Kathua „ ..	175	112	....	....	5	....	1,483	1,221	40	27	4	8	....	....	1,559	1,188	....	....	....	....
3. Udhampur „ (*including Bhadarwah*) ..	1,144	991	....	....	....	....	438	476	10	31	1	....	3	3	284	227	15	12	....	....
4. Riasi District ..	1,369	1,010	....	....	131	176	283	240	1,083	969	2	3	....	....	403	563	3	5	....	....
5. Mirpur „ ..	1,196	910	....	....	1,402	1,119	247	199	3,285	3,055	14	9	....	....	1,968	2,020	....	....	....	....
(*b*) *Jagirs.*																				
6. Poonch Jagir ..	6,096	5,506	....	....	31,365	33,828	1	1	1,817	1,638	....	....	....	....	377	358	....	....	....	....
7. Chenani „ ..	57	31	....	....	....	....	3	1	....	....	....	....	....	....	8	8	....	....	....	....
II. Kashmir Province ..	3,981	3,422	....	....	272	269	....	1	246	208	....	1	....	....	147	123	....	....	5	....
8. Srinagar (*including City*), (Kashmir South) ..	136	107	....	....	....	....	....	1	13	35	....	....	....	....	....	....	....	....	....	....
9. Baramulla (*including Lanjet*), (Kashmir North) ..	16	15	....	....	....	....	....	....	....	1	....	....	....	....	....	....	....	....	....	....
10. Muzaffarabad ..	3,829	3,300	....	....	272	269	....	....	233	172	....	1	....	....	147	123	....	....	5	....
III. Frontier Districts ..	247	162	7,126	7,013	....	....	....	....	32	14	....	....	....	....	30	20	....	....	....	....
11. Ladakh District ..	192	121	....	....	....	....	....	....	....	....	....	....	....	....	....	....	....	....	....	....
12. Gilgit „ ..	55	41	2,348	2,060	....	....	....	....	32	14	....	....	....	....	....	....	....	....	....	....
13. Frontier Ilaqas ..	....	....	4,778	4,953	....	....	....	....	....	....	....	....	....	....	30	20	....	....	....	....

TABLE XVII.

RACE, TRIBE AND CASTE.

Jammu and Kashmir Census 1931.

District, Jagir or Ilaqa.	TARAKHKHAS.		TURK.		WATTAL.				YASHKUN.		ZARGAR.						OTHERS (MINOR AND UNSPECIFIED CASTES, ETC.).			
	Muslim.		*Muslim.*		*Hindu.*		*Muslim.*		*Muslim.*		*Hindu.*		*Muslim.*		*Sikh.*		*Hindu.*		*Buddhist.*	
	Males.	Females.	Males.	Females.	Males.	Females.	Males.	Females.	Males.	Females.	Males.	Females.	Males.	Females.	Males.	Females.	Males.	Females.	Males.	Females.
	381	382	383	384	385	386	387	388	389	390	391	392	393	394	395	396	397	398	399	400
Jammu and Kashmir State ..	5,221	4,934	1,221	1,050	10	3	213	207	19,091	17,069	1,734	1,546	525	465	125	277	13,352	10,097	1,327	1,199
I. Jammu Province (*including Jagirs*) ..	....	....	39	33	....	....	213	207	....	....	1,726	1,543	259	212	121	268	11,933	9,425	231	226
(*a*) *Districts.*																				
1. Jammu District (*including City*) ..	....	....	....	....	....	....	11	2	....	....	661	584	81	55	....	1	6,588	5,408	4	5
2. Kathua „ ..	....	....	....	....	....	....	....	4	....	....	271	267	37	16	1	....	2,957	2,264	....	....
3. Udhampur „ (*including Bhadarwah*) ..	....	....	....	....	....	....	144	102	....	....	255	219	37	37	....	....	894	746	226	219
4. Riasi District ..	....	....	....	....	....	....	58	62	....	....	154	146	36	36	3	149	830	554	1	2
5. Mirpur „ ..	....	....	7	....	....	....	....	....	....	....	336	293	64	63	93	102	545	382	....	....
(*b*) *Jagirs.*																				
6. Poonch Jagir ..	....	....	32	33	....	....	....	36	....	....	21	11	4	5	24	16	119	71	....	....
7. Chenani „ ..	....	....	....	....	....	....	....	1	....	....	28	23	....	....	....	....	....	....	....	....
II. Kashmir Province ..	....	....	1,182	1,017	10	3	....	....	....	....	8	3	7	12	4	9	1,151	654	5	....
8. Srinagar (*including City*), (Kashmir South) ..	....	....	91	60	10	3	....	....	....	....	3	....	....	7	....	....	589	276	5	....
9. Baramulla (*including Langet*), (Kashmir North) ..	....	....	....	....	....	....	....	....	....	....	....	....	3	2	2	8	113	70	....	....
10. Muzaffarabad ..	....	....	1,091	957	....	....	....	....	....	....	5	3	4	3	2	1	449	308	....	....
III. Frontier Districts ..	5,221	4,934	....	....	....	....	....	....	19,091	17,069	....	....	259	241	....	....	268	18	1,091	973
11. Ladakh District ..	5,216	4,934	....	....	....	....	....	....	....	....	....	....	....	....	....	....	39	7	1,091	973
12. Gilgit „ ..	5	....	....	....	....	....	....	....	9,360	7,992	....	....	254	231	....	....	52	11	....	....
13. Frontier Ilaqas ..	....	....	....	....	....	....	....	....	9,731	9,077	....	....	5	10	....	....	177	....	....	....

TABLE XVII.

RACE, TRIBE AND CASTE.

Jammu and Kashmir Census 1931.

District, Jagir or Ilaqa.	OTHERS (MINOR AND UNSPECIFIED CASTES, ETC.)—(concluded).												REMARKS.
	Muslim.		*Sikh.*		*Jain.*		*Indian Christian.*		*Parsi.*		*Sansi.*		
	Males.	Females.	Males.	Females.	Males.	Females.	Males.	Females.	Males.	Females.	Males.	Females.	
	401	402	403	404	405	406	407	408	409	410	411	412	
Jammu and Kashmir State ..	67,208	63,138	11,904	10,359	9	7	1,100	842	3	2	78	56	
I. Jammu Province (*including Jagirs*) ..	20,123	18,267	1,781	1,220	4	6	953	740	....	....	17	24	
(a) *Districts.*													
1. Jammu District (*including City*) ..	2,960	2,579	403	292	....	....	743	577	....	....	17	24	
2. Kathua „ ..	599	403	17	10	....	....	98	71	....	....	....	....	
3. Udhampur „ (*including Bhadarwah*) ..	1,394	840	86	70	1	1	19	12	....	....	....	....	
4. Riasi District ..	3,266	2,399	184	....	....	....	18	13	....	....	....	....	
5. Mirpur „ ..	3,704	3,223	1,012	781	3	5	37	36	....	....	....	....	
(b) *Jagirs.*													
6. Poonch Jagir ..	8,200	8,814	75	67	....	....	38	31	....	....	....	....	
7. Chenani „ ..	....	9	4	....	....	....	....	....	....	....	....	....	
II. Kashmir Province ..	26,015	27,682	10,022	9,088	3	....	78	41	3	2	61	32	
8. Srinagar (*including City*), (Kashmir South) ..	815	707	2,095	1,560	3	....	49	32	3	1	20	15	
9. Baramulla (*including Langet*), (Kashmir North) ..	1,027	964	3,202	2,983	....	....	29	9	....	....	41	17	
10. Muzaffarabad ..	24,173	26,011	4,725	4,545	....	....	....	....	....	1	....	....	
III. Frontier Districts ..	21,070	17,189	101	51	2	1	69	61	....	....	....	....	
11. Ladakh District ..	931	869	60	31	....	....	49	58	....	....	....	....	
12. Gilgit „ ..	3,138	2,603	35	18	2	1	19	3	....	....	....	....	
13. Frontier Ilaqas ..	17,001	13,717	6	2	....	....	1	....	....	....	....	....	

TABLE XVIII.

VARIATION OF POPULATION OF SELECTED CASTES.

Jammu and Kashmir Census 1931.

1. Figures prior to the 1911 Census have been omitted on account of their doubtful reliability.

2. The Figures of Kashmiri Pandits include vohras (attars) numbering 1,512 persons who are in reality Kashmiri Khatris.

3. The decrease in some of the Muslim castes is counterbalanced by the abnormal increase under "Kashmiri Muslims" which include a large number of castes.

TABLE XVIII.

Variation of Population of Selected Castes.

Jammu and Kashmir Census 1931.

Tribe.	Persons. 1931.	Persons. 1921.	Persons. 1911.	Variation (Increase + Decrease —). 1921 to 1931.	Variation (Increase + Decrease —). 1911 to 1921.	Net Variation 1911 to 1931. Increase + Decrease —	Males. 1931.	Males. 1921.	Males. 1911.	Females. 1931.	Females. 1921.	Females. 1911.
1	2	3	4	5	6	7	8	9	10	11	12	13
Hindu.												
1. Brahman ..	190,441	172,078	174,145	+18,363	—2,067	+16,296	98,183	89,230	93,129	92,258	82,848	81,016
2. Chumar ..	41,189	39,090	39,094	+2,099	—4	+2,095	21,672	20,672	20,459	19,517	18,418	18,635
3. Doom ..	34,329	30,617	36,794	+3,712	—6,177	—2,465	18,400	15,870	19,400	15,929	14,747	17,394
4. Jat ..	23,371	25,861	25,194	—2,490	+667	—1,823	12,287	13,342	13,598	11,084	12,519	11,596
5. Kashmiri Pandit ..	63,088	55,055	55,279	+8,033	—224	+7,809	35,060	30,947	30,769	28,028	24,108	24,510
6. Khatri ..	20,556	18,795	16,118	+1,761	+2,677	+4,438	11,254	11,098	9,340	9,302	7,697	6,778
7. Mahajan ..	21,009	19,888	20,342	+1,121	—454	+667	10,973	11,199	11,509	10,036	8,689	8,833
8. Megh ..	70,030	78,809	75,191	—8,779	+3,618	—5,161	37,062	41,081	39,225	32,968	37,728	35,966
9. Rajput ..	158,457	141,064	144,873	+17,393	—3,809	13,584	87,339	77,327	79,445	71,118	63,737	65,428
Muslim.												
10. Arain ..	22,922	26,370	20,621	—3,448	+5,749	+2,301	12,727	15,644	11,497	10,195	10,726	9,124
11. Bafinda ..	33,872	28,162	26,830	+5,710	+1,332	+7,042	17,679	14,813	14,795	16,193	13,349	12,035
12. Balti ..	47,326	124,760	72,439	—77,434	+52,321	—25,113	23,274	61,786	40,597	24,052	62,974	31,842
13. Gujjar ..	402,781	362,107	328,003	+40,674	+34,104	+74,778	216,958	191,004	183,798	185,823	171,103	144,205
14. Jat ..	120,083	102,649	115,530	+17,434	—12,881	+4,553	62,227	52,514	58,905	57,856	50,135	56,625
15. Kashmiri Muslim ..	1,352,822	796,804	765,442	+556,018	+31,362	+587,380	730,769	428,675	391,484	622,053	368,129	373,958
16. Rajput ..	195,449	172,944	153,677	+22,505	+19,267	+41,772	101,875	84,910	78,438	93,574	88,034	75,239
17. Sayed ..	39,726	89,353	102,195	—49,627	—12,842	—62,469	20,675	47,772	54,066	19,051	41,581	48,129
18. Shin ..	14,139	15 106	11,080	—967	+4,026	+3,059	7,126	7,065	5,930	7,013	7,441	5,150
19. Yashkun ..	36,160	44,087	35,011	—7,927	+9,076	+1,149	19,091	23,373	17,965	17,069	20,714	17,046
Buddhist.												
20. Mangrik ..	34,107	33,183	35,616	+924	—2,433	—1,509	16,943	16,193	17,691	17,164	16,990	17,925

TABLE XIX.

EUROPEANS AND ALLIED RACES AND ANGLO-INDIANS BY RACE AND AGE.

Jammu and Kashmir Census 1931.

1. The figures for Cities have been included in the Districts concerned and also shown separately in accordance with instructions contained in para. 21 page 51 of the Imperial Census Code, part II.

2. The number of Armenians returned is 12 males and 1 female only.

TABLE XIX.

Europeans and Allied Races and Anglo-Indians by Race and Age.

Jammu and Kashmir Census 1931.

District, Jagir or Ilaqa.	Total.			(A) European and Allied Races (including Armenians). (A) British Subjects. All Ages.			0–13		14–16		17–23.		24–33.		34–43.		44–53.		54 & over.		(B) Others. All ages.			0–13.		14–16.		17–23.		24–33.	
	Persons.	Males.	Females.	Persons.	Males.	Females.	Males.	Females.	Males.	Females.	Males.	Females.	Males.	Females.	Males.	Females.	Males.	Females.	Males.	Females.	Persons.	Males.	Females.	Males.	Females.	Male.	Females.	Males.	Females.	Males.	Females.
1	2	3	4	5	6	7	8	9	10	11	12	13	14	15	16	17	18	19	20	21	22	23	24	25	26	27	28	29	30	31	32
1. Jammu and Kashmir State ..	321	143	178	151	69	82	2	4	1	..	6	4	10	24	19	23	19	12	12	15	47	24	23	3	1	..	..	..	..	4	5
Jammu Province (including Jagirs) ..	60	34	26	21	14	7	..	..	1	..	2	..	2	3	4	3	4	1	1	..	6	4	2	1	..	..	..	..	..	..	1
(a) *Total Districts* ..	*53*	*29*	*24*	*16*	*11*	*5*	..	..	..	..	*1*	..	*1*	*3*	*4*	*1*	*4*	*1*	*1*	..	*4*	*2*	*2*	*1*	..	..	..	..	..	..	*1*
1. Jammu District (including City) ..	42	22	20	7	6	1	..	..	..	..	1	..	..	..	2	..	2	1	1	..	4	2	2	..	..	..	..	..	..	..	1
2 Kathua District ..	..	..	..	..	..	..	..	..	..	..	..	..	..	..	..	..	..	..	..	..	..	..	..	..	..	..	..	..	..	..	..
3. Udhampur „ (including Bhadrawah) ..	1	1	..	1	1	..	..	..	..	..	..	..	..	..	..	..	1	..	..	..	..	..	..	..	..	..	..	..	..	..	..
4. Riasi District ..	1	1	..	1	1	..	..	..	..	..	..	..	..	..	..	..	1	..	..	..	..	..	..	..	..	..	..	..	..	..	..
5. Mirpur „ ..	9	5	4	7	3	4	..	..	..	..	..	..	1	3	2	1	..	..	..	..	..	..	..	..	..	..	..	..	..	..	..
(b) *Total Jagirs* ..	*7*	*5*	*2*	*5*	*3*	*2*	..	..	*1*	..	*1*	..	*1*	..	..	*2*	..	..	..	..	*2*	*2*	..	*1*	..	..	..	..	..	..	..
6. Chenani Jagir ..	..	..	..	..	..	..	..	..	..	..	..	..	..	..	..	..	..	..	..	..	..	..	..	..	..	..	..	..	..	..	..
7. Poonch „ ..	7	5	2	5	3	2	..	..	1	..	1	..	1	..	..	2	..	..	..	..	2	2	..	1	..	..	..	..	..	..	..
II. Kashmir Province ..	220	88	132	110	46	64	2	3	..	..	4	4	6	17	9	15	14	11	11	14	34	15	19	1	1	..	..	..	..	2	3
8. Baramulla District (including Langet) or Kashmir North	23	7	16	11	5	6	..	..	..	..	2	..	1	1	..	3	1	1	1	1	12	2	10	..	..	..	..	..	..	..	3
9. Srinagar District (including City) or Kashmir South ..	187	73	114	94	38	56	2	3	..	..	2	4	4	14	8	12	13	10	9	13	17	8	9	..	1	..	..	..	..	1	..
10. Muzaffarabad District ..	10	8	2	5	3	2	..	..	..	..	..	..	1	2	1	..	..	..	1	..	5	5	..	1	..	..	..	..	..	1	..
III. Frontier Province. ..	41	21	20	20	9	11	..	1	..	..	..	..	2	4	6	5	1	..	..	1	7	5	2	1	..	..	..	..	..	2	1
11. Ladakh District ..	15	8	7	3	1	2	..	..	..	..	..	..	1	..	..	1	..	..	..	1	7	5	2	1	..	..	..	..	..	2	1
12. Gilgit „ ..	16	6	10	8	2	6	..	1	..	..	..	..	..	1	2	4	..	..	..	..	..	..	..	..	..	..	..	..	..	..	..
13. Frontier Ilaqas. ..	10	7	3	9	6	3	..	..	..	..	..	..	1	3	4	..	1	..	..	..	..	..	..	..	..	..	..	..	..	..	..
Cities and Cantonments.																															
14. Jammu City (including Cantonment) ..	41	21	20	6	5	1	..	..	..	..	..	..	..	..	2	..	2	1	1	..	4	2	2	..	..	..	..	..	..	..	1
15. Jammu Cantonment ..	6	1	5	..	..	..	..	..	..	..	..	..	..	..	..	..	..	..	..	..	..	..	..	..	..	..	..	..	..	..	..
16. Srinagar City (including Cantonment) ..	184	73	111	93	38	55	2	3	..	..	2	4	4	14	8	12	13	10	9	12	16	7	9	..	1	..	..	..	..	1	..
17. Badami Bagh Cantonment ..	1	1	..	..	..	..	..	..	..	..	..	..	..	..	..	..	..	..	..	..	..	..	..	..	..	..	..	..	..	..	..

TABLE XIX.

EUROPEANS AND ALLIED RACES AND ANGLO-INDIANS BY RACE AND AGE.

Jammu and Kashmir Census 1931.

(B) Anglo-Indians.

ANGLO-INDIANS

District, Jagir or Ilaqa.	34—43.		44—53.		54 & over.		All ages.			0—3.		4—6.		7—13.		14—16.		17—19.		20—9.		30—39.		40—49.		0—59.		60—69.		70 & above.	
	Males.	Females.	Males.	Females.	Males.	Females.	Persons.	Males.	Females.	Males.	Females.	Males.	Females.	Males.	Females.	Males.	Females.	Males.	Females.	Males.	Females.	Males.	Females.	Males.	Females.	Males.	Females.	Males.	Females.	Males.	Females.
	33	34	35	36	37	38	39	40	41	42	43	44	45	46	47	48	49	50	51	52	53	54	55	56	57	58	59	60	61	62	63
I. Jammu and Kashmir State ..	6	9	6	4	5	4	123	50	73	8	7	3	8	6	7	2	1	..	6	5	7	11	10	9	6	5	9	..	11	1	1
Jammu Province (including Jagirs) ..	2	..	1	..	..	1	33	16	17	5	4	2	3	1	1	2	..	..	1	..	..	1	5	3	1	2	2	..	..	—	—
(a) Total Districts ..	*2*	..	..	..	..	*1*	*33*	*16*	*17*	*5*	*4*	*2*	*3*	*1*	*1*	*2*	..	..	*1*	..	..	*1*	*5*	*3*	*1*	*2*	*2*	..	..	—	—
1. Jammu District (including City) ..	2	..	..	..	..	1	31	14	17	3	4	2	3	1	1	2	—	..	1	..	..	1	5	3	1	2	2	..	..	—	—
2. Kathua District ..	..	..	..	..	..	..	..	..	..	..	..	..	..	..	..	..	..	..	..	..	..	..	..	..	..	..	..	—	..	—	—
3. Udhampur „ (including Bhadarwah) ..	..	..	..	..	..	..	..	..	..	..	..	..	..	..	..	..	—	..	..	..	..	..	..	..	..	..	..	..	..	—	—
4. Riasi District ..	..	..	..	..	..	..	..	..	..	..	..	..	..	..	..	..	..	..	..	..	..	..	..	..	..	..	..	..	..	—	—
5. Mirpur „ ..	..	..	..	..	..	..	2	2	..	2	..	..	..	..	..	..	..	..	..	..	..	..	..	..	..	..	..	..	..	—	—
(b) Total Jagirs ..	..	..	*1*	..	..	..	..	..	..	..	..	..	..	..	..	..	..	..	—	..	..	..	..	..	..	..	..	..	—	—	—
6. Chenani Jagir ..	..	..	..	..	..	..	..	..	..	..	..	..	—	..	..	..	..	..	..	..	..	..	..	—	..	..	..	..	..	—	—
7. Poonch „ ..	..	..	1	..	..	..	..	..	..	..	..	..	..	..	..	..	..	..	..	..	..	..	..	..	..	..	..	..	..	—	—
II. Kashmir Province ..	4	9	5	3	3	3	76	27	49	2	1	1	3	4	5	..	1	..	5	3	5	7	5	6	5	3	7	..	11	1	1
8. Baramulla District (including Langet) Kashmir North ..	1	4	1	2	..	1	..	..	..	..	..	..	..	..	..	—	..	—	..	—	..	..	..	..	—	..	..	..	..	—	—
9. Srinagar District (including City) Kashmir South ..	3	5	3	1	1	2	76	27	49	2	1	1	3	4	5	..	1	—	5	3	5	7	5	6	5	3	7	..	11	1	1
10. Muzaffarabad District ..	..	..	1	..	2	..	..	..	..	..	..	—	..	..	..	—	..	..	..	—	—	..	—	—	..	—	..	..	..	—	—
III. Frontier Province ..	..	..	..	1	2	..	14	7	7	1	2	..	2	1	1	—	..	—	..	2	2	3	—	—	—	—	..	..	—	—	—
11. Ladakh District ..	..	..	..	1	2	..	5	2	3	..	1	..	..	..	..	..	..	—	—	..	2	2	—	—	—	—	..	—	—	—	—
12. Gilgit „ ..	..	..	—	..	..	..	8	4	4	1	1	..	2	1	1	—	..	..	..	1	..	1	..	—	—	—	..	..	—	—	—
13. Frontier Ilaqas ..	..	..	..	..	..	..	1	1	—	..	..	—	..	..	..	..	..	..	—	1	—	—	..	—	..	—	—	..	—	—	—
Cities and Cantonments.																															
14. Jammu City (including Cantonment) ..	2	..	..	..	..	1	31	14	17	3	4	2	3	1	1	2	..	—	1	..	—	1	5	3	1	2	2	—	—	—	—
15. Jammu Cantonment ..	..	..	..	—	..	—	6	1	5	..	..	..	1	—	1	—	—	—	—	..	..	—	2	1	1	..	—	—	..	—	—
16. Srinagar City (including Cantonment) ..	2	5	3	1	1	2	75	28	47	2	1	1	3	4	5	—	1	..	5	3	5	7	5	7	4	3	7	—	10	1	1
17. Badami Bagh Cantonment ..	—	—	—	—	—	—	1	1	—	..	..	—	..	..	—	—	—	—	—	—	—	—	—	1	—	—	—	—	—	—	—

TABLE XX.

SUMMARY FIGURES FOR DISTRICTS.

Jammu and Kashmir Census 1931.

1. Density figures in column 10 have been shown in whole numbers, fraction below ·5 being omitted, while those above ·5 being counted as full numbers.

2. Under the Kashmir Province the old names of Districts, Kashmir North and Kashmir South, though retained within brackets for purposes of comparison with past Censuses, have been amplified by the addition of the more familiar names of Baramulla and Srinagar Districts respectively.

3. The term "others" includes population shown under 'Jains' 'Zoroastrians' and 'others' in Table XVI.

4. For purposes of comparative study, remarks against items 1, 2, 3 and 4 on the fly leaf of Table I should also be referred to.

TABLE

SUMMARY FIGURES

Jammu and Kashmir

Serial No.	District or State.	Area in Sq. miles.	*Population 1931.*			Population 1921.	*Percentage of variation.*		*Number of Persons per Sq. mile in*	
			Persons.	Males.	Females.		1921—1931.	1911—1921.	1931.	1921.
1	2	3	4	5	6	7	8	9	10	11
	Jammu and Kashmir State ..	**84,471**	**3,646,243**	**1,938,338**	**1,707,905**	**3,320,518**	**+9·8**	**+5·1**	**43**	**39**
	I.—Jammu Province (including Jagirs) ..	**12,378**	**1,788,441**	**942,815**	**845.626**	**1,640,259**	**+9·03**	**+2·7**	**144**	**135**
	(a) Total Districts ..	*10,656*	*1,390,132*	*738,267*	*651,865*	*1,277,858*	*+8·78*	*+2·7*	*130*	*122*
1	Jammu District (including City) ..	1,147	375,240	205,719	169,521	337,544	+11·16	+2·5	327	292
2	Kathua ,, ..	1,023	161,232	85,993	75,239	154,209	+4·55	+1·6	158	151
3	Udhampur .. (including Bhadrawah) ..	5,070	273,668	143,514	130,154	245,255	+11·58	+1·7	54	50
4	Riasi District ..	1,789	235,245	124,210	111,035	223,652	+5·18	+8·6	131	123
5	Mirpur ,, ..	1,627	344,747	178,831	165,916	317,198	+8·68	—1·8	212	202
	(b) Total Jagirs ..	*1,722*	*398,309*	*204,548*	*193,761*	*362,401*	*+9·9*	*+5·4*	*231*	*210*
6	Chenani Jagir ..	95	10,925	5,930	4,995	10,620	+2·87	+·3	115	114
7	Poonch ,, ..	1,627	387,384	198,618	188,766	351,781	+10·12	+5·2	238	216
	II.—Kashmir Province ..	**8,539**	**1,569,218**	**847,022**	**722,196**	**1,407,086**	**+11·52**	**+8·6**	**184**	**164**
8	Baramulla District (including Langet) or Kashmir North.	3,317	559,828	301,397	258.431	502,216	+11·47	+9·1	169	151
9	Srinagar District (including City) or Kashmir South.	2,814	771,943	419,190	352,753	688,761	+12·1	+7·7	274	245
10	Muzaffarabad District ..	2,408	237,447	126,435	111,012	216,109	+9·87	+10·7	99	90
	III.—Frontier Districts ..	**63,554**	**288,584**	**148,501**	**140,083**	**273,173**	**+5·64**	**+3·1**	**5**	**4**
11	Ladakh ..	45,762	192,138	96,259	95,879	183,476	+4·72	—1·7	4	4
12	Gilgit ..	3,112	31,002	17,752	14,150	28,706	+11·13	+19·8	10	9
13	Frontier Ilaqas ..	14,680	64,544	34,490	30,054	60,991	+5·82	+12	4	4

XX.

FOR DISTRICTS.

Census 1931.

Distribution by Religion.											
Hindu.		*Muslim.*		*Sikh.*		*Christian.*		*Buddhist.*		*Others.*	
Males.	Females.	Males.	Females.	Males.	Females.	Males.	Females.	Males.	Females.	Males.	Females.
12	13	14	15	16	17	18	19	20	21	22	23
393,699	**342,523**	**1,497,252**	**1,820,384**	**26,457**	**24,205**	**1,248**	**1,020**	**19,287**	**19,437**	**400**	**336**
353,348	**311,898**	**572,699**	**518,322**	**15,197**	**14,085**	**957**	**766**	**253**	**254**	**331**	**301**
335,098	*295,269*	*392,222*	*346,796*	*9,420*	*8,514*	*944*	*733*	*253*	*254*	*330*	*299*
118,745	98,315	82,202	67,134	3,677	3,177	765	597	4	5	326	293
64,008	56,930	21,619	18,028	268	210	98	71	......	......	......	......
80,709	75,054	62,361	54,690	178	150	20	12	245	247	1	1
41,416	37,596	82,322	73,031	449	393	19	13	4	2	......	......
30,220	27,374	143,718	133,913	4,848	4,584	42	40	......	......	3	5
18,250	*16,629*	*180,477*	*171,526*	*5,777*	*5,571*	*43*	*33*	......	......	*1*	*2*
5,034	4,375	892	620	4	......	......	......	......	......	......	......
13,216	12,254	179,585	170,906	5,773	5,571	43	33	......	......	1	2
38,847	**30,449**	**796,802**	**681,485**	**11,135**	**10,055**	**166**	**173**	**5**	......	**67**	**34**
6,286	4,420	291,786	250,957	3,248	3,012	36	25	......	......	41	17
29,871	24,229	356,863	326,668	2,303	1,694	122	146	5	......	26	16
2,690	1,800	118,153	103,860	5,584	5,349	8	2	......	......	......	1
1,504	**176**	**127,751**	**120,577**	**125**	**65**	**90**	**81**	**19,029**	**19,183**	**2**	**1**
261	58	76,849	76,539	63	34	57	65	19,029	19,183	......	......
942	93	16,727	14,014	56	29	25	13	......	......	2	1
301	25	34,175	30,024	6	2	8	3	......	......	......	......

STATE TABLE I.

AREA AND POPULATION BY TEHSILS.

Jammu and Kashmir Census 1931.

STATE TABLE I.

AREA AND POPULATION BY TEHSILS.

Jammu and Kashmir Census 1931.

Tehsils.	Area in square miles.	Number of Towns.	Number of Villages.	Number of occupied houses.	Population 1931. Persons.	Males.	Females.	1921 Both sexes.	Percentage of Variation. 1921 to 1931.	1911 to 1921.	Number of persons per square mile in 1931.
1	2	3	4	5	6	7	8	9	10	11	12
Jammu and Kashmir State ..	**84,516**	**39**	**8,903**	**671,638**	**3,646,243**	**1,938,338**	**1,707,905**	**3,320,518**	**+9·8**	**+5·1**	**43**
I.—Jammu Province including Jagirs	**12,401**	**20**	**4,544**	**350,928**	**1,788,441**	**942,815**	**845,626**	**1,640,259**	**+9·03**	**+2·7**	**144**
(a) *Total Districts* ..	*10,685*	*19*	*4,004*	*282,009*	*1,390,132*	*738,267*	*651,865*	*1,277,858*	*+8·8*	*+2·0*	*130*
Jammu District ..	**1,144**	**5**	**1,160**	**78,717**	**375,240**	**205,719**	**169,521**	**337,544**	**+11·16**	**+2·5**	**328**
1. Jammu Tehsil (inclusive of Jammu City) ..	343	2	326	20,109	132,840	76,065	56,775	119,875	+10·8	—·8	387
**Jammu City* ..	*1*	*1*	....	*8,398*	*38,474*	*23,228*	*15,246*	*31,506*	*+22·11*	*—7*	*38,474*
2. Samba Tehsil ..	327	1	323	15,478	79,181	42,042	37,139	67,287	+17·67	—3	242
3. Sri Ranbir Singh Pura Tehsil	157	1	293	17,764	82,788	44,761	38,027	76,780	+7·82	+12·8	527
4. Akhnoor Tehsil ..	317	1	218	16,968	80,431	42,851	37,680	73,602	+9·27	—1·2	254
Kathua District ..	**1,022**	**3**	**561**	**34,101**	**161,232**	**85,993**	**75,239**	**154,209**	**+4·55**	**+1·6**	**158**
5. Kathua Tehsil ..	224	2	164	9,200	43,299	24,179	19,120	40,841	+6.01	—2·6	193
6. Jasmergharh Tehsil ..	185	..	260	10,595	51,957	27,662	24,295	47,889	+8·5	+7·5	281
7. Basohli „ ..	613	1	137	14,306	65,976	34,152	31,824	65,479	+·75	+·2	108
Udhampur District ..	**5,074**	**4**	**938**	**50,381**	**278,668**	**143,514**	**130,154**	**245,255**	**+11·58**	**+1·7**	**54**
8. Udhampur Tehsil ..	383	1	196	10,238	48,880	26,083	22,797	45,668	+7·03	+2·5	128
9. Kishtwar „ ..	3,026	1	166	8,955	56,496	29,918	26,578	47,698	+18·44	+2·2	18
10. Ramban „ ..	588	..	130	11,771	71,043	37,502	33,541	62,020	+14·55	+2·9	121
11. Ramnagar „ ..	524	1	137	11,760	55,666	28,615	27,051	52,255	+6·52	+1·4	106
12. Bhadarwah „ ..	553	1	309	7,657	41,583	21,396	20,187	37,614	+10·55	+·3	75
Reasi District ..	**1,818**	**3**	**647**	**42,479**	**235,245**	**124,210**	**111,035**	**223,652**	**+5·18**	**+8·6**	**129**
13. Reasi Tehsil ..	998	2	323	19,957	106,876	56,403	50,473	100,921	+5·90	+7·6	107
14. Rampur Rajauri Tehsil ..	820	1	324	22,522	128,369	67,807	60,562	122,731	+4·59	+[illegible]·4	156
Mirpur District ..	**1,627**	**4**	**698**	**76,331**	**344,747**	**178,831**	**165,916**	**317,198**	**+8·68**	**—1·8**	**212**
15. Kotli Tehsil ..	574	1	222	22,178	102,787	54,304	48,483	94,342	+8·95	—1·9	179
16. Mirpur „ ..	355	1	289	24,024	101,102	51,554	49,548	93,381	+8·26	—4·8	285
17. Bhimber „ ..	698	2	187	30,129	140,858	72,973	67,885	129,475	+8·79	+·4	202
(b) *Total Jagirs* ..	*1,716*	*1*	*540*	*68,919*	*398,309*	*204,548*	*193,761*	*362,401*	*+9·9*	*+5·4*	*232*
Chenani Jagir ..	95	..	57	2,338	10,925	5,930	4,995	10,620	+2·87	+·3	115
Total Poonch ..	*1,621*	*1*	*483*	*66,581*	*387,384*	*198,618*	*188,766*	*351,781*	*+10·12*	*+5·2*	*239*
Haveli Tehsil ..	476	1	172	15,908	101,151	53,425	47,726	95,554	+5·85	....	212
Mendhar „ ..	476	..	98	15,210	91,807	48,194	43,613	83,248	+10·28	....	193
Bagh „ ..	319	..	112	16,536	93,956	47,642	46,314	83,883	+12·0	....	294
Sadhnoti „ ..	346	..	101	18,927	100,470	49,357	51,113	89,096	+12·76	....	290
Area of Poonch villages situated in Jammu Province) ..	4	..	....	....	....	....	....	....	....	....	....
II.—Kashmir Province ..	**8,555**	**15**	**3,542**	**267,016**	**1,569,218**	**847,022**	**722,196**	**1,407,086**	**+11·52**	**+8·6**	**183**
Kashmir North (Baramulla including Langet) ..	**3,326**	**4**	**1,390**	**92,290**	**559,828**	**301,397**	**258,431**	**502,216**	**+11·47**	**+8·1**	**168**
18. Uttarmachipura Tehsil ..	2,248	1	562	37,810	247,849	132,039	115,810	221,334	+11·98	+10·5	110
19. Baramulla „ ..	590	2	357	23,600	149,009	80,705	68,304	133,887	+11·29	+10·8	252
20. Sripratapsingh Pura Tehsil ..	488	1	471	30,880	162,970	88,653	74,317	146,995	+10·87	....	334
Kashmir South (Srinagar including City) ..	**2,822**	**9**	**1,331**	**136,896**	**771,943**	**419,190**	**352,753**	**688,761**	**+12·1**	**+7·7**	**274**
21. Tehsil Khas (excluding City) ..	732	1	217	17,[illegible]59	108,884	59,425	49,459	100,463	+8·38	+15·5	501
Srinagar City ..	11	1	....	28,525	173,573	94,793	78,780	141,735	+22·46	+8·9	15,779
22. Awanti Pura Tehsil ..	449	1	389	24,619	149,807	82,183	67,624	134,918	+11·04	+5·1	334
23. Kulgam „ ..	588	1	454	30,944	146,147	77,407	68,740	136,581	+7·0	+3·9	248
24. Anantnag „ ..	1,042	5	321	35,549	193,532	105,382	88,150	175,064	+10·55	+8·2	186
Muzaffarabad District ..	**2,407**	**2**	**771**	**37,830**	**237,447**	**126,435**	**111,012**	**216,109**	**+9·87**	**+10·7**	**99**
25. Muzaffarabad Tehsil ..	546	1	425	19,261	112,798	59,801	52,997	104,031	+8·42	+10·3	206
26. Uri „ —	520	1	230	10,544	71,570	38,250	33,320	64,641	+10·72	+8·8	137
27. Karnah „ ..	1,341	..	116	8,025	53,079	28,384	24,695	47,437	+11·89	+14·3	39
III.—Frontier Districts ..	**63,560**	**4**	**817**	**53,694**	**288,584**	**148,501**	**140,083**	**273,173**	**+5·64**	**+3·1**	**5**
Ladhakh District ..	**45,762**	**2**	**468**	**37,053**	**192,138**	**96,259**	**95,879**	**183,476**	**+4·72**	**—1·7**	**4**
28. Ladhakh Tehsil ..	29,848	1	108	8,586	34,423	17,332	17,091	33,052	+4·14	+2·9	1
29. Kargil „ ..	7,392	..	160	7,053	50,238	24,446	25,792	47,679	+5·36	—·1	7
30. Skardu „ ..	8,522	1	200	21,414	107,477	54,481	52,996	102,745	+4·60	—3·8	13
Gilgit District ..	**3,118**	**2**	**79**	**5,144**	**31,902**	**17,752**	**14,150**	**28,706**	**+11·13**	**+19·8**	**10**
31. Gilgil Tehsil ..	3,118	2	79	5,144	31,902	17,752	14,150	28,706	+11,13	+19·8	10
Frontier Ilaqas ..	**14,680**	..	**270**	**11,497**	**64,544**	**34,490**	**30,054**	**60,991**	**+5·82**	**+12**	**4**
Chillas ..	2,800	..	96	3,165	13,534	7,461	6,073	13,135	+3·03	+5·01	5
Nagar ..	1,600	..	57	2,582	13,672	7,363	6,309	14,188	—3·63	+6·3	9
Hunza ..	3,900	..	46	2,300	13,241	6,965	6,276	12,117	+9·27	+19·7	3
Punial ..	1,600	..	14	780	6,108	3,225	2,883	5,492	+11·21	+24·2	4
Ishkomam ..	1,600	—	11	365	2,986	1,611	1,375	2,753	+8·46	+36·3	2
Yasin ..	1,200	..	25	1,339	8,083	4,154	3,929	7,065	+14·4	+11·9	7
Kuh ..	480	..	11	409	2,808	1,547	1,261	2,288	+22·72	+10·9	6
Ghizar ..	1,300	..	10	557	4,112	2,164	1,948	3,953	+4·02	+8·6	3

*Excludes Railway population.

NOTE.—The figures of area given in Imperial Table I are *revised* area figures supplied by the Survey Department of the Government of India but they were not available by Tehsils and hence have not been adopted in this Table though the figures in this Table are also based on the information received from the same source excepting figures for Ladakh and Frontier Ilaqas which the Survey Department could not supply.

STATE TABLE II.

Population of Districts and Taluks by Religion and Literacy.

Jammu and Kashmir Census 1931.

1. The figures under "Others" include those of Zoroastrians.

STATE TABLE II.

POPULATION OF DISTRICT AND TALUKS BY RELIGION AND LITERACY.

Jammu and Kashmir Census 1931.

District and Taluk.	HINDUS. Brahmans. No. of Persons. Males.	Females.	No. of Literate. Males.	Females.	Other Hindus. No. of Persons. Males.	Females.	No. of Literate. Males.	Females.	Depressed Classes. No. of Persons. Males.	Females.	No. of Literate. Males.	Females.	Jains. No. of Persons. Males.	Females.	No. of Literate. Males.	Females.	Sikhs. No. of Persons. Males.	Females.	No. of Literate. Males.	Females.	Muslims. No. of Persons. Males.	Females.
1	2	3	4	5	6	7	8	9	10	11	12	13	14	15	16	17	18	19	20	21	22	23
Jammu and Kashmir State ..	133,243	120,286	31,351	1,981	170,183	141,582	31,521	3,588	90,273	80,655	836	65	319	278	219	95	26,457	24,205	5,560	906	1,497,252	1,320,384
I. Jammu Province ..	93,686	92,519	12,886	1,475	164,450	138,762	28,855	3,182	90,212	80,617	822	62	314	277	215	95	15,197	14,085	3,197	627	572,699	518,322
Jammu District ..	31,037	27,792	4,733	818	50,964	39,963	13,405	1,854	36,154	30,560	347	19	309	269	213	92	3,677	3,177	816	224	82,202	67,134
Jammu City ..	3,912	2,589	2,451	712	9,056	6,178	7,689	1,504	1,386	981	131	12	297	266	205	91	757	539	550	188	7,621	4,415
" Cantonment ..	262	81	139	10	2,166	189	945	12	60	39	1	4	8	1	6	..	10	11	8	6	1,118	229
" Tehsil ..	7,509	5,980	636	15	10,561	9,316	1,537	85	11,215	9,309	30	..	..	..	..	..	296	264	73	13	19,138	15,783
Karloop Ilaqa ..	84	100	2	..	66	48	5	..	80	82	1	..	..	..	..	..	3	3	..	..	79	67
Total Jammu Tehsil ..	*11,767*	*8,750*	*3,231*	*737*	*21,849*	*15,731*	*10,176*	*1,601*	*12,741*	*10,411*	*163*	*16*	*305*	*267*	*211*	*91*	*1,066*	*817*	*631*	*207*	*27,956*	*20,494*
Samba Tehsil ..	5,736	5,481	697	45	9,605	8,163	1,366	82	9,045	7,748	91	2	..	..	..	..	974	924	49	4	16,665	14,804
Ranbirsinghpura Tehsil ..	3,662	3,214	326	11	11,427	9,613	1,064	99	6,110	5,113	43	1	..	..	..	..	1,411	1,213	113	7	21,784	18,587
Akhnoor " ..	10,462	10,347	479	25	8,083	6,456	799	72	8,258	7,288	50	..	4	2	2	1	226	223	23	6	15,797	13,249
Kathua District ..	16,992	18,925	2,237	121	34,263	27,195	2,583	143	12,753	10,810	78	19	..	..	..	..	268	210	58	11	21,619	18,028
Kathua Tehsil ..	3,128	2,624	557	42	8,503	6,423	925	43	3,962	3,308	44	..	..	..	..	..	73	54	32	9	8,424	6,649
Jasmergarh Tehsil ..	7,977	8,062	685	22	7,249	6,086	499	24	4,672	3,738	9	13	..	..	..	..	192	154	24	1	7,564	6,249
Basohli " ..	5,887	8,239	995	57	18,511	14,686	1,159	76	4,119	3,764	25	6	..	..	..	..	3	2	2	1	5,631	5,130
Udhampur District ..	17,901	16,066	2,335	145	40,677	38,070	5,513	344	22,131	20,918	228	14	1	1	1	1	178	150	76	8	62,361	54,690
Udhampur Tehsil ..	5,957	5,455	934	75	8,702	7,614	1,990	106	5,890	5,398	58	7	1	1	1	1	63	60	33	3	5,468	4,268
Bhadrawah " ..	1,356	1,309	339	28	6,427	6,268	1,123	54	4,215	4,100	85	5	..	..	..	..	34	33	16	1	9,364	8,477
Kishtwar " ..	1,898	1,330	292	5	8,563	7,967	546	56	1,829	1,634	19	..	..	..	..	..	46	31	13	..	17,337	15,369
Ramban " ..	1,964	1,599	176	14	6,969	6,613	536	14	1,725	1,746	11	2	..	..	..	..	33	26	14	4	26,810	23,557
Ramnagar " ..	6,726	6,373	604	23	10,016	9,608	1,318	14	8,472	8,040	55	..	..	..	..	..	2	..	..	..	3,383	3,019

Riasi District ..	**14,196**	**12,635**	**895**	**50**	**16,202**	**14,545**	**1,941**	**170**	**11,016**	**10,416**	**47**	**2**	–	–	–	–	**440**	**393**	**158**	**30**	**82,322**	**73,031**
Riasi Tehsil ..	7,487	6,847	440	23	11,156	9,850	1,298	107	8,144	7,435	22	..	–	–	–	..	77	66	29	5	29,523	26,264
Rampur Rajouri Tehsil ..	6,711	5,788	455	27	5,046	4,695	643	63	2,872	2,981	5	2	..	..	–	..	372	327	129	25	52,799	46,767
Mirpur District ..	**6,844**	**6,406**	**1,488**	**251**	**17,686**	**15,317**	**3,713**	**629**	**5,690**	**5,651**	**82**	**5**	**3**	**5**	..	..	**4,848**	**4,584**	**1,190**	**287**	**143,718**	**133,913**
Kotli Tehsil ..	1,799	1,643	383	60	1,470	1,251	780	151	845	832	13	..	..	..	..	..	605	561	170	30	49,585	44,195
Bhimber „ ..	3,976	3,814	570	47	14,105	12,319	1,385	114	4,795	4,778	69	5	..	..	..	..	3,149	3,037	489	54	46,911	43,902
Mirpur „ ..	1,069	949	535	144	2,111	1,747	1,548	364	50	41	..	..	3	5	..	..	1,094	986	531	203	47,222	45,816
Poonch Jagir (*Ilaqa*) ..	**10,382**	**10,065**	**1,068**	**89**	**2,021**	**1,465**	**1,356**	**114**	**813**	**724**	**14**	**3**	**1**	**2**	**1**	**2**	**5,773**	**5,571**	**898**	**67**	**179,585**	**170,906**
Haveli Tehsil ..	1,690	1,424	275	58	1,140	865	940	102	112	89	7	..	1	2	1	2	822	697	242	44	49,651	44,639
Maindor „ ..	1,541	1,439	134	5	508	363	142	3	206	162	7	..	..	..	..	..	66	52	17	..	45,873	41,597
Bagh „ ..	686	604	93	10	142	116	56	1	35	34	..	2	..	..	..	..	3,387	3,417	357	12	43,392	42,143
Sadhnoti „ ..	6,465	6,598	566	16	231	121	209	8	460	439	..	1	..	..	..	..	1,498	1,405	282	11	40,669	42,527
Chenani Jagir ..	**742**	**630**	**130**	**1**	**2,637**	**2,207**	**344**	**28**	**1,655**	**1,538**	**26**	..	..	..	..	..	**4**	..	**1**	..	**892**	**620**
II. Kashmir Province ..	**34,265**	**27,675**	**18,264**	**482**	**4,521**	**2,736**	**1,975**	**386**	**61**	**38**	**14**	**3**	**3**	..	**3**	..	**11,135**	**10,055**	**2,287**	**258**	**796,802**	**681,485**
Kashmir South ..	**27,658**	**23,116**	**14,974**	**384**	**2,152**	**1,075**	**1,071**	**217**	**61**	**38**	**14**	**3**	**3**	..	**3**	..	**2,303**	**1,694**	**545**	**46**	**386,863**	**326,668**
Tehsil Khas ..	1,147	824	487	4	589	124	265	5	..	..	..	..	..	..	..	..	67	23	22	3	57,598	48,470
Srinagar City ..	17,306	14,546	10,490	352	1,080	639	630	199	61	38	14	3	3	..	3	..	634	236	273	40	75,583	63,181
Total Tehsil Khas ..	*18,453*	*15,370*	*10,986*	*356*	*1,669*	*763*	*895*	*204*	*61*	*38*	*14*	*3*	*3*	..	*3*	..	*701*	*259*	*295*	*43*	*133,181*	*111,651*
Awantipura Tehsil ..	2,128	1,810	856	2	11	3	10	..	..	..	..	..	..	..	..	..	1,021	969	132	2	79,023	64,842
Kulgam „ ..	2,565	2,182	1,074	6	401	260	142	3	..	..	..	..	..	..	..	..	99	88	5	1	74,342	66,208
Anantnag „ ..	4,512	3,754	2,058	20	71	49	24	10	..	..	..	..	..	..	..	..	482	378	113	..	100,317	83,967
Kashmir North ..	**5,541**	**3,948**	**2,681**	**20**	**745**	**472**	**197**	**43**	..	..	..	..	..	..	..	..	**3,248**	**3,012**	**737**	**70**	**291,786**	**250,957**
Baramulla Tehsil ..	2,035	1,411	1,061	3	353	223	8	21	..	..	..	..	..	..	..	..	1,039	845	280	26	77,249	65,803
Sri Pratapsingh Pura Tehsil ..	1,063	775	534	6	69	37	29	7	..	..	..	..	..	..	..	..	860	892	90	1	86,622	72,593
Uttarmachipura „ ..	2,443	1,762	1,086	11	323	212	160	15	..	..	..	..	..	..	..	..	1,349	1,275	367	43	127,915	112,561
Muzaffarabad District ..	**1,066**	**611**	**609**	**78**	**1,624**	**1,189**	**707**	**126**	..	..	..	..	..	..	..	..	**5,584**	**5,349**	**1,005**	**142**	**118,153**	**103,860**
Karnah Tehsil ..	110	29	89	5	81	38	32	3	–	..	..	..	..	..	..	..	226	106	58	14	27,965	24,461
Muzaffarabad Tehsil ..	589	315	360	72	1,143	866	506	107	..	..	..	..	..	..	..	–	3,881	3,915	758	114	54,183	47,899
Uri „ ..	367	267	160	1	400	285	169	16	..	..	..	..	..	..	..	–	1,477	1,268	189	14	36,005	31,500
III. Frontier District ..	**292**	**93**	**201**	**24**	**1,212**	**84**	**691**	**20**	..	..	..	..	**2**	**1**	**1**	..	**125**	**65**	**76**	**21**	**127,751**	**120,577**
Ladakh District ..	**127**	**44**	**86**	**9**	**134**	**14**	**69**	**5**	..	–	–	–	–	–	–	..	**63**	**34**	**44**	**19**	**76,849**	**76,539**
Ladakh Tehsil ..	**15**	**5**	**12**	..	**73**	**2**	**41**	**1**	–	–	–	–	–	–	–	–	**3**	–	**3**	–	**2,076**	**1,997**
Skardu „ ..	**81**	**19**	**54**	**8**	**45**	**2**	**17**	**2**	–	–	–	–	–	–	..	–	**47**	**27**	**31**	**16**	**54,245**	**52,947**

STATE TABLE II.

Population of District and Taluks by Religion and Literacy.

Jammu and Kashmir Census 1931.

District and Taluk.	Muslims. No. of Literates.		Christians. No. of Persons.		Christians. No. of Literates.		Buddhist. No. of Persons.		Buddhist. No. of Literates.		Others. No. of Persons.		Others. No of Literates.		No. of Literates. Aged 0—15.		No. of Literates. Aged 15—20.		No. of Literates. Aged 20 & over.		Literate in English.	
	Males.	Females.	Males.	Females.	Males.	Females.	Males.	Females.	Males.	Females.	Males.	Females.	Males.	Females.	Males.	Females.	Males.	Females.	Males	Females.	Males.	Females.
1	24	25	26	27	28	29	30	31	32	33	34	35	36	37	38	39	40	41	42	43	44	45
Jammu and Kashmir State ..	43,476	2,166	1,243	1,020	305	263	19,287	19,437	1,592	28	81	58	4	1	13,488	2,616	15,837	1,652	85,539	4,825	18,671	810
I. Jammu Province ..	19,952	1,447	987	766	115	67	253	254	10	..	17	24	1	..	8,129	1,927	9,101	1,261	48,823	3,767	6,876	453
Jammu District ..	4,942	846	765	597	84	46	4	5	2	..	17	24	1	..	3,151	1,096	3,806	700	17,586	2,103	3,736	387
Jammu City ..	2,388	607	328	274	77	43	4	5	2	..	..	5	..	..	1,910	896	2,205	565	9,381	1,696	2,746	362
" Cantonment ..	286	9	2	5	1	3	....	....	....	..	..	..	..	..	33	9	172	8	1,181	27	152	6
" Tehsil ..	413	25	42	14	5	....	....	....	....	..	..	..	..	..	241	32	393	21	2,060	85	358	14
Karloop Ilaqa ..	7	....	1	....	....	....	....	....	....	..	..	..	..	..	..	..	1	..	14	....	....	....
Total Jammu Tehsil ..	*3,094*	*641*	*373*	*293*	*83*	*46*	*4*	*5*	*2*	..	..	*5*	..	..	*2,184*	*937*	*2,771*	*694*	*12,636*	*1,808*	*3,256*	*352*
Samba Tehsil ..	402	32	....	....	....	....	....	....	....	..	17	19	1	..	342	51	408	33	1,856	81	191	....
Ranbirsinghpura Tehsil ..	971	114	367	287	1	....	....	....	....	..	..	..	..	..	380	55	381	48	1,757	129	202	2
Akhnur " ..	475	59	25	17	....	....	....	....	....	..	..	..	..	..	245	53	246	25	1,337	85	87	3
Kathua District ..	634	45	98	71	1	....	....	....	....	..	..	..	..	..	710	91	701	68	4,180	180	533	8
Kathua Tehsil ..	402	19	89	62	....	....	....	....	....	..	..	..	..	..	225	26	271	23	1,464	64	204	5
Jasmergarh Tehsil ..	79	3	8	6	....	....	....	....	....	..	..	..	..	..	159	12	188	15	949	36	75	2
Basohli " ..	53	23	1	3	1	....	....	....	....	..	..	..	..	..	326	53	242	30	1,767	80	254	1
Udhampur District ..	2,055	69	20	12	8	3	245	247	8	..	..	..	..	..	1,065	128	1,278	86	7,881	270	867	16
Udhampur Tehsil ..	302	33	2	1	....	....	....	....	....	..	..	..	..	..	411	61	466	38	2,441	126	421	4
Bhadrawah " ..	497	12	..	..	..	..	..	..	..	..	..	..	..	..	221	25	258	19	1,571	56	150	1
Kishtwar " ..	526	18	..	..	..	..	245	247	8	..	..	..	..	..	111	18	194	16	1,099	45	128	8
Ramban " ..	621	5	1	..	1	..	..	..	..	..	..	..	..	..	72	7	130	6	1,157	26	67	3
Ramnagar " ..	109	1	17	11	7	3	..	..	..	..	..	..	..	..	250	17	230	7	1,613	17	101	....

Riasi District ..	1,466	45	19	13	1	....	4	2	....	..	..	..	..	..	406	70	483	55	3,617	172	149	4
Riasi Tehsil ..	402	13	16	11	1	....	....	....	....	..	..	..	..	..	199	34	223	27	1,770	87	96	4
Rampur Rajouri Tehsil ..	1,064	32	3	2	....	....	4	2	....	..	..	..	..	..	209	36	260	28	1,847	85	53	....
Mirpur District ..	4,858	195	42	40	8	10	....	....	....	..	..	..	..	..	1,541	408	1,458	255	8,345	714	960	15
Kotli Tehsil ..	1,310	44	....	1	....	....	....	....	....	..	..	..	..	..	275	98	328	56	2,053	131	137	3
Bhimber „ ..	1,555	52	37	35	3	6	....	....	....	..	..	..	..	..	635	74	448	50	2,988	154	205	1
Mirpur „ ..	1,993	99	5	4	5	4	....	....	....	..	..	..	..	..	631	236	677	149	3,304	429	618	11
Poonch Jagir (*Illaqa*) ..	5,932	240	43	33	13	8	....	....	....	..	..	..	..	..	1,212	131	1,337	90	6,733	302	606	23
Haveli Tehsil ..	1,902	155	9	10	5	2	....	....	....	..	..	..	..	..	464	103	511	64	2,406	196	433	21
Mendhar „ ..	661	8	....	....	....	....	....	....	....	..	..	..	..	..	80	3	117	2	764	11	16	....
Bagh „ ..	1,262	25	....	....	....	....	....	....	....	..	..	..	..	..	225	10	228	9	1,315	31	45	....
Sadhnoti ..	2,107	52	34	23	8	6	....	....	....	..	..	..	..	..	443	15	481	15	2,248	64	112	2
Chenani Jagir ..	65	7	....	....	....	....	....	....	....	..	..	..	..	..	42	3	43	7	481	26	25	....
II. Kashmir Province ..	20,989	663	166	173	141	160	5	....	1	..	64	34	3	1	5,012	649	6,215	364	32,450	940	11,461	334
Kashmir South ..	11,807	510	122	146	108	135	5	....	1	..	23	16	3	..	3,463	486	4,176	237	20,887	572	9,420	289
Tehsil Khas ..	898	15	4	3	4	1	....	....	....	..	20	15	..	..	116	8	196	4	1,364	16	212	4
Srinagar City ..	4,979	379	118	139	104	130	5	....	1	..	3	1	3	..	2,276	424	2,533	190	11,697	489	7,998	275
Total Tehsil Khas ..	*5,877*	*394*	*122*	*142*	*108*	*131*	*5*	....	*1*	..	*23*	*16*	*3*	..	*2,392*	*432*	*2,729*	*194*	*13,061*	*505*	*8,210*	*279*
Awantipura Tehsil ..	1,554	16	....	....	....	....	....	....	....	..	..	..	..	..	209	6	337	6	2,006	8	208	2
Kulgam „ ..	1,535	65	....	2	....	2	....	....	....	..	..	..	..	..	281	24	366	22	2,109	31	227	4
Anantnag „ ..	2,841	35	....	2	....	2	....	....	....	..	..	..	..	..	581	24	744	15	3,711	28	775	4
Kashmir North ..	6,223	93	36	25	27	23	....	....	....	..	41	17	..	..	938	61	1,384	47	7,543	141	1,460	34
Baramulla Tehsil ..	1,571	27	29	22	20	20	....	....	....	..	..	..	..	..	280	23	442	17	2,218	57	647	27
Sri Pratapsinghpura Tehsil ..	1,369	8	2	3	2	3	....	....	....	..	37	17	..	..	171	4	247	3	1,606	18	207	3
Uttarmachipura „ ..	3,283	58	5	....	5	....	....	....	....	..	4	..	..	..	487	34	695	27	3,719	66	606	4
Muzaffarabad District ..	2,959	60	8	2	6	2	....	....	....	..	..	1	..	1	611	103	655	80	4,020	227	581	11
Karnah Tehsil ..	562	5	2	1	2	1	....	....	....	..	..	..	..	..	97	10	96	6	550	12	75	3
Muzaffarabad Tehsil ..	1,506	45	5	1	3	1	....	....	....	..	..	1	..	1	350	81	374	68	2,409	191	355	6
Uri „ ..	891	10	1	....	1	....	....	....	....	..	..	..	..	..	164	11	185	6	1,061	24	151	2
III. Frontier District ..	2,535	56	90	81	49	36	19,029	19,183	1,581	28	..	..	..	..	347	40	521	37	4,266	118	334	23
Ladakh District ..	1,532	27	57	65	36	28	19,029	19,183	1,581	28	..	..	..	..	187	24	278	14	2,833	78	179	13
Ladakh Tehsil ..	253	11	52	63	34	26	15,113	15,024	1,479	27	..	..	..	..	79	12	128	7	1,615	46	64	7
Skardu „ ..	786	13	....	....	....	....	63	1	4	..	..	..	..	..	36	9	85	7	771	23	77	4

STATE TABLE II.

Population of District and Taluks by Religion and Literacy.

Jammu and Kashmir Census 1931.

District and Taluk.	Hindus. Brahmans. No. of Persons. Males.	Females.	No. of Literates. Males.	Females.	Other Hindus. No. of Persons. Males.	Females.	No. of Literates. Males.	Females.	Depressed. No. of Persons. Males.	Females.	No. of Literates. Males.	Females.	Jains. No. of Persons. Males.	Females.	No. of Literates. Males.	Females.	Sikhs. No. of Persons. Males.	Females.	No. of Literates. Males.	Females.	Muslims. No. of Persons. Males.	Females.
1	2	3	4	5	6	7	8	9	10	11	12	13	14	15	16	17	18	19	20	21	22	23
Ladakh District—(continued).																						
Kargil Tehsil ..	31	20	20	1	16	10	11	2	....	....	..	..	..	..	..	..	13	7	10	3	20,528	21,595
Gilgit District ..	157	48	110	15	785	45	505	10	....	....	..	..	2	1	1	..	56	29	28	2	16,727	14,014
Gilgit Tehsil ..	157	48	110	15	785	45	505	10	....	....	..	..	2	1	1	..	56	29	28	2	16,727	14,014
Frontier Ilaqas ..	8	....	5	....	29	25	117	5	....	....	..	..	..	..	..	..	6	2	4	....	34,175	30,024
Chilas ..	6	....	3	....	196	19	106	3	....	....	..	..	..	..	..	..	2	....	1	....	7,250	6,051
Nagar ..	....	....	....	....	5	1	2	....	....	....	..	..	..	..	..	..	....	....	....	....	7,358	6,308
Hunza ..	....	....	....	....	6	2	2	2	....	....	..	..	..	..	..	..	3	....	3	....	6,956	6,274
Punjal ..	....	....	....	....	....	....	....	....	....	....	..	..	..	..	..	..	1	2	....	....	3,223	2,881
Ishkoman ..	....	....	....	....	....	....	....	....	....	....	..	..	..	..	..	..	....	....	....	....	1,611	1,375
Yasin ..	....	....	....	....	1	....	....	....	....	....	..	..	..	..	..	..	....	....	....	....	4,153	3,929
Kub ..	2	....	2	....	85	3	7	....	....	....	..	..	..	..	..	..	....	....	....	....	1,460	1,258
Ghizar ..	....	....	....	....	....	....	....	....	....	....	..	..	..	..	..	..	....	....	....	....	2,164	1,948
Total Yasin ..	2	....	2	....	86	3	7	....	....	....	..	..	..	..	..	..	....	....	....	....	7,777	7,135

STATE TABLE II.

Population of District and Taluk by Religion and Literacy

Jammu and Kashmir Census 1931.

District and Taluk.	Muslims.		Christians.				Buddhist.				Others.				No. of Literates.						Literate in English.	
	No. of Literates		No. of Persons.		No. of Literates.		No. of Persons.		No. of Literates.		No. of Persons		No. of Literates.		Aged 0—15.		Aged 15—20.		Aged 20 & over.			
	Males.	Females.	Males.	Females.	Males.	Females.	Males.	Females.	Males.	Females.	Males.	Females.	Males.	Females.	Males.	Females.	Males.	Females.	Males.	Females.	Males.	Females.
1	24	25	26	27	28	29	30	31	32	33	34	35	36	37	38	39	40	41	42	43	44	45
Ladakh District—(concluded).																						
Kargil ..	493	3	5	2	2	2	3,853	4,158	98	1	..	..	..	..	72	3	65	....	497	9	38	2
Gilgit District ..	646	23	25	13	6	5	....	....	....	..	..	..	..	..	122	12	191	9	983	34	144	7
Gilgit Tehsil ..	646	23	25	13	6	5	....	....	....	..	..	..	..	..	122	12	191	9	983	34	144	7
Frontier Ilaqas ..	357	6	8	3	7	3	....	....	....	..	..	..	..	..	38	4	52	4	400	6	11	3
Chilas ..	73	....	7	3	7	3	....	....	....	..	..	..	..	..	11	2	25	4	154	....	5	1
Nagar ..	44	2	....	....	....	....	....	....	....	..	..	..	..	..	2	....	7	....	37	2	1	1
Hunza ..	84	1	....	....	....	....	....	....	....	..	..	..	..	..	2	2	6	....	81	1	3	1
Punjal ..	90	2	1	....	....	....	....	....	....	..	..	..	..	..	10	....	10	....	61	2	....	....
Ishkoman ..	10	....	....	....	....	....	....	....	....	..	..	..	..	..	....	....	....	....	10	....	....	....
Yasin ..	23	1	....	....	....	....	....	....	....	..	..	..	..	..	3	....	1	....	19	1	....	....
Kub ..	12	....	....	....	....	....	....	....	....	..	..	..	..	..	1	....	1	....	19	....	....	....
Ghizar ..	21	....	....	....	....	....	....	....	....	..	..	..	..	..	....	....	2	....	19	....	....	....
Total Yasin ..	*56*	*1*	....	....	....	....	....	....	....	..	..	..	..	..	*4*	....	*4*	....	*57*	*1*	....	....

STATE TABLE III.

INFIRMITIES BY SELECTED CASTES, TRIBES OR RACES.

Jammu and Kashmir Census 1931.

STATE TABLE III.

INFIRMITIES BY SELECTED CASTES, TRIBES OR RACES.

Jammu and Kashmir Census 1931.

Caste, tribe or Race.	Population dealt with.			Insane.			Deaf-Mutes.			Blind.			Lepers.		
	Persons.	Males.	Females.	Persons	Males.	Females.	Persons.	Males.	Females.	Persons.	Males.	Females.	Persons.	Males.	Females.
1	2	3	4	5	6	7	8	9	10	11	12	13	14	15	16
Hindu Total ..	*591,491*	*312,930*	*278,561*	*234*	*175*	*59*	*1,169*	*753*	*416*	*1,449*	*708*	*741*	*342*	*241*	*101*
Barwala ..	5,682	3,011	2,671	1	1	..	17	11	6	12	3	9	..	..	..
Basith ..	6,213	3,071	3,142	..	..	..	4	2	2	14	4	10	7	4	3
Brahmans (exclusive of mohyals and Kashmiri Pandits ..	185,321	94,931	90,390	82	67	15	349	244	105	410	194	216	81	64	17
Chumar ..	41,189	21,672	19,517	10	5	5	90	56	34	87	44	43	12	11	1
Dhiar ..	3,165	1,555	1,610	1	1	..	8	3	5	16	8	8	3	2	1
Doom ..	34,329	18,400	15,929	12	9	3	85	55	30	53	30	23	21	16	5
Gaddi ..	11,341	5,599	5,742	2	..	2	3	..	3	10	..	10	6	..	6
Jat ..	23,371	12,287	11,084	41	31	10	178	98	80	276	135	141	23	12	11
Julaha ..	40	20	20	2	1	1	8	5	3	14	6	8	1	1	..
Khatri ..	20,556	11,254	9,302	4	4	..	12	10	2	11	11	..	..	..	..
Lohar ..	10,788	5,756	5,032	2	2	..	3	3	..	2	2	..	5	5	..
Mahajan ..	21,009	10,973	10,036	5	5	..	11	11	..	26	26	..	2	2	..
Megh ..	70,030	37,062	32,968	21	14	7	186	114	72	175	87	88	65	42	23
Rajput ..	158,457	87,339	71,118	51	35	16	215	141	74	343	158	185	116	82	34
Muslim Total ..	*2,538,656*	*1,353,022*	*1,185,634*	*1,176*	*772*	*404*	*4,520*	*2,676*	*1,844*	*4,088*	*2,106*	*1,982*	*1,668*	*1,130*	*538*
Arain ..	22,922	12,727	10,195	2	1	1	31	15	16	28	11	17	2	..	2
Bafinda ..	33,872	17,679	16,193	14	7	7	46	24	22	46	16	30	31	22	9
Balti ..	47,326	23,274	24,052	35	22	13	585	302	283	491	176	315	131	63	68
Brukpa ..	13,104	6,691	6,413	7	3	4	32	17	15	47	17	30	13	8	5
Dhund ..	17,523	8,839	8,684	4	..	4	6	..	6	6	1	5	3	1	2
Gaddi ..	76	56	20	1	1	..	5	5	..	9	9	..	9	9	..
Gujjar ..	402,781	216,958	185,823	130	89	41	342	208	134	469	241	228	391	292	99
Hajjam ..	14,504	7,578	6,926	1	1	..	6	6	..	10	10	..	6	6	..
Kashmiri ..	1,352,822	730,769	622,053	570	394	176	1,900	1,166	734	1,667	947	720	568	370	198
Kumhiar ..	12,283	6,550	5,733	7	3	4	13	8	5	20	10	10	4	4	..
Khoja ..	3,771	1,894	1,877	3	3		14	9	5	5	2	3	4	4	..
Lohar ..	16,131	8,487	7,644	12	7	5	53	36	17	34	17	17	25	19	6
Mirasi ..	7,908	4,297	3,701	..	..	..	4	4	..	3	3	..	5	5	..
Mughal ..	30,198	15,820	14,378	5	3	2	29	18	11	10	3	7	9	5	4
Pathan ..	19,288	10,554	8,734	17	13	4	25	20	5	20	8	12	8	8	..
Rajput ..	195,449	101,875	93,574	27	13	14	139	85	54	146	89	57	64	49	15
Sayed	39,726	20,675	19,051	12	11	1	27	19	8	27	13	14	11	9	2
Shin ..	14,139	7,126	7,013	1	..	1	31	13	18	6	3	3	2	1	1
Shiekh ..	28,934	15,623	13,361	55	34	21	143	92	51	123	61	62	65	42	23
Sudan ..	68,594	33,201	35,393	33	10	23	95	43	52	70	28	42	60	45	15
Tarkhan ...	14,405	7,616	6,789	13	6	7	50	26	24	40	23	17	4	3	1
Teli ..	15,834	8,221	7,613	1	1	..	16	16	..	11	11	..	1	1	..
Watal ..	420	213	207	1	..	1	11	8	3	6	4	2	1	1	..
Yashkun ..	36,160	19,091	17,069	10	4	6	227	128	99	26	13	13	11	7	4
Others ..	130,346	67,208	63,138	215	146	69	690	408	282	768	390	378	240	156	84
Buddhist Total ..	*35,654*	*17,682*	*17,972*	*5*	*1*	*4*	*27*	*12*	*15*	*84*	*42*	*42*	*7*	*5*	*2*
Mangrik ..	34,107	16,943	17,164	5	1	4	27	12	15	83	41	42	4	2	2
Rigzong ..	1,547	739	808	..	..	..	..	..	..	1	1	..	3	3	..

STATE TABLE IV.—A.

Jammu and Kashmir Census 1931.

SUBSIDIARY OCCUPATIONS OF AGRICULTURISTS—ACTUAL WORKERS ONLY.

STATE TABLE IV.—A.

Jammu and Kashmir Census 1931.

Subsidiary Occupations of Agriculturists—Actual Workers only.

(i) *Rent Receivers.*

District, Province or State.	Total No. of rent receivers (actual workers).		No. of actual workers who returned subsidiary occupations.		Subsidiary Occupations.																													
					Cultivating Owners.		*Cultivating tenants.*		*Agricultural labourers.*		*Government servants of all kinds.*		*Money lenders & grain dealers.*		*Other traders of all kinds.*		*Priests.*		*Clerks of all kinds.*		*School Masters.*		*Lawyers.*		*Estate Agents & Managers.*		*Medical Practitioners.*		*Artisans.*		*Others.*	
	Males.	Females.	Males.	Females.	Males.	Females.	Males.	Females.	Males.	Females.	Males.	Females.	Males.	Females.	Males.	Females.	Males.	Females.	Males.	Females.	Males.	Females.	Males.	Females.	Males.	Females.	Males.	Females.	Males.	Females.	Males.	Females.
Jammu and Kashmir State ..	24,688	4,411	5,698	2,515	607	50	353	45	52	9	777	5	221	4	367	14	326	17	18	..	35	..	3	..	..	..	25	..	654	106	2,255	2,265
Jammu Province including Jagirs..	13,549	3,427	2,283	1,870	336	35	197	35	37	5	285	3	155	4	108	9	114	10	1	..	9	..	..	..	..	..	15	..	162	93	814	1,670
Kashmir Province ..	3,826	447	2,035	587	249	4	151	1	14	..	270	2	60	..	242	5	199	1	17	..	20	..	3	..	..	..	10	..	102	13	698	561
Frontier Districts ..	7,313	537	1,375	58	22	11	5	9	1	4	222	..	6	..	17	..	13	..	..	..	6	..	..	..	..	..	..	..	390	..	693	34

STATE TABLE IV.—A.

Jammu and Kashmir Census 1931.

Subsidiary Occupations of Agriculturists—Actual workers only.

(ii) Farm servants and Field Labourers (Agricultural Labourers).

District, Province or State.	Total No. of Agricultural Labourers (actual workers).		No. of actual workers who returned subsidiary occupations.		Subsidiary Occupations.																															
					Rent receivers.		*Owners.*		*Cultivating tenants.*		*General labourers.*		*Village Watchmen.*		*Cattle breeders, and milkmen.*		*Mill hands.*		*Fishermen & boatmen.*		*Rice pounders.*		*Traders of all kinds.*		*Oil pressers.*		*Weavers.*		*Potters.*		*Leather Workers.*		*Washermen.*		*Blacksmiths and Carpenters.*		*Others.*	
	Males.	Females.	Males.	Females.	Males.	Females.	Males.	Females.	Males.	Females.	Males.	Females.	Males.	Females.	Males.	Females.	Males.	Females.	Males.	Females.	Males.	Females.	Males.	Females.	Males.	Females.	Males.	Females.	Males.	Females.	Males.	Females.	Males.	Females.	Males.	Females.	Males.	Females.
Jammu and Kashmir State ..	11,066	780	1,522	1,059	58	3	36	1	467	7	101	24	13	..	151	56	2	1	..	..	4	..	55	1	15	2	88	9	27	..	47	..	..	..	45	..	413	955
Jammu Province including Jagirs ..	9,196	593	1,338	1,003	46	2	13	..	444	4	80	24	11	..	141	56	1	1	..	..	..	..	50	1	11	2	88	9	27	..	47	..	..	..	43	..	336	904
Kashmir Province ..	1,562	15	159	37	10	..	23	1	23	..	17	..	2	..	5	..	1	..	..	..	4	..	5	..	4	..	..	..	..	..	..	..	..	..	3	..	63	36
Frontier Districts ..	308	172	25	19	2	1	..	..	..	3	4	..	..	..	5	..	..	..	..	..	..	..	..	..	..	..	..	..	..	..	..	..	..	..	..	..	14	15

STATE TABLE IV.—B.

Jammu and Kashmir Census 1931.

SUBSIDIARY OCCUPATIONS OF AGRICULTURISTS—ACTUAL WORKERS ONLY.

Cultivating Owners and Cultivating Tenants.

District, Province or State.	Total No. of Cultivating Owners and Cultivating Tenants. (Actual Workers).		No. of Actual Workers who returned Subsidiary Occupation.		Subsidiary Occupations.																													
					Rent receivers.		*Agricultural labourers.*		*General labourers.*		*Government servants of all kinds.*		*Money Lenders and grain dealers.*		*Other traders of all kinds.*		*Fishermen and Boatmen.*		*Cattle breeders and Milkmen.*		*Village Watchmen.*		*Weavers.*		*Barbers.*		*Oil Pressers.*		*Washermen.*		*Potters.*		*Blacksmiths & carpenters.*		*Others.*	
	Males.	Females.	Males.	Females.	Males.	Females.	Males.	Females.	Males.	Females.	Males.	Females.	Males.	Females.	Males.	Females.	Males.	Females.	Males.	Females.	Males.	Females.	Males.	Females.	Males.	Females.	Males.	Females.	Males.	Females.	Males.	Females.	Males.	Females.	Males.	Females.
Jammu and Kashmir State ..	502,704	14,604	142,278	8,949	4,193	469	1,398	63	1,233	100	3,388	5	813	24	4,822	38	407	3	546	46	110	..	901	41	481	2	163	4	70	7	515	11	871	5	122,062	8,131
Jammu Province including Jagirs ..	272,804	8,187	67,737	6,870	2,203	367	1,238	50	710	90	2,188	4	779	24	3,001	34	22	..	315	35	92	..	845	3	325	2	163	4	60	7	315	11	462	2	55,017	6,237
Kashmir Province ..	185,706	2,210	68,194	831	2,000	58	140	12	509	10	1,100	..	34	..	1,777	4	385	3	228	11	18	..	54	8	156	..	..	..	9	..	200	..	400	3	61,184	722
Frontier Districts ..	44,194	4,207	6,347	1,248	295	44	20	1	14	..	100	1	..	..	42	..	..	..	8	..	..	..	2	30	..	..	..	..	1	..	..	..	9	..	5,861	1,172

STATE TABLE V.

Showing for certain Mixed Occupations the number of Persons who returned each Occupation as their (*a*) Principal, (*b*) Subsidiary Means of Livelihood.

Jammu and Kashmir Census 1931.

STATE TABLE V.

SHOWING FOR CERTAIN MIXED OCCUPATIONS THE NUMBER OF PERSONS WHO RETURNED EACH OCCUPATION AS THEIR (a) PRINCIPAL, (b) SUBSIDIARY MEANS OF LIVELIHOOD.

Jammu and Kashmir Census 1931.

Jammu Province.

CULTIVATING OWNERS AND MONEY LENDERS.

Serial No.	District or Jagir.	*Total number of persons (actual workers) who returned occupation of Cultivating owners as their principal occupation.*		*Number of persons in the two preceding columns who returned Money-lending as their subsidiary occupation.*		*Total number of persons (actual workers) who returned occupation of Money-lenders as their principal occupation.*		*Number of persons in the two preceding columns who returned Cultivating owners, as their subsidiary occupation.*	
		Males.	Females.	Males.	Females.	Males.	Females.	Males.	Females.
1	2	3	4	5	6	7	8	9	10
1	Jammu District (including City)	14,291	212	44	2	538	13	10	—
2	Kathua District ..	8,768	180	141	....	241	9	32	—
3	Reasi ..	12,273	572	13	1	303	73	15	—
4	Mirpur ..	11,087	188	21	....	207	9	6	—

RENT RECEIVING OWNERS AND GOVERNMENT SERVANTS.

Serial No.	District or Jagir.	*Total Number of persons (actual workers) who returned occupation of Rent receiving owners as their principal occupation.*		*Number of persons in the two preceding columns who returned Government service as their subsidiary occupation.*		*Total number of persons (actual workers) who returned occupation of Government servants as their principal occupation.*		*Number of persons in the two preceding columns who returned "Rent receiving owners" as their subsidiary occupation.*	
		Males.	Females.	Males.	Females.	Males.	Females.	Males.	Females.
1	2	3	4	5	6	7	8	9	10
1	Jammu District (including City)	1,751	594	26	23	2,901	60	209	—
2	Kathua District ..	4,826	456	27	....	440	5	59	—
3	Udhampur „ ..	571	261	42	1	498	9	178	—
4	Reasi „ ..	4,965	1,422	34	....	250	14	31	—
5	Mirpur „ ..	869	473	4	....	812	31	48	1
6	Poonch Jagir ..	25	211	29	....	439	9	136	1

AGRICULTURAL LABOURERS AND GENERAL LABOURERS.

Serial No.	District or Jagir.	*Total number of persons (actual workers) who returned occupation of Agricultural labourers as their principal occupation.*		*Number of persons in the two preceding columns who returned General labourers as their subsidiary occupation.*		*Total Number of persons (actual workers) who returned occupation of General labourers as their principal occupation.*		*Number of persons in the two preceding columns who returned Agricultural labourers as their subsidiary occupation.*	
		Males.	Females.	Males.	Females.	Males.	Females.	Males.	Females.
1	2	3	4	5	6	7	8	9	10
1	Jammu District (including City)	5,133	292	24	12	2,510	619	18	—
2	Kathua „ ..	1,223	123	27	36	759	76	37	4
3	Udhampur „ ..	718	87	5	....	407	177	1	—
4	Reasi „ ..	1,318	68	34	....	84	178	2	—
5	Mirpur „ ..	713	23	3	—	667	171	1	—
6	Poonch Jagir ..	80	—	—	....	412	5,272	—	—
7	Chenani „ ..	11	....	....	....	50	....	....	....

STATE TABLE V.

Showing for certain Mixed Occupations the number of Persons who returned each Occupation as their (a) Principal, (b) Subsidiary Means of Livelihood.

Jammu and Kashmir Census 1931.

Jammu Province.

Shop-keepers and Money-lenders.

Serial No.	District or Jagir.	Total number of persons (actual workers) who returned occupation of Shop keepers as their principal occupation.		Number of persons in the two preceding columns who returned Money-lenders as their subsidiary occupation.		Total Number of persons (actual workers) who returned occupation of Money lenders as their principal occupation.		Number of persons in the two preceding columns who returned Shop-keepers as their subsidiary occupation.	
		Males.	Females.	Males.	Females.	Males.	Females.	Males.	Females.
1	2	3	4	5	6	7	8	9	10
1	Jammu District (including City)	1,038	9	16	....	538	13	20	—
2	Udhampur District ..	466	13	19	...	420	21	1	—
3	Mirpur " ..	388	38	112	...	207	9	58	—
4	Poonch Jagir ..	314	4	7	—	199	2	—	—

Oil pressers and transport by pack animals.

Serial No.	District or Jagir.	Total number of persons (actual workers) who returned occupation of Oil pressers as their principal occupation.		Number of persons in the two preceding columns who returned transport by pack animals as their subsidiary occupation.		Total number of persons (actual workers) who returned occupation of transport by pack animals as their principal occupation.		Number of persons in the two preceding columns who returned Oil-pressers as their subsidiary occupation.	
		Males.	Females.	Males.	Females.	Males.	Females.	Males.	Females.
1	2	3	4	5	6	7	8	9	10
1	Kathua District ..	179	7	5	....	134	—	3	—
2	Mirpur " ..	219	8	2	....	189	9	5	—

Goldsmith and Money-lender.

Serial No.	District or Jagir.	Total number of persons (actual workers) who returned occupation of Goldsmiths as their principal occupation.		Number of persons in the two preceding columns who returned Money-lenders as their subsidiary occupation.		Total number of persons (actual workers) who returned occupation of money lenders as their principal occupation.		Number of persons in the two preceding columns who returned goldsmith as their subsidiary occupation.	
		Males.	Females.	Males.	Females.	Males.	Females.	Males.	Females.
1	2	3	3	5	6	7	8	9	10
1	Kathua District ..	162	....	14	....	241	9	2	—
2	Mirpur " ..	338	....	4	....	207	9	2	—

Money-lenders and Priests.

Serial No.	District or Jagir.	Total number of persons (actual workers) who returned occupation of Money-lenders as their principal occupation.		Number of persons in the two preceding columns who returned Priests as their subsidiary occupation.		Total number of persons (actual workers) who returned occupation of Priests as their principal occupation.		Number of persons in the two preceding columns who returned Money-lenders as their subsidiary occupation.	
		Males.	Females.	Males.	Females.	Males.	Females.	Males.	Females.
1	2	3	4	5	6	7	8	9	10
1	Jammu District (including City)	538	13	12	...	380	14	14	....
2	Kathua " ..	241	9	9	....	332	57	17	....
3	Reasi " —	303	73	8	....	154	11	1	....
4	Mirpur " ..	207	9	1	....	136	7	1	....

STATE TABLE V.

Showing for certain Mixed Occupations the number of Persons who returned each Occupation as their (a) Principal, (b) Subsidiary Means of Livelihood.

Jammu and Kashmir Census 1931.

Jammu Province.

Carpenter and Blacksmith.

Serial No.	District or Jagir.	Total number of persons (actual workers) who returned occupation of Carpenters as their principal occupation.		Number of persons in the two preceding columns who returned Blacksmiths as their subsidiary occupation.		Total number of persons (actual workers) who returned occupation of Blacksmiths as their principal occupation.		Number of persons in the two preceding columns who returned Carpenters as their subsidiary occupation.	
		Males.	Females.	Males.	Females.	Males.	Females.	Males.	Females.
1	2	3	4	5	6	7	8	9	10
1	Jammu District (including City)	1,158	3	11	....	726	6	12	....
2	Reasi „ ..	63	9	2	....	93	....	1	....
3	Mirpur „ ..	935	2	1	....	128	1	12	....

Kashmir Province.

Hanjis (Boatmen and Fishermen.)

Serial No.	District or Jagir.	Total number of persons (actual workers) who returned occupation of Hanjis (Boatmen) as their principal occupation.		Number of persons in the two preceding columns who returned Fishermen as their subsidiary occupation.		Total number of persons (actual workers) who returned occupation of Fishermen as their principal occupation.		Number of persons in the two preceding columns who returned Hanjis (Boatmen) as their subsidiary occupation.	
		Males.	Females.	Males.	Females.	Males.	Females.	Males.	Females.
1	2	3	4	5	6	7	8	9	10
1	Kashmir South (including City)	2,499	155	37	....	534	....	24	....
2	Kashmir North ..	474	25	65	....	660	37	4	....

Hanjis and Vegetable-sellers.

Serial No.	District or Jagir.	Total Number of persons (actual workers) who returned occupation of Hanjis as their principal occupation.		Number of persons in the two preceding columns who returned Vegetable-sellers as their subsidiary occupation.		Total number of persons (actual workers) who returned occupation of Vegetable-sellers as their principal occupation.		Number of persons in the two preceding columns who returned Hanjis as their subsidiary occupation.	
		Males.	Females.	Males.	Females.	Males.	Females.	Males.	Females.
1	2	3	4	5	6	7	8	9	10
1	Kashmir South (including City)	2,499	155	15	....	620	96	2	....
2	Kashmir North ..	474	25	16	....	63	7	4	....

State Service and Agriculture.

Serial No.	District or Jagir.	Total number of persons (actual workers) who returned occupation of State service as their principal occupation.		Number of persons in the two preceding columns who returned Agriculture as their subsidiary occupation.		Total number of persons (actual workers) who returned occupation of Agriculture as their principal occupation.		Number of persons in the two preceding columns who returned State service as their subsidiary occupation,	
		Males.	Females.	Males.	Females.	Males.	Females.	Males.	Females.
1	2	3	4	5	6	7	8	9	10
1	Kashmir South (including City)	4,658	166	775	....	76,517	998	858	....
2	Kashmir North ..	821	7	309	....	74,203	668	150	....
3	Muzaffarabad ..	369	4	219	....	10,556	1,006	100	....

STATE TABLE VI.

ORGANISED INDUSTRY.

Jammu and Kashmir Census 1931.

STATE TABLE VI.

Organised Industry.

Jammu and Kashmir Census 1931.

Industry.	Total Population engaged.			Directional, Supervising and Clerical Staff.						Welfare Doctors, Compounders, School-Masters, etc.		Operatives.			
				Managers.		Supervising and Technical.		Clerical.				Adult.		Immature.	
	Persons.	Males.	Females.	Indian.	Other.	Indian.	Other.	Indian.	Other.	Indian.	Other.	Males.	Females.	Male.	Females.
1	2	3	4	5	6	7	8	9	10	11	12	13	14	15	16
Mines ..	3	3	....	....	....	3	....	....	....	....	....	....	....	....	....
Refineries of borax and other saline substances ..	3	3	....	....	....	3	....	....	....	....	....	....	....	....	....
Textiles ..	4,456	3,539	917	36	....	35	....	110	....	....	....	2,605	491	753	426
Cotton weaving mills ..	454	446	8	22	....	2	....	....	....	....	....	355	6	67	2
Cotton Carpet factories ..	1,210	622	588	5	....	18	....	22	....	....	....	421	306	156	282
Silk factories ..	1,538	1,476	62	1	....	10	....	77	....	....	....	1,166	58	222	4
Dye works ..	4	4	....	....	....	....	....	....	....	....	....	4	....	....	....
Lace and embroidery works ..	417	415	2	6	....	1	....	5	....	....	....	245	1	158	1
Shawl and fringe weaving establishments ..	828	571	257	2	....	4	....	6	....	....	....	410	120	149	137
Cotton printing works ..	5	5	....	....	....	....	....	....	....	....	....	4	....	1	....
Hides, skins and hard materials from the animal kingdom	161	144	17	6	....	....	....	....	....	....	....	102	6	36	11
Leather and leather dying works ..	159	142	17	6	....	....	....	....	....	....	....	100	6	30	11
Saddlery and harness factories ..	2	2	....	....	....	....	....	....	....	....	....	2	....	....	....
Wood ..	1,118	1,095	23	12	....	62	....	137	....	1	....	849	19	34	4
Extraction of timber and timber yards ..	997	997	....	12	....	60	....	130	....	1	....	764	....	30	....
Saw mills ..	32	32	....	....	....	2	....	6	....	....	....	22	....	2	....
Cane and basket factories ..	15	10	5	....	....	....	....	....	....	....	....	9	4	1	1
Papier Machie works ..	74	56	18	....	....	....	....	1	....	....	....	54	15	1	3

Metals ..	111	111	....	4	....	....	....	1	....	....	....	90	....	16	....
Iron and steel works ..	63	63	....	2	....	....	....	....	....	....	....	50	....	11	....
Steel trunk factories ..	16	16	....	1	....	....	....	1	....	....	....	13	....	1	....
Brass, Copper, Bronze and tin foundries ..	32	32	....	1	....	....	....	....	....	....	....	27	....	4	....
Ceramics ..	60	57	3	4	....	....	....	5	....	....	....	48	....	....	3
Brick Works ..	45	45	....	4	....	....	....	5	....	....	....	36	....	....	....
Pottery factories ..	15	12	3	....	....	....	....	....	....	....	....	12	....	....	3
Chemical products, properly so called and analogous ..	295	295	....	13	....	23	....	31	....	....	....	172	....	56	....
Match factories ..	20	20	....	1	....	7	....	5	....	....	....	4	....	3	....
Fireworks and explosives factories ..	3	3	....	....	....	....	....	....	....	....	....	3	....	....	....
Soda water factories ..	34	34	....	6	....	....	....	1	....	....	....	25	....	2	....
Oil mills ..	54	54	....	1	....	1	....	2	....	....	....	35	....	15	....
Soap factories ..	89	89	....	3	....	5	....	10	....	....	....	53	....	18	....
Chemicals, drugs, antiseptics and pharmaceutical works generally ..	92	92	....	2	....	10	....	13	....	....	....	49	....	18	....
Factories of leather and metal polishes ..	3	3	....	....	....	....	....	....	....	....	....	3	....	....	....
Food Industries ..	391	384	7	45	....	8	3	22	....	....	....	267	7	39	....
Rice mills ..	112	110	2	30	....	....	....	14	....	....	....	63	2	3	....
Flour mills ..	90	85	5	5	....	....	....	....	....	....	....	67	5	13	....
Bakeries, confectioners and chocolate factories ..	106	106	....	5	....	....	....	....	....	....	....	84	....	17	....
Slaughter houses ..	14	14	....	....	....	....	....	....	....	....	....	11	....	3	....
Sugar factories and refineries ..	15	15	....	....	....	....	....	....	....	....	....	14	....	1	....
Tobacco and Snuff factories ..	24	24	....	4	....	7	....	....	....	....	....	13	....	....	....
Water works ..	27	27	....	1	....	1	....	8	....	....	....	15	....	2	....
Wine merchants ..	3	3	....	....	....	....	3	....	....	....	....	....	....	....	....
Industries of dress and the toilet ..	1,907	1,846	61	46	....	4	....	16	....	....	....	1,371	53	409	8
Boot and Shoe factories ..	340	310	30	9	....	....	....	....	....	....	....	253	30	48	....
Hosiery factories ..	17	17	....	4	....	....	....	....	....	....	....	12	....	1	....
Tailoring works ..	274	256	18	3	....	1	....	11	....	....	....	196	14	45	4
Hat and cap factories ..	66	53	13	10	....	....	....	1	....	....	....	37	9	5	4
Darning works ..	1,210	1,210	....	20	....	3	....	4	....	....	....	873	....	310	....
Furniture Industries ..	35	35	....	....	....	8	....	7	....	....	....	17	....	3	....
Furniture factories ..	32	32	....	....	....	8	....	7	....	....	....	17	....	....	....
Tent factories ..	3	3	....	....	....	....	....	....	....	....	....	....	....	3	....

STATE TABLE VI.

ORGANISED INDUSTRIES.

Jammu and Kashmir Census 1931.

INDUSTRY.	TOTAL POPULATION ENGAGED.			DIRECTIONAL, SUPERVISING AND CLERICAL STAFF.						WELFARE DOCTORS, COMPOUNDERS, SCHOOL MASTERS, ETC.		OPERATIVES.			
				Managers.		*Supervising and Technical.*		*Clerical.*				*Adult.*		*Immature.*	
	Persons.	Males.	Females.	Indian.	Other.	Indian.	Other.	Indian.	Other.	Indian.	Other.	Males.	Females.	Males.	Females.
1	2	3	4	5	6	7	8	9	10	11	12	13	14	15	16
Building Industries ..	33	33	....	2	....	1	....	1	....	....	....	28	....	1	....
Stone and marble works ..	29	29	....	1	....	1	....	....	....	....	....	26	....	1	....
Lime works ..	4	4	....	1	....	....	....	1	....	....	....	2	....	....	....
Construction of means of transport ..	106	106	....	5	....	1	....	6	....	....	....	92	....	2	....
Motor Car works ..	106	106	....	5	....	1	....	6	....	....	....	92	....	2	....
Production and transmission of physical force ..	228	228	....	15	....	4	....	69	....	....	....	137	....	3	....
Hydro Electric works ..	228	228	....	15	....	4	....	69	....	....	....	137	....	3	....
Miscellaneous and undefined Industries ..	465	462	3	4	1	1	....	27	....	....	....	397	3	32	....
Envelope and Cardboard factories—Book-binders ..	3	3	....	....	....	....	....	....	....	....	....	3	....	....	....
Printing Presses ..	54	54	....	1	....	1	....	2	....	....	....	50	....	....	....
Photo and map producing works ..	31	31	....	2	....	....	....	9	....	....	....	20	....	....	....
Factories of musical instruments ..	60	60	....	....	....	....	....	12	....	....	....	41	....	7	....
Factories of ornaments of gold and silver ..	292	289	3	1	....	....	....	....	....	....	....	266	3	22	....
Toy factories ..	15	15	....	....	....	....	....	....	....	....	....	15	....	....	....
Unspecified Firms ..	10	10	....	....	1	....	....	4	....	....	....	2	....	3	....
Transport by Road ..	20	20	....	4	....	....	....	4	....	....	....	12	....	....	....
Motor transport ..	20	20	....	4	....	....	....	4	....	....	....	12	....	....	....
Total ..	*9,359*	*8,358*	*1,031*	*196*	*1*	*150*	*3*	*436*	....	*1*	....	*6,187*	*579*	*1,384*	*[illegible]*

STATE TABLE VII.

Jammu and Kashmir Census 1931.

The details of persons in each religion following different occupations include.—

(i) Earners, (ii) Working Dependants and (iii) Persons following an occupation as subsidiary to other.

2. The non-working dependants are not shown in this Table.

STATE TABLE VII.

DISTRIBUTION BY RELIGION IN DIFFERENT OCCUPATIONS.

Jammu and Kashmir Census 1931.

Group No.	Occupation.	Total of workers as principal occupation & dependant workers.	Total following occupation as subsidiary to other.	Distribution by Religion.						
				Hindus.	Buddhists.	Jains.	Sikhs.	Muslims.	Christians.	Tribal or others.
1	2	3	4	5	6	7	8	9	10	11
1	Non-cultivating proprietors taking rent in money or kind	44,037	8,208	20,867	168	....	955	30,254	1	....
2	Estate Agents and Managers of owners ..	24	12	31	....	....	....	5	....	....
4	Rent collectors, clerks, etc. ..	193	15	2	....	....	....	206	....	....
5	Cultivating owners ..	430,358	91,914	74,753	12,225	....	6,447	428,795	45	7
6	Tenant cultivators ..	262,860	59,313	77,536	1,878	....	3,397	239,316	46	....
7	Agricultural labourers ..	13,459	2,581	9,318	335	....	80	6,146	161	....
8	Cultivators of jhum, taungya and shifting areas ..	456	205	6	....	....	....	655	....	....
11	Cultivators of Coffee ..	3	1	....	....	....	....	4	....	....
16	Market gardeners, flower and fruit growers ..	1,139	602	88	....	....	3	1,650	....	....
17	Forest officers, rangers, guards, etc. ..	1,180	316	995	....	....	139	359	3	....
18	Wood cutters and charcoal burners ..	342	46	155	....	....	29	203	1	....
21	Cattle and buffalo breeders and keepers ..	14,436	1,443	1,136	33	....	75	14,634	1	....
22	Breeders of transport animals ..	295	87	53	....	....	....	329	....	....
23	Herdsmen, shepherds and breeders of other animals ..	46,933	2,194	14,189	268	....	811	33,851	8	....
24	Raising of birds, bees, etc. ..	10	....	10	....	....	....	....	....	....
25	Raising of silkworms ..	124	81	3	....	....	14	188	....	....
27	Fishing and pearling ..	1,453	272	40	....	....	....	1,685	....	....
28	Hunting ..	58	22	....	....	....	....	51	1	28
29	Exploitation of gold ..	40	18	....	....	....	....	58	....	....
31	Extraction of lead, silver and zinc ..	19	11	....	....	....	....	30	....	....
33	Extraction of tin and wolfram ..	4	....	1	....	....	....	3	....	....
34	Extraction of other metallic minerals ..	2	....	2	....	....	....	....	....	....
36	Extraction of Petroleum ..	1	....	....	....	....	1	....	....	....
37	Extraction of building materials ..	993	50	8	....	....	9	1,026	....	....
38	Extraction of Mica ..	5	3	....	....	....	....	8	....	....
39	Extraction of precious and semi-precious stones ..	29	1	30	....	....	....	....	....	....
42	Cotton ginning, cleaning and pressing ..	413	105	117	....	....	....	401	....	....
43	Cotton spinning, sizing and weaving ..	7,695	3,404	5,420	264	....	30	5,374	11	....
44	Jute pressing, spinning and weaving ..	13	4	2	....	....	1	14	....	....
45	Rope, twine, string and other fibres ..	84	20	2	....	....	....	102	....	....
46	Wool carding, spinning and weaving ..	2,529	934	195	....	....	2	3,261	5	....
47	Silk spinning and weaving ..	479	50	54	....	....	1	474	....	....
48	Preparation and supply of hair (Horse-hair), etc. ..	8	1	3	....	....	....	6	....	....
49	Dyeing, bleaching, printing, preparation and sponging of textiles ..	442	99	54	....	....	....	487	....	....
50	Lace, crepe, embroideries, fringes, etc., and insufficiently described textile industries ..	4,644	348	509	....	....	3	4,480	....	....
51	Working in leather ..	5,020	1,860	2,437	....	....	2	4,439	2	....
52	Furriers and persons occupied with feathers, and bristles; brush makers ..	81	7	37	....	....	....	51	....	....
53	Bone, ivory, horn, shell, etc., workers (except buttons).	17	7	18	....	....	....	3	3	....
54	Sawyers ..	1,744	378	320	....	....	5	1,797	....	....

STATE TABLE VII.

DISTRIBUTION BY RELIGION IN DIFFERENT OCCUPATIONS.

Jammu and Kashmir Census 1931.

Group No.	Occupation.	Total of workers & principal occupation & dependant workers.	Total following occupation as subsidiary to other.	Distribution by Religion.						
				Hindus.	Buddhists.	Jains.	Sikhs.	Muslims.	Christians.	Tribal or others.
1	2	3	4	5	6	7	8	9	10	11
55	Carpenters, turners and joiners, etc. ..	5,918	1,835	1,874	79	....	65	5,735	— —	— —
56	Basket makers and other industries of woody materials, including leaves and thatchers and builders working with bamboo, reeds or similar materials ..	2,576	1,034	1,524	....	— —	1	2,085	— —	— —
57	Smelting, forging and rolling of iron and other metals	933	286	420	....	....	2	797	— —	— —
58	Makers of arms, guns, etc. ..	33	2	16	....	....	....	19	— —	—
59	Blacksmiths, other workers in iron, makers of implements ..	2,524	1,008	699	114	— —	83	2,636	— —	— —
60	Workers in brass, copper and bell metal ..	725	30	59	— —	— —	31	665	— —	— —
61	Workers in other metals ..	9	2	....	....	....	....	11	— —	— —
62	Workers in mints, die-sinkers, etc. ..	17	1	....	....	....	....	18	— —	— —
63	Potters and makers of earthen-ware ..	4,151	1,895	1,104	2	....	3	4,937	— —	— —
64	Brick and tile makers ..	203	15	52	....	— —	....	153	13	— —
65	Other workers in ceramics ..	24	1	13	....	....	....	12	— —	— —
66	Manufacture of matches, fire-works and other explosives	84	17	1	....	....	....	100	— —	— —
67	Manufacture of aerated and mineral waters and ice ..	7	....	7	....	....	....	....	....	— —
68	Manufacture and refining of vegetable oils ..	2,532	1,075	16	....	....	2	3,589	....	— —
69	Manufacture and refining of mineral oils ..	23	8	....	....	....	....	31	....	— —
70	Manufacture of other chemical products ..	8	....	1	....	....	....	7	— —	— —
71	Rice pounders and huskers and flour grinders ..	1,782	477	1,434	2	....	4	819	— —	— —
72	Grain parchers, etc. ..	143	71	145	— —	....	1	68	— —	— —
73	Butchers ..	1,366	109	7	....	....	....	1,468	— —	— —
74	Makers of sugar, molasses and gur ..	2	....	2	....	....	....	....	— —	— —
75	Sweetmeat and condiment makers ..	613	97	557	— —	....	20	115	18	— —
76	Toddy drawers ..	60	7	41	....	....	....	26	— —	— —
77	Brewers and distillers ..	12	2	14	....	....	....	— —	— —	— —
78	Manufacturers of tobacco ..	51	6	54	....	....	....	3	....	— —
79	Manufacturers of opium ..	18	....	18	....	....	....	— —	— —	— —
80	Manufacturers of ganja ..	5	....	....	....	....	....	5	....	— —
81	Manufacture of other Food Industries ..	950	111	9	1	....	28	1,023	— —	— —
82	Boot, shoe, sandal and clog makers ..	3,114	1,182	2,879	12	....	11	1,394	— —	— —
83	Tailors, milliners, dress-makers and darners ..	19,932	1,665	2,309	36	2	76	19,173	1	— —
84	Embroiderers, hat-makers and makers of other articles of wear ..	2,234	86	211	— —	8	5	2,096	....	— —
85	Washing and cleaning ..	1,335	338	39	....	....	1	1,633	....	— —
86	Barbers, hair-dressers and wig-makers ..	3,900	1,248	1,123	....	....	2	4,021	2	— —
87	Other industries connected with the toilet ..	61	19	54	....	....	1	25	— —	— —
88	Cabinet-makers, carriage painters, etc. ..	76	14	28	4	....	....	57	1	— —
89	Upholsterers, tent-makers, etc. ..	3	....	....	....	....	....	2	1	— —
90	Lime burners, cement workers; Excavators and well sinkers; Stone cutters and dressers; Brick layers and masons; Builders (other than buildings made of bamboo or similar materials), painters, decorators of houses, tilers, plumbers, etc. ..	662	87	335	4	....	15	395	— —	— —

STATE TABLE VII.

Distribution by Religion in Different Occupations.

Jammu and Kashmir Census 1931.

Group No.	Occupation.	Total of workers as principal occupation & dependant workers.	Total following occupation as subsidiary to other.	*Distribution by Religion.* Hindus.	Buddhists.	Jains.	Sikhs.	Muslims.	Christians.	Tribal or others.
1	2	3	4	5	6	7	8	9	10	11
91	Persons engaged in making, assembling or repairing motor vehicles or cycles ..	8	....	3	....	1	2	1	1	—
94	Production and transmission of heat, light, electricity, motive power, etc., Gas works and electric light and power ..	2	1	2	....	....	1	—	—	—
95	Printers, engravers, book-binders, etc. ..	26	1	16	....	....	3	8	—	—
96	Makers of musical instruments ..	4	....	....	....	....	1	3	....	....
97	Makers of clocks and surgical or scientific instruments, etc.	61	4	20	....	....	1	44	....	....
98	Makers of jewellery and ornaments ..	3,414	453	1,453	13	....	150	2,251	—	....
99	Other miscellaneous and undefined industries (toy-making, taxidermy, etc.) ..	69	31	60	....	....	....	40	....	....
100	Scavenging ..	655	110	176	....	....	....	377	212	....
101	Persons concerned with aerodromes ond aeroplanes ..	4	....	1	....	....	3	....	—	—
102	Ship owners, boat-owners and their employees, officers, mariners, etc. Ships' brokers, boatmen and tow men ..	3,557	1,066	11	....	....	....	4,612	—	....
103	Persons (other than labourers) employed in harbours, docks, rivers and canals, including pilots ..	236	75	27	....	....	3	281	....	....
104	Labourers employed on harbours, docks, rivers and canals ..	426	53	135	....	....	2	342	—	....
105	Persons (other than labourers) employed on the construction and maintenance of roads and bridges ..	573	38	595	....	....	....	16	—	....
106	Labourers employed on roads and bridges ..	1,743	190	616	....	....	34	1,283	....	—
107	Owners, managers and employees (excluding personal servants) connected with mechanically driven vehicles (including trams) ..	2	....	1	....	....	1	....	—	—
108	Owners, managers and employees (excluding personal servants) connected with other vehicles ..	579	24	72	....	....	24	507	—	....
110	Pack elephant, camel, mule, ass and bullock owners and drivers ..	1,363	293	320	....	....	20	1,309	7	....
111	Porters and messengers ..	1	1	1	....	....	....	1	....	—
112	Railway employees of all kinds other than coolies ..	35	21	35	....	....	1	19	1	....
113	Labourers employed on railway construction and maintenance and coolies and porters employed on railway premises ..	21	4	....	....	....	....	25	....	....
114	Post Office, Telegraph and Telephone services ..	845	112	514	11	....	24	408	....	....
115	Bank managers, money-lenders, exchange and insurance agents, money changers and brokers and their employees	2,193	1,109	2,723	....	....	178	401	....	....
116	Brokers, commission agents, commercial travellers, ware-house owners and employees ..	82	10	43	....	....	12	37	—	....
117	Trade in piece-goods, wool, cotton, silk, hair and other textiles ..	2,091	406	1,163	26	28	192	1,088	....	....
118	Trade in skins, leather, furs, feathers, horn, etc., and the articles made from these ..	422	56	10	331	....	....	134	3	....
119	Trade in wood (not fire-wood) ..	577	129	244	....	....	15	444	3	—
121	Trade in bamboos and canes ..	1	1	2	....	....	....	....	....	....
122	Trade in thatches and other forest produce ..	184	115	270	....	....	....	29	....	....
123	Trade in metals, machinery, knives, tools, etc. ..	19	....	....	....	14	....	5	....	....
124	Trade in pottery, bricks and tiles ..	40	3	5	....	....	....	38	....	....
125	Drugs, dyes, paints, petroleum, explosives, etc. ..	31	23	34	....	1	1	18	....	....
126	Venders of wine, liquors, aerated waters and ice ..	87	6	62	8	1	3	19	....	—

STATE TABLE VII.

Distribution by Religion in Different Occupations.

Jammu and Kashmir Census 1931.

Group No.	Occupation.	Total of workers in principal occupation & dependant workers.	Total following occupation as subsidiary to other.	*Distribution by Religion.* Hindus.	Buddhists.	Jains.	Sikhs.	Muslims.	Christians.	Tribal or others.
1	2	3	4	5	6	7	8	9	10	11
127	Owners and managers of hotels, cook shops, sarais, etc. (and employees) ..	1,351	81	369	—	—	5	1,058	—	—
128	Hawkers of drink and food stuffs ..	240	24	216	....	—	—	48	—	—
129	Grain and pulse dealers ..	5,713	935	5,200	2	—	355	1,091	—	—
130	Dealers in sweetmeats, sugar and spices ..	1,312	289	721	12	—	23	845	—	—
131	Dealers in dairy product, eggs and poultry ..	814	423	105	—	....	4	1,128	—	—
132	Dealers in animals for food ..	109	13	—	....	....	—	122	—	—
133	Dealers in fodder for animals ..	386	89	297	....	—	5	173	—	—
134	Dealers in other food-stuff ..	3,197	700	1,669	4	—	103	2,121	—	—
135	Dealers in tobacco ..	215	28	141	....	—	—	102	—	—
136	Dealers in opium ..	3	1	4	....	....	—	—	—	—
137	Dealers in ganja ..	2	....	....	....	—	....	2	—	—
138	Trade in ready-made clothing and other articles of dress and the toilet (hats, umbrellas, socks, ready-made shoes, perfumes, etc.) ..	883	68	158	....	....	6	787	—	—
139	Trade in furniture, carpets, curtains and bedding ..	234	25	11	....	35	13	200	—	—
140	Trade in Hardware, cooking utensils, porcelain, crockery, glass ware, bottles, articles for gardening, etc. ..	75	7	37	....	14	3	28	....	....
141	Trade in building materials (other than bricks, tiles and woody materials) ..	16	2	13	....	....	....	4	1	—
142	Dealers and hirers, in mechanical transport motors, cycles, etc. ..	533	80	28	....	....	2	583	—	—
143	Dealers and hirers in other carriages, carts, boats, etc...	617	34	7	....	5	7	632	....	—
144	Dealers and hirers of elephants, camels, horses, cattle, asses, mules, etc. ..	1,232	244	260	12	....	22	1,182	—	—
145	Dealers in firewood, charcoal, coal, cowdung, etc. ..	1,300	639	1,361	....	2	....	575	1	—
146	Dealers in precious stones jewellery (real and imitation), clocks, optical instruments, etc. ..	69	5	23	....	28	12	11	—	—
147	Dealers in common bangles, bead necklaces, fans, small articles, toys, hunting and fishing tackle, flowers, etc.	68	13	8	....	....	3	70	—	—
148	Publishers, book-sellers, stationers, dealers in music, pictures, musical instruments and curiosities ..	24	5	18	....	....	2	9	....	—
149	Dealers in rags, stable refuse, etc. ..	13	26	2	1	....	3	33	—	—
150	General store keepers and shop-keepers otherwise unspecified ..	6,255	1,392	3,740	....	35	345	3,527	—	....
151	Itinerant traders, pedlars and hawkers (of other than food, etc.) ..	36	4	20	....	1	....	19	....	....
152	Other traders (including farmers of pounds, tolls and markets) ..	823	1,628	2,146	....	....	11	294	....	....
153	Army (Imperial) ..	829	1,007	658	....	....	44	1,130	4	....
154	Army (Indian States) ..	4,794	725	3,107	3	....	98	2,311	....	....
157	Police ..	2,576	814	1,634	3	1	108	1,644	—	....
158	Village watchmen ..	935	371	765	....	....	48	491	2	....
159	Service of the State ..	12,265	2,808	9,180	75	6	712	5,052	48	....
160	Service of Indian and Foreign States ..	138	36	....	....	1	7	157	9	....
161	Municipal and other local (not village) service ..	502	30	45	....	....	....	115	372	....
162	Village officials and servants other than watchmen ..	228	178	174	11	....	66	149	6	....
163	Priests, Ministers, etc. ..	4,281	1,070	2,675	389	....	140	2,105	45	....

STATE TABLE VII.

Distribution by Religion in Different Occupations.

Jammu and Kashmir Census 1931.

Group No.	Occupation.	Total of workers in principal occupation & dependant workers.	Total following occupation as subsidiary to other.	*Distribution by Religion.* Hindus.	Buddhists.	Jains.	Sikhs.	Muslims.	Christians.	Tribal or others.
1	2	3	4	5	6	7	8	9	10	11
164	Monks, nuns, religious mendicants ..	1,140	405	1,201	3	....	13	322	6	—
165	Other religious workers ..	2,503	954	1,284	971	....	27	1,157	18	—
166	Servants in religious edifices, burial and burning grounds pilgrim conductors, circumcisers, etc. ..	695	270	45	1	1	6	912	....	—
167	Lawyers of all kinds, including Qazis, Law Agents and Mukhtiars ..	124	38	127	....	1	1	33	—	—
168	Lawyers' clerks, petition-writers, etc. ..	455	101	494	....	—	10	52	—	—
169	Registered medical practitioners including oculists ..	280	49	156	1	....	6	164	2	—
170	Other persons practising the healing arts without being registered ..	399	87	290	16	....	10	169	1	—
171	Dentists ..	20	2	5	....	....	1	16	—	—
172	Midwives, vaccinators, compounders, nurses, masseurs, etc. ..	407	49	330	....	....	7	114	5	....
173	Veterinary Surgeons ..	21	8	5	....	....	....	24	....	—
174	Professors and teachers of all kinds ..	1,594	238	1,156	7	1	35	620	13	....
175	Clerks and servants connected with education ..	516	136	431	....	....	22	188	11	—
176	Public scribes, stenographers, etc. ..	24	3	2	....	....	3	22	....	—
177	Architects, surveyors, engineers and their employees (not being State servants) ..	25	7	13	....	....	4	15	....	....
178	Authors, editors, journalists, and photographers ..	31	1	31	....	....	....	1	....	....
180	Scientists (astronomers, botanists, etc.) ..	3	....	....	....	....	2	1	....	—
181	Horoscope casters, astrologers, fortune-tellers, wizards, witches and mediums ..	17	1	18	....	....	....	....	....	—
182	Musicians (composers and performers other than military), actors, dancers, etc. ..	797	353	201	24	....	15	910	....	....
183	Managers, and employees of places of public entertainments, race courses, societies, clubs ..	51	26	34	....	....	....	43	....	....
184	Conjurors, acrobats, recitors, exhibitors of curiosities and wild animals, etc. ..	292	181	359	....	....	1	113	....	....
185	Proprietors (other than of agricultural land), fund and scholarship holders and pensioners ..	2,672	843	2,464	....	4	583	459	5	....
186	Private motor-drivers and cleaners ..	6,075	248	4,679	....	....	170	1,457	17	—
187	Other domestic service ..	527,802	2,339	15,213	7,737	1	4,002	503,050	122	16
188	Manufacturers, business men and contractors otherwise unspecified ..	1,774	583	1,351	1	2	117	881	5	....
189	Cashiers, accountants, book-keepers, clerks and other employees in unspecified offices, ware-houses and shops	806	83	188	3	....	26	670	2	....
190	Mechanics otherwise unspecified ..	40,342	44	4,948	....	1	525	34,903	9	—
191	Labourers and workmen otherwise unspecified ..	354,120	2,116	144,869	226	117	5,700	205,110	214	—
192	Inmates of jails, asylums and alms houses ..	1,592	1	192	3	....	797	598	3	—
193	Beggars and vagrants ..	11,072	1,545	2,007	144	....	72	10,354	13	27
194	Procurers and prostitutes ..	463	4	1	31	....	....	385	....	50
195	Other unclassified non-productive industries ..	12	1	3	....	....	4	6	....	—

STATE TABLE VIII.

Territorial distribution of the Christian population by Sect and Race.

Jammu and Kashmir Census 1931.

STATE

TERRITORIAL DISTRIBUTION OF THE CHRISTIAN

Jammu and Kashmir

DISTRICT OR STATE.	ALL DENOMINATIONS.									ANGLICAN COMMUNION.									INDIA		
	Total.			Distribution by race.						Total.			Distribution by race.						Total.		
				European & allied races.		Anglo-Indian.		Indian.					European & allied races.		Anglo-Indian.		Indian.				
	Persons.	Males.	Females.	Males.	Females.	Males.	Females.	Males.	Females.	Persons.	Males.	Females.	Males.	Females.	Males.	Females.	Males.	Females.	Persons.	Males.	Females.
1	2	3	4	5	6	7	8	9	10	11	12	13	14	15	16	17	18	19	20	21	22
Jammu & Kashmir State	**2,263**	**1,243**	**1,020**	**93**	**105**	**50**	**73**	**1,100**	**842**	**576**	**275**	**301**	**43**	**63**	**18**	**49**	**214**	**189**	**770**	**421**	**349**
I. Jammu Province(including Jagirs) ..	**1,753**	**987**	**766**	**18**	**9**	**16**	**17**	**953**	**740**	**410**	**218**	**192**	**2**	**2**	**4**	**8**	**212**	**182**	**756**	**415**	**341**
(a) *Total Districts* ..	*1,677*	*944*	*733*	*13*	*7*	*16*	*17*	*915*	*709*	*410*	*218*	*192*	*2*	*2*	*4*	*8*	*212*	*182*	*749*	*415*	*334*
1. Jammu District (including City) ..	1,362	765	597	8	3	14	17	743	577	409	217	192	1	2	4	8	212	182	731	405	326
2. Kathua District ..	169	98	71	..	..	..	..	98	71	—	..	..	—	..	..	..	—	—	17	10	7
3. Udhampur (including Bhadrawah) ..	32	20	12	1	..	..	..	19	12	1	1	..	1	..	..	..	—	—	—	—	..
4. Riasi District ..	32	19	13	1	..	..	..	18	13	..	..	..	..	..	—	..	..	—	..	..	—
5. Mirpur	82	42	40	3	4	2	..	37	36	..	..	..	..	..	..	..	..	—	1	..	1
(b) *Total Jagirs* ..	*76*	*43*	*33*	*5*	*2*	..	..	*38*	*31*	..	..	..	..	..	..	..	..	..	*7*	—	*7*
4. Chenani Jagir ..	..	..	..	..	—	..	..	..	—	..	..	..	..	..	—	—	—	..	..	..	—
7. Poonch .. —	76	43	33	5	2	..	..	38	31	..	..	—	..	..	..	..	..	—	7	—	7
II. Kashmir Province ..	**339**	**166**	**173**	**61**	**83**	**27**	**49**	**78**	**41**	**144**	**46**	**98**	**34**	**53**	**10**	**38**	**2**	**7**	**14**	**6**	**8**
1. Baramulla, including Langet (Kashmir North) ..	61	36	25	7	16	..	..	29	9	7	4	3	3	3	..	..	1	—	—	—	—
2. Srinagar, including City (Kashmir South)	268	122	146	46	65	27	49	49	32	134	40	94	29	49	10	38	1	7	14	6	8
3. Muzaffarabad ..	10	8	2	8	2	..	..	..	..	3	2	1	2	1	..	..	..	—	—	—	—
III. Frontier Districts ..	**171**	**90**	**81**	**14**	**13**	**7**	**7**	**69**	**61**	**22**	**11**	**11**	**7**	**8**	**4**	**3**	—	—	—	—	..
1. Ladakh District ..	122	57	65	6	4	2	3	49	58	1	..	1	—	1	..	..	..	—	—	—	..
2. Gilgit .. —	38	25	13	2	6	4	4	19	3	11	4	7	1	4	3	3	—	—	—	—	..
3. Frontier Ilaqas ..	11	8	3	6	3	1	..	1	..	10	7	3	6	3	1	..	—	—	—	..	—

TABLE VIII.

POPULATION BY SECT AND RACE.

Census 1931.

United Church.						Lutheran.									Minor and Unspecified Protestants.									Roman Catholics.									Others.								
Distribution by race.						Total.			Distribution by race.						Total.			Distribution by race.						Total.			Distribution by race.						Total.			Distribution by race.					
European & allied races		Anglo-Indian.		Indian.					European & allied races		Anglo-Indian.		Indian.					European & allied races		Anglo-Indian.		Indian.					European & allied races		Anglo-Indian.		Indian.					European & allied races		Anglo-Indian.		Indian.	
Males.	Females.	Males.	Females.	Males.	Females.	Persons.	Males.	Females.	Males.	Females.	Males.	Females.	Males.	Females.	Persons.	Males.	Females.	Males.	Females.	Males.	Females.	Males.	Females.	Persons.	Males.	Females.	Males.	Females.	Males.	Females.	Males.	Females.	Persons.	Males.	Females.	Males.	Females.	Males.	Females.	Males.	Females.
23	24	25	26	27	28	29	30	31	32	33	34	35	36	37	38	39	40	41	42	43	44	45	46	47	48	49	50	51	52	53	54	55	56	57	58	59	60	61	62	63	64
4	8	1	1	416	340	2	2	..	2	..	..	..	..	..	369	201	168	9	12	9	9	183	147	124	82	42	10	16	17	14	55	12	422	262	160	25	6	5	..	232	154
1	2	..	..	414	339	1	1	..	1	..	..	..	..	..	158	94	64	..	..	2	2	92	62	29	18	11	2	..	6	7	10	4	399	241	158	12	5	4	..	225	153
1	..	..	..	*414*	*334*	*1*	*1*	..	*1*	..	..	..	..	..	*158*	*94*	*64*	..	..	*2*	*2*	*92*	*62*	*29*	*18*	*11*	*2*	..	*6*	*7*	*10*	*4*	*330*	*198*	*132*	*7*	*5*	*4*	..	*187*	*127*
1	..	..	..	404	326	1	1	..	1	..	..	..	..	..	66	39	27	..	..	2	2	37	25	29	18	11	2	..	6	7	10	4	126	85	41	3	1	2	..	80	40
..	..	..	..	10	7	..	..	..	..	..	..	..	..	..	47	32	15	..	..	..	..	32	15	..	..	..	..	..	..	..	..	..	105	56	49	..	..	..	..	56	49
..	..	..	..	..	..	..	..	..	..	..	..	..	..	..	30	19	11	..	..	..	..	19	11	..	..	..	..	..	..	..	..	..	1	..	1	..	..	..	..	—	1
..	..	..	..	..	..	..	..	..	..	..	..	..	..	..	15	4	11	..	..	..	..	4	11	..	..	..	..	..	..	..	..	..	17	15	2	1	..	..	..	14	2
..	..	..	..	..	1	..	..	..	..	..	..	..	..	..	..	..	..	..	..	..	..	..	..	..	..	..	..	..	..	..	..	..	81	42	39	3	4	2	..	37	35
..	*2*	..	..	..	*5*	..	..	..	..	..	..	..	..	..	..	..	..	..	..	..	..	..	..	..	..	..	..	..	..	..	..	..	*69*	*43*	*26*	*5*	..	..	..	*38*	*26*
..	..	..	..	..	..	..	..	..	..	..	..	..	..	..	..	..	..	..	..	..	..	..	..	..	..	..	..	..	..	..	..	..	—	..	..	..	..	..	..	—	—
..	2	..	..	..	5	..	..	..	..	..	..	..	..	..	..	..	..	..	..	..	..	..	..	..	..	..	..	..	..	..	..	..	69	43	26	5	..	..	..	38	26
3	6	1	1	2	1	1	1	..	1	..	..	..	..	..	73	39	34	6	7	6	3	27	24	89	58	31	8	16	10	7	40	8	18	16	2	9	1	..	..	7	1
..	..	..	..	..	..	1	1	..	1	..	..	..	..	..	11	7	4	2	1	..	..	5	3	42	24	18	1	12	..	..	23	6	..	..	..	..	..	..	..	..	—
3	6	1	1	2	1	..	..	..	..	..	..	..	..	..	60	31	29	3	5	6	3	22	21	47	34	13	7	4	10	7	17	2	13	11	2	4	1	..	..	7	1
..	..	..	..	..	..	..	..	..	..	..	..	..	..	..	2	1	1	1	1	..	..	..	..	..	..	..	..	..	..	..	..	..	5	5	—	5	..	..	..	..	—
..	..	..	..	..	..	..	..	..	..	..	..	..	..	..	138	68	70	3	5	1	4	64	61	6	6	..	..	..	1	..	5	..	5	5	—	4	..	1	..	..	—
..	..	..	..	..	..	..	..	..	..	..	..	..	..	..	116	52	64	2	3	1	3	49	58	..	..	..	..	..	..	..	..	..	5	5	..	4	..	1	..	—	—
..	..	..	..	..	..	..	..	..	..	..	..	..	..	..	21	15	6	1	2	..	1	14	3	6	6	..	..	..	1	..	5	..	..	—	—	..	..	..	..	..	..
..	..	..	..	..	..	..	..	..	..	..	..	..	..	..	1	1	..	..	..	..	..	1	..	..	..	..	..	..	..	..	..	..	..	—	—	..	..	..	..	—	—